E.C.
Environmental Law

Fourth Edition

AUSTRALIA

LBC Information Services
Sydney

CANADA and USA

Carswell
Toronto

NEW ZEALAND

Brooker's
Auckland

SINGAPORE and MALAYSIA

Sweet & Maxwell Asia
Singapore and Kuala Lumpur

E.C. Environmental Law

Fourth Edition

by

PROFESSOR LUDWIG KRÄMER
Judge at Landgericht in Kiel, LL.D.
Head of the Unit for Waste Management
in DG XI of the European Commission

Being the Fourth Edition of
E.C. Treaty and Environmental Law

LONDON
SWEET & MAXWELL
2000

Published in 2000 by
Sweet & Maxwell Limited of
100 Avenue Road, London, NW3 3PF
Computerset by J&L Composition Ltd,
Filey, North Yorkshire
Printed and bound in Great Britain by MPG Books Ltd,
Bodmin, Cornwall

No natural forests were destroyed to make this product:
only farmed timber was used and replanted.

A CIP catalogue record for this book is available from
the British Library

ISBN 0 421 590203

Preface

This book on Community environmental law summarises more than twenty-five years that I have spent on this issue. In fact, when, in 1973, the Environment and Consumer Protection Service was set up within the Commission, which later became Directorate General Environment (DG XI), I had the privilege of being an official in that Service. Community environmental policy and law has developed spectacularly since then. A general presentation of this law therefore seems appropriate.

This book is, at the same time, the fourth edition of *E.C. Treaty and Environmental Law*, which has been published since 1991. While the previous editions of the book were limited to the presentation of Community primary law, this book now includes a presentation of Community secondary environmental law. At the same time, the general chapters have been reviewed and considerably enlarged. As therefore more than half of the chapters (chapters 4 to 9) are completely new and the others rewritten, specified and detailed, the new title of the book seems justified.

I am more than aware of deficiencies, shortcomings and omissions that this book contains. Environmental law has become very broad and the integration clause of Article 6 (ex 3c) of the E.C. Treaty brings numerous aspects of transport, energy, agricultural and regional law under the heading "environment". This book deliberately limits itself on the legal aspects of integration, though it is obvious that the integration of environmental requirements into other policies largely implies political choices and the fixing of political priorities.

Community legislation and jurisprudence up to June 30, 1999 were taken into consideration, later developments only sporadically. I would be grateful for any correction that readers might suggest.

My special thanks are addressed to the team of Sweet & Maxwell, who, with a lot of patience, allowed this book to come into existence.

Ludwig Krämer
October 1999

Contents

Alphabetical Table of Cases

Numerical Table of Cases

Table of European Union Treaties and Conventions

Table of Regulations

Table of Directives

Table of Decisions

Table of Environmental Programmes

Table of International Treaties and Conventions

CHAPTER 1

Objectives, Principles and Conditions

1. THE ENVIRONMENT IN COMMUNITY LAW

1—01   The Treaty on European Union, concluded in 1991 in Maastricht[1] and amended in 1997 by the Treaty of Amsterdam,[2] does not directly mention the environment. Article 2, which describes the objectives of the European Union, states that one of its objectives is "to promote economic and social progress and to achieve balanced and sustainable development", without explaining what balanced and sustainable development is. Fortunately, however, Article 8 of this Treaty integrated in full the Treaty on the European Community into the Treaty and this E.C. Treaty mentioned in Article 2 the protection of the environment as one of the objectives of Community activity.[3] The objectives were completed by specific environmental objectives in Article 174 (ex 130r) E.C.

Neither of these provisions, though, define "environment"; nor do the other provisions of the E.C. Treaty[4] contain any definition. It follows from Articles 174(1) (ex 130r(1)) and 175(2) (ex 130s(2)) E.C. that the environment includes human beings, natural resources, land use, town and country issues, waste and water. These categories include practically all areas of the environment, in particular fauna and flora, which are part of the natural resources, and climate. The inclusion of issues concerning town and country planning underlines that the environment is not limited to natural elements, but also includes the man-made environment.

1—02   When the section "environment" was first included in the E.C. Treaty in 1987, there was already extensive secondary Community legislation adopted on the basis of three environmental action programmes and this was generally perceived as legislation on the environment. This secondary legislation covered water and air, noise and chemicals, nature conservation, waste and some measures of a general nature. Furthermore, in June 1990, shortly before the commencement of the negotiations on the Maastricht Treaty on European Union, the Community Heads of State and Government adopted a "Declaration on the Environment",[5] where they proclaimed a right to a healthy and clean environment, which included, in particular, "the quality of air, rivers, lakes, coastal and marine waters, the quality of food and drinking water, protection against noise, protection against contamination of soil, soil erosion and

---

[1] [1992] O.J. C191/1.
[2] [1997] O.J. C340/1.
[3] Art. 2: "The Community shall have as its task, by establishing a common market and an economic and monetary union and by implementing the common policies or activities referred to in Articles 3 and 3a, to promote throughout the Community a harmonious, balanced and sutainable development of economic activities, sustainable and non-inflationary growth, a high degree of convergence of economic performance, a high level of employment and of social protection, a high level of protection and improvement of the quality of the environment, the raising of the standard of living and quality of life, and economic and social cohesion and solidarity among Member States."
[4] Arts 3(k), 6, 95 (ex 100a), 161 (ex 130d), 175 and 176 (ex 130s and 130t).
[5] European Council Res. of June 15, 1990 (1990) *Bulletin of the European Communities*, para. 1.36.

desertification, preservation of habitats, flora and fauna, landscape and other elements of the natural heritage, the amenity and quality of residential areas".

It must be assumed that by using the concept "environment" in this legal, political, economic and ecological context, the authors of the Treaty have given to the term the emphasis which it had at that time in Community law. The term "environment" is thus all-embracing and includes economic, social and aesthetic aspects, the preservation of natural and archaeological heritage, and the man-made as well as the natural environment.

"Environment" in Articles 2, 3 and 174 to 176 (ex 130r to 130t) E.C. is different from the "working environment" used in Articles 95 and 138 (ex 100a and 118a) E.C., which obviously concerns the conditions at the workplace, such as air pollution, noise, risk of accidents, etc. The specific conditions of the workplace justify a different treatment of "environment" and "working environment", although in the early 1970s, Community environmental policy did not make this distinction[6] and some directives do not really differentiate between worker protection and environmental protection.[7] Working environment provisions come, therefore, under Article 138 (ex 118a) or, as the case may be, under Article 95 (ex 100a) E.C.

1—03 Doubts were sometimes raised as to whether "environment" also included animal welfare. However, wild animals are part of the natural environment, thus protection measures for wild animals—not only as a threatened species, but as living creatures—are environmental measures. The Amsterdam Treaty on European Union added a protocol to the E.C. Treaty, according to which Community policies on agriculture, transport, the internal market and research had to pay "full regard to the welfare of animals".[8] It is obvious, though, that this provision referred to domestic, not wild, animals and therefore does not contradict the interpretation given here.

The uncertainty of how to classify (wild) animal welfare became obvious when the Commission made a proposal for a directive on the protection of zoo animals. In view of the subsidiarity debate, the Commission repealed this proposal and replaced it by a proposal for a recommendation. However, the Council rearranged the text so as to be a text that was mainly concerned with protecting animals as endangered species and adopted, on that basis, a directive in 1999.[9]

Geographically, the environment mentioned in the Treaty is not limited to the Community environment, as is clear in Article 174(1) (ex 130r(1)) E.C.[10] Consequently, the Community can—and did—take measures to protect the environment outside the territory covered by the Treaty, such as measures to protect the ozone layer, combat climate change, protect endangered species in the Third World or ban the export of waste to non-industrialised countries.

1—04 The question of whether the Community should deal with matters of a purely local nature, is something to be answered under the general principle of subsidiarity. In the past, the Commission has sometimes rejected requests to take initiatives on a specific environmental problem, arguing that such matters could be better solved at local or regional level; such questions concerned, for instance, noise from nightclubs and discothèques, bicycle facilities in urban areas or noise in the vicinity of airports. However, it may well be that some day the ambient noise level

---

[6] See first environmental action programme [1973] O.J. C112/1, p. 43.

[7] See Dir. 96/82 on the prevention of industrial accidents [1997] O.J. L10/13.

[8] [1997] O.J. C340/110.

[9] Dir. 1999/22 [1999] O.J. L94/24, see for more detail para. 5–38, below.

[10] Art. 174(1), fourth indent: "(Community policy on the environment shall contribute to pursuit of the following objectives.)—promoting measures at international level to deal with regional or worldwide environmental problems."

in the neighbourhood of airports will become the subject of a Community regulation, as the Commission had already announced in 1992.[11]

There is no Community environment distinguishable from any individual, local, regional or national environment. Therefore, the Community measures need not be and are not restricted to transfrontier environmental problems. As mentioned above, the definition of "environment" is, as regards its content and its geographical extension, very wide and includes human beings, fauna and flora, soil, water, air, climate, landscape, material assets, and natural heritage.[12] Environmental law is the totality of the legal measures which try to prevent, protect and improve parts or all of the environment.

2. GENESIS AND DEVELOPMENT OF COMMUNITY ENVIRONMENTAL LAW

1—05 The original E.C. Treaty of 1957 did not contain any provision on the environment, environmental policy or environmental law. Subsequent to the discussions of the late 1960s, where the Club of Rome described the limits to growth, the European Commission announced in 1970 the necessity of establishing a Community action programme on the environment. In 1971 it submitted a first communication on Community environmental policy,[13] where it suggested the establishment of Community measures for the protection of the environment recurring, if necessary, to the possibilities for action outlined in Article 308 (ex 235) E.C. This communication was soon followed by a proposal for an environmental action programme.[14]

In 1972, the United Kingdom, Denmark and Ireland joined the Community. In the autumn of that year, the Heads of State and Government met for the first time, agreed on the necessity to take action on the environment and asked for a Community action programme.[15] Since this programme was already before the Council discussions advanced relatively quickly. France in particular considered, however, that Community action should instead take place in the form of intergovernmental co-operation. For this reason, the finally adopted programme was agreed in the form of a joint "declaration" by the Community and by the representatives of Member States meeting in Council.[16] In the same way the agreement to inform the Commission of national environmental measures which could have a direct effect on the functioning of the internal market, was made in the form of a non-binding gentleman's agreement[17]: this policy continued throughout 1973 and 1974.[18]

---

[11] COM (92) 494 of December 2, 1992.

[12] Enumeration from Dir. 85/337 on the assessment of the effects of certain public and private projects on the environment [1985] O.J. L175/40, Art. 3.

[13] Commission, First communication on a Community policy for the environment, SEC (71) 2616 of July 22, 1971.

[14] [1972] O.J. C52/1.

[15] Commission Sixth General Report (1972), p. 8.

[16] [1973] O.J. C112/1.

[17] [1973] O.J. C9/1.

[18] See Agreement of July 20, 1974 to complete the 1973 agreement [1974] O.J. C86/1; Resolution of March 3, 1974 on energy and the environment [1975] O.J. C168/2; Recommendation 75/436 of March 3, 1975 on cost allocation and action by public authorities on environmental matters [1975] O.J. L194/1; Resolution of June 24, 1975 on a second group of air pollutants which are to be studied [1975] O.J. C168/4; Resolution of July 15, 1975 on adapting Community measures to technical progress [1975] O.J. C168/5; Decision of December 8, 1975 setting up a common procedure for an inventory of information sources on the environment [1976] O.J. L31/8.

1—06   The first legally binding instruments on environmental issues were adopted in 1975, based on Article 94 (ex 100) E.C. and/or Article 308 (ex 235) E.C. The choice of measures was determined both by the environmental action programme and by the necessity of selecting areas which did not come under the responsibility of the internal market or agricultural services of the Commission. This was the case for measures in the area of water and waste.[19]

The E.C. Treaty was amended in 1985 to complete, by the end of 1992, the internal market.[20] Majority voting for internal market measures was introduced by inserting a new Article 95 (ex 100a) into the Treaty. A new section was introduced for environmental measures (Articles 174 to 176 (ex 130r to 130t)). However, such measures had to be adopted unanimously. This has led, since 1987 (the date when the Treaty amendment came into effect) to considerable discussions on the legal basis for environmental measures, which the Commission and the European Parliament often wished to base on Article 95, while the Council and Member States preferred Article 175.

When the Maastricht Treaty on European Union amended the E.C. Treaty in 1991 (it entered into effect in 1993) it introduced majority decisions in environmental matters (Article 175 (ex 130s)), though some matters remained subjected to unanimous decisions.[21]

Finally, the Amsterdam Treaty,[22] which entered into effect on May 1, 1999, introduced the codecision procedure for environmental matters (Article 175(1) (ex 130s(1))) and aligned this provision thus further to that of Article 95 (ex 100a), though the unanimity clause for some areas (Article 175(2) (ex 130s(2))) was not deleted.

3. SOURCES OF COMMUNITY ENVIRONMENTAL LAW

1—07   The broad definition of objectives of Community environmental policy, as laid down in Articles 2 and 174(1) (ex 130r(1)) E.C., hardly leaves any area of environmental policy, as it is perceived in any one of the 15 Member States, outside Community competence. Measures to realise the objectives of Community environmental policy can be based on any relevant Article of the E.C. Treaty, although Articles 174 and 175 (ex 130r and 130s) remain the most relevant provisions for Community environmental action. Thus, measures which concern agricultural aspects of environmental protection will normally be based on Article 37 (ex 43), measures on environmental aspects of transport on Article 80 (ex 84) E.C. The choice of the correct legal basis is important because the elaboration of the proposal, the participation of other Community institutions, the intensity of this participation (see Articles 250 to 252 (ex 189a to 189c)) E.C. and the residual rights for Member States are different from one provision to another.

The rules of Articles 174 and 175 are not directly applicable: while for instance, Article 27 (ex 29) states that "quantitative restrictions on imports and all measures having equivalent effect shall . . . be prohibited between Member States", no similar formulation can be found in Articles 174 or 175, stating that pollution is prohibited or that the polluter shall pay for pollution.

Articles 174 and 175 need to be formalised and made precise by secondary legislation

---

[19] See, in chronological order, Dec. 75/437 of March 3, 1975 to adhere to the Paris Convention on marine protection from land-based sources [1975] O.J. L194/5; Dir. 75/439 of June 16, 1975 on waste [1975] O.J. L194/23; Dir. 75/440 of June 16, 1975 on surface water [1975] O.J. L194/26; Dir. 75/442 of June 16, 1975 [1975] O.J. L194/23; Dir. 76/160 of December 8, 1975 on bathing water [1976] O.J. L31/1.

[20] Single European Act [1987] O.J. L169/1.

[21] [1992] O.J. C191/1.

[22] [1997] O.J. C340/1.

in order to become applicable for administrative bodies and courts or used for or against polluters.

The most relevant other provisions, on which Community environmental measures can be based are Article 95 (ex 100a) for measures aiming at the establishment and the functioning of the internal market, Article 37 (ex 43) for agricultural measures, Article 80 (ex 84) for measures concerning transport, Article 133 (ex 113) for commercial measures and Article 166 (ex 130i) on research and devlopment. Environmental measures in the energy sector are frequently based on Article 175, as there is no specific chapter on energy policy in the E.C. Treaty; otherwise Article 308 (ex 235) is used.

The choice of the correct legal basis for an environmental matter will be discussed below at paragraphs 2–69 *et seq.*, the rights of Member States under paragraphs 3–41 *et seq.* International convention to which the Community has adhered to, is part of Community law. This ranks below the primary law of the E.C. Treaty, but above secondary legislation and thus prevails over conflicting environmental directives or regulations.

1—08 The Community has adhered to a considerable number of international environmental conventions and to numerous protocols, drawn up in pursuance of these conventions. All these conventions are so-called "mixed" conventions: the competence for the subject-matter regulated by the conventions was partly in the hands of the Community and partly in the hands of Member States. Where exactly the line is drawn between Community responsibility and Member States' responsibility inevitably varies from one convention to the other.

As decisions which are based on Article 175 and transpose environmental conventions into Community law have as a consequence that Member States may, under Article 176 (ex 130t) introduce more stringent provisions in that area at national level, such decisions can never establish an exclusive Community competence for the subject-matter regulated by the convention.[23]

An international environmental convention only plays a significant role in Community law where the Community has adopted a directive or a regulation in order to transpose the content of the convention into Community law. Where there is only a Council decision to adhere to a convention, the Commission omits to enforce the content of the convention against Member States. Member States are left at their discretion to also ratify the convention and to apply it. This practice is well established, although it clearly contradicts Article 211 (ex 155) E.C., which assigns the task to the Commission to ensure that Community law is applied within the Community.[24]

1—09 The Community has adopted an important number of pieces of environmental legislation in the form of regulations, directives and non-binding recommendations. Their exact number depends on the classification of measures. Thus, for example, since at least the mid-1980s standards for air emissions or noise levels from motorised vehicles have been set and strenghthened in order to better protect the environment. Yet the two basic directives on air and noise emissions from cars had been adopted as part of a Community programme for the elimination of technical barriers to trade in the internal market. The different instruments will be further discussed below at paragraphs 2–31 *et seq.*

Environmental action programmes are, since the end of 1993, regulated by Article 175(3) (ex 130s(3)); they must now be adopted in the form of a legally binding decision. As such, their content will become a source of law in future.

---

[23] See below, para. 3–50, for a concrete case where the question of exclusive competence became relevant at Community level.

[24] E.C. Treaty, Art. 211 (ex 155): "the Commission shall . . . ensure that the provisions of this Treaty and the measures taken by the institutions pursuant thereto are applied . . .".

The five environmental action programmes which have been adopted since 1973 do not constitute a source of law. They were elaborated by the Commission and sent to the other Community institutions. The Council, together with governments from Member States, normally approved their concept and the approach in the form of a unanimously adopted (political) resolution, but carefully avoided any statement that it adopted the programme as such.[25]

4. OBJECTIVES OF ENVIRONMENTAL POLICY

(a) General remarks

1—10 Article 2 (ex B) of the Treaty on European Union[26] and Article 2 of the E.C. Treaty[27] fix the general environmental objectives of the European Union, which are completed by the specific objectives fixed in Article 174 (ex 130r),[28] since it is common understanding that the tasks of Article 2 are not an exhaustive enumeration.

The different objectives of the Treaty are not in a hierarchical order. The Community has to try to attain all its objectives. Should different objectives conflict in a specific case, then the Community institutions must try to find a compromise. Conflicts—for instance between the establishment of an internal market for goods and the need to protect the environment via the precautionary principle—are frequent. Article 6 of the E.C. Treaty,[29] which was introduced by the Treaty of Amsterdam, does not lead to a different interpretation. Indeed, any such hierarchy would have needed clearer expression in the Treaty.

The different environmental objectives do not lead to concrete requirements for legislative action. It is not possible, for instance, to deduce from the requirement of a prudent use of natural resources the right to limit land use, for instance for agricultural purposes. Nor are the objectives, in practice, enforceable. The possibility of an action under Article 232 (ex 175) against the Community, the Council or the Commission for not pursuing the environmental objectives, is theoretical, since Community institutions have a very large discretion for taking—or not taking—action.

Community action shall contribute to achieve the different objectives, as is stated in Article 174 (ex 130r) E.C. Next to Community measures there are also international, national, regional and local measures which exist to help reach the objectives. The responsibility and competence of the Community in environmental matters is thus shared with Member States, but is in no way exclusive. Whether the Community acts is generally determined by the principle of subsidiarity, Article 5 (ex 3b); in specific cases the environmental action programmes, Article 175(3) (ex 130s(3)) outline the focus for

---

[25] See, for instance, Res. of the Council and the Representatives of the Governments of the Member States, meeting within the Council of February 1, 1993 [1993] O.J. C138/1: ". . . approve the general approach and strategy of the programme towards sustainability presented by the Commission; . . .".

[26] Treaty on European Union (n. 1), Art. 2: "[The Union shall set itself the following objectives]—to promote economic and social progress and to achieve balanced and sustainable development . . ."

[27] E.C. Treaty (n. 2), Art. 2: "[The Community shall have as its task] . . . to promote throughout the Community a harmonious, balanced and sustainable development of economic activities, sustainable and non inflationary growth..a high level of protection and improvement of the quality of the environment, the raising of the standard of living and quality of life . . ."

[28] E.C. Treaty, Art. 174(1): "Community policy on the environment shall contribute to pursuit of the following objectives: preserving, protecting and improving the quality of the environment; protecting human health;—prudent and rational utilisation of natural resources; promoting measures at international level to deal with regional or worldwide environmental problems."

[29] E.C. Treaty, Art. 6: "Environmental protection requirements must be integrated into the definition and implementation of Community policies and activities referred to in Article 3, in particular with a view to promoting sustainable development." This text was earlier inserted in Art. 174(2.3) (ex 130r(2.3)) E.C.

action and the individual measures still need, in order to be adopted, the necessary majority under the different Treaty provisions.

(b) Sustainable development

1—11   The Amsterdam Treaty 1997 introduced the concept of sustainable development into Community law: the Preamble to the Treaty on European Union, Article 2 of that Treaty, as well as Articles 2 and 6 of the E.C. Treaty mention this objective without defining it. Already, Article 2 in the version of the Maastricht Treaty, had fixed as one of the Community objectives "sustainable growth", also without defining it. Both entities go back to a report which an ad hoc "World Commission on Environment and Development" chaired by G. Brundtland made in 1987 to the United Nations and which was entitled "Our Common Future". In that report, the need for economic development was emphasised which should, however, be "sustainable". Sustainable development was defined as a "development which meets the needs of the present without compromising the ability of future generations to meet their own needs".

The insertion of this concept into the Treaty, together with the other provisions on the environment, signals the commitment to ensure a prudent use of natural resources in order to take the environmental and economic interests of future generations, as those of the present ones, into account. It is the first time that future generations see their environmental interests at least mentioned in the legal context of the Treaty on European Union.

In secondary Community legislation, "sustainable development" was defined as follows[30]: "'Sustainable development' means the improvement of the standard of living and welfare of the relevant populations within the limits of the capacity of the ecosystems, by maintaining natural assets and their biological diversity for the benefit of present and future generations." This definition again seems more descriptive than precise. It demonstrates that the legal content of "sustainable development" remains more than vague, since nobody knows about the impact of present measures on future—which future?—generations. Thus, for example, it might well be argued that the use of nuclear energy, which includes the generation of radioactive waste for which no safe disposal technology exists as yet and which will continue to be hazardous for thousands of years, most certainly affects future generations and is therefore not sustainable. Another example is the gradual, progressive contamination of ground-water, which often shows its effects only decades later, when the groundwater is used. Further examples are the disappearance of fauna and flora species, urbanisation and the construction of motorways.

1—12   Community practice shows an inflationary use of the expression "sustainable" which is linked to any activity in order to give it a green colour; contents are put into the notion of "substainability", which are later derived from it. Generally, it seems impossible to determine precisely if and when future generations will be able or unable to meet their own needs. The construction of the Via Appia some 2,500 years ago has affected the siting of towns and villages; in the same way, any town siting and road construction today will affect future generations' rights to determine their own needs, i.e. their own town siting or road construction. The different provisions in the Treaty on sustainable development thus give more of a guideline to policy action than an actual legal concept.

---

[30] Reg. 3062/95 on operations to promote tropical forests [1995] O.J. L327/9, Art. 2(4).

(c) High level of protection

1—13   The objective to reach a high level of environmental protection is now enshrined in E.C. Treaty,[31] Art. 2 and is repeated in similar terms in Article 174(2.1) (ex 130r(2.1)) E.C.[32] A similar provision is to be found in Article 95(3) (ex 100a(3)) E.C.[33] Neither Article specifies what a high level of protection is: certainly, it is not the highest level one could think of.[34] A high level can probably best be determined by looking at environmental standards which Member States that normally have a high standard of environmental protection (Denmark, the Netherlands, Sweden, Finland, Austria, Germany) have set; the practice of other industrial states with a recognised strong environmental policy, such as Switzerland or Norway, may also be considered. Policy declarations, resolutions and targets can be an important indicator, especially in areas where no standards have yet been set at national or international level, or where scientific uncertainty is great. Since, Article 2 of the E.C. Treaty expressly declares the improvement of the quality of the environment to be one of the objectives of Community policy, any measure aiming at a high level must therefore aim at improving the existing situation.

The specific reference to a high level of protection no longer permits the adoption of measures which only provide for the lowest common denominator of environmental protection and lets individual Member States, which are in favour of more stringent measures, to adopt such measures by virtue of Article 176 (ex 130t) E.C. at national level. Indeed, the high level is to be achieved by the Community as a whole, not by national measures. Article 174 (ex 130r) clarifies that the interests of regions which are environmentally lagging behind shall be duly taken into account, allowing them to catch up; this again pleads for a high level, not the highest level of protection.

A high level of environmental protection cannot be enforced in court. This follows from the fact that Articles 2 and 174 (ex 130r) E.C. refer to the environmental policy as a whole, not to the individual measure adopted under that policy; also, the policy has to "aim at" a high level and can thus always argue that it is on its way towards this attainment.

1—14   In contrast to Articles 2 and 174, Article 95 (ex 100a) refers to individual measures, not to the policy in general. Where a Commission proposal is not based on a high level of environmental protection, the European Parliament has a right of action against the Commission[35] under Article 230 (ex 173). This follows from the procedural provisions of Articles 250 and 251 (ex 189a and 189b) E.C. Indeed, where the Commission has made a "high level" proposal (case A), the Council can reach a common position and adopt a proposal that lowers the protection, only by unanimity

---

[31] See n. 3 above.

[32] E.C. Treaty, Art. 174(2.1): "Community policy on the environment shall aim at a high level of protection taking into account the diversity of situations in the various regions of the Community."

[33] E.C. Treaty, Art. 95(3): "(The Commission, in its proposals concerning environmental protection) will take as a base a high level of protection taking account in particular of any new development based on scientific facts. Within their respective powers, the European Parliament and the Council will also seek to achieve this objective."

[34] See also Court of Justice, case C-233/94 *Germany v. Parliament and Council* [1997] E.C.R I-2405, para. 48 for a case of consumer protection where under Article 153 (ex 129a) E.C. a high level of protection is required: "Admittedly, there must be a high level of consumer protection . . .; however, no provision of the Treaty obliges the Community legislature to adopt the highest level of protection which can be found in a particular Member State. The reduction in the level of protection which may thereby result in certain cases through the application of . . . the Directive does not call into question the general result which the Directive seeks to achieve, namely a considerable improvement in the protection of . . . [consumers] within the Community."

[35] The Parliament has no such right against the Council, since E.C. Treaty, Art. 95(3) expressly provides that the Council shall only "seek to achieve" a high level of protection.

(Article 250 (ex 189a)); however, where the Commission has made a "low level" proposal (case B), the Council can reach a common position and finally adopt the proposal by a qualified majority, since it does not change the Commission's proposal. The Council's common position may only be challenged by an absolute majority of the European Parliament. Where this majority opinion is concurrent with the Commission's opinion, the Council must decide unanimously (case A); where this majority opinion does not concur with the Commission's opinion, the Council may decide by majority (case B).

These considerations are of theoretical character. The European Parliament has, until now, never attempted such a case against the Commission. In all situations—under Articles 95 and 175 (ex 100a and 130s) E.C.—that have occurred up until now, the practice of the Commission and the Council indicates that both institutions use the formula of a high level in its reversed order: whatever is proposed or adopted is considered to be a high level of environmental protection.

The "sanction" for not proposing or adopting measures on a high level of environmental protection is Article 176 (ex 130t) for measures under Article 175 (ex 130s) and Article 95(4) to (7): in both cases, Member States may, under certain conditions, maintain or introduce more stringent national measures. It may well be expected that the lower the level of protection the Community measure is, the greater becomes the pressure from Member States with a high level of protection to opt out of the Community environmental measure and take or maintain national measures.

(d) The specific objectives of Article 174(1) (ex 130r(1))

1—15 The four specific objectives mentioned under Article 174(1) are rather detailed in their description; but these details do not, in fact, add too much to the objective to protect the environment. They clarify that the Community protection measures are not limited to the Community territory, which, in practice, these measures never were. Measures to protect human health[36] can, as the case may be, pursue an environmental, internal market, agricultural, consumer protection or public health objective and thus be based on other Treaty provisions than Articles 174 to 176. "Natural resources" is a vague term: it probably covers the management of all resources which are found in the environment, fauna and flora, timber, minerals, air, water, soil, oil, natural gas and chemicals. Measures to prevent degradation or impairment of these resources, such as accident prevention and the safe disposal of waste, are included in the term "prudent and rational use".

Identifying the objective, eventually the main objective, of a measure is important, because the objective determines the legal base for the measure; and the decision-making procedure, the content of the measure and Member States' residual rights and obligations vary according to the legal base applicable.

5. PRINCIPLES OF ENVIRONMENTAL ACTION

(a) General remarks

1—16 The first section of the E.C. Treaty, Articles 1 to 16 of the E.C. Treaty, is entitled "Principles". It fixes the basics of the E.C. Treaty, objectives, institutional and

---

[36] The difference between "health of humans" (Art. 30 (ex 36)), "human health" (Art. 174, but also Art. 152) and "public health" (title of Art. 152) has lost its legal precision; see also Court of Justice, case C-272/80 *Biologische Produkten* [1981] E.C.R. 3277, where the Court refers to Art. 30 (ex 36) as protecting "public health".

procedural rules and a number of other provisions of a general character. As regards the environment, Articles 5 (ex 3b) on subsidiarity[37] and 6 (ex 3c) on integration[38] are of relevance.

To these general principles, Article 174(2.2) (ex 130r(2.2)) adds some specific environmental principles.[39]

It is doubtful whether all these different provisions have the same legal character. As regards the principles of Article 174(2.2) (ex 130r(2.2)) E.C., they are rather general guidelines for Community environmental policy but do not constitute binding rules of law which apply to each individual Community measure, nor do they contain an obligation to take specific measures in favour of the environment. Therefore, they could only by enforced by the European Court in very extreme cases where a systematic disregard of the principles in the policy is shown.

1—17 This reasoning is contested. German authors in particular see the principles of Article 174(2.2) as binding rules of law, which have to be respected in each individual measure.[40] The wide discretion of Community institutions, however, for taking measures would only lead to the illegality of a measure in exceptional cases because the principles had been disregarded. As can be seen, the practical results are not really different.

The discussion on principles in environmental law and policy is, to a large extent, a spill-over from discussions which take place under the auspices of public international law. In that context, principles may play an important role in contributing to the shaping of international environmental law. However, it should not be forgotten that the essential part of public international environmental law is soft law, which is not really binding on the Member States. In contrast to that, Community law is binding and capable of fixing provisions that have binding force on Member States and on private persons. In the same way as the United Nations' Declaration on Human Rights remains of high value for the international community, but is of secondary importance in Europe, where the Council of Europe's Convention on Human Rights established binding, enforceable human rights, the environmental principles in the E.C. Treaty are less important for Community environmental law, which has developed a large number of binding provisions that materialise these principles for the actual, concrete situations.

1—18 The Court of Justice has in one case interpreted Community law in the light of one of the principles of Article 174 (2.2) (ex 130r(2.2)).[41] In that judgment the Court had to decide whether a regional ban for waste imports was compatible with the Community provisions on the free circulation of goods, although waste imports

---

[37] E.C. Treaty, Art. 5: "The Community shall act within the limits of the powers conferred upon it by this Treaty and of the objectives assigned to it therein. In areas which do not fall within its exclusive competence, the Community shall take action in accordance with the principle of subsidiarity, only if and in so far as the objectives of the proposed action cannot be sufficiently acheved by the Member States and can therefore, by reason of the scale or effects of the proposed action, be better achieved by the Community.

Any action by the Community shall not go beyond what is necessary to achieve the objectives of this Treaty".

[38] E.C. Treaty, Art. 6: "Environmental protection requirements must be integrated into the definition and implementation of Community policies and activities referred to in Article 3, in particular with a view to promoting sustainable development."

[39] E.C. Treaty, Art. 174(2.2): "[Community policy] . . . shall be based on the precautionary principle and on the principles that preventive action should be taken, that environmental damage should as a priority be rectified at source and that the polluter should pay."

[40] See, for instance, A. Epiney, *Umweltrecht in der Europäischen Union* (Cologne, Berlin, Bonn and Munich, 1997), p. 108: "The above-mentioned principles are of binding nature, so that their non-respect by a specific Community measure can lead to the nullity of that measure" (author's translation); W. Frenz, *Europëisches Umweltrecht* (Munich, 1997), para. 138.

[41] Case C-2/90 *Commission v. Belgium* [1992] E.C.R. I-4431.

from other Member States were treated differently from regional waste. The Court found no discrimination in this case.[42]

The judgment was given under the 1987 version of Article 174 (ex 130r), which referred to Community action rather than to Community policy. Under that provision it could be argued that the principles of Article 174 referrred to individual measures. By contrast, the present wording of that Article considers the Community policy as a whole; it does not require that each individual Community measure take into account all the principles of Article 174(2.2). Requesting that the principles of Article 174 apply to each individual Community measure would mean that numerous measures would contradict (for instance) the polluter-pays principle, since they do not contain any provision about it.[43]

Even where the principles of Article 174 are seen as general guidelines for Community policy they have some indirect legal significance. They place an obligation on the Community to base its policy on these principles and to plan policy and measures accordingly. Moreover, observance of these principles can play an important part in deciding, case by case, whether the objectives of Article 174(1) cannot be sufficiently achieved by the Member States and are therefore capable of being better achieved by the Community (subsidiarity, E.C. Treaty, Art. 5). Where, for instance, the Community takes a measure on environmental liability, it could invoke the prevention and the polluter-pays principle to justify the Community action, under subsidiarity auspices; this example shows at the same time the limited usefulness of the principles, since Member States which oppose the measure could argue that the subsidiarity principle would not allow action to be taken at Community level.

The principles could also be used to justify the chosen legal basis—Article 95 (ex 100a), 175 (ex 130s) or another provision—for a specific measure and its content[44] and to interpret secondary Community legislation.

(b) Subsidiarity

1—19 The subsidiarity principle,[45] which is now laid down in Article 5 (ex 3b) E.C.,[46] was first inserted in 1987 into the E.C. Treaty, but in a different version[47] and limited to environmental matters. The Maastricht Treaty 1992 repealed that provision and inserted a new Article 3b into the Treaty. The Amsterdam Treaty 1997 added to

---

[42] *Ibid.*, para. 34: ". . . in order to determine whether the obstacle in question is discriminatory, the particular type of waste must be taken into account. The principle that environmental damage should as a priority be rectified at source—a principle laid down by Article 174(2) (ex 130r(2)) E.C. for action by the Community relating to the environment—means that it is for each region, commune or other local entity to take appropriate measures to receive, process and dispose of its own waste . . ." See also cases C-157/96 *R. v. Min. of Agriculture* [1998] E.C.R. I-2211 and C-180/96 *United Kingdom v. Commission* [1998] E.C.R. I-2265, where the Court interpreted the preventative principle.

[43] The judgment in case C-2/90 (n. 41 above) seems to have been influenced by some policy considerations which might explain some inconsistencies: the principle of Art. 174(2.2) was applied to a national measure, although the Article refers to Community policy; the Court did not examine whether the Belgian measure was proportional; the Court transformed the principle into a rule of law; it also justified its findings by reference to the Basel Convention on the shipment of hazardous waste, although the Community was, at the time of the judgment, not a member of that Convention, etc.

[44] See for the integration principle of Art. 6, case C-62/88 *European Parliament v. Council* [1990] E.C.R. I-1527: "[the integration requirement which] reflects the principle whereby all Community measures must satisfy the requirements of environmental protection, implies that a Community measure cannot be part of Community action on environmental matters merely because it takes account of these requirements".

[45] See, for this principle in general (without specific reference to the environment), Commission COM (93) 545 of November 29, 1993; COM (94) 533 of November 25, 1994; SEC (95) 580 of November 24, 1995; SEC (96) 2 of June 14, 1996, SEC (96) 7 of November 27, 1996.

[46] See above n. 37.

[47] E.C. Treaty, Art. 130r(4) (1987 version): "The Community shall take action relating to the environment to the extent to which the objectives referred to in paragraph 1 can be attained better at Community level than at the level of the individual Member States."

this, as an annex to the E.C. Treaty, a "Protocol on the application of the principles of subsidiarity and proportionality",[48] where, in 13 detailed points, rules were laid down on subsidiarity and proportionality. The style of this Protocol gives the impression that it was drafted less from the perspective of a European Union, but rather with the aim of containing as far as possible the threat of European integration, thus reducing the amount of power that regional or national administration had up until then.

Article 5 and its Protocol were probably inspired by the old Article 130r(4) and a preceding draft from the European Parliament on a general Treaty on European Union[49]; it establishes a general rule for all Community activity, including the environment. It is not a rule of competence but a principle which predetermines the activity of the Community[50] and, as such, has legal force. Community institutions will, when taking action, have to demonstrate for each individual measure that the conditions of Article 5 and its Protocol are actually complied with. They benefit, however, from a large amount of discretion on the question of what content a measure would have.

1—20   The discussion on subsidiarity is ongoing at Community level, in particular since the signature of the Maastricht Treaty, concentrating on the deregulation and simplification of legislation. Though Article 2 (ex B) of the Treaty on European Union provides that the "*acquis communautaire*" is to be maintained in full, political approaches were started in 1992, in the name of subsidiarity, to review existing environmental directives where Member States felt obliged to undertake clean-up investment: this discussion has been particularly intense in the water sector. In contrast to that there is hardly ever a discussion on subsidiarity when questions of Community funding for economically weaker regions are in question, where measures are considered which improve the competitivity of Community economic operators or where financial assistance for small and medium-sized enterprises is discussed.

For the environment, much depends on the interpretation given to the requirement that the objective of environmental protection cannot be sufficiently achieved by Member States and can thus be better achieved at Community level. Probably the best illustration of the practical difficulties is the discussion in the Economic and Social Committee on the proposal for Directive 96/61 on integrated prevention and pollution control.[51] The Committee discussed the pros and cons of fixing Community-wide emission limit values for industrial installations and concluded: "the subsidiarity principle, properly understood, is not inconsistent with the establishment of limit values at European level. The high level of protection in the Community called for in the E.C. Treaty can only be achieved if European limit values are set." A minority view of the Committee (eight members) stated in contrast to that: "the subsidiarity principle, properly understood, is consistent with the establishment of limit values at Member State level. The high level of protection in the Community called for in the E.U. Treaty can only be achieved if Member State limit values are set and implemented."[52]

1—21   It is not easy to establish general rules to show when environmental policy objectives can be better attained at Community level. Member States with an active environmental policy of their own may well think that measures at the level of individual Member States are a better solution. At present, there is a wide gulf between the individual Member States' national environmental policies and regulations. Member States such as Denmark, the Netherlands, Sweden, Austria and Germany are far more convinced of the need for environmental protection measures than, for

---

[48] [1997] O.J. C340/105.
[49] [1984] O.J. C77/33, Arts 55 and 59.
[50] See also Commission SEC (92) 1990 of October 27, 1992.
[51] For this Dir. see para. 4–16.
[52] [1995] O.J. C195/54 and App. II.

instance, Greece, Spain, Portugal or Italy. In some Member States environmental legislation often consists of not much more than the transposition of measures which had previously been adopted at Community level. Consequently, action at Community level is often a means of ensuring that environmental measures are taken in all 15 Member States. If, instead, it were left to the Member States to take action, generally speaking it could not be ensured that all 15 Member States would adopt the provisions. Even if they did, concepts, content and timing would rarely coincide. Where Member States take action at different times, there is once again a danger for the Community as a whole of imbalances, distortions of competition and of trade patterns, the creation of new barriers to trade, etc. Furthermore, river and sea water, air pollution, protection of fauna and flora species, climate issues, ozone layer protection, acidification, eutrophication and the management of products which have finished their useful lifetime (waste) cannot seriously be tackled at national level alone. In such cases the efforts of one Member State would easily be frustrated by the passivity of another Member State. This also would have an effect on the location of industrial undertakings, employment and quality of life, for example. Therefore, the objectives of Article 174(1) can be attained faster and more effectively by and within the entire Community, *i.e.* for the Community ecosystem as a whole.

Furthermore, it must be borne in mind that some Member States find it difficult, if not impossible, to conceive and implement measures to provide effective protection for the environment in general, and for fauna and flora in particular, since environmental protection measures are perceived as slowing down economic development. The negative effects of environmental impairment normally become more visible and therefore also politically more relevant when economic development is sufficiently advanced. Poverty is the biggest environmental pollutant; in Western Europe there is an element of economic divide between the north and the south (or the Cohesion Fund countries) to which countries of Central and Eastern Europe will have to be added shortly. In southern parts of the Community environmental awareness and readiness to act are distinctly less prevalent. Community discussions on where environmental protection can be better achieved may not leave these considerations aside, although they often occur less in Germany or the United Kingdom.

1—22   Precisely what "better" means in Article 5 is not at all clear; it could mean quicker, more effective, cheaper, more efficient, closer to the citizen (*i.e.* not too centralised), more democratic, more uniform, more consistent with measures in other parts of the industrialised world, or the global or the European Community, without these concepts being more precise. It will, therefore, have to be decided on a case-by-case basis, considering all the facts, whether or not it is better to take measures at Community level to attain the Community's environmental objectives. The aim must be to protect and improve the quality of the environment in the whole Community. Due consideration must be given to the differences in the Member States' environmental legislation, the differing awareness of environmental issues, the environmental infrastructure in Member States, the risk that national protection measures might be differently timed or formulated, the danger of relocating industrial undertakings to countries with lower standards, the possible deflection of trade and the potential changes in the competitive position within the Community and of the Community towards non-E.C. countries. The main concern is to improve the quality of the environment, to reach a high level of protection and to ensure sustainable development over the broadest possible area.

Article 5 mentions the scale or effects of the proposed action as examples where objectives can be better achieved at Community level. The 1997 Protocol also lists as "guidelines" that, where an issue has transnational aspects, actions by Member States alone would conflict with the requirements of the Treaty or "would otherwise significantly damage Member States' interests and that Community action would produce clear benefits by reason of scale or effects". The reference to Member States' interests conveniently ignores the fact that the E.C. Treaty also contains the concept of "general interest of the Community".[53]

1—23   If one tries to apply all these theoretical issues to the debate as to whether there should be Community legislation on environmental liability, the following aspects would have to be considered: there is legislation on liability in all Member States, but this differs as to questions of liability for negligence or strict liability, burden of proof, protected assets and damages; there are differences as to the application of these provisions to environmental damage; environmental damage is differently defined; *locus standi* varies; the number of cases decided by courts varies considerably among Member States; costs for economic operators are likely to increase, *e.g.* over insurance premiums; the environmental problem is not one of accidental pollution, but the progressive accumulation of pollutants in the environment; many an impairment is caused by a multitude of polluters, not by a single one; where an economic operator respects existing legislation, he should not be liable for environmental impairment, and so on. At the end of such a list, the question of whether there should be Community legislation on liability for damage to the environment or not and what content such legislation should have, is a political one, not a legal one of subsidiarity.

There are many other examples: why should, under subsidiarity auspices, the Community be competent to ban the import of furs from third countries which do not prohibit leg-hold traps but not be competent to stop bullfighting, foxhunting or cockfighting? Why should there be common measures on smog in urban zones, but not on the quality of bathing water in public swimming pools?

It is submitted that at the end of almost any discussion on a specific topic, the lawyer is placed in an inferior position behind the policy-maker and he has to weigh political, economic, social cultural, legal and environmental aspects as best he can: his decision usually remains a political decision.

(c) Integration

1—24   The present Article 6 (ex 3c) E.C.[54] had antecedents in the environmental chapter of the E.C. Treaty: the 1987 version of Article 174 (ex 130r) contained a clause on integration,[55] which was formulated in such a way that it could, using the Court of Justice's doctrine of direct effect, be applied directly. The clause was considered both too precise and too vague and was therefore replaced by a phrase that was similar to the one used now in Article 6.[56] As it was felt that some other Community policies did not sufficiently integrate environmental considerations into their policies and measures, the discussion prior to the Amsterdam Treaty on European Union focused on the request to incorporate into the chapters on agriculture, transport, competition and so on, a reference to environmental considerations. This led to the removal and slight reformulation of the provision to the present Article 6.[57]

The provision states that environmental considerations be fully taken into account

---

[53] E.C. Treaty, Art. 213 (ex 157).

[54] See n. 29.

[55] Art. 130r(2.2.) E.C. (1987 version): "Environmental protection requirements shall be a component of the Community's other policies."

[56] Art. 130r(2.3) E.C. (1993 version): "Environmental protection requirements must be integrated into the definition and implementation of other Community policies."

[57] See also Arts 151 (culture), 152 (public health) and 153(2) (consumer protection), which also contain a requirement of integration, but where this requirement was not deplaced to the first chapter of the E.C. Treaty.

in the elaboration and implementation of other Community policies. It is based on the concept that environmental requirements and, subsequently, environmental policy cannot be seen as an isolated green policy which groups specific actions on the protection of water, air, soil, fauna and flora. Rather, the environment is affected by other policies such as transport, energy and agriculture, for example. Article 6 therefore calls for a permanent, continuous "greening" of all Community policies. As mentioned above, though, Article 6 does not allow priority to be given to environmental requirements over other requirements; rather, the different objectives of the E.C. Treaty rank at the same level and the policy must endeavour to achieve all of them.

"Community policies and activities" referred to are the different policies listed in Article 3. They include all activities of the Community under the E.C. Treaty. Measures which come under the Treaty on European Union—foreign and security policy, provisions on police and judicial co-operation in criminal matters—are not covered by Article 6. Policies under the EURATOM Treaty are not included either, as the EURATOM Treaty, essentially a Treaty to promote the use of nuclear energy, is not mentioned in Article 6. The reference to "energy activities" in Article 3 of the E.C. Treaty does not really remedy this situation, since it allows specific measures in the energy sector without changing the Community responsibilities under the EURATOM Treaty.

1—25 In my opinion the Community has spent, from the beginning, too much Community money on nuclear energy in relation to renewable energy. Article 6 would allow a reversal of this policy, if the political will existed to promote renewable energies. Again, this is a question of policy, not of law: there is no legal obligation to invest an increased sum into the promotion of renewable energies.

"Environmental protection requirements" are first of all the different objectives laid down in Articles 2 and 174(1) (ex 130r(1)). Thus, the objectives of ensuring a sustainable development, of preserving, protecting and improving the quality of the environment shall also have to be considered within the framework of other policies. The principles laid down in Article 174(2.2) also form part of environmental protection requirements. Indeed, it does not make sense to apply the precautionary principle, under the environmental policy, and take action without the lastest scientific evidence of a substance's harmfulness and then take the opposite approach in the context of the internal market policy.

The Court of Justice reached the same conclusion when applying the principle of preventive action of Article 174(2) (ex 130r(2)) to the BSE ("mad cow disease") case, which had no relationship whatsoever with environmental protection issues.[58]

In the same way it would be contradictory to provide for preventive measures in environmental policy, but not to do so in other policies, thus limiting Community action to remedial measures which try to repair the environmental damage. Indeed, the greatest damage to the environment is caused by transport, agriculture, energy, industrial development and other policies, not by measures taken within the framework of environmental policy.

1—26 Indeed, the whole debate on how to classify a specific Community measure

---

[58] Cases C-157/96 R. v. Min. of Agriculture [1998] E.C.R. I-2211, paras 63–64; C-180/96 United Kingdom v. Commission [1998] E.C.R. I-2265, paras 99–100: "Where there is uncertainty as to the existence or extent of risks to human health, the institutions may take protective measures without having to wait until the reality and seriousness of those risks become fully apparent. That approach is borne out by Article 130r(1) of the E.C. Treaty, according to which Community policy on the environment is to pursue the objective *inter alia* of protecting human health. Article 130r(2) provides that that policy is to be based in particular on the principles that preventive action should be taken and that environmental protection requirements must be integrated into the definition and implementation of other Community policies."

is rather futile: whether the protection of waters from nitrates of an agricultural source, is a measure of agricultural or environmental policy should not have any influence over the principles which are taken into consideration. The same applies to a ban on asbestos fibres, the use of phthalates, pollution-abatement measures for cars, fuel or installations (*i.e.* plants). It seems rather old-fashioned to classify a specific measure as belonging to a specifiy policy, and Article 6 contributes to progressively overcoming this artificiality. Therefore, its interpretation is wide: wherever a measure is taken under the E.C. Treaty, full consideration should be given to protecting the environment.

This wide interpretation should not let us forget that environmental requirements should be taken into consideration at the formulation and implementation of policies, not of individual measures: it is true, however, that a specific policy is "implemented" by individual measures. It is therefore doubtful whether each individual measure in the internal market, agriculture or transport policy should take into consideration the environmental requirements. In any case, Community institutions have a very broad discretion in putting the principle of Article 6 into practice. Since Article 6, in contrast to its 1987 version, no longer states a fact but rather propounds the necessity of procedure for Community policy, its application in practice will depend almost entirely on the political will of Community institutions to make this provision operational. Again, only in extreme cases could it be argued that Community policies do not take into account environmental protection requirements in their definition and implementation. Normally, the wide discretion which is available under Article 6 would not make such an action successful.

To give some examples: to what extent transport policy promotes a European network of high-speed trains is a question for or against which a number of environmental and other arguments can be raised. The promotion of biomass for fuel by agricultural policy would save fossil fuels, but would at the same time promote monocultures, large-scale use of pesticides and reduce biodiversity. The integration requirement of Article 6 does not provide a useful answer to this question. Other examples are provisions to ban aeroplane flights at night, decommissioning of used platforms at sea, development of an electrical windpark in or next to a natural habitat, requirement for an environment impact assessment in all cases where a project is co-financed with Community funds, and so on. The question to what extent such measures are to be realised is in all these cases of a political, not a legal nature.

(d) Precautionary principle

1—27   The precautionary principle was inserted into Article 174(2) (ex 130r(2)) E.C. in 1993, while the prevention principle had already been present in the Treaty since 1987. Origin and content of the precautionary principle are unclear. Since no definition exists in the Treaty, the principle is open to broad interpretation. The Convention on the protection of the marine environment in the North-East Atlantic (OSPAR), to which the Community adhered,[59] describes the precautionary principle as a principle "by virtue of which preventive measures are taken when there are reasonable grounds for concern that substances or energy introduced directly or indirectly into the environment may bring about damage to human health, harm living resources, . . . even where there is no conclusive evidence of a causal relationship between the inputs and effects". The principle was mentioned in the Declaration of the United Nations Conference in Rio

---

[59] Dec. 98/249 [1998] O.J. L104/1.

de Janeiro in 1992[60] and increasingly it is understood to justify Community measures even in cases where scientific research has not yet fully shown the cause of the environmental impairment.

An example is the taking of measures to ban or restrict the circulation of substances or products such as asbestos, cadmium and phthalates: under Regulation 793/93,[61] economic operators ask that for each of these products a risk assessment be made to find out whether the environmental and human risk justifies restrictions. Applying the precautionary principle would mean that Community measures can be taken without waiting for such a risk assessment, which all too often takes a long time, is inconclusive or is interpreted differently as to the results. Another example is climate change: the Community adhered to the United Nations' Convention on Climate Change which undertakes to combat global warming, while the latest scientific evidence of manmade global warming—at least in the eyes of some—still lacks absoluteness.

1—28 Sometimes it is argued that the adoption of the precautionary principle requires a scientific assessment of risks.[62] This argument seems to stem more from political efforts to reduce the field of application of this principle as far as possible; indeed, Article 174(2) does not contain any such condition and the above-mentioned examples show the political character of these arguments: if for precautionary measures a scientific risk assessment is necessary, it would be necessary for any measure.

Similar considerations apply to other requests to limiting the application of the precautionary principle to cases where there is the possibility of an extreme, irreversible hazard, where there is a need to adopt measures urgently or to limit it to provisional measures only. None of these conditions are found in Article 174(2), which demonstrates the political rather than legal character of these arguments.

(e) Prevention principle

1—29 It is unclear to what extent the prevention principle has content independent from the precautionary principle, although the history of the principles' insertion into the E.C. Treaty suggests there is none. There seems to be no Community action which would be possible under the precautionary principle, but not under the prevention principle—and vice versa. Since both principles are, in practice, almost always used together and there is no definition for either of them in the E.C. Treaty, the added legal value of one to the other is not visible; therefore, they should be used synonymously.[63]

The precautionary/preventive action principle is of overriding importance in every serious environmental policy, since it allows or requires action to be taken at an early stage. Measures are no longer primarily meant to repair damage or impairment after it has occurred: instead, measures are to be taken earlier, to prevent impairment or damage occurring. This also makes economic sense since it is normally far more costly

---

[60] P. Sands, R. Tarasofsky and M.Weiss (eds), *Documents in international environmental law* (Manchester and New York, 1994), Vol. II, App. 49: Rio de Janeiro Declaration on Environment and Development, June 16, 1992, Principle 15 "In order to protect the environment, the precautionary approach shall be widely applied by States according to their capabilities. Where there are threats of serious or irreversible damages, lack of full scientific certainty shall not be used as a reason for postponing cost-effective measures to prevent environmental degradation."

[61] See in detail paras 6–27 *et seq.*

[62] See, *e.g.* Dir. 1999/39 on baby food [1999] O.J. L124/8, 4th considerant: "Whereas, taking into account the Community's international obligations, in cases where the relevant scientific evidence is insufficient, the precautionary principle allows the Community to provisionally adopt measures on the basis of available pertinent information, pending an additional assessment of risk and a review of the measure within a reasonable period of time."

[63] See also cases C-157/96 and C-180/96 (n. 58 above) where the Court based its reasoning that in order to combat the BSE disease, full evidence of the extent and seriousness of a risk was not required in order to take action on the prevention principle, not on the precautionary principle.

to clean up or remedy impairment after it has occurred—if any remedy is possible at all. Article 174(2) does not specify which form the preventive action should take: it is probably "better" to produce goods without cadmium, but should the existing, cadmium-containing batteries, crates, window frames, etc., be recycled or burnt with energy recovery or landfilled? No answer can be found in the prevention/precautionary principle.

(f) Rectification of damage at source

1—30   The principle that environmental damage[64] should, as a priority, be rectified at source was inserted into the Treaty in 1987. It represents wishful thinking rather than reality. Indeed, rectified environmental damage from cars—air pollution, land use, noise, traffic congestion, waste generation, etc.—at source would mean that cars would have to be abolished or at the very least absolute priority be given to public transport, the price of fuel be increased in order to reduce the use of cars, restrictions on the making of cars—maximum fuel consumption, maximum speed and so on—be imposed or other measures taken. This would have implications on production, employment and investments for which no country in the world seems to be prepared. The present technology of catalytic converters for cars is clearly an end-of-the-pipe technology but it is not seriously challenged. Similar examples could easily be given for measures regarding climate change, waste generation, forest decline, acidification or marine pollution.

It is not clear what "rectified" means. Certainly, as in all other cases, Community institutions have a large discretion as to what measures they wish to take, and the time-span and content these measures would take. Since environmental damage (impairment) often cannot really be completely rectified, it must be up to the legislature to decide how the damage (impairment), once it has occurred, can be minimised and further damage (impairment) be prevented.

As mentioned above at paragraph 1–18, the Court of Justice has justified a regional import ban for waste amongst other arguments with this principle, which leads, in the Court's opinion, to the necessity of disposing of waste as close to the place of waste generation as possible. In a similar case, the Court of Justice declared a German provision which required that the disposal of waste take place in Germany, which was compatible with the Treaty since it "reflects the pursuit of an objective which is in conformity with the principle laid down in Article 130r(2) of the Treaty that environmental damage should, as a principle, be rectified at source".[65]

1—31   As stated, the judgment in the first case seems more motivated by considerations about the division of responsibilities between the Community and Member States. It seems impossible to define a legal rule of the precision "waste shall be disposed at the closest possible place" for the principle that is here discussed. In legal literature, there remains the question over whether the principle of rectifying damage at source does not lead the Community being required, in future, to adopt, as a priority, emission limit values rather than to adopt or favour quality standards.[66] Community practice, certainly as regards air and water pollution, prefers quality standards.[67] This tendency has been more pronouncd since 1991–1992, when the

---

[64] About half of the linguistic versions of the Treaty use the word "damage", the other half "impairment".
[65] Case C-422/92 *Commission v. Germany* [1995] E.C.R. I-1097; the judgment was given when Community secondary law did not then contain a provision which allowed Member States to generally export or import wastes for disposal. The judgment therefore dealt only with primary law.
[66] H. Sevenster, *Milieubeleid en Gemeenschapsrecht* (Deventer, 1992), p. 111; J. Jans, *European environmental law* (The Hague, London and Boston, 1995), p. 22.
[67] See below, paras 7–01 and 8–01.

Community debate on deregulation, subsidiarity and flexibility started. Using the same reasoning as in the two waste judgments mentioned above, the Court of Justice could state, in conformity with the legal opinion mentioned, that the principle of rectification at source required Community legislation to be based mainly on emission standards. Also, the Court could come to the conclusion that the catalytic converter approach, which Community law had adopted to minimise car emissions, was not compatible with this principle and that cars and fuel had to be developed that generate fewer pollutants. These examples demonstrate how far the reasoning can go where the principles of Article 174(2) are turned into legal rules—leaving aside the point that at best they only constitute legal rules for the Community not for national or regional provisions.

The conclusion is that this principle well provides for Community provisions to be established which deal with import or export bans on waste, but it does not contain such provisions itself. The principle allows Community emission limit values to be preferred over quality standards, but it does not require that such an approach be taken: a ban on waste exports to developing countries[68] may be supported by this principle, but the principle does not require such a ban to be pronounced. No Member State could bring the Council before the European Court if the Council were adopting other measures; and it may be added that no Member State would have been entitled, in the absence of a Council measure on the export ban, to pronounce such an export ban unilaterally.

(g) Polluter-pays principle

1—32　This principle was introduced into the Treaty in 1987, though it has existed at Community level since 1973.[69] Its linguistic versions are quite different: while the English version states "the polluter should pay", there are six versions which affirm "the polluter pays" and the German text talks of the principle of causation. As all versions are of equal value and the principle, as for any other notion of Community law, must be interpreted autonomously by virtue of Community law and without recourse to national interpretations,[70] its content is difficult to determine: what is a polluter? A person who contaminates the environment or a person who exceeds existing limit values? Is a car driver a polluter, the car manufacturer or the producer or importer of the fuel? Furthermore, who is to pay (or should do) for emissions or damage caused? What about damage in another Member State or in a third country? Should car drivers also pay for the construction of roads? How much should be paid? Is an investment in cleaner technologies also a payment?

The questions demonstrate that the polluter-pays principle was originally an economic principle and was understood as expressing the concept that the cost of environmental impairment, damage and clean-up should not be borne via taxes by society, but that the person who caused the pollution should bear the cost. Its transfer to the E.C. Treaty has led to all sorts of anomalies which have not much to do with law. First, hardly any Community text contains provisions on who shall pay for what or any other provision which puts the polluter-pays principle into practice: if the principle were legally binding and enforceable, this would be a systematic omission that could hardly be tolerated; however, no one has as yet claimed damages from such provisions.

1—33　Secondly, if the polluter and not the taxpayer had to pay for pollution, subventions and state aids would not be in line with this principle and would have to be

---

[68] Example given by P. Pagh, *E.U.-Miljoeret* (2nd ed., Copenhagen, 1996), p. 81.
[69] Recommendation 75/436 (n. 18).
[70] See Case C-72/95 *Kraaijeveld* [1996] E.C.R. I-5403.

deleted. However, Community measures have from the very beginning accepted that undertakings and other economic operators may receive state aid and have set up general rules for such aid.[71] The same applies to Community environmental aid, which is given to Member States under the Structural Funds, the Cohesion Fund, LIFE and other budgetary titles. If the polluter-pays principle were a legally binding principle, the Cohesion Fund would certainly be partly incompatible with it[72] since it also finances clean-up measures. However, no legal writer has ever claimed any enforcement of the polluter-pays principle with regard to state aids.

In reality, in all Member States and at Community level the clean-up of the environment is seen as a task for public authorities which exists independently from the question of whether a polluter can be identified and asked to pay for pollution. Such an identification is practically impossible in cases of groundwater or coastal water pollution, forest decline, soil erosion, desertification, climate change, smog in urban areas and numerous pollution from past activities. Public authorities are thus the only ones to ensure a clean-up or to take other remedial or preventive measures to stop contamination continuing. It is not unconceivable that this practice be considered as incompatible with the polluter-pays principle.

Therefore, on the whole, the polluter-pays principle allows Community institutions to adopt measures which charge persons who cause environmental pollution to bear the cost of pollution; however, this was already available to Community institutions in order to attain the objectives of Article 174(1) of the E.C. Treaty.

6. CONDITIONS FOR ACTION

(a) General remarks

1—34   Article 174(3) (ex 130r(4)) lists a number of conditions which Community environmental policy should take into account. This obligation refers to the policy as a whole, not to each individual measure adopted at Community level. The addressee of the provision is all Community institutions. The words "taken into account" indicate that the paragraph does not contain preconditions for Community actions, which is further clarified by the fact that no details are given as to which condition is to be attained, which level of regional development requires action (or derogations) nor what data would be needed for action. No other sector of Community policy has such conditions laid down in the Treaty.

In Community practice, the four conditions only play a subordinate role. They are rarely mentioned in the preamble of legal texts; references to them are slightly more frequent in explanatory memorandums for legislative proposals. Their legal impact is hardly measurable except for the cost-benefit condition, which is used by economic operators to object to measures that would internalise the environmental costs or make the polluter pay.

(b) Available scientific data

1—35   This criterion states the obvious: it only requires that account be taken of the available data. The Community need not even order its own studies before shaping its policy or take individual measures, but may simply draw on the available data. Nor is there any need to give scientific evidence that a specific measure would be effective,

---

[71] See Rec. 75/436 (n. 18).
[72] See Reg. 1164/94 establishing a Cohesion Fund [1994] O.J. L130/1, Art. 3: "[The Fund may provide assistance for] projects resulting from measures adopted pursuant to Article 130s of the Treaty."

which is not really possible in any case. In particular, the precautionary/prevention principle allows action without definite scientific proof being available. This principle would lose much of its force if unequivocal data had to be produced before any measure could be taken.

In 1990, the European Environmental Agency was set up.[73] It is located in Copenhagen and has been operational since the end of 1993. The Agency has the task to collect, process and distribute data on the environment in order to improve knowledge of scientific and technical data. The Agency is assisted by Topic Centres on specific subjects—air, water, fauna and flora, for example—which are located in different Member States and assemble data on their specific topic. The Agency also has the task of publishing a report, at regular intervals, on the state of the Community environment.[74]

(c) Regional conditions

1—36   The provision that the environmental conditions in the various regions of the Community be taken into account is a reminder that the environment within the Community is by no means uniform, but that geographical, climatic, soil, water and other conditions vary greatly from one area to another. The provision does not require more the taking into account of divergency: for this reason some Community legislation contains specific derogations whilst other does not. Where derogations are given, they are never directly applied to a specific region, but instead to a specific Member State,[75] which well reflects the small direct influence that regions have in the decision-making procedure. Instead of giving a direct derogation for a region (a Member State), Community legislation may provide for indirect derogations, *e.g.* for less sensitive areas, for mountainous areas or small islands.

(d) Potential benefits and charges

1—37   This condition reads "advantages and charges of action or lack of action" in all Community languages except English, because it was thought, in 1987 when the provision was inserted, that "costs and benefits" were equivalent to "advantages and charges". This is obviously not the case, at least not in the political debate, where discussion on the advantages and disadvantages of Community environmental measures has been reduced, *de facto*, to the economic costs and benefits of a measure. Also since economists have, up until now, not yet developed a standardised method of how to calculate in monetary terms the environmental benefits of a measure, this debate is all too often reduced to the question of how much the envisaged measure will cost trade and industry. This development has been particularly evident in Community activity since the early 1990s and more specifically in the measures to combat air pollution in the transport sector, where the Commission justified a number of derogations with nothing more than the argument that they were not "cost-effective".

The advantages–charges factor suggests that the full range of short, medium and

---

[73] Reg. 1210/90 on the establishment of the European Environment Agency and the European environment information and observation network [1990] O.J. L120/1.

[74] So far, the Community has published six reports on the state of the environment: *State of the environment*, First Report (Brussels, Luxembourg, 1977); *State of the environment*, Second Report (Brussels and Luxembourg, 1979), *The state of the environment in the EEC* (Luxembourg, 1986); *The state of the environment in the European Community*, COM (92) 23, Vol. III of April 3, 1992; *European Environmental Agency: Environment in the European Union* (Copenhagen, 1995) *European Environmental Agency: Environment in the European Union at the turn of the century* (Luxembourg, 1999).

[75] Examples: Dir. 88/609 on large combustion plants (1988) where Spain, Portugal and Greece obtained special derogations; see also para. 8–37; Dir. 94/62 on packaging and packaging waste [1994] O.J. L365/10 where Greece, Portugal and Ireland obtained derogations; see also para. 9–49.

long-term measures be considered in an attempt to assess the effect of taking action or failing to do so. This consideration is not to be limited to economic aspects, but has to include social, employment, ecological, human and other aspects. At the end of this appraisal, if doubts still persist as to whether the measures will be sufficiently effective, the preventive action principle comes into play and, furthermore, the express mandate that the Community not only preserve but also improve the quality of the environment.

The provision gives no details of the ways and means of taking account of the potential charges and advantages. In this respect, the political resolutions adopted by the Council and the decisions on the Community environmental action programmes under Article 175(3) (ex 130s(3)) E.C. become of importance: where the Community institutions approved or adopted a programme or a number of actions of environmental measures, this will normally be sufficient proof that according to the best knowledge of the Community institutions the advantages of a specific measure outweigh the disadvantages.

(e) Economic and social development

1—38   The condition on the economic and social development of the Community as a whole and the balanced development of its regions is meant to reflect the less-developed Member States' concern that environmental protection provisions should not be imposed at the expense of economic growth. This criterion is so broadly drafted that it covers practically all economic and social development. Every Community-wide rule inevitably implies a degree of standardisation and harmonisation and cannot, therefore, take account of every individual region. Similarly, the same scientific and technical data which demonstrates a need for action may not be available in every region; however, this cannot be a decisive factor in differentiating. The Community also has the task of ensuring environmental improvement in all parts of the Community, although it is obvious that any specific measure will bring greater advantages for some regions more than others.

The Community institutions must weigh up all these factors and produce an overall assessment. At the end of the day it is up to the Council and the European Parliament to decide to what extent regional differences should lead to specific wording in the final texts adopted at Community level.

Community practice has never taken into consideration the situation of specific regions, but, as already mentioned, has from time to time given derogations to specific Member States—which mainly coincided with the so-called "Cohesion Fund-countries" (Greece, Spain, Portugal, Ireland) that were economically lagging behind. In the area of air pollution, consideration is given to developing the concept of "national emission ceilings", which would fix a certain quantity of allowed pollution emissions per Member State. As can be seen, this concept has little to do with regional differences (which could be very great between Lombardy and Calabria, Catalunya and Estremadura, Essex and Northern Ireland, Hamburg and Thüringen, etc.) but more to do with a certain renationalisation of environmental policy.

BIBLIOGRAPHY

Alonso García, E.: *Derecho ambiental de la Comunidad Europea* (Madrid, 1993), Vols I and II

Aubin, A.: *L'impact du droit communautaire de l'environnement en France* (Nantes, 1995)

Bär, S. and Kraemer, R.: *Amsterdam and the environment* (Berlin, 1997)

Baziadoly, S.: *Le droit communautaire de l'environnement depuis l'Acte Unique européen jusqu'à la Conférence Intergouvernementale* (Brussels, 1996)

Behrens, P. and Koch, H. (eds): *Umweltschutz in der Europäischen Gemeinschaft: Spannungsfelder zwischen nationalem und europäischem Gemeinschaftsrecht* (Baden-Baden, 1991)

Breier, S.: "Die Bedeutung der umweltrechtlichen Querschnittsklausel des Art. 130r Abs.2 S.2 EWG-Vertrag für die Verwirklichung des Europäischen Binnenmarktes", *Natur und Recht* (1992), p. 174

Breier, S.: "Umweltschutz in der Europäischen Gemeinschaft—eine Bestandsaufnahme nach Maastricht", *Natur und Recht* (1993), p. 457

Breuer, R.: *Entwicklungen des europäischen Umweltrechts—Ziele, Wege und Irrwege* (Berlin and New York, 1993)

Brinkhorst, L.: *Subsidiariteit en milieu in de Europese Gemeenschap. Doos van Pandora of Panacee?* (Leiden, 1992)

Burgi, M.: "Das Schutz- und Ursprungsprinzip im europäischen Umweltrecht", *Natur und Recht* (1995), p. 11

Calliess, C.: "Perspektiven für die Weiterentwicklung der Europäischen Union zu einer ökologischen Rechtsgemeinschaft", *Kritische Justiz* (1995), p. 284

Campins i Eritja, M. and Pont i Castejón, I. (eds): *Perspectives de dret comunitari ambiental* (*Bellaterra*, 1997)

Cassese, S. (ed.): *Diritto ambientale communitario* (Milan, 1995)

Cross, G.: "Subsidiarity and the environment", *Yearbook of European Law* (1996), p. 107

Chiti, M.: "Ambiente e "costituzione" europea: alcuni nodi problematici", in S. Grassi, M. Cecchetti and A. Andronio (eds), *Ambiente e diritto* (Milan, 1999), p. 131

Epiney, A.: "Einbeziehung gemeinschaftlicher Umweltschutzprinzipien in die Bestimmung mitgliedstaatlichen Handlungsspielraums", *Deutsches Verwaltungsblatt* (1993), p. 93

Epiney, A.: "Umweltrechtliche Querschnittsklausel und freir Warenverkehr: die Einbeziehung umweltpolitischer Belange über die Beschränkung der Grundfreiheit", *Natur und Recht* (1995), p. 498

Epiney, A.: *Umweltrecht in der Europäischen Union* (Cologne, Berlin, Bonn and Munich, 1997)

Epiney, A. "Die umweltpolitischen Handlungsprinzipien in Art. 130r EGV: politische Leitlinien oder rechtsverbindliche Vorgaben? Zu den Urteilen des EuGH in den Rs C-284/95, C-341/95 (Safety Hi-Tech) vom 14.7.1998", *Natur und Recht* (1999), p. 181

Fernández Sánchez de Gatta, D.: "Politica Ambiental Comunitaria en el Tratado de la Unión Europea", *Revista de Derecho Ambiental* (1994), p. 73

Fischer, K. and Freytag, E.: *Österreich und das Umweltrecht der Europäischen Union* (Vienna, 1995)

Freestone, D. and Somsen, H.: "The impact of subsidiarity" in J. Holder (ed.), *The impact of E.C. environmental law in the United Kingdom* (Chichester, 1997), p. 87

Frenz, W.: *Europäisches Umweltrecht* (Munich, 1997)

Führ, M.: "Von Rio nach Brüssel über 15 europäische Hauptstädte—Entwicklungstendenzen im Europäischen Umweltrecht", *Kritische Vierteljahresschrift für Gesetzgebung und Rechtswissenschaften* (1995), p. 335

García Ureta, A.: "La protección del ambiente a la luz del Tratado de la Unión Europea", *Revista Vasca de Administración Pública* (1992), p. 85

Gellermann, M.: *Beeinflussung des bundesdeutschen Rechts durch Richtlinien der EG—dargestellt am Beispiel des europäischen Umweltrechts* (Cologne, etc., 1994)

Glim, M.: *European environmental legislation, what does it really mean?* (Delft, 1990)

Golub, J. (ed.): *Global competition and E.U. environmental policy* (London, 1998)

Gröpl, C.: "Die Euratom auf dem Weg zu einer Umweltgemeinschaft", *Deutsches Verwaltungs-blatt* (1995), p. 322

Haigh, N., *et al.*: *Manual of environmental policy: the E.C. and Britain* (London) (looseleaf)

Hailbronner, K.: *Umweltrecht und Umweltpolitik in der Europäischen Gemeinschaft* (Linz, 1991)

Hession, M. and Macrory, R.: "Maastricht and the environmental policy of the Community: legal issues of a new environment policy", in D. O'Keeffe and P. Toomey (eds), *Legal issues of the Maastricht Treaty* (London and New York, 1994), p. 151

Holder, J. (ed.): *The impact of E.C. environmental law in the United Kingdom* (Chichester, 1997)

Holder, J.: "Safe science? The precautionary principle in U.K. environmental law" in J. Holder (ed.), *The impact of E.C. environmental law in the United Kingdom* (Chichester, 1997), p. 123

Ingelaere, F., Lavrysen, L. and Vanden Bilcke, C.: *Inleiding to het internationaal en europees milieurecht* (Brussels, 1992)

Jans, J.: *European environmental law* (The Hague, London and Boston, 1995)

Jans, J.: "State aid and Articles 92 and 93 of the E.C. Treaty. Does the polluter pay?" *European Environmental Law Review* (1995), p. 108

Jarass, H.: *Grundfragen der innerstaatlichen Bedeutung des EG-Rechts* (Cologne, Berlin, Bonn and Munich, 1994)

Kahl, W.: *Umweltprinzip und Gemeinschaftsrcht* (Heidelberg, 1993)

Kamminga, M. and Klatte, E.: "Twintig jaar EG milieubeleid en het integratiebeginsel", *Milieu en Recht* (1994), p. 2

Krämer, L.: *Focus on european environmental law* (London, 1992)

Krämer, L.: *European environmental law* (London, 1993)

Krämer, L.: *Focus on european environmental law* (London, 1997)

Krämer, L.: "Grundlagen(Grundfragen) der E.U.-Umweltverfassung, Ziele, Kompetenzen, Durchführung" in N. Reich and R. Heine-Mernik (eds), *Umweltverfassung und nachhaltige Entwicklung in der Europäischen Union* (Baden-Baden, 1997), p. 11

Krämer, L.: "Das 'hohe Schutzniveau' im EG-Vertrag", *Zeitschrift für Umweltrecht* (1997), p. 303;

Krämer, L.: *E.C. treaty and environmental law* (3rd ed., London, 1998)

Lenaerts, K.: "The principle of subsidiarity and the environment in the European Union: keeping the balance of federalism" in F. Abraham, K. Deketelaere and J. Stuyck (eds), *Recent economic and legal developments in European environmental policy* (Leuven, 1995), p. 11

Lübbe-Wolff, G.: "Präventiver Umweltschutz—Auftrag und Grenzen des Vorsorgeprinzips im deutschen und europäischen Recht" in J. Bizer and H. Koch (eds), *Sicherheit, Vielfalt, Solidarität. Ein neues Paradigma des Verfassungsrechts?* (Baden-Baden, 1998), p. 47

Mahmoudi, S.: *E.U.'s miljörätt* (Stockholm, 1995)

Martín Mateo, R.: *Protección del medio ambiente en la Europa de los ciudadones* (Valladolid, 1993)

McIntyre, O.: "Proportionnality and environmental protection in E.C. law" in J. Holder (ed.), *The impact of E.C. environmental law in the United Kingdom* (Chichester, 1997), p. 101

Moench, C.: "Der Einfluß des europäischen Rechts auf das deutsche Umweltrecht", *Kritische Vierteljahreszeitschrift* (1996), p. 214

Mortelmans, K.: *EG-milieuwetgeving* (2nd ed., Deventer, 1993)

Nijman, M.: *Le développement du principe de subsidiarité, avec une étude de cas sur la politique de l'environnemnt dans la Communauté européenne et le principe de subsidiarité* (Amsterdam, 1991)

Pagh, P.: "Unionstraktaten og milioeet", *Juristen* (1992), p. 225

Pagh, P.: *E.U. miljoeret* (2nd ed., Copenhagen, 1996)

Parejo Alfonso, L. and Krämer, L. (eds): *Derecho medioambiental de la Unión Europea* (Madrid, 1996)

Pillitu, P.: *Profili costituzionali della tutela ambientale nell'ordinamento communitario europeo* (Perugia, 1992)

Poostchi, B.: "The 1997 Treaty of Amsterdam—implications for European Union environmental law and policy making", *Review of European Community and International Environmental Law* (1998), p. 76

Rehbinder, E. and Stewart, R.: *Environment protection policy* (Berlin and New York, 1985)

Reich, N.: *Bürgerrechte in der Europäischen Union* (Baden-Baden, 1999)

Reich, N. and Heine-Mernik, R. (eds): *Umweltverfassung und nachhaltige Entwicklung* (Baden-Baden, 1997)

Renaudière, P.: "Le droit communautaire de l'environnement après Maastricht", *Aménagement-environnement* (1992), p. 70

Renaudière, P. and Van Pelt, P. (eds): *Développements récents du droit communautaire de l'environnement* (Diegem, 1995)

Rengeling, H. (ed.): *Handbuch zum europäischen und deutschen Umweltrecht* (Cologne, etc., 1998), Vols I and II

Rengeling, H. and Gellermann, M.: "Gestaltung des europäischen Umweltrechts und seine Implementation im deutschen Rechtsraum", *Jahrbuch des Umwelt- und Technikrechts* (1996), p. 1

Romi, R.: *L'Europe et la protection juridique de l'environnement* (Paris, 1990)

Rossnagel, A.: "Lernfähiges Europarecht—am Beispiel des europäischen Umweltrechts", *Neue Zeitschrift für Verwaltungsrecht* (1997), 122

Sevenster, H.: *Milieubeleid en Gemeenschapsrecht* (Deventer, 1992)

Steinberg, R.: "Probleme der Europäisierung des deutschen Umweltrechts", *Archiv des öfent-lichen Rechts* (1995), p. 549

Stockholm Environmental Institute (ed.): *Study of costs for measures in the environmental area* (Stockholm, 1999)

Thieffry, P.: *Droit européen de l'environnement* (Paris, 1998)

Vacca, M.: *La politica communitaria dell'ambiente e la sua attuazione negli stati membri* (Milan, 1992)

Vandermeersch, D.: "Twintig jaar EG-milieurecht in retrospectief: van casuistiek naar modern beleid?", *Sociaal Economisch Wetgeving* (1992), p. 532

Vohrer, M.(ed.): *Ökologische Marktwirtschaft in Europa* (Baden-Baden, 1992)

Wenzel, B.(ed.): *First Nordic Conference on E.U. environmental law* (Copenhagen, 1994)

Winter, G. (ed.): *European environmental law* (Brookfield (USA), Singapore and Sydney 1995)

Winter, G.: "On the effectiveness of E.C. administration: the case of environmental protection" [1996] C.M.L.R. 689

Zils, H.: *Die Wertigkeit des Umweltschutzes in Beziehung zu anderen Aufgaben der Europäischen Gemeinschaft* (Heidelberg, 1994)

CHAPTER 2
Actors, Instruments, Decision-making Procedures

1. ACTORS

2—01 Community environmental policy is conceived and elaborated by Community institutions, with of course, considerable input from national governments and other national actors. Community institutions contribute in differing degrees to the making of E.C. environmental policy and since Article 249 (ex 189) E.C. provides for legal instruments to carry out the Community tasks in the making of E.C. environmental law. Hereafter, the different actors will be described, followed by the instruments for the making of environmental law and the decision-making procedure.

(a) The European Commission

2—02 The Commission has the following tasks (Article 211 (ex 155) E.C.): to ensure that the provisions of the E.C. Treaty and the measures taken by the institutions pursuant thereto are applied; to formulate opinions and recommendations; to take decisions and "participate in the shaping of measures" where the Treaty so provides; to exercise the powers conferred on it by the Council for the implementation of provisions.

(i) Administrative structures

2—03 The Commission consists of 20 commissioners appointed for five years by the Council[1]: France, United Kingdom, Germany, Italy and Spain have two members, the other, smaller, Member States have one member each.[2] One of the 20 members is appointed President of the Commission and the Commission autonomously divides the general work among its members. Each ordinary member of the Commission has a private office which consists of six members who assist him in his task.

The administrative services of the Commission consist of Directorate-Generals for the different areas (*e.g.* transport, agriculture and information); at present there are some 30 Directorate-Generals, some of which, as for instance the Legal Service, are known as "Services". A General Secretariat organises the daily administration of the Commission and the Directorates-General. A member of the Commission may be responsible for several Directorates-General; conversely, one general directorate may, for different parts of its activity, be under the responsibility of several commissioners. Overall, there is a staff of some 21,000 officials, among whom are a number of national officials on secondment with the Commission for up to three years and persons

---

[1] For details of the procedure see Art. 214 (ex 158) E.C.
[2] This repartition already casts some doubt on the formulation of Art. 213 (ex 157(2)): "The members of the Commission shall, in the general interest of the Community, be completely independent in the performance of their duties. In the performance of their duties, they shall neither seek nor take instructions from any government or from any other body."

employed on a contractual basis.[3] The Commission works in the 11 languages, though in daily practice English and French dominate.

2—04   Environmental matters are mainly, but not exclusively, the responsibility of the Directorate-General for Environment, Nuclear Safety and Civil Protection (XI) which, between 1999 and 2005, is placed under the responsibility of the Swedish member of the Commission, Mrs M. Wallström. The Directorate-General comprises about 460 officials, to which a number of persons on secondment and under contract (overall some 65) have to be added; about half of these officials have a university education.[4] The 1998 budget provides for environmental expenses a sum of 140 million euro,[5] out of which 100 million euro were earmarked for the financial instrument LIFE[6] and 16 million euro as a contribution to the European Environmental Agency. However, these sums only cover the expenses coming under the management of Directorate-General XI. In 1992, the Commission estimated the total Community expenses for the environment at 600 million euro per year.

The structure and working methods of the Commission continue to be considerably affected by the original aim of the E.C. Treaty to organise a common agricultural policy, to open up national markets and to realise the four fundamental freedoms of the E.C. Treaty: free movement of goods and services, capital and labour. Environmental policy, which started in the early 1970s without an express legal basis in the Treaty, was considered an illegitimate child, and this impression only gradually began to disappear when, in 1987, it was "legitimised" by the insertion of an environmental chapter in the Treaty. The Commission's environmental activity, orientated towards achieving the objectives laid down in Articles 2 and 174(1) (ex 130r(1)) E.C., may be structured for the purpose of presentation into activities initiating new measures, activities of management and monitoring activities (monitoring activities will be discussed in detail in Chapter 11).

(ii) Commission initiatives

2—05   Under the Treaty the Commission has the right to initiate new environmental legal measures at Community level. The different environmental action programmes constituted, at least in the past,[7] a frame for initiatives, but never put limits on them. However, numerous proposals for directives or regulations which were made had never been previously announced by an environmental action programme, and initiatives which the action programmes announced were not necessarily presented. The action programmes are completed by annual working programmes which the Commission publishes every year: the published version, however, only contains the most important, new activities. Furthermore, each member of the Commission may

---

[3] Budget 1998 for the European Union [1998] O.J. L44/1 at 129.

[4] These figures may be compared to those of national environmental administration (quoted from C. Demmke, *Europäische Umweltpolitik und Nationale Verwaltungen* (Maastricht, 1998), p. 98 who collected the data from national departments): Belgium 41 (at central level), Denmark 100 (plus 1,000 in the Environmental Agency), Germany 780 (plus 1,820 in the Environmental Agency), Greece 250, Spain 500, France 2,300 (plus 6,000 in the Environmental Agencies), Ireland 480 (plus 327 in the Environmental Agency), Italy 450 (plus 5,220 in the Environmental Agencies), Netherlands 1,000, Austria 300 (plus 230 in the Environmental Agency), Portugal 3,500, Finland 300 (plus 500 in the Environmental Agency), Sweden 130 (plus 750 in the Environmental Agency), United Kingdom 3,700 (plus 2,260 in the Environmental Agency).

[5] European Parliament, Budget 1998 [1998] O.J. L44/1, Chap. B.4–3; the budget for 1999 was €195 million.

[6] Reg. 1973/92 establishing a financial instrument for the environment (LIFE) [1992] O.J. L206/1, amended by Reg. 1404/96 [1996] O.J. L181/1.

[7] Since 1993, Art. 175(3) (ex 130s(3)) E.C. provides that general environmental action programmes are adopted in the form of a decision by the European Parliament and the Council jointly. As yet, no general action programme has been prepared under this provision, though a review of the fifth programme was adopted under this new form [1998] O.J. L275/1.

have for his area of responsibility, a work programme which directs the work of the administrative services. Whether the recent Treaty provisions of Article 192(2) (ex 138b(2)) and 175(3) (ex 130s(3)) E.C. have limited the Commission's right of initiative, will be discussed below.[8]

Next to these general programmes, the Commission submits from time to time action programmes for specific sectors, such as groundwater and climate change, for example, for which the environmental Directorate-General is, as for the general environmental action programme, the file-leading department. These sectoral action programmes, which have considerably increased over the last few years, are sent to the other institutions and regularly followed by resolutions of the European Parliament and the Council, which give their comments as to the activities to be taken up. The Commission is not bound by these resolutions, although they do have considerable political influence. More general communications which the Commission submits are presented as greenbooks, whitebooks, strategy papers or else are given another name, without any specific difference between these communications; normally, they do not provide for specific legislative measures.

In view of Article 6 (ex 3c) E.C., precursors of which have appeared in similar Treaty provisions since 1987, other initiatives in other areas such as agriculture, industrial or regional policy or transport shall take into consideration the environmental require-ments. Initiatives—programmatic initiatives or individual measures—are prepared by the Directorate-General responsible, with generally close participation from the envir-onmental and other interested Directorate-Generals.

2—06   The Commission decides on all drafts as a college (*i.e.* all Commissioners decide on the drafts). In view of the shortage of staff in all its departments and the often considerable size of these (agriculture, industry, foreign trade and competition) it remains only theoretical that a proposal, which has been developed for several months or even years by the file-leading department, can still be significantly amended by other departments. The general approach, the structure and most of the detailed provisions are *de facto* carried in the form proposed by the file-leading department and are only in exceptional cases brought into question at the political level of the Commission. The shortage of staff thus makes it extremely difficult to integrate environmental require-ments into other policies on an everyday basis. Indeed, identifying the specific envir-onmental interest in the numerous discussions and preparatory meetings for decisions inside the Commission requires time and effort, which the present Directorate-General for the environment is not able to perform.

In order to improve the integration of environmental requirements within its own administration, the Commission adopted internal rules in 1993,[9] which were revised in 1997 and provide for the following: all Commission proposals shall be checked for their environmental impact; where such impact is likely, an environmental impact assessment is to be made; proposals for new legal provisions should describe and assess environmental effects and costs; the annual working programme shall take note of those planned measures which are likely to have significant environmental effects; all relevant departments shall designate contact points for integrating environmental requirements. In some departments environmental units were created; an environmen-tal network of Director-Generals was created, chaired by the Director-General for the Environment and responsible for general co-ordination between the environment and other policies; Directorate-General XI created a specific administrative unit which is in

---

[8] Para. 2–21.
[9] Written Question E-649/97 (Díez de Rivera Icaza) [1997] O.J. C367/33. The rules and their revision are not published.

charge of integrating the environment into other policies; the Commission's annual report, set up under Article 212 (ex 156) E.C. now indicates which environmental aspects have been considered in the relevant policies and what measures have been taken to make the Commission's budget more environmentally aware.

2—07 Initiatives for new legislative measures come from all sources. Council and European Parliament may, via resolutions, ask for this or that new proposal and the Council may, during the debate over or adoption of a measure, request another measure to be proposed or an existing measure to be amended. The Commissioner responsible for the environment may wish a given new proposal to be developed or the environmental Directorate-General may take the initiative. From outside the Community institutions, the initiative for action might be suggested by Member States or it might stem from international activities such as existing or new environmental conventions, or be proposed by lobby groups, researchers, environmental organisations or have other origins. In all cases, however, the college of the Commission will have to formally decide on a text which is submitted to it by its administration before there can be any question of a Commission initiative.

(iii) Administrative activities

2—08 The Commission's task to initiate new policies, strategies and individual measures is perceived as their most important aim: managing activity clearly ranks lower. One of the reasons for this is the express provision in Article 175(4) (ex 130s(4)) E.C., according to which Member States shall, as a rule, implement the measures decided at Community level. Since most of Community environmental legislation is adopted in the form of directives which are addressed to Member States, it is up to Member States to transpose these directives into national law and to ensure that these provisions are properly applied. The Commission has the task of ensuring that Community environmental directives and regulations are properly applied.[10]

Besides this, the Commission has a number of tasks attributed to it by the different environmental directives or regulations, which concern the administering of the "acquis communautaire". These tasks include:

2—09 The collection of national legislation which was adopted in pursuance of the Community provisions. Since Community environmental legislation dates back to the mid-1970s and Member States' legislation is variously amended, renewed, replaced, and often adopted at a regional level,[11] sometimes even refering to non-environmental, more general legislation, the precise knowledge about the state of environmental legislation within the Community is at times difficult to obtain.

2—10 The collection and comparison of national reports on the transposition and implementation of directives and the publication of Community implementation reports. Most of Community environmental directives and regulations provide for Member States to report regularly on the implementation measures adopted (the Commission was required to establish regular Community reports). In view of considerable deficiencies in the national reporting and, subsequently, the Commission's reports, a directive was adopted to streamline and improve the reporting.[12] Until mid-1999, however, this directive has not brought about the desired improvements.

---

[10] See paras 11–01 et seq., below.
[11] Within Member States regions have large responsibilities for legislation on environmental matters, for, e.g. in Austria, Belgium, Spain, Germany, Italy and to a lesser degree, the United Kingdom.
[12] Dir. 91/692 standardising and rationalising reports on the implementation of certain directives relating to the environment [1991] O.J. L377/48.

2—11　The collection and comparison of national clean-up or other plans for specific sectors or plants. Several directives provide for clean-up programmes for regions which are contaminated, where pollutant levels are exceeded or for industrial plants to adapt to new legal requirements. Other directives, such as on waste management or nature protection, provide for management plans. Member States are regularly obliged to send such plans or programmes to the Commission, which shall align and occasionally also compare them in order to obtain greater coherence. The number of directives asking for planning measures seems to have been on the increase since the early 1990s, although planning experience in conjunction with Community environmental law matters is anything but a success story.

2—12　Exchange of experience concerning problems with the application of environmental measures. These comprise environmental directives which regularly ask Member States to plan improvements and clean-up, to promote or impose cleaner technologies and reduce pollutant emissions. Discussion takes place on these questions as well as on how issues such as "best available technologies", licensing, inspection procedures or the interpretation of provisions in a directive are transposed into administrative practice, and furthermore, on co-operation in frontier regions or with administrations of another Member State. Often such exchanges between Member States' administrations are necessary or useful. Such an exchange also allows a transfer of environmental know-how from one administration to the other.

2—13　Information on new scientific and technical developments. Community directives also age over time and might have to be adapted due to scientific and technical developments. Most of this exchange normally takes place in the different committees for adapting directives to scientific and technical progress.

2—14　Elaboration of implementation measures. Directives may require that the Commission deal with forms and formulae, establish lists, registers, collect data, take individual decisions on national derogating measures or other technical measures to ensure a smooth application of the text.

2—15　Administration of funds. The amount of Community funding for environmental measures has considerably increased over the years. These amounts are monitored according to specific regulations which lay out the legal basis for expenditure.[13] The Commission has to collect the national programmes or projects, assess them, select the most appropriate applications and decide on the amount which it grants, assisted in this on a regular basis by a committee made up of representatives from Member States.

2—16　Exchange of data. A number of decisions require that the Commission collect data on air or water pollution and soil contamination, for example. The Commission organises the networks, the co-operation required between different parties and the related practical questions. These tasks are progressively being transferred to the European Environmental Agency which needs, however, assistance from the Commission, certainly in the beginning, combined, if necessary, with formal, binding decisions.

---

[13] See, *e.g.* Reg. 1973/92 on a financial instrument for the environment—LIFE [1992] O.J. L206/1; Reg. 1164/94 establishing a Cohesion Fund [1994] O.J. L130/1.

2—17 Participation in international discussions. Where environmental issues are discussed at international level, the Commission, beyond participation in the elaboration of conventions, etc., represents the Community, co-ordinates and aligns the position of the Member States and tries to ensure that internationally the Community speaks with one voice.

2—18 Information and promotion. The Commission is not an administrative body that can remain distanced from discussions about the organisation of Europe and its environment. It has to inform about the state of the environment, its policy and its individual measures and try to persuade, publicly, in committees or in bilateral meetings, policy-makers, interest groups, environmental organisations, the media and the public of its proposals and the Community's decisions. In so doing it is fulfilling the objective which is outlined in Article 213 (ex 157) E.C.: to promote the general interest of the Community in environmental issues.

(iv) The "satellites"

2—19 During the last decade a number of bodies have been set up to assist the Commission in its work. The most relevant of these are:

- The European Environment Agency, which was created in 1990,[14] but only became operational in 1993 due to Member States' divergencies on its seat. Attempts by the European Parliament also to mandate the Agency with tasks on controlling the application of Community environmental law failed and seem since to have been abandoned. The Agency has the task of collecting, processing and distributing information about the Community environment and publishing at regular intervals a report on the state of the environment. Thus, its advice function is not limited to the Commission, but also extends to the other institutions and to Member States. It is headed by an executive director, who is appointed by the management board; this board is composed of Member States' representatives, two Commission representatives and two scientific experts appointed by the European Parliament. Non-E.C. states, which are members of the Agency, are also represented. The Agency has a staff of about 70 persons.

  When the Agency was created there was much debate between the European Parliament and the Council over whether it should also have functions on enforcing application of Community environmental law. The compromise reached provided that this question should be decided at a later stage. The amendment of the Agency's statute, adopted in 1999, does not contain anything on law enforcement.[15]

- The European Consultative Forum on the environment and sustainable development, set up in 1993 by the Commission and reviewed in 1997,[16] consists of 32 members from business, local and regional authorities, environmental and consumer organisations, trade unions and general environmental experts. These members do not represent their respective organisations and its secretariat is ensured by the Commission. The Forum may be consulted by the Commission on any problem of Community environmental policy; however, own-initiative reports are not envisaged. To date, the impact of the opinions given by the Forum seems to have been rather limited.

---

[14] Reg. 1210/90 on the establishment of the European Environment Agency and the European environment information and observation network [1990] O.J. L120/1.
[15] Reg. 933/1999 amending Reg. 1210/90 [1999] O.J. L117/1.
[16] Dec. 93/701 [1993] O.J. L328/53; Dec. 97/150 [1997] O.J. L58/48.

- IMPEL. The fifth environmental action programme 1992 announced the creation of an implementation network with the primary task of promoting the "exchange of information and experiences and the development of common approaches at practical level, under the supervision of the Commission".[17] This network was set up under the name "IMPEL" by Member States. It is informal, acts as an inter-governmental co-operation network and tries to improve implementation of Community legislation and influence new Commission initiatives.

- The "Environmental Policy Review Group"—also an informal body. Its setting-up was announced by the fifth action programme.[18] It groups high-level officials from national environmental administrations who meet with high officials from the Commission to discuss the conception and shaping of the Commission's environmental strategies and initiatives. The Group has no secretariat of its own and its conclusions are not made public.

(b) The European Parliament

2—20   The European Parliament has played a prominent role in initiating and strengthening environmental issues at Community level since the early 1970s. Its proposals and suggestions for institutional and administrative structures, for new initiatives or proposals were very often taken up by the Commission, although sometimes after some delay. One of the reasons for this is that the European Parliament also decides—along with the Council—on the Commission's budget and thus has a subtle means of pressure at its disposal.

Parliament's opinions on proposals for directives or regulations, obviously considerably influenced by the very active Parliamentary Committee on Environment, Public Health and Consumer Protection, may be summarised as follows:

- On general environmental questions or on horizontal legislation, Parliament constantly urges the Commission and the Council to do more and provide for even better environmental protection than the Commission had proposed. There seems to be not a single Commission environmental proposal where Parliament was of the opinion that it was too ambitious, too far-reaching or too protective. Parliament generally opposed environmental agreements, environmental deregulation and other attempts to reduce environmental protection.

- Proposals of a more technical nature are only exceptionally challenged as to the approach chosen by the Commission. The amendments suggested concern the need for more and "better" environmental protection.

- Parliament not only looked for more progressive and efficient environmental legislation, but also pleaded for greater transparency in environmental matters, better access to information and greater participation of environmental organisations in the decision-making process.

- Parliament gradually managed to introduce environmental requirements into its opinions on proposals for legislative acts in agricultural and regional matters, the internal market or other policies and in this it was more advanced than the Commission or the Council.

---

[17] Fifth environmental action programme [1993] O.J. C138/5, Chap. 9.
[18] *Ibid.*

2—21   Parliament's influence on the development of environmental legislation has been constantly increased over the years. Article 192(2) (ex 138b(2)) E.C., introduced in the E.C. Treaty in 1993, gave Parliament the right to require that the Commission submit a proposal for a directive or regulation. Commission and Council are of the opinion that this right does not question the Commission's discretion to decide alone whether it submits a proposal or not. This seems incorrect since Article 192 (ex 138b) would not make much sense otherwise: the European Parliament has always had the possibility of asking for a proposal of a legal measure. Thus, the Council's and Commission's interpretation would remove the efficacy of the insertion of Article 192(2) into the Treaty. In 1994, the Parliament formally asked for a proposal of a directive on environmental liability: the Commission has not yet followed up this request.

Article 175(3) (ex 130s(3)) E.C. provides that general environmental action programmes be adopted by a joint decision of the Council and the European Parliament. Since a decision is "binding in its entirety upon those to whom it is addressed",[19] future environmental action programmes will begin to lose their guiding character and become binding. Parliament's objective therefore must be—and in fact, during the discussions on the review of the fifth environmental action programme, it was—to obtain as concrete a content of action programmes as possible. Indeed, it might be doubtful whether a provision in a decision on an environmental action programme that the Commission wished to submit, within a specific time-span, a proposal for a directive on environmental liability, can in fact legally oblige the Commission to make such a proposal; from a political point of view, however, there would be very strong pressure on the Commission to follow such a request. In any case, Parliament has, by means of Article 175(3), a possibility to significantly influence the direction of Community environmental policy and law.

2—22   In the past, a considerable part of Community legislative activity, which was subject to the "comitology" procedure (adaptation of existing provisions due to technical or scientific progress) of Article 202 (ex 145) E.C. was not accessible to the European Parliament, since the procedures for the different committees, established by the Council,[20] did not provide for its participation. In order to increase transparency and a more open procedure, the Commission made an agreement with the European Parliament at the end of 1996, in the context of budgetary negotiations; according to that agreement, members of the European Parliament shall be fully informed of the agenda of committees and may ask to attend meetings. The committee has to decide unanimously on such a request. It is as yet uncertain whether the actual participation of Parliament in the adaptation committees will take place, since some Member States veto such participation and Parliament seems to reject such non-formalised participation. In 1999, the Council revised its Decision, in order to improve co-operation with the the the Parliament.[20a]

The European Parliament does not attend meetings of the Council or of its working parties. Overall, its influence on the Council is, in the context of a specific legislative text, limited mainly for two reasons: on the one hand, the Parliament has, in environmental issues, a chiefly co-operative role, not a co-deciding function.[21] The Council is thus normally not bound to take Parliament's opinion on board. The Amsterdam Treaty introduces, as a rule, the co-decision procedure in environmental matters; this might eventually lead to an increase in Parliament's influence.

---

[19] Art. 249 (ex 189) E.C.
[20] Dec. 87/373 [1987] O.J. L197/33.
[20a] Dec. 1999/468 [1999] O.J. L184/23.
[21] See Arts 251 (ex 189b) (co-decision procedure) and 252 (ex 189c) (co-operation procedure) of the E.C. Treaty.

On the other hand, the Council frequently discusses a proposal from the Commission before the European Parliament has given its opinion. These Council discussions are often even taken as far as to lead to a political consensus in Council; then only the opinion of Parliament is waited for before the Council formally adopts its common position. Since there is a tacit agreement in Council not to change a common position if at all possible, Parliament's opinions are of limited value.

This Council practice, which is not limited to the environmental sector, seems at the very least to contradict the spirit of the Treaty which is based on the idea that the opinions of Parliament, the Economic and Social Committee and the Committee of the Regions form part of Council discussions.

(c) The Economic and Social Committee; Committee of the Regions

2—23   The Economic and Social Committee (Articles 257 *et seq.* (ex 193 *et seq.*) E.C.) is thought to represent the different non-governmental interests within the Community, although representatives of the environment are not expressly mentioned in Article 257(2) of the E.C. Treaty. At present, only one member of this Committee has indicated a specific interest in environmental matters. The Committee of the Regions (Articles 263 *et seq.* (ex 198a) E.C.) is composed of regional and local authorities).

Article 4(2) of the E.C. Treaty provides that the Economic and Social Committee and the Committee of the Regions both advise the Council and the Commission. In reality this advisory function is exercised by both Committees only after the Commission has submitted a proposal or made a communication. Nor does the Commission consult these Committees. The opinions of both Committees in environmental matters have not yet reached the point of having any significant influence on the content of Community directives or regulations.

(d) The Council

2—24   The Council, while formally one institution, meets under relatively specific headings (*e.g.* Agricultural Council, Transport Council, Social Affairs Council). In environmental matters, the Council normally meets three times under each presidency—which changes every six months—twice formally in Brussels and once informally at a place which is determined by each presidency. At the informal meetings issues of environmental policy or environmental strategy are discussed, without any decisions being made. The ministers responsible for environmental matters have Council meetings in Brussels or in Luxembourg, on agenda issues drawn up by the presidency.

The Council meetings are not public except where the Council decides otherwise; however, up until now such public meetings, introduced after 1993, have been very exceptional and do not deal with essential matters. Nor does the Council organise public hearings. Position papers from lobby groups or other organisations are only rarely distributed among Member States. Contacts with media or with representatives of vested interests are not organised by the Council: at best, meetings with the media are organised by individual Member States immediately before or after a Council meeting. Normally, however, such contact takes place at the capital of each Member State. The public is thus informed about a Member State's viewpoint in the Council or during the preparatory meetings by this Member State itself.

There is no possibility of compelling the Council to debate a proposal for a directive or a regulation presented by the Commission. The Council, therefore, can, by not discussing a Commission proposal, let this proposal become obsolete. An example is

---

[22] [1989] O.J. C452/16; see also para. 4–31.

the Commission proposal for a directive on liability for damage caused by waste which had been presented at the Council's request.[22] The Council did not discuss the proposal: finally, the Commission declared its proposal to be outdated.[23] Other examples are the proposal on chromium discharges into water or the dumping of waste at sea.[24]

2—25 Institutional co-operation between the Council and the Commission generally occurs as regards the organisation of work in Council working groups, since here the Commission has to explain and defend its proposals for legislation. This co-operation is, however, limited to organisational questions; if, when, and how often Commission proposals are discussed in Council and within the different Council working groups, is decided by each Council Presidency at its discretion. The Council working groups are normally composed of the environmental attaché of each Member State's Permanent Representation with the Community as well as of Commission officials; officials from Member States—normally from the environmental department—participate at the discretion of each Member State, mainly in cases where expert advice is needed. The meetings are presided over by an official of the Member State who holds the presidency.

Institutional co-operation between the Council and other institutions, in particular the European Parliament, practically does not exist in environmental matters. However, the increasing number of co-decision procedures will probably lead to more organisational contacts between the two institutions.[25]

(e) The European Courts (Court of Justice and Court of First Instance)

2—26 No detailed description needs to be given of the role of the European Courts in ensuring that "the law is applied" in the interpretation and application of the environmental Treaty provisions and secondary legislation (Article 220 (ex 164) E.C.). The Courts have almost always tried to interpret existing legislation in a way which is favourable to the environment and to formalise the concept of environmental law which has often been rather general and vague. Of course, there have been judgments which have been heavily influenced by political considerations.[26] However, it is usual that judgments from a supreme court will also include policy considerations and are not given in a policy-free environment.

The division of work between the Court of Justice and the Court of First Instance is decided by the Council (Article 225(2) (ex 168a(2))). At present, the Court of First Instance decides in particular on all applications from individual persons (Article 230(4) (ex 173(4)) E.C.), and in competition matters.

2—27 For a number of reasons the Commission does not automatically bring cases concerning a breach of Community law before the Court of Justice. The Court has repeatedly stated that the Commission has, under Article 226 (ex 169) a discretion as to whether it wishes to bring an action or not.[27] This may well be but in any case, the clear wording of Article 226 indicates that the Commission has no such discretion on the question over whether it begins infringement procedures or not against a Member State. Since, however, the Court of Justice has furthermore stated that the Commission

---

[22] COM (96) 399 of July 30, 1996, para. 79.

[24] See paras 7–26 and 7–30, below.

[25] See, as one rare example, the *modus vivendi* between the European Parliament, Council and Commission concrning the implementation measures for acts adopted in accordance with the procedure laid down in Art. 251 (ex 189b) E.C. [1995] O.J. C293/1.

[26] This seems to be the case with C-252/85 *Commission v. France* [1988] E.C.R. 2243 on traditional hunting; C-302/86 *Commission v. Denmark* [1988] E.C.R. 4607 on a deposit and return system for bottles; C-2/90 *Commission v. Belgium* [1992] E.C.R. I-4431 on import bans for waste; C-155/91 *Commission v. Council* [1993] E.C.R. I-939 on the legal basis for waste legislation.

[27] Cases 416/85 *Commission v. United Kingdom* [1988] E.C.R. 3127; C-234/91 *Commission v. Denmark* [1993] E.C.R. I-6273.

cannot be obliged to begin procedures under that Article,[28] the Commission's attitude of not beginning procedures under Article 226 (and thus not bringing them before the Court of Justice either) remains unchallenged.

One essential difference between the judgments given by the Court of Justice and judgments given by a national supreme court is that the Court of Justice's judgment is given in an area in which different legal cultures exist. Thus, a judgment which states that one Member State has breached Community law because it has not submitted clean-up plans, not reported on the implementation of a specific directive or not ensured that the quality of drinking water complies with the requirements of Community law, is not accepted by the administration of all Member States as obliging them to make sure that the same omission does not occur under their responsibility. Infact, Member States do not really pay much attention to an environmental judgment that was given against another Member State.

(f) Non-institutional actors

(i) Professional organisations

2—28   The representation of vested interests at Community level is probably even greater than in most capitals of Member States. Economic operators and their professional organisations discovered the common market, globalisation effects and the advantages of economies of scale a long time ago and are also well aware that Community trade needs Community legal provisions. Their influence on the shaping of Community environmental law is considerable, although only with difficulty is it capable of being demonstrated. This influence is not so much exercised by legal papers which argue this or that rule, but rather by influencing the strategic thinking inside the Commission administration. I estimate that even with Directorate-General XI, out of the 100 contacts or interlocutors which the Directorate-General has outside the national administrations, more than 90 represent vested interests. Such exchange of views is bound to have some long-term repercussions.

European professional associations are normally relatively lacking in influence, compared to their national member organisations, and the influencing of the Community decision-making persons or bodies is mirrored by similar approaches by national associations or individual members at national level.

Examples where vested interests seem to have significantly influenced the Community policy of environmental law, are in my opinion: the abandoning of integrated emission limit values for industries or sectors of industries[29]; the abandoning, as a rule, of setting emission values at Community level[30]; the establishing provisions for environmental taxes and charges at Community level; the abandoning of set emission limit values for CO_2 emissions from cars[31]; the omission to formalise, in some binding form, the polluter-pays principle; industrial standardisation; the omission to promote alternative energies and a nuclear energy policy.

(ii) Environmental organisations

2—29   Community environmental organisations suffer from a chronic shortage in manpower and financial resources which seriously affects their organisational

---

[28] Case C-247/87, *Star Fruit Company v. Commission* [1989] E.C.R. 291; C-371/89 *Emrich v. Commission* [1990] E.C.R. I-1555.
[29] See para. 4–03, below.
[30] See para. 4–16, below.
[31] See paras 8–23 *et seq.*, below.

structures. There is no overall Community umbrella organisation which contains all environmental associations. In 1998, the Commission published a list of 23 "representative" European organisations which had, presumably in 1997, received the financial assistance of 2.58 million euro from the Commission.[32] Alhough associations such as Greenpeace were not listed, the list gives a fairly good picture of the diversity of environmental organisations at Community level.

At the same time the Council adopted a decision, based on Article 175(3) (ex 130s(3)) E.C. concerning an action programme for financial assistance for environmental organisations.[33] The action programme provides for a sum of 10.6 million euro over four years and is project-based, intended for information on the environment, the analysis of environmental measures and the promotion of co-operation between environmental organisations. The amount which is made available has thus not increased but is now more strictly linked to specific activities which are supervised by the Commission.

One might wonder whether it is not time for environmental organisations to pool their limited personal and financial resources and form a Community Institute for environmental organisations or a similar body.[34] The current diversity of environmental organisations is also an obstacle to the professionalisation. An association such as the European Environmental Bureau, the umbrella environmental organisation of some 130 national organisations, has a permanent staff of six people in Brussels and is thought to cover all facets of Community environmental policy and law. Other organisations are even smaller.

Overall, the contribution of environmental organisations to Community environmental law is small, but where they do manage to highlight an issue in the public awareness, they can influence Community environmental policy and the content of some measures.

(iii) Individuals

2—30   The environmental provisions of the E.C. Treaty do not mention individual persons and, as mentioned, are not set out in such a way that they could be (under the Court of Justice's doctrine of direct effect) interpreted so that individual persons could invoke them in disputes with administrations or courts. The European Court made a major effort in increasing the position of individual persons, by declaring, in a landmark decision of 1990, that environmental measures which also aimed at the protection of human health, were to be interpreted in a way that would allow individuals to invoke these rights before courts.[35] But neither the Commission, environmental organisations nor individual persons have ever pushed this line of thinking further, for example by making proposals for introducing a right of action for individuals or their associations against environmental impairment (Commission), or by trying, via an established number of test cases in court, to explore the content and the limits of environmental rights for individuals (environmental organisations) or by trying to bring into action a "right to a clean environment" which is so often referred to by politicians.

---

[32] [1998] O.J. C85/3; furthermore, the list indicates 59 associations at national level which had received financial assistance for "information and sensibilisation" on environmental problems.

[33] Dec. 97/872 [1997] O.J. L354/25.

[34] It might be worth mentioning that the Commission budget for 1998 (n. 5) provided, under Title B3-4002, for an annual contribution of 3.1 million euro to finance the work of a European Trade Union Institute and a sum of 2.4 million for a European Trade Union Academy. The Commission spends 9.2 million euro per year on financial assistance to the European Standardisation Organisations CEN and CENELEC (Budget 1998, title B5–315).

[35] Case C-361/88 *Commission v. Germany* [1991] E.C.R. I-2567.

Community institutions, and in particular the Commission, start from the premise that the protection of the environment is the task of the public administration—as if the (Community) administration were the owner of the environment: since the (Community) administration knows best what is desirable to preserve, protect or do to improve the quality of the environment, an individual person is rather a nuisance. This basic conception is the reason why access to environmental information at Community level is so much less organised than access to environmental information at national level[36] and why there are no systematic hearings organised for the preparation of environmental legislation in order to rebalance the structural imbalance between professional and environmental organisations and why environmental organisations and individuals are simply not given the possibility to contribute to the enforcement of Community environmental provisions. In my opinion there is a basic difference between an environmental action by a professional organisation and by an environmental organisation: an environmental organisation usually does not bear in mind its own vested interests, but the general interest to protect the environment, whereas a professional organisation usually has in mind specific, vested interests, not the general interest.

It is the European Commission's fault that it generally speaking does not try to mobilise private individuals who wish to ensure a better protection of the environment, by making people participate in environmental law-making and implementing. The European Union citizenship, introduced by Articles 17 *et seq.* (ex 8 *et seq.*) E.C., is lacking in the environmental sector, where individual persons remain recipients of Community environmental law and policy, rather than being given the status of instigators.

2. Instruments

(a) Legal and political instruments

(i) General remarks

2—31   The following presentation of instruments is limited to the E.C. Treaty, since the terminology of the EURATOM Treaty corresponds to it—except, of course, the numbers of the Articles—and the CECA Treaty has not really become relevant in environmental matters.[37]

In environmental matters a number of instruments were developed which are not detailed in the central provision of Article 249 (ex 189) E.C. The main reason for this evolution is he absence of an express chapter in the E.C. Treaty on environmental policy prior to 1987.

Regulations and directives can only be adopted by the European Parliament and the Council jointly, by the Council alone or by the Commission. The Commission has, unless it adopts the measure itself, the monopoly of initiating the legislative measure in all such cases: regulations and directives may only be adopted upon proposal on the Commission.

2—32   The possibility to have directives and regulations adopted jointly by the European Parliament and the Council has only existed since 1993. As regards the environment, Articles 95 (ex 100a) for environmental provisions, in particular those

---

[36] See para. 4–42, below.

[37] Under the CECA Treaty, the concept "decision" corresponds to "regulation" in the E.C. Treaty and is also an individual decision (as in the E.C. Treaty); "recommendation" in the CECA Treaty corresponds to "directive" in the E.C. Treaty and may also be addressed to individual persons.

which are product-related, and Article 175(3) (ex 130s(3)) E.C., for the adoption of environmental action programmes, provide for this joint adoption. The Amsterdam Treaty has added to those measures which are adopted by virtue of Article 175(1) (ex 130s(1)) E.C. In a number of cases the Council alone adopts environmental-related regulations and directives, in particular under Articles 175(2), 37 (ex 43), 71 (ex 75), 93 (ex 99) and 133 (ex 113) E.C. Where the Council adopts measures by a qualified majority,[38] Member States' votes are considered according to Article 205 (ex 148) E.C.: a qualified majority needs 62 of the (at present) 86 votes. It is important to underline that the Council can only amend a Commission proposal unanimously (Article 250, (ex 189a)) E.C.

The Commission can adopt regulations or directives only where it has expressly been authorised to do so by the Treaty or by secondary Community law. The Commission is frequently authorised under Article 202 (ex 145) E.C. to decide on the adaptation of environmental regulations and directives to take account of scientific or technical progress; individual regulations or directives specify how far this authorisation can go. In environmental matters the Commission is normally assisted in such cases by a committee, which has to give an opinion on proposals for adaptation before the Commission can decide. In cases of divergency between the committee and the Commission, the decision is normally taken by the Council. Details are outlined in a Council decision of 1987, revised in 1999.[39]

Regulations, directives and decisions must "state the reasons on which they are based" (Article 253 (ex 190)). This is the aim of the considerants which precede the different texts and give, in condensed form, the reasons on which they are based. The Court of Justice uses the considerants for the interpretation of the provisions; the Court's interpretation is not too severe as regards the content of the considerants, though it sometimes happens that legal acts are voided because of a lack of reasoning.[40]

Since the entry into effect of the Maastricht Treaty in 1993 the Council, when establishing a common position, publishes, in the *Official Journal*, in summary the reasons for its common position and also why it has not adopted all the proposals by the Commission or the European Parliament.

Regulations, directives and decisions are published in the *Official Journal* of the European Community, with the exception of those which are addressed to individual Member States or individual persons (Article 254 (ex 191) E.C.).

(ii) Regulations

2—33 In environmental matters, the Community mainly acts in the form of directives: regulations are exceptional. They are normally adopted when uniform provisions are sought,[41] since regulations are of general application and shall be binding in their entirety and directly applicable to all Member States (Article 249 (ex 189) E.C.). A first group is composed of regulations which set up a specific administrative structure, such as the European Environmental Agency,[42] the financial instrument LIFE,[43] the financial assistance for environmentally friendly agricultural

---

[38] This is the case under Arts 37, 75(1) and E.C. Treaty, Art. 133.
[39] Dec. 87/373 [1987] O.J. L197/33; revision by Dec. 1999/486 [1999] O.J. L184/23.
[40] See, *e.g.* Case C-41/93 *France v. Commission* [1994] E.C.R. I-1829; Case T-105/95, *WWF v. Commission* [1997] E.C.R. II-313.
[41] Written Question E-3089 (93) (Arbeloa Muru) [1994] O.J. C358/15.
[42] Reg. 1210/90 (n. 14).
[43] Reg. 1973/92 establishing a financial instrument for the environment (LIFE) [1992] O.J. L206/1.

production[44] or the Cohesion Fund,[45] furthermore there are measures which create committees, uniform procedures and structures; examples are the provision on organic agriculture,[46] the procedures for attributing an eco-label,[47] the risk assessment of chemicals[48] and the eco-audit scheme.[49]

A second group is formed by regulations which transpose obligations of international environmental conventions into Community law. They mainly serve to organise international trade, concerning products, waste, fauna and flora species. Examples are the Regulation on ozone-depleting substances,[50] the shipment of waste[51] and the trade in endangered species.[52] Also the regulations on an import ban of whale products,[53] on the ban of leghold traps and the import of certain furs[54] and the import or export of chemicals[55] belong to this category.

2—34   Regulations do not exist in the water, air and noise sector and there are only a few in the area of nature protection, waste and chemicals. However, these last two sectors show a slowly increasing need for uniform provisions. The reasons for this might lie in the necessity of having uniform provisions before the international state or trade community, but also in the wish to avoid, within an internal market which is still developing, different provisions which could lead to competitive distortions and changes in commercial relationships.

Although regulations are directly applicable in all Member States, not all provisions of environmental regulations have this direct effect. Several regulatory provisions require an action by Member States, such as the licensing and supervision of environmental auditors,[56] the authorisation of imports, the establishment of documents or certificates,[57] the designation of competent authorities, the supervision of plants, activities or transports, the establishment of reports and the transmission of information to the Commission or to other Member States. In this way regulations seem to have more the content of a directive. Furthermore, not all provisions of a regulation are of a directly applicable nature: thus, a provision such as "Member States may apply the system provided for in Titles II, VII and VIII within their jurisdiction"[58] is of purely facultative character: similar facultative provisions can be found in other regulations.

2—35   No environmental regulation outlines details of sanctions which apply in case of non-respect of the regulation. For instance, the Regulation on the shipment of waste provides that Member States "shall take appropriate legal action to prohibit and punish illegal traffic" of waste;[59] the Regulation on the assessment of chemicals asks

---

[44] Reg. 2078/92 [1992] O.J. L215/85.

[45] Reg. 1164/94 establishing a Cohesion Fund [1994] O.J. L130/1.

[46] Reg. 2092/91 on organic production of agricultural products and indications referring thereto on agricultural products and foodstuffs [1991] O.J. L198/1.

[47] Reg. 880/92 on a Community eco-label award scheme [1992] O.J. L99/1.

[48] Reg. 793/93 on the evaluation and control of the risks of existing substances [1993] O.J. L84/1.

[49] Reg. 1836/93 allowing voluntary participation by companies in the industrial sector in a Community eco-management and audit scheme [1993] O.J. L168/1.

[50] Reg. 3093/94 on substances that deplete the ozone layer [1994] O.J. L333/1.

[51] Reg. 259/93 on the supervision and control of shipments of waste within, into and out of the European Community [1993] O.J. L30/1.

[52] Reg. 338/97 on the protection of species of wild fauna and flora by regulating trade therein [1997] O.J. L61/1.

[53] Reg. 348/81 on common rules for imports of whales or other cetacean products [1981] O.J. L39/1.

[54] Reg. 3254/91 prohibiting the use of leghold traps in the Community and the introduction into the Community of pelts and manufactured goods of certain wild animal species originating in countries which catch them by means of leghold traps or trapping methods which do not meet international humane trapping standards [1991] O.J. L308/1.

[55] Reg. 2455/92 concerning the export and import of certain dangerous chemicals [1992] O.J. L251/13.

[56] Reg. 1836/93 (n. 49), Art. 6.

[57] Reg. 338/97 (n. 52), Art. 8.

[58] Reg. 259/93 (n. 51), Art. 13(4).

[59] Ibid., Art. 26(5).

Member States to "establish appropriate legal or administrative measures in order to deal with non-compliance with the provisions of this Regulation".[60] Whether the sanction is criminal, administrative or civil, is left to the discretion of Member States. The jurisprudence of the Court of Justice only requires that national sanctions are proportional and deterrent and correspond to sanctions which are pronounced in similar cases under national law.

(iii) Directives

2—36   Directives[61] are the most frequently used instrument in Community environmental policy. The degree of detail provided for in a directive is less determined by the concept of a "directive" than by the need to attain the different objectives pursued. Thus, directives on harmonising motor vehicles rules quite often contain 50 to 80 pages of detailed rules, which outline all the details of the composition of products, test methods and so on.[62] Such detailed directives are frequent for products, but are also in the agricultural sector. In contrast to that, environmental directives tend to be of a general nature. In particular the debate over subsidiarity and deregulation and the general loss of integration capacity of the Commuity has led to environmental directives which outline general rules, framework provisions and basic requirements. Provisions on measuring methods and frequency, emission limit values, quantitative restrictions and other similar provisions are only outlined in exceptional cases. Whether this restriction is really capable of contributing to a high level of environmental protection, is doubtful; although time is too short for a definite assessment, it seems that such general provisions do not increase the added value of Community environmental law provisions and, furthermore, perpetuate differences in the level of protection among Member States.

Directives address Member States and normally oblige them to act in a certain way. Private persons, undertakings or associations cannot be obligated by a directive; however, they can acquire rights from a directive in those cases where a provision in a directive is sufficiently concrete, precise and unconditional and where the Member State has not transposed that directive completely or correctly into national law.[63]

2—37   Member States have to transpose the provisions of a directive into national law. It is up to each Member State to decide whether this is done by an Act of Parliament or regulation, whether the transposition measure is a national measure or whether several regional or even local provisions are adopted. It is only relevant that the directive's provisions are transposed for the whole territory of the Member State. The transposing measure can be incorporated in one legal act; more frequently, however, the transposition is by a number of legal measures, in particular in Member States with a decentralised federal structure.

In the area of products and waste, the definitions of a directive normally also have to be transposed in order to establish a common language. For the rest, at the very least those provisions need to be transposed which are capable of creating rights or obligations for private persons. In contrast to this, provisions which exclusively address the administration (for instance, by sending reports to the Commission to designate competent authorities) need not be transposed.

2—38   The provisions of the directive which have been transposed into national law

---

[60] Reg. 793/93 (n. 48), Art. 17; similar to the provision in Art. 6 of Reg. 2455/92 (n. 55).
[61] Art. 249 (ex 189) E.C.: "A directive shall be binding, as to the result to be achieved, upon each Member State to which it is addressed, but shall leave to the national authorities the choice of form and methods.".
[62] Dir. 97/24 on three-wheel cars has a length of 454 pages in the *Official Journal* [1997] O.J. L226/1.
[63] See further at para. 11–01, below.

must be actually applied. This follows from the very nature of a directive, which obliges Member States to achieve a certain result. It is not enough to take all practical steps to reach these objectives; indeed, the directive shows Member States how to achieve a certain result, but does not leave it at their discretion as to whether they achieve a result or not. It was for this reason that the United Kingdom was not heeded before the Court of Justice, concerning its argument that it had taken all reasonable steps to ensure clean drinking water: the Court requested that the requirements of the drinking water Directive be complied with.[64]

Amendments of directives follow the general rules. Normally, they are adopted by the same institutions which adopted the original directive; however, as pointed out, the Commission may be authorised, under Article 202 (ex 145) E.C. to amend a directive, in particular to adapt it as a result of technical or scientific progress. Furthermore, the legal basis of a directive is determined by its objective and its content, not by the legal basis of a previous directive; thus, where an environmental directive, based on Article 175 (ex 130s) is amended by a directive which has a trade-related objective, Article 133 (ex 113) may become the appropriate legal basis, and the institution which adopts the amendment may be different.

Legally, differentiations such as "umbrella directive", "daughter directive", etc., are not relevant. Such concepts only signal that the specific directive is placed in a close context with a more general directive; however, the specific directive is to be interpreted by itself, including, of course, possible references to other directives.

Directives do not become obsolete with time. Since they are legal acts, they need to be repealed expressly: in Community practice this normally takes place with the adoption of a new directive. No environmental directive has as yet been repealed without the adption of new provisions.

(iv) Decisions

2—39   Decisions[65] are rather numerous in Community environmental policy. The most frequent types of decisions are: decisions to establish a committee or another body[66]; to grant financial assistance for environmental projects under the Cohesion Fund or the financial instrument LIFE; in the context of competition policy on agreements (Article 81 (ex 85)); abuse of dominant positions (Article 82 (ex 86)) or on state aid (Articles 87 and 88 (ex 92 and 93)); on details of putting into operation specific directives or regulations[67] or establishing criteria for the attribution of an eco-label for specific product groups[68]; on the adherence of the Community to international (environmental) conventions; on environmental action programmes according to Article 175(3) (ex 130s(3)); and on Article 95(4) and (6) (ex 100a(4) and (6)) on more stringent national environmental measures.

(v) Recommendations

2—40   Commission or Council recommendations have no binding force. They play a limited role in Community environmental policy. Indeed, experience has shown that neither economic operators nor Member States are inclined to respect recommendations,

---

[64] Case C-337/89 *Commission v. United Kingdom* [1992] E.C.R. 6103.

[65] Art. 249 (ex 189) E.C.: "A decision shall be binding in its entirety upon those to whom it is addressed."

[66] See, *e.g.* Dec. 76/431 setting up a committee on waste management [1976] O.J. L115/73; Dec. 97/150 on the European Environmental Forum (n. 16).

[67] See, *e.g.* Dec. 94/904 establishing a list of hazardous waste [1994] O.J. L356/14.

[68] Under Reg. 880/92; see, *e.g.* Dec. 93/430 on ecological criteria for dishwashers [1993] O.J. L38; Dec. 98/488 on ecological criteria for soil improvers [1998] O.J. L219/39.

and the example of international organisations—OECD, Council of Europe, United Nations—which largely work with recommendations, demonstrate the very limited effective influence of non-binding environmental measures.

The Council made environmental recommendations on cost allocation,[69] on the cost of pollution control to industry[70] and on the reuse of waste paper and the use of recycled paper.[71] The Commission in particular made recommendations on birds, on environmental agreements and the use of CFCs in industry.[72] Where an environmental agreement is made at Community level, the Commission furthermore issues a recommendation taking up the content of the agreement.[73]

None of these recommendations had, as far as can be seen, any influence on Community or national environmental policy or law.

(vi) Communications

2—41 Communications, not expressly provided for in the E.C. Treaty, are legally non-binding. They are sent from the Commission to the other institutions, in particular the Council or the Parliament, and expose the Commission's position on a particular problem, they indicate orientation and discuss options which the Commission considers possible. Since the beginning of the 1990s, the number of communications on environmental matters has increased.[74]

Communications appear under different headings, as strategies, greenbooks, whitebooks, reports or communication. Legally, there is no difference. Communications may be accompanied by a draft for a Council resolution, a directive or a regulation.

(vii) Action programmes

2—42 Community environmental action programmes have been developed since the early 1970s also in reaction to the fact that the E.C. Treaty did not provide for an express legal basis for environmental measures. When such specific provisions were introduced in 1987, the practice of action programmes was maintained. Action programmes were, legally, communications by the Commission to other Community institutions, which set out for a period of four to five years, the objectives, principles and priorities of Community action which the Commission envisaged. The Court of Justice confirmed that the environmental action programmes did not contain legally binding or enforceable provisions.[75] Action programmes were followed by (political) resolutions by the Parliament and the Council. Between 1973 and mid-1998, five environmental action programmes were agreed at Community level.[76] Their main effect was essentially political. They achieved a large consensus among Member States on objectives and priorities of Community environmental policy, and since the majority

---

[69] Recommendation 75/436 [1975] O.J. L194/1.
[70] Recommendation 79/3 [1979] O.J. L5/28.
[71] Recommendation 81/972 [1981] O.J. L355/56.
[72] Recommendations 75/66 [1975] O.J. L21/24 (birds); 96/733 [1996] O.J. L33/59 (environmental agreements); 89/349 [1989] O.J. L89/56; 90/437 and 90/438 [1990] O.J. L227/26 and 30 (CFC); for these last recommendations see also para. 8–60.
[73] See Dec. 98/480 on environmentally sound use of household detergents [1998] O.J. L215/73.
[74] Number of Commission communications on environmental issues; figures from: *Bulletin of the European Union* 1991–1997 (author's own counting): 1991: 1; 1992: 4; 1993: 1; 1994: 3; 1995: 3; 1996: 7; 1997: 4 communications.
[75] Case C-142/95P *Rovigo* [1996] E.C.R. I-6669.
[76] First environmental action programme 1973–1976 [1973] O.J. C112/1; second environmental action programme (1977–1982) [1977] O.J. C139/1; third environmental action programme 1982–1986 [1983] O.J. C46/1; fourth environmental action programme 1987–1992 [1987] O.J. C328/1; fifth environmental action programme 1993–2000 [1993] O.J. C138/5.

of Member States did not have a national environmental policy, the measures agreed and adopted at Community level often influenced environmental policy within Member States.

Since the end of 1993, environmental action programmes have had to be adopted by way of a joint decision by the European Parliament and the Council (Article 175(3) (ex 130s(3))). This has as a consequence that future environmental action programmes will contain legally binding provisions.[77]

2—43 Action programmes under Article 175(3) must at least outline priority objectives for Community action, provide for measures to achieve these objectives and contain a time period within which the measures are taken. The right for initiative for such a programme rests with the Commission, and no other institution can oblige it to submit such a programme.

Community action programmes may oblige the Commission to make proposals for specific measures, with the consequence, in the case of failure to do so, of an action—by the Council and also by the European Parliament—under Article 232 (ex 175) E.C. It is true that the Commission normally has the monopoly for legal initiatives and cannot be compelled to make a proposal. However, primary and secondary law contain a number of exceptions to this rule[78] and there is no provision in Community law which would oppose such an exception. In contrast to this, it does not seem possible to oblige the Council or the Member States to take specific measures: in both cases, a concrete content—such as, for instance, that the use of certain substances or products will be banned from a specific date onwards—contradicts the form of an action programme; such measures would require a directive or a regulation and would be adopted in respect of the procedures foreseen for those instruments.

The new provision of Article 175(3) creates new possibilities for the European Parliament to influence the legislative programme of the Community and to see proposals for legislative measures presented. Parliament's interest must therefore be to have environmental action programmes as concrete as possible, whereas the interests of the Commission and the Council must be to keep the programme as general and loosely drafted as possible. This difference of interest was very notable in the Commission's proposal for a review of the fifth action programme and Parliament's position on it.[79] The final Decision on this review contains objectives and principles, but not actions.[80]

(viii) Resolutions

2—44 Nor does the Treaty consider resolutions. These are political resolutions adopted by the Council, with or without a proposal from the Commission. Environmental resolutions are agreed upon unanimously; it is true that no vote is taken, but the Council redrafts the text until a consensus of all Member States is reached.

Resolutions often constitute the Council's reaction on a Commission communication concerning an environmental issue. However, the Council is not obliged to react to such communications. Where it adopts a resolution, this shows the Commission's political or legal leanings without being legally binding.

---

[77] See Dec. 2179/98 on the review of the fifth environmental action programme [1998] O.J. L275/1.
[78] See, e.g. Art. 208 (ex 152) E.C.; an example in secondary law is Art. 1(5) of Dir. 91/689 on hazardous waste [1991] O.J. L377/20 which requests the Commission to make a proposal on hazardous household waste.
[79] Commission, [1996] O.J. C140/5. European Parliament [1996] O.J. C362/112.
[80] See Dec. 2179/98 (n. 77 above).

(ix) Environmental agreements

2—45 Environmental agreements, *i.e.* agreements between Community institutions and private business,[81] are not mentioned in Article 249 (ex 189); since the Community may only act within the limits of powers conferred upon it (Article 6 (ex 3c)), it is doubtful whether they are at all capable of regulating substantive parts of Community environmental policy. As the European Parliament, the Economic and Social Committee and the Committee of the Regions have institutional rights and guarantees to take part in the Community decision-making procedures, environmental agreements, which set these rights aside, are legally not permissible. For this reason the Commission declared that it could only make non-binding environmental agreements at Community level.[82]

Apart from that, procedures for the making of such agreements—who should negotiate in the name of the Community—and the follow-up—how and by whom the agreement would be monitored, enforced, sanctioned, applied to free-riders, such as importers and third country producers—are not clear, nor are they answered by the Commission's communication.[83] Since Member States would have to monitor and enforce agreements, their participation in the negotiation procedure is inevitable. However, it is then not clear where the advantage is with regard to a directive which is negotiated and decided in Council.

2—46 Furthermore, problems under competition policy—Articles 81 and 82 (ex 85 and 86)—are not really solved. Agreements among competitors may come under Article 81, even where public authorities participate in such agreements. As regards measures which have an impact on imports, international trade provisions may also be applicable.

In conclusion, it seems that (Community) environmental agreements may contribute to the protection of the environment in those cases where legally binding measures are also effective; however, in those parts of the Community where environmental directives are almost or not at all effective, environmental agreements are not likely to have a greater effect.

Community legal policy tries to circumvent these obstacles: in the case of an environmental agreement on CO_2 emissions from cars, negotiations took place between the Commission and economic operators on what might by an acceptable offer from the car industry; Council and Parliament were informed of the state of negotiations. At the end of such negotiations a statement might be issued or there might be a recommendation from the Commission, a Council resolution or another non-binding declaration in the sense that there is no need for binding measures at Community level, since there is a voluntary commitment by the car industry.[84]

2—47 A second way consists in negotiations between the Commission and one or more professional organisations on an improvement in environmental performance. At the end of these negotiations, the European professional organisations make a commitment to the Commission. The Commission adopts a recommendation based on Article 211 (ex 155) E.C., which recommends that those environmental commitments be followed, which the professional organisation had agreed to accept. An example of

---

[81] Dir. 94/62 on packaging and packaging waste [1994] O.J. L365/10, Art. 3(12) gives a definition of "voluntary agreements", though such agreements play no role in that Directive: "'Voluntary agreements' shall mean the formal agreement concluded between the competent public authorities of the Member State and the economic sectors concerned, which has to be open to all partners who wish to meet the conditions of the agreement with a view to working towards the objectives of this Directive."

[82] Communication on environmental agreements, COM (96) 561 of November 27, 1996.

[83] *Ibid.*

[84] See also para. 8–24, below.

this model which does not contain any form of "agreement" (*i.e.* some form of a contract) is the use of detergents, where the Commission made a recommendation in 1998.[85]

Underlying both types of environmental agreement is the Commission's commitment not to make proposals for a directive or a regulation. It is as yet unclear to what extent Member States feel bound by the Commission's recommendation. On general aspects of environmental agreements, the Commission made a communication and a recommendation, in 1996, on the implementation of directives by environmental agreements, but seems to have given greater consideration to environmental agreements at national than at Community level.[86]

(b) Instruments to influence the behaviour of undertakings and individual persons

2—48 Community provisions contain a number of provisions which aim at influencing the behaviour of undertakings or individual persons towards a better environment. Since the great majority of Community environmental law is made in the form of directives, these provisions do not directly address these private persons; they normally address instead Member States and ask them to "transmit" these messages via their national provisions, to the addressees. The most important instruments that exist under Community environmental law are the following.

(i) Obligation of notification

2—49 In a number of cases, private persons are obliged to notify the authorities of a Member State of a certain activity or practice. Thus, persons who intend to put new chemical substances on the Community market have to notify public authorities of their intention and submit certain documents referring to the tests of that substance: they may put the substance on the market only 60 days after that notification.[87] Where a chemical, whose use in the Community is prohibited or restricted, is to be exported into a third country for the first time, this intention must be notified 30 days before the export takes place; the intention behind this provision is to inform the third country.[88] A notification obligation also exists for the contained use of genetically modified micro-organisms[89] and the deliberate release of genetically modified organisms[90]; sometimes in these two instances, however, the notification is followed by an express authorisation. Directive 86/609 on animal testing[91] details notification obligations for experiments on animals or the details of persons conducting such experiments; establishments which use animals shall be registered, however, Member States may also arrange for permits instead. Also, the production, processing and import of organic agricultural products must be notified.[92]

---

[85] Recommendation 98/480 [1998] O.J. L215/73; see also the recommendations on CFCs 89/349, 90/437 and 90/438 (n. 72) which followed the same pattern, but became obsolete because of the evolution in the sector of ozone-depleting substances.

[86] COM (96) 561 (n. 82); Recommendation 96/733 (n. 72).

[87] Dir. 67/548 on the classification, packaging and labelling of chemical substances [1967] O.J. L196/1, Art. 7 *et seq.*; see further at para. 6–26, below.

[88] Reg. 2455/92 on the export and import of certain chemicals (1992) O.J. L251/13, Art. 4; see also para. 6–65, below.

[89] Dir. 90/219 on the contained use of genetically modified micro-organisms [1990] O.J. L117/1, Arts 8 and 10.

[90] Dir. 90/220 on the deliberate release into the environment of genetically modified organisms [1990] O.J. L117/15, Arts 5 *et seq.*

[91] Dir. 86/609 on the protection of animals used for experimental and other scientific purposes [1986] O.J. L358/1.

[92] Reg. 2092/91 (n. 46).

As regards installations, notification is required for any industrial activity during which certain chemicals are used or produced; notification has to inform the authorities of the substances used, the plant and possible risks of accidents.[93] Furthermore, malfunctions or breakdowns of the functioning of installations sometimes requires notification.[94]

Regulation 793/93 finally contains a notification obligation for manufacturers or importers of chemical substances which exists *vis-à-vis* the Commission (rather than, as is more usual, *vis-à-vis* the Member State).[95] Where these persons produce or import chemicals in quantities of more than 1,000 tonnes per year, they have to inform the Commission thereof and provide it with details on these substances.

All these obligations for information or notification are intended to inform the authorities responsible in due time, in order to allow them to take appropriate, and if necessary preventive, action.

(ii) Authorisation

2—50   Authorisation is organised in very different ways in Member States. It is thus usual that Community legislature limits itself to requiring that certain activities have an environmental authorisation[96] (sometimes the word "permit" is used,[97] without there being any legal difference) and to setting out conditions for this authorisation.

First, a number of new installations need an authorisation for discharges into the environment. Directive 96/61[98] has to some extent harmonised the permits and the conditions thereof; however, this is only for some bigger installations. Authorisation for existing installations has to be adapted to this Directive's requirements by 2007. It is also envisaged that the authorisation for discharges into water under Directives 76/464 on water discharges,[99] 88/609 on large combustion plants[1] and 84/360 on air emissions from industrial plants[2] shall gradually be adapted to the provisions of Directives 96/61 which will thus eventually become a framework directive. In the waste sector, all installations which recover, collect, treat or dispose of waste, need an authorisation[3].

2—51   A second area deals with the authorisation to impair the environment. Besides the discharge from installations which are mentioned above, the artificial enrichment of groundwater is mentioned,[4] as is the discharge of waste-water from urban waste-water treatment plants; the discharge of sewage sludge into surface waters also needs an authorisation (but this is forbidden as of the end of 1998).[5] Product-related authorisation concern the placing on the market of pesticides,[6] biocides[7] and the

---

[93] Dir. 96/82 on the control of major accident hazards involving dangerous substances [1997] O.J. L10/13, Art. 6.

[94] Dir. 88/609 on the limitation of emissions of certain pollutants into the air from large combustion plants [1988] O.J. L336/1, Art. 8; Dir. 89/369 on the prevention of air pollution from any municipal waste incineration plant [1989] O.J. L163/32, Art. 8.

[95] Reg. 793/93 on the evaluation and control of the risks of existing substances [1993] O.J. L84/1.

[96] See, *e.g.* Dir. 76/464 on the discharge of pollutants into water [1976] O.J. L129/23; Dir. 80/68 on discharges to groundwater [1980] O.J. L20/43.

[97] See for instance Dir. 96/61 on integrated pollution prevention control [1996] O.J. L257/26; Dir. 75/442 on waste [1975] O.J. L194/47.

[98] Dir. 96/61 (n. 97).

[99] Dir. 76/464 (n. 96).

[1] Dir. 88/609 on the limitation of emissions of certain pollutants into the air from large combustion plants [1988] O.J. L336/1.

[2] Dir. 84/360 on the combating of air pollution from industrial plants [1984] O.J. L188/20.

[3] Dir. 75/442 (n. 97).

[4] Dir. 80/68 (n. 96), Art. 5.

[5] Dir. 91/271 on urban waste water [1991] O.J. L135/40, Arts 12 and 14.

[6] Dir. 91/414 on the placing of plant protection products on the market [1991] O.J. L230/1.

[7] Dir. 98/8 concerning the placing of biocidal products on the market [1998] O.J. L123/1.

release of genetically modified organisms into the environment.[8] Also the import and export of ozone-depleting substances[9] and of endangered species of fauna and flora[10] fall into this category.

There is no general rule on the conditions which accompany the authorisation. Early directives established very detailed conditions,[11] which were, however, not really controlled. The new Directive 96/61 also provides for detailed conditions, such as emission limit values or equivalent parameters, the best available techniques, measurement frequency and methodology, suitable requirements for controlling emissions and measures for other than normal operating conditions. However, the condition requirements are vaguely formulated and leave a lot of discretion to Member States.

2—52   In contrast to earlier directives, Directive 96/61 does not provide for limited authorisation; it only requires that the authorisation be regularly reviewed.

The procedure requirements for authorisation are few and far between. Directive 96/61 requires a written application with a number of minimal indications and a non-technical résumé of the documentation. The application has, for an appropriate length of time, to be made available to the public to enable it to comment. An environmental impact assessment is only required for certain specific projects, but not as yet for spatial planning and programmes.[12] This Directive provides that the public must be given "the opportunity to express an opinion" on the project, which is really a way of understanding, the author has the right of an individual to a clean and healthy environment. A hydrogeological examination is also required before the discharge of pollutants into groundwater is authorised.[13]

Directive 96/61 also provides that authorisation be made available to the public; most other directives concur with this requirement. No details are set out and checking on whether the conditions for authorisation continue to be complied with or not has been reduced in recent directives. While Directive 76/464 and its subsequent different daughter directives outlined detail control requirements, Directive 75/440 on the quality of surface water[14] was even completed by a specific "control" directive[15] and the directives on air quality standards also contain detailed measurement and control provisions,[16] while Directive 96/61 limits itself to stating that the "conditions of the permit are complied with". As if the devil were not in the detail!

(iii) Interdiction and obligation to act

2—53   Community environmentally relevant interdictions have been pronounced essentially in the product-related legislation. The most important provision is Directive 76/769[17] which is continuously amended to include further restrictions. Besides that, every measure which fixes limit values, implicitly contains the interdiction on exceeding

---

[8] Dir. 90/220 (n. 90).

[9] Reg. 3093/94 on ozone-depleting substances [1994] O.J. L333/1.

[10] Reg. 338/97 on trade in endangered species [1997] O.J. L61/1.

[11] See, e.g. Dir. 80/68 (n. 96) which requires methods of discharge, essential precautions, monitoring arrangements and monitoring groundwater to be detailed.

[12] Dir. 85/337 on the assessment of the effects of certain public and private projects on the environment [1985] O.J. L175/40.

[13] Dir. 80/68 (n. 96), Arts 5 and 7.

[14] Dir. 75/440 concerning the quality required of surface water intended for the abstraction of drinking water in the Member States [1975] O.J. L194/26.

[15] Dir. 79/869 concerning the methods of measurement and frequencies of sampling and analysis of surface water intended for the abstraction of drinking waters in the Member States [1979] O.J. L271/44.

[16] Dir. 80/779 (SO$_2$ in the air) [1980] O.J. L229/30; 82/884 (lead in the air) [1982] O.J. L378/15, 85/203 (NOx in the air) [1985] O.J. L87/1.

[17] Dir. 76/769 relating to restrictions on the marketing and use of certain dangerous substances and preparations [1976] O.J. L262/201.

these values. Other interdictions and restrictions are found in numerous directives, such as the ban on certain pesticides,[18] on certain heavy metals or other substances in products, on the discharge of used oils into water[19] or on the non-authorised disposal of waste.[20] Most of these interdictions leave the provision of not respecting them in extraordinary circumstances.

Occasionally, Community law itself authorises Member States to establish a ban. General authorisation so far are found in Articles 95(4) (ex 100a(4)) and 176 (ex 130t) E.C. Further elements exist in secondary law under the so-called safeguard clause: these clauses give the possibility of temporarily prohibiting a product even though it complies with Community requirements. Such a ban provokes a Community control procedure which ends either with a Community prohibition or an invitation to the acting Member State to repeal its ban. Specific authorisation for Member States to issue bans exist for ordinary leaded petrol,[21] for using sewage sludge where certain concentrations of heavy metals are exceeded[22] and for importing/exporting hazardous waste for disposal purposes.[23]

2—54 Community environmental law only rarely provides for general national derogations of a ban. An example is the possibility of hunting certain birds in specified Member States.[24] Considerably more often, it happens that a Member State may grant a derogation of a ban in a specific case.

Obligations to act are also rather few and far between. They concern, for instance, obligations to keep registers, to measure emissions, to hand over waste to an authorised undertaker, to discharge air emissions via a chimney, etc. Never are sanctions provided: these are left to national legislation.

Directive 96/61 sets out "basic obligations" for the operator of an installation which comes under that Directive,[25] which probably has a placebo effect because they serve no useful purpose. Also Directive 96/82 obliges the operator of a plant to take all necessary measures to prevent accidents. There are no take-back obligations for consumer durables (cars, packaging, batteries); national take-back schemes are possible. Deposit and return systems are likewise possible at national level, but have not yet beein introduced at Community level. Obligations to ensure financial security only exist for the shipment of hazardous waste to another Member State[26]: no insurance obligation exists.

2—55 There is no obligation for an undertaking to mandate a person to look into environmental issues. Directive 82/501 contained the obligation for an undertaking coming under that Directive to designate a specific person in charge of security and to implement the accident prevention and evacuation plans.[27] However, Directive 96/82 deleted this provision altogether.[28]

Community environmental law does not acknowledge an express requirement to connect the supply of water, electricity or fuel or to deliver waste or waste water to a specific place. However, such an obligation implicitly underlies the Directive on urban

---

[18] Dir. 79/117 on the interdiction of certain plant protection products [1979] O.J. L33/36.
[19] Dir. 75/439 on used oils [1975] O.J. L194/31, Art. 4.
[20] *Ibid.*, Art. 4.
[21] Dir. 87/416 [1987] O.J. L225/33.
[22] Dir. 86/278 on the use of sewage sludge in agriculture [1986] O.J. L181/6, Art. 5.
[23] Reg. 259/93 on the shipment of waste [1993] O.J. L30/1, Art. 4.
[24] Dir. 79/409 [1979] O.J. L103/1. Art. 7(3) and annex II(2).
[25] Dir. 96/61 (n. 97), Art. 3: For instance: "'no significant pollution is cause; energy is used efficiently"; the necessary measures are taken to prevent accidents and limit their consequences" and so on.
[26] Reg. 259/93 (n. 51), Art. 27.
[27] Dir. 82/501 on accident prevention [1982] O.J. L230/5; see also case C-190/90 *Commission v. Netherlands* [1992] E.C.R. I-3265.
[28] Dir. 96/82 (n. 93), Art. 11.

waste water.[29] Member States may make provision for such an obligation, however not for waste which may be recovered.

Obligations for remedial action, following an action that impaired the environment, do not exist in Community environmental law. Regulation 259/93 provides for an obligation to take back waste which has been illegally shipped to another Member State.[30] Liability obligations only exist for damage caused by defective products[31]; this Directive also applies to damage caused by waste, although this is contested.[32]

(iv) Information, appeals, warnings

2—56   Community environmental law and policy contain numerous addresses and appeals to citizens to behave in a way which is environmentally more beneficial. A good example is the Council resolution on the fifth environmental action programme,[33] where the Council declared that "many current forms of activity and development are not environmentally sustainable" and that "the achievement of sustainable development calls for significant changes in current patterns of development, production, consumption and behaviour"; this implied "a sharing of responsibility at global, Community, regional, local and even personal level". No visible effect has ever been noticed as a result of such appeals.

Since 1992, the Community has tried to re-educate consumers' and users' behaviour towards environmentally "better" products, by establishing an E.C. eco-label.[34] Since industry opposes the system, the work advances very slowly and the system also has to compete with differing national systems, so its effects have been up until now only very limited. The eco-audit scheme[35] has had more success, at least in the northern Member State; it tries to persuade undertakings to improve their environmental management and thus reduce environmental impairment.

The Community has never issued warnings against environmentally dangerous products. A recent recommendation to be careful with toys for small children that contain PVC with certain phthalates,[36] obviously aims more at protecting health than the environment. Under Directive 92/72,[37] Member States are obliged to warn the population of each individual Member State where certain levels of ozone concentration are exceeded, a way to replace remedial action by warnings.

Generally, the effect of Community appeals and information is not essentially greater than that of corresponding national measures. It is correct that Community institutions have, at least in part, greater credit with the population in environmental matters; however, this is balanced by a greater distance towards the ordinary citizen.

(v) Financial assistance

2—57   Up until now, no Community provision has provided for financial advantages of environmentally "better" products. Member States oppose such rules, since environmental protection is of different importance in the different Member States, and they are afraid of competitive disadvantages. Thus, a Commission proposal to introduce a price differentiation between leaded and unleaded petrol and thus accelerate the

---

[29] Dir. 91/271 (n. 5).
[30] Reg. 259/93 (n. 51), Arts 25 and 26.
[31] Dir. 85/374 on product liability [1985] O.J. L210/29.
[32] See also para. 4–32.
[33] [1993] O.J. C138/1.
[34] Reg. 880/92 (n. 47).
[35] Reg. 1836/93 (n. 49).
[36] Recommendation 98/485 [1998] O.J. L217/35.
[37] Dir. 92/72 on air pollution by ozone [1992] O.J. L297/1.

introduction of catalytic converters and lead-free petrol[38] was rejected: such differentiation was subsequently introduced at national level. In the same way the attempt failed to introduce general financial advantages for the introduction of cars with catalytic converters; the final compromise only allowed such encouragement for a limited period of time. Attempts in this direction seem to have been largely abandoned since then.

(vi) Subventions

2—58   National subventions (state aids) are in principle prohibited (Article 87 (ex 92) E.C.), but are in practice in all Member States. The total amount of state aids per year is about 94 billion euro,[39] the amount of environmental aid is not known. Since 1974 the Commission has fixed a Community framework for environmental aids, which was last reviewed in 1993.[40] This framework fixes the conditions under which the Commission normally considers environmental aid compatible with the Treaty. The regular amount is 15–30 per cent of the total investment. Financial encouragements to consumers to acquire environmentally "better" products do not fall into this scheme as long as the aid does not advantage individual undertakings.

Community subventions are particularly granted under the Structural Funds and the Cohesion Fund. The Structural Funds aim at balancing the situation of economically disadvantaged regions, including rural areas (Article 158, (ex 130s) E.C.). The Member States entitled to receive funds establish programmes which are approved by the Commission; the individual projects are then realised under the responsibility of the Member State. The priorities and the taking of environmental measures is largely left to the discretion of each Member State.

The Cohesion Fund co-finances individual projects in the environmental and transport sector in those Member States where the gross national product significantly lies below the Community average. Until 1999 this was the case for Greece, Spain, Portugal and Ireland. Both funds also co-finance projects which contribute to the implementation of obligations under Community environmental law, such as the construction of sewers, waste-water treatment plants, waste disposal or recovery installations or nature protection projects. There are several other Community aid programmes, in particular in the sectors of energy, research or agriculture.

As mentioned, there have been up until now no fiscal advantages granted by Community measures. Likewise, there are as yet no Community rules on environmental charges.[41]

(vii) Tradable certificates; bubbles

2—59   Environmental certificates are used as tokens, which, against payment, are issued by the public authorities and give the right to input into the environment the quantity of pollutants indicated by the token. These certificates are tradable.

As yet, there are no Community tradable certificates. However, the Kyoto Protocol to the United Nation Convention on Climate Change[42] provides, internationally, for the introduction of tradable certificates. It is thus possible that the Community will introduce a tradable certificate system for air emissions.

Under Regulation 3093/94 producers of ozone-depleting substances have the

---

[38] [1984] O.J. C178/5.
[39] Written Question E-2530/96 (Amadeo) [1997] O.J. C83/22.
[40] [1994] O.J. C72/3.
[41] See for more details para. 4–28.
[42] See for more details para. 8–54.

possibility, granted by the Commission, of marketing specific quantities of ozone-depleting ore to use themselves. Such rights may be transferred to other Community producers of the same substance; the Commission is to be informed of any such transaction.[43] The essential difference to certificates is the fact that this provision deals with a product for which limitations already exist and that the general objective of all these provisions is to progressively reduce and finally completely end the production of such substances.

The bubble concept requires, within a specific geographical area that total pollution quantities are taken into account. Within this total quantity, the different emittors may emit differing quantities of pollutants. Community law provides for a bubble concept in Directive 88/609 on emissions from large combustion plants,[44] where total quantities for SO_2 and NOx-emissions have been set for each Member State. These total quantities were to be reduced in two or three stages. It was left to Member States to distribute nationally the total quantities for emissions.

2—60   A form of bubble concept was incorporated into the Convention on the transit of the Alps between Austria and the Community.[45] Trucks which crossed the Alps via Austria were charged with "eco-points"; the number of points varied according to the truck's pollution emissions. Member States obtained a total number of carriages which they had to attribute on the individual trucks. The total number of eco-points was to be reduced by 60 per cent during the 12-year period of the Convention. This agreement became incorporated in the Austrian Accession Treaty when Austria joined the Community in 1995.[46]

The Community envisages, in future, providing for national emission ceilings for some air pollutants.

3. DECISION-MAKING PROCEDURE

(a) Elaboration of a legislative measure[47]

(i) Commission proposal

2—61   The Commission has, as mentioned, the monopoly on taking initiatives for legal action, although there is at least a political, if not a legal, obligation to take such initiatives under Article 192(2) (ex 138b (2)) and Article 175(3) (ex 130s(3)) E.C.[48] It is at the Commission's discretion to decide what form, objective and content its proposal for a legislative act shall take and what preparatory work is undertaken. Normally, a comparative assessment of national legislation is made as well as one or several studies on the scientific, technical, economic and environmental aspects of a subject and estimations about the impact of the planned measures undertaken. Draft proposals are prepared by the technical units inside the Directorate-General responsible, not by a central "drafting unit".

Consultations with Member States at an administrative level generally start with a

---

[43] Reg. 3093/94 (n. 9), Art. 4(10).
[44] Dir. 88/609 [1988] O.J. L336/1.
[45] Agreement between the European Economic Community and the Republic of Austria on the transit of goods by road and rail [1992] O.J. L373/6; Reg. 3637/92 on a system of distribution of rights of transit (ecopoints)for heavy goods vehicles with a laden weight of over 7.5 tonnes registered in a Member State transiting through Austria [1992] O.J. L373/1.
[46] Accession Treaty, Protocol 9 [1995] O.J. L1/1.
[47] See generally: Interinstitutional Agreement on common guidelines for the quality of drafting of Community legislation [1999] O.J. C73/1.
[48] See para. 2–05, above.

first draft of a directive, which is frequently accompanied by background documents which explain the approach chosen, indicate the options and raise other matters that might be of interest. Practice varies as to whether at this stage of the drafting a consensus is sought with other departments inside the Commission before a draft is sent to a wider audience.

2—62   Such discussions hardly ever take the form of bilateral discussions with Member States (which would take place in the different capitals rather than in Brussels): they are limited to particularly "important" Member States and they are mainly made to consult on the approach to be taken or the strategy to be adopted. Multilateral discussions on draft proposals for environmental directives between the Commission's administration and Member States' officials always take place. These meetings are convened in Brussels on invitation by the Commission administration which chairs them. Officials from interested Commission departments participate. The invitation to these meetings is addressed to the Permanent Representation of Member States with the Community and asks them to designate experts to attend the meeting. The experts need not come from environmental administration or even administration at all.

As environmental law often is technical and has a limited number of national rules to take into consideration, only one or two of such multilateral meetings of experts are usually needed to reach a consensus. In areas where more general problems are touched upon, discussions inside the Commission and with Member States' experts may take a long time. Thus, while the Commission services drafted 23 texts for a proposal on environmental impact assessment[49] before the text could become an official proposal for a directive and be sent to the Council, the directive on liquid beverage containers[50] had almost as many drafts in the preliminary stage alone.

2—63   Parallel to those meetings with governmental experts, discussions with organisations from trade and industry and environmental organisations take place. No systematic consultation is organised, although the Commission services prefer consultation with European organisations over national bodies or even individual companies. The sheer number of professional organisations guarantees them a greater chance of consultation, compared to environmental organisations which are under-represented at Community level and lack resources, know-how and expertise in successful lobbying.

At the end of the consultation process a draft text emerges which the Directorate-General responsible takes back into the Commission in order to start the formal adoption phase. The draft, together with an explanatory memorandum,[51] is sent to all interested Directorates-General and in all cases to the Legal Service with the request for approval. There will be different positions (which of course are also influenced by outside lobbying) with an attempt to reach a compromise text. The revised text then goes into the approval procedure of the Commission itself. At cabinet level, attempts are made to find, if necessary, a political compromise on outstanding questions. If the

---

[49] Dir. 85/337 [1985] O.J. L175/40; for more details see para. 4–10, below.
[50] Dir. 85/339 [1985] O.J. L176/18; see also para. 9–49, below.
[51] Internal Commission rules have largely standardised the content of the explanatory memorandum, though each text is adapted to the specific subject matter; as an example, the proposal for a directive on end of life vehicles, COM (97) 358 of July 9, 1997, might be quoted which contains the following headings: 1. Introduction; 2. Problems addressed in this proposal; 3. The fifth environmental action programme; 4. Environmental objectives; 5. Internal market and economic objectives; 6. Economic assessment; 7. Situation in Member States; 8. Developments at international level; 9. Subsidiarity and proportionality; 10. Legislative and administrative simplification; 11. Imports from third countries; 12. Consistency with other Community policies; 13. Consultation with stakeholders; 14. Legal basis; 15. Data/scientific bases; 16. Content Article by Article; 17. Impact of the proposal on business with special reference to small and medium-sized enterprises.

cabinets succeed, the 20 Commissioners normally approve the draft by way of written procedure. Where they do not succeed, the draft is discussed orally: a majority of 11 Commissioners is necessary to have a draft adopted as a formal Commission proposal. It may happen that a text is not capable of being approved by the Commission, though this is rather unusual in environmental matters.

The official Commission proposal for a directive or a regulation is published in the *Official Journal* of the European Communities, part C. The explanatory memorandum, which is not an integral part of the proposal, is made available to the public in the form of an official COM-document. The text of the proposed act is drafted in all 11 languages, while the explanatory memorandum is usually produced in only English, French and German.

(ii) European Parliament, ECOSOC and Committee of the Regions

2—64   The Commission's proposal is transmitted to the Council, which passes the text on to the European Parliament, the Economic and Social Committee and the Committee of the Regions, which all give opinions on the text. These opinions are prepared within committees, under the responsibility of a rapporteur for the proposal, who is selected from the committee's members. Commission officials attend committee meetings, answer questions and explain reasons for the options taken. Their attitude is marked by the necessity to "defend", if possible, the Commission's proposal.

There is no standard practice for how the rapporteurs assemble the necessary know-how to prepare their report and the draft opinion. Both are mostly prepared by means of informal contacts with persons or groups which are politically or professionally close to the rapporteur's political party or group; formal written consultation with groups or public hearings in the Parliament are exceptional and almost never take place in the other two bodies.

In Parliament the Environmental Committee votes on the draft opinion and all amendments which were presented by members of the Committee. Then the text goes to Parliament's plenary, where again amendments to the draft opinion may be tabled. The opinion is voted upon and is, after adoption, published in the *Official Journal*. The Committee's report is not published, but is available from the European Parliament.

2—65   Since 1979, when the European Parliament became elected by general elections, there has been agreement between the Commission and the Parliament that the Commission would take on board amendments suggested by the Parliament wherever possible. Obviously, such a vague clause which raises difficulties in practice, does not satisfy Parliament, which is of the opinion that all amendments to proposals should be accepted by the Commission. It sometimes uses procedural means (delays or refusals to vote, extensive discussions between the rapporteur and the Commission's services or the president of the Environmental Committee and the Commissioner for environmental issues) in order to compel the Commission to accept its amendments.

The procedure in the Economic and Social Committee and the Committee of the Regions is similar; also their adopted opinions are published in the *Official Journal*.

(iii) Council procedure

2—66   At Council level the Commission's proposal is first examined by a working group, which normally takes up its work without having the opinion of the other institutions. The frequency of meetings depends on whether the presidency wishes to get ahead with the proposal[52]; whereas some proposals are immediately taken up, others might wait for years or not be discussed at all. The working party starts with a general discussion and then passes through each individual article. After having revised the proposal and listed all objections to its different provisions in detail, the working group's chair sends the text to the Committee of Permanent Representatives (COREPER). He may also do so when he wishes to receive political instruction on questions which the working group feels unable to solve. The report sent to COREPER contains the new text proposal, accompanied by remarks, reservations, suggested compromise solutions or declarations by Member States.

COREPER meets once a week and deals with practically all questions of Community policy. In environmental matters, COREPER tries to concentrate discussions on Commission proposals in one or two meetings which take place in preparation of Council meetings on environmental matters. After discussion of the environmental proposal as it emerged from the working group the text is either sent back to the working group with further instructions or—where an agreement by the Council seems possible—it is sent to the Environmental Council for decision or for political guidance on basic issues. COREPER prepares the Council agenda, though the final decision on it is made by the presidency of the Council.

2—67 The Council may only take a decision where the opinions of the other institutions, in particular that of the European Parliament, have been given; and in all cases the Council must decide unanimously where it amends a Commission proposal (Article 250 (ex 189a) E.C.). The Council's decision in environmental matters consists in the adoption of the Commission's proposal, where the Parliament has only a consultative function—mainly Articles 175(2)(ex 130s(2)) in environmental matters and 37 (ex 43) in agricultural-environmental matters—or where Parliament has either not proposed amendments or the Council adopts all amendments proposed by the European Parliament.[53] In other environmental cases, the Council establishes a common position which is then submitted to the European Parliament for a second reading. If Parliament agrees to the common position or does not decide, the common position becomes the adopted act; if Parliament rejects the common position with an absolute majority, the proposal is rejected. If the Council agrees to all amendments which Parliament has proposed in the second reading the legal act is so adopted. If this is not the case, a Conciliation Committee is convened which consists of 15 members of the Council and the same number of members from Parliament; the Commission participates, but is not a member as such. Where a compromise is reached, that compromise normally becomes the adopted legal act. Where no compromise is reached, the proposal is considered rejected.

Details of this co-decision procedure, which is the normal procedure in environmental matters since the entering into effect of the Amsterdam Treaty, are laid down in Article 251; Article 252 (ex 189c) provides for some different procedures for the co-operation procedure, which, however, no longer applies in environmental matters.

2—68 The co-decision procedure is complicated and can hardly be called a legislative procedure in which citizens have much input. It is marked by the effort to place more influence on the legislative procedure to the European Parliament, the only elected Community institution, without significantly reducing the decision-making power of Member States who meet in Council.

---

[52] As an example, Dir. 96/59 on PCB/PCT [1996] O.J. L243/31 may be quoted, which took eight years between the Commission's proposal and the adoption by the Council; in contrast to that, Dir. 96/61 on integrated prevention and pollution control [1991] O.J. L257/26, was adopted within two years.
[53] Art. 251(2) (ex 189b(2)) E.C.; this procedure was changed by the Amsterdam Treaty 1997.

The co-decision procedure is the normal procedure for decisions in environmental matters, as follows from Article 175(1) in the Amsterdam Treaty. However, since Article 6 of the E.C. Treaty requires that environmental requirements are taken into consideration when measures in other Communities are adopted, measures which aim at protecting or improving the evnronment need not necessarily be based on Article 175(1). Rather, Article 175(2), Article 174(4) for international envionmental matters, Article 37 (ex 43) for agricultural matters, Article 80 (ex 84) on transport, Article 93 (ex 99) on taxation, Article 95 (ex 100a) on the internal market, Article 133 (ex 113) on commercial matters or Article 172 (ex 130o) on research may also be applicable.

(b) The choice of the legal basis

(i) General principles

2—69   The question of which legal basis is to be applied has been the subject of a number of clarifying judgments by the Court of Justice. The Court did not favour a double legal base for legal acts, because in particular the European Parliament's rights of participation in the decision-making procedure were different under both provisions.[54] It is not certain whether this judgment would still be the same today when in particular the most important provisions for environmental measures, Articles 175(1) (ex 130s(1)) and 95 (ex 100a) now both provide for the co-decision procedure. In particular the Council adopts measures that are based on several Treaty provisions.[55]

The Court of Justice stated at several occasions that the choice of the legal basis for a Community measure was not left to the discretion of the Community institutions, but had to be based on objective criteria, in particular the stated objective and the content of the measure.[56] Furthermore, the Court was of the opinion that where a measure pursued two objectives at the same time, which had exactly the same weight in that matter, preference had to be given to the legal basis that ensured greater participation of the European Parliament. The Court does not decide how to proceed when the participation procedure for the European Parliament is the same, but considers other matters—such as, for instance, those following both from Article 95(4) to (8) (ex 100a(4) to (8)), and from Article 176 (ex 130t) E.C. In my opinion, Article 95 would prevail in such a case because it leads, in reality, to a greater degree of integration.

2—70   Where two or more objectives of an environmental measure had a different emphasis, the Court applied the theory of the "centre of gravity": it looked at the legislative measure as a whole as well as at its different provisions. Where the measure primarily aimed at the protection of the environment, Article 175 was applied; where the main emphasis was placed on ensuring the free movement of goods, Article 95 was the appropriate legal basis, even in cases where the measure also aimed, secondly, at the protection of the environment.[57] Similar reasonings were applied when other Treaty provisions such as Articles 37 or 133 were considered against Article 175.

The Court summarised its jurisprudence as follows[58]:

---

[54] Case C-300/89 *Commission v. Council* [1991] E.C.R. I-2867.
[55] See, *e.g.* Dec. 94/800 on adhering to the Uruguay agreements [1994] O.J. L336/1,which was based on (old) Articles 43, 54, 57, 66, 75, 84, 99, 100, 100a, 113, 235; Dec. 98/487 on an agreement with the United States on humane trapping methods for animals [1998] O.J. L219/24, which was based on (old) Articles 113 and 100a.
[56] Case C-233/94 *Germany v. Parliament and Council* [1997] E.C.R. I-2405.
[57] Cases C-155/91 *Commission v. Council* [1993] E.C.R. I-939; C-187/93 *European Parliament v. Council* [1994] E.C.R. I-2857; C-164 & 165/97 *European Parliament v. Council*, judgment of February 25, 1999, not yet reported.
[58] Cases C-164 & 165/97 (n. 57 above), para. 14.

"it is necessary, in order to determine the appropriate legal basis, to consider whether the measures in question relate principally to a particular field of actions, having only incidental effects on other policies, or whether both aspects are equally essential. If the first hypothesis is correct, recourse to a single legal basis is sufficent . . . ; if the second is correct, it is insufficient and the institution is required to adopt the measure on the basis of both the provisions from which its competence derives . . . However, no such dual basis is possible, where the procedures laid down for each legal basis are incompatible with each other . . ."

This theory seems to give good results in most cases. However, its concept raises a number of problems:

- **2—71** Whether the objective of a directive or a regulation is the protection of the environment or the achievement of the internal market and the free flow of goods, is not at all clear. It is worth mentioning in this regard that the basic Directive on emission standards for cars was adopted as part of the Community programme to eliminate technical barriers to trade, *i.e.* with the objective of establishing a common market for cars.[59] The fact that a Member State presses for more stringent environmental standards for cars does not detract from the fact that the Community provision is primarily designed to maintain the free circulation of goods and to lay down stringent environmental standards to prevent a disturbance of the internal market. However, it may equally be the objective of a Community provision to take on board the motives of the environmentally conscious Member State and improve the quality of the environment. These reasons for a Community provision may be supplemented by others, such as protection of consumers, protection of the national or European motor industry, an attempt to shut out imports from third countries, or economic, transport or commercial policy reasons.

  In case C-302/86, Denmark had prohibited the use of metal cans as containers for beer and some soft drinks. The primary objective of the ban was, apparently, the protection of the environment, especially since the ban was part of a series of measures to avoid and reduce waste from packaging materials. The ban, however, undoubtedly implied competitive disadvantages for suppliers of beer and soft drinks from other Member States, as cans are lighter and cheaper to transport. The Danish drink industry was therefore a main beneficiary from the ban. It is impossible to ascertain with certainty what the specific primary objective of the Danish measure was, as tax, health, import of raw materials (aluminium and steel) and other considerations may also have played a part. In the same way, a Community measure prohibiting cans could also have several objectives, such as the maintenance or restoration of uniform provisions on cans within the Community; correction of a solo initiative by a Member State; protection of the environment from cans; promotion of the glass and plastic industry; a reduction in dependence on raw material imports; or for economic policy reasons.

- **2—72** The introduction of Community car emission standards, which required the introduction of catalytic converters, was motivated by increased air pollution. This was the reason stated in the Directives, which were partly an amendment of Directive 70/220 and partly independent directives[60]; mention was also made of internal market considerations—however, this was in a very marginal form. Directive

[59] Dir. 70/220 [1970] O.J. L76/1.
[60] Dir. 88/6 [1988] O.J. L36/1; Dir. 88/436 [1988] O.J. L214/1; Dir. 89/458 [1989] O.J. L226/1; Dir. 91/441 [1991] O.J. L242/1; Dir. 93/59 [1993] O.J. L186/21; Dir. 94/12 [1994] O.J. L100/42.

91/173 on restrictions of the use of pentachlorophenol (PCP)[61] was constructed in a similar way: the Commission was notified by Germany of restrictions on the use of PCP. On its proposal, the Council adopted Directive 91/173 which severely restricted the use of PCP in the Community, stating in the Directive that the main objective was to reduce the environmental and human health risk of PCP. Directive 91/157 limits the content of dangerous substances in batteries and accumulators.[62] Its primary objective, as it appears in the preamble and the text of the Directive, is the reduction of dangerous substances in the environment.

In all these cases, to which others could be added, the directives were based on Article 95—correctly in my opinion. If, however, one were taking the theory of the "centre of gravity" seriously, all these directives would have had to be based on Article 175, since their primary objective, as indicated in their text, was the protection of the environment. In particular, where a substance or a product is banned or its use restricted, it is almost always not the case that the primary objective will be the functioning of the internal market.

• 2—73   The theory of the centre of gravity of a specific measure is not as clear as it might appear. A good example is case C-300/89,[63] relating to Directive 89/428 on the harmonisation of programmes for the reduction of waste from the titanium dioxide industry,[64] where both the Council and the Commission agents based their arguments before the Court of Justice on the primary objective of Directive 89/428. However, while the Commission agent (attorney) saw the primary objective of the Directive as the creation of equal competitive conditions for the titanium dioxide industry and thus wanted to have Article 95 established as the correct legal basis, the Council agent saw as its primary objective the protection of the environment and pleaded for Article 175 as the appropriate legal basis. The Court, in that specific case, did not concur with that theory at all and decided, for other reasons, in favour of Article 95.

2—74   The conclusion from all this is that the wording of the preamble and the articles of a legal act cannot be decisive on their own, particularly as it is a Community institution—it is the Council, in fact, which determines the wording, in cases of co-decisions together with the European Parliament. Preambles are normally adopted without much discussion. However, the Council is also obliged to respect the provisions of the Treaty. It cannot turn away from it just by arranging the wording of a legislative measure. The relevant criterion must therefore be, whether—independent from the wording of the measure—uniformity is necessary to achieve the Treaty's objective. Indeed, as follows from Article 14 (ex 7a) E.C., the Community has the objective of achieving the free movement of goods and services as quickly as possible. This objective requires uniform rules. For this reason, Community instruments laying down common product standards must come under Article 95 (ex 100a). This provision also applies when the measure contains common provisions of a restrictive nature, such as bans, restrictions on use, or maximum concentration levels, for example. If such measures were based on Article 175, the effect arising from Article 176 (ex 130t) would be that the Community's objective of achieving free circulation of goods or, more generally, of completing the internal market, would never be attained. The legal basis of a measure which affects the environment and the circulation of goods should therefore be chosen with a view to permitting achievement of both objectives, namely

[61] Dir. 91/173 [1991] O.J. L85/34.
[62] Dir. 91/157 [1991] O.J. L78/38.
[63] Case C-300/89 (n. 54).
[64] Dir. 89/428 [1989] O.J. L201/56.

completion of the internal market (Article 14) and improvement of the quality of the environment (Article 175). The better provision for both these objectives is Article 95.[65] Since Article 6 (ex 3c) E.C. requires that environmental requirements must be integrated into other Community policies, the choice of this legal basis is not really a risk for the environment.

The Council seems, at present, to apply Article 175 as a basis for harmonisation of product-related measures, in cases where it does not wish to proceed to toal harmonisation under Article 95. This approach neglects Article 14 of the E.C. Treaty, which expressly requires measures that lead to the achievement of the internal market. Article 14 is so clear and unambiguous that there is no room for having product-related measures adopted under Article 175. Article 14 and, more generally, the whole Treaty is also binding on the Council. In conclusion, therefore, all product-related measures must, under the present E.C. Treaty, be based on Article 95 of the E.C. Treaty, with the exception, though of Article 37 (ex 43), which is *lex specialis* to Article 95, as appears from Article 32 (ex 38) E.C.[66]

(ii) Nature protection

2—75 Nature conservation measures are a specific problem. Fauna and flora species are not products under the E.C. Treaty, as is obvious from Article 30 (ex 36) E.C.: if they were to be treated as products, their mentioning in Article 30, which constitutes an exception to Article 28 (ex 30), would not be justified. It also appears from Article 95(4) (ex 100a(4)) E.C. Treaty that measures for the protection of the health and life of animals and plants are different from product-related measures: under certain conditions, Member States may take such measures, while they are not allowed to do so to protect products.

The Council has therefore quite rightly based nature protection measures on Article 175(1),[67] including provisions on trade in endangered species. An exception is Regulation 3254/91 on the ban of leghold traps and the import of certain furs from specified non-E.C. countries, which the Council based on Articles 175(1) and 133 (ex 113) E.C. jointly.[68]

Measures on biotechnology also belong to nature conservation measures. Genetically modified organisms as well as genetically modified micro-organisms remain organisms, thus living entities. The fact of basing the deliberate release of genetically modified organisms on Article 95[69] only indicates that the borderline between life and non-life has been lost.

(iii) Waste

2—76 Another specific problem is the legal basis for waste measures. Waste is a physical object and as such is capable of being traded between Member States. International legislation has, in the last 10 years, started to differentiate between waste which is destined for recovery and waste which is destined for final disposal. The reason for this is that a buyer might have an interest in acquiring waste which has an economic

---

[65] The insertion of Arts 95(4) to (8) by the Amsterdam Treaty 1997 does not challenge these conclusions. It is true that Article 95 is now closer to the system of Articles 175 and 176; however, any measure under Article 95(4) to (8) needs authorisation from the Commission. It is thus subjected to a specific control to see whether it brings into question the objectives of the internal market.

[66] Art. 32(2) (ex 38(2)) E.C.: "Save as otherwise provided in Articles 33 to 38, the rules laid down for the establishment of the common market shall apply to agricultural products."

[67] Prior to 1987, the Council had used Art. 308 (ex 235) as the legal basis.

[68] Reg. 3254/91 [1991] O.J. L308/1; see also paras 5–36 *et seq.*, below.

[69] Dir. 90/220 (n. 90).

value; by contrast, the owner of waste which is destined for disposal would normally be willing to pay for such a disposal.

The Court of Justice decided that waste should come under Article 28 (ex 30) E.C., whether it was recoverable or not.[70] The Court justified this decision by pointing out that waste was the subject of commercial transactions and that it was in practice impossible to differentiate between recoverable and non-recoverable waste. The Court added, however, that "waste has a special characteristic. The accumulation of waste, even before it becomes a health hazard, constitutes a threat to the environment because of the limited capacity of each region or locality for receiving it".

2—77   Although waste is a product, the Court held, in another judgment, that Directive 91/156[71] on waste was rightly based on Article 175.[72] In this judgment, the Court recurred to the theory of the "centre of gravity", the primary objective: it saw the Directive as aiming primarily at the protection of the environment and only dealing in an ancillary way with aspects of the internal market. This choice of legal basis was further confirmed in case C-187/93,[73] where the Court again recurred to the theory of "centre of gravity" and held that Regulation 259/93 on the shipment of waste[74] was correctly based on Article 175.

The Council based directives on batteries[75] and on packaging and packaging waste[76] on Article 95. This approach seems to suggest that the Council considers Articles 175 and 95 as being equally capable of being used for product-related waste standards and that it chooses the legal basis according to the relative emphasis on free circulation or protection of the environment expressed in each directive. As mentioned, the Treaty provisions are not at the disposal of the Council and the obligation to complete the internal market as quickly as possible excludes having recurrence to Article 175 at the Council's discretion.

2—78   A closer look at Directive 94/62[77] illustrates the problem. The Directive is based on Article 95. Of the first 12 considerants, 10 deal with environmental objectives and two with environmental and internal market issues; not one considerant deals exclusively with internal market issues. Article 1 indicates the objective of the Directive, indicating as the first objective the protection of the environment.[78] Articles 9 and 10 provide for essential requirements which packaging has to comply with. Article 18 stipulates that packaging which satisfies the Directive's provisions shall not be impeded from circulating within the Community.

It is difficult to see how the main aim of this Directive, according to its objective and content, could be the achievement of the internal market rather than the protection of the environment. All the Court's criteria plead for Article 175 as the legal basis.

---

[70] Case C-2/90 *Commission v. Belgium* [1992] E.C.R. I-4431: "waste, whether recyclable or not, should be regarded as a product the movement of which must not in principle, pursuant to Article 30 EEC, be impeded."

[71] Dir. 91/156 on waste [1991] O.J. L78/32.

[72] Case C-155/91 *Commission v. Council* [1993] E.C.R. I-939.

[73] Case C-187/93 *European Parliament v. Council* [1994] E.C.R. I-2857.

[74] Reg. 259/93 (n. 23).

[75] Dir. 91/157 [1991] O.J. L78/38.

[76] Dir. 94/62 [1994] O.J. L365/10.

[77] *Ibid.*

[78] *Ibid.*, Art. 1: "1. This Directive aims to harmonise national measures concerning the management of packaging and packaging waste in order, on the one hand, to prevent and impact thereof on the environment of all Member States as well as of third countries or to reduce such impact, thus providing a high level of environmental protection, and, on the other hand, to ensure the functioning of the internal market and to avoid obstacles to trade and distortion and restriction of competition within the Community.

2. To this end this Directive lays down measures aimed, as a first priority, at preventing the production of packaging waste and, as additional fundamental principles, at reusing packaging, at recycling and other forms of recovering packaging waste and, hence, at reducing the final disposal of such waste."

Jans is of the opinion that a directive which contains a free-movement clause, such as the one of Article 18 of Directive 94/62, leads to the application of Article 95; more generally, a waste directive which contains product standards is to be based on Article 95. Advocate-General Tesauro, in his Opinion on case C-155/91,[79] held that waste directives concerning specific items of waste or waste from specific industrial sectors (such as batteries, packaging waste or waste from the titanium dioxide industry) are to be based on Article 95, since in such cases the competitive element of an act at Community level is dominant. In contrast, waste measures which tackle the problem of waste generally were to be based on Article 175, since their primary objective was environmental protection.

2—79 It is not quite clear whether the Court of Justice, in case C-155/91, implicitly adhered to that concept. It has the disadvantage that the impact of a "general" directive or regulation on a specific sector of industry might be as great as the impact of a "specific" directive: the borderline between general acts and specific acts is not at all clear, particularly if one remembers that, for instance, "general" Directive 75/442 is accompanied by Decision 94/3 which contains a detailed list of wastes which come under that Directive;[80] that "general" Directive 91/689 on hazardous waste is accompanied by Decision 94/904 which details which wastes are hazardous,[81] and that "general" Regulation 259/93 on the shipment of waste contains a long list of waste, the export of which to third countries is banned or the shipment of which within the Community is or may be otherwise restricted.[82]

In conclusion there is not yet a clear, convincing way to classify waste-related measures under either Article 175 or 95. The Council favours Article 175, because of the existence of Article 176 (ex 130t), and the Court of Justice generally accepts this approach. It is to be expected that in future most waste legislation will be based on Article 175, also because the European Parliament no longer has more participation rights under Article 95 than under Article 175 and is thus unlikely to push for the application of Article 95.

(iv) Other environmental measures

2—80 Standards for industrial installations, production-related standards and environmental production standards concern air emissions or water discharges from installations, conditions for landfill sites and accident-prevention measures in industrial plants for example. Installations do not circulate freely within the Community, but the products produced in them do. Environmental standards for plants may have an impact on costs and affect the competitive position of a manufacturer. This is therefore relevant for the establishment and functioning of the internal market which also includes competition free from distortion (Article 95(4)).[83] The risk of distortion of competition increases as environmental standards become more stringent, unless uniform provisions prevail throughout the Community. If the objectives "completion of the internal market" and "improvement of the quality of the environment" are to be attained simultaneously throughout the Community, provisions relating to production standards or to plants must be based on Article 95.

The Council instead bases all production-related directives on Article 175 and the

---

[79] Case C-155/91 (n. 72 above), Advocate Tesauro's Opinion, para. 10.
[80] Dec. 94/3 [1994] O.J. L5/15.
[81] Dec. 94/904 [1994] O.J. L356/14.
[82] Reg. 259/93 [1993] O.J. L30/1; see also para. 9–36, below.
[83] Case C-300/89 *Commission v. Council* [1991] E.C.R. I-939.

Commission now follows the same line in its proposals. This practice seems doubtful. Different environmental standards for the production of goods will lead to different competitive situations, the more cost-intensive such standards are, the greater the competitive distortion becomes. It might be acceptable to have differences between one Member State and another of 1 or 2 per cent in the production costs, when the differences are due to different environmental standards. However, where such differences reach 5, 10 or more per cent of the production costs[84] these differences must be eliminated through the adoption of uniform standards, thus by measures based on Article 95. In other words, the dividing line between Articles 95 and 175 is not fixed once and for all: it is flexible, and the more stringent the environmental standards are—always bearing in mind the requirement of a high level of environmental protection—the more it is necessary to base the measure on Article 95.

2—81   Basing production-related environmental measures on Article 175 also bears the political risk that Member States who place low priority on environmental issues will inevitably try to ensure that standards fixed at Community level are low, arguing that Member States with a developed environmental policy could always, under Article 176, adopt more stringent protective measures. But a tendency towards lower Community environmental standards is bound to increase discrepancies within the Community and will thus be, from an environmental point of view, counterproductive. Indeed, even environmentally conscious Member States will be reluctant to adopt stricter measures as this would lead to a competitive disadvantage of installations on their territory.[85] Finally, it should be mentioned that the debates at Community level on environmental standards such as air emissions or water discharges or even on quality standards, never centre on the issue of how much pollution of the pollutant the environment can tolerate; the discussion instead focuses on the question of what standards can reasonably be imposed on the polluting industries or other polluters. This demonstrates that the competitive aspect—which comes under Article 95—is in question, not the protection of the environment—which comes under Article 175.

Perhaps the progressive elimination of significant differences in the procedures and the legal consequences between Articles 95 and 175 by the Amsterdam Treaty will lead to some reconsideration of these questions.

2—82   The Council's practice might be summarised as follows:

(a) Measures of a general nature are based on Article 175. Examples: access to information, environmental impact assessment, ecoaudit, measures related to installations;

(b) Nature conservation: all measures based on Article 175. Exception: ban on leghold trap and fur trade: Articles 175 and 133 (ex 113);

(c) Products: measures based on Article 95. Exceptions: authorisation for pesticides: Article 37; ozone-depleting substances, contained use of genetically modified micro-organisms: Article 175;

(d) Water measures are all based on Article 175;

(e) Air pollution measures are based on Article 175. Exceptions: emissions from cars and motorcycles, composition of petrol and gas: Article 95; emissions from aeroplanes: Article 80 (ex 84);

---

[84] In case C-300/89 (n. 83) these differences reached 20 per cent of the production costs.
[85] Such a trend is already visible at the discussion on the introduction of a CO_2 tax at national level.

(f) Noise measures are based on Article 95. Exception: noise from aeroplanes: Article 80 (ex 84);

(g) Waste measures are based on Article 175. Exception: packaging and packaging waste, batteries, waste programmes from titanium dioxide industry: Article 95.

(c) The different legal bases

(i) Measures under Article 175(1) (ex 130s(1))

2—83 Legal decisions—regulations, directives, decisions or recommendations—under Article 175(1) are taken by Council and Parliament jointly, according to the procedure of Article 251 (ex 189b) E.C. The consultation of the Economic and Social Committee and of the Committee of the Regions is mandatory. Council and Parliament must be in possession of a proposal by the Commission.

Article 175(1) is completed by Article 175(5), introduced in 1993. This provision has its origin in the idea, particularly stressed by the less wealthy Member States, that if the protection of the environment were in the general interest of the Community, then the Community should pay for such measures. The provision stipulates that it is the Council which must, together with the measure which it adopts, decide on the specific measures that countries must make. The following conditions must be fulfilled. The Community measure must be adopted by virtue of Article 175(1). This condition prevents a single Member State from vetoing the adoption of a Community measure until the state has obtained a temporary derogation of financial assistance; there must be a request from a Member State that costs are disproportionate. This condition leads to an examination of the request by the Council, *i.e.* by all other Member States, and the Commission; thus, trivial requests will more easily be detected. The costs must be deemed to be inappropriate for the public authorities. It is thus not the cost of the measure itself which will be examined, but rather the cost impact on public authorities; where these authorities have the possibility of charging private undertakings (where they can make the polluter pay, in particular) Article 175(5) is not applicable.

2—84 The Council decision,[86] which needs a qualified majority, may consist of temporary derogations or financial support from the Cohesion Fund. The possibility of granting a temporary derogation to some Member States existed well before the Maastricht Treaty and was used in a number of cases. This provision demonstrates that non-compliance with environmental provisions brings an economic advantage to the non-complying Member State.

The financial support from the Cohesion Fund, which is not limited to the Member States beneficiary of the Cohesion Fund,[87] is not further specified. It may consist of a lump sum or in regular payments over a longer period, or the financing of an investment programme.

Paragraph 5 is introduced by the words "without prejudice to the principle that the polluter should pay". In view of this wording, it could well be argued that non-compliance with Community environmental legislation is a breach of the polluter-pays principle. By mid-1999, Article 175(5) had not been applied even once by the Council.

---

[86] Since Art. 175(5) mentions that the decision is to be taken "in the act adopting that measure" and Art. 175(1) provides for joint Council and Parliament decisions, the form of the decision under Art. 175(5) is equally a co-decision between Parliament and Council.
[87] At present, until 2005, Greece, Spain, Portugal and Ireland.

(ii) Decisions on programmes, Article 175(3) (ex 130s(3))

2—85   Article 175(3) provides for co-decision majority procedures and also for the adoption of "general action programmes setting out priority objectives to be attained".[88] The initiative for Article 175(3) lies with the Commission, which cannot be obliged to submit a proposal for a decision on an action programme.[89] An action programme may be limited to a specific sector of environmental policy; it need not cover the whole range of activities.[90]

(iii) Decisions under Article 175(2) (ex 130s(2))

Article 175(2) provides for the adoption of some measures by unanimous decisions. The provision is an exception to Article 175(1) and has therefore to be interpreted narrowly. The European Parliament, the Economic and Social Committee and the Committee of the Regions are to be consulted.

2—86   **Fiscal provisions**   Provisions of a fiscal nature normally come under Article 93 (ex 99) E.C., which expressly provides for unanimous decisions. Article 93 provides for harmonisation of fiscal legislation to the extent that it is necessary for the establishment and functioning of the internal market. Article 175(2) clarifies that fiscal measures are also permitted in order to achieve the objectives of environmental protection (Article 174(1)). Fiscal measures touch the core of national sovereignty. It is therefore understandable that Member States who did not accept majority decisions under Article 93 were not ready to accept such majority decisions for eco-taxes.

Since the provision only mentions the fiscal character of a measure, acts which provide for environmental charges, environmental fees or an environmental fund for covering damage of the environment do not come under Article 175(2).[91] For a measure to come under Article 175(2), the fiscal content must be the primary objective of the Community measure. Environmental provisions on taxes which form an additional part of another set of rules that are not primarily of a fiscal nature, may be the subject of majority decisions.[92] The dividing line between this provision and Article 93 is the same as between Article 175(1) and Article 95 (ex 100a) E.C.[93]

2—87   **Town and country planning and land use**   Measures for town and country planning and land use also have to be adopted unanimously. The provision in particular leaves infrastructural planning decisions to the autonomous decision of each Member State, since it gives to each state, via the unanimity requirement, a veto against Community planning decisions which affect its territory. It is consistent with this understanding that the provision of the E.C. Treaty, which deals with planning measures for infrastructures, also requires unanimous decisions: Article 156(2) (ex 129d(2)) E.C. concerns the planning of trans-European networks for transport, telecommunications and energy infrastructure; it provides for the elaboration of Community (non-binding) guidelines for such networks, which may be adopted only with the approval of the Member State concerned.

---

[88] See also para. 1–09, above.
[89] See, however, Art. 192 (ex 138b) E.C. and para. 2–21, above.
[90] See, e.g. the proposal for a groundwater action programme [1996] O.J. C355/1.
[91] J. Jans, *European environmental law* (The Hague, London and Boston, 1995), p. 36; P. Pagh, *EU miljoeret* (2nd ed., Copenhagen, 1996), p. 120; A. Epiney, *Umweltrecht in der Europäischen Union* (Cologne, Berlin, Bonn and Munich, 1997), p. 57.
[92] See, e.g. the tax provisions in the different directives on car emissions, para. 4–30, below.
[93] See para. 3–38, below.

Article 175(2) mentions town and country planning, land use and the management of water resources.[94] Under this heading come infrastructure projects such as cities, ports, roads, railways, airports, dams and so on: such projects shall not be decided by a Council majority, but shall be determined with the consent of the affected Member State.

2—88 Measures of a general nature and measure of waste management do not fall under this provision and are therefore to be decided according to the general rule of Article 175(1). The mentioning of measures of a general nature signals that such measures also concern town and country planning, land use and management of water resources; otherwise, this part of the notion would make no sense, since such measures would have come under Article 175(1) anyway. The difference between measures of a general and of a specific nature derives from the objective of the derogation of Article 175(2): Member States shall not be compelled against their will to build a new airport, a railway line, a port or another infrastructure project at a specific place. Instead they should determine where the project would be effected and what dimension it would have.

Thus, Directive 91/271 on urban waste water, which requests Member States to build waste-water treatment plants,[95] would not have to be adopted under Article 175(2) but under Article 175(1): indeed, each Member State remains free to decide how many installations are to be built and where they are to be placed. In the same way, Directives 79/409 on the conservation of wild birds and 92/43 on the conservation of natural habitats and of wild fauna and flora[96] are of a general, not a specific, nature. No Member State is obliged to designate a specific habitat under these directives as natural habitat even where the wealth of natural biodiversity sometimes leads to a reduction in the unlimited discretion of Member States; also, the land use in designated areas is not regulated; the requirement to abstain, within habitats, from significant disturbance of protected species is not a measure of land use, but rather a general nature conservation measure.[97]

Other measures of a general nature are, for instance, provisions on the environmental impact assessment for projects or plans[98] or measures which require clean-up activities for certain areas which are particularly polluted by air contaminants or water discharges. Waste management projects concern in particular landfill provisions, but there are also measures to clean up contaminated soil.

2—89 **Energy matters** Unanimous decisions are finally required for "measures significantly affecting a Member State's choice between different energy sources and the general structure of its energy supply". Measures which come under this provision are, for instance, measures which lead to the abandoning, for environmental reasons, of nuclear energy or of lignite or coal that has too high a sulphur content. Conversely, however, a Community measure not to allow the import of petrol from third countries and to rely primarily on nuclear energy throughout Community territory would need unanimity in Council.

In contrast to this, the decision to adhere to the United Nations Convention on

---

[94] See as regards the interpretation of "managment of water resources", para. 7–03, below.

[95] Dir. 91/271 concerning urban waste water treatment [1991] O.J. L135/40; this Directive is a "water", not a "waste" directive; for details see para. 7–32, below.

[96] Dir. 79/409 [1979] O.J. L103/1; Dir. 92/43 [1992] O.J. L206/7.

[97] See for more details, L. Krämer, E.C. Treaty and environmental law (3rd ed., London, 1998), para. 3.22. Epiney (n. 91), p. 58 is of the opinion that Dirs 79/409 and 92/43 presumably come under Art. 175(2); in the same sense Frenz, Europäisches Umweltrecht (Munich, 1997), para. 86; Jans (n. 91), p. 37 leaves the meaning of "general nature" open.

[98] See para. 4–15, below.

Climate Change[99] was rightly based on Article 175(1), not on 175(2), of the E.C. Treaty. Indeed, the Convention does not impose specific measures which affect energy supply nor ask Member States to change their choice of energy sources. Finally, it does not impose the introduction of fiscal measures either, such as the introduction of an energy tax. What measures are taken at Community level in order to comply with the requirements of the Convention need thus to be decided by another measure, but this has not been prejudged by the decision to adhere to the Convention.

While in all these cases of Article 175(2), the Council decides unanimously, it may decide to take majority decisions in the future in this area. The provision is of a rather theoretical nature; indeed, it has existed in a different form[1] since 1987, but has not gained in importance: there has not been one sector in which the Council has introduced majority decisions.

(iv) Decisions on co-operation with other countries (Article 174(4) (ex 130r(4)) E.C.)

2—90 Article 174(4) (ex 130r(4)) gives express competence to the Community to conclude international environmental agreements (conventions), which are then binding on the institutions of the Community and on Member States (Article 300(7) (ex 228(7))). Details are laid down in Article 300.

Agreements are negotiated by the Commission, which needs an express negotiating mandate from the Council; this mandate is given by the Council, on the proposal of the Commission, without the participation of the European Parliament. During the negotiation period, the Commission continuously consults with a special committee composed of Member States' representatives. In practice, Member States also participate in the negotiation of agreements at international level, since such agreements also come into the competence of Member States; in fact, the influence of Member States, at least some of them, is often greater than that of the Commission during these negotiations.

The decision to adhere to an international agreement is taken by the Council, upon a proposal from the Commission. The correct legal basis for the decision is Article 174(4) together with Article 300 of the E.C. Treaty. The Council instead bases its decision on Article 175(1) or (2), together with Article 300; consultation of the Economic and Social Committee and the Committee of the regions does not take place.

2—91 The Council practice is not convincing. Indeed, Article 300(3) provides for a specific provision as regards the participation of the European Parliament and the absence of participation of the Economic and Social Committee and the Committee of the Regions. If Article 175(1) were to apply there would be a conflict between Articles 175(1) and 300(3) as regards these two Committees, nor could this conflict be solved by applying the legal principle that the specific provision prevails over the general provision, because Article 175(1) might well be the more specific provision since it only applies to the environment. Instead, Article 174(4) together with Article 300 is the correct legal basis.[2]

The Commission, therefore, rightly based its proposal to adhere to an amendment of the Basel Convention on the shipment of hazardous waste on Articles 174(4) and 300(4); the same legal basis was chosen for the proposal to adhere to the international

---

[99] Dec. 94/69 [1994] O.J. L33/11.

[1] Between 1987 and 1993, all envrionmental measures under Art. 175 of the E.C. Treaty had to be adopted unanimously.

[2] In the same sense case C-268/94 *Portugal v. Council* [1996] E.C.R. I-6177; this case concerned the legal basis of Art. 181 (ex 130y), which has the same wording as Art. 174(4).

Convention on transboundary effects of industrial accidents.[3] The Council has not yet changed its above-mentioned practice.

(v) Decisions based on other Treaty provisions

2—92 As mentioned, Community acts affecting the environment may be based on Treaty provisions other than Articles 174 and 175. This applies to those environmental provisions where the "centre of gravity"[4] lies in policy area other than environmental policy. The most relevant provisions are as follows:

2—93 Decisions in the agricultural sector (Article 37 (ex 43) E.C.) Article 37 provides that the Council, in working out and implementing the common agricultural policy, adopts legislation by a qualified majority. Numerous measures in agricultural policy affect air and soil, water, fauna, flora and the landscape. Examples include the use of fertilisers and pesticides, drainage and irrigation measures, land use, discharge of substances, animal waste, the production and marketing of agricultural products, for example. The objective of the rules adopted by virtue of Article 37 is the establishment of a common agricultural policy among Member States, which includes the production of uniform products and unified production and marketing conditions.

Since 1988 it has been accepted that measures under Article 37 may also protect human health.[5] When the Court of Justice had to decide on the relationship between Article 175 (ex 130s) and Article 37 (ex 43), it applied a similar reasoning to its 1988 judgment. The environmental case concerned the ban on drift-nets for fishing which the Council had established by Regulation 345/92.[6] Some fishermen contested the legality of that ban, arguing, amongst other things, that the regulations should also have been based on Article 175, which provided, at that time, for unanimous decisions. The Court held that the Regulation's principal objective was the protection of living marine resources and that this was an objective of the common fishery policy; thus, the appropriate legal basis was Article 37. According to the Court, the application of Article 175 was not necessary because environmental requirements had to be integrated into other policies anyway.[7]

2—94 All legislation on agricultural pesticides is now to be based on Article 37 since that provision prevails, as mentioned above, at paragraph 2–74, over Article 95. This is accepted for the placing on the market of such pesticides,[8] but there is room for doubt as regards the ban of pesticides. Indeed, Directive 79/117, which first provided for the ban on some pesticides, was based on Article 95 (ex 100) E.C. However, this legislation was adopted prior to the above-mentioned Court decision in case 68/86. Today, that legal basis would be replaced by Article 37, exactly because there is the new Treaty provision that environmental requirements must be integrated into other policies and measures under such policies. The Court's reasoning in case C-405/92 thus also applies in the case on banning pesticides.

Legal debate has taken place over which legal basis should apply to measures that protect forests against fire or against air pollution. The Council originally adopted such measures on the basis of Articles 37 and 308 (ex 43 and 235),[9] as there were no environmental provisions in the Treaty in 1986. Amendments of 1989 were based on

---

[3] [1997] O.J. C197/12 and [1997] O.J. C267/60.
[4] See para. 2–70, above.
[5] The landmark decision was case C-68/86 *United Kingdom v. Council* [1988] E.C.R. 855.
[6] Reg. 345/92 [1992] O.J. L42/15.
[7] Case C-405/92 *Mondiet v. Islais* [1993] E.C.R. I-6133.
[8] Dir. 91/414 (n. 6).
[9] Reg. 3528/86 [1986] O.J. L326/2.

Articles 37 and 175 (ex 43 and 130s).[10] In 1997, the Council adopted further amend-ments, basing them exclusively on Article 37.[11] The European Parliament submitted both Regulations 307/97 and 308/97 to the Court of Justice, arguing among other things that the Council had wished to exclude the co-operation of the European Parliament in the elaboration of these Regulations, which had become mandatory under Article 175(1) since 1993. The Court considered Article 175 as the appropriate legal basis as it was of the opinion that the protection of forests against fire and atmospheric pollution was primarily an environmental measure and did not establish rules on the production and marketing of agricultural products.[12] This reasoning is all the more convincing if one considers that the Commission co-finances reforestation projects after fire damage under the Cohesion Fund (which may co-finance environ-mental, but not agricultural projects).

The question whether environmental measures which are adopted under Article 37, under Article 176 (ex 130t), allow Member States to take more stringent measures, will be discussed below at paragraphs 3–69 *et seq.*

2—95   Decisions in the transport sector (Article 80 (ex 84))   The common trans-port policy, Articles 70 to 80 (ex 74 to 84) of the E.C. Treaty, tries to set common conditions for transport within the Community and beyond: such conditions may have a very considerable impact on the environment.

Both Articles 71 and 80 (ex 75 and 84) now provide, as a rule, for majority decisions by virtue of Article 251.[13] For that reason, the most relevant question is whether Article 176 can be applied to measures adopted under Article 80; again, this question will be discussed below at paragraphs 3–69 *et seq.*

2—96   Decisions regarding the internal market   Article 95 outlines the fulfilment of the objectives set out in Article 14 (ex 7a),[14] *i.e.* the progressive establishment of the internal market. Its wording clarifies that it can also be the legal basis for measures aiming at the protection of the environment. Indeed, finding the demarcation line between Articles 95 and 175 (ex 130s) was one of the biggest legal problems of the past. The Amsterdam Treaty has brought the two provisions much closer to one another, so that usually, only some differences exist concerning the procedures and consequences of maintaining or introducing more stringent national environmental measures than those agreed at Community level.

The Treaty itself does not contain criteria for making a clear distinction between Articles 95 and 175. Article 95 wishes to achieve the internal market. Articles 174 to 176 aim at the protection of the environment at a high level; the provisions do not contain anything explicit that could be described as the "free movement of goods". On the contrary, Article 174 explicitly indicates that different measures are both possible and necessary to protect the environment at a high level.

As Article 95 is concerned with goods and services; provisions which affect trade in such goods and services should, as mentioned above, be allocated primarily to Article 95. Provisions which contribute to the attainment of one of the objectives specified in

---

[10] Reg. 1613/89 [1989] O.J. L165/8.

[11] Reg. 307/97 [1997] O.J. L51/9; see also Reg. 308/97 [1997] O.J. L51/11, which was based on Art. 37 and amended Reg. 2158/92 [1992] O.J. L217/3, which had been based on Arts 37 and 175.

[12] Cases C-164 & 165/97 (n. 57, above).

[13] See, however, Art. 71(3) where unanimity is required where a measure "would be liable to have a serious effect on the standard of living and on employment in certain areas and on the operation of transport facilities".

[14] Art. 14(2): "The internal market shall comprise an area without internal frontiers in which the free movement of goods, persons, services and capital is ensured in accordance with the provisions of this Treaty."

Article 174 should primarily be assigned to Article 175. As a consequence of the arguments on the choice of the legal basis given above, at paragraphs 2–69 *et seq.* the Council should have based the Regulation on ozone-depleting substances[15] and the Regulation on export and import of certain dangerous chemicals[16] on Article 95, since they both deal with product standards.

2—97 Decisions on commercial matters (Article 133 (ex 113)) Decisions in the area of commercial policy are taken by the Council by a qualified majority (Article 133(4)); the European Parliament does not participate. The provisions on commercial policy establish exclusive Community competence, which means that there is no longer a Member States' commercial policy. In the past, however, the importance of Article 113 for environmental issues was diminished as a result of differences about its meaning. Whereas the Commission considered Article 133 relevant for all commercial provisions and international agreements, the Council applied Article 133 only in those cases where the measure in question did not pursue any other than a commercial objective. This Article 133 was, where a trade-related measure also aimed at the protection of the environment, according to the Council, not relevant; other provisions applied instead, particularly Article 175. In practice therefore, Article 133 is not applied to environmental matters, at least not without Article 175.

The respective interpretations might have been influenced by the fact that Article 133 gives exclusive competence to the Community, whereas, under Articles 174 to 176 (ex 130r to 130t), the competence is shared between the Community and Member States. The European Parliament is not entitled to challenge, under Article 230 (ex 173) E.C., the Council's practice[17] and the Commission does not challenge it.

2—98 It is not logical to draw the dividing line between Articles 95 and 175 according to the "centre of gravity" theory, and then not to follow this theory for trade-related matters. Indeed, modern commercial agreements often include environmental rules which may or may not contribute to the "harmonious development of world trade" (Article 131 (ex 110)); there is no reason for the unduly restrictive interpretation given to Article 133 by the Council.

The judgment of the Court of Justice in case C-62/88 seems to confirm the Commission's interpretation.[18] There the Court held that a commercial measure which also concerned environmental protection issues, could well be based on Article 133 alone, since environmental requirements had to be integrated into other Community policies. However, these legal considerations have not changed the Council's practice. The Commission has not decided to seek clarification before the Court on the interpretation of Article 133. The longer the present Council practice is accepted *de facto*, the less likely it is that it will be questioned by the Court of Justice. Commercial measures and international commercial agreements which also aim at the protection of the environment, will therefore probably continue to be all based on Article 175; perhaps by way of compromise, Article 133 is added.

2—99 Decisions on research matters (Article 172 (ex 130o)) Article 172 provides that the Council unanimously decides on measures under Article 171 (ex 130n)—the establishment of joint undertakings or any other structure for the execution of Community research, technological development and demonstration programmes—

---

[15] Reg. 3093/94 (n. 9).
[16] Reg. 2455/92 [1992] O.J. L251/13.
[17] See case C-18/93 (n. 73).
[18] Case C-62/88 *Greece v. Council* [1990] E.C.R. I-1527.

and by majority on measures for the implementation of multi-annual research programmes. Multi-annual research framework programmes are adopted under Article
166 (ex 130i).

Thus, decisions on research and development programmes in the area of the environment are taken on the basis of Article 172. Article 175 (ex 130s) does not apply since
Article 163(3) (ex 130f(3)) has solved this potential conflict by stipulating: "All
Community activities under this Treaty in the area of research and technological
development, including demonstration projects, shall be decided on and implemented
in accordance with the provisions of this Title."

(vi) Decisions under the new flexibility provisions

2—100   The Amsterdam Treaty has introduced a new form of decision-making, the
so-called "flexibility" procedure. This procedure is laid down both in Articles 43 to 45
(ex K15 to K17) of the Treaty on European Union and also in a new Article 11 of the
E.C. Treaty. It is not limited to environmental matters.

The underlying rationale of the procedure is that some Member States might wish to
advance more rapidly than the Community as a whole. Nothing currently prevents
them from concluding a bilateral or multilateral international Convention, which
would then be governed by public international law and not constitute Community
law—although, of course, such obligations would have to respect the Member States'
obligations under the Treaty on European Union.

2—101   The flexibility provisions now offer a new possibility to those Member
States that want to proceed more quickly: they may, under certain conditions[19] laid
down in Articles 43 to 45 (ex K15 to K19) of the Treaty on European Union, make use
of the institutions, procedures and mechanisms laid down by the Treaties.

For any such co-operation, the Member States in question need an express authorisation from the Council. The Council may only act on a proposal from the Commission which has its own discretionary power to decide whether it wishes to submit a
proposal to the Council or not.[20]

The Council shall decide on the authorisation to co-operate by a qualified majority
vote, after consultation with the European Parliament. Each Member State has a right
to oppose voting if there are "important and stated reasons of national policy".[21] In
such a case, the matter is submitted to the European Council for a unanimous decision,
which means that individual Member States have a veto right.

2—102   The measure adopted under the flexibility procedure "shall be subject to
all the relevant provisions of this Treaty". The question once so controversial under
Article 293 (ex 220) E.C.—whether the conventions adopted under that provision
were part of Community law or were measures of public international law—is

---

[19] These conditions are the following: the co-operation is aimed at furthering the objectives of the European
Union; it respects the principles of the Treaties; it is only used as a last resort; it concerns at least a majority
of Member States; it does not affect the measures adopted so far by virtue of the Treaties; it does not affect
those Member States which do not participate; it is open to all Member States; it is authorised by the
Council.

Art. 11 of the E.C. Treaty adds to this the following conditions: the co-operation does not concern areas of
exclusive Community competence; it does not affect Community policies, actions or programmes; it does not
afffect citizenship or create discrimination; it remains within the limits of the Community powers under the
E.C. Treaty; and—this provision will be very relevant in environmental matters—it does not constitute
discrimination or a restriction of trade between Member States and does not distort the conditions of
competition between Member States.

[20] See Art. 11(2) of the E.C. Treaty: "In the event of the Commission not submitting a proposal, it shall
inform the Member States concerned of the reasons for not doing so."

[21] Art. 11(2) of the E.C. Treaty.

answered in the case of the flexibility procedure: they are Community law. Indeed, the Commission, which must make a proposal for a "flexibility" measure, can only propose measures that are mentioned in Article 249 (ex 189) E.C., *i.e.* a regulation, directive or a decision. As regards the flexibility procedure, the decision-making in Council, the consultation of or the co-decision with the European Parliament, and the transposition of the measure into national law, its monitoring by the Commission under Article 211 (ex 155) and the possible judicial control under Articles 211 *et seq.* (ex 169 *et seq.*)—all follow Community law provisions. This leaves no room for the application of provisions of public international law.

2—103   In order to illustrate the impact of the flexibility provisions on the environment, the fictitious example of a directive on environmental liability may be given. Under Article 11 of the E.C. Treaty, a majority of Member States could request the Commission to submit a proposal for such a directive. The Commission could then ask the Council to authorise the use of the "institutions, procedures and mechanisms of the Treaty". The Council would normally decide on this proposal by a qualified majority.

The procedure of substance has to be distinguished from the flexibility procedure. The Commission would make a proposal for a directive on environmental liability, following the institutional procedures of Article 175(1). The directive would be adopted by a qualified majority of those Member States that participate in the co-operation. If, later, another Member State would like to be party to the Community co-operation procedure, "the Commission shall decide on it and on possible arrangements as it may deem necessary".

Nothing would prevent the Commission, during its discussions in Council on a proposal which was intended to cover all Member States, from submitting to the Council a proposal for authorising the flexibility procedure. Indeed, despite the somewhat unclear wording of Article 11(2) of the E.C. Treaty,[22] the start of the procedure does not depend on the initiative of a majority of Member States. It is up to the Commission to ensure that the flexibility procedure does not put at risk the coherence of the Community.

2—104   Article 11 of the E.C. Treaty does not provide for the elaboration of a proposal by Member States. Indeed, the reference to the Treaty provisions also has the consequence that the Council may only act upon a proposal from the Commission, as is also foreseen in Article 175(1). In particular, Article 249(1) (ex 189(1)) provides that the Council may only unanimously amend a proposal from the Commission. This provision would be set aside if the Council could also decide upon a proposal from Member States.

In conclusion, co-operating Member States have the choice to recur either to forms of public international law, or to establish, within the E.C. framework, Community law.

BIBLIOGRAPHY

Bocken, H. and Ryckbost, D. (eds): *L'élaboration et l'application des directives européennes en matière d'environnement* (Ghent, 1990)

Calliess, C. and Wegener, B. (eds): *Europäisches Umweltrecht als Chance: die Umweltpolitik der EG und die Einflussmöglichkeiten der Umweltverbände* (Taunusstein, 1992)

---

[22] Art. 11(2) of the E.C. Treaty: "Member States which intend to establish closer co-operation as referred to in paragraph 1 may address a request to the Commission, which may submit a proposal to the Council to that effect."

Cameron, J.: "Introduction of group action on the European level: how can interest groups use E.C. law to protect the environment" in M. Führ and G. Roller (eds), *Participation and litigation rights of environmental associations in Europe* (Frankfurt/Main, 1991), p. 141

Demmke, C.: "Umweltpolitik im Europa der Verwaltungen", *Die Verwaltung* (1994), p. 49

Demmke, C. (ed.): *Europäische Umweltpolitik und nationale Verwaltungen* (Maastricht, 1998)

Dibout, P.: "Fiscalité européenne et environnement", *Revue des affaires européennes* (1995), p. 31

Díez de Vellasco Vallejo, M.: *Aspectos jurídicos de la protección del medio ambiente en la Comunidad Europea y en especial la contribución de su Tribunal de Justicia* (Granada, 1991)

Everling, U.: "Umweltschutz durch Gemeinschaftsrecht in der Rechtsprechung des EUGH" in P. Behrens and H. Koch (eds), *Umweltschutz in der Europäischen Gemeinschaft* (Baden-Baden, 1991), p. 29

Fehr, H. and Van der Stelt-Scheele, D.: "The E.C. environmental policy in relation to the E.C. structural funds: a critical analysis of its application", *European Environmental Law Review* (1992), pp. 121 and 143

Frenz, W.: "Subjektiv-öffentliche Rechte aus Gemeinschaftsrecht vor deutschen Verwaltungs-gerichten", *Deutsches Verwaltungsblatt* (1995), p. 408

Führ, M. Roller, G. (eds): *Participation and litigation rights of environmental associations in Europe: current legal situation and practical experience* (Frankfurt/Main, 1991)

Gale, L.: "Citizen and NGO participation in policymaking and enforcement of environmental Community law" in M. Campins i Eritja and I. Pont i Castejón (eds), *Perspectives de dret comunitari ambiental* (Bellaterra, 1997), p. 515

García Ureta, A.: "En busca de la línea divisoria entre los artículos 100a y 130s del Tratado CE: reflexiones a la luz de los asuntos C-300/89, C-155/91 y C-187/93", *Revista vasca de adminis-tracion publica* (1995), p. 607

Gebers, B. and Robesin, M. (eds): *Licensing procedures for industrial plants and the influence of E.C. procedures* (Frankfurt/Main, 1993)

Giesberts, L.: "Die CO_2-/Energiesteuer der EG. Anmerkungen zum geänderten Richtlinien-vorschlag der Europäischen Kommissio", *Recht der Internationalen Wirtschaft* (1995), p. 847

Golub, J. (ed.): *New instruments for environmental protection in the E.U.* (London, 1998)

Grube, C.: "Decision-making in E.C. environmental law" in B. Wenzel (ed.), *First Nordic conference on E.U. environmental law* (Copenhagen, 1994), p. 45

Henke, J.: "EUGH und Umweltschutz", *Die Auswirkungen der Rechtsprechung des Gericht-shofs der Europäischen Gemeinschaften auf das Umweltschutzrecht in Europa* (Munich and Florence, 1992)

Hilf, M.: "Umweltabgaben als Gegenstand von Gemeinschaftsrecht und-politik", *Neue Zeits-chrift für Verwaltungsrecht* (1992), p. 105

Hoffmann-Riem, W. and Schneider, J. (eds): *Umweltpolitiche Steuerung in einem liberalisierten Strommarkt* (Baden-Baden, 1995)

Hubschmid, C. and Moser, P.: "The co-operation procedure in the E.U.: why was the European Parliament influential in the decision on car emission standards?", *Journal of Common Market Studies* (1997), p. 225

Kahl, W.: "Der EUGH als 'Motor des europäischen Umweltschutzes'?", *Thüringer Verwaltungs-blätter* (1994), pp. 225 and 256

Kahl, W.: "Stellung und Funktion von Umweltagenturen—eine rechtsvergleichende Typologie", *Jahrbuch des Umwelt- und Technikrechts* (1996), p. 119

Khalastchi, R. and Ward, H.: "New instruments for sustainability: an assessment of environ-mental agreements under Community law", *Journal of Environmental Law* (1998), p. 257

Klocke, U.: *Klimaschutz durch ökonomische Instrumente* (Baden-Baden, 1995)

Koppen, I.: "The role of the European Court of Justice in the development of the European

Community environmental policy", *European University Institute Working Paper* 92/18 (Florence, 1993)

Krämer, L.: "Participation of environmental organisations in the activities of the EEC" in M. Führ and G. Roller (eds), *Participation and litigation rights of environmental associations in Europe* (Frankfurt/Main, 1991), p. 129

Krämer, L.: "Die Rechtsprechung des Gerichtshofs der Europäischen Gemeinschaften zum Umweltrecht 1992 bis 1994", *Europäische Grundrechte Zeitschrift* (1995), p. 45

Krämer, L.: "Die Rechtsprechung der EG-Gerichte zum Umweltrecht 1995 bis 1997", *Europäische Grundrechte Zeitschrift* (1998), p. 309

Kromarek, P.: "La Cour de Justice des Communautés européennes et l'environnement", *Jurisclasseur-environnement*, Fasc. 1120 (Paris, 1992)

Ladeur, K.: "Die Europäische Umweltagentur und die Perspektiven eines europäischen Netzwerks der Umweltverwaltungen", *Natur und Recht* (1997), p. 8

Macrory, R.: *Environmental citizenship and the law: repairing the European road* (London, 1996)

Peeters, M.: "Towards a European system of tradable pollution permits", *Tilburg Foreign Law Review* (1993), p. 117

Renaudière, P.: "Le cinquième programme d'action communautaire à mi-parcours", *Aménagement-Environnement* (1996), p. 65

Ruffert, M.: *Sujektive Rechte im Umweltrecht der Europäischen Gemeinschaft* (Heidelberg, 1996)

Ryland, D.: "The European Environmental Agency", *European Environmental Law Review* (1994), p. 138

Scherer, J.: "Grenzen und Schwächen der legislatorischen Rechtsvereinheitlichung im europäische Umweltrecht", *Kritische Vierteljahresschrift für Gesetzgebung und Rechtswissenschaft* (1995), p. 197

Steinberg, R.: "Zulassung von Industrieanlagen im deutschen und europäischen Recht", *Neue Zeitschrift für Verwaltungsrecht* (1995), p. 209

Voss, U.: "Die Rechtsprechung des Europäischen Gerichtshofes zum Umweltschutz" in C. Demmke (ed.), *Europäische Umweltpolitik und nationale Verwaltungen* (Maastricht, 1998), p. 163

Wägenbaur, R.: "Zwölf Thesen zum Thema 'Umweltvereinbarungen'" *Europäische Zeitschrift für Wirtschaftsrecht* (1997), p. 645

Wasmeier, M.: *Umweltabgaben und Europarecht* (Munich, 1995)

Wegener, B.: "Rechte des Einzelnen", *Die Interessentenklage im europäischen Umweltrecht* (Baden-Baden, 1998)

Winter, G.: "Das Umweltrecht der Europäischen Union unter dem Druck der globalen Konkurrenz" in N. Reich and R. Heine-Mernik (eds), *Umweltverfassung und nachhaltige Entwicklung in der Europäischen Union* (Baden-Baden, 1997), p. 33

Zuleeg, M.: "Umweltschutz in der Rechtsprechung des Europäischen Gerichtshofs", *Neue Juristische Wochenschrift* (1993), p. 31

CHAPTER 3
Community Powers and Member State Powers

1. GENERAL ASPECTS ON THE DIVISION OF COMPETENCE IN ENVIRONMENTAL MATTERS

3—01 The objective of Community environmental policy and law is the preservation, protection and, over all, the improvement of the quality of the environment within the European Union. This objective, however, is also that of Member States' environmental policy and law. The protection and preservation of the environment is a fundamental part of the general interest of the Community[1] and of Member States. Because it is in the general interest, the environment, like the non-commercial assets listed in Article 30 (ex 36) E.C., cannot be left unprotected: as long as the Community fails to take action on a given environmental issue, the Member States retain their powers to adopt provisions to protect and preserve the environment, provided, of course, that these measures are compatible with the general rules laid down in the E.C. Treaty. When the Community takes action, this by no means removes Member States' powers to take environmental measures, although such powers then no longer apply to the particular subject governed by Community legislation, in so far as this has been regulated.

Since the protection of the environment is in the general interest of the Community, the Community is "competent",[2] i.e. responsible for taking legal provisions in order to protect it. In doing so, the Community has, of course, to take into consideration the principles which the Treaty provides for such action, in particular the subsidiartiy principle.[3] Where a Community environmental legal rule conflicts with a national legal rule, Community law prevails, according to the established case law of the Court of Justice.[4] The reason for this is obvious: if the national legal rule prevailed, the Community legal provision would apply only in those Member States which had not taken legal measures. Then, the Community legal rule would not be a rule which applied throughout the Community, but only in those parts of it where no national measures had been taken. Also, the Community measure could at any moment be reduced in its application by a subsequent national measure, which would create quite considerable legal uncertainty. Such legal uncertainty would also be created by differences over the question of whether or not the national measure really is in question or

---

[1] See already case 240/83 *Procureur de la Republique v. Assoc. de Défense de Bruleurs de Huiles Usagées* [1985] E.C.R. 531, para. 13: "environmental protection . . . is one of the Community's essential objectives".
[2] This concept is used in Art. 174(4) (ex 130r(4)) and, more generally, in Art. 5 (ex 3b) E.C.
[3] E.C. Treaty, Art. 5: "The Community shall act within the limits of the powers conferred upon it by this Treaty and of the objectives assigned to it therein. In areas which do not fall within its exclusive competence, the Community shall take action . . . only if and in so far as the objectives of the proposed action cannot be sufficiently achieved by the Member States . . ."
[4] Cases 6/64 *Costa v. ENEL* [1964] E.C.R. 1265; 106/77 *Simmenthal* [1978] E.C.R. 629; C-213/89 *Factortame* [1990] E.C.R. I-2466; C-184/89 *Nimz* [1991] E.C.R. I-297.

not. As the national law would mainly be interpreted by national courts, inevitable discrepancies would follow.

3—02   It is therefore now uncontested that, in the case of conflict, Community (environmental) law prevails over national law. From this it follows that Community environmental law cannot be amended by subsequent national law. In other words, the rule *lex posterior derogat legem anteriorem* (the later legal provision prevails over the earlier provision) does not apply to the relationship between E.C. law and national law.

Both the Community and Member States are thus responsible, "competent" or empowered to take action on environmental issues. In view of the unlimited scope of the term "environment" in the E.C. Treaty, this holds true for all environmental issues. The Treaty assigns no particular area of environmental legislation exclusively to the Community or exclusively to Member States. As can be seen from Article 176 (ex 130t), this similarly applies to subjects already covered by Community legislation. Consequently, the inter-relationship between the Community's and the Member States' competence is flexible, dynamic and complementary.

3—03   It follows from the above-mentioned Article 5 (ex 3b) of the E.C. Treaty that Community environmental action is dependent on certain circumstances which have to be fulfilled. Community institutions decide themselves whether this is the case. In the case of dispute, the matter has to be decided by the Community Court of Justice, which has to ensure, under Article 220 (ex 164) that the provisions of the Treaty are respected.[5] The logical consequence of Article 5 (ex 3b) is that in cases where the Community has not taken action to protect, preserve or improve the quality of the environment, Member States are free to do so. Their competence to deal with environmental issues is unlimited. They can do whatever they wish in whatever form they wish to ensure environmental protection. Limitations to this right to protect—or not to protect—the environment stem from:

- Member States' own, national rules, such as for instance, rules on local government and rules for regional responsibility in environmental matters for example;

- rules of international law, such as existing international Conventions or other written or unwritten rules of international law;

- rules of Community law.

The first two limitations are not dealt with in this book, which deals with Community law. As regards the third limitation, the E.C. Treaty itself constitutes a set of provisions that may limit national environmental measures. Indeed, the E.C. Treaty contains a number of provisions that limit the Member States' possibilities of action. These different limitations will be discussed later.

2. MEMBER STATES' MEASURES IN THE ABSENCE OF COMMUNITY MEASURES

(a) National environmental measures that affect imports: Articles 28 and 30 (ex 30 and 36) E.C.

3—04   Article 28 (ex 30) provides that all "quantitative restrictions on imports and all measures having equivalent effect" shall be prohibited between Member States;

---

[5] Art. 220 of the E.C. Treaty: "The Court of Justice shall ensure that in the interpretation and application of this Treaty the law is observed."

Article 29 (ex 34) E.C. mirrors this provision by stating that "quantitative restrictions on exports, and all measures having equivalent effect, shall be prohibited between Member States".

From these provisions Article 30 (ex 36) makes an exception; this provision reads as follows: "The provisions of Articles 28 and 29 shall not preclude prohibitions on imports, exports . . . justified on grounds of . . . the protection of health and life of humans, animals or plants; . . . Such prohibitions or restrictions shall not, however, constitute a means of arbitrary discrimination or a disguised restriction on trade between Member States." Article 30 thus does allow certain trade restrictions. The Court of Justice has declared, on a number of occasions, that Article 30 is an exception to the principle of Article 28 and must therefore be narrowly interpreted.[6] In particular, according to the established case law of the Court of Justice, the grounds for restricting trade by virtue of Article 30 constitute an exhaustive list and may not be extended.

The protection of the environment is not listed in Article 30 as a possible justification for restrictions to the free circulation of goods of Article 28. Therefore, only such national environmental measures that aim at the "protection of health and life of humans, animals and plants" could be justified by Article 30. Such measures concern, for instance, provisions on banning or restricting the use of substances or products which are dangerous to health; measures to limit the presence of pollutants in drinking water or in the air; measures to regulate the marketing of pesticides or biocides, for example.

3—05   However, there are numerous environmental measures which cannot be considered to protect the health and life of humans, animals or plants. Such measures include environmental label schemes, eco-management systems, environmental taxes and charges, measures to prevent the generation of waste, environmental impact measures, deposit-and-return schemes, environmental liability or environmental information and education. For other measures, finally, it is doubtful whether they can really be considered to protect health and life; such measures are, for instance, provisions to reduce the noise level of cars, the designation of fauna or flora habitats, emission limit values from installations, licensing procedures or measures to protect the ozone layer or to combat global warming.

The criterion that defines whether or not a measure aims at the protection of health or life is the relationship of the measure to health effects, *i.e.* its "proximity" to health effects. Thus, the Court of Justice decided that the shipment of recoverable waste oils did not pose a threat to the life and health of humans to justify the application of Article 30.[7]

Another example might be the restriction on the use of CFCs and other ozone-depleting substances in order to protect the ozone layer. Damage to the ozone layer may increase skin cancer for humans and may have other health effects on humans, animals and plants. However, this possibility is remote and indirect. Therefore, national measures to restrict the use of ozone-depleting substances cannot really be justified on the basis of Article 30.

3—06   Fortunately enough, however, this problem of subsuming environmental measures under Article 30 has lost its relevance. Indeed, the Court of Justice in 1979 adopted a landmark decision on Article 28.[8] The Court declared that in the absence of Community legislation, a national restriction on the free circulation of goods from

---

[6] Cases 29/72 *Marimex* [1982] E.C.R. 1309; 113/80 *Commission v. Ireland* [1981] E.C.R. 1625; C-205/89 *Commission v. Greece* [1991] E.C.R. I-1361.

[7] Case C-203/96 *Dusseldorp* [1998] E.C.R. I-4075, para. 47.

[8] Case 120/78 *Rewe v. Bundesmonopolverwaltung* ("Cassis de Dijon") [1979] E.C.R. 649.

other Member States had to be accepted to the extent that it was necessary to satisfy mandatory requirements such as the necessity for fiscal controls, fair trading practices and consumer protection, and added that there might be other mandatory requirements. The Court added further that the national measure taken in order to satisfy such a mandatory requirement had to be non-discriminatory and proportional:

> "in the absence of common rules relating to the marketing of the products in question obstacles to free movement within the Community resulting from disparities between the national laws must be accepted in so far as such rules, applicable to domestic and imported products without distinction, may be recognised as being necessary in order to satisfy mandatory requirements recognised by Community law. Such rules must also be proportionate to the aim in view. If a Member State has a choice between various measures for achieving the same aim, it should choose the means which least restricts the free movement of goods."[9]

In 1988, the Court recognised that the protection of the environment was a mandatory requirement which could justify restrictions on the free circulation of goods.[10] In this case the Commission had attacked a Danish national measure, which introduced a deposit-and-return system for drink containers. The Commission considered that the system could not be justified by Article 30 and that it was incompatible with Article 28. It was followed in its assessment by the Advocate General, but not by the Court of Justice.

3—07 As regards the application of Article 30, there was practically no dispute: it was not really possible to consider a deposit-and-return system to protect the health or life of humans; Article 30 was therefore not discussed by the Court. Instead, the Court held that Denmark was entitled to introduce a deposit-and-return system, since such a system aimed at the protection of the environment, which was an objective of general Community interest. Denmark, according to the Court, was entitled to set up an efficient system of waste prevention and such a system required the introduction of a deposit-and-return scheme even though the practical circumstances might make it more difficult for non-Danish producers and traders to comply with the system.

The recognition of the environment as a mandatory requirement under Article 28 was confirmed in later Court judgments[11] without the Court sharply distinguishing between justification under Articles 30 (health grounds) and 28 (grounds to satisfy a mandatory requirement). Thus, while national environmental measures may restrict the free circulation of goods on either of these grounds, the limits to such national measures follow from the Treaty provisions and from the limits drawn by the very detailed and sophisticated case law of the Court.

3—08 **The necessity for action** The first problem is whether a Member State may adopt any measure to protect the environment which seems appropriate or whether it may only adopt some measures, which are "necessary". The Court itself has contributed to this debate by not accepting, in case 302/86, a Danish measure which obliged economic operators to use only authorised standardised containers. The Court stated[12]: "It is undoubtedly true that the existing system for returning approved containers ensures a maximum rate of reuse and therefore a very considerable degree

---

[9] Wording from case 302/86 *Commission v. Denmark* [1988] E.C.R. 4607.

[10] *Ibid.*

[11] Cases C-2/90 *Commission v. Belgium* [1992] E.C.R. I-4431; C-131/93 *Commission v. Germany* [1994] E.C.R. I-3303.

[12] Case 302/86 (n. 9), paras 20 and 21.

of protection of the environment. Nevertheless, the system for returning non-approved containers is capable of protecting the environment". This seems to indicate that the Court is of the opinion that a "very considerable degree" of environmental protection is not necessary and therefore not allowed, only a "reasonable" degree of environmental protection—whatever that may be—is permitted. In other words, it is not a Member State which decides on the necessary degree of the environmental protection but Community law (as interpreted by the Court) which determines what is necessary (or reasonable). This reasonableness is measured against the interest in free circulation of goods as there is no other factor to consider.

The underlying principle of this approach is that Community law provides for the free circulation of goods which is of paramount importance. Restrictions on the free circulation of goods are allowed only where they are necessary; in other words, measures to protect the environment are possible where their importance is greater than that of free circulation of goods. This leads to the conclusion that the free circulation of goods, in the event of any conflict with environmental (national) measures, will prevail.

3—09   This conclusion, however, is not compatible with the division of competence for the protection of the environment. The protection of the environment is of general Community interest. It is expressly mentioned in the seventh indent of the Preamble and indirectly, via the notion of "sustainable development", in Article 2 of the Treaty on European Union. Nothing indicates that it is less important than other objectives, in particular the free circulation of goods. On the contrary, the rule of Article 6 of the E.C. Treaty that environmental protection requirements must be integrated into the definition and implementation of all other policies is unique in the whole Treaty; nowhere in the Treaty is the same said of the free circulation of goods. Furthermore, Commission proposals in the area of the internal market must be based on a high level of environmental protection and the European Parliament and the Council must try to achieve such a level (Article 95(3) (ex 100a(3)) E.C.). This is the only provision in the E.C. Treaty which contains quality requirements for individual measures. Finally, Article 95 (4) to (8) and Article 176 allow Member States, once a Community measure has been taken, to maintain or to introduce more protective environmental measures at national level. Article 95(5) to (8) only applies to environmental measures not to all non-economic assets of Article 30, as is the case with Article 95(4).

All these provisions clearly show the importance that the Treaty attaches to the protection of the environment. In view of this importance, which has been growing continuously and achieved recognition in the different Treaty amendments of 1987, 1993 and 1997, it cannot be considered that only a reasonable degree of environmental protection is allowed to restrict the free circulation of goods. Rather, it is the Member States which decide on the amount of environmental protection which they wish to ensure.

3—10   There are two other arguments which plead against a limitation for environmental measures to "reasonable" measures. First, Article 95(5) to (8) of the E.C. Treaty, which was newly introduced by the Amsterdam Treaty 1997, outlined provisions for the Member States to introduce new environmental measures at national level once a Community harmonisation measure under Article 95(1) had been adopted. These measures are not limited to reasonable measures, as will be discussed below; rather, the criteria for the national measures are whether the measure constitutes an arbitrary discrimination, a disguised distortion of trade or whether they hamper the functioning of the internal market. It is not consistent to ask for only reasonable measures under Article 30 where no Community measure exists, and not to ask for only reasonable measures under Article 95 (ex 100a).

On the other hand, the only instance which could decide what is reasonable is the Court of Justice—and in the pre-litigation stage, the European Commission. But what criteria could be used, if there is no Community legislation? The E.C. Treaty gives no clarification of what is reasonable or not.

3—11   To give a specific example: In the early 1990s Denmark limited the noise level from electrical windmills that are used for energy production; the standards are stricter, the closer the windmill is installed to residential areas. France protested against this measure, arguing that the sale and export of French windmills to Denmark would be hampered by the Danish measure.

It seems obvious that nobody outside Denmark can really decide whether a noise level of 50 decibels is reasonable for the Danish environment and Danish citizens and whether a noise level of 40 decibels is unreasonable. The environmental conditions are specific in each case. No element in the Treaty allows the establishing of Community criteria for such an assessment and as there is no Community legislation on windmills or on acceptable noise levels for citizens Community law cannot decide what is reasonable or not in Denmark.

Similar reasons argue in favour of the noise levels for pleasure boats to be allowed, which Sweden introduced. In view of the thousands of lakes—independently from the endless miles of shoreline—with numerous small islands in Sweden, it would not be possible to allow the marketing of pleasure boats but prohibit their use in all or in parts of Sweden if they exceed a certain noise level. Also the level of permitted noise cannot, in the absence of Community provisions, be determined by a manufacturer or authorising body from another Member State—or by the Community.

3—12   Another example is a restriction on the use of Karlstad airport which Sweden has pronounced for some noisy aeroplanes, although Directive 92/14[13] provided that these aeroplanes were allowed to be used until the year 2002. It is clear that not every aeroplane which circulates within the Community may use any airport that exists. Indeed, Member States implicitly regulate access to airports by regulating the number and length of the runways, the size of the airports, landing and take-off times, for example. If the neighbourhood is residential or is an ecologically valuable habitat this may lead to the conclusion that specific aeroplanes may not use specific airports. The most obvious example is the supersonic aeroplane, Concorde, which may not land at most Community airports. In the same way as it is possible to prohibit the use of certain roads for trucks—or indeed for cars generally—without impeding the free circulation of cars, it is possible to prohibit the use of certain airports for certain aeroplanes. It is not clear who else other than the Swedish authorities could determine whether the local environmental conditions at Karlstad make it necessary or not to restrict the landing or take-off of noisy airplanes at it. Directive 92/14 is not relevant since aeroplanes which conform to that Directive are allowed to use Swedish airports, except, perhaps, Karlstad airport.

The Commission based its decision against the Swedish restriction not on Article 28 (ex 30), but on secondary Community legislation, Regulation 2408/92 and Directive 92/14,[14] and decided that these provisions gave any air transport carrier a right to access to any Community airport.[15] If that secondary Community legislation indeed went so far, and I doubt this, the above-mentioned considerations, which start from the assumption that it is not covered by secondary legislation, are obsolete.

---

[13] Dir. 92/14 on the limitation of the operation of aeroplanes covered by Part II, Chap. 2, vol. 1 of annex 16 to the Convention on International Civil Aviation (2nd ed.) [1992] O.J. L76/21.

[14] Reg. 2408/92 [1992] O.J. L240/8; Dir. 92/14 (n. 13, above).

[15] Dec. 98/523 [1998] O.J. L233/25.

3—13   For restrictions in the free circulation of goods which affect human health and therefore come under Article 30, the Court of Justice has already come to the same decision. In case C-125/88,[16] it was faced with a Dutch measure concerning the use of a pesticide "Improsol"; the question was whether such a national measure did not unduly restrict the free circulation of that pesticide which was used in other Member States. The Court found that pesticides constituted "significant risks to the health of humans and animals and to the environment" and then continued: "It is therefore for the Member States, pursuant to Article 36 (ex 42) of the Treaty and in the absence of full harmonization in this matter, to decide at what level they wish to set the protection of the life and health of humans." This judgment has been confirmed by several other judgments on pesticides and Member States' measures to restrict their use.

It is not really imaginable that the Member States themselves set the degree of protection which they wish to ensure for measures to protect the environment which concern the health and life of humans, animals and plants (Article 30), but that for measures to protect the environment which concern other environmental values and thus come under Article 28, the Member States are limited to reasonable measures.

3—14   Jans[17] is of the opinion that the Court of Justice, in environmental matters, differentiates between matters which come under Article 30 and for which no reasonableness test applies, and environmental measures which come under Article 28; for such measures, a reasonableness test is to be applied. He takes this conclusion from a case decided by the Court of Justice[18] where the Court considered waste to constitute an environmental problem, even where waste did not, as yet, constitute a health problem. Jans seems to agree to this reasoning.[19]

Epiney,[20] Thieffry[21] and Frenz[22] do not discuss this question. Pagh[23] leaves the question largely open. He is of the opinion that a case-by-case examination is necessary to weigh the national environmental measure against the requirement of Community law on the free circulation of goods.

This is certainly correct: the freedom to set national environmental standards does not allow protectionist measures to be taken or measures to be taken which are not really necessary to protect the local, regional or national environment. These issues will be discussed later. It still remains, however, that there are no specific, autonomous criteria for assessing whether national environmental measures are necessary (reasonable) or not. It is up to Member States to establish the degree of environmental protection at local, regional or national level which they consider appropriate. In this, however, Member States must take into consideration the state of science at international and Community level, such as the statements of the World Health Organisation or the Community scientific committees, for example; the greater the scientific certainty about the risk of a substance is, the less is the discretion of the Member State.

---

[16] Case C-125/88 *H. Nijman* [1989] E.C.R. I-3533.

[17] J. Jans, *European environmental law* (The Hague, London and Boston, 1995), pp. 213 and 228.

[18] Case C-2/90 *Commission v. Belgium* [1992] E.C.R. 4431.

[19] Jans (n. 17), p. 228: "the conditions for applying Article 36 [now Article 30] are not the same as those for applying the rule of reason . . . the protection of the life and health of humans, animals and plants is not the same as 'protection of the environment'".

[20] A. Epiney, *Umweltrecht in der Europäischen Union* (Cologne, Berlin, Bonn and Munich, 1997), pp. 115 *et seq.*

[21] P. Thieffry, *Droit européen de l'environnement* (Paris, 1998), pp. 196 *et seq.*

[22] W. Frenz, *Europäisches Umweltrecht* (Munich, 1997), pp. 226 *et seq.*

[23] P. Pagh, *E.U. miljoeret* (Copenhagen, 1996), para. 4.3.4.

3—15   Non-economic grounds   The discretion of Member States is further limited by the provisions of the Treaty. When establishing its jurisdiction on the mandatory requirements which justified, under Article 28, a restriction on the free circulation of goods, the Court of Justice stated that such measures were not allowed to be discriminatory or disproportionate and had to be applied indistinctively to national and to imported products. As can be seen, the two criteria of non-discrimination and proportionality are taken from Article 30(2) of the E.C. Treaty,[24] but apply both to measures which are examined under Article 30, and to measures assessed, under the *Cassis de Dijon* jurisdiction, under Article 28.

To these limits has to be added the proviso that Article 30 itself only refers to non-economic criteria, as can be concluded from Article 95(10) (ex 100a(10)); this limitation also applies under Article 28, as the Court of Justice has clarified: "aims of a purely economic nature cannot justify barriers to the fundamental principle of the free movement of goods".[25] With this argument, the Court of Justice rejected an argument by the Dutch Government that restrictions to the shipment of waste were necessary to enable a Dutch waste recovery installation to operate in a profitable manner with sufficient material at its disposal and to ensure it a sufficient supply of recoverable waste.

3—16   Discriminating measures   A discrimination or, as Article 30(2) (ex 36(2)) puts it, an arbitrary discrimination exists when goods from other Member States are subject to conditions which are, directly or indirectly, stricter than those on domestic goods. Since the Court of Justice also takes into consideration indirect discrimination, practically every national environmental measure will have to be weighed in the balance as to whether it factually leads to a different treatment of domestic or imported goods or not.

In case 302/86[26] the Commission had tackled the Danish deposit-and-return system by arguing that the mandatory use of reusable containers for drinks and beers indirectly discriminated against imported goods: reusable containers—mainly glass bottles—were considerably heavier in weight than containers made of plastic or other material. Therefore, the costs of transporting them to Denmark and, in their empty state, back to the country of origin, were higher than necessary and created indirect discrimination. If a foreign producer or trader wanted to avoid transport, it had to set up a deposit-and-return system of its own which would be costly.

3—17   The Court did not discuss questions of discrimination. Since it rejected the Commission's application, it must be presumed that it did not consider the increased transport costs or the difficulties involved in the setting-up of a deposit-and-return system to be sufficiently relevant as to constitute indirect discrimination.

In case C-2/90,[27] the Wallonian Government's import ban on waste from other Member States was tackled by the Commission, which argued that waste from other Member States was not more harmful than waste generated in Wallonia. The Court rejected that argument. It held that waste, while coming under Article 28 (ex 30) of the E.C. Treaty, had special characteristics. As there was an obligation to dispose of waste as close as possible to the place where it was produced in order to keep the transport of waste to as little as possible, which followed from Article 174(2) (ex 130r(2)) E.C.,[28]

---

[24] See above, para. 3–04.
[25] Case C-203/96 *Dusseldorp* (n. 7, above), para. 44.
[26] Case 302/86 (n. 9).
[27] Case C-2/90 (n. 11).
[28] See above, para. 1–30.

the different treatment between Wallonian waste and imported waste did not constitute, in the opinion of the Court, an arbitrary discrimination.[29]

Another case, which has been submitted to the Court but not yet decided, is the
Danish ban on metal cans, introduced in the early 1980s. The Commission had
considered that this measure was taken in order to protect the (Danish) environment,
and had therefore not condemned this ban before the Court of Justice; the attempts of
the United Kingdom, as a third-party intervenor, to have this ban discussed in case
302/86, failed for procedural reasons, since a third-party intervenor may not enlarge the
object of litigation before the Court beyond the limits which the main applicant has
established by its application.[30]

3—18   If it is correct that a Member State, in the absence of Community provisions, itself establishes the necessity or degree of protection of the environment which
it wishes to achieve at national level, then it is in principle up to the Danish
authorities to decide whether they wish to have metal cans in their environment.
Such metal cans made from aluminium or steel take more natural resources to
produce, are not reusable, constitute litter in the environment when they are thrown
away and reduce the efficiency of reuse systems, which a Member State may have set
up.

Compared to this, however, might be an Irish draft regulation of 1988, which aimed
at prohibiting metal cans, however, only for beer.[31] In this case, many of the environmental arguments in favour of such a ban are not really valid, since they would apply,
in the same way, to metal cans for soft drinks. The Commission was therefore of the
opinion that environmental reasons could not have caused the Irish Government to
consider a ban on metal cans for beer, but that this ban constituted an attempt to
reduce the import of British beer. Confronted with this argument, Ireland withdrew its
draft regulation.

3—19   In Denmark, the ban of metal cans was limited to beer and some soft drinks.
Other soft drinks, such as iced tea, were allowed to be marketed in metal cans; also, of
course, metal cans are used in Denmark for fruit and vegetable preserves and other
food products. While fruit and vegetable containers might not really be comparable to
drink containers, this is certainly the case with, for instance, iced tea or chocolate
drinks. It is thus very much a question of weighing up the different aspects of the
Danish ban in order to come to a decision whether or not it is discriminating. Also, it
should be pointed out that, in 1994, a Community Directive on packaging and packaging waste was adopted, which provides for the free circulation of packaging containers that comply with the requirements of this Directive.[32] Any decision on the Danish
ban would therefore take into consideration that Directive and not Article 28 (ex 30) of
the E.C. Treaty. In view of this new legislation, the Commission appealed, in 1999 to
the Court of Justice.

In 1993, the Netherlands set up a national Covenant on Tropical Hardwoods,
which provided that, after 1995, only timber from sustainably managed forests was to
be traded or processed in the Netherlands. The Covenant, an environmental agreement, was signed by the Dutch Government, the timber trade and timber processing
industry, trade unions and environmental organisations. It was intended to introduce a
Dutch approval mark in order to distinguish sustainably produced timber from other
timber. Since the Covenant was actively supported and signed by the Dutch Government,

---

[29] See for a critical comment L. Krämer, *European environmental law casebook* (London, 1993), p. 77.
[30] Case 302/86 (n. 9).
[31] See L. Krämer, *E.C. Treaty and environmental law* (London, 1998) para. 4.58.
[32] Dir. 94/62 on packaging and packaging waste [1994] O.J. L365/10; see also para. 9–49, below.

it must be considered a national public measure[33] and therefore be assessed under Article 28.

The discrimination problem lies in the fact that the Covenant refers to timber imports from tropical timber only; other hardwood-producing countries, such as Canada and Russia (Siberia) are not covered. It is not really clear why such differentiation is made; environmental reasons require the same treatment in both cases. The Dutch Covenant therefore seems to be discriminatory.

3—20   Some German Länder had adopted, in the 1980s, smog regulations which provided for restrictions on the use of private cars in the case of smog. Cars equipped with catalytic converters could, during the first stage of smog alert, circulate whereas cars without a catalytic converter could not. The Commission stated that this measure discriminated against car producers from other Member States, since the Community provisions valid at that time had considered the emissions from cars to be equivalent, whether or not the cars were equipped with catalytic converters. According to the Commission, foreign manufacturers were more severely affected by the German measures than German producers.

There is no E.C. legislation on smog and, therefore, Member States were free to decide on measures in the case of an extraordinary situation such as smog. Since cars with catalytic converters emit fewer pollutants than cars without such converters, and since all manufacturers were producing, at the time of the German measure, cars with catalytic converters, no discrimination can be seen in the smog-regulations, which, in any case, were measures to deal with a temporary situation. When the Commission changed its policy in 1987 and began working towards Community emission limit values which required catalytic converter equipment, it filed the case against Germany.

These examples might have shown how much depends, in an assessment upon whether a Member State's measure constitutes an arbitrary discrimination of products from other Member States or not, on the factual situation. A detailed case-by-case analysis of any specific case is therefore necessary.

3—21   **Disproportionate measures**   The second requirement set up by the Court of Justice was the proportionality requirement where it must be examined whether there are other measures available which restrict the free circulation of goods less severely than the measure which was taken.

The proportionality requirement became relevant in case C-131/93 where Germany had prohibited the import of living crayfish in order to protect the health and life of indigenous crayfish species.[34] The Court did not contest Germany's right to take such measures; however, it argued that Germany could have taken other, less restrictive steps, such as health controls for crayfish imports from other Member States, licensing requirements for putting living crayfish into German waters, for example. The Court also came to this conclusion because Germany had been rather generous in granting derogations from the import ban and had itself, in such cases, put similar conditions on the import authorisation.

3—22   In case 302/86[35] the Court considered the Danish measure on only allowing approved drink containers to be part of the Danish deposit-and-return system to be incompatible with Article 28 (ex 30); a Danish measure to allow some derogations for importers of small quantities was considered disproportionate. The Court did not

---

[33] Private measures would have to be assessed as to their compatibility with the E.C. Treaty, against Arts 81 and 82 (ex 85 and 86) E.C.

[34] Case C-131/93 *Commission v. Germany* [1994] E.C.R. I-3303.

[35] Case 302/86 (n. 9).

explain what other, less restrictive, measures Denmark could have taken; its judgment is instead confined to the statement that "a very considerable degree of protection of the environment" is not really nessary to protect the environment. This seems to have the hallmark of a political statement.

In case C-2/90,[36] the Court did not discuss at all whether or not the Belgian measure to ban waste imports was disproportionate: as Belgium had argued that the measure was taken in order to react to a suddenly increased import of waste and as the judgment was given nine years after the taking of the measure, there could well have been reasons to discuss the proportionality requirement.

In its Decision 98/523[37] the Commission considered the limitation of access to Karlstad airport to less noisy aeroplanes disproportionate, except as regarded a night curfew between 22.00 and 07.00 hours. The Commission argued, amongst other things, that the airport was situated in a sparsely populated area away from the city centre and that it accounted for a rather low traffic volume. The Commission requested that the Swedish authorities demonstrate the need to take the noise-restriction measures.

3—23   There is a lot of discussion on questions of burden of proof, burden of evidence, and so on. However, this rule of procedure simply means that in a dispute attempts must be made from the Commission, other parties, private bodies and Member States to clarify the facts as far as possible. The more substantiated the arguments from one side are, the more detailed those from the other side have to be. Only at the end of this process, where factual aspects remain open, can there be a question of who is to have the charge that a factual aspect has not been clarified.

It has already been pointed out that environmental protection reasons are, under the E.C. Treaty, not subordinated to considerations of free circulation of goods. In an assessment under Article 28 (ex 30), whether the consideration of free circulation of goods or the protection of the environment prevail, Member States have an amount of discretion as to the degree at which they wish to fix the protection of the environment. It is difficult to understand why a night curfew should comply with the principle of necessity and proportionality but a limitation on access to the airports to less noisy aeroplanes does not. Anyway, this issue cannot be solved by shifting the burden of proof.

3—24   Also, how difficult the proportionality principle is to apply in practice may be demonstrated by the question of product bans. Member States have pronounced a considerable number of bans of products; besides those mentioned on metal cans (Denmark) or pesticides (Netherlands), one could mention the restriction on phosphates in detergents (Italy—1988), or the Austrian ban of polybromated biphenyls (PBB), non-biodegradable plastic bags (some local authorities in Italy), lead capsules for alcoholic beverages (Germany, Netherlands), waste shredding machines (Germany) or lead-containing ammunition (Denmark, the Netherlands) and PVC.

The argument that a ban is not allowed where other means are available which less restrict the free circulation of goods must not be overused. Indeed, as has been already mentioned, the Court of Justice had expressly recognised the right of Member States to ban pesticides which had not been the subject of Community secondary legislation.[38] It would theoretically always be possible to argue that a strict licensing system together with control and surveillance mechanisms would reach more or less the same result, but be less restrictive than a total ban. The Court's jurisdiction to allow the complete ban of pesticides by Member States means in practice that the Court grants them a

---

[36] Case C-2/90 (n. 11).
[37] Dec. 98/523 (n. 15).
[38] Case 125/88 (n. 16).

considerable amount of discretion to decide on what measures they consider appropriate. Following the same line of reasoning, the Court of Justice accepted that the fixing of noise emission limit values for aeroplanes was the most effective and most appropriate means of combating noise emissions from aeroplanes; indeed, investments in construction around airports were normally very cost-intensive. Establishing noise emission limit values was therefore not disproportionate.[39]

3—25   This reasoning also applies to the German ban on waste shredding machines, on which the Commission has not yet taken a decision. Waste shredding machines cut biological waste into small pieces, which are then disposed of together with ordinary waste water.

German law provides that waste must first of all be recovered; this conforms to the Community waste hierarchy which is laid down in Directive 75/442.[40] Disposing of waste by shredding it and discharging it into water contradicts this principle. Furthermore, the pipes for waste water would be charged with the mud freight, filtering would become more difficult and costly, waste water treatment stations would incur increased costs, and so on. It would therefore certainly be possible to prohibit waste disposal together with waste water without banning the shredding machines. In order to find out whether the marketing of waste shredding machines might be prohibited as well, the import of such machines into Germany would have to be considered and the possibility of controlling the ban on using these machines and of disposing of the waste via the waste water flow. Since such a ban could probably never be effectively controlled, a ban on marketing shredding machines appears not to be disproportionate.

3—26   Italy, the United Kingdom, Denmark and Sweden took measures, in 1996–1997, to prohibit the marketing of self-chilling cans. These are metal cans for drinks which contain hydrofluorocarbons (HFCs), a cooling gas, which is spread between the wall of the can and the drink, in such a way that the can functions as a mobile mini-refrigerator, chilling the content of the can.

HFC is a greenhouse gas, used as a substitute to CFC; it is considered, in global warming terms, to have a global warming potential of 11,700 (CO_2 has a global warming potential of 1).[41] It is not yet regulated by international agreements or Community legislation, but was identified, under the Kyoto Protocol (1998), as one of the greenhouse gases. Its extensive use would undermine efforts in other sectors to reduce CO_2 emissions and thus combat climate change. Therefore, national bans on HFC or on products and equipment that contain HFC are justified under Article 28 (ex 30).

As regards the Italian ban of phosphates in detergents, it is not clear what less restrictive measure could reduce the eutrophication of rivers, lakes and coastal waters. The same applies to the Danish and Dutch ban on lead-containing ammunition which aims at reducing the presence of lead in the environment. If Denmark and the Netherlands consider that there is too much lead in the environment, that ducks and birds might eat that ammunition, then a ban appears appropriate since equally effective measures, which restrict the free flow of goods, are not available. The Commission has not taken any legal action against these three Member States. Similar considerations apparently also influenced the Commission in the case of biodegradable plastic bags, which were also accepted.[42] In the case of lead capsules for alcoholic

---

[39] Case C-389/96 *Aher-Waggon* [1998] E.C.R. I-4473.

[40] Dir. 75/442 on waste [1975] O.J. L194/23; amended by Dir. 91/156 [1991] O.J. L78/32.

[41] See para. 8–57, below.

[42] An Italian judge had asked the Court of Justice whether such a ban was compatible with Community law, but omitted to ask for its compatibility with Article 28 of the E.C. Treaty. The Court therefore only assessed its compatibility with Dir. 75/442 (n. 40, above) and found no problem with this Directive, case 380/87 *Enichem v. Cinisello-Balsamo* [1989] E.C.R. 2491.

beverages, the Community thought it appropriate to adopt Community regulations in order to provide for a complete phasing-out of such capsules.[43]

3—27   In 1999, the Netherlands issued draft legislation which considerably restricted the use of chlorinated paraffins. This measure was a follow-up of a decision taken within the framework of the Paris Convention of 1995,[44] aiming at progressively reducing paraffin in order to prevent marine pollution. The Commission did not object to this restriction on the free circulation of goods.

A similar case is the Austrian ban on PBB. PBB is suspected to cause serious health or environmental problems; however, the definitive scientific evidence on the risk of PBB has not yet been determined. The Commission considered that the OECD had recommended, at international level, that the marketing and use of PBBs be stopped and decided to accept the Austrian ban. This example shows that in the case of conflict between the free circulation of goods (Article 28 (ex 30) of the E.C. Treaty) and environmental protection, the precautionary principle of Article 174(2) (ex 130r(2)) may apply and lead to preference being given to measures which aim at environmental protection.

As mentioned above in paragraphs 1–27 *et seq.* there are attempts, in particular from economic operators, to limit the application of the precautionary principle also as regards national measures and to require, for its application, that there be scientific uncertainty, a possibility of severe and irreversible hazard, a need to adopt measures urgently and that national legislation is of a provisional nature only. All these conditions are interpreted to be part of the Court's requirement of proportionality which is thus very considerably extended.

3—28   The precautionary principle may also be relevant in cases which concern national measures to restrict or ban the use of PVC. PVC is a plastic product which is mainly used in construction materials, packaging, cars, toys and office equipment. When incinerated, however, it is thought to generate dioxins and furans; its recycling as well as its disposal is particularly difficult. The question is whether Member States may, in view of the complications of waste incineration and disposal, restrict the use of PVC products or of certain substances (phthalates or heavy metals) in PVC. In application of the precautionary principle and in the absence of Community measures, it is well within the discretion of Member States to restrict or prohibit the use of PVC; it is not clear what less restrictive measure would be available.[45]

In another case, Greece prohibited the import of diesel cars for private use, arguing that the heavy air pollution in Athens and Thessaloniki required such a measure. It seems obvious that a total import ban on private diesel cars in order to combat air pollution in two regions is disproportionate.

Upon the request of the Commission, Greece amended its legislation and prohibited the use of diesel cars in Athens and Thessaloniki. Such a measure may be proportional, if the air pollution in these two regions is primarily due to the use of diesel cars. However, it seems rather unlikely that the air pollution is no more due to diesel and petrol-driven cars, than it is to do with industrial emissions, other economic activity and household heating. As long as a significantly higher participation of diesel cars emissions is not established, the restriction on the use of diesel, but not on petrol-driven, cars is discriminatory; furthermore, the measure as such is disproportional, since it appears that it is not capable of reaching the objective, *i.e.* the reduction of environmental pollution.

---

[43] See, *e.g.*, Reg. 3280/92 [1992] O.J. L327/3.
[44] Paris Convention for the protection of the marine environment in the North-East Atlantic (OSPAR), see Dec. 98/249 [1998] O.J. L104/1; see also para. 7–38, below.
[45] As regards PVC, see para. 6–52 below also.

3—29   In 1998 Denmark announced draft national legislation which intended to limit considerably the marketing of lead in Denmark, and of products which contained lead; these products were expressly listed in an annex. Products which complied with Community directives were exempted from this ban.

The essential question in this case is whether Denmark is entitled, in the absence of Community law, to decide that it does not wish to see lead in its environment. In my opinion, this is indeed the case and it cannot be argued, in the name of proportionality, that less restrictive measures could be taken.

3—30   **Protecting the environment outside the national territory**   It has been argued in legal texts that a Member State's environmental measure under Article 28 (ex 30) of the E.C. Treaty may also be taken in order to protect the environment outside its own jurdsdiction. The Court of Justice has not yet formally decided on this issue. The first argument which is relevant in this context is the fact that the requirements of environmental protection are not limited to the Community territory. If the point of departure defended in this Chapter is correct—that in the absence of Community measures, the task of ensuring environmental protection is with Member States—it cannot seriously be argued that such measures are not allowed under Articles 28 or 30 (ex 30 or 36) of the E.C. Treaty. Indeed, measures to combat climate change or to protect the ozone layer, tropical forests, elephants, whales, tigers or rhinos do affect the environment outside the Community territory—and yet have been taken by the Community, without ever having seriously been questioned under Article 28.[46] In the absence then of such Community measures this competence is with Member States.

The possibility of protecting the environment outside the national jurisdiction of a Member State finds its limits in the general Treaty provisions, in particular in that of Article 10 (ex 5) E.C.[47] Thus, the protection of the environment in another Member State will normally have to be left to that other Member State. However, the individual case will have to be weighed carefully. For instance, where a Member State decides to enact a national import ban on ivory in order to protect the African elephant,[48] this measure also affects the imports of ivory from other Member States. And yet this measure may be upheld under Article 28 where the principles of non-discrimination and proportionality have been respected.

A similar reasoning may apply for the protection of an endangered species that lives in another Member State. Normally, it would be, under Article 10 of the E.C. Treaty, up to that Member State to protect this species. But there may be circumstances where such a measure is not taken, for political, economic or other reasons. In such a case, another Member State may decide to take measures to protect that species. An example is the German ban of the mid-1980s on imports for products made from *corallium rubrum*: *corallium rubrum* is a coral which lives in the Mediterranean and which is used in some Member States to produce jewellery. Weighing the arguments, the Commission did not see in that import ban a breach of Germany's obligations under Article 28/30 (ex 30/36) of the Treaty.[49]

---

[46] In case C-284/95, *Safety Hi-Tech* [1998] E.C.R. I-4301 the Court of Justice assessed the validity of Community measures to protect the ozone layer against Article 28 of the E.C. Treaty, but found no breach of the Treaty provisions; see also paras 8–60 *et seq.*, below.

[47] E.C. Treaty, Art. 10: "Member States shall . . . abstain from any measure which could jeopardise the attainment of the objectives of this Treaty."

[48] Reg. 2496/89 [1989] O.J. L240/5 introduced a Community-wide import ban on ivory. However, a number of Member States had already decided, at national level, to introduce such a ban prior to the Community action.

[49] Since then, *corallium rubrum* has been the subject of Community measures to restrict its trade, see Reg. 338/97 on the protection of species of wild fauna and flora by regulating trade therein [1997] O.J. L61/1.

The Court of Justice has not accepted export restrictions which France and the Netherlands[50] had introduced for specific wastes and for which they had invoked, amongst other arguments, the necessity of protecting the environment in other Member States. The Court considered that nothing indicated that the other Member States did not or could not protect themselves and their environment.

In case C-169/89,[51] the Court decided that the Netherlands could not lawfully prohibit the marketing of a bird which had been legally marketed in the United Kingdom. The details of this judgment appear questionable, but will not be discussed here,[52] since the judgment mainly dealt with the interpretation of Directive 79/409 on the conservation of wild birds.

3—31   In conclusion, Member States may, in the absence of Community provisions on specific products, take those measures to protect the environment against the risk arising from the products which they consider appropriate. However, Articles 28 and 30 of the E.C. Treaty and the very sophisticated and detailed case law of the Court of Justice require that a very careful assessment is made between the environmental advantage and the restriction of the free circulation of goods. Any national measure which restricts the circulation of goods must be based on non-economic considerations to protect the environment. It may not constitute an arbitrary discrimination between national producers and traders and producers or traders from other Member States. The national measure must be capable of reaching the envisaged aim and not go beyond what is necessary to reach it.

The different criteria—arbitrary discrimination, proportionality, a non-economic objective—leave a considerable amount of discretion to the Court of Justice, which is the final place for deciding on the legality of the national environmental measure. Therefore, a case-by-case assessment is necessary, which carefully considers all aspects of a national measure.

(b) National measures affecting exports

3—32   Similar requirements apply to measures which concern the export of products. Article 29 (ex 34) E.C. prohibits quantitative restrictions on exports as well as measures having an equivalent effect; Article 30 (ex 36) constitutes an exception to this principle and allows export restrictions, amongst other things for reasons to protect life and health of humans, animals or plants. The Court of Justice interpreted Article 29 (ex 34) in a way that this prohibition "concerns all national measures which have as their specific object or effect the restriction of patterns of exports and thereby . . . provide a special advantage for national products or for the domestic markets".[53]

A frequent way of prohibiting exports is the requirement to deliver waste to specific (national) plants. The Court of Justice considered that such an obligation constituted an indirect export ban and was therefore incompatible with Article 29 (ex 34).[54] In some contradiction to these judgments is the decision in case C-422/92 where the Court of

---

[50] Case 172/82 *Inter-Huiles* [1983] E.C.R. 555: "The environment is protected just as effectively when the oils are sold to an authorised disposal or regenerating undertaking of another Member State as when they are disposed of in the Member States of origin"; case 118/86 *Nertsfoederfabriek* [1987] E.C.R. 3883; the case concerned poultry waste.

[51] Case C-169/89 *Gourmetterie van den Burg* [1990] E.C.R. 2143.

[52] See for more details L. Krämer, *European environmental law casebook* (London, 1993), p. 149.

[53] Case 172/82 (n. 50).

[54] Cases 172/82 (n. 50); C-37/92 *Vanacker* [1993] E.C.R. I-4947; 118/86 *Nertsvoederfabriek* [1987] E.C.R. 3883.

Justice declared that the requirement to dispose waste generated in Germany only in that country was compatible with Community law.[55]

It should be noted that on the one hand waste is a product of a specific nature which may have as a consequence that different provisions apply.[56] On the other hand, the Community adopted, in 1993, new and specific provisons on the shipment of waste within the Community, which have been substituted for previous provisions.[57] Member States may, under these provisions, oblige waste generators or holders to deliver their waste to specific plants, provided that the activity is a disposal activity. However, where waste is shipped for recovery to another Member State, it is not possible to prohibit such a shipment by a provision which obliges the waste holder to supply it to a specific waste disposal or recovery plant. Such a provision contradicts Article 29 (ex 34) and the above-mentioned Regulation 259/93.

Apart from waste issues, there has not yet been any Court decision to allow or disallow export restrictions for environmental purposes. In practice therefore, the export ban for environmental purposes does not play a significant role.

(c) Measures under other policies

(i) Agricultural policy

3—33   Community agricultural policy is a common policy. Its concept is that the Community has exclusive competence in agricultural matters and also that the subsidarity principle of Article 5 (ex 3b) E.C. does not apply. Member States' measures in environmental matters that would affect the common agricultural policy and its legislation are therefore not allowed. Instead, Member States may only take measures where the Community has not taken action; such measures are under a permanent threat of being replaced by Community action. An example is the setting up of national criteria for organic farming and food therefrom: as the Community has regulated this matter,[58] there is no competence for national measures in this area.

Measures which had been taken in the past include, in particular, the ban on certain agricultural pesticides. Since 1991, this subject has been regulated at Community level by Directive 91/414[59]; however, since the implementing provisions have not yet all been elaborated, the Community de facto accepts that Member States continue to maintain national bans or restrictions of the marketing or use of pesticides. Once the Community system is fully established, this practice will have to be abandoned.

Environmental measures which Member States may take under these restricted conditions concern, for instance, measures concerning the handling of manure, the limitation of the size of industrial feedstock installations, irrigation measures, action on the management of water resources and limiting the use of fertilisers or the number of cattle per km^2.

(ii) Transport policy

3—34   Transport policy (Articles 70 to 80 (ex 74 to 84) E.C.) is also, under the E.C. Treaty, a common policy, though it is much less complete than the common agricultural policy. For this reason, Member States' environmental measures have a much greater

---

[55] Case C-422/92 Commission v. Germany [1995] E.C.R. I-1097; in that judgment, the Court did not expressly discuss Article 29 but examined the German legislation under Dir. 84/631 on the shipment of waste [1984] O.J. L326/31.
[56] See para. 2–76, above.
[57] Reg. 259/93 [1993] O.J. L30/1.
[58] Reg. 2092/91 [1992] O.J. L198/1; see for more details para. 10–10, below.
[59] Dir. 91/414 [1991] O.J. L230/51.

possibility of adopting environmental measures affecting transport. An important limitation, however, is Article 72 (ex 76), which prohibits direct or indirect discrimination of carriers from other Member States. In 1992, the Court of Justice had to decide on a tax on the use of roads by heavy goods vehicles which Germany had introduced.[60] While this road tax was the same for all carriers, Germany had, at the same time, provided for a reduction in the motor vehicle tax to the same amount; thus, the charge of the tax on the use of roads only affected carriers from other Member States. The Court did not accept the German Government's argument that the tax on the use of roads had an environmental objective because it was intended to increase the rate of goods transported by railway. Instead, it was of the opinion that there was no encouragement for German carriers to move to railway transport and that, therefore, the effect of the German measures contradicted Article 72 (ex 76).

Member States may therefore take, in the absence of Community measures, non-discriminatory environmental measures, as regards, for instance, provisions on night flights at airports, taxes or charges on the use of roads of all types of cars or provisions on ships. Since the Community has, up until now, not taken many measures to integrate environmental requirements into the transport policy, Articles 70 *et seq.* leave, in theory, large scope for national measures, although Member States do not seem enclined to make extensive use of this possibility.

(iii) State aids

3—35   Under the E.C. Treaty, a state aid is a measure which provides a company or business with an economic or financial advantage, which must be granted by the state or through state resources; it must favour certain undertakings or the production of certain goods and it must affect the trade between Member States (Article 87 (ex 92) E.C.). State aids are in principle prohibited. The intention of granting state aid has to be notified to the Commission (Article 88(3) (ex 93(3))) in order to allow the assessment of its compatibility with the E.C. Treaty, as Article 87(2) and (3) (ex 92(2) and (3)) allows state aids under certain conditions.

The connection with the Treaty's provision on competition needs to be underlined. Indeed, where consumers or users receive financial advantages to buy environmentally better products, there is normally no question of a state aid, since financial benefits are not given to particular firms. Where this is the case, aid may be authorised where it is granted without discrimination and does not exceed 100 per cent of the extra environmental costs. Small amounts of aid—up to 100,000 ECU per firm over a period of three years—are considered not to affect trade and need not be notified to the Commission.[61]

3—36   In the same way, financial assistance which is granted to every undertaking is not aid, but may, of course, be seen as such where the receiving companies are in competition with other companies that do not have access to this assistance.

The Commission has, since 1974, established guidelines for national aid with environmental objectives,[62] which were fundamentally reviewed and also published in 1994.[63] Legally, these guidelines are a communication to Member States and the other institutions, which indicate the criteria which the Commission uses to exercise its discretion for authorising national aids.

---

[60] Case C-195/90 *Commission v. Germany* [1992] E.C.R. I-3141; see also case C-195/90R *Commission v. Germany* [1990] E.C.R. I-3351, which dealt with interim measures.

[61] Commission, 26th report on competition policy (1996) (Luxembourg, 1997), p. 59.

[62] Commission, 4th report on competition policy (Brussels and Luxembourg, 1975), para. 175; 10th report on competition policy (Brussels and Luxembourg, 1981), para. 222; 16th report on competition policy (Brussels and Luxembourg, 1986), para. 259.

[63] Guidelines for state aid for environmental purposes [1994] O.J. C72/3.

The basis for authorising national environmental aid is now Article 88(3c)[64]; however, in specific cases, Articles 88(3a) or (3b) might be applicable.

3—37   Aid for investment—in land, buildings, plants and equipment—can be authorised up to 15 per cent gross of the eligible costs where aid is given in order to help firms adapt to new mandatory standards. For small and medium-sized enterprises, an extra 10 per cent may be allowed. In keeping with the polluter-pays principle, no aid should normally be given to cover the costs of complying with mandatory standards in new plants. Aid to encourage firms to attain significantly higher than the mandatory standards may be authorised up to 30 per cent of the eligible costs, plus, for small and medium-sized enterprises, an extra 10 per cent. These figures also apply where no mandatory standards or other legal obligations exist to protect the environment.

Aid for information activities, training and advisory services, where any part falls within the notion of "aid" under Article 87(1) (ex 92(1)) at all, "are normally exemptible" from that provision. Operating aids which relieve firms of costs resulting from the pollution or nuisance which they cause will be approved by the Commission only in exceptional cases; such cases could exist in the field of waste management or temporary relief from new environmental taxes. Examples are tax relief for CO_2–SO_2 taxes for some undertakings in Denmark, the Netherlands and Sweden, or tax relief for groundwater and waste taxes in the Netherlands.[65]

These provisions thus open up a very large range of possibilities to financially assist companies which invest in clean technologies or otherwise improve the environment. Examples of state aids of the last few years concern investments in the reduction of CO_2 emissions and in renewable energies,[66] aid for the development of a new, cleaner car,[67] industrial waste management,[68] energy-saving measures[69] and alternative energies.[70]

(iv) Taxes and charges

3—38   Member States' possibilities of adopting environmental taxes and charges are equally great. They find their limitation in Article 90 (ex 95) which is limited to goods and which prohibits any direct or indirect discrimination. The very existence of this provision shows that national fiscal measures are not to be assessed under Article 28 (ex 30). Indeed, Article 90 is lex specialis to Article 28 (ex 30).[71] The essential difference between the two provisions is that Article 90 prohibits discriminating taxation measures, but does not refer to disproportionate taxes; and as the primary function of taxes is to ensure income there cannot be question of environmental taxes only being allowed for non-economic reasons. Hence, Member States may fix taxes on whatever topic they wish and at whatever level they wish, as long as they do not discriminate against products from other Member States. No notification of a national measure to the Commission is necessary under Article 90.

Denmark had fixed the registration tax on new vehicles at between 105 and 180 per cent of the net sales price. The Commission was of the opinion that this provision was

---

[64] Art. 88(3c) "[The following may be considered to be compatible with the common market:] aid to facilitate the development of certain economic activities or of certain economic areas, where such aid does not adversely affect trading conditions to an extent contrary to the common interest."
[65] Commission, 25th report on competition policy (1995) (Brussels and Luxembourg, 1996), paras 83 et seq., para. 206; (1996) 12 Bulletin of the European Union, para. 1.3.77.
[66] (1996) 5 Bulletin of the European Union, para. 1.3.42.
[67] (1996) 7–8 Bulletin of the European Union, para. 1.3.74.
[68] (1997) 4 Bulletin of the European Union, para. 1.3.83.
[69] (1997) 9 Bulletin of the European Union, para. 1.2.36.
[70] (1997) 11 Bulletin of the European Union, para. 1.3.77 and (1998) 4, para. 1.2.50.
[71] Cases 74/76 Iannelli and Volpi [1977] E.C.R. 557; C–78–83/90 Compagnie Commerciale de l'Ouest [1992] E.C.R. I-1847.

incompatible with Article 90, since it impeded the free movement of goods. However, the Court of Justice decided that Article 90 only applied where tax measures were meant to protect domestic production; and since Denmark did not have a national car production industry there was no question of a breach of Article 90 (ex 95).[72] Article 28 could, in such a case, become applicable only where a tax is so high that the import of products from other Member States would be effectively barred. Even in such cases a national tax may be compatible with Article 28, namely in those cases where a Member State has environmental grounds for raising such a tax. Where for instance, a Member State would not like to see a Concorde aeroplane, a pesticide, metal cans or other products on its market or in its environment, it would be entitled, instead of prohibiting the use of that product, to levy a high, disuasive tax on the product.

3—39   National eco-taxes, on CFCs, energy use, packaging, groundwater and so on, are to be examined initially under Article 90, not under Article 28. Besides the objective of creating income, they aim at influencing economic operators', users', consumers' and tax-payers' behaviour to reduce pollution, ensure prudent use of natural resources and encourage a preference for environmentally friendly products.

In 1993, Belgium adopted legislation providing for an environmental tax on a number of products, in particular packages for drinks, disposable cameras and razors, batteries, pesticides and paper. Products on which the tax was levied had to carry a distinctive sign, showing that they were ecotaxed. The Court of Justice considered the tax to come under Article 90[73]; however, since the distinctive sign was to be applied on the products, it directly affected the circulation of goods and had therefore to be assessed under Article 28.

In 1996, France informed the Commission of its intention to introduce tax incentives for biofuels. The Commission at first refused to accept the French measures, since they protected French products and thus were in conflict with Article 90.[74] France then amended its legislation; the Commission was of the opinion that the new system eliminated any discrimination between the types of vegetable matter or crops which produce the biofuel and between French producers and those from other Member States. It therefore approved of the system. A private company has in the meantime attacked this decision before the Court, arguing that discrimination still exists.[75]

3—40   A number of German local authorities taxed single-use packaging, in order to promote reusable packaging. The Commission, seized with complaints from several economic operators, decided in 1996, that no infringement of the Treaty provisions was visible. In the meantime, these taxes were held to be incompatible with internal German law.

In 1997, the Commission made a communication to the other institutions, in which it discussed environmental taxes and levies in the internal market.[76] The Communication examined several aspects of eco-taxes, with the implicit intention of bringing as many of the national taxes and levies under the control of Article 28 of the E.C. Treaty as possible. This is understandable since with the progressive elimination of technical barriers to trade by Article 28, barriers with similar effect may result by virtue of the introduction of national taxes and charges.

---

[72] Case C-47/88 *Commission v. Denmark* [1990] E.C.R. I-4509.
[73] Case C-13/96 *Bic* [1997] E.C.R. I-1753.
[74] Dec. 97/542 [1997] O.J. L226/26.
[75] Case T-184/97 *BP Chemicals v. Commission* [1997] O.J. C252/36.
[76] COM (97) 9 of January 29, 1997 [1997] O.J. C224/4.

Eco-taxes are a useful tool in the promotion of environmentally sound behaviour; they help to keep environmentally unwelcome products off the market.[77] Member States have always used taxes to influence the behaviour of economic operators or private persons; examples are the taxation of petrol and diesel, of spirits and cigarettes, water, electricity and heating. Examples of past eco-taxes are differential taxes for leaded and unleaded petrol, tax relief for nuclear energy, natural gas, lignite or coal, or landfill taxes. Since eco-taxes are being used increasingly in the north of the Community, but have until now been used only rather infrequently in the south,[78] their divisive effect increases Community differences rather than promoting integration and cohesion.

3. Existence of Community legislation and the taking of national measures

(a) General aspects

3—41 As mentioned above, Member States' competence to deal with environmental measures does not end once the Community has adopted an environmental measure. However, it is "superseded" by the Community measure, to the extent that the Community measure reaches. Member States' possibility of acting therefore depends both on the content of the Community legislative act, and on the legal basis on which that legislative act was based.

In order to assess the legal content of a Community measure, it is important to examine exactly what the measure intends to cover. For instance, the Community measure might, for product standards, cover only the standards for those products which participate in the trade between Member States, but leave the standards for products which remain on the national market to Member States. Community terminology speaks, in such cases, of optional harmonisation, since Member States may decide to set up two different types of standards for products.[79] In contrast to this, total harmonisation exists where a Community measure intends to set standards for all products which are put into circulation within the Community, whether they cross a border or not.[80] Partial harmonisation only concerns some products, but not all of a given type.[81] Minimum harmonisation sets standards at Community level, but leaves the possibility to Member States to fix more stringent requirements.[82] Combinations of these types of harmonisation are possible; thus, a Community directive may well fix standards for some products only (partial harmonisation), deal with all products that are on the Community market (total harmonisations) and leave Member States the possibility to adopt more stringent standards (minimum harmonisation).

The second aspect finds its source in the E.C. Treaty itself. Indeed, the Treaty provides for differences in Member States' rights according to the legal basis on which a Community environmental measure is grounded. These different situations will therefore be discussed later.

---

[77] See also European Environmental Agency: Environmental taxes, implementation and environmental effectiveness (Copenhagen, 1996).

[78] The annex to COM (97) 9 (n. 76) lists, for October 1996, 22 eco-taxes in Denmark, 20 in Sweden, 19 in Finland, but only 4 in Greece, 7 in Italy and 8 in Spain.

[79] Examples are the limit values for noise emissions from construction equipment, see para. 8–80, below.

[80] Examples are the limit values for air emission from cars since 1988, see para. 8–18, below.

[81] An example is Dir. 79/117 on the ban of certain pesticides, see para. 6–40, below.

[82] Examples are standards for waste incineration plants, see para. 8–41, below.

(b) Rights under Article 176 (ex 130t) E.C.

3—42   Where a Community measure was based on Article 175 (ex 130s), the relationship between the Member States' and the Community's right to legislate is governed by Article 176 (ex 130t).[83] The provision only refers to protective measures and it may thus be doubtful whether measures that aim at preserving or improving the quality of the environment (see Article 174 (ex 130r)) are also covered. However, such a differentiation would make no sense, all the more since no clear distinction can be drawn between protective, preserving and improving measures. "Protective measures" must therefore be interpreted as including all measures adopted under Article 175.

Article 176 says nothing about the form which the Community provision under Article 175 must take. It is therefore irrelevant whether the provision is set out in a directive, a regulation or a decision—for instance, whether to adhere to an international convention—whether the measure was the provision was adopted unanimously or by majority vote, whether it is a partial or an optional or a total harmonisation measure.

3—43   Article 176 only allows stricter measures to be taken. Consequently, the Member States may not adopt different measures from those adopted by the Community. On the contrary: the more stringent measure must follow the same direction and come closer than the Community to attaining the objectives of Article 174 (1) of the E.C. Treaty. It is important that the rules adopted by the individual Member State are of the same type as the Community provisions, because then the Community and other Member States have the possibility of catching up and aligning with the more protective measure taken by one Member State, re-establishing in this way uniform legislation throughout the Community.

For example, if the Community decides in a measure based on Article 175, to halve the production and consumption of chlorofluorocarbons (CFCs) because of its ozone-depleting potential, any Member State may still propose an outright ban on the production and consumption of CFCs. However, it may not ban, on the basis of Article 176, the use of aerosol cans which contain CFC gas: this is not a more stringent protective measure, but another, different measure: an aliud. The legality of such a measure is therefore determined according to general Treaty provisions, in particular by Articles 28 and 30 (ex 30 and 36).

If the Community introduces a system of strict liability for environmental damage, but limits the amount of compensation payable to a certain limit, each Member State may impose strict liability and provide for unlimited compensation. However, it may not provide for unlimited liability for damage caused by negligence instead, since this is a different system. Nor could the Member State in that case, argue that experience had shown that certain industrial activities too often give cause for environmental liability and then prohibit that specific industrial activity.

When the Community introduced an eco-label for products and took a flower as its symbol, it expressly allowed Member States to maintain their national eco-label systems.[84] Without this express authorisation, Member States would not have been able, based on Article 176, to maintain their national systems. Indeed, the symbols as well as the selection and assessment criteria being different, these national systems are not "more protective" systems under Article 176, but rather different systems.

A more protective system is a system which establishes stricter limit values for the

---

[83] Art. 176 of the E.C. Treaty: "The protective measures adopted in common pursuant to Article 175, shall not prevent any Member State from maintaining or introducing more stringent protective measures. Such measures must be compatible with this Treaty. They shall be notified to the Commission."

[84] Reg. 880/92 [1992] O.J. L99/1; see para. 4–34, below.

emission of pollutants into the environment, which reduces emissions more quickly than the Community measure or which regulates, for emissions from an industrial plant, more pollutants than the Community measure.

The nationally more protective measures must be compatible with the Treaty. Consequently, they may not conflict with any provision of the Treaty, particularly with the provisions on the free circulation of goods or on undistorted competition. The measures must not constitute a means of arbitrary discrimination or a disguised restriction on trade between Member States (Articles 28 and 30 (ex 30 and 36)). Reference to the Treaty means, of course, reference to the interpretation given to the different Treaty provisions, by the Court of Justice in particular. Therefore, a national, more protective measure may neither be discriminatory nor disproportionate with regard to the objective that is pursued with it. Protectionism is still protectionism, even if the aim is to protect the environment.

3—46   "Treaty" refers also to secondary Community law, since this is based on the E.C. Treaty.[85] This theory is contested mainly by German writers[86] who argue that otherwise the right to take more protective measures would be undermined by Community secondary legislation and become meaningless. However, this opinion does not take into consideration the fact that Community secondary legislation is also based on the Treaty. As regards Article 30 (ex 36) E.C., it is well established Court jurisdiction, and in the meantime is no longer contested, that this provision no longer applies where the Community has adopted secondary legislation—whether such Community measures were based on Articles 95 (ex 100a), 175 (ex 130s) or any other provision.

Furthermore, it has already been discussed above[87] that the Council considers Articles 95 (ex 100a) and 175 (ex 130s) as being equally valid grounds on which to base legislation and that it differentiates the legal basis, supported in this by the Court of Justice and the Commission, according to the "centre of gravity" of a measure. This means that up to 49 per cent of a measure that is based on Article 175 may be provisions which deal with internal market issues. If Member States could in such cases introduce, under Article 176 (ex 130t), more stringent protective measures, the whole system that was set up by the secondary Community legislation would fall apart. This would contradict the objectives of Articles 14 (ex 7a) and 95 (ex 100a), which try to set up and maintain an internal market system, where goods may circulate freely.

3–47   The problem is of considerable practical importance. For example, Regulation 880/92, based on Article 175, introduced a Community eco-label.[88] The Community criteria for attribution of an eco-label are set for product groups by Community decisions which are based on Regulation 880/92 and, finally, on Article 175 of the E.C. Treaty. The specific decisions, to grant the eco-label for a specific product, are made at national level.[89] It seems an impossible idea to establish Community-wide criteria for specific product groups and then, when a producer asks a national authority to obtain the eco-label, inform him that the Member State in question has adopted more protective provisions so that he could not obtain the eco-label. Such a solution would be all the more contradictory as the same producer could obtain the eco-label in another Member State that had not adopted such "more protective measures" and

---

[85] See, also Jans, *European environmental law* (n. 17, above), p. 104; Pagh, *E.U. Miljoeret* (n. 23, above), p. 242; *contra* Epiney, *Umweltrecht in der Europäischen Union* (n. 20, above), p. 126 quoting other German authors.

[86] Also see on this point, para. 1–13.

[87] See paras 2–69 *et seq.*, above.

[88] Reg. 880/92 [1992] O.J. L99/1.

[89] For more details see para. 4–34.

could then circulate his product freely within the Community. Thus, within one and the same Member State, products could circulate with the same eco-label, but with different eco-criteria: this result is absurd.

Another example is the regulation on the shipment of waste, which is based on Article 175.[90] The regulation establishes lists of non-dangerous (green) and hazardous (amber and red) waste, for which different surveillance and control systems as regards shipments apply. Green list waste may be shipped practically without restriction. The question is whether Member States are allowed, under Article 176, to classify a green list waste as amber list waste and then apply stricter controls to such shipments.

A last example again concerns the shipment of waste. Regulation 259/93 differentiates, for hazardous wastes, between shipments that are made for disposal and shipments that are made for recovery purposes. While Member States may prohibit shipments of hazardous waste for disposal altogether,[91] they may object to shipments for recovery only in seven specific cases which are listed in Article 7(4a) of Regulation 259/93. The last of these cases allows objection to shipments, "if the ration of the recoverable and non-recoverable waste, the estimated value of the materials to be finally recovered or the cost of the recovery and the cost of the disposal of the non recoverable fraction do not justify the recovery under economic and environmental considerations". Could a Member State, invoking Article 176, also generally prohibit shipments of waste for recovery?

3—48   The answer must be in the negative. Indeed, there is no sense in differentiating between waste for disposal and waste for recovery at all, if Member States could adopt provisions which would lead to an equal treatment of waste in both cases. Why should there be the necessity for very carefully considering environmental and economic aspects of a waste shipment under Article 7(4a) of Regulation 259/93, if a Member State could ensure, as a general rule, that shipments of waste would be prohibited even if the weighing up of arguments showed that such a shipment was environmentally sound? Listing seven grounds for objecting to waste shipments in Article 7(4a) and then admitting an unlimited number of supplementary objections does not really make sense.

This question was submitted to the Court of Justice in case C-203/96.[92] The Court found that neither Regulation 259/93 nor Directive 75/442 on waste[93] allowed the application of the principles of self-sufficiency and proximity to shipments of waste for recovery. However, it did not answer the question of whether Article 176 allowed such an application and, thus, whether Member States could go beyond Regulation 259/93 by invoking Article 176. Instead, it examined the grounds invoked by the Dutch Government for its national measure which went beyond Regulation 259/93 and found that the justification—to ensure the continuity of supply of Dutch undertakings and increased risks for the environment by waste shipments—did not justify, in this specific case,[94] the restriction under Article 30 (ex 36) E.C.

3—49   This judgment might well be claimed by both sides. Indeed, if a Member State could have have recourse to Article 176 and generally object to waste shipments, an examination of whether such a restriction is contrary to Article 29 (ex 34) E.C. would not have been necessary. On the other hand, if the objections listed in Article 7(4a)

---

[90] Reg. 259/93 [1993] O.J. L30/1.

[91] Ibid., Art. 4(3a).

[92] Case C-203/96 Dusseldorp (n. 7, above).

[93] Dir. 75/442 as amended by Dir. 91/156 [1991] O.J. L78/32.

[94] It is not clear why the Court entered into the discussion of this specific case, although it was a question which was put to the Court under the procedure of Art. 234 (ex 177) E.C.

of Regulation 259/93 were exhaustive, should the Court have entered into an examination of supplementary objection grounds?

In my opinion, it should first of all be noted that the problem only appears as regards product standards, where the Community principle of free circulation of goods interferes. Indeed, where Community secondary legislation establishes limit values for emissions from installations, or quality standards for concentrations of pollutants in water, there is general agreement that Member States may, on the basis of Article 176, set stricter provisions at national level.

3—50   As regards product-related secondary Community legislation, the solution lies in the necessity of reading the two criteria of Article 176 (ex 130t) together—*i.e.* "more protective measure" and "compatible with the Treaty": any Community environmental legislation, including the legislation that is based on Article 175 (ex 130s) must respect the provisions of Articles 28 and 30 (ex 30 and 36)—this is established case law of the Court of Justice.[95] Thus, Community legislation also has to respect the principles of non-discrimination and proportionality which form part of the interpretation of Articles 28 and 30,[96] although the Community legislature enjoy a large degree of discretion as to how to draft legislation in a specific case. The more the Community legislature has weighed up the different economic, ecological, social, political and other arguments in detail and has elaborated detailed, balanced and sophisticated provisions (such as decisions on eco-label criteria, waste lists, objection grounds) the more the principles of Articles 28 and 30 are "filled up"; in the case of a total harmonisation—on this notion see paragraph 3–41—there is thus no room left for the principles of Articles 28 and 30 (ex 30 and 36). Then when a Member State, based on Article 176 of the E.C. Treaty, wants to take more protective measures, its legislative discretion is reduced in proportion to the concretisation which Community secondary legislation has given to the balance between environmental and economic interests in a specific situation. A national measure which deviates from the solutions set by Community secondary legislation would thus be disproportionate and therefore not compatible with the Treaty.

This solution is largely in line with that of Jans,[97] who is of the opinion that in cases of total harmonisation of a specific measure, Member States would not be allowed to take more protective measures under Article 176.

The problem has only been seen in practice in one case up until now. Directive 87/416 allows Member States to prohibit the use of leaded petrol, but requires that the intention of such a ban be published and notified to the Commissions six months in advance.[98] Germany wanted, based on Article 176, to disregard the six-month delay and ban leaded petrol four months after notification. Finally, however, it accepted the Commission's opinion in this matter—an insistence that the six-month delay be respected, which safeguarded the interests of producers, importers, traders and users of petrol and cars.

Measures adopted under Article 176 must be notified to the Commission. There is no time-limit for such notification and the measures must not be notified to the Commission in draft form. However, where the national measure comes into the field of application of Directive 98/34,[99] the obligation to notify the measures in draft form certainly exists. Indeed, that Directive provides that all product-related measures shall be notified to the Commission in draft form in order to allow an examination of

---

[95] Cases 15/83 *Denkavit Nederland* [1984] E.C.R. 2171; C-51/93 *Meyhui* [1994] E.C.R. I-3879; C-284/95 *Safety Hi-Tech* [1998] E.C.R. I-4301.
[96] See paras 3–04 *et seq.*, above.
[97] Jans (n. 17), p. 104.
[98] Dir. 87/416 [1987] O.J. L225/1.
[99] Dir. 98/34 laying down a procedure for the provision of information in the field of technical standards and regulations [1998] O.J. L204/37. This Directive replaces Dir. 83/189 [1983] O.J. L109/8.

whether or not they could create new barriers to trade. Therefore, where a more
protective measure could have an influence on Article 28 (ex 30) of the E.C. Treaty,
the Commission must be notified of it in draft form. Under Directive 98/34, there is
then a standstill period of at least three months during which the Commission and all
other Member States may question the compatibility of the draft measure with Article
28 or secondary Community legislation. Omitting to notify the Commission of the
draft makes the national provision unenforceable.[1]

Article 176 does not contain any procedural provisions for checking whether the
national measure fulfils the conditions that are laid down in Article 176 (ex 130t).
Where the Commission is of the opinion that a national measure is not a more
protective, but a different measure (an "aliud"), or where it believes that the measure
is not compatible with primary or secondary Community law, it has, in the last
instance, to recur to procedures under Article 226 (ex 169) E.C. The same possibility
is open to any Member States under Article 227 (ex 170) E.C.

(c) Rights under Article 95(4) to (8) (ex 100a(4) to (8)) E.C.

(i) General aspects

3—52   Article 95(4) to (8) (ex 100a(4) to (8)) deals with the right of Member States
to maintain existing or introduce new legislative measures where the Community has
legislated on the legal basis of Article 95.

Article 95 was introduced, as Article 100a, into the Treaty in 1987. Its paragraph 4
allowed Member States, in the case of decisions according to that provision and under
certain conditions, to "apply" diverging national legislation. Between 1987 and 1997,
the Commission took three decisions under Article 95(4)[2]; in one case, the Court of
Justice issued a judgment.[3] On two notifications from the Netherlands, dated 1992 and
concerning restrictions on the use of cadmium and pentachlorophenol, the Commission had, by mid-1999, not yet decided; it has, however, tolerated the application of the
reductions in the Netherlands, which was not quite in line with the Court's judgment
in case C-41/93.

In case C-319/97,[4] the Court decided that where the Commission failed to take a
decision within a reasonable time, a Member State could only take action under Article
231 (ex 175) E.C., but had, in the meantime, to apply the Community measure. In view
of the six-month rule, introduced by the Amsterdam Treaty as of May 1, 1999,[5] this
judgment will probably not have far-reaching effects.

The Amsterdam Treaty modified Article 95 considerably, and, more specifically,
provided for the possibility for Member States to maintain or introduce national
measures after the Community had adopted a measure under Article 95. The extensive
legal discussion on Article 95 (ex 100a) which took place between 1987 and 1997, is
therefore of only limited value now. The new version of Article 95 has ended the legal
battle over whether "apply" in the previous version was to be understood as "continue
to apply"—this has always been the Commission's understanding—or was equivalent
to "maintain or introduce".

---

[1] Case C-194/94 *CIA Security International* [1996] E.C.R. I-2201.
[2] [1992] O.J. C334/8 (*Pentachlorophenol Germany*); [1994] O.J. L316/43 (*Pentachlorophenol Germany*);
[1996] O.J. L68/32 (*Pentachlorophenol Denmark*).
[3] Case C-41/93 *France v. Commission* [1994] E.C.R. I-1829.
[4] Case C-319/97 *Kortas*, judgment of June 1, 1999, not yet reported.
[5] See para. 3–62, below.

(ii) Maintaining national legislation (Article 95(4) (ex 100a(4)))[6]

3—53 For a Member State to maintain national environmental legislation, according to Article 95(4) despite Community legislation, a number of conditions must be fulfilled:

(a) the Community must have adopted a harmonisation measure;

(b) a Member State must deem it necessary to maintain its national legislation on grounds that relate to the protection of the environment;

(c) the Member State notifies the Commission of these provisions as well as of the grounds for maintaining them;

(d) the Commission approves of the national measures (Article 95(4)).

These different conditions will be examined one by one.

3—54 **Adoption of a harmonisation measure** The wording of Article 95(4) (ex 100a(4)) only speaks of measures taken by the Council or the Commission, not by the Community. However, this is obviously incomplete. Indeed, it follows from Article 95(1) that measures under Article 95 are adopted by way of co-decision (Article 251 (ex 189b)) E.C.; and Article 254 (ex 191) expressly states that measures under Article 251 are adopted by the European Parliament and the Council jointly. The omission of any mention of the European Parliament, which is also found elsewhere in the Treaty,[7] makes it necessary to understand the wording of Article 95(4) as referring to the Community. The express inclusion of measures taken by the Commission clarifies that the adaptation of Community measures to scientific or technical progress by way of a committee procedure (Article 202 (ex 145) EC), which are frequently taken by the Commission, may also lead to the right of Member States to maintain national legislation; such cases may well occur where technical annexes of directives are adapted to technical progress.

"Harmonisation measures" are measures adopted under Article 95 of the E.C. Treaty. Such a measure need not have been adopted by majority decision[8]; even in the case of a unanimous decision, the right of a Member State to maintain its national legislation exists. It is not contradictory to vote in favour of a Community measure and then decide to maintain more stringent national legislation. Indeed, a Member State may well vote in favour of a Community measure because it wishes to see the level of environmental protection increased throughout the Community, even if the Community measure does not go as far as its own national legislation.

3—55 **Necessity of maintaining national legislation** It is doubtful whether any national legislation can be maintained. These doubts stem from Article 95(7),[9] which

---

[6] Art. 95(4) of the E.C. Treaty: "If, after the adoption by the Council or by the Commission of a harmonisation measure, a Member State deems it necessary to maintain national provisions on grounds of major needs referred to in Article 30, or relating to the protection of the environment or the working environment, it shall notify the Commission of these provisions as well as the grounds for maintaining them."

[7] See, e.g. Arts 71 (transport), 153 (consumer protection) and 175 (environment).

[8] Prior to the amendment made to Art. 95 by the Amsterdam Treaty, Art. 100a(4) contained a requirement that the Council must have decided by qualified majority.

[9] Art. 95(7) of the E.C. Treaty: "When . . . a Member State is authorised to maintain or introduce national provisions derogating from a harmonisation measure, the Commission shall immediately examine whether to propose an adaptation to that measure."

demonstrates the aim of the Treaty legislature to ensure that uniform legislation applies throughout the Community. Therefore, the Community measure shall, if at all possible, be adapted to that of the derogating Member State in order to ensure the continuous free circulation of goods in the Community's internal market.

These questions will be discussed below, when the Commission's options are examined for approving or of refusing the Member State's maintaining its national legislation. It is certain that a Member State may notify any national measure under Article 95(4); it is not necessary that the legislation adopted at national level. Regional measures may also be notified.

3—56 Notification and justification of the national measure   The Member State which wishes to maintain its national legislation must formally inform the Commission of its intention to do so. There is no time-limit for this notification; terms that require such notification to be addressed to the Commission within a specific timespan after the adoption of the Community legislation or within the timespan which was provided for in the Community measure for transposition into national legislation, have not been retained. Usually, therefore, a Member State is free to notify the Commission when it seems fit to do so.

However, it is clearly in the self-interest of the notifying Member State to notify as early as possible. On the one hand, provisions of Community law prevail over national law and may have a direct effect, even where they are not transposed into national law.[10] On the other hand, the notification puts into operation a six-month delay within which a decision on the national measure must be taken (Article 95(6) (ex 100a(6)).)

3—57   And, finally, the Court of Justice has decided[11] that a Member State may only apply its national legislation which deviates from the Community harmonisation measure, once it has received an approving decision from the Commission.[12] It is doubtful whether this decision, which was made *obiter* in a case, where the Treaty text did not yet differentiate in Article 95, between "apply" and "maintain". Indeed, it would constitute a considerable disturbance of economic operations and administrative practice if a Member State would have to suspend the application of national legislation which might have existed for years, and wait for a Commission decision. The reasonable, and largely logical, consequence is therefore to consider the Court's statement remaining valid only for the cases of Article 95(5), *i.e.* for cases where new national legislation is introduced. Anyway, the uncertainty of the described legal situation suggests that the Member State has a strong interest in trying to obtain the Commission's decision as quickly as possible and before the transposition period for the harmonisation measure has ended.

The notifying Member State will also have to give the grounds for its decision to maintain national legislation. It has to indicate the factual and legal aspects in sufficient detail to allow the Commission to reach a decision on the notification within six months. The requirement of providing the grounds for the decision is new and constitutes, without doubt, a considerable supplementary burden for the notifying Member State.

3—58 Commission approval   The Commission must "approve" of the environmental measure; this wording of Article 95(6) is more precise than the previous version

---

[10] See para. 11–27, below.

[11] Case C-41/93 (n. 3), para. 30.

[12] See *ibid.*, Opinion of Advocate General Tesauro, para. 9, who argues that this interpretation is the only one which is compatible with the supremacy of Community law and which avoids legal insecurity.

which provided that the Commission should "confirm" the national measure, since it is now clear that the approval must be made in the form of a decision under Article 249 (ex 189) E.C.

Approval has to be given if the national measure does not constitute a "means of arbitrary discrimination or a disguised restriction on trade between Member States". This wording is identical to that of Article 30(2) (ex 36(2)) E.C. Thus, the interpretation of Article 30(2) may be used to interpret this provision. Arbitrary discrimination or disguised trade restrictions are cases of abuse, where a formally legitimate objective—the protection of the environment—is used to discriminate against goods from other Member States or to pursue protectionist goals.

3—59   To these two goals, which were already contained in the previous versions of Article 95, a third one has been added: the national measure "shall not constitute an obstacle to the functioning of the internal market".

It is clear that any national measure which is maintained, despite a harmonisation measure taken by the Community, constitutes an obstacle to the functioning of the internal market; the two bans on pentachlorophenol in Germany and Denmark, on which the Commission had decided, constitute a clear example, since products containing that substance were not allowed to circulate in these countries. It is thus not quite clear what the provision intends to achieve.

3—60   Where, for instance, the Community decides to create a uniform eco-labelling system throughout the Community, such a measure would have to be based on Article 95 (ex 100a). Supposing that Germany then wanted to maintain its national eco-symbol, which is a blue angel—and not a flower, as is the Community symbol—could this be done by invoking Article 95(4)? The answer seems clearly to be in the negative. Indeed, it is possible to have either a system based on the flower or on the blue angel, but one cannot have both systems inside an internal market. In fact, the German system, in this example, would be a different system. Also, it is not clear what the environmental grounds would be which would make it "necessary" to maintain the blue angel system; greater efficiency cannot be a valid ground, because the Community system is just meant to create an equivalent system. In conclusion, thus, the maintaining of the blue angel system would be a different system where the environmental grounds that make its maintenance necessary are not visible.

Where the Community provides for certain limit values for noise emissions from coaches, any more stringent national limit value would, if properly enforced, create an obstacle to the free circulation of coaches and would thus have to be disallowed. This solution could be avoided where the Member State that wishes to maintain the more stringent national emission limit values would at least allow the circulation of coaches on its territory, which are registered in other Member States and only occasionally circulate within the Member State with the more stringent values. This consideration demonstrates that the assessment of whether the maintaining of a national measure is necessary, requires a detailed consideration of the pros and cons so doing under internal market and ecological auspices. Sevenster[13] goes so far as to generalise this position: she is of the opinion that the necessity of considering whether the national measure constitutes an obstacle is a badly drafted expression of the proportionality principle.

3—61   In conclusion, the new addition to Article 95 (ex 100a) does not mean that the national environmental measure cannot under any circumstances constitute an obstacle to the free circulation of goods. It is only meaningful when it is completed by a word such as "inadequate" or "inappropriate". This would mean that, in each

---

[13] H. Sevenster, *European yearbook of environmental law* (Oxford, 1999), p. 116.

individual case, the Commission would have to weigh up the protection of the environment against seeing the internal market function properly. Thus, a national measure must be proportional to the objective pursued by it; where a less restrictive measure is available, the Member State may be asked to recur to that measure even where this would mean a change in its national rules. Also, a measure that constitutes a significant obstacle to the functioning of the internal market and where the environmental advantage is insignificant, could be rejected by the Commission.

This interpretation would bring the principle of proportionality from Article 5 (ex 3b) into the assessment process of Article 95(6): while it is legitimate to protect the environment and not to see the national level of environmental protection lowered by a harmonisation measure from the Community, the national measure must not go beyond what is necessary to achieve appropriate environmental protection.

3—62 Procedure The Commission is required to approve—or reject—the national decision to maintain national legislation within six months of notification; in particularly complex cases it may prolong this period by a maximum of six months more. This provision was introduced by the Amsterdam Treaty and is, no doubt, a reaction to the fact that some national notifications under Article 95(4) had not been decided upon in more than six years.

It is not possible to prolong this delay, for instance when the Commission argues that the Member State's decision has not been sufficiently argued. The Commission may then refuse to authorise the measure; but it may not ask for further documentation, evidence or other justification, since this would create guidelines for the six-month period—which clearly it cannot do.

The time given for approval may appear short. It should be noted, however, that the legal and environmental situation in the different Member States has normally been discussed at Community level during the elaboration of the harmonisation measure. The subject-matter of national legislation is thus not entirely new to the Commission.

3—63 The sanction for failing to decide within six months is tough: the national measure "shall be deemed to have been approved". The national measure has, in such a case, an effect on all other Member States as well as on all economic operators, even though they did not have the possibility of influencing the speed of decision-making within the Commission. Where a Member State is of the opinion that the Commission has made a wrong decision, either by approving or rejecting the national maintaining decision within six months or by letting the six-month period elapse, it may bring the matter before the Court of Justice directly (Article 95(8)). The procedure is governed by Article 230 (2) (ex 173(2)) if the action is directed against the Commission, and by Article 227 (ex 170) E.C. if the action is directed against another Member State. The two-month delay of Article 230(5) starts, in the case of the absence of a Commission decision within six months, at the end of this six-month period.

Private operators may take action against the Commission under Article 230(4) if they are directly and individually concerned by the decision, for instance when their exports or imports are affected. They may also try to conform to the Community harmonisation measure and, where they see their trade affected, bring the matter before the competent national court and then ask for a preliminary ruling by the Court of Justice under Article 234 (ex 177) E.C., in order to have the Commission's decision checked.

(iii) Introducing new national legislation

3—64 The new provision of Article 95(5) (ex 100a(5)) clarifies that Member States may, under certain conditions, introduce new legislation in cases where the Community has adopted a harmonisation measure.[14] This provision ended a longlasting dispute among legal writers as to whether the word "apply" in the previous version of Article 95(4) also allowed the introduction of new measures. Between 1987, when that old provision had been introduced, and 1997, no Member State had asked to be allowed to introduce new legislation under the old Article 100a(4) of the E.C. Treaty. The possibility of introducing new measures exists only for measures relating to the environment and the working environment. The different grounds of Article 30 (ex. 36) which allow Member States, under Article 95(4) to maintain existing more stringent national provisions, may not be invoked for the introduction of new measures.

The conditions for introducing new national environmental measures are relatively strict. They are the following:

(a) the new national measure must be based on new scientific evidence;

(b) the problem must be specific to the Member State that wishes to introduce the measure;

(c) the problem must have arisen after the adoption of the harmonisation measure.

The three conditions must be fulfilled cumulatively. Their likely effect will make it very rare for a Member State to demonstrate the necessity to opt out of the common Community measure, although the acting Member State has a certain amount of discretion to assess whether the new situation requires the opting out of the Community measure ("deems it necessary"). Its decision is, in turn, assessed by the Commission and, in case of litigation, by the Court of Justice.

3—65 **New scientific evidence** New scientific evidence must consist of studies, reports or other documentation, showing that there is a real risk to the environment and that, therefore, it is necessary to introduce a more protective national measure. It is not easy to comply with this criterion. For instance, the fact that benzene, an additive in petrol, is carcinogenic, has been known for years; thus, a Member State would not be allowed to lower the maximum admissible content of benzene in petrol below the level that was fixed by the Community. It might be argued that the cancer statistics which show the effects of benzene, constitute "new evidence". This seems doubtful; in any case, however, such a discovery would not be specific to an individual Member State, but would concern the whole of the Community. For such cases, the new formulation of Article 95(3) (ex 100a(3)) suggests that the Commission make a new proposal for a harmonisation measure "taking account in particular of any new development based on scientific facts".

To take another example: the continuing global climate problem would not justify a Member State introducing national standards for air emissions from cars which deviate from Community standards; again, this is neither a "new" scientific evidence nor is the problem specific to one Member State alone.

Scientific evidence is new where the Community legislature was not able to take it into account at the moment of adopting the harmonisation measure. The word

---

[14] Art. 95(5) of the E.C. Treaty: ". . . if, after the adoption by the Council or by the Commission of a harmonisation measure, a Member State deems it necessary to introduce national provisions based on new scientific evidence relating to the protection of the environment or the working environment on grounds of a problem specific to that Member State arising after the adoption of the harmonisation measure, it shall notify the Commission of the envisaged provisions as well as the grounds for introducing them."

"evidence"[15] will have to be interpreted broadly and will be considered to include data, the accumulation of existing studies which bring to light a specific problem, and other factual aspects.

3—66   Specific problem   The condition that the problem must be specific to a Member State is probably the most difficult to comply with. Indeed, since Article 95 (ex 100a) refers to the internal market and thus mainly to product-related measures, it is difficult to imagine the effects of a product causing environmental problems that are specific to the national territory of a single Member State. Neither would the effect of a product on global warming, on the ozone-layer, or on water or fauna and flora be sufficient, since, normally, all these effects affect more than one Member State.

When the Commission decided to allow Denmark to apply more restrictive measures on the use of the biocide pentachlorophenol (PCP), it declared that PCP easily migrated to groundwater, that Denmark took most of its drinking water from groundwater and that therefore Denmark should be allowed to deviate from the Community harmonisation measure.[16] The decision to allow Germany to deviate from the harmonisation measure was essentially justified by the argument that Germany had built a lot of buildings after 1945 and had extensively used PCP for wood preservation.[17] This may be the case; however, in most Member States drinking water is taken from groundwater, and the use of PCP for wood preservation was widespread in the Community, although not necessarily as widespread as in Germany. Taking the criterion seriously would mean that in either case, the new Article 95(5) would not allow the introduction of new national legislation in derogation from the Community measure. More generally, a derogation under that provision could not be granted where an environmental problem appeared in several Member States.

The result is not as strange as it might appear at first sight: indeed, under Article 95(3) the Commission is obliged to examine whether a new proposal for Community action shall be made; furthermore, where a concrete risk for man or the environment becomes apparent, national action under the safeguard clause of Article 95(9) remains possible.[18]

3—67   New problems   The condition that the problem must have arisen after the adoption of the harmonisation measure may concern cases in which health or environmental effects of a specific problem become evident, such as the effect of a biocide, a pesticide or another chemical product which suddenly shows serious environmental problems in a specific region to have been caused. A simple change in the environmental policy in a Member State would not justify the introduction of new legislation. In the same way, this condition would not be fulfilled where an environmental problem—gradually or suddenly—appears before the adoption of the harmonisation measure and the Member States wishes to introduce "opt out" legislation after the adoption of the harmonisation measure.

3—68   Procedure   The procedure for measures under Article 95(5), including the time delays, verification, approval or rejection of the national measure, is the same as in the case of the maintaining of a national measure. In the case of the introduction of

---

[15] At least in some Community languages the word which is used has the connotation of "findings", such as in Dutch (gegevens), German (Erkenntnisse), Portuguese (novedades) and French (preuves).
[16] Commission, Dec. 94/783 [1994] O.J. L316/43.
[17] Commission, Dec. 96/211 [1996] O.J. L68/32.
[18] See para. 3–71, below.

new legislation, however, the standstill period stipulated by the Court of Justice[19] will apply; thus, a Member State may only introduce its legislation after the Commission has approved of it. For the rest, reference is made to paragraph 3–62, above.

(d) Rights under other Treaty provisions

3—69   Where a Community environmental measure was based on Treaty provisions other than Articles 175 (ex 130s) or 95 (ex 100a), it is doubtful whether Member States also have the possibility of maintaining or introducing stricter national environmental measures. This applies in particular to measures based on Articles 37 for agricultural policy measures (ex 43), 71 or 80 on transport policy measures (ex 74 or 84), 93 on tax measures (ex 99) or 133 on commercial policy measures (ex 113).

German legal writers have developed, since 1987, a concept according to which the E.C. Treaty contains a legally binding principle according to which environmental protection within the Community must be optimised. The reasoning is based on several provisions and principles of the Treaty, in particular Articles 176, 95(4), 100b(2),[20] and Article 6. The definition varies. Zuleeg, who later acted as judge at the European Court of Justice and who "invented" that principle, defined it as "the right of Member States to maintain or introduce more protection of the environment, even where the Community has adopted a measure to protect the environment".[21] Other authors, while following Zuleeg in his approach, go even further; some declare that in the case of conflict between environmental objectives and objectives under other policies priority should, in the case of doubt, be given to the environmental objective. Others even suggest that, for Community environmental measures, the Treaty provision which optimises environmental protection be used as a legal basis, and this is usually Article 175 (ex 130s).

3—70   For the question with which we are here concerned, these writers suggest that, generally speaking, Member States be granted the rights under Article 176, whatever the legal base was on which the Community measure had been based. However, the legal concept is unconvincing. Indeed, it is not clear why the principle of optimising protection should just apply to environmental protection and not to the protection of human health, the respect of human rights and fundamental freedoms or to any of the values which are mentioned in Article 30 where the environment is not mentioned. If ever the authors of the E.C. Treaty had in mind any such principle, they could have inserted it in the Treaty at one of the Treaty amendments in 1993 or 1997.

Furthermore, where a Community environmental measure in the sector of agricultural policy is based on Article 37 (ex 43) it is not clear at all that Article 176 (ex 130t) is the more protective provision with regard to Article 95 (ex 100a). The concept of optimising environmental protection is incapable of explaining why Member States' residual rights have been organised differently under Articles 176 and 95, although there would have been the possibility of finding a single, optimising solution. Also, the concept is more motivated, it seems, by concerns about national sovereignty than on environmental optimisation, since it cares little for those Member States which do not have an elaborated, consistent, national environmental policy.

As none of the Treaty provisions on which an environmental action can be based contain provisions similar to those of Articles 176 and 95, the conclusion must be that

---

[19] Case C-41/93 (n. 3) and para. 3–57, above.
[20] This Article was deleted by the Amsterdam Treaty.
[21] M. Zuleeg, "Vorbehaltene Kompetenzen der Mitgliedstaaten der Europäischen Gemeinschaft auf dem Gebiet des Umweltschutzes", *Neue Zeitschrift für Verwaltungsrecht* (1987), p. 280 (author's translation).

these provisions are exceptions to the general rule that Community measures cannot be derogated from by Member States, unless Community law expressly so provides. Their application to measures which had been adopted by virtue of Articles 37, 71, 93 or 133 of the E.C. Treaty is therefore not possible; all the more so since it would not be clear whether Article 176 or 95 should apply in a specific case.

(e) Rights under safeguard clauses

3—71   The safeguard clauses of both Articles 174(2.4) (ex 130r(2.4)) and 95(9) (ex 100a(9)) E.C. apply where secondary Community legislation expressly contains a provision which enables Member States to take safeguard measures. However, both provisions require a specific provision in secondary Community legislation; they do not directly give rights to Member States.

The specificity of safeguard clauses is that they allow Member States to object to the marketing or the circulation of goods even in those cases where these products comply with the requirements which have been laid down at Community level. This basic consideration leads to the consequence, expressed in both provisions of Articles 174(2.4) and 95(9) that the national safeguard measures may only be provisional, limited in time and subject to a decision by the Community as to its compatibility with Community law.

3—72   Safeguard clauses in Community environmental legislation existed long before Articles 174(2.4) and 95(9) were introduced into the Treaty. A considerable number of Community directives or regulations contained safeguard clauses which allowed Member States to deviate, for health or environmental reasons, from Community standards. The conditions for having recourse to a safeguard clause were practically always the same:

- an express provision in the corresponding Community directive or regulation;

- a formal notification by a Member State that it had evidence that a product, while complying with the requirements of the directive/regulation, constituted a hazard for man or the environment and that therefore the circulation of the product was restricted or suspended;

- justifications for the national decision taken.

The Commission then had to proceed to consultation with the other Member States and to take, on a regular basis by the committee procedure instituted by virtue of Article 202 (ex 145) E.C., a Community decision. Such a decision could consist of adapting the Community harmonisation measure to the requests of the notifying Member State, or in informing the Member State that his safeguard measure was not justified and had to be abandoned.[22]

BIBLIOGRAPHY

Auvret-Finck, J.: "L'avis 2/91 relatif à la Convention n° 170 de l'OIT", *Cahiers de droit européen* (1995), p. 443

Barents, R.: "Milieu en de interne markt", *Tijdschrift voor Europees en Economisch Recht* (1993), p. 5

---

[22] See, *e.g.* Dec. 90/420 [1990] O.J. L22/49, informing Denmark that a specific substance which Denmark had declared carcinogenic by way of a safeguard measure, was in reality not carcinogenic.

Becker, U.: *Der Gestaltungsspielraum der EG-Mitgliedstaaten im Spannungsfeld zwischen Umweltschutz und freiem Warenverkehr* (Baden-Baden, 1991)

Bennett, G.: *The internal market and environmental policy in the Federal Republic of Germany and the Netherlands* (Arnhem, 1989)

Breier, S.: "Die öffentliche Beschaffung umweltfreundlicher KFZ und Kraftstoffe aus europarechtlicher Sicht", *Umwelt- und Planungsrecht* (1995), p. 128

Breier, S.: "Die Organisationsgewalt der Gemeinschaft am Beispiel der Errichtung der Europäischen Umweltagentur". *Natur und Recht* (1995), p. 516

Breuer, R.: "Umweltrechtliche und wirtschaftslenkende Abgaben im europäischen Binnenmarkt", *Deutsches Verwaltungsblatt* (1992), p. 485

Chalmers, D.: "Environmental protection and the Single Market: an unsustainable development. Does the E.C. Treaty need a Title on the environment?", *Legal Issues in European Integration* (1994), p. I-65

Churchill, R. and Kütting, G.: "International environmental agreements and the free movement of gods in the EC: the case of the Montreal Protocol", *European Environmental Law Review* (1995), p. 329

Epiney, A.: "Die Maßstabsfunktion des Art. 30 EGV für nationale umweltpolitische Maßnahmen", *Zeitschrift für Umweltrecht* (1995), p. 24

Epiney, A.: "Umweltrechtliche Querschnittsklausel und freier Warenverkehr: die Einbeziehung umweltpolitischer Belange über die Beschränkung der Grundfreiheit", *Natur und Recht* (1995), p. 497

Epiney, A. and Furrer, A.: "Umweltschutz nach Maastricht. Ein Europa der drei Geschwindigkeiten?", *Europarecht* (1993), p. 369

Fallon, M.: "Les ecotaxes et le droit communautaire" in CEDRE (ed.), *L'introduction des ecotaxtes en droit belge* (Brussels, 1994), p. 33

Grabitz, E. and Zacker, C.: "Scope for action by the E.C. Member States for the improvement of environmental protection under EEC Law: the example of environmental taxes and subsidies" [1989] C.M.L.R. 423

Hey, C. and Jahns-Böhm, J.: *Ökologie und freier Binnenmarkt* (Freiburg and Frankfurt/M., 1989)

Jans, J.: "Europeesrechtelijke grenzen aan nationaal milieubeleid", *Sociaal-economische wetgeving* (1989), p. 217

Jans, J.: "State aid and Articles 92 and 93 of the E.C. Treaty. Does the polluter pay?", *European Environmental Law Review* (1995), p. 108

Joseph, T.: "Preaching heresy: permitting Member States to enforce stricter environmental laws than the European Community", *Yale Journal of International Law* (1995), p. 227

Krämer, L.: "Environmental protection and Article 30 EEC Treaty" *Common Market Law Reports* (1993), p. 111

Mahmoudi, S.: "EG-medlemskap och strängere nationella miljöutgärder", *Svensk Juristtidning* (1993), p. 419

Middeke, A.: "Der Kompetenznormenkonflikt umweltrelevanter Gemeinschaftsakte im Binnenmarkt", *Deutsches Verwaltungsblatt* (1993), p. 769

Middeke, A.: *Nationaler Umweltschutz im Binnenmarkt* (Berlin, 1992)

Nettesheim, M.: Die völkerrechtlichen Vertragsschlußkompetenzen der Europäischen Gemeinschaft und ihrer Mitgliedstaaten im Bereich des Umweltschutzes", *Europarecht* (1993), p. 340

Pagh, P.: "Miljoegarantien efter PCP.dommen", *Ugeskrift for Retsvaesen* (1994), p. B276

Palme, C.: *Nationale Umweltpolitik in der EG. Zur Rolle des Art. 100a IV im Rahmen einer europäischen Umweltgemeinschaft* (Berlin, 1992)

Pieper, S.: "Gemeinschaftsrechtliche Anforderungen an Umweltsonderabgaben unter Berücksichtigung ihres Aufkommens", *Die Öffentliche Verwaltung* (1996), p. 232

Quick, R.: "Der Gemeinschaftsrahmen für staatliche Umweltschutzbeihilfen", *Europäische Zeitschrift für Wirtschaftsrecht* (1994), p. 620

Scherer, J.: *Umweltrecht: Handelshemmnis im EG-Binnenmarkt; Umweltrecht in der Praxis* (1992), p. H.1, 76

Schröder, M.: "Zusammenwirken von Gemeinschaftsrecht und nationalem Recht auf dem Gebiet der Umweltabgaben" in P. Kirchhoff (ed.), *Umweltschutz im Abgaben- und Steuerrecht* (Cologne, 1993), p. 87

Schröer, T.: *Die Kompetenzverteilung zwischen der europäischen Wirtschaftsgemeinschaft und ihren Mitgliedstaaten auf dem Gebiet des Umweltschutzes* (Berlin, 1992)

Scott, J.: "Environmental compatibility and the Community's structural funds: a legal analysis", *Journal of Environmental Law* (1996), p. 99

Thiel, J.: *Umweltrechtliche Kompetenzen in der Europäischen Union* (Bochum, 1995)

Vorwerk, A.: *Die umweltpolitischen Kompetenzen der Europäischen Gemeinschaft und ihrer Mitgliedstaaten nach Inkrafttreten der Einheitlichen Europäischen Akte* (Munich, 1990)

Wiegand, B.: "Bestmöglicher Umweltschutz als Aufgabe der Europäischen Gemeinschaften", *Deutsches Verwaltungsblatt* (1993), p. 533

Ziegler, A.: *Trade and environmental law in the European Community* (Oxford, 1996)

CHAPTER 4

Horizontal Measures

The Community has adopted or envisaged a number of provisions which try to regulate situations which have as a common feature that they go beyond one specific medium (for example, water, air) or a specific situation. They have little in common amongst themselves.

1. TOWN AND COUNTRY PLANNING; LAND USE

4—01 Article 175(2) (ex 130s(2)) provides that measures concerning town and country planning and land use require unanimous adoption in Council. The provision thus stems from the idea that such measures may also be taken at Community level. Until now, though, with one exception no such measures have been taken. The Commission has issued some communications which concern basic aspects of town and country planning,[1] the urban environment,[2] integrated coastal zone management[3] and wetlands.[4]

The exception concerns accident prevention from industrial establishments: Article 12 of Directive 96/82[5] requires that Member States ensure that the objectives of preventing major accidents and limiting the consequences of such accidents are taken into account in their land-use policies: in the long term there will have to be appropriate distances between such establishments and residential areas, areas of public use and natural sensitivity or interest. The implementation of these provisions is to be ensured by consultation procedures.

4—02 Apart from this exception the different measures mentioned and other, similar measures instead aim at focusing the attention on some specific aspects of development within the European Union or showing the environmental problems of specific developments, rather than determining legal measures for intended town and country planning or land use. Indeed, these measures do not announce or propose new legal measures at all to contribute to the solution of problems. They have to be viewed alongside the Community's policies which affect planning and land use, in particular regional and agricultural policy. Sometimes the communications also serve to start a discussion over whether Community financial assistance for some specific topics should be envisaged, notably in the framework of the Structural Funds. Also, measures concerning the protection of the architectural and natural heritage of the

---

[1] Commission, Europe 2000: perspectives of future town and country planning of the Community, COM (90) 544 of November 27, 1990; Commission, Europe 2000: outlook for the development of the Community's territory COM (91) 452 of November 7, 1991.

[2] Commission, Green Paper on the urban environment, COM (90) 218 of July 6, 1990 and Council Res. of January 28, 1991 [1991] O.J. C33/4; see further Court of Auditors, Special Report on urban environment [1994] O.J. C383/1; Commission, Communication on urban development in the European Union, COM (97) 197 of May 6, 1997.

[3] Commission, Communication on integrated coastal zone management, COM (95) 511 of November 29, 1995.

[4] Commission, Communication on the wise use and conservation of wetlands, COM (95) 189 of May 29, 1995

[5] Dir. 96/82 on the control of major-accident hazards involving dangerous substances [1997] O.J. L10/13.

Community[6] increasingly come under the culture provision Article 151 (ex 128) E.C.[7]

2. MEASURES RELATING TO SPECIFIC ECONOMIC SECTORS

4—03 At the beginning of Community environmental policy in the 1970s, there was a general consensus on the necessity of regulating environmental emission from specific industrial installations.[8] Although the general usefulness of this concept was confirmed in 1987,[9] it has not led to many concrete results.

(a) Titanium dioxide

4—04 In 1978 the Council adopted Directive 78/176 on waste from the titanium dioxide industry.[10] The origins of this Directive go back to discharges of waste in the early 1970s, from a Montedison factory at Scarlino (Italy) into Mediterranean waters, which caused concern in Corsica and led to discord between Italy and France. The Directive's main aim is the progressive reduction of pollution caused by waste from the titanium dioxide (TiO_2) industry. The manufacture of titanium dioxide, which is a white pigment used principally in paints, normally results in a larger quantity of waste than product. Until recently, this waste was dumped in the sea or into coastal waters, causing considerable environmental concerns. Directive 78/176 only fixed general obligations on Member States to promote the prevention of waste generation and its recycling and processing. For this purpose, Member States had to set up pollution reduction programmes which had to contain reduction targets; relatively precise provisions were made for the content of these programmes.

Following a provision laid down in Article 7 of Directive 78/176, the Council adopted, in 1982, a directive on the monitoring of TiO_2-installations.[11] Another provision of Directive 78/176 requested the Commission to submit proposals for harmonising the targets fixed in the different national waste reduction programmes. With some delay, these programmes were transmitted, and the Commission made a proposal in 1983 for a directive, suggesting uniform reductions in discharges largely irrespective of the waters into which the discharges were made. As, prior to 1987, all environmental measures at Community level had to be adopted unanimously and the United Kingdom did not agree to uniform emission standards,[12] it vetoed the proposal in Council. In 1987, the Commission resubmitted the proposal, basing it now on Article 95 (ex 100a). The Council adopted the proposal as Directive 89/428,[13] but based it on Article 175 (ex 130s) E.C., which provided for unanimous decisions. On request of the Commission the Court of Justice declared the Directive void, since it

---

[6] See Rec. 74/65 on the protection of the architectural and natural heritage [1975] O.J. L21/22; Res. of the Council and of Member States meeting in Council on the conservation of the European architectural heritage [1986] O.J. C320/1.

[7] Dec. 2228/97 on an action programme for the conservation of cultural heritage [1997] O.J. L305/31.

[8] See first environmental action programme [1973] O.J. C112/1 at p. 20, where measures for the paper and pulp industry, the iron and steel industry and the manufacture of titanium dioxide are announced and measures for the chemical, leather, food and textile industry are envisaged.

[9] See fourth environmental action programme [1987] O.J. C328/1 at no. 3.4.

[10] Dir. 78/176 [1978] O.J. L54/19.

[11] Dir. 82/883 on procedures for the surveillance and monitoring of environments concerned by waste from the titanium dioxide industry [1982] O.J. L378/1.

[12] See for the history and development of E.C. legislation in the TiO_2 sector, N. Haigh, *Manual of Environmental Policy: The E.C. and Britain* (looseleaf) (London, 1994), Chap. 4.9.

[13] [1989] O.J. L201/56.

was of the opinion that it should have been based on Article 95.[14] The Commission submitted a new text, which was then adopted by virtue of Article 95.[15]

4—05   Directive 92/112 prohibited the dumping by ship or aircraft of wastes from the TiO_2 industry by June 1993 and provided for uniform reduction measures for waste discharges into waters in other ways, differentiated according to the technological process used. Also the limit values for air emissions—fixed for SOx and dust and chlorine—were differentiated according to the industrial process, not to the receiving environment.

The implementation of the different directives raised some problems since the titanium dioxide industry exists only in some Member States. The Commission, however, was of the opinion that TiO_2 waste could also be transferred from one Member State to another and that therefore all Member States had to transpose the directives into national law. Belgium was condemned twice for not having adopted the necessary legislative measures for transpose Directive 78/176.[16] A Commission announcement to take Court action against Belgium for not having transposing Directive 92/112, was averted when Belgium transmitted implementation measures in 1996—with a three-year delay.

4—06   Reports on the implementation of Directive 78/176 had to be published every three years, from 1981 onwards. Three such reports were published, in 1983, 1986 and 1989.[17] However, while Article 14 of Directive 78/176 requested that the Commission "shall report . . . on the application of this Directive", the three reports limited themselves to reproducing the national reports, without any comment, evaluation or criticism. Directive 91/692[18] required that the reports on the Directive's application should form part of the triannual comprehensive reports on the application of water directives. The first report, due for 1997, has not yet been published.

Overall evaluation of Directive 78/176 is difficult. The progressive reduction of the discharge of TiO_2 waste into sea and coastal waters was more influenced by debate from international conventions and North Sea Conferences and by the technological possibility of recycling TiO_2 waste which has been progressively developed over the past 20 years. The existence of Directive 78/176 may have pushed for more research for such solutions. The different legal provisions to progressively reduce waste from the production of TiO_2 were impossible to monitor and thus had little effect.

(b) Other industrial sectors

4—07   In 1975, the Commission made a proposal for a directive on the reduction of water pollution caused by wood pulp mills.[19] The proposal limited itself to proposing emission limit values for some water contaminants. Since some at least of the Member States were opposed to E.C.-wide uniform limit values for emissions into the environment, the proposal was not discussed in Council and has in the meantime become obsolete. In 1980 the Commission announced that it would not submit more proposals

---

[14] Case C-300/89 *Commission v. Council* [1991] E.C.R. I-2867.

[15] Dir. 92/112 [1992] O.J. L409/11.

[16] Case C-68/81 *Commission v. Belgium* [1982] E.C.R. 153; C-227–230/85 *Commission v. Belgium* [1988] E.C.R. 1.

[17] The reports do not appear to have formally been approved by the European Commission. The titanium dioxide industry, prevention and progressive reduction of pollution: First triannual report, XI/695/83 (1983) May; Second triannial report (1986) August; Third triannial report (1989) September.

[18] Dir. 91/692 standardising and rationalising reports on the implementation of certain Directives relating to the environment [1991] O.J. L377/48.

[19] [1975] O.J. C99/2.

for specific industrial sectors because of "obvious differences of opinion within the Council".[20] In 1992 it intended making a proposal for a directive on environmental pollution by the paper industry, but abandoned this idea in 1995.[21]

The sector-orientated approach was partly used with the adoption of daughter directives for Directive 76/464,[22] such as for instance Directive 82/176 on limit values and quality objectives for mercury discharges by the chlor-alkali electrolysis industry.[23] As will be further explained below,[24] this Directive, like all other daughter directives, set emission limit values and quality objectives, leaving it to Member States to use one or other approach. Directives 89/369[25] and 89/429[26] on municipal waste incinerators only concern air emissions, the same approach that was taken by Directive 88/609 on large combustion plants.[27] In contrast to this, Directive 94/67 on the incineration of hazardous waste[28] regulates emissions into the air and the water which stems from these installations.[29]

(c) Asbestos

4—08   There is a far-reaching ban for (new) asbestos to be placed on the market. Though several Member States decided on a total ban on asbestos products, the Commission did not take action against them; instead, it prepared for a total ban on asbestos at Community level.[30] As regards asbestos which is already on the market (and in the environment), the Council adopted Directive 87/217 which tried to create integrated provisions for asbestos.[31] The Directive provides for general requirements to reduce asbestos emissions into the air, into the waste water and to minimise the risk to humans and the environment by the demolition of asbestos-containing buildings, during transport and in the disposal. Generally, the best available technology not entailing excessive costs shall be used. For air emissions, a general emission limit value of 0.1 mg per cubic metre is fixed, small installations may obtain derogations.

As regards water discharges from the production of asbestos cement, the Directive requires a complete recycling of waste water; however, where this is "economically not practicable" an emission limit value shall have to be respected. A similar approach is used for the production of asbestos paper. For waste generation no emission limit values were set.

4—09   The Directive was to be transposed into national law by the end of 1988. In 1997 the Commission reported that the Directive was not completely transposed in

---

[20] Commission, Progress made in connection with the environment action programme and assessment of the work to implement it, COM (80) 222 of May 7, 1980, p. 5.
[21] See Written Question 1491/91 (Van Hemeldonck) [1992] O.J. C242/4 and Written Question E-2849/95 (De Coene) [1995] O.J. C109/11.The Commission justified this attitude by reference to the proposal for Dir. 96/61 which contained a new approach. This Directive will be discussed below at para. xxx.
[22] Dir. 76/464 on pollution caused by certain dangerous substances discharged into the aquatic environment of the Community [1976] O.J. L129/23.
[23] Dir. 82/176 [1982] O.J. L81/29.
[24] See paras 7–23 et seq., below.
[25] Dir. 89/369 on the preservation of air pollution from new municipal waste incineration plants [1989] O.J. L163/32.
[26] Dir. 89/429 on the reduction of air pollution from existing municipal waste incineration plants [1989] O.J. L203/50.
[27] Dir. 88/609 on the limitation of emissions of certain pollutants into the air from large combustion plants [1988] O.J. L336/1.
[28] Dir. 94/67 on the incineration of hazardous waste [1994] O.J. L365/34.
[29] See proposal for an amendent of Dir. 94/67 [1997] O.J. C13/6.
[30] See para. 6–38, below.
[31] Dir. 87/217 on the prevention and reduction of environmental pollution by asbestos [1987] O.J. L85/40.

Portugal and badly applied in Belgium and the United Kingdom.[32] The Commission had, under Directive 91/692 to report on the implementation of Directive 87/217 by mid 1998.

The Directive's loose drafting and the absence of constant monitoring of its application in and by Member States seems to have had as a consequence that its real effect is limited.

For the rest, asbestos fibres are classified as carcinogens.[33] Six asbestos fibres and products which contain such fibres are forbidden within the Community. A seventh, chrysotil, was forbidden in 14 product groups, before, finally, that fibre was also forbidden in 1999.[34] The Commission had accepted, until 1999, that Member States might adopt more stringent provisions although the different Community measures were aimed at ensuring the free circulation of asbestos within the Community.

3. ENVIRONMENTAL IMPACT ASSESSMENT

4—10   A Directive on the assessment of the effects of certain public and private projects on the environment was adopted in 1985 and substantially amended in 1997.[35] It requests that public authorities, before they give development consent for specific public and private projects, mainly concerning infrastructure, make an assessment of the direct and indirect effects which the project may have on humans and the environment. Specific procedural provisions are laid down for such an assessment, such as the requirement for the developer to submit factual information on the project and its likely impact, the participation of environmental administrative bodies and the possibility for the "public concerned" to express an opinion. The decision on the application shall take into consideration all these comments.

For a first group of projects such as large oil refineries, large thermal power stations, radioactive waste disposal installations, motorways, lines for long-distance railway traffic, larger airports, for example, listed in annex I to the Directive, an environmental impact assessment always has to be made. For a second group of projects (annex II) an environmental impact has to be made where the project is likely to have significant effects on the environment by virtue, in particular, of its nature, size or location. Member States have a considerable amount of discretion in deciding whether a project has such a significant impact or not.

4—11   The Court of Justice has given a wide interpretation to the provisions of Directive 85/337[36]; its jurisprudence on annex II projects may have contributed to the new provision in Article 4 which now requires Member States to either examine on a case-by-case basis whether an environmental impact assessment is to be made or fix thresholds beyond which projects of annex II have to be made the subject of an assessment.

Directive 85/337 has been implemented in all Member States, although some with considerable delays and not all conforming to the Directive's requirements. On the date required for implementation (July 4, 1988), five Member States had notified the Commission of their transposing measures[37]; Luxembourg did not transpose the Directive until 1994.[38] In 1998, the Commission mentioned that the transposing

---

[32] Commission, 14th report on monitoring application of Community law (1996) [1997] O.J. C332/1 at p. 182.
[33] Commission, Written Question P-591/96 (Féret) [1996] O.J. C183/39.
[34] Dir. 1999/77 [1999] O.J. L207/18.
[35] Dir. 85/337 [1985] O.J. 175/40; amended by Dir. 97/11 [1997] O.J. 73/5.
[36] Case C-72/95 *Kraaijeveld* [1996] E.C.R. I-5403.
[37] Written Question 1744/90 (Harrison) [1991] O.J. C28/30.
[38] Case C-313/93 *Commission v. Luxembourg* [1994] E.C.R. I-1279.

legislation in Spain, Ireland, Greece, Italy, Portugal, Belgium and Germany still did not conform with Community law.[39]

4—12   A particular problem is the application of the Directive's requirements in practice: in 1996 the Commission mentioned that most of the complaints, petitions and infringement procedures which it dealt with concerned Directive 85/337.[40] The main concerns are the policy decision to realise a project independently from its, potentially very negative, impact on the environment, the environmentally poor quality of the impact assessment,[41] the beginning of the realisation of the project prior to the impact assessment, arbitrary exclusions of making an assessment for an annex II project and omissions to consult properly the public concerned.[42] The transboundary effects of a project are to be discussed and solved in a way which involves international co-operation more than planning in the European Union.

Directive 85/337 has undoubtedly influenced the development of consent procedures in all Member States, by imposing the taking into consideration of environmental aspects into this procedure. In a number of cases, the almost total discretion given to local or other authorities to authorise a project was capable of being challenged in the name of the environment. This influence is likely to grow progressively.

4—13   The main problems of the Directive are:

- its loose drafting and the large discretion given to administrations often lead to the non-application of some of its principles, such as for instance Article 5(1) or annex III;

- the Directive does not oblige a developer to study or have studied alternatives to a project;[43]

- the administration is not in any way obliged to avoid and/or minimise the negative effects of a project on the environment, but may give development consent also where very serious negative effects are to be expected;

- the impact assessment need not, according to general understanding, be made in writing, though it is difficult to see how on can describe ("describe" is the word used in Article 3) the effects of a project otherwise than in writing;

- no regular Commission report on the application of Directive 85/337 is foreseen.[44]

Commission attempts in the 1980s to have an environmental impact assessment made for any project which is co-financed by Community funds (in particular the Structural Funds or the Cohesion Fund) failed, as the main receiving Member States argued that this would be discriminatory. This is hardly convincing since the taxpayers

---

[39] Commission, Monitoring application of Community law, 15th report (1997) [1998] O.J. C250/1 at p. 175.

[40] Commission, Monitoring application of Community law, 13th report (1995) [1996] O.J. C303/1 at p. 50.

[41] See, *e.g.* Commission, Joint Research Centre: An analysis of environmental impact studies on installations for the treatment and disposal of toxic and dangerous waste in the E.U. (Brussels, Luxembourg 1996), which examined 28 impact studies.

[42] See also case C-396/92 *Bund Naturschutz Bayern v. Stahnsdorf* [1994] E.C.R. I-3717; C-431/92 *Commission v. Germany* [1995] E.C.R. I-2189; C-133/93 *Commission v. Belgium* [1996] E.C.R. I-2323; C-72/95 *Kraaijeveld* [1996] E.C.R. I-5403.

[43] See Dir. 85/337 (n. 35) Annex III, No. 2: "Where appropriate, an outline of the main alternatives studied by the developer" may be asked for.

[44] The implementation report required under Article 11(3) of Dir. 85/337 has been published (COM (93) 28 of April 2, 1993), but mainly deals with the formal transposition into national law, not with practical application; Dir. 91/692 standardising and rationalising reports on the implementation of certain directives relating to the environment, [1991] O.J. L377/48 omitted to provide for regular reports on Dir. 85/337.

in the different Member States are certainly entitled to be assured that their money is properly used in the distribution of Community funds.

4—14   During the intergovernmental discussions on the Maastricht Treaty on the European Union, the United Kingdom in particular suggested that Community measures should undergo an environmental impact assessment. The Intergovernmental Conference limited itself, however, to a declaration in the Final Act of the Conference. As this did not lead to Commission proposals being preceded by an environmental impact assessment, the Intergovernmental Conference for the Amsterdam Treaty 1997 adopted the following declaration[45]:

> "The Conference notes that the Commission undertakes to prepare environment impact assessment studies, when making proposals which may have significant environmental implications."

The first studies of this kind are to be expected in 1999.

4—15   Directive 85/337 only applies to specific projects. In 1997, the Commission submitted a proposal for a directive "on the assessment of the effects of certain plans and programmes on the environment".[46] The proposal suggests that plans[47] set up by administrative bodies and plans adopted by way of legislative procedure shall have to undergo an environmental impact assessment; for that purpose, the authority shall prepare an environmental statement and then proceed to the appropriate consultations.

The Commission based its proposal on Article 175(1). However, since the proposal expressly intends to cover town and country planning plans, there are grounds for believing that the appropriate legal basis is Article 175(2), which requires unanimous decisions. The choice of the legal basis will depend upon which plans are finally covered by the measure. Anyway, it remains to be seen whether the Council and the European Parliament will be able to agree to this proposal which certainly aims at better integrating environmental requirements into administrative planning, but at the same time reduces administrative discretion.[48]

4. INTEGRATED POLLUTION PREVENTION AND CONTROL

4—16   Directive 76/464[49] provided that Community-wide emission limit values for the industrial discharge of some dangerous substances into the water were to be fixed, based on the "best technical means available". As regards air emissions from industrial installations, Directive 84/360[50] stipulated that for new installations permits should be issued for preventing air pollution, based on the best available technology not entailing excessive costs; for existing installations, Member States had to "implement policies

---

[45] Declaration No. 12 [1997] O.J. C340/133; see also European Parliament, Res. of November 5, 1998 [1998] O.J. C359/1 which requested (pt 5) the Commission to provide for a systematic environmental impact assessment for all new relevant proposals.
[46] [1997] O.J. C129/14; explanatory memorandum in COM (96) 511 of December 4, 1996; amended proposal [1999] O.J. C83/13.
[47] Plans and programmes under the proposal include town and country planning plans as well as programmes in sectors such as transport (including transport corridors, port facilities and airports), energy, waste management, water resource management, industry (including extraction of mineral resources), telecommunications and tourism.
[48] See European Parliament [1998] O.J. C341/18.
[49] Dir. 76/464 on pollution caused by certain dangerous substances discharged into the aquatic environment of the Community [1976] O.J. L129/23; for details of this Directive, see para. 7–23, below.
[50] Dir. 84/360 on the combating of air pollution from industrial plants [1984] O.J. L188/20. For details of this Directive, see para. 8–35, below.

and strategies, including appropriate measures, for the gradual adaptation of existing plants . . . to the best available technology".

The putting into operation of the principle of progressively introducing the best available technology largely failed, among other reasons, because no consensus was reached as to which technology, in any given case, was the best available technology. Under Directive 76/464, the Community emission standards were fixed by way of a political compromise, not by having recourse to an analysis and application of the best available technology. Under Directive 84/360, technical notes were elaborated and published to determine what constituted, for specific sectors of industry, the best available technology. However, these notes did not seem to have had a significant impact, since they had no binding legal nature and their observation was neither monitored nor made known. Both directives, therefore, did not lead to a significant change in technologies used in industrial installations.

4—17   In an attempt to improve this situation and, at the same time, to deregulate, decentralise and take into consideration the subsidiarity principle of the E.C. Treaty, the Council adopted, in 1996, Directive 96/61 concerning integrated pollution prevention and control,[51] which will become applicable, for new installations, in 1999: existing installations shall comply with its requirements by 2008. The Directive concerns a number of large industrial installations which are listed in an annex I.

For some time the Commission had also pursued the idea of a similar, though less stringent, directive for smaller industrial installations. However, in 1997, environmental ministers of Member States concluded that from an environmental point of view, there was no reason to apply environmentally less stringent standards to small enterprises.[52] Therefore, plans for a directive on integrated pollution prevention and control for small industrial installations have been shelved, at least for the moment.[53]

The Directive provides that as a rule emission limit values are to be fixed at local level in the individual permits[54]; instead of that, Member States may provide for such emission limit values in "general binding rules", provided that the same results are achieved.

4—18   Permits for installations must include emission limit values for pollutants which are likely to be emitted from the installation into water, air or land. The emission limit values "shall be based on the best available techniques". A technique is available when it is "developed on a scale which allows implementation in the relevant industrial sector, under economically and technically viable circumstances, taking into consideration the costs and advantages, whether or not the techniques are used or produced inside the Member State in question as long as they are reasonably accessible to the operator" (Article 3(11)); thus, the best available technique depends also on economic considerations. The permit itself shall take into account when fixing

---

[51] Dir. 96/61 [1996] O.J. L257/26; Commission proposal [1993] O.J. C311/6, the explanatory memorandum in COM (93) 423 of September 14, 1993; opinion of the Economic and Social Committee [1994] O.J. C195/54; opinion of the European Parliament [1995] O.J. C18/82; Commission amendment [1995] O.J. C165/9; Council common position (with explanation of the positions adopted) [1995] O.J. C87/8; European Parliament, second opinion [1996] O.J. C166/89.

[52] President's conclusions, informal meeting of E.U. Environmental Ministers, Amsterdam April 18–20, 1997, para. 3: "Environmental requirements should be related to the nature and magnitude of environmental pollution and not to the size of the enterprise. Therefore, in principle similar requirements should apply to larger and smaller enterprises." The conclusions are not published; the reference is taken from M. Pallemaerts, "Production, toxics and transnational law: an inquiry into the effectiveness of international and European Community environmental law", *Proefschrift* (Brussels, 1998), p. 337.

[53] Written Question E-1667/97 (Bowe) [1997] O.J. C391/116.

[54] See Dir. 96/61 (n. 51), recital 8: "the objective of an integrated approach to pollution control is to prevent emissions into air, water or soil wherever this is practicable, taking into account waste management, and, where it is not, to minimize them . . .". Attention is drawn to the word "practicable" which also includes, in Community legislative language, economic considerations.

the emission limit values "the technical characteristics of the installation concerned, its geographical location and the local environmental conditions" (Article 9(4)).

These provisions will most likely lead to different emission limit values being fixed for the same type of industrial installation, according to its location, its economic situation and other circumstances; this will affect competition between installations. Also, one may expect that the bargaining for lower limit values will increase, since the threat will exist that the installations will look for a site elsewhere with more favourable permit conditions. The possibility that Member States may fix generally binding limit values—a provision which was inserted into the text especially at the request of Germany—is of limited assistance; indeed, the competition among installations within an internal market is likely also to be effective across national frontiers, not only within Member States.

4—19 Member States shall send to the Commission every three years "the available representative data on the limit values" and "if appropriate", the best available techniques (Article 9). Where this exchange of information allows "a need for Community action" to be identified, Community-wide emission limit values shall be set for installations covered by Directive 96/61. In the absence of such Community emission limit values those that exist at present shall apply as minimum standards. Where an envionmental quality standard requires stricter conditions than those which could be achieved by the use of best available techniques, additional measures shall have to be taken (Article 10).

To what extent Directive 96/61 will lead to a high level of protection of the environment as a whole, an objective which is announced in several provisions, will have to be seen. It is to be welcomed that all installations covered by the Directive must have a permit and that this permit must fix emission limit values. However, since numerous local circumstances including the economic situation of the individual installation are to be taken into account, there is a considerable risk of bargaining over the different conditions for values, which is made all too easily at the expense of the environment that has no bargaining power. The Directive has not provided that there be a central register for all permits and their conditions, although such a register would have been easy to set up in the computer age. Rather, the Commission will regularly publish an inventory of the principal emissions and sources of pollution "based on the data supplied by the Member States" (Article 15(3)), although Member States do not have an obligation to transmit such data beyond the above mentioned "representative data on the limit values laid down by specific category of activities . . . and, if appropriate, the best available techniques from which those values are derived" (Article 16(1)).

4—20 Individuals themselves can set up a register of permits and conditions, since the decision on a permit, "including at least a copy of the permit and any subsequent updates, must be made available to the public" (Article 15(1)); the organisational capacity for such a private register would, however, presumably only be available within environmental organisations, environmental agencies and institutes.

In order to implement Directive 96/61 the Commission arranged a five-year work programme to establish, for all types of installations covered by the Directive, the breadth of guidance documents ("BREF"—Best Available Technique Reference Document) which describe the best available technique for each specific process: these documents are to be published. This approach is similar to the one under Directive 84/360[55] and it will be seen to what extent it contributes to some harmonisation of production standards in the future. Generally, the approach reflects the political

---

[55] See para. 4–16, above.

decision by the Community not to harmonise production standards: combustion and waste incineration installations[56] are an exception to this approach.

The effects of Directive 96/61 will therefore largely depend on the political will of Member States to reach a high level of environmental protection—and of the Commission's determination to enforce such a high level.

5. ENVIRONMENTAL AUDITING

4—21 In 1993 the Council adopted Regulation 1836/93, which establishes a voluntary system of eco-auditing for industrial installations (EMAS).[57] An industrial company which wishes to participate in the scheme for its sites (one at a time or all together) must establish an environmental policy for that site which must provide for the respect of all existing environmental provisions and a continuous improvement of the environmental performance. The site must then be submitted to an environmental review which concerns the environmental conditions such as water and energy use, waste treatment and so on. The company then has to develop an environmental programme for all activities on the site in order to reach its policy objectives and must ensure that at management level the necessary measures are taken to realise the programme. The site then shall be audited, either by auditors belonging to the company or by external auditors.

The company finally has to make an environmental statement on its activity on the site, its policy, programme, strategy and management system. This statement is validated by an independent, accredited verifier and published; the site is then listed in a register. The company is allowed to inform in its correspondence and papers (but not on products, in product advertising and packaging) of its participation in the EMAS scheme.

4—22 Although participation in the scheme is voluntary, a company which decides to join in must comply with all the requirements of EMAS. At the end of 1997, the EMAS scheme was fully operational in all Member States, except Greece and Portugal. By February 1998, some 1,800 sites had been registered with the Commission to participate in the system, more than two-thirds of them in Germany, and with much less enthusiasm in the southern parts of the Community.[58]

About 40 per cent of all plants which participate in the scheme are small and medium-sized companies, though the costs of participation are sometimes not insignificant. For the time being, the idea of having specific, less stringent provisions adopted for small and medium-sized companies is not being pursued, mainly for the reasons mentioned above, at paragraph 4—17. Some Member States have started to apply the system to other areas than the industrial sector, such as tourism, transport, public administration, local authorities or retail trade.

4—23 For the participating company there are clear advantages in the environmental performance and its improvement: better motivation of the personnel and improved competitiveness. Credit institutes and insurance companies start considering making their intervention dependant on the existence of an auditing scheme, for example.

At international level, EMAS is competing with ISO 14001, an International

---

[56] See paras 8–35 et seq., below.

[57] Reg. 1836/93 allowing voluntary participation by companies in the industrial sector in a Community eco-management and audit system [1993] O.J. L168/1; Commission proposal [1993] O.J. C120/3; Opinion of the European Parliament [1993] O.J. C42/44.

[58] [1998] O.J. C254/63: Germany—1,286 sites; Austria—125; Sweden—106; U.K.—52; Denmark—64; France—21; the Netherlands—20; Spain—14; Finland—11; Belgium—5; Ireland—4; Italy—3; Luxembourg—1; Portugal and Greece—none.

Environmental Management Standard (EMS), developed in 1996 by the International Standardisation Organisation (ISO). This voluntary standard differs from EMAS in particular in that it applies worldwide, is open to the participation of all economic sectors and also refers to products, not only to sites. Furthermore, there is no necessity for a company to comply with all environmental regulations. Finally, the publication of an environmental statement is not necessary; the company needs not respect transparency as regards its environmental performance.

The Commission has recognised those elements of ISO 14001 which are equivalent to EMAS[59]; thus, a company may use ISO 14001 as a first step towards adherence to EMAS and thus avoid duplication of work. Nevertheless, a number of companies, in particular in the United Kingdom, have opted for ISO 14001 rather than adhering to the EMAS scheme.[60]

4—24   A general assessment of the efficiency of the EMAS scheme seems not yet to be possible. For this reason too, efforts by some national administrations to lower the requirements in permit conditions, where the installations comply with EMAS, seem more influenced by deregulation efforts rather than by the aim of improving the environment.

At the end of 1998 the Commission made a proposal for a general review of Regulation 1836/93, which in particular will allow administrations and other organisations to participate in the system.[61]

6. ACCIDENT PREVENTION

4—25   In 1976, a serious industrial accident occurred in Seveso (Italy), where dioxin was emitted into the air: some 600 people had to be evacuated from their homes and about 2,000 were treated for dioxin poisoning. Subsequently, the Community drew up and adopted, in 1982, a directive on accident prevention from industrial installations.[62] Following two major accidents in Bhopal (India—1984, where more than 2,500 people were killed) and Basel (Switzerland—1986, where a massive pollution of the Rhine occurred) this Directive was amended twice in 1987 and 1988.[63] A complete revision took place in the early 1990s, which finally led to the adoption of Directive 96/82[64] which replaces Directive 82/501.

The structure and concept of Directive 82/501 have largely been maintained. The new Directive aims at preventing major industrial accidents which involve dangerous substances and at limiting the consequences of such accidents. The Directive concerns establishments where dangerous substances are present in quantities that are laid down in an annex. The operator of the establishment has to produce a safety report[65] which gives details of the establishment, the dangerous substances present, possible major

---

[59] Dec. 97/265 [1997] O.J. L104/37.

[60] Bundesumweltamt (Germany) gives the following figures as of February 1998: U.K.—650 facilities, Germany—390, the Netherlands—230, Sweden—155, Finland—90, Austria—80, France—64.

[61] [1998] O.J. C400/7.

[62] Dir. 82/501 on the major accident hazards of certain industrial activities [1982] O.J. L230/1; Commission proposal [1979] O.J. C212/4; Opinion of the European Parliament [1980] O.J. C 175/48; Opinion of the Economic and Social Committee [1980] O.J. C182/25.

[63] Dir. 87/216 [1987] O.J. L85/36; Dir. 88/610 [1988] O.J. L336/14.

[64] Dir. 96/82 (see n. 5, above); Commission proposal [1994] O.J. C106/4; Opinion of the European Parliament [1995] O.J. C56/80; Opinion of the Economic and Social Committee [1994] O.J. C295/83; common position of the Council (with explanations) [1996] O.J. C120/20; Dec. of the European Parliament [1996] O.J. C261/24.

[65] The requirements of the safety report are laid down in Art. 9; in contrast to it, Art. 7 requires an operator to draw up a document on its accident prevention policy without detailing the requirements for that document. Art. 7(3) then states: "This Article shall not apply to the establishments referred to in Article 9." Since Art. 9 contains no such reference, the operator seems to have the choice between Art. 7 and Art. 9.

accidents and, an innovation with regard to Directive 82/501, the management systems available. This last requirement is justified by the fact that "analysis of the major accidents reported in the Community indicates that the majority of them are the result of managerial and/or organizational shortcomings". Establishments must furthermore have an internal emergency plan and must inform the public authorities in such a way that they are able to draw up an external emergency plan. Persons—inside and outside an establishment—who are likely to be affected by an accident must be informed of the safety measures and of the requisite behaviour in the event of an accident. After an accident, the operator has to provide comprehensive information to the authorities on the accident and on the measures taken to prevent recurrence.

4—26 Directive 96/82 provides for detailed rules on the inspection of the establishments by competent authorities, which is a very innovative provision. Likewise, it introduces national and Community reporting provisions, which did not exist before.[66]

In 1995, a report on the 10-year functioning of Directive 82/501 was published[67] which reported a total of 178 accidents having been notified to the Commission between 1984 and 1993, whereas there were estimated to have been between 500 to 800 accidents during that period. In 30 accidents people were killed, 20 accidents also had environmental consequences; however, it is recognised that information about the ecological consequence of accidents is still scarce and that long-term environmental consequences were not detailed at all.

The Directive does not cover pipelines,[68] transport activities, military establishments, hazards created by ionising radiation,[69] mines, quarries and boreholes and waste landfills. Since it is based on Article 175(1) (ex 130s(1)) E.C., Member States are of course free to extend its application to such installations.

4—27 Overall, the system which had been set up by Directive 82/501 and which is improved and finetuned by Directive 96/82 seems to work well, though it is obviously not possible to assess the exact impact of the prevention measures. The accident-prevention scheme of Directive 82/501 was taken over by a number of third countries and co-generated the International Convention on Transboundary Effects of Industrial Accidents, signed in Helsinki on March 18, 1992, to which the Community adhered in 1998.[70] A Commission announcement for an accident prevention initiative on nuclear installations, made shortly after the nuclear accident in Chernobyl,[71] was not followed by definite action.

7. Taxes and Charges

4—28 The first environmental action programme of 1973 pleaded in favour of economic instruments in the shaping of environmental policy.[72] Subsequent

---

[66] The Commission published one report on the application of Dir. 82/501 in Member States, COM (88) 261 of May 18, 1988.

[67] K. Rasmussen, *The experience with the major accident reporting system from 1984 to 1993* (Luxembourg, 1995); see also C. Kirchsteiger (ed.), *Lessons learnt from accidents* (EUR 17733) (Ispra, 1998).

[68] It is estimated that there are some 150,000 km gas transmission, 31,000 km oil and 10,000 km chemical pipelines within the European Union.

[69] This clause means that nuclear installations which process dangerous substances are covered by the Directive; as regards the safety of nuclear installations generally see European Parliament Res. of September 17, 1992 [1992] O.J. C284/111.

[70] Dec. 98/685 [1998] O.J. L326/1.

[71] Fourth environmental action programme [1987] O.J. C328/1, paras 4.3.8 and 4.6.4.

[72] The first environmental action programme [1973] O.J. C112/1, p. 31: "careful analysis should be made of the economic instruments which can be used in the context of an environment policy, their various functions, the advantages and drawbacks of using them, their relative effectiveness with regard to the objectives in view and their compatibility with the rules of cost allocation."

programmes repeated the usefulness of developing economic instruments and the fourth environmental action programme was the first to mention that, besides legal provisions taxes, charges and tradable pollution permits could also be an appropriate instrument for improving or preserving the quality of the environment.[73] In order to combat climate change, the Commission made a proposal in 1991 for the Community-wide introduction of a combined CO_2 energy tax.[74] The proposal was based on Articles 93 and 175(1) (ex 99 and 130s(1)) E.C., which both required, in 1991, unanimous decisions in Council. This unanimity could not be reached since a number of Member States, in particular the United Kingdom, opposed for fundamental reasons the adoption of taxes and charges at Community level. The Commission therefore amended its proposal in the sense that Member States remained free to decide whether they wanted to introduce a CO_2 energy tax; where they so decided, they had to comply with certain conditions fixed in the proposal.[75]

This proposal, which again requires a unanimous adoption in Council, had not been adopted by mid-1999.

4—29 In view of the obvious difficulties linked with this proposal, the Commission has not yet made any other proposal for the introduction of an eco-tax. Scattered in directives or regulations there exist references that taxes or charges will be fixed at Community level[76]; however, such provisions neither have legal effect nor do they restrict the possibility of Member States deciding on their own to introduce eco-taxes or charges.

However, taxes and charges play a considerable role in the environmental policy of Member States. Since they aim to influence, via pricing, the economic behaviour or economic operators and others, their competitiveness and market position, the Community cannot remain unconcerned about developments at national level. Therefore, Community measures with regard to national eco-taxes instead try to limit their use.

4—30 The most obvious example is the provisions in the car sector. When the catalytic converter for cars was introduced, the Netherlands and Germany in particular thought of promoting the introduction of cars with catalytic converters by means of tax incentives. The objection of other Member States that were afraid of a competitive disadvantage, finally led to a provision which has since then become standard for car emission directives[77]:

"Member States may make provision for tax incentives for the vehicles covered in this Directive. Such incentives shall meet the provisions of the Treaty as well as the following conditions:

- they shall apply to all domestic car production and to vehicles imported for marketing in a Member State and fitted with equipment allowing the European standards to be met in 1992 to be satisfied ahead of time,

- they shall cease upon the date set in Article 2(3) for the compulsory entry into force of the emission values for new vehicles,

---

[73] Fourth environmental action programme [1987] O.J. C3128/1, no. 2.5.1.
[74] [1992] O.J. C196/1.
[75] COM (95) 172 of May 10, 1995.
[76] See, *e.g.* Dir. 94/10 on packaging and packaging waste [1994] O.J. L365/10, Art. 15: "Acting on the basis of the relevant provisions of the Treaty, the Council adopts economic instruments to promote the implementation of the objectives set by this Directive. In the absence of such measures, the Member States may, in accordance with the principles governing Community environmental policy, *inter alia*, the polluter-pays principle, and the obligations arising out of the Treaty, adopt measures to implement those objectives."
[77] Text from Dir. 89/458 [1989] O.J. L226/1, Art. 3.

- they shall be of value, for each type of vehicle, substantially lower than the actual cost of the equipment fitted to meet the values set and of its fitting on the vehicle."

A Commission communication of 1997 tried to determine generally the limits for "environmental taxes and charges in the Single Market".[78] Recommendations for optimising environmental taxes and charges are not given, probably because there are also diverging opinions within the Commission.

8. ENVIRONMENTAL LIABILITY

4—31   There are no Community provisions specifically on environmental liability. As regards damage caused by waste, the Commission proposed in 1976 a liability provision in its proposal on hazardous waste,[79] which failed to be adopted by the Council. In 1982–1983 the scandal of the "Seveso barrels"[80] caused the Commission to submit a proposal to the Council for a regulation on the shipment of waste, which included a liability clause.[81] The Council could not agree on this clause, but committed itself to deciding on waste liability before the end of 1988.[82] The Commission submitted a proposal for a directive in 1989,[83] which it amended in 1991.[84] The Council did not discuss the proposal. Thus in 1996, the Commission declared that it considered its proposal obsolete.[85]

In 1986, subsequent to the Sandoz accident in Basel (Switzerland), the Council asked the Commission to consider whether it was appropriate to introduce a system of environmental liability. In pursuance thereof, the Commission submitted a greenbook on environmental liability.[86] The European Parliament organised a hearing on this question and then asked, under Article 192 (ex 138b) E.C., for the drawing-up of a proposal for a directive.[87] The Commission announced a whitebook in 1995, which is scheduled for 1999.[88]

4—32   There is a Community directive on product liability, which introduces strict liability for damage caused by defective products.[89] Liability is limited to bodily injury and to economic loss which has been suffered by a private consumer.

It is doubtful whether the concept of "product"[90] includes waste. In my opinion

---

[78] COM (97) 9 of March 26, 1997; see also Commission, Database on environmental taxes in the European Union Member States, plus Norway and Switzerland. *Evaluation of environmental effects of environmental taxes* (Luxembourg, 1999).

[79] [1976] O.J. C194/2.

[80] They concerned 41 barrels of waste that was contaminated with dioxins and stemmed from the industrial accident in Seveso 1976 (see above). The companies responsible had handed over these barrels to a French one-man transport company, which had shipped them outside Italy and had hidden them for some time.

[81] [1983] O.J. C186/3.

[82] Dir. 84/631 on the supervision and control within the European Community of the transfrontier shipment of hazardous waste [1984] O.J. L326/31, Art. 11: "The Council shall . . . determine not later than September 1988 the conditions for implementing the civil liability of the producer in the case of damage or that of any other person who may be accountable for the said damage and shall also determine a system of insurance."

[83] [1989] O.J. C251/3; explanatory memorandum in COM (89) 282 of September 15, 1989.

[84] [1991] O.J. C192/6; explanatory memorandum in COM (91) 219 of June 27, 1991.

[85] Commission, Communication on the review of the Community strategy for waste management, COM (96) 399 of July 30, 1996, para. 79.

[86] Commission, Greenbook on remedying environmental damage [1993] O.J. C149/12.

[87] [1994] O.J. C149/6.

[88] [1995] O.J. C225/6, p. 26.

[89] Dir. 85/374 on the approximation of laws, regs and administrative provisions of the Member States concerning liability for defective products [1985] O.J. L210/29

[90] Dir. 85/374 (n. 63), Art. 2: "all movables, with the exception of primary agricultural products and game".

this is indeed the case, since the concept of waste is an economic one. Also, the Court of Justice considered waste to come under the concept of "goods" under Article 28 (ex 30) E.C.[91] It is not clear why a defective physical object, which causes damage just by changing the name from "goods" to "waste", all of a sudden should not make its producer liable. There are as yet no decisions from the courts on this subject.

Community Regulation 2027/97[92] concerns the liability of air companies in cases of accident. It does not deal with environmental liability.

4—33   It does not seem very likely that the Community will legislate, in the foreseeable future, on environmental liability issues. Leaving aside the difference of opinions among Member States and the heavy opposition of economic operators to any liability system, the concept of compensating for environmental damage seems too far removed from environmental needs. In short, the environment is sick, rather than suffering from specific, punctual disasters (or accidents). The liability concept, which stems from compensation for bodily injury and was extended to economic loss, and later to damages for pain and suffering, only adapts with difficulty to progressive deterioration, legalised contamination and the disappearance of species. This is the reason why, until now, national environmental liability legislation had only limited success. Since the discussion on similar questions does not really take place at Community level, there is little probability that effective legislation can be set up.[93]

9. ENVIRONMENTAL LABELLING

4—34   In 1992, the Community adopted a regulation on an eco-label award scheme[94] with the aim of promoting products which have a reduced environmental impact during their entire life cycle and give better information to consumers. Participation in the scheme is voluntary. The regulation created an eco-logo—a flower consisting of a corolla of petals in the form of the 12 E.C. stars surrounding an E (for Europe)—which is to be given to products which satisfy certain environmental criteria. These criteria are fixed at Community level for specific product groups while the attribution of the label to the individual product is decided by the competent authorities of each Member State. The regulation fixes selective criteria, organises the consultation with interest groups and other relevant matters for the functioning of the scheme. Recital 7 states: "while existing or future independent award schemes can continue to exist, the aim of this Regulation is to create the conditions for ultimately establishing an effective single environmental label in the Community".

The system had difficulties to overcome in order to succeed. Indeed, it met with the opposition of economic operators from the very beginning, who opposed the idea that some 15, 20 or 30 per cent of products of a specific type should be allowed to bear an official label which qualified them to be "better". Such objections formed themselves at national level in countries that were afraid of competition from other Member States, but reached the Community level. Furthermore, procedures for determining criteria were very long and complicated; consumers barely knew about the logo, so that

---

[91] Case C-2/90 *Commission v. Belgium* [1992] E.C.R. 1I-4431.
[92] Reg. 2027/97 on liability of air companies in case of accidents [1997] O.J. L285/1.
[93] See also L. Krämer, "Environmental liability at Community level", pp. 138 *et seq.* in L. Krämer, *Focus on European environmental law* (2nd ed., London, 1997).
[94] Reg. 880/92 [1992] O.J. L99/1.

producers did not have much to gain from using the logo, which was not inexpensive. National eco-label systems—in particular the blue angel in Germany, the Nordic green swan in Scandinavia, etc.—were well established, better known and accepted and quicker at producing results. Finally, third countries complained that the scheme created barriers to international trade.

4—35 Typical controversies concerned questions over whether the use of recycled paper should be rated as environmentally favourable: wood-producing countries were of course not of this opinion. The United States was of the opinion that, if criteria concerning the production methods were taken into consideration, this would mean that the European Community wanted to impose its production standards on third countries. Community producers were of the opinion that production or social standards in third countries were not adequately taken into account, and that this privileged imports.

These and other circumstances led to the result that, by the end of 1998, criteria for 21 products had been established and about 230 products had, E.C.-wide, received the E.C. eco-label.[95] Denmark even turned away from the E.C. system and back to the Scandinavian eco-label system, while Austria, Netherlands, France, Spain, Italy and Greece set up or considered setting up national eco-label schemes. The status of the eco-label is still very slight; neither economic operators nor environmental or consumer groups are enthusiastic. A discussion on a major revision of the scheme has started, the outcome of which is not yet certain.[96] For the foreseeable future, it seems unlikely that Member States will be prepared partly or completely to abandon their national schemes in favour of the Community eco-label scheme.

4—36 Agricultural products which come from specific ecological production—the conditions of which have been very meticulously laid down, in order to avoid abuses— may bear the label "organic product".[97] Products from organic production have reached a market share of about 5 per cent within the Community, although the differences among Member States are considerable. Agricultural product imports may bear the statement "organic product" where the production methods have expressly been recognised as being equivalent to the requirements of Regulation 2092/91 which was the case, up until 1997, for some deliveries from Argentina, Australia, Hungary, Israel and Switzerland. In 1999, the Council adopted an amendment in order to have animal farming included in the Regulation.[98]

Directive 92/75 was adopted after the attempts to conclude voluntary agreements with producers that had gone on for a decade, had failed.[99] The Directive laid down specific provisions for the labelling of energy consumption of household products.[1] The labels determined are very sophisticated and precise.[2] Their influence on consumers' purchasing behaviour is as yet uncertain.

A number of other environmental labels, which concern products, will be discussed below at paragraphs 6–55 et seq.

---

[95] At the same time, the German blue angel scheme covered some 80 product groups and 4,200 products, the Scandinavian green swan system some 35 product groups and 800 products.

[96] Commission proposal for a revision of Reg. 880/92 [1997] O.J. C114/9; amended [1999] O.J. C64/14.

[97] Reg. 2092/91 [1991] O.J. L198/1. This regulation is constantly modified and finetuned; also, it must be noted that no other language uses the word "organic" but instead the equivalent of "ecological" (or "biological").

[98] Reg. 1804/99 [1999] O.J. L222/1.

[99] See Economic and Social Committee [1995] O.J. C155/19.

[1] Dir. 92/75 on the indication by labelling and standard product information of the consumption of energy and other resources by household appliances [1992] O.J. L297/16.

[2] Until the end of 1997, energy labels were fixed for the following products: Household electrical refrigerators and freezers and their combinations, Dir. 94/2 [1994] O.J. L45/1; household washing machines, Dir. 95/12 [1995] O.J. L136/1; household electrical tumble driers, Dir. 95/13 [1995] O.J. L136/28; household washer-driers, Dir. 95/60 [1995] O.J. L266/1; household dishwashers, Dir. 97/16 [1997] O.J. L1118/1.

10. NOTIFICATION OF DRAFT NATIONAL ENVIRONMENTAL LAW

4—37 Directive 98/34,[3] which is based on Articles 95, 284 and 37 (ex 100a, 213 and 43) E.C., aims at the removal or reduction of any barriers which national legislation might create to the free movement of goods. It requests Member States to notify the Commission of product-related legislation already in the draft stage; where a restriction on use or a ban on a substance is in question, the Member State is asked to add, "if available", data on production, substitution products as well as "in appropriate cases" the conclusions of a risk evaluation, made in accordance with the principles of Regulation 793/93.[4] The national draft measure is sent to all other Member States and the notifying Member States may adopt the draft measure only after a period of three months after notification. Where the Commission or one Member State indicates that the draft measure may create barriers to the free movement of goods, the standstill period is extended to six months. Where the Commission indicates its intention to propose a legally binding Community measure or the fact that there is already a proposal on the subject-matter in question before the Council, the standstill period is 12 months. In cases of urgency, the standstill delays do not apply. Also, there exist technical specifications to which fiscal or financial measures are linked and certain voluntary agreements where a state is a contracting party and has to be notified, although there are specific provisions for the standstill periods.[5]

Where a Member State adopts a national measure without having previously notified it under Directive 98/34, this provision is unenforceable on economic operators, and national courts are obliged not to apply the national measure in question.[6] This "sanction", which follows from the direct effect of the Directive's provisions, is very effective since penalties or other sanctions which were pronounced under the national measure, are also not valid. Where a Member State adopts a measure, even though it was informed of potential trade barriers, the normal instruments under Articles 226 and 227 of the E.C. Treaty will have to be used to see this breach of the Member State's obligations stated.[7]

4—38 Since Directive 98/34 has an extremely wide field of application, it has *de facto* replaced an information standstill agreement in environmental matters which was adopted, in 1973, in the form of a gentlemen's agreement.[8] The Commission's announcement in 1987 to draft legislation on a standstill procedure in environmental matters[9] was never realised.

Directive 98/34 affects numerous environmental measures; measures which fix

---

[3] Dir. 98/34 laying down a procedure for the provision of information in the field of technical standards and regulations [1998] O.J. L204/37; this Dir. constitutes a consolidated version of Dir. 83/189, which was repealed. The issues of European technical standardisation are discussed at para. 6–68, below.

[4] Reg. 793/93 [1993] O.J. L84/1; see also para. 6–28, below.

[5] See in particular case C-13/96 *Bic* [1997] E.C.R. I-1753, where the Court of Justice held that a Belgian eco-tax legislation which requested the products affected by the eco-tax to bear a distinctive sign, had to be notified under Dir. 98/34.

[6] Case C-194/94 *Security International v. Signalson* [1996] E.C.R. 2201.

[7] See also Commission [1998] O.J. C281/3 which indicates that in 1997 900 national draft regulatory measures were notified under Dir. 98/34, out of which 63 may be qualified as environmental measures; in July 1997, 83 infringement procedures were pending against Member States because of a breach of their obligations under Dir. 83/189, see Written Question P-2214/97 (Peijs) [1998] O.J. C45/159.

[8] Agreement of the representatives of the Governments of the Member States meeting in Council on information for the Commission and for the Member States with a view to possible harmonisation throughout the Communities of urgent measures concerning the protection of the environment [1973] O.J. C9/1; amendment [1974] O.J. C86/2.

[9] Fourth environmental action programme [1987] O.J. C328/1, para. 2.1.7.

quality standards for the air or the water normally do not come under the field of application of the Directive: likewise, nature protection measures are not affected. In the same way, measures on the storage of products or on industrial installations are normally not notifiable. As Member States are afraid of the possibility of seeing their national measure not being enforceable, they tend to notify draft measures, even where this might not be necessary. The checking of whether potential trade barriers exist is mainly influenced by internal market considerations; there is only a summary con- sidering of environmental aspects against trade considerations.

The only other provision where Member States are obliged to notify draft environ- mental legislation to the Commission is Article 16 of Directive 94/62.[10] This provision also aims at preventing trade barriers by national packaging provisions. The procedure is that of Directive 98/34.

11. ACCESS TO ENVIRONMENTAL INFORMATION

4—39   In 1990 the Council adopted Directive 90/313 on the freedom of access to information on the environment.[11] This Directive gives a right to any natural or legal person[12] to accede to information relating to the environment which is held by public authorities or by "bodies with public responsabilities for the environment and under the control of public authorities"; the person seeking information does not have to prove an interest in the information. The notion of "information relating to the environment" is very broadly defined,[13] and it is difficult to see any aspect of the environment which is excluded from the definition—perhaps with the exception of radioactivity aspects. Permits for installations or activities come under it, as well as statistics, data on monitoring, inspecting and emissions.

The individual is given the right against public authorities; the principle is not limited to environmental administrations, but also includes, for example, transport authorities, agriculture authorities, public research institutes, agencies and so on. The authorities need only supply information which is "available", but are not obliged to start collecting information themselves. They may charge reasonable costs for the supply of the information—but not for the refusal of it.

4—40   Access to information may only be refused in certain circumstances, which are listed in Article 3(2) of the Directive:

- the confidentiality of the proceedings of public authorities;

- public security;

- matters *sub judice* or under inquiry or which are the subject of preliminary inves- tigation procedures;

- commercial and industrial confidentiality;

---

[10] Dir. 94/62 on packaging and packaging waste [1994] O.J. L365/10.

[11] Dir. 90/313 on the freedom of access to information on the environment [1990] O.J. L156/58; Commission proposal [1988] O.J. C335/5; European Parliament Opinion [1989] O.J. C120/231.

[12] This is the wording of Art. 3(1); recital 6 of the Directive only has "any natural or legal person throughout the Community". As this restriction is not found in the Arts of Dir. 90/313, it is irrelevant.

[13] See Art. 2(a): "'information relating to the environment' shall mean: any available information in written, visual, aural or database form on the state of water, air, soil, fauna, flora, land and natural sites, and on activities (including those which give rise to nuisances such as noise) or measures adversely affecting, or likely so to affect these, and on activities or measures designed to protect these, including administrative measures and environmental management programmes".

- confidentiality of personal data;

- material which was given to the administration without a legal obligation to do so;

- material, the disclosure of which would risk damage to the environment.

The supply of unfinished documents or internal communications may also be refused where too-general requests are asked or where the request is "manifestly unreasonable".

Reasons for the refusal must be given in all cases. A person whose request has been refused or ignored may seek judicial or administrative review under national provisions.

4—41 All Member States have taken measures to transpose the requirements of the Directive into national law. At the end of 1997, legislation in Belgium, Germany, Netherlands, Portugal and Spain was considered not to be in conformity with the Directive.[14]

Also, there are numerous attempts to not grant access to information in individual cases. The most frequent issues are the charging of prohibitively high costs, wide interpretation of the refusal grounds, in particular the concept of "commercial and industrial confidentiality" and the commencement of inquiries or investigation procedures.[15]

The Directive ensures, as the title and its provisions indicate, freedom of access to information: thus it places access to information in the context of a human right. It is for this reason that the right is given not just to E.U. citizens, but to everybody, including associations. The omission to require proof of a specific interest constitutes for many local, regional and national administrations a change from traditional concepts in the relationship with the citizen, and some time will be needed before this concept is fully accepted.

4—42 Directive 90/313 is addressed to Member States and therefore does not apply to Community institutions. When making the proposal for a directive, the Commission announced that it would take initiatives to apply the directive's principles to the Community institutions.[16] Such initiatives have not been taken.

In 1998, a United Nations Convention on access to information, public participation and access to justice in environmental matters was held for signature in Aarhus (Denmark). If ever the Community were to adhere to this Convention, considerable changes as regards access to environmental information would have to follow.

Following a Communication from the Commission[17] and based on a joint Code of Conduct,[18] the Council[19] and the Commission[20] adopted, in 1993/1994, decisions concerning the access of the public to documents; since then, almost all of the other Community bodies and agencies have adopted similar decisions.[21] Their common feature is that they are of a general nature, not limited to information relating to the environment. Furthermore, they only relate to documents, not to other information; also, it is not entirely clear to what extent they confer a right of access to

---

[14] Commission, 15th annual report on monitoring the application of Community law (1997) [1998] O.J. C250/1 at p. 177.

[15] See, as an example for the most recent refusal, case C-321/96 *Mecklenburg* [1998] E.C.R. I-3809.

[16] Commission, COM (88) 484 of November 28, 1988; see also legislative work programme for 1994, COM (93) 599 of November 28, 1993, no. 241.

[17] Commission, Public access to documents of the institutions [1993] O.J. C156/5.

[18] Code of Conduct concerning public access to Council and Commission documents [1993] O.J. L340/41.

[19] Dec. 93/731 on public access to Council documents [1993] O.J. L340/43; see also Dec. of February 27, 1996 [1996] O.J. C74/3 on fees for such access.

[20] Dec. 94/90 on public access to Commission documents [1994] O.J. L46/58.

[21] See Special Report of the European Ombudsman [1998] O.J. C44/10.

documents.[22] The reasons for refusing access are drafted in a rather loose way, giving the administration wide discretion. In the case of refusal to grant access, judicial action may be taken under Article 230 of the E.C. Treaty, since the different decisions confer at least such a right for judicial control to persons.[23]

12. ACCESS TO JUSTICE

4—43   There are no Community provisions on access to Community or to national courts in environmental matters. Commission's announcements in the fifth environmental action programme and in the 1992 working programme[24] to submit a proposal for a directive on access to justice in environmental matters has not been followed up; a working document elaborated by outside experts, in 1992, and which included a draft directive on access to justice,[25] was not taken over. The adoption of a directive for access to justice in consumer matters[26] has not yet led to similar initiatives for environmental organisations.

In June 1998 the Community and Member States signed the Aarhus Convention on access to information, public participation in decision-making and access to justice in environmental matters which had been prepared in the framework of the United Nations Economic Commission for Europe. This Convention also provides for access to justice provisions for individuals and environmental organisations. To what extent this Convention will be made operational by legislation adopted at Member State level or whether there will be any Community initiative, is as yet unclear. Individuals and environmental organisations thus have access to Community courts under the provisions of Article 230(4) (ex 173(4)) where Community measures are addressed to them or where they are directly and individually concerned. This is particularly the case where secondary Community law grants them "rights". The cases mentioned under Directive 90/313 and on the different decisions by Community institutions and bodies, and which were mentioned above, certainly do give such rights: the different measures expressly refer to that Treaty provision.

4—44   Another such "right" is found in the Directive on environmental impact assessment.[27] Article 6(2) of that Directive requests Member States to ensure that during the environmental impact procedure, "the public concerned is given the opportunity to express an opinion before the project is initiated". This provision thus gives a participation right to individuals and environmental organisations. And where this right is disregarded, individuals and organisations have a right to take judicial action. Normally, such action is to be brought before a national court, but a case, where action to the European courts is, in my opinion, possible, is case T-585/93,[28] where the applicants argued that the Commission had funded projects without proper environmental impact assessment. The application was dismissed as inadmissible, but both the applicants and the Court omitted to discuss Article 6(2) of Directive 85/337. The

---

[22] Until the end of 1997 the Court (Court of First Instance) had not yet clearly determined the content of the applicants' rights under these decisions, but instead limited itself to requesting individualised, specific justification for any refusal, see, e.g. case T-105/95 WWF v. Commission [1997] E.C.R. II-313 .
[23] Case T-194/94 Carvel and Guardian Newspapers v. Council [1995] E.C.R. II-2765; case T-105/95 (n. 22, above).
[24] Fifth environmental action programme [1993] O.J. C138/1, Chap. 9: "Individuals and public interest groups should have practicable access to the courts . . .".
[25] See for this text Environmental Law Network International, Newsletter 1/1994, pp. 7 et seq.
[26] Dir. 98/27 [1998] O.J. L166/51; this Directive is based on Art. 95 (ex 100a) E.C.
[27] Dir. 85/337 on the assessment of the effects of certain public and private projects on the environment [1985] O.J. L175/40; amendment Dir. 97/11 [1997] O.J. L73/5.
[28] Case T-585/93 Greenpeace and Others v. Commission [1995] E.C.R. II-2205.

appeal was rejected with the argument that both actions, the one against improper application of Directive 85/337 and the one against the Commission's funding, "are based on the same rights afforded to individuals by Directive 85/337, so that in the circumstances of the present case those rights are fully protected by the national courts which may, if need be, refer a question to this Court for a preliminary ruling under Article 177 of the Treaty".[29]

I would rather see the object of litigation to be different in the two cases. Indeed, the national court has no possibility of checking whether the Commission acted legally, and this cannot be decided by way of a preliminary question, either. Denying the right of access to the courts in such cases means that the Commission's acts for financing projects in practice cannot be attacked in court at all.

4—45 Whether in other cases of secondary environmental law environmental organisations may invoke Article 230(4) is doubtful. A general right of action in the name of the environment is incompatible with the structure of the judicial system under Articles 220 *et seq.* (ex 164 *et seq.*); it would not normally be available under the E.C. Treaty, but under national courts.

Access to national courts depends on the national legal system, in particular the judicial system, and is therefore not discussed here.

BIBLIOGRAPHY

Basse, M.: "Environment impact assessment (EIA)" in B. Wenzel (ed.), *First Nordic conference on E.U. environmental law* (Copenhagen, 1994), p. 93

Collier, U. (ed.): *Deregulation in the European Union: environmental perspectives* (London and New York, 1997)

Dawkins, K.: *Ecolabelling: consumer's rights to know or restrictive business practice?* (Minneapolis, 1995)

Decaesteker, J.: "Les instruments financiers de la Communauté Européenne en matière d'environnement" in M. Campins i Eritja and I. Pont i Castejón (eds), *Perspectives de dret comunitari ambiental* (Bellaterra, 1997), p. 57

Delbeke, J. and Bergman, H.: "Environmental taxes and charges in the E.U." in J. Golub (ed.), *New instruments for environmental policy in the E.U.* (London and New York, 1998), p. 242

Eiderström. E.: 'Ecolabels in E.U. environmental policy" in J. Golub (ed.), *New instruments for environmental policy in the E.U.* (London and New York, 1998), p. 190

Falke, J.: "Standardization by professional organisations" in G. Winter (ed.), *Sources and categories of European Union law* (Baden-Baden, 1996)

Führ, M. and Roller, G. (eds): *Participation and litigation rights of environmental associations in Europe* (Frankfurt, Bern, New York and Paris, 1991)

Führ, M.: "Betriebsorganisation als Element proaktiven Umweltschutzes", *Jahrbuch des Umwelt- und Technikrechts* (1993), p. 145

Gispert Pi, I.: "Instrumentos fiscales y reforma ecológica de la fiscalidad en la Unión Europea" in M. Campins i Eritja and I. Pont i Castejón (eds), *Perspectives de dret comunitari ambiental* (Bellaterra, 1997), p. 73

Golub, J. (ed.): *New instruments for environmental policy in the E.U.* (London and New York, 1998)

Hager, G.: "Europäisches Umwelthaftungsrecht Zeitschrift für europäische Politik", (1997), p. 9

Hey, C. and Taschner, K. (eds): *EEB Industry Handbook* (Brussels, 1998)

---

[29] Case C-321/95P *Greenpeace v. Commission* [1998] E.C.R. I-1651.

Köck, W.: "Vollzugsaspekte des Öko-Audit-Systems" in N. Reich and R. Heine-Mernik (eds), *Umweltverfassung und nachhaltige Entwiclung in der Europäischen Union* (Baden-Baden, 1997), p. 149

London, C.: "Instruments économiques et droit communautaire", *Revue juridique de l'environnement* (1998), p. 31

Martín Mateo, R.: *Nuevos instrumentos para la tutela ambiental* (Madrid, 1994)

Möllers, T.: "Qualitätsmanagement, Umweltmanagement und Haftung", *Der Betrieb* (1996), p. 1455

Morena Molina, A.: "Puesta en funcionamento del derecho comunitario del medio ambiente. Acceso a la información. Acceso a la justicia" in L. Parejo Alfonso and L. Krämer (eds), *Derecho medioambiental de la Unión Europea* (Madrid, 1996), p. 141

Moreno Molina, A.: "La empresa y el derecho de la Unión Europea en el medio ambiente. Autorización. Evaluación de impacto ecologico. Prevention de accidentes. Control integrado de la contaminación. Eco-auditoria. Eco-etiqueta" in L. Parejo Alfonso and L. Krämer (eds), *Derecho medioambiental de la Unión Europea* (Madrid, 1996), p. 169

Pont i Castejón, I.: "El etiquetado ecológico y las auditorías ambientales" in M. Campins i Eritja and I. Pont i Castejón (eds), *Perspectives de dret comunitari ambiental* (Bellaterra, 1997), p. 415

Rehbinder, E.: "Environmental regulation through fiscal and economic incentives in a federalist system", *Ecology Law Quarterly* (1993), p. 57

Rehbinder, E.: "*Locus standi*, Community law and the case for harmonization" in H. Somsen (ed.), *Protecting the European environment: enforcing E.C. environmental law* (London, 1996), p. 151

Robinson, J.: "Environmental impact assessment and Community law" in M. Campins i Eritja and I. Pont i Castejón (eds), *Perspectives de dret comunitari ambiental* (Bellaterra, 1997), p. 371

Sakse, D.: "Envionmental legislation in Member States. Notification and 'standstill' obligations in Community law" in B. Wenzel (ed.), *First Nordic conference on E.U. environmental law* (Copenhagen, 1994), p. 53

Schäfer, E.: *Individualrechtsschutz im Umweltrecht* (Vienna, 1998)

Ward, H.: "Trade and environmental issues in voluntary eco-labelling and life-cycle analysis", *Review of European Community and International Environmental Law* (1997), p. 131

Zetter, J.: "Environment impact assessment: has it had an impact?" in J. Holder (ed.), *The impact of E.C. environmental law in the United Kingdom* (Chichester, 1997), p. 257

Zierock, K. and Salomon, N.: "Die Umsetzung des Artikels 16 Abs.2 der EG-IVU-Richtlinie auf internationaler und nationaler Eben", *Zeitschrift für Umweltrecht* (1998), p. 27

Zöttl, J.: *Integrierter Umweltschutz in der neuesten Rechtsentwicklung* (Baden-Baden, 1998)

CHAPTER 5

Biodiversity and Nature Conservation

5—01 Nature conservation measures within the European Community were, until about the mid-1980s, influenced by the fact that the majority of Member States were of the opinion that nature protection came in their exclusive competence. Since environmental legal acts had, prior to 1987, to be taken unanimously, this attitude considerably influenced the number and the content of the measures adopted; indeed, Member States favoured the negotiation and conclusion of international conventions; another consequence was that all nature conservation measures that the Council was ready to adopt were based on Article 308 (ex 235) E.C.

When Article 175 (ex 130s) was introduced into the Treaty to give an explicit environmental competence to the Community which included nature conservation, matters only gradually changed. The main reasons were that Member States were very keen to keep their responsibility in land use planning matters, which they saw at least partly threatened by Community nature conservation measures; that transfrontier management of wildlife and nature protection was hardly practised; and that national and Community enforcement mechanisms for nature conservation measures were structurally too weak to properly enforce the different provisions, never mind initiating new measures.

1. GENERAL MEASURES

(a) International conventions

5—02 The Community has adhered to a number of international conventions which aim, as a general objective, at the protection of nature or of parts of it. For several cases, however, the Community has not taken measures of secondary Community law to implement these international conventions. In law, an international convention to which the Community adheres becomes part of Community law; as regards the hierarchy, the provisions of the convention rank between primary and secondary Community law. The application and enforcement of the provisions of the convention is shared between the Community and its Member States, according to their internal divisioning of competence.

In practice, the application and enforcement of international environmental conventions to which the Community has adhered without adopting a regulation or directive to implement its provisions in Community law, does not take place as far as the Community level is concerned. Rather, the Commission leaves it to Member States to apply the provisions of the convention. As a consequence, the decision to adhere to the international environmental convention is marked by the participation of the Community, but as such does not bring an added value to the protection of the environment.

5—03   The following environmental conventions belong to this group of conventions on nature protection:

(a) Bonn Convention of June 23, 1979 on the conservation of migratory species of wild animals[1];

(b) Rio de Janeiro Convention of June 5, 1992 on biological diversity[2];

(c) Salzburg Convention of November 7, 1991 on the protection of the Alps[3];

(d) Geneva Convention of February 26, 1994 on tropical wood[4];

(e) Paris Convention of June 17, 1994 on combating desertification.[5]

On biological diversity, the Community adopted a communication on a Community strategy for biological diversity[6] which contained four areas of activity: on conservation and sustainable use of biological diversity, on the sharing of genetical resources, on research, control and exchange of information and on education, training and sensitivisation. No specific legislative measures were intended; instead, the objectives of the strategy were to be reached within the context of the different ongoing Community activities.[7]

5—04   Concerning forests, in 1998 the Council adopted, for the first time, a resolution on a Community forest strategy underlining that the Treaty did not provide for a specific common forest policy and that therefore the responsibility for forest policy rested with Member States.[8] The Council mentioned the international efforts to protect tropical and other forests, referred to E.C. measures regarding forests and encouraged a prudent intensification of activities concerning forests.

(b) Land use and soil protection

5—05   There are no general Community measures which directly concern soil protection, although agricultural measures generally may have an impact on land use.[9] A regulation from 1992 provided for financial assistance to farmers who voluntarily agree to substantially reduce the use of fertilisers or pesticides, to use organic farming methods, to set aside land—for at least 20 years—for environmental purposes, or to pursue other ways of environmentally acceptable farming practices.[10] By mid-1997, 1.35 million agreements had been signed with farmers under this regulation, covering 22.3 million hectares or 17 per cent of the Community-utilised agricultural area.[11] The use of some pesticides has been prohibited throughout the Community by virtue of Directive 79/117.[12]

---

[1] Dec. 82/461 [1982] O.J. L210/10.
[2] Dec. 93/626 [1993] O.J. L309/1.
[3] Dec. 96/191 [1996] O.J. L61/31.
[4] Dec. 94/493 [1996] O.J. L208/1.
[5] Dec. 98/216 [1998] O.J. L83/1.
[6] COM (1998) of February 4, 1998.
[7] See also Commission, First report on the implementation of the Convention on biological diversity by the European Community (Luxembourg, 1998) European Parliament, Res. of October 20, 1998 on biodiversity [1998] O.J. C341/41.
[8] Res. of December 15, 1998 [1999] O.J. C56/1.
[9] The Commission's communication on sustainable agriculture [1999] O.J. C173/2 indicates that some 156 million hectares of soil are suffering from water or wind erosion and that soil erosion is increasing (pt 2.3).
[10] Reg. 2078/92 on agricultural production methods compatible with the requirements of the protection of the environment and the maintenance of the countryside [1992] O.J. L215/85.
[11] Commission, First report on biodiversity (n. 7), p. 50.
[12] Dir. 79/117 prohibiting the placing on the market and use of plant protection products containing certain active substances [1979] O.J. L33/36; this Directive is updated at regular intervals.

In 1995, the Commission launched an Integrated Coastal Zone management demonstration programme.[13] This programme, however, only explores ways for an effective management; it does not affect decisions on land use, which are taken at the level of Member States.

5—06   It is clear that the progressive ban on uncontrolled discharges to rivers, lakes or coastal waters also contributes to the protection of land. The siting of industrial installations or infrastructure measures is decided by Member States at their discretion; eventual negative impacts on the environment, demonstrated for instance by an environmental impact assessment,[14] do not restrict this right.

Directive 79/409[15] requires Member States to classify the most suitable territories as special protection areas for some particularly threatened bird species. Within these areas, they shall take "appropriate steps to avoid pollution or deterioration of habitats or any disturbances affecting the birds, in so far as these would be significant".[16]

In individual cases, this can lead to restrictions of the use of land: in case C-355/90,[17] the construction of roads and other infrastructure measure within a birds' habitat was declared incompatible with Article 4 of Directive 79/409; that specific habitat had not been classified under that provision even though it should have been. In case C-44/95,[18] the United Kingdom had classified a specific area under Article 4, but had exempted a specific part, since it considered that at a later stage this part could be needed for the extension of a nearby commercial port. The Court of Justice held that this was not allowed, although, obviously, it did not commit itself on the compatibility of the port extension with the designation of the habitat.

5—07   A similar provision to Article 4 of Directive 79/409 was introduced in an Article of Directive 92/43.[19] However, in reaction to Court jurisdiction, which was considered too restrictive, a provision was inserted that despite its negative effects a measure could be carried out "for imperative reasons of overriding public interest".[20] This provision is likely to facilitate considerably the carrying out of measures even in a classified habitat, in particular in the light of the Commission's wide interpretation of Article 6 (4).[21]

Directive 75/442[22] prohibits the unauthorised discharge or dumping of waste and Directive 86/278[23] prohibits, under certain conditions, the use of sewage sludge on certain land, in particular where there are overly high concentrations of heavy metals, on grassland or forage crops, on soil in which fruit and vegetable crops are growing and on ground for the cultivation of fruit and vegetable crops which are normally eaten raw.

5—08   There are no specific Community provisions for combating soil erosion[24]

---

[13] COM (95) 511 of October 31, 1995; progress report COM (97) 744 of January 12, 1998.

[14] See more closely Chap. 4, para. 4–10 of this book.

[15] Dir. 79/409 on the conservation of wild birds [1979] O.J. L103/1.

[16] Ibid., Art. 4 (4).

[17] Case C-355/90 Commission v. Spain [1993] E.C.R. I-4221 (Santona).

[18] Case C-44/95 RSPB [1996] E.C.R. I-3805 (Lappel-Bank); see also case C-57/89 Commission v. Germany [1991] E.C.R. I-883 (Leybucht).

[19] Dir. 92/43 on the conservation of natural habitats and of wild fauna and flora [1992] O.J. L206/7, Art. 6(2): "Member States shall take appropriate steps to avoid, in the special areas of conservation, the deterioration of natural habitats and the habitats of species as well as disturbance of the species for which the areas have been designated, in so far as such disturbance could be significant in relation to the objectives of this Directive."

[20] Ibid., Art. 6(4).

[21] Commission, Opinion of April 27, 1995 [1995] O.J. C178/3; Opinion of December 18, 1995 [1996] O.J. L6/14.

[22] Dir. 75/442 on waste [1975] O.J. L194/47, as amended by Dir. 91/156 [1991] O.J. L78/32, Art. 4(2).

[23] Dir. 86/278 on the protection of the environment and in particular of the soil, when sewage sludge is used in agriculture [1986] O.J. L181/6, Arts 5 and 7.

[24] Written Question P-135/98 (Díez de Rivera) [1998] O.J. C223/123.

although Community funds may assist national measures. The same can be said with regard to questions of desertification.[25]

Any land use measure by the Community would have to be adopted by virtue of Article 175(2) (ex 130s(2)). In legal texts, it is sometimes argued that this provision also applies to amendments of Directives 79/409 and 92/43. However, both directives concern general measures which give a specific status to land, but do not directly deal with the use of the land. Indeed, land use is not outlined in a specific way by either directive. The correct legal basis is therefore Article 175(1).

(c) Habitat protection

5—09   The Dobris 1998 Report stated: "Data, particularly about plants and vertebrates and some insect groups such as butterflies, indicates a continuing impoverishment of European natural and semi-natural habitats, which in turn has led to severe declines in the populations and, subsequently, the distribution of a very wide number of species."[26]

(i) Birds' habitats

5—10   In 1979 the Community adopted Directive 79/409 on the conservation of wild birds,[27] following considerable public pressure in favour of such a measure. That directive aimed at comprehensive protection of all wild birds within the Community and outlined detailed provisions, in particular on hunting, capturing and trading of birds. Member States were required to take necessary measures "to preserve, maintain or re-establish a sufficient diversity and area of habitats" for all birds (Article 3) by the creation of protected areas or biotopes and the upkeep, management and re-establishment of biotopes. For some 180 particularly threatened bird species they were asked to classify habitats as special protection areas for the conservation of these species (Article 4). The different designated habitats were to form a "coherent whole",[28] which met the protection requirements for birds all over the Community. Inside these special protection areas, appropriate conservation measures had to be taken.

5—11   The provision of Article 3 has, as far as can be seen, not led to any significant change at national level; the provision was scarcely monitored by the Commission.[29] As regards Article 4, designation of special protection areas advanced only slowly. While the directive required the classification to be done by 1981, the following actual development took place[30]:

1986: 309 areas covering 1.4 million hectares

1990: 450 areas covering 3.6 million hectares

---

[25] See also European Parliament, Res. of September 16, 1993 [1993] O.J. C268/148.

[26] European Environmental Agency, *Europe's environment, the second assessment* (Copenhagen, 1998), p. 222.; see also p. 233: "Many of the changes observed in the populations and richness of species have resulted from changes to habitats. In general, they indicate a continuing impoverishment of European habitats."

[27] Dir. 79/409 (n. 15).

[28] *Ibid.*, Art. 4(3); the French and German texts talk of a "coherent network", which is certainly more precise.

[29] See Commission, Information sur l'application de la directive 79/409/CEE (Brussels and Luxembourg 1990), p. 35 *et seq.*

[30] Commission, Information (n. 29) p. 46; Commission, Second report on the application of Directive 79/409/CEE on the conservation of wild birds, COM (93) 572 of November 24, 1993, p. 115; Commission (DG XI) Natura 2000 newsletter, May 1996, p. 6; Natura 2000 newsletter, February 1998, p. 6 and November 1998, p. 6.

1996: 1,351 areas covering 4.3 million hectares

1998: 1,842 areas covering 13 million hectares

The Commission stated in 1991 and again in 1998 that only Denmark and Belgium had fully complied with their obligations under Article 4 of Directive 79/409[31]; the situation in France, Italy, Luxembourg and Finland was declared, in 1998, to be not satisfactory; in the other Member States as incomplete.[32] In 1996, the Commission appealed to the Court of Justice, since the Netherlands had not classified a sufficient number of habitats under Article 4; the Court agreed with the Commission and found that the Netherlands were in breach of its obligations flowing from Directive 79/409.[33]

In a number of other cases, the Commission tried to ensure through legal proceedings the habitat status of specific zones where it was of the opinion that Member States had not fully complied with their obligations. These procedures are rather time-consuming, in particular where the dispute has to be decided by the Court of Justice.[34]

(ii) Fauna and flora habitats

5—12   Habitats are also protected by virtue of the provisions of Directive 92/43.[35] The procedure of designating these habitats is slightly different from that of Directive 79/409. First of all, Member States should establish national lists of sites which are important for the conservation of habitat types or fauna or flora species; where the Commission disagrees, the matter is finally decided by a unanimous Council decision. Out of these national lists, the Commission, in agreement with the Member State concerned, establishes a list of sites of Community importance. Member States shall then, within six years, designate the sites on this list as Special Area of Conservation, which form, all together, "a coherent European ecological network" or Natura 2000.[36] By the end of 1997, Belgium, Germany, Greece, France and Finland had not even transposed the Directive into national law: Germany and Greece have therefore been condemned by the Court of Justice.[37] The Commission has started legal proceedings under Article 226 (ex 169) E.C. against 11 Member States.[38]

The national lists had to be drawn up by June 1995. In April 1996, five Member States had transmitted complete national lists, two others partial lists. By early 1998 all Member States with the exception of Luxembourg had submitted national lists,

---

[31] Commission, 8th report on monitoring application of Community law (1990) [1991] O.J. C338/1, p. 220; Commission, Natura 2000 Newsletter, February 1998, p. 6.

[32] Commission, Natura 2000 (n. 30), p. 6; there is a certain contradiction between these statements and the fact that the Commission declared, in 1995, that the designation of habitats under Article 4 was unsatisfactory "in particular" in the Netherlands, Greece, Luxembourg, Ireland, Germany, Italy and the United Kingdom, and that it declared in 1996 that there was progress as regards the United Kingdom and Ireland, but no or almost no progress in Germany, Greece and the Netherlands. See Commission, 13th report on monitoring application of Community law (1995) [1996] O.J. C303/1 at p. 54 and 14th report on monitoring application of Community law (1996) [1997] O.J. C332/1 at p. 64.

[33] Case C-3/96 Commission v. Netherlands [1998] E.C.R. I-3031; WWF, Spotlight on Natura 2000 No. 4/1997, p. 8 reports that the Commission stated during a public hearing before the Court that proceedings had been initiated against the Netherlands, because these had not, contrary to other Member States, "shown any interest in settling the matter bilaterally".

[34] See, e.g. cases C-57/89 Commission v. Germany [1991] E.C.R. I-883; C-355/90 (n. 17 above;) C-44/95 RSPB [1996] E.C.R. I-3805; C-166/97 Commission v. France, judgment of March 18, 1999, not yet reported.

[35] Dir. 92/43 on the conservation of natural habitats and of wild fauna and flora [1992] O.J. L206/7; Commission proposal [1988] O.J. C247/3; European Parliament Opinion [1991] O.J. C75/12; Economic and Social Committee Opinion [1991] O.J. C31/25.

[36] The special protection areas classified under Dir. 79/409 are also included in this network.

[37] Cases C-329/96 Commission v. Greece [1997] E.C.R. I-3749; C-83/97 Commission v. Germany [1997] E.C.R. I-7191.

[38] Commission, Monitoring application of Community law—15th report (1997) [1998] O.J. C250/1, p. 178.

although the lists for Finland, Germany, France, Ireland and Austria were incomplete[39]: none of the Member States had fully complied with the Directive's requirements. The setting up of a list of sites of Community importance, which was due for June 1998, will thus be considerably delayed.

5—13　One of the main reasons for delay in the setting up of national lists was the provision of Article 6(2) of Directive 92/43, which requested Member States to avoid "the deterioration of natural habitats and the habitats of species as well as disturbance of the species for which the areas have been designated, in so far as such disturbance could be significant in relation to the objectives of this Directive". Although this provision was completed by the above-mentioned provision of Article 6(4) and although the first Commission decisions even showed a wide interpretation of this exemption,[40] there was considerable concern at local level in many Member States that, on a site which would come under Directive 92/43, economic or leisure activities would severely be restricted. Under pressure from hunters, fishermen, farmers and other groups, France went even so far, in the summer of 1996, as to freeze its work on a national list for several months, arguing that it was neither clear who would finance the managing of the habitats[41] nor exactly what activities would be forbidden within a habitat.[42]

The question of what is allowed and what is not allowed in a designated habitat is one of the most intricate ones. Bird hunting in a habitat is often accepted—although heavily contested by environmental organisations. Other economic measures such as irrigation, urbanisation and road construction are often undertaken within habitats without systematic monitoring by local, regional, national or Community authorities. Generally, economic development prevails over conservation, and cases where the development of a project was stopped because of the existence of a habitat or a threatened species, are extremely rare in the Community. The Commission attempted twice to have a rule adopted that all projects listed in annex II of the environmental impact assessment Directive[43] should, before development consent is given, be preceded by an environmental impact assessment; however, the Council twice rejected this approach.[44]

5—14　The dilemma is that, on the one hand, it is hardly possible to transform designated habitats into nature museums, where no change may take place; this is the reason why local people or authorities so often oppose designation of a habitat. On the other hand, the Commission itself[45] stated that almost everywhere in Western Europe habitats and nature protection sites are shrinking slowly, but dramatically, due to road and other infrastructure construction, urbanisation, intensive farming activity, irrigation and holiday and leisure activities.[46]

---

[39] Commission, Natura 2000 newsletter, 4/1996, p. 6, 2/1998, p. 8 and 11/1998, p. 6; Written Question P-305/98 (Böge) (1998) O.J. C223/163.

[40] See para. 5–07, above; further A. Nollkaemper, "Habitat protection in European Community law: evolving conceptions of a balance of interests" Journal of Environmental Law (1997), p. 271; W. Wilts, "La protection des habitats naturels en droit communautaire" Cahiers de droit européen (1994), p. 398.

[41] As regards financing of habitats and the coresponding conservation measures, see Art. 8 of Dir. 92/43.

[42] Commission, Written Question P-2422/96 (Eisma) [1997] O.J. C60/76 and press release of July 31, 1996, IP/96/759.

[43] Dir. 85/337 on the assessment of the effects of certain public and private projects on the environment [1985] O.J. L175/40.

[44] Commission, proposal for Dir. 92/43 [1988] O.J. C247/7, Art. 10; proposal for Dir. 97/11 [1994] O.J. C130/8; the Council's decision is found in Dir. 97/11 [1997] O.J. L37/5, recital 10.

[45] Commission, Communication on rational use and conservation of wetlands, COM (95) 189 of May 29, 1995.

[46] Perhaps the most eloquent example is the French habitat Camargue which lost, between 1942 and 1984, about 1,000 hectares per year of its natural surface, see A. Tamisier, Camargue, milieux et paysages évolution de 1942 à 1984 (Arles, 1992).

With all the delays and difficulties in designating habitats and conserving them, Directives 79/409 and 92/43 constitute the first promising attempt in Western Europe to conserve nature protection sites. As such, they go far beyond what individual Member States had done at national level in this area. The experience of 20 years of application of Directive 79/409, which has neither led to sufficient designation of habitats and adequate conservation measures nor generally stopped the shrinking of individual habitats, does not promote optimism. In Western Europe, which is a small area that is densely populated, that has great economic activity and an impressive transport infrastructure network, nature is in retreat because it disturbs demographic and economic evolution. For this reason, in almost all cases, where economic interests in building a bridge, a port, an airport, a motorway or a new high-speed train clash with the environmental interests of preserving a habitat, the environmental interests lose. It is not likely that the application of Directive 92/43 will significantly change this situation.

5—15   As regards other areas than habitats belonging to Natura 2000, Directive 92/43 invites Member States, to "encourage the management of features of the landscape which are of major importance for wild fauna and flora" (Article 10); the Directive mentions rivers, field boundaries, ponds and small woods as examples. This invitation is not more than a recommendation to Member States.

Habitats of wild flora and fauna species are also protected under Article 4 of the Berne Convention on the conservation of European wildlife and natural habitats of 1979, to which the Community had adhered by a decision of 1981.[47] However, as is explained above,[48] the Commission does not monitor the application of international conventions to which the Community has adhered, but leaves their application entirely to Member States: an exception is only made in those cases where the Community enacts legislation which transposes the convention requirements into Community environmental law. In those cases, the implementation of the transposing act is monitored under Article 211 (ex 155) E.C.; indeed, the Commission justified the proposal for Directive 92/43 amongst others with the argument that it transposed the Berne Convention into Community law.

5—16   A specific problem is that of (habitats of) species which are protected under the Berne Convention, but not under Directives 79/409 or 92/43; an example of this is the badger. Supposing a Member State were infringing the obligation adequately to protect the badger's habitat: would this constitute a breach of the Community's obligations under the Convention?

In my opinion the Community undertakes, by adhering to an international convention, to ensure that the convention is respected all over the Community territory. E.C. Member States are obliged, under Article 10 (ex 5) E.C., to take all measures in order to allow the Community to respect this obligation; such an obligation even exists where a Member State itself is not a contracting party of the convention and the Commission has the obligation to ensure, under Article 211 (ex 155) E.C., that Member States fulfil their obligations.

(iii) Habitats for fish

5—17   Directives 78/659[49] tried to protect the habitats of fish. Member States were asked to designate fresh waters to support fish life. For these waters they had to

---

[47] Dec. 82/72, of December 3, 1981 [1982] O.J. L38/1.
[48] See above, para. 5–02.
[49] Dir. 78/659 on the quality of fresh waters needing protection or improvement in order to support fish life [1978] O.J. L222/1.

establish programmes which had to ensure that the waters corresponded to specific quality requirements which were laid down in the Directive. A similar approach was followed by Directive 79/923 for shellfish.[50]

Both directives completely failed to reach their objective.[51] The main reasons were that Member States were also allowed to designate waters which already complied with the requirements so that no clean-up programme was necessary. Furthermore, the number of waters which were to be designated was not fixed which led several Member States to designate only very few waters. A decision by the Court of Justice in 1988, stipulating that Member States had to designate and clean up waters throughout their territory,[52] did not lead to substantial changes. Italy was condemned in 1988 and again in 1994, because it had not transposed Directive 78/659 into national law[53]; and in 1996, the Court found that Germany had not designated any waters under both Directives.[54] Finally, the Commission did not monitor the application of these directives closely.

(d) Financial measures to support nature conservation

5—18   The different Community financial means, given to Member States in particular in the context of the agricultural or regional policy, may also contribute, as the case might be, to the conservation of nature; examples are the setting aside of land or the construction of walls alongside a road. However, the main purpose of such measures is not the protection of the environment, but rather the achievement of an objective of agricultural or regional policy.

This also applies to the financial assistance given under Regulation 2078/92[55] which aims at ensuring income to farmers who practise environmentally responsible farming practices. The regional policy objective is also visible with the financial means which are made available under the Cohesion Fund,[56] which finances transport and environment projects in Spain, Greece, Portugal and Ireland and which disposed, between 1993 and 1999, of 15.15 billion euro, more or less half of which was being earmarked for the environment. Such environmental projects are, in particular, projects for water supply infrastructure, waste water treatment, waste treatment and disposal installations. Nature conservation measures are only very exceptionally considered as contributing to a regional development.

5—19   One of the principal objectives of the financial instrument LIFE, which was set up in 1992 and reviewed in 1996, is the protection of "habitats and of nature".[57] LIFE disposed, between 1992 and 1995, of 400 million euro and had, between 1996 and 1999, 450 million euro at its disposal. 46 per cent of these sums (1992 to 1995: 45 per cent) co-financed up to 50 per cent projects that protect habitats under Directives 79/409 and 92/43 and contributed to the creation of Natura 2000. Between 1992 and 1997, the Commission received 1,308 requests to support nature protection measures, with a

---

[50] Dir. 79/923 on the quality required of shellfish waters [1979] O.J. L281/47.
[51] See for the factual details Commission, Quality of fresh water for fish and of shellfish water; summary report on the state of application of the Directives 78/659 and 79/923 (Luxembourg, 1995) (EUR 14118).
[52] Case C-322/86 Commission v. Italy [1988] E.C.R. 3995.
[53] Ibid.; case C-291/93 Commission v. Italy [1994] E.C.R. I-859.
[54] Case C-298/95 Commission v. Germany [1996] E.C.R. I-6747.
[55] Reg. 2078/92 (n. 10, above).
[56] Reg. 1164/94 setting up a Cohesion Fund [1994] O.J. L130/1.
[57] Reg. 1973/92 establishing a financial instrument for the environment [1992] O.J. L206/1; Commission proposal [1991] O.J. 44/4; the explanatory memorandum, COM (91) 28 of January 31, 1991 contains detailed figures on Community expenditure for the environment prior to 1991. Reg. 1404/96 [1996] O.J. L181/1 brought significant amendments to the original text.

total amount of 1,328 million euro. Until the end of 1998, 347 projects were cofinanced, with an amount of 283 million euro.[58]

Since the timespan imposed on Member States to submit national lists for habitats under Directive 92/43[59] elapsed in 1996, LIFE now only co-finances projects for sites which have been listed in these national lists or, in the case of bird habitats, have already been classified under Directive 79/409. The Community funds are mainly used to buy or to hire the ground—most of the acquisition is done by local or regional nature conservation groups or bodies—to assist in the establishment of national, regional or local inventories or to pay for conservation or improvement measures at the site.[60] In 1999, the Commission proposed a new regulation to replace the existing provisions.[61]

5—20 The Community also finances measures to protect forests. As regards tropical forests, a regulation of 1995[62] provides for 200 million euro (from 1996 until 1999) to assist in sustainable forestry and generally in sustainable development measures. It also plans to assist in the development of an international labelling system for tropical wood that stems from sustainable forestry.[63]

As regards forests within the Community, the Council adopted, in 1986, a Regulation on the protection of forests against atmospheric pollution.[64] Contrary to its slightly misleading title, this Regulation provides for the setting up of inventories for forest damage, a network in order to obtain a coherent network of data, and regular national reports on that data. A Regulation of the same year on the protection of forests against fire was later replaced.[65] The measures provide for technical and financial assistance to prevent forest fire, in particular in the Mediterranean area.[66] In 1993, the Commission reported that it had spent, between 1983 and 1993, more than 1 billion euro on the conservation, improvement and protection of Community forests.[67]

2. PROTECTION OF THREATENED SPECIES

(a) Fauna and flora species

5—21 Directive 92/43[68] establishes a general system of protection for Community endangered species, which it lists (in Latin only) in an annex; since the Directive is based on Article 175 (ex 130s), Member States may, at national level, provide for other species to be protected. Deliberate capture or killing is prohibited, and deliberate disturbance, taking eggs or deterioration or destruction of breeding sites or resting places of fauna species are prohibited. Derogations are, under relatively loosely drafted

---

[58] COM (97) 633 of December 12, 1997; Nature 2000, February 1999, p. 2; see also Commission, COM (95) 135 of April 12, 1995: Progress report on implementation of the LIFE Regulation and evaluation of the action by the Community relating to the environment ACE, MEDSPA, NORSPA and ACNAT.

[59] See para. 5–12, above.

[60] See generally Commission, "LIFE in action. Demonstration projects for Europe's environment. 96 success stories" (Luxembourg, 1998).

[61] [1999] O.J. C15/4.

[62] Reg. 3062/95 on measures concerning tropical forests [1995] O.J. L327/9; the Reg. is based on Arts 175 and 179 (ex 130s and 130w) E.C.

[63] See generally on tropical forests, Commission, Communication on the role of the Community in the conservation of tropical forests [1989] O.J. C264/1.

[64] Reg. 3528/86 [1986] O.J. L326/2.

[65] Reg. 3529/86 [1986] O.J. L326/5; Reg. 2158/92 on protection of the Community's forests against fire [1992] O.J. L217/3.

[66] The Committee of the Regions indicated in its opinion of October 15, 1997 [1998] O.J. C64/27, at pt 2.1.18, that out of the 300,000 to 500,000 hectares of forest which are burnt every year in the Community, 97 per cent concern Spain, France, Italy, Greece and Portugal.

[67] Commission, Written Questions E-2077/93 and E-2495/93 (Kostopoulos) [1994] O.J. C255/28.

[68] Dir. 92/43 (n. 35).

provisions, possible (Article 16). Reports on derogations granted shall be sent to the Commission every two years; however, the experience with the similar derogation provision of Article 9 of Directive 79/409 does not inspire optimism. And it is surprising to find that the Commission's comments on these national derogations shall only be submitted to the Committee under Directive 92/43, but shall not be published (Article 9(2)[69]).

(b) Birds

5—22   Directive 79/409 lists in an annex some 180 particularly threatened bird species which require special protection measures. The most important of these measures are the designation of special protection areas under Article 4[70] and the taking of conservation measures within these areas. The list of threatened bird species has constantly been prolonged, in particular due to the subsequent accession of Greece, Spain, Portugal, Austria, Finland and Sweden to the Community. In 1997, the Commission decided for the first time to delete a species, the cormorant, from the list of threatened species, in particular due to pressure from fishermen.[71]

Directive 79/409, however, does not only protect threatened birds, but all wild birds within the Community; the reason for this overall protection was most likely the fact that "a large number of wild birds . . . are declining in number".[72] The Directive thus provides for restrictive measures such as hunting times restrictions, prohibitions on killing or capturing birds or on the taking of eggs. Furthermore, it bans a number of means for large-scale or non-selective capture or killing of birds (snares, limes, hooks, mirrors, explosives, nets, traps or motor vehicles). Derogations are possible "where there is no other satisfactory solution" (Article 9).

5—23   Directive 79/409 meant to improve the conditions of birds in Western Europe. This also implied a considerable change in people's habits. Apart from the designation of birds' habitats, the different provisions, including hunting provisions, proved difficult to enforce.[73] In particular, but not restricted to, France and Mediterranean countries, hunting is perceived by hunters, farmers and others, as a human right. National hunting provisions often did not correctly transpose the Directive[74]; hunting seasons were generously allowed and little restricted. To what extent the hunting of migrating birds, which Article 7(4) of the Directive expressly forbids, has really diminished, in particular in southern Europe—nobody can argue that it has stopped in reality—is very doubtful.

In 1998, the French Parliament adopted legislation which extended the hunting period for birds into the time of migration and breeding, in deliberate and open

---

[69] See also Commission, 8th report on monitoring application of Community law (1990) [1991] O.J. C338/1, p. 220, where the Commission stated that the reports on the derogations under Dir. 79/409 were so general that they did not allow any control.

[70] See para. 5–06, above.

[71] Dir. 97/49 [1997] O.J. L223/9.

[72] Dir. 79/409 (n. 15), second considerant.

[73] Cases C-247/85 *Commission v. Belgium* [1987] E.C.R. 3073; C-262/85 *Commission v. Italy* [1987] E.C.R. 3073; C-412/85 *Commission v. Germany* [1987] E.C.R. 3503; C-236/85 *Commission v. Netherlands* [1987] E.C.R. 3989; C-252/85 *Commission v. France* [1988] E.C.R. 2243; C-169/89 *Gourmetterie van den Burg* [1990] E.C.R. 2143; C-334/89 *Commission v. Italy* [1991] E.C.R. 93; C-345/92 *Commission v. Germany* [1993] E.C.R. I-1115; C-435/92 *Association des Animaux v. Préfet Maine et Loire* [1994] E.C.R. I-69; C-149/94 *Ministère public v. Vergy* [1996] E.C.R. I-299; C-202/94 *V. D. Feesten* [1996] E.C.R. I-355; C-10/96 *Ligue belge des oiseaux* [1996] E.C.R. I-6775.

[74] See the different cases on national hunting rules: C-339/87 *Commission v. Netherlands* [1990] E.C.R. 851; C-288/88 *Commission v. Germany* [1990] E.C.R. 2721; C-157/89 *Commission v. Italy* [1991] E.C.R. 57; C-435/92 (n. 73); C-118/94 *WWF v. Veneto* [1996] E.C.R. I-1451. In 1990, some 20 infringement procedures were running against Member States for incorrect transposition of the hunting provisions, see Commission, 8th report (n. 69), p. 220.

defiance of Directive 79/409. In 1999, France was condemned by the European Court of Human Rights because some of its hunting provisions were in conflict with the individual right of property. Whether this will lead to a review of the French legislation remains to be seen.

5—24   Generally, implementation of Directive 79/409 has been slow. The fact that in 1996, 15 years after its entering into effect, the Commission signalled 18 running proceedings against Member States,[75] is significant, but is only one element. Another element is the lack of data transmitted by Member States which has as a consequence that the Commission by 1998 had only published two of the five composite reports which it should have published under Article 12(2) of the Directive.[76]

The conclusion after 20 years of operation of Directive 79/409[77] is that it has undoubtedly had positive effects. Its legally binding provisions, which markedly contrast with international conventions that are considered as soft law and are neither enforceable nor enforced, have alerted administrations concerned, public opinion and research and caused them seriously to consider the state of birdlife in Europe. Habitats have been designated and concern for ensuring the survival of the different species of birds has been raised. No international convention was capable of achieving similar results, in particular as the Commission acted and continues to act as a co-ordination and enforcement body. Some species of birds have increased in number. The problems of applying the Directive are those which apply to nature conservation generally: the overall decline of birds has not yet been stopped in Western Europe.

(c) Trade restrictions

5—25   The Community is not a member of the Convention on International Trade in endangered species of fauna and flora (CITES) of 1973, since that Convention is, at present, only open to states, not to international institutions. A 1983 amendment of the Convention, which would enable the Community to adhere, has not yet been ratified by a sufficient number of contracting states.[78] The Community transposed the provisions of that Convention into Community law in 1982 and updated its own provisions by a Regulation of 1997.[79]

Regulation 338/97 only deals with conservation measures. Provisions in earlier regulations and also in the Commission's proposal for Regulation 338/97,[80] which aimed at dealing with questions of public safety and animal welfare, were removed from the final version of the Regulation, which led, at the same time, to the taking of Article 175 (ex 130s) E.C. as a legal basis, rather than Articles 95 and 133 (ex 100a and 113) E.C., as proposed by the Commission.

5—26   The Regulation treats the Community as one territory. It introduces a differentiated system of protection. Annex A contains all endangered species which are under the total protection of the CITES Convention and, in addition, a number of

---

[75] Commission, 14th report on monitoring application of Community law—1996 [1997] O.J. C332/1 at p. 178.
[76] Commission (nn. 29 and 30).
[77] See N. de Sadeleer, "Bilan d'une décennie d'efforts législatifs en droit communautaire de la protection de la nature" in P. Renaudière and P. van Pelt (eds), *Développements récents du droit communautaire de l'environnement* (Diegem, 1995), pp. 199 *et seq.* (at p. 259); C. Mayr, "Vierzehn Jahre EG-Vogelschutzrichtlinie. Bilanz ihrer Umsetzung in der Bundesrepublik Deutschland", *Berichte zum Vogelschutz* 31 (1993), p. 13; P. Pagh, "EU's beskyttelse af vilde fugle og fisk: indgribende betydning for arealanvendelsen", *Ugeskrift for Retsvaesen* (1997), pp. 511 *et seq.*
[78] CITES Convention of March 3, 1973 [1982] O.J. L384/8; see also Written Question E-2183/96 (*Bloch v. Blottnitz*) [1996] O.J. C365/89.
[79] Reg. 338/97 on the protection of species of wild fauna and flora by regulating trade therein [1997] O.J. L61/1; this Reg. replaced Reg. 3626/82 [1982] O.J. L384/1.
[80] [1992] O.J. C26/1.

other species which are considered threatened under the stricter criteria of the Regulation. Trade in these species for primarily commercial purposes is prohibited; also, within the Community only very narrow derogation possibilities exist. The Commission's proposal generally to prohibit any possession of species listed in annex A was not accepted by the Council.

Annex B contains species which are not actually threatened by trade, but trade in these species should take place under strict conditions in order to avoid them becoming threatened. Again, the regulation goes considerably beyond the requirements of the CITES Convention. Importing these species into the Community requires an import licence from the country of destination, which must be presented at the time of importation.

5—27   The import of species listed in annex C into the Community is subject to the presentation of an import notification rather than a licence. Finally, annex D includes species that are imported into the Community in such quantitites that an import notification is considered necessary.

All annexes can be amended by way of a committee procedure, which allows a speedy reaction to decisions of the contracting parties of the CITES Convention.[81]

Prior to adopting the different CITES Regulations since 1982, the Community had already, in 1981, adopted a regulation to protect whales.[82] The regulation strictly prohibited, without derogation, the commercial import of whale and other cetacean meat, bones, fats and oils, leather and furs. Since this ban was in line with international decisions on the protection of whales, this regulation, which was later largely superseded by the provisions of Regulation 3626/82,[83] raised few concerns.

(d) Other measures

5—28   Among the other measures to be mentioned, capturing methods for capturing animals should be particularly noted. Directives 79/409 and 92/43 both contain a specific annex to prohibit the use of large-scale or non-selective capturing methods, without having been able to stop completely the use of such means within the Community, in particular for bird hunting.

Regulation 894/97, which replaces a number of earlier legislative acts, prohibits the use of fishing driftnets of more than 2.5 km in length.[84] This ban applies to most Community waters and outside these waters to ships showing the flag of a Member State or registered in a Member State. Specific provisions apply to the Baltic Sea, where driftnets up to 21 km in length may be used.[85] Regulation 894/97 also prohibits driftnets altogether for tuna fishing in Portuguese or Spanish waters, following a ban that these two Member States have pronounced. The reason for these bans is the non-selective character of capturing with driftnets, which may reach 50 km in length; originally, the problem started worldwide, when dolphins were captured during the fishing of tuna. Besides this problem, the use of driftnets leads to overfishing and has already created a serious depletion of fish resources worldwide and in Community waters.

---

[81] See last Commission Reg. 2473/98 [1998] O.J. L308/18.
[82] Reg. 348/81 on common rules for imports of whales or other cetacean products [1981] O.J. L39/1.
[83] Reg. 3626/82 (n. 79).
[84] Reg. 894/97 on technical measures to preserve fish resources [1997] O.J. L132, p. 1, Art. 11. The reg. is based on Art. 37 (ex 43) E.C.
[85] Reg. 1866/86 [1986] O.J. L162/1.

3. Animal welfare

(a) Animal welfare and the E.C. Treaty

5—29   Animal welfare concerns animals as living beings. It tries to protect animals independently from the question of whether a species is endangered or not. It is obvious that such a concept is strongly influenced by ethical, religious and similar considerations. The E.C. Treaty treats animals differently from goods, as appears clearly in Article 30 (ex 36), which allows restrictions for the free circulation of goods in order to protect life and safety of animals and plants; furthermore, trade measures for animals are based on Article 175 (ex 130s) or, in agricultural matters, on Article 37 (ex 43), rather than on Article 95 (ex 100a) E.C.

At Community level, the idea that animals could or should have rights of their own, or that trees should be important in their own right, has never seriously been discussed: such considerations appear too distant from the concept of nature in particular in Roman law Member States. A mention of consideration for animals in the fourth environmental action programme 1987[86] did not lead to the development of a coherent approach.

5—30   Attempts by animal welfare groups, supported in this also by the European Parliament,[87] to have a specific provision on animal welfare inserted into the E.C. Treaty, were not successful. At the conclusion of the Maastricht Treaty, a declaration was made by the Intergovernmental Conference that animal welfare aspects should be taken into consideration in the context of some Community policies.[88] The Amsterdam Treaty on European Union added a Protocol to the Treaty, which provided that Community policy should fully take animal welfare into consideration in its policies on agriculture, transport, internal market and research.[89] It is not quite clear why environmental policy was not mentioned. Anyway, the Protocol allows the interpretation that in other policies animal welfare issues should be considered where appropriate.

Wild animals are part of the natural resources; measures to protect them, to provide for their welfare when captured and so on, are environmental measures. Indeed, the preservation and protection of natural resources is not limited to protecting endangered species, but applies to all natural resources. Measures regarding wild animals, even where they do not belong to an endangered species, therefore come under Articles 174 to 176 (ex 130r to 130t) E.C. This approach was recognised in 1999, when the Community adopted a Directive on the keeping of wild animals in zoos, based on Article 175.[90]

5—31   The main legal problem is that the rules of international trade, established by the General Agreement of Tariffs and Trade (GATT) and the World Trade Organisation (WTO), are generally interpreted as prohibiting measures which restrict trade because of the production methods used. Debate about these issues is not very thorough, as the

---

[86] Fourth environmental action programme 1987–1992 [1987] O.J. C328/1, no. 5.1.9: "An improvement in the quality of life also entails respect for animals in the Member States and in the Member States' dealings with the rest of the world. The regular debates concerning the hunting of seal pups should not conceal the many questions raised by the exploitation of animals in Europe: the use of animals for experiments, factory farming, trading in animals and the processing of animals for consumption. The Commission will examine all possible steps which it can take in this connection."

[87] See European Parliament, Res. of January 21, 1994 [1994] O.J. C44/206; the European Parliament in particular wanted animals to be no longer called, within the context of agricultural policy, "agricultural products".

[88] [1992] O.J. C191/1, Declaration No. 12.

[89] [1997] O.J. C340/110.

[90] See para. 5–38, below.

examples of products made by working children or those produced in jail demonstrate. The discussion on environmentally sustainable production methods—an example is the consideration on import restrictions for tropical wood that does not stem from sustainable production—has only just started. The Community has, since the early 1990s, begun to take measures in order to prevent possible conflicts with WTO or trading partners, which might end in formal WTO proceedings. This explains why the full implementation of animal welfare measures is often delayed.

(b) Tests on animals

5—32   Directive 86/609[91] limits the use of animals for experimental or scientific purposes, in order in particular to avoid unnecessary experiments and "to avoid distress and unnecessary pain and suffering to the experimental animal". The Directive lays down detailed provisions on the authorisation of animal testing, the persons responsible for experiments, the keeping of animals, the establishments, etc.; detailed guidelines for accommodation and care of animals are annexed to the Directive. Particular restrictions apply to endangered animals.

Whether the Directive applies where animals are used to "produce", for instance a secretum, blood or anti-bodies, etc., is doubtful. Article 3(a) declares the Directive to be applicable for "the development, manufacture, quality, effectiveness and safety testing of drugs, foodstuffs and other substances or products". The above-mentioned examples come, in my opinion, under the "manufacture of substances or products". In contrast to this, the Commission and at least some Member States do not apply the Directive where experiments on animals are made in order to make animals "produce" something. To date there has not been any court interpretation of this.

5—33   Animals may not be used where another scientifically satisfactory method of obtaining the result sought is reasonably and practically available (Article 7(2)). This provision gives wide discretion to researchers and administrations, since "practically" also includes questions of time and costs of the experiment.[92]

The Directive was transposed with some delay by Belgium, Italy and Portugal (all in 1992). In 1995, the Commission stated that Ireland and Luxembourg had not yet transposed the Directive.[93] In 1997, Sweden had not yet notified transposition measures and the legislation in Belgium, Luxembourg and Portugal was considered to incorrectly transpose the Directive.[94] Only four Member States were thought to have fully transposed the Directive. A particular problem is the use of stray dogs and cats in the laboratories of some Member States.

5—34   In 1994, the Commission published a report on the number of animals used for experimental purposes under Directive 86/609.[95] The figures for 1991[96] indicate that more than 12 million animals had been used, out of which 8,409 were primates. A

---

[91] Dir. 86/609 on the approximation of laws, regulations and administrative provisions of the Member States regarding the protection of animals used for experimental and other scientific purposes [1986] O.J. L358/1; the Directive is based on Art. 94 (ex 100) E.C., since at the time of its adoption, neither Art. 95 (ex 100a) nor Art. 175 (ex 130s) existed.

[92] See also Written Question E-2607/96 (Dury) [1997] O.J. C72/63.

[93] Written Question E-2783/94 (Pollack) [1995] O.J. C145/16; this contradicts the—in itself contradictory—statement in Commission, 12th report on monitoring application of Community law (1994) [1995] O.J. C254/1 at p. 110 that all Member States had notified implementation measures, but that Court proceedings were pending against Luxembourg for not having notified transposition measures.

[94] Commission, 15th report on monitoring application of Community law (1997) [1998] O.J. C250/1, p. 176.

[95] COM (95) 195 of May 27, 1994.

[96] Belgium and Luxembourg did not send figures; data from Italy, the U.K. and Portugal (for 1992) was not complete. Also, not all the data is comparable.

second report has not yet been published, although under the Directive such reports are due every three years.

Since neither reliable data is available nor any agreed method of calculating this data exists, the target fixed by the Commission in 1992, to halve the number of animals used in testing by the year 2000, will be difficult to verify. The extent to which economic considerations influence the discussion on these matters is demonstrated by the fact that the Commission had already suggested in 1989 that the Community adhere to the Council of Europe Convention for the protection of vertebrate animals used for experimental and other scientific purposes.[97] The Community had, by mid-1999, not yet decided on this proposal; one of the main reasons is that the Convention requires the annual transmission of statistical data, while Article 26 of Directive 86/609 only provides for transmission of such data every three years.

In 1993, the Directive on cosmetic products was amended with a view to ban, as of January 1, 1998, cosmetic products containing ingredients or combinations of ingredients tested on animals.[98] However, in April 1997, the Commission delayed this date till June 30, 2000, arguing that satisfactory and recognised alternative testing methods were not yet available.[99]

(c) Seal pups

5—35 Beginning in 1982, the killing of baby seals, particularly in Canada, attracted considerable attention from the Western European media. The European Parliament asked for an import ban on baby seal fur[1] and environmental organisations urged action. Although the Council strongly doubted the possibility of adopting a Commission proposal to ban imports of baby seal fur,[2] it finally adopted such an import ban for two years.[3] After an initial prolongation for four years, the import ban was extended, in 1989, for an undetermined time.[4]

The Directive does not argue that seals are an endangered species. For that reason alone, it is more than doubtful whether an import ban on furs and other seal products can be justified because of the killing methods.

(d) Leghold traps

5—36 Regulation 3254/91 prohibits, as of January 1, 1995, the use of leghold traps within the Community.[5] Leghold traps are considered non-selective[6] and cruel (not "humane"). Bans or restrictions on the use of leghold traps are in use in about 60 states all over the world.[7]

While this ban is undisputed, the Commission had—subsequent to a petition of 272

---

[97] [1989] O.J. C200/8.

[98] Dir. 93/35 [1993] O.J. L151/32.

[99] See Written Question E-1385/98 (Muscardini) [1998] O.J. C402/123.

[1] European Parliament, Res. of [1982] O.J. C87/87 and March 11, 1982 [1982] O.J. C267/47.

[2] Res. of [1983] O.J. C14/1; France, the U.K., Belgium, Denmark and Greece were reported to have opposed measures since these would be motivated by purely moral motives.

[3] Dir. 83/129 concerning the importation into Member States of skins of certain seal pups and products derived therefrom [1983] O.J. L91/30.

[4] Dir. 85/444 [1985] O.J. L259/70 and Dir. 89/370 [1989] O.J. L163/37.

[5] Reg. 254/91 prohibiting the use of leghold traps in the Community and the introduction into the Community of pelts and manufactured goods of certain wild animal species originating in countries which catch them by means of leghold traps or trapping methods which do not meet international humane trapping standards [1991] O.J. L308/1.

[6] According to figures quoted by ECOSOC, Opinion of April 26, 1990 [1990] O.J. C168/32, no. 1.6.3, about 10 per cent of animals caught in leghold traps are caught unintentionally.

[7] Written Question 1936/88 (Zarges) [1989] O.J. C255/15.

Members of the European Parliament—proposed and the Council had adopted an import ban on the fur of 13 animal species (beaver, otter, coyote, wolf, lynx, bobcat, sable, raccoon, musk rat, fisher (*martes pennanti*), badger, marten and ermine) from those countries which continued to use leghold traps.[8] The import ban was to come into effect in 1995[9]; the Council expected that by then internationally "humane trapping standards" would be agreed.

5—37   However, this was not to be the case. In particular, the United States, Canada and Russia heavily opposed the import ban, arguing that it was contrary to the rules of the GATT/World Trade Organisation and disadvantaged indigenous populations. In view of this, the Commission proposed, in December 1995, to replace the import ban by a mandate to be given to the Community in order to negotiate an agreement with third countries on humane trapping standards.[10] The Council did not adopt the proposal, but agreed to negotiations. In 1997 an agreement with Canada and Russia was reached, in 1998 an agreement with the United States.[11] They provide essentially for the fixing of some trapping standards and the phasing out, within four years, of some leghold traps for two species, without containing a legally enforceable commitment of this kind. Regulation 3254/91 has not yet been amended. Thus, for other third countries, the import ban entered into effect on December 1, 1997.[12]

(e) Animals in zoos

5—38   In 1991, the Commission proposed a directive on the keeping of animals in zoos, of which there are about 1,000 within the Community.[13] Following the extensive discussion on subsidiarity and deregulation which followed the signing of the Maastricht Treaty on European Union in 1991, the proposal was listed, by the Edinburgh summit meeting of the European Council, as one of the instruments for which the subsidiarity clause should apply; this meant that the Community should leave the matter to Member States to deal with. The Commission thus withdrew its proposal and replaced it by a proposal for a Council recommendation which contained detailed guidelines on the accommodation and care of animals in zoos.[14]

The European Parliament and the Economic and Social Committee both pleaded in favour of a directive. The Council first agreed unanimously on a common position concerning a recommendation. However, upon the instigation of the United Kingdom, which completely changed its position adopted in 1992 at the Edinburgh summit, it changed the principal objective of the instrument, to make it an instrument for the conservation of biodiversity; the detailed rules on accommodation and care of animals were deleted. Zoos were mainly considered to have a role in the conservation of biodiversity. They had to have a permit and were to be regularly inspected by the national competent authorities.

---

[8] The Commission's proposal [1989] O.J. C134/5 did not contain a ban on leghold traps, since such a ban had been proposed in the directive on habitats [1988] O.J. C247/3); since it thus only contained an import ban, it was based on Art. 133 (ex 113). The Council Regulation is based on Arts 133 and 175 (ex 113 and 130s) E.C.

[9] Subsequently, there was a controversy whether the ban did indeed become effective. Art. 3(1) of Reg. 3254/91 stipulates: "The introduction into the Community of the pelts . . . shall be prohibited as of 1 January 1995, unless the Commission . . ." (states that in a third country leghold traps or inhumane trapping methods are forbidden). This wording indicates, in my opinion without any legal doubt, that the ban became effective as of January 1, 1995, since the Commission has not made any such statement.

[10] [1996] O.J. C58/17.

[11] Dec. 98/487 [1998] O.J. L219/24; the Decision was based on Arts 133 and 95 (ex 113 and 100a) E.C.; see also European Parliament [1998] O.J. C210/31, which had rejected the agreement.

[12] See Dir. 97/602 [1997] O.J. L242/64; see also Written Question E-294/98 (Pollack) [1998] O.J. C223/160.

[13] [1991] O.J. C241/14.

[14] COM (95) 619 of December 12, 1995.

On this basis, a Directive was adopted in 1999 based on Article 175(1) (ex 130s(1)) E.C.[15]

BIBLIOGRAPHY

Adams, C.: "Die Kennzeichnung lebender Wirbeltierarten nach der EG-Durchführungsverordnung", *Natur und Recht* (1998), p. 14

Alvarez Baquerizo, C. and Gonzalez Vela, V.: "La directiva de habitats", *Revista de Derecho Ambiental* (1992), p. 57

Baldock, D.: "The legal status of Special Protection Areas for the protection of wild birds", *Journal of Environmental Law* (1992), p. 139

Ballosteros, M.: "The Habitats Directive: pressure on governments essential", *Metamorphosis, The EEB Newsletter* 10/1998, p. 3

Beurier, J.: "Le droit de la biodiversité", *Revue juridique de l'environnement* (1996), p. 5

Birnie, P.: "The case of the Convention on Trade in Endangered Species", in R. Wolfrum (ed.), *Enforcing environmental standards: economic mechanisms as viable means?* (Berlin, etc., 1996), p. 233

Birnie, P.: "The European Community and preservation of biological diversity" in M. Bowman and C. Redgwell (eds), *International law and the conservation of biological diversity* (London, 1995), p. 71

Bowman, M.: "The Ramsar Convention comes of age", *Netherlands International Law Review* (1995), p. 1

Bowman, M.: "The protection of animals under international law", *Connecticut Journal of International law* (1989), p. 487

Boudant, J.: "La préservation communautaire des oiseaux et la chasse en France: le temps des recours", *Recours de droit rural* (1990), p. 373

Coffey, C. (ed.): *Implementing the Habitats Directive in marine and coastal areas* (Luxembourg, 1998)

de Benito, J.: "Nuevas orientaciones en la protección de la naturaleza en Espana por imperativos del derecho comunitario" in M. Campins i Eritja and I. Pont i Castejón (eds), *Perspectives de dret comunitari ambiental* (Bellaterra, 1997), p. 315

de Sadeleer, N.: "Les conflits d'intérêts portant sur la protection des milieux naturels en droit communautaire", *Revue juridique de l'environnement* (1993), p. 351

de Sadeleer, N.: "La directive 92/43 concernant la conservation des habitats naturels ainsi que de la faune et de la flore sauvages: vers la reconnaissance d'un patrimoine naturel de la Communauté européenne", *Revue du Marché Commun et de l'Union Européenne* (1993), p. 24

de Sadeleer, N.: "Bilan d'une décennie d'efforts législatifs en droit communautaire de la protection de la nature" in P. Renaudière and P. van Pelt (eds), *Développements récents du droit communautaire de l'environnement* (Diegem, 1995), p. 199

de Silguy, R.: "Les oiseaux migrateurs et l'Europe", *Gazette du Palais* (1993), p. 30

de Silguy, R.: "Migrateurs et Europe; évolution juridique récente", *Gazette du Palais* (1995), p. 4

Elsworthy, S.: "Crated calves and crazy cows: live animals and free movement of goods" in J. Holder (ed.), *The impact of E.C. environmental law in the United Kingdom* (Chichester, etc., 1997), p. 303

Emonds, S.: "Die neue EG-Artenschutzverordnung und das geltende nationale Artenschutzrecht. Drohender Verstoß gegen EG-Recht?", *Natur und Recht* (1997), p. 26

---

[15] Dir. 1999/22 on the keeping of wild animals in zoos [1999] O.J. L94/24.

Epiney, A.: "Vogel- und Habitatschutz in der EU. Mitgliedstaatliche Beurteilungsspielräume bei der Ausweitung von Schutzgebieten und der Anwendung der Schutzregime", *Umwelt- und Planungsrecht* (1997), p. 293

Erbguth, W. amd Stollmann, F.: "Die Bindung der Verwaltung an die Vorgaben der FFH-Richtlinie", *Deutsches Verwaltungsblatt* (1997), p. 45

Feddersen, C.: "Recent E.C. environmental legislation and its compatibility with WTO rules: free trade or animal welfare trade", *European Environmental Law Review* (1998), p. 207

Fernández de Casadevante, C.: "El incumplimiento del derecho comunitario en las Marismas de Santona", *Revista de Instituciones Europeas* (1994), p. 137

Fisahn, A.: "Die Konvention über die biologische Vielfalt und die Flora-Fauna-Habitat-Richtlinie der EU", *Zeitschrift für Umweltrecht* (1996), p. 3

Freestone, D.: "The Leybucht Dikes case", *Water Law* (1991), p. 153

Freestone, D.: "The enforcement of the Wild Bird Directive" in H. Somsen (ed.), *Protecting the European environment: enforcing E.C. environmental law* (London, 1996), p. 229

Freytag, C. and Iven, K.: "Gemeinschaftsrechtliche Vorgaben für den nationalen Habitatschutz", *Natur und Recht* (1995), p. 109

García Ureta, A.: *Protección de hábitats y de especies de flora y fauna en derecho comunitario europeo* (Basauri, 1997)

Gellermann, M.: "Rechtsfragen des europäischen Habitatschutzes", *Natur und Recht* (1996), p. 548

Harrems, N.: "The leghold trap regulation and potential pitfalls during the Dutch Presidency of the E.U.", *European Environmental Law Review* (1998), 7

Harte, J.: "Nature conservation: the rule of law in European Community law", *Journal of Environmental Policy* (1997), p. 168

House of Lords Select Committee of the European Communities, *Protection of wild birds 1993/94*, 11th report (London, 1994)

Iven, K.: "Schutz natürlicher Lebensräume und Gemeinschaftsrecht", *Natur und Recht* (1996), p. 373

Jarza Bandarra, N.: "La protection de l'espace et politiques agri-environnementales", *Revue du Marché Commun et de l'Union Européenne* (1994), p. 444

Krämer, L.: "The interdependency of Community and Member State activity on nature protection within the European Community", *Ecology Law Quarterly* (1993), p. 25

Malafosse, J.: "Législation sur la chasse et application de la directive de la CEE sur les oiseaux sauvages", *Environmental Policy and Law* (1981), p. 7

Martín Mateo, R.: "La protección de la fauna y la flora", *Revista Vasca de Administración Publica* (1995), p. 647

Mathews, G.: *The Ramsar convention on wetlands. Its history and development* (Gland, 1992)

Mayr, C.: "Vierzehn Jahre EG-Vogelschutzrichtlinie. Bilanz ihrer Umsetzung in der Bundesrepublik Deutschland", *Berichte zum Vogelschutz* (1993), p. 13

Nollkaemper, A.: "Habitat protection in European Community law: evolving conceptions of a balance of interests", *Journal of Environmental Law* (1997), p. 271

Ong, D.: "The Convention on international trade in endangered species (CITES, 1973): implication of recent developments in international and E.C. environmental law", *Journal of Environmental Law* (1998), p. 291

Pagh, P.: "E.U.'s beskyttelse af vilde fugle og fisk: indgribende betydning for arealanvendelsen", *Ugeskrift for Retsvaesen* (1997), p. 511

Pallemaerts, M.: "Van de stranden van Blackpool tot de moerassen van Santona: plaatsgebonden verplichtingen in het milieurecht", *Tijdschrift voor Milieurecht* (1994), p. 19

Purdue, M.: "The impact of E.C. environmental law on planning law in the United Kingdom" in

J. Holder (ed.), *The impact of E.C. environmental law in the United Kingdom* (Chichester, etc., 1997), p. 231

Redman, M.: "European Community planning law", *Journal of Planning and Environmental Law* (1993), p. 999

Reid, C.: "Nature conservation law" in J. Holder (ed.), *The impact of E.C. environmental law in the United Kingdom* (Chichester, etc., 1997), p. 199

Riechenberg, K.: "La directiva sobre la protección de las aves salvajes: un hito en la política comunitaria del medio ambiente", *Revista de Instituciones Europeas* (1990), p. 369

Schmidt-Räntsch, A.: "Besitz und Vermarktung von geschützten Tieren und Pflanzen nach der Vollendung des EG-Binnenmarktes", *Natur und Recht* (1992), p. 49

Schmitz, S.: "Habitatschutz für Vögel? Zur unmittelbaren Wirkung der FFH-Richtlinie der EU", *Zeitschrift für Umweltrecht* (1996), p. 12

Somsen, H.: "Member States' obligations under Directive 79/409", *Water Law* (1993), p. 209

Thomson, G.: "La Communauté européenne et le paysage", *Revue juridique de l'environnement* (1993), p. 541

Untermaier, J.: "Des petits oiseaux aux grands principes", *Revue juridique de l'environnement* (1988), p. 466

Untermaier, J.: "La politique et le droit communautaires de protection de la nature et de la vie sauvage" in M. Campins i Eritja and I. Pont i Castejón (eds), *Perspectives de dret comunitari ambiental* (Bellaterra, 1997), p. 303

Van der Zwiep, K. and Backes, C.: *Integrated system for conservation of marine environments* (Baden-Baden, 1994)

Wilkins, A.: *Animal welfare in Europe* (London, 1997)

Wils, W.: "The Birds Directive 15 years later: a survey of the case law and a comparison with the Habitats Directive", *Journal of Environmental Law* (1994), p. 220

Wils, W.: "La protection des habitats naturels en droit communautaire", *Cahiers de droit européen* (1994), p. 398

Winter, G.: "Der Säbelschnäbler als Teil fürs Ganze", *Natur und Recht* (1992), p. 21

CHAPTER 6

Products

1. GENERAL QUESTIONS

6—01   There is no consistent and coherent Community policy on products. Most of the product-related measures adopted meant to establish common rules for the establishment and functioning of the internal Community market and thus enable the free circulation of goods. Aspects of health, safety, consumer protection and, at a later stage, environmental protection, were not systematically tackled at Community level, but were, rather, left to be regulated at Member State level; hence, common rules became necessary in order to ensure a level playing field. The so-called "new approach" to product standards' harmonisation, introduced in the 1980s, where Community legislation only fixes the essential requirements for a product, leaving the details to industrial standardisation by European standardisation organisations, has not changed this situation. Indeed, these "essential requirements" normally refer to health and safety aspects of a product, but not to its impact on the environment.

Different scientific committees, which the Commission had set up in the 1970s, have played some role in determining the effects of products on man and the environment. Only the Scientific Committee on Human Consumption has achieved, in the past, an authoritative reputation; some of the other committees do not seem to have always been completely neutral towards vested interests. In 1997, following the BSE scandal (where concern was voiced that the Commission had hidden information on "mad cow disease" and its influence on humans), the Commission restructured the different scientific committees, renamed them and placed them under the responsibility of the Commissioner on consumer affairs. Thus, the Scientific Committee for the Toxicity and Ecotoxicity of Chemical Substances became the Scientific Committee for Toxicity, Ecotoxicity and the Environment, without, however, changing its previous responsibilities.[1]

6—02   At international level and, in particular, within the context of the World Trade Organisation, attempts are being made to accept restrictions to trade only to the extent that it is scientifically proven that this or that product or production method presents a risk for human health or for the environment, despite the fact that there are no internationally recognised methods for "measuring" risk. It was for this reason that the European Community "lost" in a dispute where the Community ban of hormones and artificial growth promoters in meat and meat products was in question. The Community was not able to prove that the use of such hormones presented a risk to human health that justified a ban, including an import ban of hormone-treated meat.[2]

At Community level, the Commission has made a number of statements that any measure that restricts the free circulation of goods would, in future, be based on risk assessment and on a cost-benefit analysis, though there are at present no generally

---

[1] Dec. 97/579 [1997] O.J. L237/18.
[2] World Trade Organisation, Complaint by the United States and Canada, Decision WT/DS 26/12 and WT/DS 48/10 of January 16, 1998; see also the Commission's call for submission of new scientific evidence for a risk assessment of the effects of certain substances that are used as growth promoters in animals: [1999] O.J. C56/17.

recognised standards for risk assessments and cost-benefit analyses.[3] These two elements were introduced, somewhat surprisingly, into the Commission's policy for making proposals for Community legislation on chemicals—including heavy metals. The monitoring of national legislation is, in law, less systematic; the Commission tries to ensure that this systematic risk assessment review and cost-benefit analysis are undertaken when national measures are involved.[4]

6—03   This policy of requiring that any action on the restriction of use of a substance is preceded by a risk assessment contradicts the precautionary and prevention principles of Article 174 (ex 130r) E.C., which ask E.C. institutions to act even in cases where there is scientific uncertainty as to the harmfulness of a substance for humans or the environment. In the case of doubt, these principles suggest Community action, so that, in the case of an error, free trade is affected rather than human health or the environment: where a product or a substance is suspected to be dangerous, it is appropriate to act and not to wait for definitive scientific evidence.

The Commission itself has not systematically provided for a risk assessment on specific substances, in particular in those cases either where public opinion was concerned about the risks of a substance for humans or when Member States took action to restrict the use of a substance. Cases dealt with since 1997, where the results of a risk assessment were not available before Community legislative action was started, concern phthalates,[5] asbestos,[6] greenhouse gases[7] and ozone-depleting substances,[8] not to mention the different restrictions on the emission of pollutants into the air or the water. Requesting in all cases a risk analysis and a cost-benefit analysis neglects the fact that the environment suffers from the presence of too many pollutants. Accident prevention and remediation procedure should not be the first priority[9]; rather, the primary aim should be to reduce the placing of environmentally hazardous substances into the environment.

6—04   The Court of Justice has confirmed the possibility for preventive action, without putting as a condition that a risk assessment or cost-benefit analysis must be undertaken beforehand.[10] Nothing else can apply to the protection of the environment, all the more as the Court of Justice, in its judgment C-180/96, expressly referred to the necessity of preventive action, laid down in Article 174(2) (ex 130r) E.C.

In future, it is to be expected that the battle will continue between supporters of a wide application of the precautionary and prevention principle in order to promote an active, environmentally sound Community product policy, and the supporters of an umhampered circulation of goods.

There is also no systematic attempt at Community level to phase out toxic or environmentally hazardous substances, where less harmful substitutes exist. Interestingly

---

[3] Interestingly enough, Dir. 94/60 [1994] O.J. L365/1, where Council and European Parliament mention such necessities for the first time, has different wording; indeed, recital 8 of this Directive reads: "Whereas the said proposal from the Commission will take account of the risks and advantages of the substances newly classified as well as of the Community legislative proposals on risk analysis."

[4] See in this regard Art. 8(1) of Dir. 98/34 [1998] O.J. L204/37 and para. 4–37, above.

[5] See below, para. 6–53.

[6] See above, para. 4–09 and below, para. 6–38

[7] See below, para. 8–54.

[8] See below, para. 8–60.

[9] Seen under this general approach, Directives 76/769 and 79/117, which ban or restrict the use of certain products or substances, may be considered as "accident-remediation" directives, reacting to consumer accidents that have occurred or to "accidents" that consist of Member State promoting national legislation that impinges on the free circulation of goods.

[10] Case C-180/96 *United Kingdom v. Commission* [1998] E.C.R. I-2265; see also para. 1–29, above, for the Court's remarks; see, furthermore, European Parliament Res. of October 20, 1998 [1998] O.J. C341/31 on endocrine disruptors.

enough, a decision to reduce the discharge of persistant, toxic or bioaccumulative substances within 25 years to near-zero levels, was taken in 1995 by the North Sea Conference in Esbjerg (Denmark); however, this decision was limited to only some Member States.[11] The United Kingdom opposed the decision, which is not binding, and the European Commission has never made an attempt to introduce corresponding Community legislation.

6—05   Economic operators and the United Kingdom had favoured an approach that would incorporate scientific risk assessment. However, the ministerial declaration of the Esbjerg Conference stated that the precautionary principle was the "guiding principle" for ensuring a sustainable, sound and healthy North Sea ecosystem and that risk assessment was only a tool, not a prerequisite, for future action.[12]

This absence of a systematic approach is well illustrated by the example of chemicals (chemical substances and preparations, pesticides, genetically modified organisms, etc.) in the environment. Community efforts concentrate on the attempts to find a balance between health and safety of humans on the one hand, and on the free circulation of goods, their export and import on the other hand. The fact that chemicals—in the form of emissions, products, wastes, residues and so on—exist everywhere in the environment and constitute considerable risks for wildlife, soil, fresh and marine waters, or buildings, has not really led to an attempt systematically to phase out chemicals which constitute particular risks to the environment. The fact that the environment suffers from the presence of too many pollutants is clearly neglected.

6—06   At national level, an environmentally oriented product policy only exists in some Member States, a situation that is obviously strongly influenced by the Treaty provisions on the free circulation of goods and the interpretation that, under these provisions, a product that is lawfully produced and marketed in one Member State must in principle also be allowed to circulate in other Member States. It should be noted, though, that this general provision does not prevent the introduction of an environmental product policy at Member State level. Indeed, the Court jurisdiction regarding the interdependency between Article 27 (ex 29) E.C. and environmental protection may be summarised in the statement that in the absence of Community provisions concerning a product a Member State may adopt any environmental provision it wishes, as long as there is no discrimination of producers and traders from other Member States, and as long as the national measure is not disproportionate to the environmental objective pursued. Member States are therefore, in particular, entitled systematically to try to eliminate hazardous substances or parts from products, especially where other substances or parts are available which are less harmful to the environment.

Product policy inevitably affects health and safety, consumer protection and environmental protection, aspects which cannot clearly be dissociated from each other. Where genetically modified products or BSE are discussed, concern for the health and safety of humans prevail, and while environmental policy, under Article 174 (ex 130r) E.C. also contributes to public health, environmental concerns play a secondary role in such discussions. This reflects an anthropocentric view of problems, which cares less for the environment as such, caring only to the extent that it affects humans.[13]

---

[11] Belgium, Denmark, France, Germany, Netherlands, Sweden, and Norway and Switzerland.
[12] See Environmental Watch—Western Europe, June 16, 1995, p. 2.
[13] As a typical example see Dir. 89/392 on machinery [1989] O.J. L183/9, which establishes in Art. 2 essential requirements for the health and safety of persons or domestic animals and goods, but nothing on the protection of the environment.

2. THE COMPOSITION AND MARKETING OF PRODUCTS

6—07   Environmental directives and regulations have established some lists of substances or products[14] that were considered dangerous for the environment, frequently taking their lead from international environmental conventions. Directive 76/464 created a blacklist of substances and products, which were selected because of their toxicity, persistence and bioaccumulation[15]; a second list of substances was fixed, which have "a deleterious effect on the aquatic environment".[16] For list I, a priority list of 129 substances was then agreed, which should be regulated by Community emission standards[17]; until today, only 17 substances had been regulated. No new provisions are envisaged. Directive 84/360 on air emissions[18] contained another list of pollutants that were to be considered; no indication was given as to how these substances and products had been selected. The pollutants were not systematically tackled. Another list of air pollutants was laid down in Directive 96/62 on ambient air quality,[19] and on pollutants in general in Directive 96/61 on integrated prevention and pollution control.[20]

6—08   All these lists had no influence on product-related provisions adopted at Community level, but were, rather, aimed at framing Community policy for the limitation of the emission of pollutants into the environment. Restrictions concerning the composition of products are mainly found in Directive 76/769[21] which has, up to the end of 1998, been amended 16 times.[22] Any further ban or restriction of use of a substance or a product is introduced by way of adding such restrictions to the Directive's annex. Commission attempts to have restrictions introduced by way of an (accelerated) committee procedure, failed; thus, the procedure for introducing a further restriction follows the rules of Articles 95 and 251 (ex 100a and 189b) E.C., and normally takes at least two years.

Most initiatives for amending Directive 76/769 come from Member States, which introduce bans or restrictions of substances or products in order to protect, in particular, man or the environment. This then initiates the procedure under Directive 76/769, since the Commission wishes to preserve the unity of the internal market, which requires uniform product standards.

(a) Detergents

6—09   The first provisions that regulated the composition of products concerned products where diverging national provisions risked the creation of barriers to the free circulation of goods. Thus, from 1973, a Directive prohibited the placing on the market of detergents which were less than 90 per cent biodegradable[23]; since that

---

[14] Community terminology is not consistent. Sometimes, the word "substances" is used, where clearly a preparation, *i.e.* a mixture or composition of two or more substances, is meant.
[15] Dir. 76/464 on pollution caused by certain dangerous substances discharged into the aquatic environment of the Community [1976] O.J. L129/23, in particular Art.6 and annex, list I.
[16] *Ibid.*, annex, list II.
[17] Council Res. of February 1983 [1983] O.J. C46/17. For details on the monitoring of Directive 76/464, see paras 7–23 *et seq.*
[18] Dir. 84/360 on the combating of air pollution from industrial plants [1984] O.J. L188/20; for more details see paras 8–35 *et seq.*
[19] Dir. 96/62 on ambient air quality [1996] O.J. L296/55.
[20] Dir. 96/61 on integrated pollution prevention and control [1996] O.J. L257/26.
[21] Dir. 76/769 [1976] O.J. L262/201.
[22] Dir. 97/56 amending Dir. 76/769 for the sixteenth time [1997] O.J. L333/1; see also common position for a seventeenth amendment [1999] O.J. C18/43.
[23] Dir. 73/404 on the approximation of the laws of the Member States relating to detergents [1973] O.J. L347/51.

Directive had to be adopted unanimously and no real consensus was reached as to whether a percentage of 80 or 90 per cent should apply, a compromise was found that the detergent could be placed on the market, as long as the harmonised test methods showed that it is biodegradable by 80 per cent.[24]

(b) Gas oil, petrol and diesel fuel

6—10   The combustion of fuels releases pollutants that contaminate the environment—the damage caused by one tonne of sulphur dioxide is estimated at 4,000 euro.[25] Measures concerning the composition of fuels concentrated on the reduction of pollutants. As Member States had different perceptions of environmental problems, it is not surprising that such differences reappeared when fuels were regulated.

Thus, when gas oil provisions were harmonised, the sulphur content of gas oil was considered too high by some, but not by other, Member States. Directive 75/716[26] defined gas oil and then fixed two levels of sulphur content: for gas oil type A, a level of 0.5 per cent—later 0.3 per cent—of sulphur content was fixed, and for gas oil type B 0.8 per cent—later 0.6 per cent—of sulphur content. Type B gas oil was only to be used in zones where gas oil contributed only a little to atmospheric pollution or where such air pollution was low. The United Kingdom designated its whole territory as zone B; only the road system was considered zone A, a repartition of zones that neither corresponded to the wording nor the spirit of the Directive, nor was it capable of reaching its environmental objective, i.e. reducing the content of sulphur in the atmosphere.

6—11   In 1985, the Commission reported that the actual average sulphur content of gas oil in the Community was 0.34 per cent and that refinery costs would only increase significantly where the content was reduced below 0.2 per cent.[27] Directive 87/219,[28] which was based on Article 94 (ex 100) E.C., therefore deleted the differentiation between type A and B gas oil; it introduced a general level of 0.3 per cent of sulphur content.[29] However, Member States were allowed to require the use of gas oil with a sulphur content of 0.2 per cent in regions with high pollution or "where damage to the environment or to the national heritage caused by total sulphur dioxide emissions requires" a lower sulphur content than 0.3 per cent; it was clear that such a provision was not really ensuring common standards.

In 1991, the Commission found that Belgium, Germany, Denmark, Luxembourg and the Netherlands applied the 0.2 per cent limit.[30] Directive 93/12, based on Article 95 (ex 100a) E.C., generalised this approach and applied the sulphur content level of 0.2 per cent throughout the Community.[31]

Diesel fuels that contain too much sulphur create problems for the use of catalytic converters in diesel cars. In order to remedy this, and to reduce air pollution, Directive 93/12 introduced a level of 0.2 per cent sulphur as of the end of 1994 and 0.05 per cent as of the end of 1996; the Directive stated expressly that this was necessary in order to

---

[24] Dir. 73/405 on the approximation of the laws of the Member States relating to methods of testing the biodegradability on non-ionic surfactants [1973] O.J. L347/53; subsequently, Directives 82/242 [1982] O.J. L109/1 and 82/243 [1982] O.J. L109/18 completed the provisions for testing methods.

[25] Commission, COM (1997) 88 of March 12, 1997, p. 44.

[26] Dir. 75/716 [1975] O.J. L307/22.

[27] Commission [1985] O.J. C205/3.

[28] Dir. 87/219 [1987] O.J. L91/19.

[29] The Directive was no longer to apply to gas oil used by shipping and for processing in the refining industry (Art. 1).

[30] COM (91) 154 of June 10, 1991.

[31] Dir. 93/12 on the sulphur content of certain liquid fuels [1993] O.J. L74/81.

reach the emission limit values fixed in other Community provisions. However, in a proposal of 1997,[32] which was based on Article 175 (ex 130s) E.C., the Commission suggested allowing Greece and Spain (for the Canary Islands) to use gas oil with more than 0.2 per cent, because it was of the opinion that the level of 0.2 per cent could have significant economic consequences and that it had a minimal effect upon human health and the environment. The Commission rejected the request from the European Parliament to use Article 95 (ex 100a) E.C. as a legal basis, because it thought that this was incompatible with the cost-effectiveness approach[33]—hardly a legally acceptable argument.

6—12   The Council confirmed Article 175(1) as the legal basis for the Directive.[34] It fixed the maximum permissible sulphur content in gas oil at 0.2 per cent as of July 1, 2000 and at 0.1 per cent as of January 1, 2008. Member States were allowed to use, until 2013, gas oil with a sulphur content between 0.1 and 0.2 per cent, if the quality standards of Directive 80/779 were respected and the emissions did not lead to an exceeding of the critical quantities in other Member States. Furthermore, Spain (for the Canary Islands), France (for its overseas departments), Greece and Portugal (for Madeira and the Acores) were allowed, for an unspecified time, to use gas oil with a higher sulphur content than 0.2 per cent.

As regards heavy fuels, the Commission published, in 1997, figures according to which most sulphur dioxide emissions in the Community stemmed from the burning of coal (62.9 per cent), heavy fuel (18.4 per cent), gas oil/diesel (7.0 per cent) and refinery fuels (6.5 per cent).[35] As part of the Community strategy to combat acidification, Directive 1999/32[36] reduced the sulphur content of heavy fuel oils as of 2003 to 1 per cent. However, Member States obtained the possibility of allowing the use of heavy fuels with a sulphur content of up to 3 per cent, provided that the air-quality standards for sulphur dioxide laid down in Directive 80/779[37] and other Community provisions, were respected and that the contribution to transboundary pollution was negligible.[38] Furthermore, combustion plants covered by Directive 88/609[39] may use fuel with a higher sulphur content, provided that the total emissions of all such plants in a Member State do not exceed 1,000 mg/m^3 of sulphur dioxide for new plants and 1,700 mg/m^3 for existing plants.

6—13   It should be noted that the respect of quality standards under Directive 80/779 is not really monitored, that it is not indicated for how much time compliance with standards must have existed, whether transboundary pollution also refers to non-E.C. regions and how this kind of pollution is assessed.

Finally, Directive 98/70,[40] adopted at the end of 1998, fixed the maximum sulphur content of diesel fuel (and petrol) at 350 mg/kg; this level was to be reduced to 50 mg/kg by 2005. Member States were allowed to introduce more stringent requirements for sensitive areas, subject to Community authorisation.

---

[32] COM (97) 88 of March 12, 1997 [1997] O.J. C190/9; amended [1998] O.J. C259/98

[33] COM (1998) 385 of July 8, 1998.

[34] Dir. 1999/32 [1999] O.J. L121/13.

[35] COM (91) 154 (n. 30, above).

[36] Dir. 1999/32 (n. 34, above).

[37] Dir. 80/779 [1980] O.J. L229/30.

[38] The figures published in COM (97) 88 (n. 32, above), p. 46 on the average sulphur content in 1995 indicate where this derogation might apply. At the same time, the figures show which Member States tried, in the past, to reduce the sulphur content of heavy fuels as follows (expressed in per cent): Belgium 1.0; Denmark 1.0; Germany 1.2; Greece 2.7; Spain 1.0–3.5; France 2.1; Ireland 2.0; Italy 1.53; Luxembourg 0; Netherlands 2.2; Austria 0.96; Portugal 0; Finland 1.1; Sweden 0.3; United Kingdom 2.18.

[39] Dir. 88/609 on the limitation of emissions of certain pollutants into the air from large combustion plants [1988] O.J. L336/1.

[40] Dir. 98/70 [1998] O.J. L350/58

Member States were likewise divided on the lead content of petrol. Directive 78/611[41] fixed the lead content to 0.4 grams per litre, but allowed Member States to lower this level down to 0.15 grams. Until 1986, Ireland was allowed to apply a level of 0.64 grams. The reason for this split standard was the fact that Germany had already introduced, as of 1976, a lead content of 0.15 grams, and was not prepared to go back on this decision.

6—14   In the early 1980s, campaigns on reducing the lead content in the air—for health reasons in the United Kingdom, for environmental reasons (Waldsterben—the problem of dying forests) in Germany—led the European Council to ask for the introduction of lead-free petrol,[42] which was proposed in May 1984 and adopted in March 1985, almost a record time.[43]

The Directive required Member States to "take the necessary measures to ensure the availability and balanced distribution within their territories of unleaded petrol from 1 October 1989" (Article 3). Unleaded petrol was defined as petrol that contained less than 0.013 grams of lead per litre, leaded petrol as containing between 0.15 and 0.40 grams of lead per litre. Member States were also authorised to prohibit leaded regular petrol,[44] which eliminated the free circulation of such petrol within the Community.

6—15   Other content requirements for petrol concerned the benzene content, which was fixed at 5 per cent, the minimum motor octane number (85) and the minimum research octane number (95) of unleaded petrol.

The vague wording of Article 3 made any monitoring of the effective introduction of unleaded petrol practically impossible. It was the Member States' policy and the mineral oil companies that determined the speed of the introduction of unleaded petrol. Generally, this introduction advanced more quickly where a Member State had introduced a tax differentiation between leaded and unleaded petrol.[45]

6—16   At the end of 1998, Directive 85/210 was replaced by Directive 98/70, which was based on Article 95 (ex 100a) E.C.[46] This Directive prohibits the marketing of regular leaded petrol as of January 2000, reduces the benzene content to 1.0 per cent and contains a number of other specifications for unleaded petrol.

The different provisions on diesel and petrol fuel, based sometimes on Article 95, sometimes on Article 175 (ex 130s), and containing numerous derogations, transitions and authorisations for Member States' derogations, illustrate well the changing motivations behind the Community approach, which varies between environmental protection and internal market considerations. Recently, Article 175 seems to have been favoured.[47] The different provisions do not concern the composition of fuel for cars generally. There are numerous additives that are added to petrol in order to influence its quality, which may later, in the form of emissions, enter the environment.[48] Directive 94/60,[49] which

---

[41] Dir. 78/611 [1978] O.J. L197/19.

[42] See (1993) 6 Bulletin of the European Communities, 1.5.15

[43] Dir. 85/210 on the approximation of the laws of the Member States concerning the lead content of petrol [1985] O.J. L96/25; Commission proposal [1984] O.J. C178/5.

[44] Dir. 87/416 [1987] O.J. L225/33.

[45] See European Environmental Agency, Environmental taxes: implementation and environmental effectiveness (Copenhagen, 1996), p. 30 ("The tax differentiation schemes for fuels have been particularly successful") and p. 55 (annex II, where the Agency reports on the Swedish tax differentiation for leaded petrol). The Commission had proposed such a tax differentiation [1984] O.J. C178/5, but the Council had considered this to be a question for Member States alone.

[46] Dir. 98/70 [1998] O.J. L350/58.

[47] It may be expected that the entry into effect of the Amsterdam Treaty on May 1, 1999 will lead to a stabilisation in the choice of the legal basis.

[48] See Written Questions 1426/92 (Glinne) [1992] O.J. C309/41 and 2245/92 (Alber) [1993] O.J. C141/26, where the Commission admits that it does not have a policy on additives in fuels.

[49] Dir. 94/60 [1994] O.J. L365/1.

provides, amongst other things, for a ban on chemical substances and preparations which are classified as carcinogenic, mutagenic and/or teratogenic under Directives 67/548 and 88/379, even provides for an express derogation for such substances that come under Directive 85/210 or are used as fuels in cars or other machines.

No Community or international provisions exist at present for bunker fuels, which are used in ships. They contain a high level of SO_2 (4.5 per cent or more) and the reduction of this content would be a very cost-effective measure.[50] The Commission suggested not taking action at E.C. level, but rather waiting for the Convention on Maritime Pollution (MARPOL) to take decisions on designating the Baltic Sea and parts of the North Sea[51] as sensitive areas where ships would be required to use bunker fuels with a sulphur content of 1.5 per cent. Such measures have not yet been taken and are not expected, in any case, to become effective before 2005.

(c) Cars

6—17   There are no Community environmental provisions on the making of cars. It is, however, the case that numerous provisions exist that decide on the air emissions from cars, although it is left to car manufacturers to decide how they intend to comply with the emission standards, whether they install a catalytic converter, and use an electro motor or another motor with a low consumption of fuel and thus generate only low emissions. Also, for instance, there is no provision to require the fitting of existing cars with catalytic converters. In the same way, the noise levels from cars are fixed in the form of emission-limit values, but do not require the use of particular materials, designs or tyres, etc., in order to comply with these values.

6—18   Sometimes the different objectives pursued in the car sector contradict each other. Thus, a reduction of the weight of cars, which would lead to less fuel consumption, might contradict the objective of increased safety of passengers. The increased use of plastic materials, which make a car lighter, could make the recycling of end-of-life vehicles more difficult.

The Community never considered imposing certain product standards on cars, such as, for instance, a maximal fuel consumption, the use of certain materials or fuels or a top speed for cars. The proposal for a directive on end-of-life vehicles[52] provides for an article on waste prevention, but suggests measures for promotion and encouragement as regards car design and production, recycled materials and hazardous substances in cars; another provision indirectly reduces the use of lead, mercury, cadmium and hexavalent chromium, by stipulating that these substances shall not be shredded, put into landfills or incinerated. Finally, the proposal provides for cars to be 85 per cent recyclable by 2015, which again will have an impact on the composition of cars.

(d) Packaging

6—19   Directive 94/62 on packaging and packaging waste[53] provides for a reduction of the total metal content of four heavy metals—cadmium, lead, mercury and polyvalent chromium—in three steps by the year 2001. The Directive does not fix methods for the measuring of this content.

Specific requirements for the composition of packaging are not laid down. There

---

[50] COM (97) 88 (n. 32, above) p. 49.
[51] "Due to lack of data, the emissions from ships in the Mediterranean area were not included in the analysis": *ibid.*, p. 15.
[52] [1997] O.J. C337/3.
[53] Dir. 94/62 [1994] O.J. L365/10.

is, however, an interesting combination of the new approach system for product harmonisation and environmental requirements: Member States are obliged to accept onto their markets all packaging that complies with the essential requirements of Directive 94/62, which are laid down in annex II. They include the provision that "packaging shall be designed, produced and commercialised in such a way as to minimise its impact on the environment when packaging waste or residues from packaging waste management operations are disposed of", that packaging "shall be so manufactured that the presence of noxious and other hazardous substances and materials . . . is minimised with regard to their presence in emissions, ash or leachate when . . . packaging waste are incinerated or landfilled". These provisions would easily allow a Member State, which so wishes, to prohibit PVC packaging, to restrict the use of aerosols or to provide for other restrictions on the use of packaging; this would raise difficulties, since Directive 94/62 is based on Article 95 (ex 100a) E.C., which aims at ensuring the free circulation of packaging.

6—20   CEN (see paragraph 6–69) was charged with elaborating European standards for the essential requirements for packaging. It will be interesting to observe to what extent these and other essential requirements will be enshrined in industrial standards: if the requirements are taken seriously, some forms of packaging will have to disappear from the market; if they are not followed, Member States might find a justification for taking national measures.

By the end of 1997, Belgium, Greece, Ireland, Portugal, Luxembourg, Finland and the United Kingdom had not yet transposed the Directive into national law.[54]

(e) Products that contain heavy metals

6—21   A number of other Community directives or regulations limit the content of heavy metals in products. Without attempting to be exhaustive, the following examples may be given. Directive 91/157[55] prohibits the use of certain batteries, where the mercury levels fixed in the Directive are exceeded; an amendment, enlarging this ban, is in preparation. Lead carbons and lead sulphates may not be used in paints[56]; some derogations are allowed for the restoration of works of art and historic buildings.[57] Mercury, arsenic or organostannic compounds[58] may not be used to prevent the fouling by micro-organisms (plants or animals) of boats, in fish or shellfish farming and in the preservation of wood.[59] Cadmium and its compounds are banned from use as colourants or stabilisers for different products; also cadmium plating is forbidden in a number of expressly defined products[60]; a further restriction of cadmium use is in preparation. Finally, nickel is prohibited for use in products which come in contact with the human skin.[61]

6—22   As can be seen, the restrictions are anything but systematic. Only for cadmium and its compounds has the Commission made a specific communication and obtained Council agreement in the elimination, where possible, of cadmium from the environment.

---

[54] Commission, Monitoring application of Community law—15th report (1997) [1998] O.J. C250/1, p. 180.
[55] Dir. 91/157 on batteries and accumulators containing certain dangerous substances [1991] O.J. L78/38; amended by Dir. 98/101 [1999] O.J. L1/1.
[56] Dir. 76/769 on the approximation of the laws, regulations and administrative provisions of the Member States relating to restrictions on the marketing and use of certain substances and preparations [1976] O.J. L262/201 with subsequent amendments, annex I, nos 17 and 18.
[57] As regards lead, see also Written Question E-0837/96 (Muscardini) [1996] O.J. C297/35.
[58] For these substances see Written Question 1139/89 (Adam) [1990] O.J. C328/4.
[59] Dir. 76/769 (n. 56), nos 19, 20 and 21.
[60] Ibid., no. 24.
[61] Ibid., no. 28.

Cadmium is a good example as regards the Community approach to substances. The first environmental action programme designated cadmium, together with other substances, as a substance that should be examined as a priority, because of its toxicity and its effect on human health and on the environment.[62] The Council confirmed in 1975 that an examination into the effects of cadmium on water was already ongoing and asked for an examination of air emissions of cadmium.[63] In 1981 the Commission asked the Consultative Scientific Committee on the toxicity and ecotoxicity of chemical compounds for an opinion on cadmium, which recommended the reduction of cadmium emissions wherever possible.[64] In 1987, the Commission sent a communication to the Council, in which it listed 20 directives which limited the use of cadmium, suggested an action programme consisting of nine points to eliminate cadmium from the environment[65] and announced that it would, within two years, submit proposals for all nine points. The Council approved the strategy.[66] In 1991, the Council adopted a directive to reduce the cadmium content as colourant, stabiliser or surface coating for a number of products,[67] and this Directive is to be reviewed "at regular intervals" (the first review being in 1997).

6—23   Nevertheless, the Commission considered it necessary to include cadmium and its different compounds into its priority lists for existing chemicals,[68] which were established under Regulation 793/93[69] and which are designed to assess the effects of substances on man and the environment; as indicated in paragraphs 4–10 et seq., such an assessment takes several years.

The main source of the presence of cadmium in the environment is the cadmium content of fertilisers that are used in agriculture. Community law does not contain limit values for cadmium concentrations in fertilisers,[70] but the national legislation of the three acceding Member States—Sweden, Austria and Finland—did. The Accession Treaty therefore provided that this legislation could be maintained for four years; in the meantime, a re-examination of the Community provisions would take place. Since an agreement on Community-wide values could not be reached, the derogation clause was prolonged until the end of 2001.[71]

This sequence of events shows that a systematic Community approach as regards cadmium simply does not exist; similar conclusions have to be drawn for other heavy metals such as lead, mercury and chromium.

(f) Products containing ozone-depleting substances

6—24   In order to protect the ozone layer, the Community has adopted a number of measures as regards ozone-depleting substances.[72] The Montreal Protocol[73] deals with such substances, but only indirectly touches the question of products that contain

---

[62] First environmental action programme [1973] O.J. C112/1, p. 13.

[63] Res. of June 24, 1975 [1975] O.J. C168/4.

[64] Scientific Consultative Committee on the toxicity and ecotoxicity of chemical compounds, opinion of April 1981, published in *Activity Report 1979–1983* (EUR 9246) (Luxembourg, 1984), p. 37.

[65] Commission, "Environmental pollution by cadmium. Proposal for an action programme", COM (87) 165 of April 21, 1987.

[66] Res. of January 25, 1988 [1988] O.J. C30/1.

[67] Dir. 91/338 amending, for the tenth time, Directive 76/769 [1991] O.J. L186/59.

[68] See Reg. 143/97 [1997] O.J. L25/13, nos 2 and 3.

[69] Reg. 793/93 on the evaluation and control of the risks of existing substances [1993] O.J. L84/1.

[70] Dir. 75/116 on fertilisers [1975] O.J. L24/21.

[71] Dir. 98/97 [1999] O.J. L18/60.

[72] See below, paras 8–60 et seq.

[73] Montreal Protocol of September 16, 1987 on substances that deplete the ozone layer; the Protocol was adhered to by the Community by Dec. 88/540 [1988] O.J. L297/8.

ozone-depleting substances.[74] It is true, though, that Article 2(11) of the Protocol allows contracting parties to "take more stringent measures" than those required by the Protocol. These provisions, incidentally, also apply to "products produced with, but not containing" ozone-depleting substances.

The Community could thus, by virtue of the Montreal Protocol, which has been transposed into Community law by Regulation 3093/94,[75] take measures to prohibit products that contain ozone-depleting substances or that had been produced with the help of such substances, without infringing, in my opinion, provisions of the World Trade Organisation.[76] However, it has not yet done so, but has instead limited its measures to the substances themselves. Only in 1998 was a proposal made for the ban of some ozone-depleting substances in some products.[77]

6—25   Several Member States did pronounce bans on products which contained ozone-depleting substances: Luxembourg prohibited the use of CFCs and HCFCs in air-conditioning equipment for buildings. The Community did not intervene, accepting the factual breach of the common-market provisions. The legal construction which was used was that the Community provisions on ozone-depleting substances had been based on Article 175 (ex 130s) E.C.[78] This allowed Member States to recur to Article 176 (ex 130t) E.C. and adopt more stringent measures, although this Article expressly requires that any measure taken must be compatible with the Treaty provisions (and therefore also with Article 27 (ex 29) E.C.). Furthermore, banning products that contain ozone-depleting substances is not a more stringent measure than the banning of such substances; however, it is another measure (or aliud) that may not be taken under Article 176.

(g) Chemical substances and preparations

6—26   Chemicals, in the form of substances, preparations, pesticides, fertilisers, pharmaceuticals, cosmetics and food additives, are extensively regulated at Community level, since for all these products uniform rules are necessary to establish a common market. Pharmaceuticals, cosmetics and food additives will not be discussed in this book, since health issues prevail and environmental elements are peripheral in these sectors. Community legislation on substances and preparations (a preparation is a mixture of several substances) is based on Article 95 (ex 100a) E.C. and tries to achieve total harmonisation; this means that national legislation on chemicals that diverges from existing Community provisions is, in principle, not allowed.

For legislation on chemicals, four basic steps can be distinguished, which can be found in the different Community measures: (1) data collection on the different chemicals; (2) priority setting for regulating chemicals; (3) risk assessment of the chemical; (4) risk management (limiting use and emissions, etc.). It is a question of political choice, whether—pending the execution of these four steps for the individual chemical—the chemical is to be allowed to be used without restrictions, to what extent the burden of proof for the harmlessness of a chemical is on its manufacturer or importer or on the public authorities, to what extent the precautionary principle is to apply, and so on.

---

[74] Art. 4(3) of the Protocol provides for rules to be elaborated that prohibit the import of products containing ozone-depleting substances from states that are not party to the Protocol; Art. 9(1b) invites research and development of alternatives to products that contain ozone-depleting substances.
[75] Reg. 3093/94 [1994] O.J. L333/1.
[76] The Community adhered to WTO by Dec. 94/800 [1994] O.J. L336/1.
[77] [1998] O.J. C286/6, Art. 5.
[78] See, lastly, Reg. 3093/94 (n. 75, above).

(i) Existing chemical substances

6—27   As regards chemical substances, Community legislation differentiates between new and existing chemicals. Existing chemicals are those that were on the Community market on September 18, 1981[79]; these existing chemicals—exactly 100,106 substances—are listed in the EINECS inventory.[80] Their manufacturer or Community importer, by virtue of Directive 67/548,[81] has to classify, pack and label them according to their hazard potential and may then trade them freely in the Community. The Community tries, by way of a Committee procedure that is described in detail in Directive 67/548, to provide progressively for a statutory classification of these substances, by assessing their risk for man and the environment; where such a risk is identified, the substance is placed into annex I of Directive 67/548. That annex lists the name of the substance, the category of danger attributed to the substance,[82] the label and indications assigned to the substance, risk phrases, which indicate the nature of the special risk, and safety phrases indicating the recommended safety precautions. Furthermore, it lists the concentration limits of a substance contained in a preparation which is necessary to qualify that preparation as dangerous under Directive 88/379.[83]

6—28   By the end of 1998, annex I contained some 3,000 substances,[84] a considerable achievement, but small compared to the volume of more than 100,000 substances on the market and the time—some 30 years—which was needed for this classification; 1,500 other substances were considered, after examination, not to be hazardous. In order to accelerate the procedure, Regulation 793/93[85] was introduced. It provides that manufacturers or E.C. importers must inform the Commission of which substances they produce or import in quantities of 1,000 tons or more and provide information on those substances, such as on their toxicity or ecotoxicity, carcinogenicity and "any other indication relevant to the risk evaluation of the substance".

On the basis of that information, Community priority lists for about 110 substances were established, for which an evaluation of their risk to humans or the environment seemed urgent[86]; a specific regulation laid down principles for the assessment of risks to man and the environment, subdivided into human health (toxicity), human health (psycho-chemical properties) and environmental considerations.[87] For each substance on the priority list, a Member State was appointed rapporteur for the evaluation. These evaluations end with the suggestion by the reporting Member State that either no risk-reduction measures beyond those already applied are necessary, that there is a need for further information and/or testing, or that the available information justifies a Community ban or restriction of use of the chemical. On the basis of the national report, the Community will decide, by way of committee procedure, on the "results of

---

[79] This date is the date on which Dir. 79/831 ([1979] O.J. L259/10), which amended Dir. 67/548 on the classification, labelling and packaging of dangerous substances ([1967] O.J. L196/1) for the seventh time, entered into effect.

[80] [1990] O.J. C146A/4.

[81] Dir. 67/548 (n. 79, above).

[82] Ibid., Art. 2 fixes the following 15 categories of danger: explosive, oxidising, extremely flammable, highly flammable, flammable, very toxic, toxic, harmful, corrosive, irritant, sensitising, carcinogenic, mutagenic, toxic to reproduction and dangerous to the environment. "Dangerous to the environment" is defined as "substances and preparations which, were they to enter the environment, would present or may present an immediate or delayed danger for one or more components of the environment".

[83] Dir. 88/379 on the approximation of the laws, regulations and administrative provisions of the Member States relating to the classification, packaging and labelling of dangerous preparations [1988] O.J. L187/14. This Directive is now being replaced by Dir. 1999/45 [1999] O.J. L200/1.

[84] See last amendment Dir. 98/73 [1998] O.J. L305/1.

[85] Reg. 793/93 (n. 69, above).

[86] Regs 1179/94 [1994] O.J. L131/3; 2268/95 [1995] O.J. L231/18; 143/97 [1997] O.J. L25/13.

[87] Reg. 1488/94 [1994] O.J. L161/3.

the risk evaluation" and, if necessary, on "an appropriate strategy for limiting those risks".

6—29 By mid-1999, no risk assessment has been completely finished and therefore no Community decision under this new procedure has yet been taken; the anticipation is that, in future, about five to ten such assessments will be completed every year. This is not really surprising, since the—non-binding—guidance document on how to make a risk evaluation comprises about 700 pages.[88] The low figure of risk assessments that can be finished per year[89] shows how unreasonable it would be to make the result of a risk assessment a condition for banning a substance or restricting its use. It was thus quite right that the Community, until now, has never accepted such a request from economic operators.

What is further lacking in the present risk assessment procedure is the possibility of indicating that the available information is convincing enough to justify measures by way of precaution,[90] though the last scientific evidence of the detrimental effects of the substance is not yet available. This is all the more necessary, as there will never be a complete consensus on scientific arguments.[91]

(ii) New chemical substances

6—30 Substances which were, on September 18, 1981, not yet placed on the Community market and therefore were not included in the EINECS inventory, are new substances. Such substances must, subject to a number of exceptions laid down in Directive 67/548, be notified to the competent authority of the Member State where the substance is produced or—in the case of a manufacturer outside the Community—where the notifier is established, at least 60 days before the substance is placed on the market. This notification must be accompanied by a technical dossier, a proposal for the classification and labelling of the substance and a proposal for a safety data sheet. The technical dossier must include the results from testing the substance; the number and intensity of the tests vary depending on the quantity of the substance to be marketed. The test procedures are laid down in annex V of Directive 67/548, which contains 17 test methods for the determination of physico-chemical properties, 38 for the toxicity for humans and only 12 test methods for testing the (aquatic) ecotoxicity of a substance. Where the notifier learns, after notification, of new effects of the substance on humans or the environment, he must, at his own initiative, inform the competent authority of this.

Upon receipt of the notification the national competent authority checks whether it conforms with the requirements of the Directive, informs the notifier of its conclusions and carries out a risk assessment of the notified substance, which identifies the risk for humans and the environment linked to the marketing of the substance.

6—31 In this regard, Directive 93/67[92] states: "the assessment of risks should be

---

[88] Commission, "Technical guidance document in support of Commission Directive 93/67 on risk assessment for new notified substances and Commission Regulation 1488/94 on risk assessment for existing substances", Parts I–IV (Luxembourg, 1996).

[89] Reflections on how to accelerate the procedure have started: see Written Question E-0616/98 (Schleicher) [1998] O.J. C310/103; and in particular Commission, Working Document on the operation of Directives 67/548, 88/379, 76/769 and Reg. 793/93: SEC (1998) 1986 of November 18, 1998.

[90] On the precautionary principle, see above, para. 1–27.

[91] At present, there is no complete scientific consensus on, for instance, ozone-layer depletion, climate change, the causes of forest decline, the BSE impact, the effects of hormones in meat or the impact of genetically modified organisms on the environment.

[92] Dir. 93/67 laying down the principles for assessment of risks to man and the environment of substances notified in accordance with Directive 67/548 [1993] O.J. L227/9; this Directive is supported by a series of technical guidance documents on risk assessment, which comprise, overall, some 700 pages.

based on a comparison of the potential adverse effects of a substance with the reason-ably foreseeable exposure of man and the environment to that substance; . . . the assessment of risks to man should take account of the physico-chemical and toxico-logical properties of a substance; . . . the assessment of risks to the environment should take account of the environmental effects of a substance".[93] It also defines "hazard identification",[94] such as the toxicity or carcinogenicity of a substance, and "risk characterisation",[95] which is the likelihood of harm.

The competent national authority sends information to the European Commission consisting of a summary of the notification dossier, a proposal for the classification and labelling, a proposal for the inclusion of the substance in the European list of notified chemical substances (ELINCS—European List of Notified Chemical Sub-stances) and the conclusions of the risk assessment. The Commission forwards copies of this information to the competent authorities of all other Member States.

6—32 Any other Member State may ask for details of the dossier or suggest further tests. The final decision on the classification, packaging and labelling of the substance is decided by committee procedure; the Committee may, of course, also decide not to classify a substance as dangerous. By the end of 1998, some 2,100 new substances had been notified and, where appropriate, classified, placed into annex I of Directive 67/548 and registered in ELINCS. The Commission regularly publishes the list of notified substances.

Directive 67/548 has been implemented by all Member States; the different daughter directives inserting substances into annex I or otherwise adapting the Directive to technical progress—by the end of 1998 there were 25 such adaptations[96]—were quite regularly transposed with some delay,[97] which raises the question whether the Directive should not rather be transformed into a regulation. Indeed, Member States' residual possibilities to adopt more stringent requirements than those of the Directive are extremely small.[98]

(iii) Chemical preparations

6—33 Dangerous chemical preparations—the mixture of several chemical sub-stances—are mainly regulated by Directive 88/379,[99] which deals with the classifica-tion, packaging and labelling of preparations that contain at least one dangerous substance or are otherwise considered dangerous. It is estimated that there are more than 7 million chemical preparations on the market; nobody knows the exact number. Directive 88/379 does not provide for a notification of new chemical preparations prior to their placing on the market. At present, the Directive does not have a classifying category "dangerous for the environment"; it largely refers to Directive 67/548 as regards test methods, etc., but calculates the health hazards with the help of specific

---

[93] Dir. 93/67 (n. 92, above), considerants 4 to 6.

[94] Ibid., Art. 2(2a): "hazard identification' is the identification of the adverse effects which a substance has an inherent capacity to cause".

[95] Ibid., Art. 2(2d): "'risk characterisation' is the estimation of the incidence and severity of the adverse effects likely to occur in a human population or environmental compartment due to actual or predicted exposure to a substance, and may include 'risk estimation', i.e. the quantification of that likelihood".

[96] See last Dir. 98/98 [1998] O.J. L355/1.

[97] For details, see Commission, 14th Report on monitoring application of Community law (1996) [1997] O.J. L332/1; Belgium was found responsible for not having transposed directives on chemical substances into national law since 1994; see joined cases C-218–222/96 Commission v. Belgium [1996] E.C.R. I-6817, case C-135/96 Commission v. Belgium [1997] E.C.R. I-1061; joined cases C-313, 356 & 358/86 Commission v. Belgium [1997] E.C.R. I-2953; see also case C-238/95 Commission v. Italy [1996] E.C.R. I-1451.

[98] See the landmark decision of the Court of Justice, case C-278/85 Commission v. Denmark [1987] E.C.R. 4069.

[99] Dir. 88/379 (n. 83, above).

formulae, using individual concentration limits. A comprehensive review of the Directive was adopted in 1999.[1]

(iv) Restrictions on marketing and use

6—34   Where a Member State considers that a substance or a preparation, while complying with the requirements of Directives 67/548 or 88/379, poses a risk to humans or the environment, the state may impose restrictions on its circulation or prohibit it. The Commission must be notified of such measures. A Community procedure is then opened, which leads to a Community-wide decision, taken by a qualified majority.[2]

Where a substance or a preparation which is not yet regulated at Community level poses, according to the opinion of a Member State, a risk to humans or the environment, the Member State may ban or restrict its marketing or use. It has, however, to notify its draft measure to the Commission, which examines the compatibility of the national measure with the provisions on the free circulation of goods[3] and checks, at the same time, whether Community measures are necessary in order to preserve the unity of the internal market.

6—35   The different measures taken at Community level to ban or restrict the use of chemical substances and preparations, either on the above-mentioned "initiative" by a Member State or at the Commission's initiative, are normally[4] assembled in Directive 76/769.[5] The Directive is based on Article 95 (ex 100a) E.C. The restrictions are laid down in an annex to the Directive, which has, up to the end of 1998, been amended 17 times, providing for restrictions on 42 substances or groups of substances and covering about 900 individual substances.[6] The specific bans or restrictions of use are the subject of very complex discussions at Community level, where the various different economic interests frequently had a decisive influence on the outcome of the discussions. Most of the bans or restrictions of use are influenced by health considerations; environmental concerns play only a subordinate role.

Until now, Directive 76/769 has restricted: PCBs and PCTs[7]; several chemical substances that are used in ornamental objects, sneezing powders, artificial snow, etc.[8]; benzene in toys[9]; fire retardants[10]; asbestos[11]; lead in paint and anti-fouling applications[12]; pentachlorophenol[13]; cadmium[14]; Tris and nickel in contact with the skin[15];

---

[1]   Dir. 1999/45 (n. 83).
[2]   See for this safeguard procedure, para. 3–71, above.
[3]   The procedure is laid down in Dir. 98/34 [1998] O.J. L217/18; for details see paras 4–37 et seq., above.
[4]   See, however, the restrictions for pesticides (paras 6–21 et seq., below), ozone-depleting substances (para. 8–60, below), heavy metals in packaging or in batteries (para. 6–44, above), etc.
[5]   Dir. 76/769 (n. 21, above).
[6]   This rather large figure should be considered with caution. Indeed, most of the insertions into annex I of Dir. 76/769 were placed there because a great number of chemical substances were classified, under Dir. 67/548, as carcinogenic and the Council took a basic decision that such substances should not be sold to consumers. The number of "regular" restrictions on use of substances is relatively small.
[7]   Dir. 76/769 (n. 21); Dir. 82/828 [1982] O.J. L350/34; Dir. 85/467 [1985] O.J. L269/56; Dir. 91/339 [1991] O.J. L186/64 (which concerns Ugilec 21 and 141 and DBBT, which are PCB substitutes); Dir. 89/677 [1989] O.J. L398/19.
[8]   Dir. 79/663 [1979] O.J. L197/37; Dir. 83/264 [1984] O.J. L147/9; Dir. 94/48 [1994] O.J. L331/7; Dir. 97/64 [1997] O.J. L315/13
[9]   Dir. 82/806 [1982] O.J. L339/55;
[10]   Dir. 83/264 (n. 8).
[11]   Dir. 83/478 [1983] O.J. L263/33; Dir. 85/610 [1985] O.J. L375/1; Dir. 91/659 [1991] O.J. L363/1.
[12]   Dir. 89/677 (n. 7).
[13]   Dir. 91/173 [1991] O.J. L85/34.
[14]   Dir. 91/338 [1991] O.J. L186/59.
[15]   Dir. 79/663 [1979] O.J. L197/37; Dir. 94/27 [1994] O.J. L188/1. Directive 94/27 on nickel has not yet become effective, since CEN has not yet produced the necessary standards for testing methods.

carcinogens, teratogens and mutagens[16]; creosotes and some chlorinated solvents[17]; and hexachlorethane.[18]

6—36 Amendments of Directive 76/769 must be adopted in the form of a special Council and Parliament Directive, which is a slow and laborious procedure considering the risk that many chemicals pose. Past attempts by the Commission to introduce a simplified procedure[19] only succeeded in so far as existing restrictions may be adapted by way of committee procedure. As mentioned already, the adoption of Regulation 793/93[20] has not yet led to a quicker decision-making procedure.

There is no attempt being made systematically to restrict the marketing or use of harmful chemicals, on condition of the availability of substitutes. On questions from members of the European Parliament, the Commission has de facto admitted this situation.[21] Rather, the Directive's annex is normally amended where the Community measure endeavours to take up a ban or restriction that had previously been initiated by a Member State at national level, where an accident demonstrates the need to take action or where the results of national research, a new assessment of available data, public concern, etc., make action appropriate. This explains why most of the amendments to the annex of Directive 76/769 appear to be of a patchwork nature and not to deal with the most important substances or products.

6—37 Moreover, the Commissions has tried, since 1994,[22] to propose amendments of Directive 76/769 only where a "targeted" risk analysis and a cost-benefit analysis ("advantages and drawbacks") justify such action. These conditions de facto slow down any action for restricting the use of chemicals, particularly as the risk analysis is focused more on aspects of human health and much less on environmental concerns; furthermore, environmental concerns are, by definition, of non-economic nature and all attempts objectively to measure the economic value of environmental assets or impairments have not succeeded so far.

It is impossible to differentiate, as regards measures under Directive 76/769, between measures to protect human health and measures to protect the environment. Indeed, it appears already from the wording of Article 174 (ex 130r) E.C. that environmental measures also aim at protecting human health. Furthermore, substances may be banned or restricted in use in one Member State because that state mainly considers their negative effect on the environment, whereas another Member State considers their effect on human health; examples of this are lead, cadmium or PCB.

6—38 The Community measures for restricting the use of chrysotile asbestos—the only asbestos fibre the use of which had remained permissible at Community level—applied to about 40 per cent of all asbestos-containing products. Since some Member States considered these measures insufficient, they progressively banned all asbestos products at national level. Instead of taking action against these—until now nine—Member States for not complying with the requirements of Directive 76/769, the Commission prepared a total ban of such asbestos at Community level, which was finally adopted in 1999.[23]

---

[16] Dir. 94/60 [1994] O.J. L365/1; Dir. 97/56 [1997] O.J. L333/1, which lists some 800 carcinogens.
[17] Dir. 94/60 (n. 16).
[18] Dir. 97/16 [1997] O.J. L116/31.
[19] Commission proposal for a directive, COM (83) 556 of September 9, 1983 and [1990] O.J. C30/89.
[20] Reg. 793/93 (n. 69).
[21] See Written Questions 2098/85 (Staes) [1986] O.J. C137/12 (on HCH, lindane and bromophos); 2695/85 (Schmid) [1986] O.J. C299/16 (on paradichlorbenzole); 632/88 (Glinne) [1989] O.J. C132/31 (on impregnating sprays); 778/89 (Schmid) [1990] O.J. C125/14 (on azo-colours); E-2336/91 (Glinne) [1994] O.J. C140/1 (on parathion).
[22] Since the adoption of Dir. 94/60 (n. 16).
[23] See Written Question P-591/96 (Féret) [1996] O.J. C183/39, where the Commission again accepts that the national initiatives distort the internal market: Environmental Watch, February 6, 1998, p. 1; Dir. 1999/77 [1999] O.J. L207/18.

When Directive 91/173 introduced limitations on the use of pentachlorophenol, Germany notified its intention under (ex) Article 100a(4) E.C. to maintain a total ban for this product. The Commission accepted this ban; however, on the request of France, the Court of Justice annulled that decision, because it had not been sufficiently justified.[24] The Commission then took a second decision,[25] which was not contested. Now the Amsterdam Treaty has considerably amended the former Article 100a(4) E.C., by sharpening the different requirements.

6—39   At international level, discussions are going on within the framework of the Geneva Convention on Long Range Transboundary Air Pollution[26] to have a number of persistent organic pollutants[27] controlled, reduced or eliminated. These substances at present include aldrin, chlordane, chlordecone, DDT and dieldrin. The Protocol is likely to be opened for signature in 1999. It is as yet uncertain whether the Community will adhere to the Protocol and how and when it will put into operation the requirements flowing out of it.

(h) Pesticides and biocides

6—40   Pesticides in Community terminology are subdivided into agricultural (plant protection products) and non-agricultural (biocides) pesticides. As regards agricultural pesticides, of which some 20,000 with about 700 active substances are thought to be on the market, Directive 91/414 deals with the authorisation for their placing on the market[28]; Directive 79/117 with the ban of certain pesticides[29]; Directive 78/631 concerns the classification, packaging and labelling of dangerous pesticides[30]; and a number of directives deal with pesticide residues on and in fruit and vegetables, cereals and foodstuffs of animal origin.[31]

(i) Plant protection products

6—41   Directive 91/414, proposed by the Commission in 1976 and adopted, based on Article 37 (ex 43) E.C. in 1991, regulates the placing on the market of plant protection products (agricultural pesticides). The Directive differentiates between products that have to authorised by the individual Member States and the active substances for such products (which are authorised by the Community). An agricultural pesticide may only be authorised to be placed on the market if it contains an active substance that is listed—and is thus authorised Community-wide—in Directive 91/414.[32] The Directive fixes a

---

[24] Case C-41/93 *France v. Commission* [1994] E.C.R. I-1829.
[25] Dec. 94/783 [1994] O.J. L316/43; see also Dec. 96/211 [1996] O.J. L68/32 concerning more restrictive measures in Denmark.
[26] The Community adhered to the Convention by Dec. 81/462 [1981] O.J. L171/11.
[27] These so-called "POPs" are defined as organic compounds that possess toxic characteristics, are persistent, are liable to bioaccumulate, are prone to long-range transboundary atmospheric transport and deposition and can result in adverse environmental and human health effects at locations near and far from their sources.
[28] Dir. 91/414 concerning the placing of plant protection products on the market [1991] O.J. L230/1.
[29] Dir. 79/117 prohibiting the placing on the market and use of plant protection products containing certain active substances [1979] O.J. L33/36.
[30] Dir. 78/631 on the approximation of the laws of the Member States relating to the classification, packaging and labelling of dangerous preparations (pesticides) [1978] O.J. L206/13.
[31] Dir. 76/895 relating to the fixing of maximum levels for pesticide residues in and on fruit and vegetables [1976] O.J. L340/26; Dir. 86/362 on the fixing of maximum levels for pesticide residues in and on cereals [1986] O.J. L221/37; Dir. 86/363 on the fixing of maximum levels for pesticide residues in and on foodstuffs of animal origin [1986] O.J. L221/43; Dir. 90/642 on the fixing of maximum levels for pesticide residues in and on certain products of plant origin, including fruit and vegetables [1990] O.J. L350/71.
[32] Extensive transition periods ensure that pesticides may continue to be marketed, even where the Community authorisation of the active substance is not yet finished.

number of conditions for the authorisation of pesticides, such as the requirement that the pesticide may not have unacceptable effects on plants, does not have damaging effects on the health of humans or animals or on the groundwater[33] or does not have unacceptable effects on the environment in general.

The authorisation is valid for the Member State for which it was requested. However, Member States are also obliged to recognise a pesticide that was authorised in another Member State on their own territory, provided the "relevant agricultural, plant health and environmental (including climatic) conditions" are comparable in the regions concerned; the applicant has to demonstrate this comparability. Supplementary conditions may be linked to such a recognition.

6—42 Active substances are assessed, as regards their effects, by a Community mechanism. Applicants must submit detailed dossiers, which are examined and assessed, on the basis of a Member State's report, by the Standing Committee on Plant Health[34]; the substance is, after a positive decision, registered in annex I of Directive 91/414. At present, annex I provisionally contains 90 active substances, which the Commission has decided to examine by way of priority.[35] The programme for examining existing active substances is to be finished by the year 2003; no final inclusion into annex I—which is normally made for a period of 10 years—has yet taken place. In the meantime, the Commission and Member States accept that some pesticides are banned or not authorised in one Member State,[36] but are permitted to be used in other Member States, which is clearly not compatible with considerations of free circulation of pesticides, but also cannot be prevented.

Where the examination reveals that the requirements for an E.C.-wide authorisation of the active substance are not fulfilled, the Commission takes a decision, addressed to the Member States, asking them to repeal all authorisation for pesticides that contain that active substance.[37]

Directive 91/414 was progressively transposed into national law, though Greece and Germany were condemned by the Court of Justice for not having transposed it in time[38]; Austria, too, was late in transposing it.

(ii) Biocides

6—43 The Directive on the authorisation of non-agricultural pesticides (biocides), was adopted in 1998, on the basis of Article 95 (ex 100a) E.C.[39] It concerns pesticides

---

[33] Dir. 94/43 ([1994] O.J. L227/31), which inserted annex VI into the Directive, limited this examination to the effects of the pesticide on groundwater which was used for the production of drinking water. The Court of Justice considered this to be a significant amendment of Directive 91/414, on which the Council should have consulted the European Parliament, case C-303/94, *European Parliament v. Council* [1996] ECR I-2943; thus, Dir. 94/43 was replaced by Dir. 97/57 [1997] O.J. L265/87.

[34] This Committee was set up by Dec. 76/894 [1976] O.J. L340/25.

[35] Reg. 3600/92 [1992] O.J. L366/10; Reg. 933/94 [1994] O.J. L107/8; this regulation also lists the producers which had applied for the authorisation of the pesticide.

[36] See, for instance, Written Question 2600/88 (Megahy) [1989] O.J. C276/30, where the Commission stated that captan is banned in one Member State, dinoseb in seven, methylbromid restricted for use in three, parathion in two and phosdrin in four Member States. Another well-known case is that of Atrazina, which is banned in several Member States, but authorised in others.

[37] See, for example, Dec. 95/276 [1995] O.J. L170/22, repealing the authorisation for pesticides containing the active substances ferbam and azinphosetyle; Dec. 98/269 [1998] O.J. L117/13 repealing the authorisation for pesticides containing the substance dinoterb; this substance was listed mutagenic in Dir. 97/56 (n. xxx), no. 31; Dec. 98/270 [1998] O.J. L117/15 repealing the authorisation for pesticides containing the substance benvalerat.

[38] Case 380/95 *Commission v. Greece* [1996] E.C.R. I-4837; C-137/96 *Commission v. Germany* [1997] E.C.R. I-6749.

[39] Dir. 98/8 concerning the placing of biocidal products on the market [1998] O.J. L123/1; Commission proposal [1993] O.J. C239/3; Opinion, European Parliament [1996] O.J. C141/176.

such as disinfectants, preservatives, pest-control products, anti-foulants and insecticides—overall, some 15,000 products. These products are grouped in 23 product types, which constitute an exhaustive list for the Directive's application.

The structure of this Directive is very similar to that of Directive 91/414. New active substances will be authorised by the Community and inserted into a positive list (annex I). The evaluation will be based on the report of a Member State, which acts as rapporteur and which will receive data from the applying manufacturer. Existing active substances will be assessed as to whether they can be inserted into annex I; it is thought that this review programme will take 10 years.

Biocidal products will continue to be authorised by the different Member States, on the basis of common principles which are laid down in the Directive. Authorisations given in one Member State must in principle be recognised by other Member States.

(iii) Ban of plant protection products

6—44 Bans and restrictions of use of agricultural pesticides are, at present, regulated by Directive 79/117, which is based on Article 94 (ex 100) E.C. and which contains a positive list of pesticides that are banned for use within the Community.[40] This list is regularly updated. Member States are, however, entitled temporarily to authorise the use of the banned pesticides for specific purposes.

The list enumerates, among others, aldrin, dieldrin, chlordan, DDT, heptachlor and hexachlorbenzol. With the progressive coming into effect of Directive 91/414 and its positive list of active substances, Directive 79/117 will lose its importance for the Community internal market.

(i) Products from biotechnology

6—45 Community legislation on biotechnology and products derived from biotechnology, which started in the mid-1980s, is scattered, because (in particular in the areas of agriculture and food on the one hand, and of pharmaceuticals on the other hand) numerous directives fix specific provisions for certain products; these provisions are not presented here, since they concern the sectors of agriculture, consumer protection, health or industrial policy. As regards the environment, two basic directives, on the contained use of genetically modified micro-organisms[41] and on the deliberate release of genetically modified organisms,[42] were adopted in 1990. A third directive, on the legal protection of biotechnological inventions, was adopted in 1998, after 10 years of discussion at Community level.[43] This Directive is based on Article 95 (ex 100a) E.C. It provides for the protection of such inventions by national patent law of Member States and completes these provisions with a number of common rules.

Directive 90/219 on the contained use of genetically modified micro-organisms[44] is based on Article 175 (ex 130s) E.C. It defines micro-organisms as any microbiological entity, cellular or non-cellular, capable of replication or of transferring genetic material; this definition shows that the Directive deals with living beings, which are, for economic reasons, treated as chemicals. The Directive divides contained-use operations into those which are for teaching, research, development or non-industrial or non-commercial purposes and which are of small scale (type A operations) and other

---

[40] Dir. 79/117 prohibiting the placing on the market and use of plant protection products containing certain active substances [1979] O.J. L33/36.

[41] Dir. 90/219 [1990] O.J. L117/1.

[42] Dir. 90/220 [1990] O.J. L117/15.

[43] Dir. 98/44 [1998] O.J. L213/13.

[44] Dir. 90/219 (n. 41).

(type B) operations. Before an installation is used, a notification has to be made to the competent authorities, which describes the work, the scale of the operation and an "assessment of the contained uses as regards the risks to human health and the environment that may occur". The amount of information to be notified depends, furthermore, on the type of micro-organisms and the operations to be carried out. If new aspects become known, which might affect the risk, this information must also be conveyed. Also, information on any accident—"any incident involving a significant and unintended release . . . which could present an immediate or delayed hazard to human health or the environment"—that has occurred, has to be given to the authorities.

6—46   The competent authorities shall examine the completeness of the information received. In certain cases, operations may not begin before consent is given; in other cases, a waiting period of 60 to 90 days must be respected. The authorities may put conditions for the operations to be carried out, may provide a consultation of "groups or the public" and may generally take all measures that they consider necessary.

Directive 90/219 was transposed on time only by Belgium, Denmark, Germany, Netherlands and the United Kingdom.[45] Greece and Luxembourg have since been condemned by the Court of Justice for not having transposed the Directive[46]; in the intervening period, all Member States, except Luxembourg, transposed the Directive; as regards Belgium, Germany and Portugal, the transposition has not completely conformed to the requirements of the Directive.[47]

6—47   Since, in particular, economic operators considered several provisions of the Directive too restrictive—including the "small scale" requirement—a major amendment of the Directive was adopted in 1998.[48] The different procedures were simplified; notably the procedures for the risk assessment of the operation were specified in more detail, and the number of micro-organisms that come into the lower categories of risky organisms was considerably increased. It is likely that the infringement procedures for partial conformity, started under Directive 90/219, will become redundant with this revision.

Directive 90/220,[49] which is based on Article 95 (ex 100a) E.C., deals with the deliberate release into the environment of genetically modified organisms (GMOs) and of products that contain such organisms. The Directive distinguishes between releases for research and development purposes and the placing on the market of products containing GMOs. A deliberate release for research and development must be notified in advance to the competent authority of the Member State in which the release is to take place, and be accompanied by a technical dossier; this dossier shall contain, amongst other things, information on the interactions between the GMO(s) and the environment, on monitoring, control, waste treatment and emergency response plans, and an impact and risk evaluation posed by the GMO for human health or the environment. The notification is sent, in summary form, to the European Commission, which transmits it to all other Member States. The competent authority may consult "groups or the public" on the deliberate release; it has to assess the notification, consider eventual observations by other Member States and has to consent to the release or reject the notification within 90 days.

6—48   Also, where a product containing GMOs is intended to be placed on the

---

[45] Commission, 10th report on monitoring application of Community law (1992) [1993] O.J. C233/1 at p. 186.

[46] Case C-170/94 *Commission v. Greece* [1995] E.C.R. I-1819; case C-312/95 *Commission v. Luxembourg* [1996] E.C.R. I-5143.

[47] Commission, 14th report (n. 97), p. 183

[48] Dir. 98/81 [1998] O.J. L330/13.

[49] Dir. 90/220 (n. 42).

market, there shall be prior notification accompanied by a detailed technical dossier, indications for use and handling as well as proposals for labelling and packaging. The notification is examined, including the environmental risk assessment and the recommended precautions related to the safe use of the product. Within 90 days, the notification is either rejected or forwarded to the Commission with a favourable opinion. The Commission distributes the notification to the other Member States. If no objection is raised within 60 days, the competent authority that received the notification shall, in writing, give consent to the placing on the market. In this case, the product may be placed on the market within the whole of the Community. Informing or consulting with the public is foreseen neither for the Commission nor for the competent authority.

Where a Member State raises an objection—which must be reasoned—the decision on the placing of the market of the product is taken by the competent authority of the Member State, after a positive Commission decision, taken by way of a committee procedure (Article 21 of Directive 90/220). In view of the considerable objections against the deliberate release of genetically modified organisms from several Member States and from the public, the Commission proposed—and has practised since 1997—that all applications for a release against which an objection is raised be submitted to the different scientific committees set up by the Commission.[50]

6—49   Where, subsequent to the scientific committee's advice, the Commission makes a proposal that conforms with the application of the notifying Member State, and aims at authorising the marketing of the product, this proposal cannot be rejected by the committee, since this would, because of Article 250 (ex 189a) E.C., require unanimous opinion of the committee. The same is true where the committee does not take a decision and the matter is then referred to the Council: the Council may, by qualified majority, approve the Commission's proposal for a decision, but may only reject it by unanimity.

Directive 90/220 was transposed with delay by Greece, Spain, France, Ireland, Italy, Luxembourg and Portugal.[51] Greece and Luxembourg were condemned by the Court of Justice for not having transposed the Directive[52]; by the end of 1996, all Member States except Luxembourg had transposed the Directive; legislation in Belgium, Germany and Portugal did not completely conform to the Directive's requirements.[53]

6—50   Up to the end of 1997, some 600 experimental releases into the environment had taken place, about half of them on colza seedlings.[54] The Commission even adopted a decision for a simplified procedure concerning the release of genetically modified plants.[55] A number of decisions on placing products containing GMOs on the market were taken,[56] although sometimes 13 of the 15 Member States objected.[57] The political, environmental and scientific differences among Member States on the placing

---

[50] See Dec. 97/579 [1997] O.J. L237/18 setting up the scientific committees; see also Written Question E-4222 (Schleicher) [1998] O.J. C310/15.
[51] Commission, 10th report (n. 45), p. 187
[52] Case C-170/94 (n. 46); case C-312/95 (n. 46).
[53] Commission, 14th report (n. 97), p. 183.
[54] Written Question E-3154/97 (Watts) [1998] O.J. C134/99.
[55] Dec. 94/730 [1994] O.J. L292/31.
[56] See, for instance, Dec. 96/281 [1996] O.J. L107/10; Dec. 97/98 [1997] O.J. L31/69; Dec. 97/392 [1997] O.J. L162/38; Dec. 98/291 [1998] O.J. L131/26; Dec. 98/292 [1998] O.J. L131/28; Dec. 98/293 [1998] O.J. L131/30; Dec. 98/294 [1998] O.J. L131/32.
[57] See European Parliament, Res. of April 8, 1997 [1997] O.J. C132/29, Environmental Watch, July 3, 1996, which reports that only France had supported the proposal to allow the marketing of maize; yet later the Commission authorised the marketing, since the Council was not able to reach unanimity for rejection (Dec. 97/98 (n. 56)).

of the market of genetically modified products, which mainly stem from concerns on the long-term environmental and health effects of such products and which are supported by large parts of the public, also became visible, when Austria and Luxembourg provisionally prohibited the placing on the market of genetically modified maize despite a Commission decision to the contrary.[58] France banned the use of such maize for crops,[59] and this controversy is still pending.

In order to mitigate concerns of consumers and public opinion, the Council adopted a regulation on novel food,[60] which requires food products that contain GMOs to be authorised E.C.-wide or—where there the risk is less great—notified and bear a corresponding label, insofar as differences to normal food products can scientifically be detected. Standards for the concrete application of these labelling provisions were lacking until mid-1999; furthermore, a number of food additives are not covered by the legislation. The overall effect of Regulation 258/97, therefore, is limited.

6—51   The Commission also made a proposal for amending several provisions of Directive 90/220, in order to draw conclusions from the Directive's application, to include some ethical considerations in the objectives of the Directive, to improve the safety and risk assessment, systematically to consult its scientific committees and to meet public concern by a number of other procedural measures.[61] This proposal is still under discussion.

The problem with genetically modified organisms is that once they are released into the environment they cannot be taken back. From that angle, the public request, based on the precautionary principle, to err on the side of caution, is more than understandable. However, it seems that in view of the worldwide development and expansion of this new technology—in particular in agriculture, food and pharmaceuticals—the large-scale introduction of genetically modified organisms into the environment is no longer reversible.

(j) PVC

6—52   Polyvinyl chloride (PVC) is a chemical preparation that is at present produced in quantities of about 5 million tonnes per year within the Community. It is mainly used as building material (about 55 per cent), packaging (14 per cent), and in toys, cars, pipes, etc. More than half of the PVC consists of chlorine, an irritant that is not found in other plastic raw material. In order to ensure the specific properties of PVC, the use of additives—plasticisers and stabilisers—is necessary. The main plasticisers are phthalates, of which several hundred exist. The Community classified DEHP, the most commonly used phthalate, as not carcinogenic, but did not take a final classification decision on its other dangerous properties.[62] At present, DEHP and two other phthalates are subject of a risk evaluation of Regulation 793/93. Phthalates are suspected to have long-term negative effects in the aquatic environment and to be endocrine disruptors, which may disturb the hormone system of mammals and humans. Stabilisers used in PVC are mainly lead and cadmium (both toxic and bioaccumulative) and organo-tin compounds (which are considered toxic to the aquatic environment). Substitutes, mainly on the basis of barium-zinc or calcium-zinc, exist, but are less often used, for economic reasons. Manufacturing of PVC creates some

---

[58] Dec. 97/98 (n. 56) and Written Question P-1187/97 (Raschhofer) [1997] O.J. C373/82.
[59] Written Question E-0832/97 (Rauti) [1998] O.J. C45/8.
[60] Reg. 258/97 [1997] O.J. L43/1; see also Commission Reg. 1813/97 [1997] O.J. L257/7.
[61] [1998] O.J. C139/1.
[62] Commission Dec. 90/420 [1990] O.J. L222/49.

environmental problems; however, the main problems occur during its use, incineration (which generates hydrochloric acids, residues with high concentrations of heavy metals and dioxins) and landfill (where a risk of leaching of heavy metals exist). Recycling of PVC proves, at present, extremely difficult.

6—53   There is little Community legislation on PVC. Directive 86/280[63] establishes water-emission limit values for 1.2-dichlorethane (EDC), another additive of PVC; however, no air-emission standards have ever been fixed for this substance or for other componants of PVC. Cadmium is limited for use in many PVC applications. As regards incineration, Directive 94/67 on the incineration of hazardous waste fixes air-emission standards, particularly for dioxins[64]; however, PVC waste is not classified as hazardous waste and no dioxin standards as yet exist for the incineration of non-hazardous waste.

A Community recommendation of 1998 suggested to Member States that they take the necessary measures in order to ensure a high level of health protection of toys destined to be put in the mouth by small children and which contained certain phthalates.[65] The Commission did not specify what such necessary measures were. Before and after this recommendation, some Member States adopted measures to prohibit the use of some phthalates in toys.

6—54   A number of Member States and third countries have looked into the question whether, in view of its environmental effects at the waste stage, it would not be appropriate to restrict the use of PVC generally. In its proposal on the directive for end-of-life vehicles, the Commission made some remarks on this point.[66] Should a restriction on the use of PVC ever come into force, this would constitute the first Community measure with regard to a product in view of its behaviour in the waste stage. Since any restriction of the use of PVC is heavily opposed by economic operators, such Community action is not very likely to succeed. Rather, it may be expected that measures are taken against some PVC additives—cadmium, lead and phthalates—and not against PVC itself.

3. ENVIRONMENTAL LABELLING

6—55   The Community has developed a number of environmental labels[67] that either signal to consumers or users that the product bears some risk for the environment, that it was produced in a specific way, or that it has some specific characteristics with regard to the environment.

(a) Chemicals that are dangerous for the environment

6—56   Directive 67/548[68] on dangerous chemical substances was amended in 1979 to include a label "dangerous to the environment". The label consists of a symbol showing a dead fish beached beside a dead tree, both in black on a yellow-orange

---

[63] Dir. 86/280 [1986] O.J. L181/16.

[64] Dir. 94/67 [1994] O.J. L365/34.

[65] Rec. 98/485 [1998] O.J. L217/35.

[66] [1997] O.J. C337/3: "the Commission will consider the evidence regarding the environmental aspects relating to the presence of PVC in waste streams; on the basis of this evidence, the Commission will review its policy regarding the presence of PVC in waste streams".

[67] See also the definition of the International Standardisation Organisation ISO for environmental labels: "A logo or a symbol attached to a product which is awarded by a third-party, agency or non-governmental organisation and which is based on multiple criteria and lifecycle analysis." A second type of eco-labels includes claims of single attributes, such as "energy efficient".

[68] Dir. 67/548 (n. 79).

background; the symbol is accompanied by phrases on the special risks (R-phrases) and on the safe use of the substance (S-phrases). By the end of 1997, some 175 substances were labelled with the symbol "dangerous for the environment".[69] This seems few substances; however, some thousand substances from petrol refining, such as aromatic hydrocarbons, naphta, extracts and distillates, which are classified "toxic", do not bear this label, though they obviously appear to be dangerous for the environment. This is also true of substances where the indication "may cause cancer" is obligatory. Thus, it must be presumed that the testing methods for allowing a proper classification are not yet completely developed. Furthermore, the label is not mandatory for toxic substances (Article 23 of Directive 67/548).

Among the risk phrases (R-phrases) developed under Directive 67/548, the following phrases specifically refer to environmental risks: "very toxic to aquatic organisms" (R 50); "toxic to aquatic organisms" (R 51); "harmful to aquatic organisms" (R 52); "may cause long-term adverse effects in the aquatic environment" (R 53); "toxic to flora" (R 54); "toxic to fauna" (R 55); "toxic to soil organisms" (R 56); "toxic to bees" (R 57); "may cause long-term adverse effects in the environment" (R 58); "dangerous for the ozone layer" (R 59); "very toxic to aquatic organisms, may cause long-term adverse effects in the aquatic environment" (R 50/53); "toxic to aquatic organisms, may cause long-term adverse effects in the aquatic environment" (R 51/53); "harmful to aquatic organisms, may cause long-term adverse effects in the aquatic environment" (R 52/53). These phrases are obviously centred on damage to the aquatic environment. This corresponds to the above-mentioned fact that testing methods for measuring the ecotoxicity of chemical substances are not yet very numerous.

6—57 Safety phrases (S-phrases) that refer to the environment include: "do not empty into drains" (S 29); "dispose of this material and its container at hazardous or special waste collection point" (S 56); "use appropriate container to avoid environmental contamination" (S 57); "this material and its container must be disposed of as hazardous waste" (S 60); "avoid release to the environment. Refer to special instructions/safety data sheets" (S 61).

Austria had, when acceding to the Community in 1995, national symbols "do not put into drains" and "do not put into the waste bin". Under the Accession Treaty, it was allowed to maintain this legislation until 1999[70]; however, it has not yet persuaded the other Member States to adopt these symbols at Community level.

The symbol "dangerous for the environment" has existed, until now, only for chemical substances; most of those are used in industrial processes, but are not sold to consumers. For chemical preparations, which are principally available to consumers/users, no symbol "dangerous for the environment" as yet exists, but it is planned to introduce such a symbol at Community level in the near future.

Pesticides labelling is not included in the present labelling requirements for dangerous preparations: there is some pressure from economic operators to see pesticide labelling be more dependent on risks from exposure under field conditions rather than on the product's intrinsic hazards. If this suggestion were followed, this would signify a decisive change in the Community's legislative approach.

---

[69] Dir. 94/69 adapting Dir. 67/548 for the 21st time to technical progress [1994] O.J. L381/1; Dir. 96/54 adapting Dir. 67/548 for the 22nd time to technical progress [1996] O.J. L248/1.
[70] Accession Treaty between Austria, Sweden and Finland and the European Community [1994] O.J. C241/1, annex VIII (p. 305).

(b) Separate collection

6—58 Directive 91/157 on batteries[71] contains a symbol indicating "separate collection" of batteries, which consists of a roll-out container crossed through, accompanied by an indication of which heavy metal is involved (Hg for mercury, Cd for cadmium or Pb for lead). This symbol is to be placed on batteries only and indicates that they are subject to separate collection, and shall not be put in a normal wastebin. The roll-out container crossed through corresponds to the symbol used in Austria for all separate collection requirements.[72]

Under Directive 91/689,[73] the Community has to consider elaborating a directive on hazardous household waste. Reflections within the Commission are to extend the symbol used in Directive 91/157 to all household items which, as waste, shall be collected separately and not be put into normal wastebins.

(c) Eco-labelling

6—59 As described in more detail in paragraphs 4–34 *et seq.*, above, the Community has, since 1992, developed a system for voluntary participation in an eco-labelling scheme.[74] The symbol of the scheme is a stylised flower, the crown of which consists of stars and where the centre constitutes an "E". The system coexists with national eco-label schemes, which is probably the main reason why the less-known Community label is so rarely used.

(d) Label on organic agricultural production

6—60 Regulation 2092/91[75] instituted the option for agricultural products that stem from organic farming to bear the word "organic", provided the conditions laid down in the regulation are fulfilled.[76]

There are, to date, no labels or other distinctive signs for biological pesticides.[77]

(e) Recyclable packaging

6—61 Under Directive 94/62 on waste and packaging waste[78] the Commission made a proposal for the marking of packaging that is reusable or recyclable.[79] The symbols consist of different round circles. The proposal attempts to create new, specific Community symbols. Since economic operators orient themselves more and more to the U.S. system for labelling of packaging that also is promoted through international standardisation organisations, the adoption of a specific Community symbol for reusable/recyclable packaging is not very likely.

(f) Energy labelling

6—62 The Community discussion on the labelling of energy consumption of electrical household appliances started about 20 years ago. However, attempts to

---

[71] Dir. 91/157 on batteries and accumulators containing certain dangerous substances [1991] O.J. L78/38, as amended by Dir. 93/86 [1993] O.J. L264/51.
[72] See above, para. 6–57.
[73] Dir. 91/689 on hazardous waste [1991] O.J. L377/20.
[74] See for more details above, para. 4–34.
[75] Reg. 2092/91 on organic production of agricultural products and indications referring thereto on agricultural products and foodstuffs [1991] O.J. L198/1.
[76] See for more details below, para. 10–10.
[77] Written Question E-1761/97 (Mulder) [1998] O.J. C76/53.
[78] Dir. 94/62 [1994] O.J. L365/10.
[79] [1996] O.J. C382/10.

obtain solutions via industrial standardisation and voluntary agreements with manufacturers failed.[80] This has led the Community to develop, since the early 1990s,[81] environmental labels for electrical household appliances, which are—somehow too narrowly—called energy labels. Indeed, the labels indicate, according to national standards or other provisions fixed in the annexes and in a graphically fixed scheme:

- the energy consumption, marked on a seven-point scale, whether the appliance is "more efficient" or "less efficient"[82];

- the (washing, drying or cleaning, etc.) performance, expressed on a seven-point scale from higher to lower;

- the water consumption expressed in litres per cycle;

- the noise level, expressed in dB(A).

Until now, such energy labels have been fixed for refrigerators, freezers and their combinations,[83] washing machines,[84] electric tumble driers,[85] combined washer-driers[86] and dishwashers.[87]

The label is relatively detailed and provides for a considerable amount of information to consumers. Its actual efficiency is very difficult to assess.

(g) Labelling of products containing genetically modified organisms

6—63 In order to meet public concern within the Community regarding the placing on the market of products that contain genetically modified organisms, the Community adopted, in 1997, a regulation[88] that provides food labels to indicate that the food contains genetically modified organisms; however, this requirement only applies to those cases where differences between such food products and normal food products can be scientifically detected. Since this label neither covers all products nor all products that contain genetically modified organisms—estimations indicate that 90 per cent of all food products will not be covered by the labelling requirements—it will not allow consumers systematically to avoid such products. The large-scale introduction of products which contain genetically modified organisms cannot be stopped by such a measure; at best it will be slowed down.

(h) Car fuel labelling

6—64 The Commission made a proposal, based on Article 175 (ex 130s) E.C., that all new passenger cars at the point of sale bear a label on the official fuel consumption and their average carbon dioxide emissions[89]; the amended proposal also provides for the handing out of a brochure to the consumer informing him of fuel economy data,

---

[80] See Economic and Social Committee [1995] O.J. C155/19, no. 2.7.
[81] Dir. 92/75 on the conservation of energy and other resources by household appliances [1992] O.J. L297/16.
[82] The German, Danish, Greek, Italian, Finnish and Swedish labels mention instead "high consumption" or "low consumption"; the Dutch label mentions "efficient" and "inefficient".
[83] Dir. 94/2 [1994] O.J. L45/1.
[84] Dir. 95/12 [1995] O.J. L136/1.
[85] Dir. 95/13 [1995] O.J. L136/28.
[86] Dir. 96/60 [1996] O.J. L266/1.
[87] Dir. 97/17 [1997] O.J. L118/1.
[88] Reg. 258/97 (n. 60).
[89] Commission, Proposal for a directive relating to the availability of consumer information on fuel economy in respect of the marketing of new passenger cars [1998] O.J. C305/2; amended [1999] O.J. C83/1.

the 10 cars with the lowest carbon dioxide emissions and advising him or her on driving habits to lower fuel consumption.

4. IMPORTS AND EXPORTS OF PRODUCTS

(a) Imports

6—65   Community legislation generally provides that products that are placed on the Community market must comply with Community legal requirements. This rule applies to practically all products that are imported into the Community.

For some agricultural products, also, the production methods are fixed by Community provisions. Where this is the case, the agricultural directives or regulations normally provide that the import into the Community is authorised, provided the production methods in the exporting countries are equivalent to those of the Community. An example of this is Article 11 of Regulation 2092/91 on organic farming,[90] which authorises the marking as "organic" for products from third countries, too, provided that country is on a Community list of authorised countries and provided that a number of other conditions are fulfilled. For meat imports, the Community has even set up a system of controlling, on a worldwide scale, the hygienic conditions in slaughterhouses of third countries; where these conditions are considered equivalent, the slaughterhouse is taken up in a Community list of installations from which meat imports are authorised.

No such provisions exist for industrial products. Regulation 2455/92[91] provides that where a third country notifies an E.C. Member State of the export to the Community of a chemical substance that is banned or restricted in use in that third country, that notification shall be sent to the Commission and hence to all other Member States. The regulation does not provide for any other follow up; neither does it provide for any systematic notification of third countries to the Commission nor to Member States. In substance, thus, no import requirements for industrial or chemical products exist at present.[92] By the end of 1996, 311 import notifications on chemicals from third countries were made; import quantities are not known.[93]

(b) Exports

6—66   Exports of the Community follow the international voluntary principle of "prior informed consent" (PIC).[94] Regulation 2455/92, which makes this principle mandatory for the Community exporters—at present, no other country in the world has a mandatory PIC system—also refers to exports from the Community of chemicals that are "banned or severely restricted on account of their effects on human health and the environment". Chemicals which come under the Regulation are mainly added subsequent to amendments of Directives 76/769 and 79/117[95]; by mid-1998 39 groups of substances that cover more than 200 chemicals were listed in annex I. The exporter of chemicals that are covered by the Regulation shall notify his intention to export a

---

[90] Reg. 2092/91 (n. 75).

[91] Reg. 2455/92 concerning the export and import of certain dangerous chemicals [1992] O.J. L251/13.

[92] See also para. 5–25 as regards import restrictions on endangered fauna and flora species.

[93] Commission, Report on the operation of Regulation 2455/92, COM (1998) 245 of April 28, 1998.

[94] Regulation 2455/92 (n. 91), Art. 2(7), defines as follows: "prior informed consent (PIC) means the principle that international shipment of a chemical which is banned or severely restricted in order to protect human health or the environment should not proceed without the agreement, where such agreement exists, or contrary to the decision of the designated national authority of the importing country".

[95] Dir. 76/769 (n. 21); Dir. 79/117 (n. 40).

product for the first time to the competent authority of the Member State where he is established at least 30 days before the export takes place. The competent authority has to give to that exporter an Export Reference Number (ERN), which is attributed, for each first export, by the European Commission[96]; it must also ensure that the authorities of the import country receive all appropriate information 15 days prior to the export. Subsequent exports of the same chemical need not be notified, but shall make reference to the ERN. Up to mid-1997, some 550 notifications for first-time exports had taken place.[97]

6—67 The export itself is not prohibited or limited; nor is it dependent on a reaction from the importing country. The PIC principle only requires that the third country has the opportunity to react, not that it react. An export ban for products which are banned within the Community was considered excessive, since it was argued that the climatic, economic and environmental conditions can differ from one country to another, as can the pest problems for which a pesticide may be used.

These arguments[98] will have to be weighed against the fact that administrations in third countries do not always seem to be able fully to assess the impact of chemicals which it is intended are to be imported. Also, the World Health Organisation estimates that every year a considerable number of persons suffer acute unintentional poisoning as a result of the misuse of pesticides; no figures exist for environmental damage caused by chemicals the use of which is banned or restricted within the Community. These arguments plead, in my opinion, rather in favour of an export ban for chemicals that are banned within the Community or, at least, for an express import authorisation given by third countries. The Commission rejects an export ban, in particular with the argument that the sovereignty of the importing countries would need to be respected.[99]

Attempts to elaborate a worldwide PIC convention on the export and import of chemicals which are banned or restricted are fairly advanced and likely to lead to the conclusion of such a convention in 1999.

5. INDUSTRIAL STANDARDISATION

6—68 Environmental requirements for products—as for processes—may be fixed by legislative regulation, such as, for instance, for emissions from cars. They may also be fixed by industrial technical standards, which are elaborated by private standardisation organisations and the result of which is a technical indication for some product characteristics.

Industrial standards are, by definition, not mandatory. Legally, they constitute a recommendation of the authors to follow the indications laid down in the standard. Their degree of recognition depends on the readiness of producers to apply the standard. Public authorities often support the application of standards, for instance by providing in legislation that standards must be complied with or by not laying down specifications in regulations, but referring to (private) standards, etc.

At Community level, there are no specific Community standardisation organisations.

---

[96] The administrative responsibility for the export/import notification procedure is in the hands of the European Chemicals Bureau, which was set up by Commission Dec. 92/585 in Ispra (Italy).
[97] Commission (n. 93), p. 18. 309 of these came from the United Kingdom, 65 from Spain, 49 from Germany and 46 from Italy.
[98] See also Commission (n. 93) with further discussion of the actual system.
[99] See Written Question E-2054/97 (Iversen) [1998] O.J. C60/79.

Rather, the three organisations that exist are international bodies, which went, right from their beginnings, beyond the borders of the European Community. All three organisations have close relations with national standardisation bodies on the one hand, and with international bodies on the other hand, which include arrangements to avoid the duplication of work.

6—69 CEN (Comité Européen de Normalisation; European Committee for Standardisation) was created in 1961. It is an association under Belgian law, the members of which are national standards institutions of Western European countries and, since 1992, associate members in the form of organisations that represent economic and social interests at European level and which fulfil certain conditions as regards representativity and objectives. About half of CEN's budget is provided for by E.C. funds.

The CEN secretariat is located in Brussels. Since 1989, CEN has had an agreement with the International Standardisation Organisation (ISO), which allows one of the two organisations to allow the other to take the lead on a specific standardisation project. This allows the avoidance of different standards being elaborated at global (ISO) and European (CEN) level.[1]

CEN standards are prepared by technical committees—at present numbering about 300. Programme committees and technical sector boards have the task of providing for co-ordination among these committees. Since the early 1990s, CEN has established a Programming Committee on the "Environment", which, in turn, has set up a working group on "Environmental Aspects in Product Standards"; this group has the task of looking into the environmental aspects of general product standards and to give guidance and make recommendations to standards writers.

6—70 CEN differentiates between direct and indirect standardisation work. Direct standardisation concerns items such as environmental assessment methods; measurement methods for environmental properties of chemicals; pollution control methods and equipment; environmental management tools; and methods for the evaluation of environmental effects of products. Indirect standardisation aspects deal with the environmental aspects of general product standards.

CENELEC (Comité Européen de Normalisation Electrotechnique; European Committee for Electrotechnical Standardisation) began its work in the early 1960s. Since 1972 it has been located in Brussels. Its members are national electrotechnical committees. It elaborates standards in the area of electrical and electronic equipment and roughly one-third of its budget is provided by the European Community. About three-quarters of all CENELEC standards are parallels of international electrotechnical standards.

ETSI (European Telecommunications Standards Institute) was created in 1988 for the telecommunications sector.

6—71 For the Community, industrial standardisation is of growing importance for environmental issues, since the Community opted, in the early 1980s, for a "new approach" to the approximation of national legal rules,[2] by which the Council "emphasizes the importance and desirability of the new approach which provides for reference to standards—primarily European standards, but national ones if need be, as a transitional measure—for the purposes of defining the technical characteristics of products". The same resolution laid down four "fundamental principles" for the new approach:

---

[1] In pursuance of this agreement, CEN decided not to prepare separate environmental management systems, but to adopt the standards ISO 14001 and 14004 prepared by ISO; ISO has also taken the lead for standards on life-cycle assessments.

[2] The definition of "new approach" was first used in COM (85) 19 of January 31, 1985 and Council Resolution of May 7, 1985 ([1985] O.J. C136/1: On a new approach to technical harmonisation and standards).

- "legislative harmonization is limited . . . to the adoption of the essential safety requirements (or other requirements in the general interest) with which products put on the market must conform";

- the task of drawing up the technical specifications of products is done by industrial standardisation organisations,

- these technical standardisations maintain their status of voluntary standards;

- products which conform to harmonised standards are presumed to conform to the essential requirements established by a directive.

6—72   A number of product-related directives have been elaborated since the mid-1980s according to the new approach.[3] However, the essential requirements, laid down in these directives, practically never deal with environmental issues. Thus, the impact of these directives on the environment is limited: indeed, since the protection of the environment is also an essential requirement of Community policy,[4] the omission of the regulation of environmental issues in the context of essential requirements at Community level means that Member States are free to adopt environmental measures at national level as regards these products.

The new approach is certainly not applied systematically. For a number of areas, European standards do not as yet exist, and large sectors such as food and pharmaceuticals, cars and chemicals are not covered by it at all. Its main area of application is the mechanical sector.

6—73   Up to the middle of the midle of 1999, the only environmental directive adopted under the new approach has been the Directive on packaging and packaging waste.[5] This Directive, which is based on Article 95 (ex 100a) E.C., contains an annex which lays down essential requirements for packaging. Thus, packaging shall be:

- so manufactured that the packaging volume and weight is limited to the minimum adequate amount to maintain the necessary level of safety, hygiene and acceptance for the packed product and for the consumer;

- designed, produced and commercialised in such a way as to permit its reuse or recovery, including recycling, and to minimise its impact on the environment when packaging waste or residues from packaging waste management operations are disposed of;

- manufactured so that the presence of noxious and other hazardous substances and materials is minimised with regard to their presence in emissions, ash or leachate, when packaging or residues are incinerated or landfilled.

Whether these provisions will be capable of fulfilment in specific, clear standard requirements, remains to be seen.

6—74   Where the standards do not, in part or in full, comply with the essential requirements of the Directive, the only "sanction" is that the Commission could refuse to recognise them as harmonised standards. This would have as a consequence that the

[3] In particular Dir. 73/23 on low voltage equipment [1973] O.J. 77/29; Dir. 87/404 on pressure vessels [1987] O.J. L220/48; Dir. 87/378 on toy safety [1987] O.J. L187/1; Dir. 89/106 on construction products [1989] O.J. L40/12; Dir. 89/392 on the safety of machines [1989] O.J. L183/9; Dir. 90/396 on appliances burning gaseous fuels [1990] O.J. L196/15; Dir. 92/42 on new hot-water boilers fired with liquid or gaseous fuels [1992] O.J. L167/17; Dir. 94/62 on packaging and packaging waste [1994] O.J. L365/10.
[4] Case 240/83 *Procureur de la République v. Association de Désense de Bruleurs* [1985] E.C.R. 531.
[5] Dir. 94/62 on packaging and packaging waste (n. 5).

presumption—laid down in Article 11(2) of Directive 94/62—according to which a packaging that complies with the standards also complies with the requirements of the Directive would not apply. Member States are then not obliged to admit a packaging on their market that they consider not to comply with the essential requirements, even where the packaging complies with the standards. This would mean that, for instance, Denmark might continue to refuse metal cans on its market with the argument that they do not comply with essential requirements. Other candidates for national measures could be PVC packagings, aerosols or—more generally—plastic or non-biodegradable packagings, where in each case it could be argued that the packaging does not comply with the essential requirements of Directive 94/62.

Obviously, these considerations depend on the determination of Member States to ensure that the essential requirements, laid down in Directive 94/62, really are respected and that they are prepared, eventually, to pursue a national policy as regards packaging.

6—75   The problems of standards for packaging illustrate well the general environmental difficulties with industrial standardisation: the problem how industrial standards can be made greener is not yet solved. Indeed, at national level, public authorities can participate and—in Member States such as Germany or Austria—do participate in the working group that elaborates the technical standard. Their representative may bring into the discussion on the elaboration of a standard environmental aspects and influence the taking into consideration of the general interest. Where they do not succeed in this attempt, they may suggest governmental regulation on the subject covered by the standard, which makes the national standard more or less obsolete.

At Community level, the representatives of economic operators in CEN/CENELEC write their own standards and are hardly influenced at all by environmental organisations, which are too weak and financially too feeble to organise themselves structurally at Community level. Commission officials do not, in practice, participate in the working groups of CEN or CENELEC, and written contributions, if they are made at all, do not significantly influence the making of standards. Until now, no horizontal structures have existed, which would—if instigated in time—change this situation. Despite all discussion on the integration of environmental requirements into industrial standardisation, nothing significant has changed during the last 15 years. Most of the reflections on such new structures aim at the increased participation of environmental organisations in the discussion and decision-making process of CEN and, to a lesser degree, of CENELEC. Other measures discussed are an environmental impact assessment for the subject covered by a standard; the results of this assessment would be incorporated into each CEN standard.

BIBLIOGRAPHY

Anselmann, N.: "Die Bezugnahme auf harmonisierte technische Regeln im Rahmen der Rechtsangleichung" in P. Müller-Graff (ed.), *Technische Regeln im Binnenmarkt* (Baden-Baden, 1991)

Bennett, G. (ed.): *De uitvoering van EG-milieurichtlijnen toegespitst op milieugevaarlijke stoffen* (Zwolle, 1989)

Churchill, R. and Kütting, G.: "International environmental agreements and the free movement of goods in the E.C.: the case of the Montreal Protocol", *European Environmental Law Review* (1995), p. 329

Devos, J.: "Legal Aspects" in *Ullmann's Encyclopedia of Industrial Chemistry* (Weinheim, 1995), Vol. B7, p. 299

Fuchs, W. and Rapsch, A.: "Das deutsche Gentechnikrecht im Lichte quantitativer Vorgaben europarechtlicher Provenienz", *Die öffentliche Verwaltung* (1991), p. 873

Fuehr, M.: *Reform der europäischen Normungsverfahren* (Darmstadt, 1995)

Furrer, A. and Bölscher, V.: "Technische Normen im Spannungsfeld zwischen Umweltschutz und freiem Binnenmarkt", *Zeitschrift für Umweltrecht* (1998), p. 3

Gebers, B. and Jendroska, J. (eds): *Environmental control of products and substances* (Düsseldorf, 1989)

Ginzky, H.: *Saubere Produkte, schmutzige Produktion. Eine Untersuchung zu Importbeschränkungen wegen umweltschädigender Produktionsnormen* (Düsseldorf, 1997)

Goldenmann, G.: "Transboundary transfer of goods" in G. Winter (ed.), *European environmental law. A comparative perspective* (Aldershot, Brooklyn, Sydney and Singapore, 1996), p. 341

Handl, G. and Lutz, R. (eds): *Transferring hazardous technologies and substances: the international legal challenge* (London, Dordrecht and Boston, 1989)

Hunter, R.: "Standardization and the environment", *International Environmental Reporter* (1993), p. 185

Jans, J., Mortelmans, K., Sevenster, H. and Temmink, H.: *Zo sterk als de zwakste schakel: Nederlands produktgericht milieubeleid in Europees en internationaalrechtelijk verband* (Amsterdam, 1993)

Joerges, C., Falke, J., Micklitz, H. and Brüggemeier, G.: *Die Sicherheit von Konsumgütern und die Entwicklung der Europäischen Gemeinschaft* (Baden-Baden, 1988)

Joerissen, J.: *Möglichkeiten und Probleme bei der Verfolgung und Sicherung nationaler und EG-weiter Umweltschutzziele im Rahmen der europäischen Normung (Büro für Technikfolgen-Abschätzung beim Deutschen Bundestag)* (Bonn, 1996)

Joerissen, J.: *Produktbezogener Umweltschutz und technische Normung* (Berlin, 1997)

Lavrysen, L.: "Recent developments in EC policy and law relating to chemicals", *Europarättslig Tidskrift* (1999), p. 285

Leskien, D.: "Gentechnologie und Patentrecht. Zum neuen Richtlinienvorschlag der Europäischen Kommission", *Zeitschrift für Umweltrecht* (1996), p. 299

Marburger, P. and Enders, R.: "Technische Normung im Europäischen Gemeinschaftsrecht", *Jahrbuch des Umwelt- und Technikrechts* (1994), p. 333

Micklitz, H.:"International regulation and control of the production and use of chemicals and pesticides", *Michigan Journal of International Law* (1992), p. 653

Micklitz, H., Roethe, T. and Weatherhill, S. (eds): *Federalism and responsibility—a study on product safety and practice in the E.C.* (London, 1994)

Moreno Molina, A.: "Productos chimicos, biotechnologia, acuerdos voluntarios" in L. Parejo Alfonso and L. Krämer (eds), *Derecho medioambiental de la Unión Europea* (Madrid, 1996), p. 273

Müller-Graff, P. (ed.): *Technische Regeln im Binnenmarkt* (Baden-Baden, 1991)

Nicolas, F. (with J. Repussard): *Common standards for enterprises* (Luxembourg, 1995)

Pagh, P.: "Farlige stoffer og EF-retten", *Ugeskrift for Retsvaesen* (1991), p. B353

Pagh, P.: "Miljoegarantien efter PCP-dommen", *Ugeskrift for Retsvaesen* (1994), p. B276

Pallemaerts, M.: *Production, toxics and transnational law: an inquiry into the effectiveness of international and European Community environmental law* (Brussels, 1998)

Rehbinder, E.: "Das Konzept des anlagen- und produktbezogenen EG-Gentechnikrechts", *Zeitschrift für Umweltrecht* (1999), p. 6

Rengeling, H. (ed.): *Umweltnormung* (Berlin, 1998)

Roethe, T.: "Management von Gefahrstoffrisiken in Regelungsausschüssen der Europäischen

Gemeinschaft" in G. Winter (ed.), *Risikoanalyse und Risikoabwehr im Chemikalienrecht* (Düsseldorf, 1995), p. 115

Rossnagel, A.: "Europäische Techniknormen im Lichte des Gemeinschaftsrechts", *Deutsches Verwaltungsblatt* (1996), p. 1181

Schenek, M.: *Das Gentechnikrecht der Europäischen Gemeinschaft* (Berlin, 1995)

Schweizer, R. and Calame, T.: "Das Gentechnikrecht der EG", *Recht der Internationalen Wirtschaft* (1997), p. 34

Vieweg, K.: "Technische Normen im EG-Binnenmarkt" in C. Müller-Graff (ed.), *Technische Regeln im Binnenmarkt* (Baden-Baden, 1991), p. 57

Vitzthum, W. and Schenk, M.: "Die Europäisierung des Gentechnikrechts" in R. Hrbek, T. Oppermann and J. Starbatty (eds), *Integration Europas und Ordnung der Weltwirtschaft* (Baden-Baden, 1993), p. 47

Winter, G.: "Regelungsmasstäbe im Gefahrstoffrecht", *Deutsches Verwaltungsblatt* (1994), p. 913

Winter, G.: "Maßstäbe der Chemikalienkontrolle im deutschen Recht und im Gemeinschaftsrecht" in G. Winter (ed.), *Risikoanalyse und Risikoabwehr im Chemikalienrecht* (Düsseldorf, 1995), p. 1

CHAPTER 7
Water Protection

1. COMMUNITY WATER POLICY AND LAW

7—01   Community water policy and law is about 25 years old. It has undergone considerable changes and is at present about to be changed again. In its first phase, Community policy was fixed on two objectives; on the one hand, it set quality requirements for specific water uses, such as surface waters, groundwater, bathing or drinking water; on the other hand, it tried to limit discharges of pollutants into the water. In 1988, an interministerial meeting on water policy endeavoured to lay down the principles of a more coherent water policy[1]; however, the objectives identified at this seminar only very partially materialised.

The European Council in Edinburgh, in December 1992, fixed a number of orientations for Community policy and declared, amongst other things, that the Council took note of the Commission's intention to simplify, consolidate and adapt Community environmental legislation.[2] Nowhere was this statement taken more seriously then in the water sector, probably also because the United Kingdom, which had presided over the Edinburgh Council, had just received a judgment from the Court of Justice, which obliged it to make considerable investments in cleaning up drinking water.[3] Subsequent to this Council, and on the repeated insistence of the European Parliament,[4] the Commission published a communication in 1996 on the "European Community Water Policy".[5] This communication fixed as objectives of Community water policy:

- a secure supply of drinking water;

- sufficient quality and quantity of water resources to meet other economic requirements;

- to protect and sustain the good ecological state and functioning of the aquatic environment environment and meet the water needs of wetland and terrestrial ecosystems and habitats;

- the management of water so as to prevent or reduce the impact of floods and droughts.

7—02   These objectives obviously refer to fresh and coastal water rather than, for instance, to oceans. They are targeted to meet, first of all, human needs. The communication stated that the "environmental quality objectives approach" and the "emission limit values approach" were complementary and not contradictory. It

---

[1] It is significant that the conclusions of this seminar were never published; a short report is found in (1988) *Bulletin of the European Communities*, para. 2.1.175; the Council adopted a resolution on the follow-up of the seminar [1988] O.J. C209/3.
[2] See (1992) 12 *Bulletin of the European Communities*, p. 18.
[3] Case C-337/89, *Commission v. United Kingdom*, judgment of November 24, 1992 [1992] E.C.R. I-5973.
[4] See in particular European Parliament, Res. of October 23, 1996 [1996] O.J. C347/80.
[5] COM (96) 59 of February 21, 1996.

continued by stating that quality objectives could either fix common parametric values applicable in all Member States or could be expressed in a form such that common criteria for the establishment of parameters and values were fixed at Community level, but that the values were established at national level, in order "to allow flexibility to adapt to the very different environmental conditions in different parts of the Community". The Commission clearly indicated that it preferred this approach.

The European Parliament was of the opinion that the communication clearly failed in its objective to present a coherent overall concept and requested that the review of water policy should in no way lead to a lowering of standards; as a minimum the fixing of strict and uniform emission standards was necessary.[6]

7—03　As regards legal questions, the first water directives and other measures were regularly based on Articles 95 and 308 (ex 100a and 235) E.C. Since 1987, Article 175 (ex 130s) has become the legal basis for environmental measures, including those on the protection of waters. Such measures requested unanimous decisions, until the Maastricht Treaty introduced, in 1993, majority decisions into Article 175 (ex 130s) E.C. This amendment of the Treaty, however, brought some uncertainty as to the correct legal basis for such measures. Indeed, while Article 175(1) (ex 130s(1)) E.C. provided for majority decisions—with the entry into force of the Amsterdam Treaty in 1999, these will be adopted by way of co-decision between Council and European Parliament—paragraph 2 provided for unanimous decisions by the Council for the "management of water resources".

It is not clear how this notion is to be understood and how measures under Article 175(2) (ex 130s(2)) E.C. shall be differentiated from other measures in the area of water policy, which come under paragraph 1. The wording of the different linguistic versions of Article 175 does not help much, since all versions use expressions similar to "management of water resources".[7] The Dutch version of the Treaty is the only one to add "quantitative" before the word "management". It must be noted, though, that the Treaty does not talk of "water management", but only of management of water resources, which is clearly a narrower concept.

7—04　Past Community measures give little assistance. Where the various Community environmental action programmes mentioned the management of resources or of water resources, they included both quantitative and qualitative aspects.[8] Decision 85/338 on environmental data collection[9] differentiated between water quality and water resources. Regulation 1210/90 on the European Environmental Agency made a distinction, in Article 3(2), between "water quality, dangerous substances and water resources".[10]

The Commission based all its proposals on water measures, both on the quality of bathing or drinking water and on general water measures, on Article 175(1) (ex 130s(1)) E.C., without discussing the alternative of paragraph 2.[11] The Council adhered to the Convention for the protection of the Danube by Decision 97/825,[12] which was based on Article 175(1) (ex 130s(1)) E.C. Against that decision, Spain introduced an application to the Court of Justice, arguing that the decision should have been based on

---

[6] European Parliament, Res. of October 23, 1996 [1996] O.J. C347/80; see also Economic and Social Committee [1996] O.J. C30/5; Committee of the Regions [1997] O.J. C34/30.

[7] German: "Bewirtschaftung der Wasserressourcen"; French: "gestion des ressources hydrauliques"; Dutch: "waterbeheer"; Danish: "forvaltning af vandressourcerne".

[8] See fifth environmental action programme [1993] O.J. C138/5, para. 5.4.

[9] Dec. 85/338 [1985[O.J. L176/14.

[10] Reg. 210/90 [1990] O.J. L120/1.

[11] [1994] O.J. C112/3 (bathing water); 1995] O.J. C131/95 (drinking water); [1997] O.J. C184/20 (framework directive).

[12] Dec. 97/825 [1997] O.J. L342/18.

paragraph 2 of Article 175 (ex 130s) E.C.[13] The Court will probably not decide before the year 2000.

7—05   Jans[14] considers a restrictive interpretation of paragraph 2 "reasonable". Pagh seems to consider the provision as referring to quantitative aspects and to discharges into water.[15] Epiney is of the opinion that "management of water resources" only concerns methods of water use which contain an element of spatial planning; emission limit values or quality standards are not covered by this provision.[16] She comes to this conclusion by pointing to the other categories in paragraph 2—town and country planning, land use—which also deal with spatial planning issues.

Limiting the concept of "management of water resources" to quantitative aspects would certainly bring it closer to the concept of land use, since it would then concern the question of "water use". It is, however, doubtful whether quantitative and qualitative aspects can really be so clearly separated from each other. One underlying reason for the insertion of the concept of management of water resources into the Treaty might also have been that the repartition (the apportioning of a river's water where it crosses a border between Member States) of water resources between diverging Member States implies delicate political decisions that should not be taken by majority voting, as that would thus eventually produce a decision against the will of one of the affected Member States.

7—06   The decisive point is, in my opinion, the following. The general provision of Article 175 (ex 130s) E.C. is in paragraph 1: environmental measures are to be taken by majority. The derogations from this rule, which are laid down in paragraph 2, must therefore be interpreted narrowly. It would have been easy to refer in Article 175(2) (ex 130s(2)) E.C. to "water legislation", in the same way as this paragraph refers to "waste legislation". The sophisticated wording "management of water resources" in fact shows that only a specific part of all water legislation was to be covered. This analysis correlates with the fact that the text was drafted by the Dutch presidency of the Intergovernmental Conference/Council at the end of 1991: in the Netherlands there is a Department for Transport en Waterstaat that deals with quantitative water aspects, whereas the Department for the Environment deals with qualitative water aspects. The addition of the word "quantitatief" in the Dutch version of the Treaty points to the fact that the text of the Treaty was meant to maintain the distinction between quantitative and qualitative aspects. The conclusion is therefore that mere qualitative aspects of water policy are to be decided by majority decisions. "management of water resources" is thus equivalent to "water use" and aims at quantitative aspects.

7—07   In its efforts to give greater coherence to measures on water protection and, at the same time, to follow the trend towards deregulation and the abandoning of precise provisions, the Commission submitted, in 1994, a proposal for a directive on the ecological quality of water.[17] The proposal suggested a good ecological water quality for all surface water in the Community. Member States were to identify the sources of pollution and to fix objectives in order to reach this good ecological quality. They were then to elaborate integrated programmes to reach the objectives. Particularly remarkable is that each Member State was to decide what it understood by "good ecological quality" and was to decide what objectives were to be fixed. The proposal limited itself to fixing rather general criteria for this ecological quality.

---

[13] Case 36/98 *Spain v. Council* (not yet decided).

[14] J. Jans, *European environmental law* (New York, London and Boston, 1995), p. 38.

[15] P. Pagh, *EU miljoeret* (Copenhagen, 1996), p. 121.

[16] A. Epiney, *Umweltrecht in der Europäischen Union* (Cologne and Berlin, 1997), p. 58

[17] [1994] O.J. C222/6; explanatory memorandum COM (93) 680 of June 15, 1994.

The proposal met with little enthusiasm in the European Parliament, which continued to press for a more coherent approach to water policy.[18] The Commission accepted this request and presented, on the one hand, a communication on water policy[19] and, on the other hand, a proposal for a directive "establishing a framework for Community action in the field of water policy".[20] This proposal, which was based on Article 175(1) (ex 130s(1)) E.C., stated as its objective the setting up of a framework in order to prevent further deterioration, to protect and improve aquatic and terrestrial ecosystems and to promote sustainable water consumption based on long-term protection of available water resources.

7—08   Member States were to identify river basins, where appropriate jointly with other Member States. They were to analyse, for each river basin, the status of the water, and to draw up an economic analysis; furthermore, they were to draw up management plans in order to achieve "good" water and groundwater quality and comply with all standards and objectives by 2010; these timescales could be extended under certain conditions. Specific provisions were to apply for protected habitats. The proposal also stated that, by 2010, "Member States shall ensure full cost recovery for all costs for services provided for water uses overall and by economic sectors, broken down at least into households, industry and agriculture."

The proposed "river basin approach" is new at Community level, though it was already practised in a number of Member States. It remains to be seen how it will work in regionalised Member States or in transfrontier situations. The proposal again allows Member States themselves to set what exactly defines "good" quality and thus which measures they will take in order to improve the surface and groundwater quality. This will probably lead to different results from one Member State to another. The proposal does not contain elements of emission limit values and/or quality objectives. Therefore, the lower the notion of "good quality" is fixed by a Member State, the less effort will have to be taken to improve the water or to reduce pollution.

7—09   In the past, complaints have been made about the considerable asymmetry between the Community provisions on the quality of drinking water, where very stringent maximal admissible concentration values apply,[21] and the Community provisions on other waters (surface water, groundwater)—the so-called raw water—where no, or only rather lax, standards applied. This policy had, as a consequence, that drinking water production plants had to clean the water and to make the corresponding investments, a policy that favours end-of-the-pipe investment rather then to address the reduction of discharges. It cannot be expected that the present proposal for a framework directive will reorient the Community water policy.

Though the Council discussed the proposal at several occasions, no formal decision had been reached by mid-1999, since the European Parliament only gave its opinion on the proposal in February 1999, suggesting 122 amendments of the Commission proposal.[22] To what extent the proposal, once it is adopted, will modify existing Community water law, is not yet open to prediction. The proposal suggests that five

---

[18] European Parliament, Res. of October 23, 1996 (n. 4).

[19] See para. 7–01, above.

[20] [1997] O.J. C184/20; explanatory memorandum COM (97) 49 of February 26, 1997; amendment of the proposal [1998] O.J. C16/14 and [1998] O.J. C108/94.

[21] See below, para. 7–10.

[22] [1999] O.J. C150/388. This delay was due to the fact that, under the Amsterdam Treaty, measures under Article 175(1) (ex 130s(1)) E.C. are to be adopted by way of co-decision, which gives greater influence to the Parliament on decisions. The Amsterdam Treaty entered into effect on May 1, 1999.

water directives should be repealed.[23] Council's and Parliament's final decisions are still outstanding.

2. QUALITY MEASURES

(a) Drinking water

7—10   Directive 80/778, adopted in 1980, five years after the proposal of the Commission, limited the presence of undesirable substances in drinking water.[24] The Directive was based on Articles 95 and 308 (ex 100a and 235) E.C. The Directive fixed maximum admissible concentrations for 67 substances in drinking water, and gave non-mandatory guide values for some of them; Member States had to take the necessary measures to ensure compliance with the concentrations. On request of the United Kingdom Government, which had argued that Directive 80/778 only requested Member States to take "all practicable steps" to comply with the Directive's standards, the European Court stated expressly that Member States were not only obliged to make an effort, but were obliged to reach the specific result that was required by the Directive.[25]

The Directive allowed derogations from its standards:

- where the nature and structure of the ground had as a consequence a "natural enrichment" of the water (Art. 9(1a));

- in cases of exceptional meteorological conditions (Art. 9(1b));

- in emergencies (Art. 10).[26]

7—11   The monitoring requirements, laid down in Directive 80/778, were weak. Annex II fixed requirements as to the minimum frequency of analyses, which depended on the quantity of water distributed and the population concerned; however, for toxic parameters such as lead, mercury and chromium, for example, the frequency was left at the discretion of Member States. Member States had no obligation to publish monitoring results or to report to the Commission. A reporting obligation was introduced by Directive 91/692[27]; the first report was due in 1997, but has not been published.

Member States were given five years (until 1985) to clean up their drinking water; they were entitled to ask for a longer delay, but none did so. Member States transposed the Directive[28] into national law, though mostly with some delay. Compliance with the Directive's requirements posed considerable problems, since the drinking water often contained more pollutants than were accepted by the Directive. Member States then either set other, less stringent, parameters, allowed more generous derogations, or

---

[23] Dir. 75/440 on surface water [1975] O.J. L194/26; Dir. 78/659 on fishing waters [1978] O.J. L222/1; Dir. 79/869 on measuring methods for surface water quality [1979] O.J. L271/44; Dir. 79/923 on shellfish water [1979] O.J. L281/47; Dir. 80/68 on groundwater [1980] O.J. L20/43.

[24] Dir. 80/778 relating to the quality of water intended for human consumption [1980] O.J. L229/11.

[25] Case C-337/89, *Commission v. United Kingdom* [1992] E.C.R. I-6103.

[26] As to this definition, see case C-237/90 *Commission v. Germany* [1992] E.C.R. I-5973, where the German opinion was rejected that exceeding of the nitrate parameter through agricultural activity could be considered an emergency situation.

[27] Dir. 91/692 on standardising and rationalising reports on the implementation of certain directives relating to the environment [1991] O.J. L377/48.

[28] See generally on the implementation of Dir. 80/778, C. Demmke, *Die Implementation von EG—Umweltpolitik in den Mitgliedstaaten. Umsetzung und Vollzug der Trinkwasserrichtlinie* (Baden-Baden, 1994).

ignored it when some parameters were, during longer or shorter time periods, exceeded. Another way of getting around the Directive consisted in not measuring polluting concentrations in water or not making the measuring results public. The Commission's taking court action against some Member States[29] did not have general, lasting results. In practice, drinking water in large parts of the Community does not yet comply with the Directive's requirements; the parameters that are most frequently exceeded are nitrates, pesticides, coliforms and heavy metals.

7—12   Overall, the Directive introduced, for the first time, objective standards for drinking water in all Community Member States, oriented investments and led to a considerable, though slow, improvement of drinking water quality. Its long-term impact cannot easily be overestimated.

Since there were difficulties in complying with the Directive's requirements, considerable pressure was put on the Commission to lower the standards, in particular as regards pesticides, where the agrochemical and agroindustrial industry were particularly active. In 1995 the Commission made a proposal for replacing Directive 80/778 by a new directive,[30] which the Council adopted in 1998.[31] The main reasons stated to justify the new text were the necessity of adapting the existing provisions to scientific and technological progress and to take account of the subsidiarity principle. The new Directive clarifies that its requirements must be complied with at the point of entry of the water into the domestic distribution system, a point which had long been in dispute between water suppliers and water users. The provisions on monitoring compliance were made more precise, the possibilities for derogations enlarged, and a number of other changes introduced, including the requirement to publish a report every three years on the quality of drinking water (Article 13). As regards the maximum admissible concentrations, the level for lead was lowered from 50 microgrammes to 10 microgrammes per litre, with a transition period of 15 years.[32] No change was brought to the pesticide parameter.[33]

Directive 98/83 will replace the existing Directive 80/778 in 2003.

(b) Bathing water

7—13   In 1975 the Council adopted, on the basis of Articles 94 and 308 (ex 100 and 235) E.C., a Directive on the quality of bathing water,[34] which fixed, for coastal and for fresh-water zones, quality requirements for bathing waters. A bathing water was a water where bathing was authorised or not prohibited and traditionally practised by a large number of bathers. Parameters were fixed for total coliforms, faecal coliforms, mineral oils, surface active substances, phenols and a number of other pollutants. The values that were fixed for these parameters were not to be exceeded; in some cases, non-binding guide values were fixed. Member States were given 10 years to comply

---

[29] See cases C-42/89 *Commission v. Belgium* [1990] E.C.R. 2821; C-237/90 (n. 26), C-337/89 (n. 3), C-340/96 *Commission v. United Kingdom*, judgment of April, 24, 1999, not yet reported; C-49/97 *Commission v. France* (case not yet decided).

[30] [1995] O.J. C131/5; explanatory memorandum COM (94) 612 of January 4, 1995; amendment [1997] O.J. C213/8.

[31] Dir. 98/32 on the quality of water intended for human consumption [1998] O.J. L330/32.

[32] The overall costs for replacing lead pipes, which was considered necessary in order to allow this new parameter to be respected, were estimated at 70 billion euro: Commission, Explanatory memorandum (n. 30, above), p. 12 [1997] O.J. C20/121.

[33] In 1992, the Commission had declared that the existing parameters for pesticides were adequate and that it did not intend to amend them: Written Question 2534/91 (Lauga) [1992] O.J. C126/30; the proposal of 1995 (n. 30, above) had suggested the deletion of the collective pesticide parameter of 0.5 micrograms. See also the European Parliament's opposition to this proposal: [1997] O.J. C20/121.

[34] Dir. 76/160 [1976] O.J. L31/1.

with the Directive's requirements; they could obtain derogations for some bathing waters, which only the United Kingdom requested and obtained. Member States had to report annually on the quality of their bathing water; and since 1985, the Commission has published an annual report on the quality of bathing water in the Community,[35] the only directive for which this was done. In 1997, 13,129 coastal zones and 6,177 fresh water zones were monitored under the Directive.

All Member States transposed the Directive into national law, though in part with considerable delays.[36] In order not to have to invest too heavily into the clean up of waters, bathing waters, in particular, that qualified for the Directive were not designated or the measuring of the parameters was not done or the results were not published. The number of bathing waters has steadily increased since 1985, and the sampling frequency and intensity as well as the quality of waters has improved. The 1997 report indicated that about 1,100 (6.7 per cent) coastal bathing waters and 1,250 (20.2 per cent) fresh-water bathing waters did not comply with the Directive's requirements.

7—14 Overall, the Directive has, within its 24 years of existence, caused a significant improvement of bathing-water quality. To this contributed the fact that annual reports were published and that a private organisation had launched a "blue flag" campaign,[37] which identified high-quality bathing waters and beaches, and finally that, in general, the data on bathing-water quality found its way into tourism considerations. This also caused local authorities to publish data, invest in water improvement and to make specific efforts to comply with the Directive's requirements.

7—15 In 1994, the Commission made a proposal to replace Directive 76/160 by a new directive.[38] It justified this by the need to take into account subsidiarity questions, the need to simplify the text and by scientific and technical progress. The new proposal was based on Article 175 (ex 130s) E.C. The Commission suggested the replacement of some parameters by others, which better reflected water quality; it specified more accurately the measuring requirements and frequency and suggested that a bathing water that complied with all requirements could be qualified as "excellent". Where a water did not comply with the requirements, Member States had to take measures in order to make them comply "as soon as possible". Thus, non-compliance was no longer to constitute a breach of the directive, but rather activated the obligation to improve the water quality; if this provision were adopted, it would constitute a late victory for the United Kingdom in its dispute with the Commission.[39]

The proposal had not been discussed in Council by mid-1999. It is likely to be repealed by the Commission and substituted by another proposal.

(c) Groundwater

7—16 At the end of 1979, the Council adopted a directive on groundwater quality,[40] based on Articles 94 and 308 (ex 100 and 235) E.C. The Directive aimed

---

[35] See most recent Commission report, "Quality of bathing water (1997 bathing season)" (Luxembourg, 1998).
[36] On transposition and compliance, see cases C-72/81 *Commission v. Belgium* [1982] E.C.R. 183; C-96/81 *Commission v. Netherlands* [1982] E.C.R. 1791; C-56/90 *Commission v. United Kingdom* [1993] E.C.R. I-4109; C-92/96 *Commission v. Spain* [1998] E.C.R. I-505; C-198/97 *Commission v. Germany* (not yet decided).
[37] On the "blue flag" campaign, see Written Question P-3144/97 (Díez de Rivera) O.J. C117/155; Commission, 1997 report (n. 35), p. 9; Written Question P-1421/98 (Díez de Rivera) [1998] O.J. C402/130.
[38] [1994] O.J. C112/3; explanatory memorandum COM (94) 36 of February 16, 1994; amended [1998] O.J. C6/9.
[39] See above, para. 7–10.
[40] Dir. 80/68 on the protection of groundwater against pollution caused by certain dangerous substances [1980] O.J. L20/43.

to prevent groundwater pollution and to eliminate the consequences of pollution, as far as possible. It established a list I of substances that were considered toxic, persistant or bioaccumulative, and a list II that groups together substances that "could have a harmful effect on groundwater". The direct discharge of list I substances was prohibited, and the indirect discharge—discharge after percolation through the ground or the subsoil—of that list was subject to investigation and authorisation. Discharges of list II substances were subject to investigation and authorisation. Thus, in substance, Member States could at their discretion authorise discharges, without being limited by emission limit values or quality standards. Furthermore, the Directive dealt with details of the authorisation procedure. No provision for informing of the public was provided for and no comprehensive report by Member States on the implementation of the Directive was foreseen.

The Directive also regulated artificial enrichment for the purposes of groundwater management—thus, in practice, for drinking water purposes—which were only allowed "if there is no risk of polluting the groundwater" and contained a rather severe provision on the leachates from existing landfills[41]; both these provisions, however, were, in practice, virtually ignored by Member States and not seriously monitored by the Commission.

7—17   Member States were slow in transposing and enforcing the Directive; Belgium, the Netherlands and Italy were condemned by the Court of Justice for incomplete transposition,[42] and Germany for having transposed the Directive by administrative circular.[43] In 1997, the Commission was informed that Sweden and Portugal had not yet transposed the Directive and that legislation in Ireland and Germany did not conform to the Directive's requirements.[44] The Commission did not monitor the practical application of the Directive in Member States, probably mainly due to lack of information on such application. Instead, it stated "since its adoption it has become clear that the long-term challenges facing groundwater are increasingly related to diffuse pollution and to unsustainable levels of water abstraction, neither of which is adequately covered by the Directive".[45] In the same year, it submitted, based on Article 175(3) (ex 130s(3)) E.C., a proposal for a decision on an action programme for integrated groundwater protection and management, which suggested the ensuring of an integrated planning and monitoring of groundwater, a strict framework for abstracting groundwater and the tackling of diffuse pollution sources—that is, in particular, agricultural activity and the taking care of groundwater pollution by sewage sludge.

The Council and European Parliament have not yet decided on the proposal.[46] The Commission indicated its intention to have the future water framework directive[47] also cover groundwater so that a specific groundwater directive would no longer be necessary.

---

[41] Dir. 80/68 (n. 40), Art. 14: "As regards discharges . . . already occurring at the time of notification of this Directive, the Member States may stipulate a period not exceeding four years . . . on expiry of which the discharges in question must comply with this Directive."

[42] Court of Justice, cases C-1/86 *Commission v. Belgium* [1987] E.C.R. 2797; C-291/84 *Commission v. Netherlands* [1987] E.C.R. 3483; C-360/87 *Commission v. Italy* [1991] E.C.R. I-791. In 1993, Belgium was even condemned a second time, under Article 228 (ex 171) E.C. for not having complied with the first judgment: case C-174/91 *Commission v. Belgium* [1993] E.C.R. I-2275.

[43] Case C-131/88 *Commission v. Germany* [1991] E.C.R. I-825.

[44] Commission, "Monitoring application of Community law" (1996) [1997] O.J. C332/1, p. 179; the Commission there indicates that legislation in Portugal is not conforming to the requirements of the Directive. However, in case C-183/97 *Commission v. Portugal* [1998] E.C.R. I-4005 Portugal was condemned for not having transposed the Directive.

[45] COM (96) 59 of February 21, 1996, annex point 1.7.

[46] [1996] O.J. C355/1.

[47] See above, para. 7–07.

(d) Nitrates in water

7—18 Directive 91/676, adopted in 1991 and based on Article 175 (ex 130s) E.C., tries to protect waters against pollution by nitrates and thereby to combat eutrophication.[48] It was almost the first directive that provided for measures against pollution from agricultural activity.

"Waters" is not defined and thus refers to fresh water as well as to coastal and marine waters. Member States had to designate vulnerable zones in their territories according to criteria fixed by the Directive; the decisive criterion was whether the nitrate content of the water exceeded or risked exceeding 50 mg per litre or whether the waters were eutrophic. For these vulnerable zones, Member States had to establish action programmes, for which the Directive fixed some measures, amongst which were the necessity of prohibiting the use of certain fertilisers during certain periods and restricting the amount of livestock manure applied to the land per year to not more than 170 kilograms of nitrogens, though some transitional periods were allowed.

7—19 Furthermore, Member States had to establish a code of good agricultural practice "to be implemented by farmers on a voluntary basis" with the objective of reducing nitrate pollution, for which the Directive gave a number of possible ("should contain") provisions. Member States had to report on the implementation every four years and the Commission had to establish a summary report.

Member States had to transpose the Directive into national law by the end of 1993. One year later, only Denmark, France and Luxembourg had done so[49]; by the end of 1996, 13 Member States were reported to have transposed the Directive,[50] but at the end of 1997, the Commission found that only Denmark, France, Luxembourg and Spain had fully complied with their requirements.[51] At the end of 1996, action under Article 226 (ex 169) E.C. was running against nine,[52] one year later against 13 Member States, for lack of national transposition legislation or for incorrect or incomplete transposition of the Directive. Only Sweden and the United Kingdom had finished the designation of vulnerable zones; Denmark, Germany, Luxembourg and Sweden had drawn up action programmes for these zones. Codes of practice for good agricultural practice were lacking in Belgium, Portugal and Spain.[53] The Commission, in its implementation report on Directive 91/676, considered the situation "unsatisfactory".[54]

It is too early definitely to assess the effects of the Directive; however, to date the results seem to have been rather limited.[55]

---

[48] Dir. 91/676 concerning the protection of waters against pollution caused by nitrates from agricultural sources [1991] O.J. L375/1.

[49] Commission, Twelfth report on monitoring application of Community law (1994) [1995] O.J. C254/1, p. 134; the information given in the annual reports is, however, contradictory: thus, while the 12th report indicates that Finland has transmitted national transposition measures, the 14th report [1997] O.J. C332/1, p. 185, indicates that Finland has not transmitted national measures; other inconsistencies concern Belgium, Spain, the Netherlands, Italy and Greece. Written Question E-1744/97 (Apollinário) [1997] O.J. C391/100 gives further information.

[50] Commission, Fourteenth report on monitoring application of Community law (1996) [1997] O.J. C332/1, p. 185, the exceptions being Netherlands and Finland. See, however, Court of Auditors Special Report 3/98 concerning the implementation by the Commission of E.U. policy and action in the field of water pollution [1998] O.J. C191/1, which reports (n. 9) that Directive 91/676 had not yet been transposed by Austria and Finland.

[51] Commission in Court of Auditors Report (n. 50), p. 35.

[52] Commission, Fourteenth report (n. 50) p. 185; three cases have in the meantime been submitted to the Court of Justice, against Greece (C-173/97), Italy (C-195/97) and Portugal (C-227/97).

[53] Written Question E-1744/97 (n. 49).

[54] COM (97) 473 of October 1, 1997.

[55] See also Court of Auditors (n. 50), paras 29–37 for the Bretagne region; the European Parliament (Res. of October 20, 1998 [1998] O.J. C341/35) declared itself "shocked" and concerned about the lack of implementation of the Directive.

(e) Other directives

(i) Surface water

7—20   Directive 75/440, based on Articles 94 and 308 (ex 100 and 235) E.C., concerned the quality of surface water that was used for the production of drinking water.[56] It asked Member States to divide their surface waters according to their quality into three classes—class 3 was not allowed to be used for drinking-water purposes—and to identify all sampling points in a given water. At these sampling points they had to set quality values for a number of pollutants that were specified in the Directive. In order to ensure a "continuing improvement" of the surface-water quality which was to be achieved within 10 years, they had to draw up a systematic plan of action, including a timetable. Some derogations and exceptions were allowed. A specific Directive fixed the methods of measurement and frequencies of sampling and analysis for surface water.[57] A requirement to report on the application of the Directive was not foreseeen and was only introduced in 1991[58]; thus far, no report on the implementation of the Directive has been published.

Generally, it seems not exaggerated to state that most Member States considered the Directive as a recommendation. In particular, the clean-up plans were hardly ever drawn up and never transmitted to the Commission. The Commission, while belatedly taking some legal action against Member States,[59] did not really monitor the application of the Directive, but instead turned its attention to Directive 80/778 on drinking water.[60] Thus, the move to reduce discharges into surface waters was turned to treat water in order to obtain drinking water.

(ii) Fresh fish water

7—21   Directive 78/659[61] fixed quality standards for fresh fish water. Member States had to identify those waters, which came under the Directive and had then to draw up clean-up programmes in order to make the fish waters conform, within five years, to the quality values of the Directive.

The Directive suffered from the fact that Member States themselves assigned which waters were to be submitted to the Directive; they often designated waters that were unpolluted or did not designate waters that were too polluted. The Commission published, in 1995, a report on the application of the Directive; however, that report limited itself to reproducing the Member States' reports without any assessment and only added a disclaimer: "publication of the report does not mean the Commission accept that the requirements of the directives are being fully met in all Member States".[62]

In 1991, the Commission reported that only three Member States had transmitted

---

[56] Dir. 75/440 concerning the quality required of surface water intended for the abstraction of drinking water in the Member States [1975] O.J. L194/26.

[57] Dir. 79/869 [1979] O.J. L271/44.

[58] Dir. 91/692 (n. 27).

[59] Cases C-73/81 *Commission v. Belgium* [1982] E.C.R. 189; C-209/89 *Commission v. Belgium* [1991] E.C.R. I-2581; C-58/89 *Commission v. Germany* [1991] E.C.R. I-4983; C-214/97 *Commission v. Portugal* (not yet decided).

[60] See Commission statement in COM (96) 59 (above, n. 5), annex point 1.1: "This is an old Directive, adopted before the Drinking Water Directive. The parameters and classifications are now out of date and it makes little or no contribution to the safety of drinking water now that the Drinking Water Directive exists. Its value in protecting future sources of drinking water is unproven."

[61] Dir. 78/659 on the quality of fresh water needing protection or improvement in order to support fish life [1978] O.J. L222/1.

[62] "Quality of fresh water for fish and for shellfish water" (Brussels and Luxembourg, 1995).

clean-up programmes.[63] A judgment by the Court of Justice, that Member States had to designate fish waters all over their territory, not only in some regions,[64] only had limited effect: Italy was, in 1994, condemned a second time[65] and in 1996 the Court found that Germany had not designated any fish water[66]—18 years after the adoption of the Directive! In the absence of systematic monitoring of this Directive by the Commission, its effects remain modest.

(iii) Shellfish water

7—22 Directive 79/923[67] had a similar construction to Directive 78/659: Member States had to designate waters to which the Directive applied, then had to draw up pollution reduction programmes in order to make these waters conform to the quality requirements that the Directive had fixed. Again, implementation was slow: in 1991, four Member States had drawn up programmes[68] and the Commission monitoring was neither systematic nor whole-hearted.[69] The Commission is now of the opinion that Directive 91/492,[70] which fixes health conditions for the production and placing on the market of live bivalve molluscs, made Directive 79/923 redundant.[71]

3. REDUCTION OF DISCHARGES INTO WATER

(a) Dangerous substances

(i) Directive 76/464

7—23 Directive 76/464, adopted in 1976 on the basis of Articles 94 and 308 (ex 100 and 235) E.C., fixed the framework conditions for discharges of dangerous substances into waters.[72] The Directive established two lists of substances and groups of substances. List I contained substances considered toxic, persistant or bioaccumulative,[73] list II other polluting substances.[74] The Directive required all discharges which contained list I or list II substances to be authorised. The authorisations had to lay down emission limit values for these substances.

Article 6 stipulated that the Community would lay down emission limit values for list I substances "taking into account the best technical means available". At the same time, the Council was to adopt quality standards on the basis of concentrations in living organisms and in sediment. The emission limit values were to apply all over the Community "except in cases where a Member State can prove to the Commission . . . that the quality objectives . . . are being met and continuously maintained". The

---

[63] Commission, Eighth report on monitoring application of Community law (1990) [1991] O.J. C338/1, p. 218.

[64] Case C-322/86 Commission v. Italy [1988] E.C.R. 3995.

[65] Case C-291/93 Commission v. Italy [1994] E.C.R. I-859.

[66] Case C-298/95 Commission v. Germany [1996] E.C.R. I-6747.

[67] Dir. 79/923 on the quality required of shellfish waters [1979] O.J. L281/47.

[68] Commission, Eighth report (n. 63), p. 218; see also the implementation report mentioned in n. 62, above.

[69] See, for instance, Court of Justice, case C-225/96 Commission v. Italy [1997] E.C.R. I-6887, where the Commission had applied to the Court for absence of legislation in Italy in 1996, 17 years after the adoption of the Directive.

[70] Dir. 91/492 [1991] O.J. L268/1.

[71] Commission, COM (96) 59 (n. 5), annex point 1.6.

[72] Dir. 76/464 on pollution caused by certain dangerous substances discharged into the aquatic environment of the Community [1976] O.J. L129/23.

[73] Organohalogens, organophosphorous and organotin compounds, carcinogenics, mercury, cadmium, mineral oils and hydrocarbons and persistent synthetic substances.

[74] In particular, heavy metals, biocides, silicon compounds, cyanides, fluorides, ammonia, nitrites and all list I substances, for which no Community emission limit values have been fixed.

Commission had to report to the Council on cases where the quality standards were used; the Council should review every five years the cases where the quality objective method had been applied.

7—24   For list II substances, Member States had to establish programmes in order to reduce water pollution, and set timetables for their implementation. The programmes had to include quality objectives for water; individual authorisations had to be issued in such a way that these quality objectives could be respected. No publication of the programmes was foreseen; however, they had to be sent to the Commission, which had to make regular comparisons.

The Directive's provisions on emission limit values and quality standards constituted a compromise between the United Kingdom and the other—by then eight—Member States, which was necessary, since the Directive had to be adopted unanimously. The United Kingdom opposed the fixing of Community emission limit values, arguing that local environmental conditions were too different.[75] Rivers in the United Kingdom were short and quick-flowing and, at the coast, the tide would quickly wash away any eventual polluting discharge. While the other Member States pleaded in favour of common measures, they finally accepted the compromise, indicating in a statement that they would introduce only to emission limit values.

7—25   Under the Directive, emission limit values and quality objectives were fixed for 17 substances. At least in the beginning, only the United Kingdom recurred to the quality standards approach. At no time, though, did the Commission report to the Council asking for its review. Rather, the Commission and the other Member States accepted that two different approaches were practised within the Community. Also, the formula of using the best technical means available, remained a dead letter: instead, the values were fixed on the basis of a political compromise.

The Directive was a complete failure as regards list II substances. No Member State established programmes for them in order to reduce pollution; no Member State fixed quality objectives, either. Finally, it has clearly been impossible to undertake regular comparisons of Member States' pollution reduction programmes.

In 1992, the Commission reported that it had started 40 infringement procedures under Article 226 (ex 169) E.C. against Member States, for not complying with the requirements of Directive 76/464.[76] The new evolution in water law, which started with the Edinburgh summit meeting,[77] led to a complete standstill in the monitoring of Directive 76/464—except as regards the procedures under Article 226 (ex 169) E.C. that were progressively submitted to the Court of Justice.[78] In 1996, the Court of Justice found that Italy had not even yet transposed the requirement of prior authorisation for discharges into Italian law as regards existing installations.[79]

---

[75] See on the history of this controversy in particular, N. Haigh (ed.), *Manual of environmental policy: the E.C. and Britain* (looseleaf, London), at chapters 3.9 and 4.8.

[76] Written Question 1496/91 (van Hemeldonck) [1992] O.J. C202/7.

[77] See above, para. 7–01.

[78] The first ever judgment on Dir. 76/464 was given on June 11, 1998, 22 years after its adoption; this case, joined cases C-232 & 233/95 *Commission v. Greece* [1998] E.C.R. I-3343, concerned the absence of programmes for two Greek waters. In 1996 and 1997 the Commission brought actions to the Court against Luxembourg (C-206/96 [1998] E.C.R. I-3368), Spain (C-214/96 [1998] E.C.R. I-7661), Italy (C-285/96 [1998] E.C.R. I-5935), Germany (C-184/97), Belgium (C-207/97 [1999] E.C.R. I-275) and Greece (C-384/97), essentially for absence of pollution reduction programmes for list II substances. Commission, 14th report (n. 50), p. 178 lists 15 other procedures in course under Article 226 (ex 169) E.C.

[79] Case C-168/95 *Arcaro* [1996] E.C.R. I-4705.

(ii) Daughter directives

7—26   Subsequent to the framework that had been set up by Directive 76/464, the Community fixed emission limit values and quality standards for list I substances. To that end, the Commission established a list of 129 substances under list I, to which the Council agreed in a resolution.[80] A proposal for a directive on quality standards for a list II substance (chromium) was made,[81] but was not adopted by the Council.

As regards the list I substances, the emission limit values were expressed either in micrograms or milligrams per litre of water discharged or grams per kilogram or tonne of substances produced. The allowable discharges varied according to the nature of the water (inland surface water, estuary water, coastal water or territorial sea water). Normally, methods for measurements were fixed. Quality standards again varied according to the nature of the water. They were expressed as the arithmetic mean of the results of concentrations in water obtained over a year, but the number of measurements taken was left to Member States. The Commission had to establish comparative assessments report on the implementation of the daughter directives.[82]

7—27   Emission limit values and quality standards were fixed for mercury,[83] cadmium,[84] HCH (lindane),[85] carbon tetrachloride, DDT, pentachlorophenol, aldrin, dieldrin, endrin, isodrin, hexachlorobenzene, hexachlorobutadiene, chloroform, 1,2–dichloroethane, TRI, PER and trichlorobenzene.[86] As an example, Directive 83/513 on cadmium discharges[87] can be quoted in more detail. It fixed emission limit values for zinc mining, lead and zinc refining, the cadmium metal and non-ferrous metal industry, the manufacture of cadmium compounds, pigments, stabilisers and batteries, and for electroplating. A footnote requested Member States to fix emission limit values for other industrial sectors and, in particular, the production of phosphoric acid and/or phosphatic fertilisers from phosphatic rocks.[88]

Member States had to institute a monitoring procedure to check whether the actual discharges complied with the emission standards. That procedure had to provide for the taking and analysis of samples and for measurement of the flow of the discharge and the quantity of cadmium handled. A sample representative of the discharge over a period of 24 hours had to be taken. The quantity of cadmium discharged over a month then had to be calculated on the basis of the daily quantities of cadmium discharged. These monitoring requirements did not specify whether the industrial installation itself was to monitor its discharges, nor whether public authorities were ever to check the private monitoring system.

---

[80] Res. of February 7, 1983 [1983] O.J. C46/17.

[81] [1985] O.J. C351/33.

[82] Dir. 82/176 on limit values and quality objectives for mercury discharges by the chlor-alkali electrolysis industry [1982] O.J. L81/29, Art. 5(2); Dir. 83/513 on limit values and quality objectives for cadmium discharges [1983] O.J. L291/1, Art. 5(2); Dir. 86/280 on limit values and quality objectives for discharges of certain dangerous substances included in list I of the annex to Dir. 76/464 [(1986) O.J. L181/16, Art. 6.

[83] Dir. 82/176 (n. 82) and Dir. 84/156 on limit values and quality objectives for mercury discharges by sectors other than the chlor-alkali electrolysis industry [1984] O.J. L74/49.

[84] Dir. 83/513 (n. 82).

[85] Dir. 94/491 on limit values and quality objectives for discharges of hexachlorocyclohexane [1984] O.J. L274/11.

[86] Dir. 86/280 (n. 82), amended by Dir. 88/347 [1988] O.J. L158/35 and Dir. 90/415 [1990] O.J. L219/49.

[87] Dir. 83/513 (n. 82).

[88] Ibid., annex I, nn. 1 and 4: "Limit values for industrial sectors not mentioned [in this Directive] will, if necessary, be fixed by the Council at a later stage. In the meantime the Member States will fix emission standards for cadmium discharges autonomously in accordance with Directive 76/464. Such standards must take into account the best technical means available and must not be less stringent than the most nearly comparable limit value in this Annex . . . The absence of such limit values [for phosphatic rock utilisation] does not release the Member States from their obligation under Directive 76/464 to fix emission standards for these discharges."

7—28 The Commission did not systematically monitor the application of the different daughter directives by, for instance, spot checks, asking Member States for data or comparing the monitoring procedures and the actual measuring results reached. Comparative reports were never made; no attempt was made to find out what kind of emission limit values were fixed for the different industrial installations, whether they were expressly mentioned in the directives or not. Legal action against Member States was only taken where national legislation had not been adopted[89] or where a Member State had transposed the directives by administrative circulars rather than by binding legislation.[90]

Apart from such legal action, monitoring work on these daughter directives as well as on setting new emission limit values and quality standards has, since 1990, come to a standstill, without an express decision by the Council or the Commission. The causes for this are not clear: indeed, all published programmes, resolutions, press releases and communications pleaded instead in favour of accelerating and intensifying work at Community level. It can only be presumed that the subsidiarity discussion which had started with the adoption of the Maastricht Treaty on European Union in 1993 is the reason for this standstill. The Commission is of the opinion that Directive 96/61 and the water framework directive, once adopted, will in future ensure adequate standards for discharges.[91]

(b) Emissions from industrial installations

7—29 The Community measures on emissions, including water discharges, from the titanium dioxide industry have already been discussed.[92] As regards water discharges from incinerators for hazardous waste, the Commission proposed a directive where it suggested emission limit values for, in total, 15 pollutants.[93] Generally, however, the sector-oriented approach, where emission limit values are fixed for a specific industrial sector, has been abandoned with the adoption of Directive 96/61.[94] This policy change, however, creates a problem, since Directive 96/61 only applies to certain large industrial installations, whereas water contamination depends on the quantity of discharges, which may also stem from smaller plants.

Directive 96/61 will require the fixing of emission limit values[95] in the individual permits for installations that come under the Directive. The pollutants covered are those "likely to be emitted from the installation in significant quantities, having regard to their nature and their potential to tranfer pollution from one medium to the other (water, air and land)". Special attention shall be given to fixing emission limit values for 12 "main polluting substances", which are listed in annex III.[96]

---

[89] Cases C-213/97 *Commission v. Portugal* [1998] E.C.R. I-3289 on failure to transpose Dir. 86/280 and Dir. 88/347; C-208/97 *Commission v. Portugal* [1998] E.C.R. I-4017 on failure to transpose Dir. 84/156.
[90] Case C-262/95 *Commission v. Germany* [1996] E.C.R. I-5729.
[91] See below, para. 7–29.
[92] See paras 4–04 *et seq.* above.
[93] [1998] O.J. C13/6.
[94] Dir. 96/61 [1996] O.J. L257/26; where the Community regulates specific installations, it is likely to consider the water discharges in this context, see Dir. 94/67 on the incineration of hazardous waste (para. 8–49).
[95] To this, Article 9(3) of Dir. 96/61 adds: "Where appropriate, limit values may be supplemented or replaced by equivalent parameters or technical measures."
[96] 1. Organohalogen compounds and substances which may form such compounds in the aquatic environment; 2. Organophosphorous compounds; 3. Organotin compounds; 4. Substances and preparations which have been proved to possess carcinogenic or mutagenic properties or properties which may affect reproduction in or via the aquatic environment; 5. Persistent hydrocarbons and persistent and bioaccumulable organic toxic substances; 6. Cyanides; 7. Metals and their compounds; 8. Arsenic and its compounds; 9. Biocides and

(c) Dumping of waste; discharge of offshore installations

7—30   Legally speaking, the discharge of waste is no different from any other discharge into water; the terminology "dumping" stems from international conventions, which wanted to give a specific definition to the discharge of waste from ships and called this practice dumping. Under Community waste legislation, the unauthorised "abandonment, dumping or uncontrolled disposal" of waste into the environment, and thus also into waters, is prohibited[97]; this means that Member States may authorise the discharge of waste into waters at their discretion.

In 1976, the Commission made a proposal on the dumping of waste at sea[98]; it made another proposal in 1985.[99] However, these proposals were not extensively discussed in Council, since Member States preferred to see questions of marine pollution discussed in the context of international conventions, rather than at Community level. At present, therefore, waste discharge into water, in particular discharge from ships, is not regulated by Community provisions.

7—31   Identical considerations apply to the discharge of ships themselves and of offshore installations. At the end of their useful lifetime, they become waste. Their discharge into waters thus follows the same rules. After the Brent Spar incident—in 1995, an oil company had tried to sink a rig into the sea, but had abandoned its plans after massive public protests in some (northern) Member States—the Commission considered the elaboration of a directive on the decommissioning of offshore installations.[1] However, it abandoned these plans in view of the resistance from Member States; the decommissioning of offshore installations was then addressed within the framework of the OSPAR Convention.[2]

(d) Waste water

7—32   In 1991, the Community adopted a directive on urban waste water,[3] based on Article 175 (ex 130s) E.C. The Directive aimed at reducing the pollution of surface waters with nutrients, in particular nitrates and phosphates from urban waste water, and thus to combat eutrophication. It applied to domestic waste water and the mixture of domestic waste water with industrial waste water and/or run-off rainwater. The Directive required Member States to provide, by the end of 2005, a sewerage system for all agglomerations consisting of more than 2,000 people; agglomerations of more than 15,000 people have to be equipped with such a system by the end of the year 2000. These requirements concerned 17,351 agglomerations (figures for Italy not included); the financial investments in the 14 Member States were estimated, in 1998, at 130 billion euros.[4]

Before the waste water enters such a collecting system, it must undergo secondary treatment; this requirement is to be complied with by the end of 2005, and by the year 2000 for agglomerations of more than 15,000 people. Furthermore, Member States

---

plant health products; 10. Materials in suspension; 11. Substances which contribute to eutrophication (in particular, nitrates and phosphates); 12. Substances which have an unfavourable influence on the oxygen balance (and can be measures using parameters such as BOD, COD, etc.).

[97]   Dir. 75/442 on waste as amended by Dir. 91/156 [1991] O.J. L78/32, Art. 4 (2).

[98]   [1976] O.J. C40/3.

[99]   [1985] O.J. C245/23.

[1]   Written Question E-2084/95 (Méndez de Vigo) [1996] O.J. C9/15.

[2]   See below, para. 7—38.

[3]   Dir. 91/271 concerning urban waste water treatment [1991] O.J. L135/40; amended by Commission Dir. 98/15 [1998] O.J. L67/29.

[4]   Commission, Implementation of Dir. 91/271, COM (98) 775 of January 15, 1999, p. 26; when the Directive was adopted, these costs had been estimated at 40 to 60 billion euros. The Court of Auditors (n. 50), paras 3 and 5, had estimated these costs, in 1998, at 201 billion euros for nine Member States.

had to designate sensitive areas for which more stringent treatment requirements were to apply; such areas are waters that are found to be eutrophic, that are intended for the production of drinking water and could contain more than 50 milligrams of nitrates per litre, and areas where more than secondary treatment is necessary to comply with the Directive. Member States were also allowed to designate their whole territory as a sensitive area. They could also consider certain areas as less sensitive areas (marine waters), for which less stringent requirements applied. The discharge of sludge from treatment installations into waters had to be phased out by the end of 1998.

7—33   Member States had to establish programmes for the implementation of Directive 91/271 and to publish, every two years, situation reports on the disposal of urban waste water and sludge.

Overall, it was estimated that by 2005 about 40,000 water treatment plants were to be constructed or renewed; to this had to added the construction of sewerage systems.[5]

The Directive had to be transposed into national law by mid-1993. By the end of 1994, only Denmark, France and Luxembourg had done so.[6] In 1996, the Court of Justice condemned Greece, Germany and Italy for not having transposed the Directive into national law[7]; by the end of 1998, all Member States except Italy had transposed the Directive into national law. In Greece and Austria, the transposition was considered not in conformity with the Directive's requirements. The designation of sensitive zones, considerably delayed, was not completely in conformity in several Member States and was lacking, at the end of 1998, in Italy and Greece; Denmark, Luxembourg, the Netherlands, Finland and Sweden had designated their whole territory as a sensitive area.[8]

7—34   By the end of 1996, seven Member States had not yet submitted their implementation programmes to the Commission; at the end of 1998 these programmes had arrived, except for Italy.[9] Italy (for Milan) and Belgium (for Brussels) indicated that they could not respect the Directive's timescales. The United Kingdom and Portugal extensively designated less sensitive areas around their coasts; Spain and Greece also *de facto* recurred to this practice. By the end of 1997, nine Member States had established provisions for the pretreatment of biodegradable waste waters from the food industry.

At the end of 1998, procedures under Article 226 (ex 169) E.C. were running against Italy (Art. 228 (ex 171)), Greece, Belgium and Spain.

4. OCEANS AND RIVERS

(a) Oceans

7—35   Though the Community environmental policy also has as its aim to contribute to the solution of global or regional environmental problems (Article 174 (ex 130r) E.C.), it has not developed a consistent policy to reduce marine pollution. There is not one single Community environmental measure which expressly protects the marine environment, though a number of the above-mentioned directives also apply

---

[5] Court of Auditors (n. 50) paras 3 and 5.

[6] Commission, Twelfth report on monitoring application of Community law (1994) [1995] O.J. C254/1, p. 128.

[7] Cases C-161/95 *Commission v. Greece* [1996] E.C.R. I-1979; C-297/95 *Commission v. Germany* [1996] E.C.R. I-6739; C-302/95 *Commission v. Italy* [1996] E.C.R. I-6765.

[8] Commission (n. 4), p. 8.

[9] Court of Auditors (n. 50), para. 17; this report also contains detailed information on the practical implementation of Directive 91/271 and the intervention of Community funds.

to marine waters. Even in those directives, the Community has, in its political and legal activity, only considered the seas adjacent to Community territory, in particular the North Sea, the Baltic Sea and the Mediterranean Sea, and to a lesser extent the Atlantic Ocean. A different approach as regards the environment was only taken in the context of the Common Fishery Policy, where the Community also took an interest in fish—the "natural resources"—in West Africa, the Caribbean Sea and the Antarctic waters; it was also dealt with within the framework of the Common Transport Policy.

The Community has adhered to the following international conventions concerning the marine environment, most of which having been completed by a number of protocols to which the Community normally also adhered:

- Paris Convention on the prevention of marine pollution from land-based sources[10];

- Barcelona Convention on the protection of the Mediterranean Sea against pollution[11];

- Bonn Agreement for co-operation in dealing with pollution of the North Sea by oil and other harmful substances[12];

- Co-operation Agreement for the protection of the coasts and waters of the north-east Atlantic against pollution[13];

- Helsinki Convention on the protection of the marine environment of the Baltic Sea area[14];

- Helsinki 1992 Convention on the protection of the marine environment of the Baltic Sea[15];

- Paris Convention for the protection of the marine environment in the north-east Atlantic (OSPAR)[16];

- Montego Bay Convention on the law of the sea.[17]

7—36 With the adhering of the Community to these international conventions, their legal provisions became part of Community law. However, for each negotiation of a protocol to a convention or any other amendment, the Commission needs a mandate from the Council in order to negotiate in the name of the Community; for the signing of such a protocol, the same procedure applies.[18]

The reasons why Member States object to the taking of Community directives or regulations on environmental problems facing the sea, have never been expressly specified. They are presumed to be the following.

7—37 (1) International conventions are normally adopted unanimously. It is true that, during the last few years, public international law has developed the habit that amendments may, under certain conditions, be adopted by majority decisions; however, this possibility remains largely theoretical. Instead, the principle of

---

[10] Dec. 75/437 [1975] O.J. L194/5.
[11] Dec. 77/85 [1977] O.J. L240/1.
[12] Dec. 84/358 [1984] O.J. L188/7.
[13] Dec. 93/550 [1993] O.J. L267/20.
[14] Dec. 94/156 [1994] O.J. L73/1.
[15] Dec. 94/157 [1994] O.J. L73/19.
[16] Dec. 98/249 [1998] O.J. L104/1.
[17] Dec. 98/392 [1998] O.J. L179/1.
[18] Art. 300 (ex 228) E.C.

international conventions remains based on consensus. Each contracting state thus has the right to veto decisions.

In contrast to that, Community environmental measures are normally adopted by qualified majority, which allows measures to be taken against the will of an objecting Member State.

(2) The initiative for measures at international level is, jointly or severally, in the hands of contracting states. This allows a fairly direct influence of the international agenda. For the Commission to negotiate, in the name of the Community, at international conventions, a mandate is necessary under Article 300(1) (ex 228(1)) E.C. In contrast to that, initiatives for measures at Community level are taken by the Commission, which has the monopoly on this.

(3) At international level, media attention and the participation of environmental organisations is normally relatively limited. At Community level, the increasing importance of the European Parliament and its co-decision function make quasi-confidential discussions and decisions practically impossible.

(4) For years, France and the United Kingdom have also discharged radioactive materials, which stemmed from military or private activity, into the sea. In the name of national sovereignty, such activities were always considered to remain outside the area of Community competence. This attitude has probably caused these two countries, but also other Member States where the situation was similar—though not necessarily concerning radioactive matters—not to accept Community environmental initiatives to protect seas. Generally, a number of Member States continue to consider the seas as a big sewer system, where discharges are all too often allowed to take place.

7—38 The statement that the international conventions become, with the adherence of the Community, part of Community environmental law is legally correct. It is, however, rather theoretical, since the monitoring of these conventions is not ensured by the Commission, but by the secretariat of the different conventions. At no time has the Commission tried, with regard to the different decisions incorporating the conventions into Community law, to "ensure that the provisions of this Treaty and the measures taken by the insitutions pursuant thereto are applied",[19] and thus to control the effective implementation and enforcement of these conventions. Unless there is a specific Community directive or regulation that reproduces the content of the international convention, it is left to Member States to decide if and to what extent they transpose the provisions of the conventions into their national legal order and apply them. The Commission has never explained why it applies this self-restraint. The Court of Justice has not yet had to interpret Community environmental law in the light of diverging provisions of an environmental convention to which the Community is a party.

This situation leads to different legal situations and, hence, to different pollution situations for the different seas. To give an example, the meetings under the OSPAR Convention dealt, in 1996, with the following subjects, with a view to take binding OSPAR decisions: best available technologies to be used in the PVC industry; best available technology to be used in the aluminium industry; phase out of hexachloroethane; phase out of coal tar for coating; phase out of the chlorine bleaching

---

[19] Art. 211 (ex 155) E.C.

process in pulp industries; control the use and discharge of chemicals used in the offshore industry.

7—39   Most, if not all, of these measures will be decided sooner or later by the competent OSPAR authorities. In contrast, it is highly unlikely that in the context of the Barcelona Convention on the Mediterranean Sea similar subjects will be raised at all, not to mention the taking of binding decisions.

At the same time, this list of subjects indicate the impact that OSPAR decisions have or might have on the Community. Indeed, the ban of products or processes will impinge on the free circulation of goods and the competitive situation of undertakings.

In the case of hexachloroethane, the potential conflict was solved, not without complications, by the adoption of a Community Directive which took over the phasing out of that substance.[20] Another approach was taken in the Brent Spar incident: while the Commission had first considered making a proposal for a Community directive on offshore installations, it finally rejected this approach with legally unconvincing arguments[21] and left the decision to OSPAR, which reached, in 1998, a political agreement. The Commission then proposed to approve, by way of a Decision, this decision by OSPAR, without, however, proposing an amendment of E.C. law in order to introduce provisions on offshore installations that were binding on all E.C. Member States.[22]

7—40   It must be assumed that the Commission definitely abandoned its plan for a directive on offshore installations because that proposal would have been rejected in the same way as the proposal for a directive on the dumping of waste at sea. However, de facto this evolution also risks leading to a loss of the Commission's right of initiative for Community action. Rules neither on subsidiarity nor deregulation can solve this problem of non-Europe for which a legal and political price is to pay.

The Commission also submitted proposals to approve other OSPAR decisions, on a new annex V to the OSPAR Convention,[23] the disposal of radioactive waste,[24] and on emission limit values from the production of vinyl chloride monomers.[25] Once these proposals are adopted, they will be binding on those Member States which are members of OSPAR, but not for all Member States.

(b) Rivers

7—41   The Community is a member of the following international conventions regarding rivers:

- Bonn Convention for the protection of the Rhine against chemical pollution[26];

---

[20] Dir. 97/16 [1997] O.J. L116/31.

[21] Commission Communication on removal and disposal of disused offshore oil and gas installations, COM (1998) 49 of February 18, 1998, para. 6.2: "The disadvantage of this approach [a directive] is that only E.C. and EEA Member States would be bound to the common approach whereas other third countries with which we share the Seas concerned would not be bound to implement the same or similar measures without the Community taking the initiative to negotiate and adopt such rules in the relevant regional seas Conventions. Although this approach would have the advantage of applying to all E.C. Member States immediately, i.e. also to those Member States outside OSPAR—namely Austria, Greece and Italy—it would only apply to Norway after a Decision of the EEC Joint Committee. It could also be interpreted as prejudicial to Community interest in other OSPAR policies if the Commission were to be seen to press ahead separately for action via E.C. legislation rather than via the newly ratified OSPAR Convention. Furthermore it could be seen as an attempt to exclude Norway from negotiations on any final policy."

[22] Proposal for a Council decision [1999] O.J. C158/10.

[23] [1999] O.J. C158/1.

[24] [1999] O.J. C158/8.

[25] [1999] O.J. C158/19.

[26] Dec. 77/586 [1977] O.J. L240/35.

- Regensburg Agreement on co-operation on management of water resources in the Danube basin[27];

- Magdeburg Convention on the International Commission for the protection of the Elbe[28];

- Sofia Convention on co-operation for the protection of the Danube[29];

- Wroclaw Convention on the International Commission for the protection of the Oder against pollution.[30]

7—42   The legal situation as regards rivers is similar to that of seas. While the different conventions became, with the Community decisions to adhere to them, part of Community law, they are *de facto* treated, by the Community and by the Commission, as instruments of public international law. In particular, the Commission does not monitor the adoption of measures to incorporate the conventions into national law and their application in practice. Thus, the question that was put some years ago, particularly by Dutch lawyers, "Who shall clean up the Rhine river—the Rhine Commission or the European Community?", is in reality answered for the Rhine and for the other rivers that are the subject of conventions: it is not the Community, but the different secretariats of the conventions, which are in charge of combating river pollution.

The question of water resources goes beyond river water, since it might also apply to groundwater resources. To date, though, there has been not one single provision in Community water law which deals with quantitative aspects of water resources. The discussion taking place at present between Spain and Portugal on the Spanish plan for water management is mainly to be examined under general principles of public international law, including, perhaps, general aspects of Community law such as the principle of co-operation among Member States, which might be derived from Article 10 (ex 5) E.C.

BIBLIOGRAPHY

Bache, I. and McGillivray, D.: "Testing the extended gatekeeper: the law, practice and politics of implementing the Drinking Water Directive in the United Kingdom" in J. Holder (ed.), *The impact of E.C. environmental law in the United Kingdom* (Chichester, 1997), p. 147

Berggren, E. and Taams, R.: "De Cockerill-zaak: de betekenis van een vergunning en een Europees richtlijn voor lozingen in de Maas", *Tijdschrift voor Milieu-Aansprakelijkheid* (1995), p. 46

Bernauer, T.: "Protecting the Rhine river against chloride pollution" in R. Keohane (ed.), *Institutions for environmental aid: pitfalls and promise* (Cambridge, Mass., 1996)

Bodiguel, M.: *La qualité des eaux dans l'Union européenne—pratiques d'une réglementation commune* (Paris, 1996)

Breier, S.: "Das Schicksal der Titandioxid-Richtlinie", *Europäische Zeitschrift für Wirtschaftsrecht* (1993), p. 315

Breuer, R.: "EG-Richtlinien und deutsches Wasserrecht", *Wirtschaft und Verwaltung* (1990), p. 79

Breuer, R.: "Der Entwurf einer EG-Wasserrahmenrichtlinie", *Neue Zeitschrift für Verwaltungsrecht* (1998), p. 1001

---

[27]   Dec. 90/160 [1990] O.J. L377/28.
[28]   Dec. 91/598 [1991] O.J. L321/25.
[29]   Dec. 97/825 [1997] O.J. L342/18.
[30]   Dec. 1999/257 [1999] O.J. L100/20.

Delwing, P.: *Umsetzungsprobleme des EG-Wasserrechts. Dargestellt für das Abwasserrecht der Bundesrepublik Deutschland* (Baden-Baden, 1995)

Demmke, C.: *Die Implementation von EG-Umweltpolitik in den Mitgliedstaaten. Umsetzung und Vollzug der Trinkwasserrichtlinie* (Baden-Baden, 1994)

De Sadeleer, N.: "Pollution des eaux: protection des eaux intérieures" in M. Campins i Eritja and I. Pont i Castejón (eds), *Perspectives de Dret Comunitari Ambiental* (Barcelona, 1997), p. 215

Forster, M.: "Enforcing the Drinking Water Directive", *Land Management and Environmental Law Report* (1991), p. 56

Frees, C.: "Massnahmen und rechtliche Möglichkeiten der EG zur Bekämpfung und Verhütung von Öltankerunfällen vor ihren Küsten", *Natur und Recht* (1992), p. 16

Haigh, N. (with G. Bennett, P. Kromarek and T. Lavoux): *Comparative report: water and waste in four countries* (London, 1986)

Howarth, W. and Somsen, H.: "The E.C. Nitrates Directive", *Water Law* (1991), p. 149

IJlstra, T.: "L'action communautaire dans les Commission de Paris et d'Oslo" in J. Lebullinger and D. Le Morvan (eds), *La Communauté et la mer* (Paris, 1990), p. 381

Jessurun d'Oliveira, H.: "Die EWG und die Verslzung des Rheins", European University Institute, Florence, Working Paper 88/334 (San Domenico, 1988)

Kolkmann, J.: *Die EG-Trinkwasserrichtlinie: die Nitrat- und Pestizidgrenzwerte im deutschen Umweltrecht* (Berlin, 1991)

Krämer, L.: "Le déversement des déchets en mer et le droit communautaire", *Revue du Marché Commun* (1988), p. 328

Krämer, L.: "Protection of the marine environment in Community law" in L. Krämer, *Focus on European environmental law* (London, 1997), p. 259

Lübbe-Wolff, G.: "Die Bedeutung des EG-Rechts für den Grundwasserschutz" in J. Behrens and H. Koch (eds), *Umweltschutz in der Europäischen Gemeinschaft* (Baden-Baden, 1991), p. 127

Macrory, R.: "European Community water law", *Ecology Law Quarterly* (1993), p. 119

Möbs, H.: "Gewässerschutz in Deutschland und der Europäischen Gemeinschaft—divergierende Zielsetzungen?" in P. Behrens and H. Koch (eds), *Umweltschutz in der Europäischen Gemeinschaft* (Baden-Baden, 1991), p. 112

Nollkaemper, A. "Improving compliance with the international law of marine environmental protection: the role of the European Union" in J. Golub (ed.), *Global competition and E.U. environmental policy* (London and New York, 1998), p. 85

Pallemaerts, M.: *Production, toxics and transnational law: an inquiry into the effectiveness of international and European Community environmental law* (Brussels, 1998)

Pluge, W.: "Die Politik der Europäisierung auf dem Gebiet der Gas- und Wasserwirtschaft", Universität des Saarlandes, Vorträge, Reden und Berichte aus dem Europa-Institut, no. 278 (Saarbrücken, 1993)

Prat, J.: "The role and activities of the European Communities in the protection and the preservation of the marine environment of the North Sea" in D. Freestone and T. IJlstra (eds), *The North Sea: perspectives on regional environmental co-operation* (London, 1990), p. 101

Sands, P. and Blatch, C.: "Estuaries in European Community law: defining criteria", *International Journal of Marine and Coastal Law* (1998), p. 1

Somsen, H.: "E.C. water directives", *Water Law* (1990), p. 93

Suman, D.: "Regulation of ocean dumping by the European Economic Community", *Ecology Law Quarterly* (1991), p. 559

Van der Zwiep, K. and Backes, C.: *Integrated system for conservation of marine environments* (Baden-Baden, 1994)

Vennekens-Capkova, J.: "Dangerous substances: chameleons in water policy" in D. Freestone and

T. IJlstra (eds), *The North Sea: perspectives on regional environmental co-operation* (London, 1990), p. 150

Vitzthum, W. and Imperiali, C. (eds), *La protection régionale de l'environnement marin* (Paris, 1992)

Warren, L.: "The impact of E.C. environmental law on law and practice relating to marine and coastal waters" in J. Holden (ed.), *The impact of E.C. environmental law in the United Kingdom* (Chichester, 1997), p. 167

Ziehm, C.: *Europäisches Grund- und Trinkwasserschutzrecht und die Implementation in Deutschland und Frankreich* (Baden-Baden, 1998)

CHAPTER 8
Air Pollution

1. AIR POLICY AND LAW

8—01 There is no coherent, overall Community air pollution strategy. The first environmental action programmes of the Community mentioned air pollution, its causes and its effects on the environment, but actions were dispersed, incoherent and limited to specific pollution sources, in particular to emissions from passenger cars. The turning point came at the beginning of the 1980s, when the state of the forests, particularly those in Germany and central Europe, raised considerable concern. The subject of air pollution was discussed, in 1983, by the heads of state and government who suggested effective action against acid rain and air pollution.[1] This led, in the same year, to proposals for a general directive on air pollution from industrial installations,[2] for a directive on large combustion plants[3] and for a directive for quality objectives for NOx.[4] Other measures concentrated on the introduction of a catalytic converter for cars, which has been discussed since 1984 and has been progressively introduced since 1988 for new cars; since 1993, all new cars have had to be equipped in this way.

Since the mid-1980s, the depletion of the ozone layer and climate change entered more and more into the foreground of discussions. Successive strategies to combat the greenhouse effect, climate change and acidification were launched, without, however, being integrated into one overall strategy on air pollution.

8—02 This absence of a general strategy is due to a number of causes. First, air emissions stem in particular from the combustion of fuels, and the energy policy within the Community on the use of energy—nuclear energy, oil, gas, coal and lignite—varies considerably, depending also on the national availability of energy sources. Secondly, air emissions cannot be regarded separately from other environmental problems; while, for instance, nuclear energy does not emit significant quantities of air pollutants, it has numerous other environmental and other disadvantages, such as the technological risk, waste treatment and disposal problems, the siting of installations and decommissioning of installations, and acceptance by the population. Also, nuclear energy is not economically competitive within the European Community—with the exception of France, where investments in the past have been heavily subventioned by state aid. Thirdly, air emission quantities largely depend on the level of economic development, which continues to vary considerably between Member States and makes common solutions difficult. Fourthly, and perhaps foremost, there seems to be no readiness in Western European society seriously to question present lifestyles, particularly private passenger and truck transport.

Renewable energies have only recently become the subject of concentrated attention[5] and continue to play a subordinate role within the Community.

---

[1] (1993) 3 *Bulletin of the European Communities*, para. 1.5.2.
[2] [1983] O.J. C139/5.
[3] [1984] O.J. C49/1.
[4] [1983] O.J. C258/3.
[5] Commission, "Energy for the future: renewable sources of energy", Greenbook, COM (96) 576 of November 20, 1996; White paper for a Community strategy and action plan, COM (97) 599 of November 26, 1997.

8—03   At international level, Community participation in the discussions on the framework of the United Nations conventions on climate change and long-range transboundary air pollution has intensified, illustrating well the global nature of environmental (air pollution) problems. Strategy considerations during the last few years seem to concentrate more on compliance with international commitments than with reducing the quantities of pollutants that are emitted into the air. It is, however, too early to come to a conclusion on this.

Within the Community, besides the specific measures on ozone-depleting substances and on emissions from cars, action taken on emissions from industrial installations, though more scarce and limited, has slowed down since the early 1990s, also due to increasingly successful representation of vested interests. In discussions in the early 1990s on integrated pollution prevention and control, which led to the adoption of Directive 96/61,[6] the idea was shaped of the Community establishing quality standards for air emissions, while the permits for the individual installation would set air emission conditions, if necessary. Quality standards were also advocated by Directive 96/62[7] and are the subject of proposals of daughter directives under this Directive.[8] The establishing of air quality standards seems to be, at least at present, the governing principle for E.C. environmental policy, where concepts such as tradable air pollution certificates, bubbles and national emission ceilings are also emerging. These concepts are mainly imported from the worldwide discussions on climate change, where states are attributed general reduction targets. A less intensively pursued thread of Community policy leads to the elaboration of emission standards for installations, in particular in the area of incineration installations[9] and the continuation of the application of the Directive to large combustion plants.[10]

2. AIR QUALITY VALUES

8—04   There are only a few binding air quality values which have been set at Community level so far, and at national level binding air quality values have rarely been set at all.

(a) Sulphur dioxides, lead and nitrogen oxides

8—05   In the early 1980s, the Community adopted three directives which fixed air quality values for four pollutants: sulphur dioxide, suspended particulates, lead and nitrogen dioxide.[11] Guide values for these pollutants, with the exception of lead, were also laid down. The terminology—"limit values"—is somewhat misleading, since the proximity to emission limit values is too close; therefore throughout this book the terminology "air quality values" will be used.

The air quality values for sulphur dioxide differed between yearly averages (80 to 120

---

[6] Dir. 96/61 on integrated prevention and pollution control [1996] O.J. L257/26; see para. 4–16, above.

[7] Dir. 96/62 on ambient air quality assessment and management [1996] O.J. L296/55.

[8] Proposal for a directive relating to limit values for sulphur dioxide, oxides of nitrogen, particulate matter and lead in ambient air [1998] O.J. C9/6.

[9] Dir. 89/369 on the prevention of air pollution from new municipal incineration plants [1989] O.J. L163/32; Dir. 89/429 on the reduction of air pollution from existing municipal waste incineration plants [1989] O.J. L203/50; Dir. 94/67 on the incineration of hazardous waste [1994] O.J. L365/34.

[10] Dir. 88/609 on the limitation of emissions of certain pollutants into the air from large combustion plants [1988] O.J. L336/1.

[11] Dir. 80/779 on air quality limit values and guide values for sulphur dioxide and suspended particulates [1980] O.J. L229/30; Dir. 82/884 on a limit value for lead in the air [1982] O.J. L378/15; Dir. 85/203 on air quality standards for nitrogen dioxide [1985] O.J. L87/1.

micrograms), winter averages (130 to 180 micrograms) and yearly averages, measured in 24-hour intervals (250 to 350 micrograms) per cubic metre; these last values were not to be exceeded for more than three consecutive days during a year. Directive 80/779 fixed sampling and analysis methods; since Member States could not agree on one single method, two of them were fixed "which are not completely equivalent" (Art. 10(4)). In 1989, Directive 89/427 eliminated this duality.[12]

For lead, the air quality value—2 micrograms per cubic metre—and a sampling method for measuring the concentration of lead in the air were established. The air quality value for nitrogen dioxide was 200 micrograms per cubic metre; Directive 85/203 set detailed calculation provisions, rules on the monitoring of concentrations and a reference method for analysis.

8—06 The air quality values were not to be exceeded throughout the territory of Member States. However, the choice of fixing the number and location of measurement stations was left at the discretion of Member States. Also, Member States had the possibility of designating zones where the limit values were exceeded or likely to be exceeded. The Member State had to notify the Commission of these zones and to submit a plan for reducing air pollution in order to comply with the air quality values "as soon as possible"[13] and not later than 1989 (lead), 1993 (sulphur dioxide and suspended particulates) and 1994 (nitrogen dioxide).

The different provisions proved in practice[14] so complicated that compliance with the directives' air quality values could not be enforced. The possibility that Member States could place measurement stations de facto wherever they wanted, the general imprecisions of the instruments, the option of placing the instruments close or far from a road, at 0.50 metres or 2 metres above ground, the yearly averages, the communication of data with considerable delay and other factors had as a consequence that a failure to respect the values was hardly ever found, when a Member State was tolerant. The best example might be Athens in Greece, where pollution levels are so high that in the past several decades the Greek Government has taken numerous steps to reduce emissions. Yet, the Commission never undertook action against Greece to have the air quality values respected.

8—07 Some zones, where air quality values were exceeded or likely to be exceeded, were designated, but clean-up plans were not systematically submitted to the Commission; instead, Member States tended to call whatever action they undertook a clean-up plan under Article 3 of the different three directives. The Commission neither published nor monitored such plans and in no case was formal action against a Member State undertaken because the clean up was not achieved "as soon as possible". Generally, it appears that Member States exceeded the air quality values of the directives in a not insignificant number of cases, without intervention from the Commission.[15] As at national level, disputes on exceedance of air quality values are very rare, and hence I conclude that compliance with air quality values cannot be and is not really enforced.

---

[12] Dir. 89/427 [1989] O.J. L201/53.

[13] Dir. 80/779 (n. 11), Art. 3(2); Dir. 82/884 (n. 11), Art. 3(2); Dir. 85/203 (n. 11), Art. 3(2), which uses the words "as quickly as possible.

[14] See Commission, First annual report on the implementation of Directive 80/779, COM (85) 368 of July 12, 1985; second annual report on the implementation of Directive 80/779, COM (88) 142 of March 24, 1988; first annual report on the implementation of Directive 82/884, SEC (90) 1842 of January 10, 1990; report on the state of implementation of ambient air quality directives, COM (95) 372 of July 26, 1995.

[15] See data in COM (95) 372 (n. 14), pp. 49 et seq.

8—08   Number of measuring stations in 1990[16]:

Member State	SO$_2$	Particulates	Lead	NOx
Belgium	66	109	60	18
Denmark	29	18	23	15
Germany	424	387	142	372
France	232	262	72	112
Greece	30	40	1	31
Ireland	52	53	—	4
Italy	382	251	24	137
Luxembourg	5	13	3	5
Netherland	123	62	21	60
Portugal	51	54	—	19
Spain	556	534	37	151
United Kingdom	229	299	26	12

8—09   Overall, it may be said that where Member States were willing and prepared to reduce air pollution by the four regulated pollutants, the directives constituted a valuable yardstick; however, where Member States were not willing, it was hardly ever possible to compel them to do so, by reducing inputs into the environment or by cleaning up existing contamination. The added value of the directives was therefore limited.

The Court of Justice was only seized with questions of formal transposition of the three directives, which confirms the thesis of the unenforcability of air quality values. It held that Member States were obliged to adopt legislation that transposed the directives; they could not satisfy themselves with administrative circulars, in particular because the air quality values were also intended to protect the health of individuals and thus gave them individual rights to see these values respected.[17] Furthermore, Member States were obliged to transpose into national law the requirement that in frontier regions co-operation with regional authorities of neighbouring Member States had to be considered[18]—a judgment which has largely remained a dead letter.

8—10   Member States hardly ever recurred to the guide values laid down in Directives 80/779 and 85/203, nor did they establish more stringent values in sensitive areas (Article 4 of the different directives). Generally, Member States treated the minimum requirements of the directives rather as though they were maximum requirements.

Sulphur dioxide emissions within the Community rose till 1980 and than fell sharply. The Community fixed, in its fifth environmental action programme, a reduction of SO$_2$ emissions, by the year 2000, of 35 per cent of the 1985 emissions; this objective was reached in 1995.[19] Nitrogen oxide emissions have remained more stable, due in particular to the increase in transport. The fifth environmental action programme fixed a 30 per cent reduction in NOx emissions between 1990 and 2000; by 1995, an 8 per cent reduction had been achieved, and it is not likely that the objective will be reached. Lead emissions have been reduced, mainly because of the introduction of lead-free petrol. No information is available on suspended particulates.

8—11   All three directives were applicable over all the territory of Member States as

---

[16] Figures from *ibid.*; the figures for Greece are from 1995; the figures for Ireland and Portugal are unofficial.
[17] Cases C-361/88 *Commission v. Germany* [1991] E.C.R. I-2567; C-59/89 *Commission v. Germany* [1991] E.C.R. I.2607; C-13/90 *Commission v. France* [1991] E.C.R. I-4327; C-14/90 *Commission v. France* [1991] E.C.R. I-4331; C-64/90 *Commission v. France* [1991] E.C.R. I-4335.
[18] Case C-186/91 *Commission v. Belgium* [1993] I-851.
[19] European Environmental Agency, *Europe's environment, the second assessment* (Copenhagen, 1998), no. 4.7.

of January 1, 1994, without the possibility of exceeding the fixed values in specific zones. However, in summer 1994 the Commission made a proposal for a new framework directive on air quality values, which the Council adopted in 1996.[20] This Directive fixes a number of principles for future air quality values that are to be elaborated for certain air pollutants.[21] These quality values are not to be exceeded "once attained". However, Directive 96/62 allows, under certain conditions, tolerance margins, which may well lead to exceeded values. Member States shall determine those areas in which the air quality values are exceeded. For those areas, they shall set up clean-up plans which will allow the air quality values to be respected within a timespan that is fixed by the Member State itself. The plans must contain a certain amount of minimum information which is specified in annex IV of Directive 96/62 and must be "accessible to the public". The plans, as well as reports on the progress achieved under them, shall be sent to the Commission, which shall publish the list of zones that are affected and "regularly check the implementation of the plans or programmes".

For other pollutants that are not expressly mentioned, Directive 96/62 announced that air quality values and, where appropriate, alert thresholds would be fixed in subsequent daughter directives. Alert thresholds are values with levels "beyond which there is a risk for human health from brief exposure and at which immediate steps shall be taken by Member States"; where these values are exceeded, the population should be informed in an appropriate way.

8—12 Other provisions of Directive 96/62 deal with general rules on the assessment of air quality, general requirements for air quality measures and measures for zones where the air quality values are not exceeded. Directive 96/62 entered into effect in March 1998; its framework character will make it operational only when the different provisions for the individual pollutants have been adopted. It will have to be seen to what extent the general provisions will be derogated from.

A daughter directive to set air quality values for sulphur dioxide, oxides of nitrogen and nitrogen dioxide, particulate matters and lead was adopted in 1999.[22] The Directive aims at progressively replacing Directives 80/779, 82/884 and 85/203. It fixes binding limit values for the different pollutants. A proposal for a directive on limit values for benzene and carbon monoxide (CO) was made in 1999.[23] The proposed limit value for benzene is 5 micrograms per cubic metre, averaged over the calendar year, with a margin of tolerance of 100 per cent at the moment of entry into force of the Directive and a linear reduction, so that by 2010 the margin of tolerance is zero. For CO, the proposed limit value is 10 milligrams per cubic metre (averaged over eight hours) and a 50 per cent margin of tolerance, which is to be reduced to zero by 2005.

(b) Tropospheric ozone

8—13 Tropospheric ozone, in contrast to the ozone at higher altitudes (stratospheric ozone), is the ozone generated near ground level; it is an aggressive pollutant with considerable risks for humans—in particular the respiratory functions—and the

---

[20] Dir. 96/62 (n. 7).

[21] Before the end of 1997, the Commission was to make proposals for sulphur dioxide, nitrogen dioxide, fine particulate matter, suspended particulate matter, and lead. Before March 1998 a proposal was to be made for tropospheric ozone; and before the end of 1999, proposals for benzene, carbon monoxide, polyaromatic hydrocarbons, cadmium, arsenic, nickel and mercury. For this last group of pollutants, no air quality values exist as yet.

[22] Dir. 1999/30 [1999] O.J. L163/41. Proposal [1998] O.J. C9/6; explanatory memorandum COM (97) 500 of October 8, 1997; amended proposal COM (1998) 386 of July 8, 1998; common position [1998] O.J. C360/99.

[23] [1999] O.J. C53/8.

environment. It is a secondary pollutant, formed by the reaction by precursors such as volatile organic compounds (VOCs) and oxides of nitrogen (NOx); ozone formation is increased in warm sunny conditions (summertime smog).

The World Health Organisation has fixed, under health auspices, a guide air quality value value of 120 micrograms per cubic metre of air, which should not be exceeded.[24] At Community level, Directive 92/72[25] sets thresholds for ozone concentrations in the air.[26] However, these values need not be respected and Member States are not required to provide for pollution abatement measures; rather, the values trigger the need to inform or warn the affected population and serve as indicators for the protection of vegetation and human health.

8—14 Directive 92/72 was transposed with a delay by a number of Member States.[27] The number of days where the thresholds were exceeded was considerable in the Community.[28] Data on ozone concentrations within the Community, in particular in urban centres, are not complete, but indicate a trend towards rising concentration levels.[29]

In view of this fact, it is unlikely that the future daughter directive on air quality values for tropospheric ozone will retain the WHO values, since it seems likely that it will not be possible to respect these values by the year 2015. Rather, it is likely that the Commission will orient itself towards setting a target—thus not binding—value which states that the WHO level of 120 micrograms per cubic metre should not be exceeded, by the year 2010, during more than 25 to 35 days per year. It remains to be seen how this discussion evolves in the future.

(c) Other pollutants

8—15 There are no other fixed air quality values at Community level. Directive 84/360[30] established a list of the most important pollutants[31]; Directive 96/62 on ambient air quality established another list.[32] Directive 96/61 on integrated pollution and prevention control requested permits for industrial installations that had to contain emission limit values for pollutants that were likely to be emitted, and established yet another list of air pollutants.[33] The Commission's strategy on

---

[24] 6,000 $\mu g/m^3$ for the protection of vegetation.

[25] Dir. 92/72 on air pollution by ozone [1992] O.J. L297/1.

[26] 110 $\mu g/m^3$ as health protection threshold; 200 $\mu g/m^3$ as vegetation protection threshold; 180 $\mu g/m^3$ as population information threshold and 360 $\mu g/m^3$ as population warning threshold. Measuring time and conditions vary for these thresholds.

[27] According to Commission, 14th report on monitoring application of Community law (1996) [1997] O.J. C332/185, measures had been taken for delayed transposition against France, Italy, the Netherlands, Portugal and Finland; against Greece, the matter was submitted to the Court of Justice in 1996 (case C-331/96).

[28] In 1994, there were more than 3,100 episodes where the threshold of 180 $\mu g/m^3$ was exceeded. See also European Environmental Agency (n. 19), no. 5.3.4: "The threshold [110 $\mu g/m^3$] was exceeded in all E.U. countries in 1994–96, in some cases very frequently . . . the health protection threshold . . . was exceeded three times more often than the population information threshold . . . It is difficult to judge whether the population information threshold is of any real benefit to the public."

[29] See also J. Beck, M. Kzyzanowski and B. Koffi, Tropospheric ozone in the European Union. The consolidated report (Luxembourg, 1999)

[30] Dir. 84/360 on the combating of air pollution from industrial plants [1984] O.J. L188/20.

[31] Ibid., annex II: "Sulphur dioxide and other sulphur compounds; oxides of nitrogen and other nitrogen compounds; carbon monoxide; organic compounds, in particular hydrocarbons (except methane); heavy metals and their compounds; dust; asbestos (suspended particulates and fibres), glass and mineral fibres; chlorine and its compounds; fluorine and its compounds."

[32] Dir. 96/62 (n. 7), annex I: "Sulphur dioxide, nitrogen dioxide; fine particulate matters such as soot; suspended particulate matters; lead; ozone; benzene; carbon monoxide; poli-aromatic hydrocarbons; cadmium; arsenic; nickel; mercury."

[33] Dir. 96/61 (n. 6), annex III: "Sulphur dioxide and other sulphur compounds; oxigens of nitrogen and other nitrogen compounds; carbon monoxide; volatile organic compounds; metals and their compounds; dust; asbestos; chlorine and its compounds; fluorine and its compounds; arsenic and its compounds; cyanide and its compounds; substances and preparations which possess carcinogenic or mutagenic properties."

acidification[34] identified, after SO_2 and NOx, ammonia (NH_3) as a generator of acidification.

The Commission is preparing a proposal for a directive that sets national emission ceilings for certain pollutants. A formal proposal is likely to be made in 1999. The intention is to provide for such national emission ceilings for sulphur dioxide, nitrogen oxides, volatile organic compounds (VOCs) and ammonia. The ceilings would be expressed in kilotonnes per year and per Member State, and would have to be complied with by a given year. Member States would have to take measures in order not to exceed the ceilings; whether these measures are regulatory or fiscal, addressed to installations, products, infrastructure or others, would be left to the discretion of Member States.

8—16   National emission ceilings were already fixed, for SO_2 and NOx, for emissions from large combustion installations.[35] They were generally recommended by the Commission's acidification strategy.[36] The question as to how compliance will be monitored and what will happen in cases where the ceilings are exceeded, are still under discussion. My opinion is that such ceilings are unenforceable and therefore constitute—de facto—guidelines.

If one looks at the Community air quality values generally, one has to conclude that the respect of these values, though they are legally binding, is neither enforced by the Commission nor enforced by individuals. It is true that the Court of Justice had paved the way for such enforcement by individuals by stating that "whenever the exceeding of the limit values could endanger human health, the persons concerned must be in a position to rely on mandatory rules in order to be able to assert their rights."[37] However, the absence of measuring stations and, in particular, of available data on air quality (data are made publicly available months or even years later, if they are made available at all) leads to the de facto situation that Community air quality values constitute policy guidance standards rather than legal instruments. This situation is obviously even more apparent, where directives do not even require Member States to respect the air quality standards and to take measures where they are exceeded, as is the case with Directive 92/72, which only requires information to be given to the public.

3. POLLUTION EMISSIONS FROM MOBILE SOURCES (PRODUCTS)

8—17   Pollution emission limit values from products were, historically, the first Community measures on air pollution. The purpose of these first provisions was, however, not to combat air pollution, but to ensure the free circulation of products.[38] The efforts undertaken by the Community to reduce air emissions from products, in particular from means of transport, were not at all systematic. They concentrated on cars, since it became more and more obvious that individual passenger transport is the main generator of air emissions within the Community. Measures to combat air

---

[34] Commission, Communication on a Community strategy to combat acidification, COM (97) 88 of March 12, 1997.
[35] Dir. 88/609 (n. 10); see also below, para. 8–37.
[36] Commission, COM (97) 88 (n. 34).
[37] Case C-361/88 Commission v. Germany [1991] E.C.R. I-2567, para. 16; see also L. Krämer, European environmental law casebook (London, 1993), pp. 367 et seq.
[38] See Dir. 70/220 on measures to be taken against air pollution by emission from motor vehicles [1970] O.J. L176/1, 2nd and 3rd considerants: "a regulation of 31 March 1969 on the composition of exhaust gases emitted from petrol engines of motor vehicles was published in France . . . those provisions are liable to hinder the establishment and proper functioning of the common market; . . . it is therefore necessary that all Member States adopt the same requirements . . .".

emissions from trucks, from railways, aeroplanes and ships were much less intense and less systematic.

As regards the air polluting substances contained in fuels—for example, lead in petrol and sulphur in diesel fuel—see paragraph 6–10, above.

(a) Air emission from cars

8—18 Community measures to reduce air emissions from cars started in 1970. These measures concentrated on emission limit values, and, since the early 1980s, when the dying forests signalled the need for more stringent measures, on the fuels used by cars. Consequently, they were based on Article 100 (now 94), and since 1987 on Article 100a (now 95) E.C.[39]

The adoption of stringent measures that influence the design of the car, for instance by imposing the construction of cars that do not exceed a maximum speed limit—for instance, 100 kilometres per hour—or which do not burn more than a certain amount of fuels per 100 kilometres,[40] were never seriously discussed, probably because such considerations were considered to be much too interventionist. Beginning in the early 1990s, directives also stated that progress in reducing air emissions from cars is countered by the increase in the car fleet and the number of kilometres driven by each individual car, so that the overall reduction of air emissions is, at best, extremely small.

8—19 The Community did not take measures to introduce taxes or charges for cars according to their emissions into the environment; neither did it take any measures for Community-wide tax incentives in order to promote the marketing or use of less-polluting cars, as basic objections against Community tax measures made such an approach impossible. Since the late 1980s, the Community has accepted that Member States can grant tax incentives for less-polluting cars, albeit under very restrictive conditions[41] that made this instrument almost worthless. Indeed, only temporary incentives were allowed, during the transition period of the directive that reduced air emissions. Only incentives for new cars were permitted; incentives for the retrofitting of existing cars were not. This, for instance, made it impossible to give incentives for the retrofitting of existing cars with catalytic converters. If one considers that the lifetime of a car is at least 12 years and that standards that required the use of catalytic converters were only made mandatory for all new cars as of January 1, 1993, one can easily see that by the year 2005, when all cars must be equipped with catalytic converters, the reduction in air emissions will have been eaten up by the traffic increase.

8—20 Measures to reduce air emissions from cars have, since the early 1980s, been prepared by the Commission's so-called Auto/Oil Programme, which set up working groups where the European associations of the car and petrol industries were invited to "make available their considerable know-how and expertise".[42]

---

[39] See, however, below, para. 8–24.

[40] See, however, European Parliament, Res. of April 10, 1997 [1997] O.J. C132/170, where the Parliament requests that new cars do not consume more than 5 litres of petrol (4.5 litres of diesel) per 100km as of January 1, 2005 and not more than 3 litres of petrol or diesel as of January 1, 2010. The Commission concluded, in 1998, an agreement with the car industry on these issues, see below.

[41] See, for instance, Dir. 94/12 [1994] O.J. L100/42, Art. 3, which repeats the standard formula for such conditions for national tax incentives: "they shall apply to all new vehicles offered for sale on the market of a Member State which comply in advance with the requirements of Directive 70/220, as amended by this Directive; they shall be terminated with effect from the mandatory application of the emission values laid down in Article 2(3) for new motor vehicles; for each type of motor vehicle, they shall be for an amount lower than the additional cost of the technical solutions introduced to ensure compliance with the values set and of their installation on the vehicle."

[42] COM (96) 248 of June 18, 1996, p. 44; this remark refers to the Auto/Oil Programme which started in 1992 and had the task of developing an "objective assessment of the most cost-effective package of measures to reduce emissions . . .".

Member States were kept informed of the discussions, in informal meetings. Four specific meetings were organised to inform the "Members of the European Parliament"—thus not the Parliament itself—of the work carried out. Other interested groups were not consulted.[43]

The Auto/Oil Programme tried to find combined solutions concerning the emission from cars, the quality and composition of fuels, and new emission control technologies, on a "cost-effective"[44] basis. Proposals for fixing emission limit values by the Commissions were based on the results of this programme. Of course, these proposals can be—and were—criticised for not being based on an objective assessment, but rather on an assessment which conformed to the interests of these two industrial sectors. In any case, it seems unlikely that the Commission could develop policies and proposals which would be against the interests of these two industrial sectors. Also, the documents and data published do not really allow for a critical examination as to whether the suggested measures really constitute the best environmental protection potential or whether they are just a compromise between diverging interests.

8—21   In the early 1970s, different directives were adopted for petrol- and diesel-driven cars. Later, this differentiation was abandoned, in the same way as was the differentiation between passenger cars, light and heavy commercial vehicles and trucks. Furthermore, recent directives have already announced the adoption of new provisions that are aimed at further strengthening the emission limit values and which enter into details as to what such new proposals shall contain.[45] The numerous overlapping directives and proposals which contain extensive technical details, measurements, control and test rules and the lack of consolidating these texts have led to a situation in which the legal provisions lack transparency and cannot really be checked by people other than specialist experts. This is strengthened by the fact that changes to previous provisions are normally signalled by expressions such as "40 per cent reduction", "70 per cent reduction", and so on; and it adds to confusion that such reductions are calculated by including, in addition, the reduction in the fuel composition or changes in test methods.

Directive 70/220 set, in 1970, limit values for carbon monoxide and unburnt hydrocarbon emissions.[46] In 1977, limit values for nitrogen oxides were established.[47] The values for these three pollutants were progressively reduced by different directives.[48] In 1989, more stringent emission limit values for gaseous pollutants were introduced and progressively extended to all passenger cars. Emissions from diesel engines were fixed in 1972 and progressively reduced.[49] All emission limit values are the subject of an almost permanent review discussion.

---

[43] *Ibid.*, p. 90.

[44] See the criticism of the European Parliament on the way in which this cost-effectiveness was calculated without taking into consideration social costs and environmental costs: Res. of February 18, 1998 [1998] O.J. C80/92.

[45] See, as an example, Dir. 94/12 relating to measures to be taken against air pollution by emissions from motor vehicles and amending Directive 70/220 [1994] O.J. L100/42, Art. 4.

[46] Dir. 70/220 [1970] O.J. L76/1.

[47] Dir. 77/102 [1977] O.J. L32/32.

[48] Dir. 74/290 [1974] O.J. L159/61; Dir. 78/665 [1978] O.J. L223/48; Dir. 83/351 [1983] O.J. L197/1; Dir. 88/76 [1988] O.J. L36/1; Dir. 89/458 [1989] O.J. L226/1; Dir. 91/441 [1991] O.J. L242/1; Dir. 94/12 (n. 41).

[49] Dir. 72/306 [1972] O.J. L190/1; Dir. 88/77 [1988] O.J. L36/33; Dir. 91/542 [1991] O.J. L295/1.

8—22   The present emission limit values (g/km) are as follows[50]:

	Carbon monoxide (CO)		Hydrocarbons HC		NOx		Particulates Pt
	Petrol	Diesel	Petrol	Diesel	Petrol	Diesel	Diesel
Passenger cars	2.3	0.64	0.2	—	0.15	0.50	0.08
Commercial vehicles							
—up to 1,250 kg	2.3	0.64	0.2	—	0.15	0.50	0.05
—1,250–1,700kg	4.17	0.80	0.25	—	0.18	0.65	0.07
—above 1,700 kg	5.22	0.95	0.29	—	0.21	0.78	0.10

8—23   The biggest surprise in these values is the absence of an emission limit value for carbon dioxide (CO_2), the gas which is held to be primarily responsible for climate changes and designated as such under the Kyoto Protocol on Climate Change.[51] In 1990 CO_2 emissions from passenger cars accounted for about 45 per cent of transport CO_2 emissions and about 12 per cent of total CO_2 emissions in the European Union; a 20 per cent increase is expected by 2000 and a 36 per cent increase by 2010.[52]

In 1993, the Commission had announced a proposal for a directive on an emission limit value for CO_2 for cars[53] and found support from the European Parliament.[54] In 1996, the Commission suggested introducing financial incentives to lower fuel consumption, to introduce a labelling scheme for fuel consumption of cars, to conclude an environmental agreement with the car industry to reduce CO_2 emissions from cars and to promote research and development[55]; at the same time, it started discussions with car manufacturers on an agreement. It is not clear what particular reasons have been pleaded for having an environmental agreement just for CO_2,[56] but not for the other above-mentioned pollutants.

8—24   In summer 1998, the Commission announced[57] that it was ready to accept the offer by ACEA (Association des constructeurs européens d'automobiles), which groups together 11 European car manufacturers, to limit the CO_2 emissions for new cars which are brought into circulation in the Community from 2008 onwards to 140 grammes per kilometre. This offer was different from what the Council had wished to see reached (120 grammes per kilometre by 2005 or, at the latest, by 2010). The agreement that was subsequently made consisted, in legal terms, of:

- a commitment by ACEA[58];

- a recommendation by the European Commission, addressed to ACEA[59];

- an exchange of letters between the Commission and ACEA.

---

[50] Dir. 98/69 [1998] O.J. L350/1, annex; these values apply to cars put into circulation after January 1, 2000; more stringent values will apply after 2005.

[51] See below, para. 8–54.

[52] See for the overall emission of CO_2 within the European Union, Written Question E-2572/96 (Amadeo) [1997] O.J. C83/30.

[53] Commission, Legislative programme 1994, COM (93) 588 of November 24, 1993, para. 241.

[54] European Parliament Res. of October 27, 1993 [1993] O.J. C315/160.

[55] COM (95) 689 of December 20, 1995; Commission Communication on transport and CO_2; COM (1998) 204 of March 31, 1998.

[56] European Parliament Res. of February 19, 1998 [1998] O.J. C80/227, pt. 14.

[57] Commission, COM (1998) 495 of July 29, 1998.

[58] Published as annex to *ibid.*

[59] Commission Rec. 1999/125 [1999] O.J. L40/49.

8—25   The commitment states that as long as ACEA's promises are kept, ACEA is assuming "that this commitment provides complete and sufficient substitute for all new regulatory measures to limit fuel consumption or CO_2 emissions, and for any additional fiscal measures in pursuit of the CO_2 objectives of this commitment"; this expresses the expectation that the Community legislature—possibly also the national legislature—will not take regulatory measures to reduce CO_2 emissions from cars during the lifetime of the agreement. The commitment is, furthermore, based on several assumptions—amongst others, that non-ACEA car manufacturers will commit themselves to equivalent CO_2 reduction efforts. The agreement provides for a framework for a future monitoring procedure, which includes the statement that the Commission's official reports on the monitoring results will not refer to individual companies' achievements, in order to avoid competition being distorted.

The Commission entered into the agreement once the Council had signalled its endorsement of the reduction targets and the European Parliament had reluctantly accepted the deal. The Committee of the Regions and the Economic and Social Committee had no say in the matter. Furthermore, the agreement was made with ACEA alone. In summer 1999, the Commission signalled that an equivalent agreement with Japanese car manufacturers was imminent; discussions with Korean manufacturers continued.

The agreement refers to the Community market, not to cars which are marketed in other parts of the world, though such a restriction would normally also be the consequence of any regulatory measure.

8—26   The implementation and enforcement of the different adopted emission limit values does not seem to pose problems in view of the small number of car manufacturers and importers on the Community market. It should be stressed, however, that all emission limit values only apply to new cars, that is, those which have been put on the market after the entering into effect of the different provisions.[60] Since cars have an average lifetime of more than 12 years, this period of 12 years has to be added in order to work out when the Community car fleet will fully comply with the the Community values. And the monitoring of compliance with the emission limit values during the lifetime of a car is monitored rather differently within the different Member States of the Community.

(b) Air emissions from aeroplanes, ships and machines

8—27   There are no Community emission limit values for ships and aeroplanes. Both sectors are, in part, regulated by global organisations (cartels), the International Maritime Organisation (IMO) and the International Civil Aviation Organisation (ICAO).

In 1998 the Commission submitted, for the first time, a proposal on the limitation of emissions for civil subsonic aeroplanes.[61] The proposal only concerned nitrogen oxides and did not contain an emission limit value, but only a formula for calculating such emissions. The Commission mentioned in the explanatory memorandum[62] that ICAO had set up a working group to suggest reductions for nitrogen dioxide emissions worldwide, but that ICAO had not been able to agree on the proposals. Thus, the Commission took over the proposals made by the ICAO working group.

8—28   The proposal is based on Article 80(2) (ex 84(2)) E.C., which is a surprising

---

[60] See also Commission proposal for a Council decision on the monitoring of CO_2 emissions of new passenger cars [1998] O.J. C231/6; amendment [1999] O.J. C83/9.
[61] [1998] O.J. C108/14.
[62] COM (97) 629 of December 3, 1997.

legal basis since all emission limit values for cars and commercial vehicles have been based on Article 95 (ex 100a) E.C. It differentiates between larger and smaller aeroplanes; for the smaller aeroplanes a less severe regime is proposed. Small aeroplanes are not covered by the proposal, because, as the Commission explained, the ICAO proposals did not include small aeroplanes. The calculations for the limit values are based on a worldwide average of aeroplanes, since this was the method of calculation by ICAO.

Only aeroplanes registered in the Community are submitted to the proposal. Furthermore, existing aeroplanes are not covered by the proposal: only new engines manufactured after the end of 2007 shall undergo the restriction, which will lead, as estimated by the Commission, to an overall reduction of 16 per cent of nitrogen dioxide emissions; at the same time, the Commission estimates an increase of nitrogen oxide emissions by aeroplanes by around 6 per cent per annum till the year 2010. Taking all these figures and estimations together, the value of the proposal of effectively reducing nitrogen dioxide emissions from airplanes and making an effective contribution to the protection of the environment becomes doubtful.

8—29   There has been, to date, no Community provision to regulate air pollution emissions from ships. Internationally, the pollution from ships is discussed in the context of the Convention for the prevention of pollution from ships (MARPOL), to which the Community is not a signatory. While some measures have been taken in that context, no measures have as yet been adopted at Community level. Discussion has taken place as to amending Directive 93/12[63] in order to reduce the sulphur content of bunker oil, which is used by ships, and/or to introduce environmentally differentiated shipping dues. Both actions, if ever it were decided to realise them, are not likely to be in effect before 2005.

It should be pointed out that there are also no emission limit values for other ships, in particular those for internal navigation and sport boats. For sport boats the Commission announced the elaboration of Community provisions.[64]

8—30   As regards machines, the Community adopted, in 1997, for the first time, a Directive[65] which set air emission limit values for machines other than passenger and commercial vehicles, airplanes and ships; it thus concerns machinery such as compressors, forestry equipment, road-maintenance equipment, snow-plough equipment, aerial lifts, mobile cranes and ground supports in airports. The Directive is based on Article 95 (ex 100a) E.C. and concerns machinery which is type-approved after 1997; existing non-road mobile machinery is thus not affected.

8—31   The emission limit values are introduced in two steps (1998 and 2000) and are differentiated according to the power of the engine. They were fixed as follows (g per kWh):

	Carbon monoxide (CO)	Hydrocarbons (HC)	Nitrogen oxides (NOx)	Particulates (PT)
Step I	5.0–6.5	1.3	9.2	0.54–0.85
Step II	3.5–5.5	1.0–1.5	6.0–8.0	0.2–0.8

The Directive envisages that further measures will be taken after the year 2000.

---

[63] Dir. 93/12 on the sulphur content of certain combustible fuels [1993] O.J. L74/81; for this Directive, see also para. 6–11.
[64] Written Question E-1698/97 (Oomen-Ruiten) [1998] O.J. C21/83.
[65] Dir. 97/68 relating to measures against the emissions of gaseous and particulate pollutants from internal combustion engines to be installed in non-road mobile machinery [1998] O.J. L59/86.

(c) Emissions of volatile organic compounds (VOCs)

8—32 Volatile organic compounds (VOCs) are generated from the handling of (motor) gasoline; this gasoline is stored before being distributed, which can take place by pipeline, road trucks, rail cars and by barge and ships. After that distribution, the gasoline is discharged to a storage tank. During all these stages of loading/unloading, the gasoline generates VOCs. VOCs are among the precursors of photochemical oxidants such as tropospheric ozone, a potential greenhouse gas.[66] Some VOCs that are emitted are classified as toxic, teratogenic or carcinogenic.

In 1990, the Community emitted some 14.2 million tonnes of VOC, some 7.47 million tonnes (52.5 per cent) of mobile sources and about 6.74 million tonnes (47.5 per cent) of stationary sources. The biggest emitting sectors are road transport with 5.89 million tonnes (41.5 per cent), solvent use with 4.09 million tonnes (28.7 per cent) and the extraction and distribution of fossil fuels with 1.04 million tonnes (7.3 per cent).

8—33 Directive 91/441 and other directives on motor vehicle emissions[67] had already introduced a number of measures to reduce VOC emissions from motor vehicles, the main source of such emissions, without fixing emission limit values. It is estimated that these measures will reduce VOC emissions from road transport by about one third.

Council Directive 94/63[68] followed the same line; it deals with the VOC emissions resulting from the storage of petrol and its distribution from terminals to service stations, and requires Member States to make sure that the conditions laid down in the Directive and its annexes are complied with. The Directive is based on Article 95 (ex 100a) E.C.; It also applies to road trucks, which is the reason why it is mentioned in this chapter; yet it also applies to stationary sources and allows Member States to fix more stringent provisions (Arts 3(3) and 4(3)). The discussion of limiting VOC emissions from other stationary sources will be discussed below, paragraph 8–50.

8—34 Contrary to what its title provides, this Directive does not contain any emission limit values, but rather lays down requirements for storage installations at terminals (stationary petrol tanks, annex I), for loading and unloading of mobile containers at terminals (annex II), for loading and storage installations at service stations and terminals, where the intermediate storage of vapour is carried out (annex III) and specifications for bottom-loading, vapour collection and overfill protection of European road tankers (annex IV). As mentioned, it is thus a measure that affects both mobile and stationary sources of VOC generation. Interestingly, the emission of VOCs from the charging of ships is only covered by a non-committing statement in a recital.[69]

---

[66] See above, para. 8–13.
[67] Dir. 91/441 [1991] O.J. L242/1; Dir. 91/542 [1991] O.J. L295/1; Dir. 93/59 [1993] O.J. L186/21; Dir. 94/12 [1994] O.J. L100/42.
[68] Dir. 94/63 on the control of volatile organic compound (VOC) emissions resulting from the storage of petrol and its distribution from terminals to service stations [1994] O.J. L365/24.
[69] Dir. 94/63 (n. 68), recital 6: "On grounds of international standardisation and of safety during the loading of ships, standards must be drawn up at International Maritime Organisation level for vapour control and recovery systems to apply to both loading installations and ships, whereas the Community must therefore endeavour to ensure that the necessary provisions are introduced into the Marpol Convention during the current revision of Marpol due to be completed in 1996; whereas in the event that the Marpol Convention is not so revised, the Community, after discussion with its major trading partners, should propose appropriate measures to apply to ships and port installations servicing ships."

4. AIR EMISSIONS FROM INSTALLATIONS

(a) Framework provisions

8—35   Community law contains only very few provisions which relate to installations, since it is thought that products that circulate within the Community should be exposed to uniform rules, but that installations do not circulate freely. Neither has the fact that products which leave installations compete with each other, nor has the knowledge that water discharges and air emissions[70] from installations circulate and pollute transnationally, changed this attitude.

Following the discovery of dying forests in the early 1980s, the Community discussed air pollution at a summit of heads of state and governments in 1983. In 1984, it adopted a framework directive on air emissions from industrial installations,[71] which it based on Articles 94 and 308 (ex 100 and 235) E.C. The Directive introduced a general authorisation procedure for all installations which belonged to a positive list that was defined in an annex. The authorisation could only be given where "all appropriate preventive measures against air pollution have been taken, including the application of the best available technology, provided that the application of such measures does not entail excessive costs" and that the plant did not cause "significant air pollution" (Article 4), in particular from a number of pollutants which were mentioned in an annex.[72] The Council committed itself to fix, "if necessary", emission limit values based on the best available technology not entailing excessive costs. For existing installations, "Member States shall implement policies and strategies, including appropriate measures, for the gradual adaptation" of these plants.

8—36   Directive 84/360 was transposed into national law by all Member States, but had a rather limited effect. The very loose drafting did not push for changes in the practice that had existed up to then. The "best available technology not entailing excessive costs" proved to be an empty formula that did not require measures to reduce air emissions. Efforts at Community level to elaborate non-binding technical papers of what constituted, for a specific industrial sector, best available technology, had no visible effect on the permitted practice in Member States, particularly as the cost element remained decisive in each specific case.

Also, no measures are known which were imposed, by virtue of Directive 84/360, on existing installations in order gradually to lead to air emission reductions. Since on the one hand Member States were allowed to take more stringent measures than those laid down in the Directive and, on the other hand, no action was taken against a Member States for lack of action, one here finds another example where the added value of Community legislation to environmental protection is small.

(b) Large combustion plants

8—37   Combustion plants account for 63 per cent of SO_2 emissions and 21 per cent NOx emissions in the Community. In 1988, the Council adopted a Directive to reduce air emission from large combustion plants.[73] The Directive applies to new and existing combustion plants—"any technical apparatus in which fuels are oxidized in order to use the heat thus generated"—with 50 MW or more thermal input. New combustion

---

[70] It is this transboundary circulation of air emissions which creates, under the commerce clause, federal competence for air emissions in the United States.

[71] Dir. 84/360 on the combating of air pollution from industrial plants [1984] O.J. L188/20.

[72] See the list in n. 31, above.

[73] Dir. 88/609 on the limitation of emissions of certain pollutants into the air from large combustion plants [1988] O.J. L336/1.

plants have to comply with emission limit values for sulphur dioxide, oxides of nitrogen and dust:

8—38 Sulphur dioxides[74]

Solid fuels:	up to 100 MW:	2000 mg/m^3
	500 MW and over:	400 mg/m^3
Liquid fuels:	up to 300 MW:	1700 mg/m^3
	500 MW and over:	400 mg/m^3
Gaseous fuels in general:		35 mg/m^3
Liquefied gas:		5 mg/m^3
Low calorific gases, coke oven gas, blast-furnace gas		800 mg/m^3

Nitrogen oxides

Solid fuels in general:	650 mg/m^3
Solids with less than 10% volatile compounds:	1300 mg/m^3
Liquid fuels:	450 mg/m^3
Gaseous fuels:	350 mg/m^3

Dust

Solid fuels:	up to 500 MW:	50 mg/m^3
	500 MW and over:	100 mg/m^3
Liquid fuels:		50 mg/m^3
Gaseous fuels:		5 mg/m^3
—Blast furnace gas		10 mg/m^3
—Gases produced by steel industry		50 mg/m^3

8—39 Several derogations from these values are foreseen, in particular for plants that burn indigenous fuels (lignite); furthermore, Spain obtained a special derogation to authorise new plants which exceed the SO$_2$ values.

Directive 88/609 further provided that Member States were entitled to require appropriate design specifications from plants (Article 7), a right which Member States had anyway; that Member States should fix the height of the stacks that were to discharge the air emissions "in such a way as to safeguard health and the environment" (Article 10), a provision which is more declamatory than legally enforceable, because the causal link between stack height, air emissions and health and environment protection cannot be established definitively. A general provision on measuring methods left the details for monitoring compliance to Member States, according to a number of general guidelines (Article 13 and annex IX).

8—40 For existing combustion plants, the Directive introduced national emission ceilings for sulphur dioxide and nitrogen oxides. Calculated on the basis of emissions in the year 1980, Member States had to lower[75] their total emissions of sulphur dioxide from combustion plants in three stages till 2003, and of nitrogen oxides in two stages till 1998.

The Directive was transposed into national law by all Member States, sometimes with a delay.[76] No formal action was started by the Commission because a new or an

---

[74] The emission limit values for SO$_2$ in annexes III and IV are given in graphics, which provide for a linear reduction between 100 (50) MW and 500 MW; whether this form of fixing emission limit values complies with the requirements of legal certainty is doubtful.

[75] Greece, Ireland and Portugal were allowed to increase their SO$_2$ and NOx emissions.

[76] Commission, Monitoring application of Community law 8th report [1991] O.J. C338/1, p. 166; 9th report [1992] O.J. C250/1, p. 127: Belgium (1992), France (1991), United Kingdom (1991), Greece (1993), Ireland (1992), the Netherlands (1991) and Portugal (1991) were late in transposing the Directive.

existing plant did not comply with the Directive's requirement, which is not surprising. Indeed, by its very nature, the monitoring of Member States' compliance with the overall reduction in the emission of pollutants is practically impossible, all the more so since the only information on actual emissions stems from Member States themselves and the emission quantities only refer to existing combustion plants that come under the Directive.[77] The emission data submitted by Member States up to 1993 show that the ceilings have been respected everywhere, with exceptions for sulphur dioxide emissions in Greece in 1993 and nitrogen oxide emissions in Portugal in the same year.

In 1998, the Commission made a proposal for amending Directive 88/609, which aimed, in particular, at the inclusion of some new installations into the Directive's requirements and at a reduction of the above-mentioned emission limit values for sulphur dioxide, nitrogen oxides and dust.[78]

(c) Waste incineration installations

8—41   In 1989, the Community adopted two directives on municipal waste incineration plants.[79] The directives fixed general conditions for the authorisation and functioning of such incinerators, such as the minimum temperature (850°C for two seconds). Requirements for the design of installations were rather vague and largely corresponded to the requirements in Directive 88/609.

8—42   The following emission limit values were fixed for new waste incineration plants (mg/m^3):

Pollutant	Less than 1 tonne/h	1 to 3 tonnes/h	3 tonnes/h or more
Total dust	200	100	30
Lead, chromium copper, magnesium	—	5	5
Nickel, arsenic	—	1	1
Cadmium, mercury	—	0.2	0.2
Hydrochloric acid (HCl)	250	100	50
Hydrofluoric acid (HF)	—	4	2
Sulphur dioxide (SO$_2$)	—	300	300

8—43   Furthermore, during operation, the concentration of carbon monoxide (CO) must not exceed 100mg/m^3 and the concentration of organic compounds (expressed as total carbon) must not exceed 20 mg/m^3 in the combustion gases. Some possibilities for derogations have been fixed, for specific circumstances.

Existing waste incinerators—those which already existed on December 1, 1990—have a number of specific requirements (derogations). Since 1996, those with a capacity of more than six tonnes of waste per hour shall comply with the requirements for new incinerators, as mentioned above. For waste incinerators with a capacity of less than one tonne of waste per hour, the total dust emisssions are fixed at 600 mg/m^3; for plants between 1 and 6 tonnes per hour the total dust emissions is 100 mg/m^3.

---

[77] It is worth mentioning that emissions from new plants (those put into operation after 1987) represented, in 1993, less than 2 per cent of total emissions from large combustion plants.

[78] [1998] O.J. C300/6.

[79] Dir. 89/369 on the prevention of air pollution from new municipal waste incineration plants [1989] O.J. L163/32; Dir. 89/429 on the reduction of air pollution from existing municipal incineration plants [1989] O.J. L203/50.

8—44 Pollutant	Capacity	
Total dust	less than 1 tonne/h: 600 mg/m^3	1 to 6 tonnes/h: 100mg/m^3
Carbon monoxide during operation	100 mg/m^3	

No emission limit values were fixed for other pollutants; and some derogations are fixed for specific circumstances.

8—45   Directive 89/369 was transposed by all Member States except Italy,[80] though sometimes with a delay.[81] The situation is more or less the same as regards Directive 89/429.[82] There are no reports on practical compliance with the directives' requirements that have been published, and no formal action was undertaken by the Commission against a Member State for practical non-compliance.

A proposal to update the two directives is at present being discussed in Council and European Parliament.[83]

In 1994, the Council adopted a Directive on installations for the incineration of hazardous waste,[84] which entered into effect at the beginning of 1997; for existing installations, it shall be applicable from mid-2000 onwards. The Directive is based on Article 175 (ex 130s) E.C. As regards hazardous waste, the Directive refers to Directive 91/689 on hazardous waste,[85] though it provides for some remarkable derogations by not covering certain combustible liquid wastes, hazardous wastes generated and disposed of offshore by the oil and gas industries that are incinerated on board the offshore installations, municipal waste (though such waste may well be hazardous) and, furthermore, incinerators for animal carcasses and non-hazardous infectious clinical waste.

8—46   Hazardous waste incinerators, including industrial installations such as steel works, power plants or cementeries, which co-incinerate wastes together with other fuels, have to obtain permits. A permit may only be granted where the plant's design and operation prevents air pollution as far as is appropriate. The types and quantities of waste which may be incinerated must be specified in the permit. A number of provisions are less stringent for the co-incineration of waste than for their incineration in specialised plants—as if this difference would matter for health or the environment!

The wastes which are to be incinerated must be described as regards "the physical and, as far as practicable, the chemical composition" and as regards their hazard characteristics; it is not quite clear why the addition of practicability has been made. The operator of the plant has to take representative samples, "unless inappropriate".

8—47   The incineration of hazardous waste shall be "as complete as possible"; for that purpose, a number of conditions—combustion at a temperature of at least 850°C, or 1100°C if there are more than 1 per cent halogenated organic substances incinerated or oxygen content of 6 per cent—are fixed. There are a number of other conditions for the oxygen content, the burners, the start-up and shut-down processes and the carbon monoxide concentrations in the combustion gases.

Emission limit values are different according to whether they are daily average or half-hourly average values as far as the following pollutants are concerned:

[80] The Court of Justice found in 1996 that Italy had not yet transposed Directive 89/369: case C-237/95 *Commission v. Italy* [1996] E.C.R. I-3071.
[81] Directive 89/369 was transposed with a delay by Belgium, Spain, Greece, Ireland and Luxembourg: see Commission, Monitoring application of Community law, 9th report [1992] O.J. C250/1, p. 128.
[82] Delays in transposing Directive 89/429 occurred in Belgium, Spain, Greece, Italy, Luxembourg and the United Kingdom.
[83] [1998] O.J. C372/11.
[84] Dir. 94/67 on the incineration of hazardous waste [1994] O.J. L365/34.
[85] Dir. 91/689 on hazardous waste [1991] O.J. L377/20.

8—48 Pollutant	Emission limit values (mg/m^3)
Total dust	10–30
Total organic carbon	10–20
Hydrogen chloride (HCl)	10–60
Hydrogen fluoride (HF)	1–4
Sulphur dioxide (SO$_2$)	50–200

For dioxins and furans, an emission limit value of 0.1 nanograms/m^3 was established; for heavy metals, the following values were fixed:

Cadmium (Cd) and thallium (Tl)	0.05 (0.1)
Mercury (Hg)	0.05 (0.1)
Antimony (Sb), arsenic (As) Lead (Pb), chromium (Cr), cobalt (Co), copper (Cu), manganese (Mn), nickel (Ni), vanadium (V), tin (Sn)	total 0.5 (1)

The figures concern new plants, the figures in brackets existing plants.

8—49   The Directive further contains provisions on the waste generated by the incineration, the discharge of aqueous waste into waters, measurement requirements, frequency and measurement techniques.

By the start of 1997, only Germany and Luxembourg had transposed the Directive into national law; by 1998, the Directive was also transposed by Sweden, France, the Netherlands and Spain.[86]

The Council is trying to bring all provisions on waste incinerators, whether for municipal or hazardous waste, into one single directive, using the proposal for updating the directives on the incineration of municipal waste for this purpose.[87]

(d) Volatile organic compounds (VOCs) from stationary sources

8—50   The Commission had planned, in 1993/1994, to submit a proposal for a directive on VOC emissions resulting from refuelling operations at service stations. Since it was not able to submit such a proposal, seven Member States—most of them with a more active environmental policy—adopted national measures[88]; in view of this development, the Commission provisionally abandoned its plans.[89]

In 1999, the Council adopted Directive 1999/13 on emissions of VOCs from solvent-using industries,[90] which was a follow-up to Directive 94/63.[91] The Directive, which is based on Article 175(1) (ex 130s(1)) E.C., describes the industrial activity—not the installation—which is covered; thus, for instance, coating processes, coil coating, dry cleaning, printing, manufacturing of pharmaceutical products, vehicle refinishing, or wood and plastic lamination are covered. For the different activities, thresholds and emission limit values are set, based on the solvent consumption, the emission limit (milligrams of organic carbon per cubic metre) and the diffuse/total emission limit, expressed as a percentage of solvents input.

8—51   Member States shall ensure compliance either by incorporating the Directive's requirements into the individual permit or by general emission regulations.

---

[86] Commission, Monitoring application of Community law, 14th report (1996) [1997] O.J.C332/1, p. 187.
[87] Commission proposal [1998] O.J. C372/11; see also below, para. 9–13.
[88] Denmark, Germany, Italy, Luxembourg, the Netherlands, Austria and Sweden.
[89] See Written Question E-1666/97 (Bowe) [1998] O.J. C21/80.
[90] Dir. 1999/13 [1999] O.J. L85/1; proposal [1997] O.J. C99/32.
[91] See, above para. 8–32; as mentioned, that Directive also partly covered stationary sources.

Instead of transposing and applying the emission limit values fixed by the Directive, Member States may set up reduction plans for the existing installations that come under the Directive. These plans must reach a result equivalent to the emission limit values. They have to be submitted to the Commission. Where the Commission decides that the measures are insufficient, a negotiation procedure with the Member State in question is foreseen. The final decision is, however, taken by the Commission and is binding upon the Member State, though the Commission only has enforcement tools under Article 226 (ex 169) E.C

Individual operators shall have to comply with the emission limit values or the national reduction plans. However, the emission limit values for diffuse emissions may not be respected by an undertaking that can prove that it is technically and economically impossible to respect them.[92]

8—52 The whole alternative option for ensuring compliance presumes that national plans for clean-up of management can be monitored as regards their compliance, a presumption that is not supported by past experience with clean-up plans.

Installations which are permitted or those which undergo a "substantial change" after April 2001 shall have to comply with the Directive's requirements after the entry into effect of the Directive (in 2001); existing installations must reach compliance by 2007.

The Directive's measures, together with those mentioned above,[93] do not lead to a reduction in VOC emissions in 1999 by 30 per cent with compared to 1990, a commitment which the Community underwent when it signed, in 1992, a Protocol elaborated in the framework of the Convention on long-range transboundary air pollution, of which the Community is a member[94]; therefore, the Community has, to date, not adhered to this Protocol.

(e) IPPC installations

8—53 As mentioned above,[95] Directive 96/61[96] will progressively introduce the principle that emission limit values for industrial installations will be fixed for each individual installation and take into account its geographical, technical and economic specifications. To what extent this Directive will, in future, influence the different directives presented above, is as yet uncertain; likewise it is not clear to what extent the Community will adopt provisions concerning emission limit values for those installations which are not covered by Directive 96/61.

5. CLIMATE CHANGE

(a) General aspects

8—54 Climate change issues appeared in the Community environmental action programmes only rather recently. In the first instance, the Community looked into the question of CFCs, which were first suspected to be the cause of ozone depletion in 1947; in 1980 regulations on CFCs were taken, which were progressively extended and strengthened.[97] The third action programme, for the years 1982–1986, mentioned that the Commission "will continue to study the effects of certain chemicals, such as

---

[92] Dir. 1999/13 (n. 90), Art. 5(3.a) and (3.b).
[93] See para. 8–32.
[94] Dec. 81/462 [1981] O.J. L171/53.
[95] Above, paras 8–03 and 4–20.
[96] Dir. 96/61 concerning integration of pollution prevention and control [1996] O.J. L257/26.
[97] Dec. 80/372 [1980] O.J. L90/45; Dec. 82/795 [1982] O.J. L329/29; Reg. 3322/88 [1988] O.J. L297/1; Reg. 594/91 [1991] O.J. L67/1; Reg. 3093/94 on ozone-depleting substances [1994] O.J. L333/1.

chlorofluorocarbons, on the ozone layer, in the stratosphere and on the climate".[98] The fourth action programme (1987–1992) continued to perceive the climate problem mainly as a problem of CFCs and mentioned, somewhat marginally, that the Community environment research programme covered, amongst other things, "climatology and natural hazards, addressing long-term problems, such as possible climatic changes due to an increase of the CO_2-concentrations in the atmosphere".[99]

8—55   The fifth action programme dedicated a whole section to climate change. It identified carbon dioxide (CO_2), chlorofluorocarbons (CFCs), nitrous oxide (N_2O) and methane (CH_4) as the main agents responsible for climate change and identified the origins of these gases: CO_2 stemmed mainly from burning fossil fuels (energy sector, industry and transport) and deforestation; CFCs entirely stemmed from industrial production; methane gases mainly came from agriculture (cattle and certain crops), energy (natural gas leakages) and waste sites; no statement was made on N_2O.[1] Since the end of the 1980s, the Commission has also made a considerable number of communications to the other institutions in order to establish a Community policy on the different pollutants.[2]

In 1990, the Council agreed, in a non-binding commitment, to stabilise CO_2 emissions by the year 2000 at their 1994 level.[3] In 1998, it declared that CO_2 emissions would probably increase, between 1995 and 2000, by 3 per cent.[4]

8—56   The Community has, with the Member States, adhered to the New York Convention of 1992 on Climate Change.[5] It regularly reports on Community strategies and measures to fight global warming.[6] In 1998, in a Protocol to the Climate Change Convention, agreed in Kyoto, six substances were agreed worldwide as being primarily responsible for climate change: carbon dioxide (CO_2), methane (CH_4), nitrous oxide (N_2O), hydrofluorocarbon (HFC), perfluorocarbon (PFC) and sulphur hexafluoride (SF_6). The European Community and its Member States committed themselves to reducing the emissions of these six gases by 8 per cent from 1990 levels in the period 2008–2012.

8—57   In 1990, the last year for which, at present, data are available, the Community emitted the following quantities of these six gases into the air (expressed in 1000 tonnes)[7]:

Carbon dioxide (CO_2)	GWP[8]:	1	3,285,620
Methane (CH_4)	GWP :	24.5	24,671
Nitrous oxides (N_2O)	GWP :	320	928
Hydrofluorocarbon (HFC)	GWP :	11,700	37,000
Perfluorocarbon (PFC)	GWP :	6,500–9,200	7,000
Sulphur hexafluoride (SF_6)	GWP :	23,900	14,000

---

[98] Third European Community policy and action programme on the environment (1982–1986) [1987] O.J. C46/1, no. 21.

[99] Fourth environmental action programme (1987–1992) [1993] O.J. C328/5, no. 6.3.

[1] "Towards sustainability. A European Community programme of policy and action in relation to the environment and sustainable development" [1993] O.J. C138/5, no. 5.1.

[2] Beginning with COM (89) 656 of January 16, 1989: "L'effet de serre et la Communauté".

[3] (1990) 10 Bulletin of the European Communities, no. 1.3.77.

[4] Dec. 98/352 [1998] O.J. L159/93; in its Resolution of July 8, 1996 [1996] O.J. C224/1, the Council had estimated the increase between 1995 and 2000 at 5 to 8 per cent. Comparisons with the base year of 1990 are not possible.

[5] Dec. 94/69 [1994] O.J. L33/11.

[6] See SEC (95) 451 of March 30, 1995; COM (96) 217 of June 11, 1996.

[7] COM (96) 91 of March 14, 1996, p. 4; as regards the precision of these figures see Written Question E-1206/97 (Amadeo) [1997] O.J. C373/86.

[8] Global Warming Potential (GWP), is expressed in figures which make the different greenhouse gases comparable. The GWP figures are taken from COM (96) 91 (n. 7), p. 6, since there they refer to international calculations; COM (98) 353 of June 3, 1998, p. 8 indicated a GWP for methane of 21 and for N_2O of 310; COM (96) 557 of November 15, 1996, p. 6 indicated a GWP for methane of 62.

8—58 A Commission communication tried to find a Community consensus on the ways to comply with the international Kyoto commitments.[9] However, at its meeting of June 1998, the Council agreed, without the Commission having made any corresponding proposal, that the 8 per cent commitment should and would be reached, if the following reductions of emissions were made by Member States (in per cent)[10]:

Austria	− 13.0
Belgium	− 7.5
Denmark	− 21.0
Finland	0.0
France	0.0
Germany	− 21.0
Greece	+ 25.0
Ireland	+ 13.0
Italy	− 6.5
Luxembourg	− 28.0
Netherlands	− 6.0
Portugal	+ 27.0
Spain	+ 15.0
Sweden	+ 4.0
United Kingdom	− 12.5

8—59 This consensus, which intends to give legally binding form to the United Nations' decision, demonstrates the will of Member States not to let Community integration prevail too much over national sovereignty in external matters. Indeed, it is obvious that motor vehicle emission reductions or emissions from agriculture cannot be decided at a national level, but need, as in the past, Community-wide solutions. The Council's quasi-intergovernmental decision therefore gives instructions rather than guidelines to the Commission to initiate Community measures which allow the Member States' commitments to be honoured; this considerably reduces the Commission's right of initiative. This interdependency is further illustrated by the fact that, of course, national policies—for example, on the introduction of a tax on CO_2 or emission reductions from cars—are influenced by the existence or absence of a Community measure.[11]

All this international discussion on a percentage reduction of emissions should not forget the uncertainty as to what is really needed for protecting the environment. It is less than certain that an 8 per cent reduction of greenhouse gas emissions by 2012, as committed to by industrialised countries in Kyoto, will stop global warming. Indicators, indeed, seem to point to this not being the case. Law is, to that extent, at the service of policy, since it is not able to formulate the rights or the needs of the environment; as nobody in fact knows when climate change caused by anthropogenic causes will be brought to a halt, the formula "sustainable development" is not of any help at all.

---

[9] Commission, "Climate change—towards a European Union post-Kyoto strategy", COM (98) 353 of June 3, 1998.
[10] (1998) 6 *Bulletin of the European Union*, para. 1.3.141.
[11] See, for instance, Commission COM (96) 91 (n. 7), p. 10: "The Nordic countries which have C_2O taxes in place would like to increase these taxes further to fully exploit the potential of the measure, but they are reluctant to do so for reasons of competitiveness, unless a similar tax is introduced at the Community level."

(b) Ozone depletion

8—60   At an international level, ozone-depleting substances are regulated by the Montreal Protocol on substances that deplete the ozone layer, to which the Community adhered[12] and which is regularly updated. Regulation 3093/94,[13] which replaced earlier regulations and which will itself be replaced by new provisions in the near future,[14] transposes the provisions of the Protocol into Community law, though it goes further than the Protocol. The Regulation is based on Article 175 (ex 130s) E.C., though Article 95 (ex 100a) would have been the more correct legal basis, as the Regulation deals with product-related standards.

8—61   The Regulation provides for the following bans or restrictions:

CFCs 11, 12, 113, 114, 115	No production as of January 1, 1995;
Other fully halogenated CFCs	No production as of January 1, 1995;
Halons	No production as of January 1, 1994;
Carbon tetrachloride (CCl4)	No production as of January 1, 1995;
1,1,1-trichloroethane ($C_2H_3Cl_3$)	No production as of January 1, 1996;
Methyl bromide (CH_3Br)	75% of the production of 1991 as of January 1, 1998;
Hydrobromofluorocarbons (HBFCs)	No production as of January 1, 1996.

8—62   The import of such substances into the Community is, in certain quantities, possible; the quantities are controlled and set by the Commission.[15]

The production of hydrochlorofluorocarbons (HCFCs) is not controlled. The supply of HCFCs—that is, the placing on the market or the use of HCFCs by producers for their own use—has been frozen since 1995, and shall be progressively reduced and phased out as of January 1, 2015. The use of HCFCs is prohibited, but exceptions are made for certain uses; the number of these exceptions will be gradually reduced over time.

The Regulation provides for detailed rules on import of ozone-depleting substances from third countries; export of such substances to third countries that have not adhered to the Montral Protocol is prohibited. The Council also has the right to regulate the import of products which were produced with the help of such substances, though they do not contain them; to date, no such provisions have been adopted.

8—63   Undertakings are obliged to inform the Commission in detail on production, processing, recycling, uses and other data on ozone-depleting substances. The Commission may ask national authorities to make investigations as regards these substances.

The industrial gases hydrofluorocarbons (HFCs) are not covered by Regulation 3093/94 or, indeed, by any other piece of Community legislation. HFCs were developed largely as alternatives to CFCs, when these were progressively banned under the Montreal Protocol.

---

[12] Dec. 88/540 [1988] O.J. L297/8; the Montreal Protocol was elaborated in the context of the Vienna Convention of 1985 on the protection of the ozone layer, to which the Community also adhered by Dec. 88/540.

[13] Reg. 3093/94 (n. 97).

[14] See Commission proposal for a new regulation, COM (1998) 398 of August 14, 1998 [1998] O.J. C286/6; amended [1999] O.J. C83/4.

[15] See, for instance, Dec. 96/261 [1996] O.J. L89/30.

(c) Greenhouse gases

8—64   In 1991 the Commission adopted a Communication on measures to combat global warming,[16] which suggested, essentially, three types of measures; these measures were, in later years, prolonged and adapted, and continue to constitute the frame within which Community activities are grouped. Besides these measures, there are obviously programmes and measures at national level, which need to be taken into consideration.

(i) Energy conservation and energy technology

8—65   In order to promote better energy conservation and use, the Community adopted several programmes for the demonstration and dissemination of cleaner and more efficient energy techniques.[17]

Directive 93/76, which was based on Articles 175 and 308 (ex 130s and 235) E.C., aimed at improving energy efficiency in housing, cars and industrial installations and promoting public investment schemes[18]; the Council stated in this regard that the residential and tertiary sectors accounted for nearly 40 per cent of final energy consumption. It requested Member States to draw up and implement programmes for:

- the energy certification of buildings;

- the billing of heating, air-conditioning and hot water costs on the basis of actual consumption;

- third-party financing for energy-efficiency investments in the public sector;

- thermal insulation of new buildings;

- regular inspections of boilers;

- energy audits of undertakings with high energy consumption.

8—66   Details for drawing up such programmes were entirely left to Member States. The Directive entered into effect at the end of 1994. By the end of 1996, only France, Denmark, the Netherlands and the United Kingdom had informed the Commission of transposition measures.[19]

Council Decision SAVE II provided for financial assistance for energy-saving measures till the year 2000.[20] Two other decisions provided for financial support for energy-saving measures and renewable sources of energy[21]; the Decision to promote alternative energies was prolonged till the end of 1999, though with remarkably little financial support.[22]

---

[16] COM (91) 249 of September 25, 1991; in later Community documents, this Communication is regularly quoted under the number SEC (91) 1744 of October 14, 1991.
[17] Dec. 91/565 concerning the promotion of energy efficiency in the Community [1991] O.J. L307/34; Dec. 93/500 concerning the promotion of renewable energy sources in the Community (ALTENER) [1993] O.J. L235/41; Dec. 94/911 adopting a specific programme of research and technological development, including demonstration, in the field of environment and climate (1994 to 1998) [1994] O.J. L361/1; Dec. 96/737 on financial assistance for energy-saving measures (SAVE II) [1996] O.J. L335/50.
[18] Dir. 93/76 to limit carbon dioxide emissions by improving energy efficiency (SAVE I) [1993] O.J. L237/28; see also Commission proposal COM (92) 182 of June 26, 1992, which had suggested considerably stronger measures.
[19] Commission, Monitoring application of Community law (1996) [1997] O.J. C332/1, p. 191.
[20] Dec. 96/737 [1996] O.J. L335/50.
[21] Dec. 91/565 and Dec. 93/500 (n. 17).
[22] Dec. 98/352 (ALTENER II) [1998] O.J. L159/53: for the next two years the financial support given is 22 million euro.

At the end of 1997, the Commission adopted a Whitebook on renewable sources of energy,[23] where it was suggested, in particular, to increase the percentage of renewable energies from its present level of 6 per cent to 12 per cent by 2010. This political intention would require a whole series of measures, such as price differentiation between conventional and renewable energy sources, labelling, research and development measures, financial assistance, and so on; most of these measures would have to be taken at the level of Member States. Also, organic waste—that is, waste from agriculture, which is often called, in euphemistic terms, "biomass"—cannot really be considered a renewable source of energy, as its landfill and its incineration cause the same problems as the disposal of other waste.

The Council welcomed the intention to double the percentage of renewable energies; it took up the differentiation, made by the Commission, between biomass and waste, and suggested the making of concrete proposals.[24]

(ii) Monitoring mechanisms

8—67   The Community adopted a Decision to monitor CO_2 emissions and other greenhouse gases[25]; these other greenhouse gases were not named in the Decision. Member States were asked to limit CO_2 emissions and regularly to report on such emissions. In 1999, this Decision was amended to include now "all anthropogenic greenhouse gas emissions".[26] The Commission regularly reports under this Decision, evaluating the national programmes to limit greenhouse gas emissions.[27]

It is remarkable that these reports contain no data on the three gases hydrofluorocarbons (HFCs), perfluorcarbons (PFCs) and hexafluorides (SF_6). The proposal for an amendment of Decision 93/389, which is at present under discussion in the Council, provides for the first time for the collection of data on these gases.[28]

(iii) Fiscal measures

8—68   In 1992, the Commission proposed a directive for a tax on fossil fuels, the tax level to be to 50 per cent of the energy content and to 50 per cent of the carbon content of the energy product; the amount suggested was up to $10 per barrel of oil.[29] The proposal was based on Articles 93 and 175 (ex 99 and 130s) E.C. and thus needed the unanimity of the Council. The proposal was to depend on other OECD states also introducing a similar tax or taking equivalent measures (Article 1(2)). Since the negotiation in Council showed that it was impossible to reach unanimity, the Commission amended its proposal.[30] Under the new proposal, Member States remained free to introduce, or not, a carbon/energy tax. If they did so, they were to comply with the structural requirements fixed in the proposal. The proposal is still under discussion in the Council.

(iv) Carbon dioxide (CO_2)

8—69 CO_2 emissions in the Community account for approximately 80 per cent of all greenhouse gas emissions by the Community; they were estimated, in 1995, at

---

[23] COM (97) 599 (n. 5).
[24] Council, Res. of June 8, 1998 [1998] O.J. C198/1; see also Res. of June 27, 1997 [1997] O.J. C210/1, where the target of doubling the percentage of renewable energy had already been announced.
[25] Dec. 93/389 [1993] O.J. L167/31.
[26] Dec. 1999/296 [1999] O.J. L117/35.
[27] See COM (94) 67 of March 10, 1994; COM (96) 91 of March 14, 1996.
[28] [1996] O.J. C314/11.
[29] [1992] O.J. C196/1.
[30] COM (95) 172 of May 10, 1995.

3,047.6 million tons.[31] They stem from (in million tonnes): electricity and heat, 946.4; energy branch, 143.4; industry, 523.4; household, 630.9; transport 803.5 (railway, 8.5; road, 677.9; air, 96.5; inland navigation, 20.6). If trends remain unchanged, an increase in the order of 40 per cent is expected by 2010.

In the early 1990s, the Commission made two communications on reducing CO_2 emissions,[32] where it suggested, in essence, a directive on energy efficiency,[33] a programme on renewable energies,[34] a carbon/energy tax[35] and a monitoring mechanism on CO_2 and other greenhouse gases.[36] Discussions aimed at setting an emission limit value for CO_2 from cars were quickly abandoned. Instead, the Commission suggested a strategy on reducing CO_2 emissions from cars, which provided for: (a) an environmental agreement with the car industry on such a reduction; (b) fiscal measures in the context of vehicle taxation; (c) a consumer information scheme on fuel consumption of cars; and (d) improved research and development for reducing fuel consumption.[37] The Council agreed on this strategy without, however, the measures on restructuring the national tax systems for cars.[38] In 1998, the agreement with the car industry on CO_2 emission reductions was made.[39] The European Parliament had in vain requested the elaboration of a directive on emission limit values for CO_2 in cars.[40]

8—70   In addition, the Commission published a communication on CO_2 reductions in the transport sector,[41] where it confirmed the earlier strategy and suggested the following measures:

Road freight	Information programmes, promotion of voluntary actions, better management practices;
Passenger cars	Environmental agreement with the car industry; consumer information;
Rail freight	Guidelines on improving existing railway infrastructure;
Public passenger transport	Communication on how to promote public transport;
Shipping	Reference to International Maritime Organisation measures;
Air transport	Communication on optimising air transport management systems.

As can be seen, no legally binding measures are envisaged. The Commission considered that, in order to halve increases in CO_2 emissions from transport by 2010, the following actions were "crucial": (1) action on passenger car fuel economy; (2) progress with fair and efficient pricing in transport; (3) the completion of the internal market in rail transport; (4) better integration of the various modes of transport, both in freight and in passenger transport, into intermodal transport systems. Whether this is realistic is doubtful.

---

[31] Commission, COM (1998) 204 of March 31, 1998, annex 1; the figures given above, para. 8–57, are slightly different, mainly due to calculation differences; for a detailed discussion of CO_2 emissions, see in particular COM (96) 217 (n. 6).

[32] COM (91) 249 (n. 16) and COM (92) 246 of June 1, 1992.

[33] This Directive was adopted in 1993 as Directive 93/76, see para. 8–65 above.

[34] This programme was adopted by Dec. 93/500, see para. 8–65, above.

[35] This proposal is still under discussion, see para. 8–68, above.

[36] This Decision was adopted in 1993, see above, para. 8–67.

[37] COM (95) 689 of December 20, 1995.

[38] (1996) 6 *Bulletin of the European Union*, no. 1.3.142.

[39] See above, paras 8–24 *et seq*.

[40] Resolution of February 19, 1998 [1998] O.J. C80/227, no. 14.

[41] Commission, "Transport and CO_2, developing a Community approach", COM (1998) 204 of March 31, 1998.

(v) Methane

8—71 Methane emissions in the Community count for about 24.5 million tonnes per year.[42] They are expected to decrease by 2010 by about 10 per cent, due in particular to a decrease in agricultural activity and in coal mining. Increases are anticipated in emissions from landfills and from activities in the oil and gas sector.

10.5 million tonnes (44.7 per cent) of all Community methane emissions come from agriculture; the main sources of these are digestion of ruminant livestock (cattle and sheep) with 30 per cent and livestock manure with 14.7 per cent. The Community expects that the number of animals in the Community will decrease anyway by 2010, so that specific measures to reduce methane emissions from agriculture have neither been taken nor are at present envisaged.

8—72 Emissions from waste treatment and disposal count for 7.3 million tonnes (32 per cent). 30.8 per cent of them stem from landfills, 0.7 per cent from waste water treatment (sludge). A Directive on landfills was adopted in 1999.[43] The Directive provides for a reduction in the disposal of organic waste in landfills; however, it will only be fully operational by the year 2016 at the earliest.

Methane emissions from energy are about 5.3 million tonnes per year (23.3 per cent). They stem from coal mining, storage, gas production and distribution, combustion and transport. No specific legally binding measures are envisaged at present, since a decrease in coal production is expected anyway; as for gas, it is thought that an increase in the frequency with which gas pipes are checked for leakages could halve the actual emissions from this source.

(vi) The other four greenhouse gases (N_2O, HFC, PFC and SF_6)

8—73 The other four greenhouse gases identified by the Kyoto Protocol have not, to date, had the specific attention of the Community. About 928,000 tonnes of nitrous oxides (N_2O) are produced annually in the Community. It is generated during fuel combustion (14 per cent), transport, in particular by the use of catalysts in cars (4 per cent), agriculture (41 per cent), waste (1 per cent), land use change and forestry (2 per cent) and industrial processes (37 per cent). There are not yet any legal measures announced to reduce N_2O emissions. Official figures for the other three gases do not exist. The estimations for emissions are given above, in paragraph 8–57. There is no specific action proposed or decided to directly reduce such emissions, though indirectly many measures might influence such emissions.

6. NOISE AND ELECTROMAGNETIC WAVES

(a) General aspects

8—74 Data on noise levels within the Community are limited and fragmented. The Commission estimated in 1996 that almost 80 million people in the Community "suffer from noise levels that scientists and health experts consider to be unacceptable" (above 65dB(A)) and that an additional 170 million citizens are living in areas where the noise levels are such as to cause serious annoyance during the daytime (55–65dB(A)).[44] In 1990, about 17 per cent of the population in selected Member States—Denmark, Germany, Portugal, the Netherlands and France—was exposed to transport noise

---

[42] Commission, Strategy paper for reducing methane emissions COM (96) 557 of November 15, 1996.
[43] Dir. 1999/321 [1999] O.J. L182/1; see in more detail below, para. 9–14.
[44] COM (96) 540 of November 4, 1996, pp. 1a and 3.

greater than 65dB(A), while about 8 per cent of the urban population are exposed to outdoor noise at a level greater than 70dB(A). The main source of outdoor noise is road traffic, followed by neighbourhood and aircraft noise.[45]

A Community strategy to reduce noise levels within the Community was announced almost twenty years ago, in the context of the different environmental action programmes,[46] but has not yet materialised. In 1996, the Commission published a Greenbook, "Future noise policy", where it identified noise as one of the principal local environmental problems.[47] One of its main targets is to prepare the basis for a network to measures noise levels throughout the Community.

8—75   Measures to reduce noise levels have, until now, concerned noise emissions of certain products. The main objective of these directives consists in assuring their free circulation within the Community and to make sure that this circulation is not hampered by different noise standard levels at national level. For this reason, the directives set noise emission levels only for those (new) products that are implicated in intra-Community trade; by contrast, Member States may set independent noise standards for products intended exclusively for the domestic market.[48] They may also provide for specific standards for the use of the products in sensitive areas.

All noise levels fixed in the specific directives are based on the work of international standardisation organisations. They fix noise levels for products that are put on the market for the first, time but contain no provisions on noise emissions throughout the lifetime of a product.

(b) Transport

8—76   Motor vehicle noise emissions have been regulated since 1970, when noise emission limit values were introduced.[49] This Directive was based on Article 94 (ex 100) E.C. Later amendments were introduced, mainly when technical progress had already led to a practical reduction of noise levels[50]; since 1987, such amendments have been based on Article 95 (ex 100a) E.C. The following standards were fixed (in dB(A))[51]:

Vehicle category	1972	1982	1988/1990	1995/1996
Passenger car	82	80	77	74
Urban bus	89	82	80	78
Heavy lorry	91	88	84	80

This legislation led, in practice, to a reduction in actual road traffic noise levels of 1 to 2dB(A), due mainly to the significant growth in traffic and a slow replacement of older,

---

[45] European Environmental Agency, *Environment in the European Union (1995)* (Copenhagen, 1995), chapter 4.6.

[46] See second environmental action programme [1977] O.J. C139/1, pts 67 *et seq.*; fourth environmental action programme [1987] O.J. C328/5, pt 4.5.

[47] COM (96) 540 (n. 44); see also European Parliament Res. of June 10, 1997 [1997] O.J. C200/28.

[48] As regards noise emissions from cars, this so-called "optional harmonisation approach" was abandoned by Dir. 92/97 [1992] O.J. L337/1, which introduced the total harmonisation approach: all vehicles which are put into circulation within the Community must comply with the Directive's requirements.

[49] Dir. 70/157 [1970] O.J. L42/16.

[50] See, for instance, Dir. 77/212 [1977] O.J. L66/33, 2nd recital: "whereas for the protection of the general public from noise nuisance, suitable measures are required to reduce the noise level of motor vehicles; whereas such a reduction has been made possible by the technical progress in motor vehicle construction"; similar observations are made in Dir. 81/334 [1981] O.J. L131/6, 1st recital; Dir. 84/372 [1984] O.J. L196/47, 1st recital; Dir. 84/424 [1984] O.J. L238/31, 2nd recital.

[51] COM (96) 540 (n. 44), p. 30.

noisier vehicles; in "addition, the test procedure (ISO R362) doesn't reflect realistic driving conditions and without a regular inspection procedure to ensure maintenance of the acoustical design features the noise levels of the vehicle may increase over time".[52]

8—77 For two- and three-wheelers, emission limit values have existed since a Directive of 1978,[53] which was amended several times and provided for a reduction of around 3dB(A). Again, the limit values only apply to new motorcycles.

Directive 92/97 called for measures addressing the noise caused by tyres on road, which includes the use of noise-absorbing asphalts. A proposal concerning the admissible noise levels from tyres was made in 1998.[54]

Aircraft noise has, since 1979, been regulated by a number of directives,[55] which were based on Article 80 (ex 84) E.C. and which apply, at Community level, standards set by the International Civic Aviation Organisation (ICAO); the ICAO levels depend on the aircraft weight and number of engines. The Community directives do not fix emission limit values, but refer to the provisions laid down by the ICAO. Directive 92/14 provided for a ban, as of 1995, of civil subsonic aeroplanes which did not comply with the ICAO "chapter 3" requirements, or with the "chapter 2" requirements, but were not more than 25 years old.[56] A number of aeroplanes from airline companies from third world countries were exempted from these provisions, because European airlines had sold these planes to the third world countries prior to 1995. A number of other derogations were also foreseen.

8—78 In 1998, the Commission proposed a ban on registration of aeroplanes which had been modified in order to comply with the "chapter 3" requirements, the so-called "hush-kitted" aircraft.[57] As this requirement hits, in particular, older aeroplanes that are used in the United States or by United States companies, there were excited discussions as to whether this requirement *de facto* discriminated against the United States. Under the political pressure from that country, which threatened retaliation measures and also argued that some hush-kitted aircraft were less noisy than modern aircraft (Airbus), the Council Regulation that finally adopted the proposal,[58] postponed the entry into effect of the measure for a further year (May 2000) in order to avoid a trade dispute. From April 1, 2002, hush-kitted aircraft will be prohibited at Community airports, unless they were operated at Community airports before May 2000.

It is likely that the reduction of aeroplane noise that was caused by the different directives is outweighed by the increase in the size of the individual aircraft and, in particular, the rapid growth of air traffic.[59]

8—79 A Community Whitebook on transport policy of 1992 announced Community measures to fix acceptable noise levels in the vicinity of airports.[60] This announcement has been left without any follow-up.

No Community provisions exist for railways. A proposal for a directive, submitted in 1983, was withdrawn by the Commission in 1993. The introduction of high-speed trains in the Community, also promoted by the rules on trans-European networks (Articles 154–156 (ex 129b–129d) E.C.) in the Maastricht Treaty of 1993, has not led to a change in this situation.

---

[52] COM (96) 540 (n. 44), p. 7.
[53] Dir. 78/1015 [1978] O.J. L349/21.
[54] [1998] O.J. C30/8.
[55] Dir. 80/51 [1980] O.J. L18/26; Dir. 89/629 [1989] O.J. L363/27.
[56] Dir. 92/14 [1992] O.J. L76/21, amended by Dir. 98/20 [1998] O.J. L107/4.
[57] [1998] O.J. C329/98.
[58] Reg. 925/1999 [1999] O.J. L115/1.
[59] The Commission (n. 44), p. 4, expects an increase in air traffic by 2010 of 180 per cent.
[60] Commission, "Whitebook on a Community strategy on sustainable mobility" COM (92) 494 of December 2, 1992.

(c) Construction machines

8—80   A number of Community directives regulate the noise level of construction machinery, specifically compressors,[61] tower cranes,[62] welding generators,[63] power generators,[64] handheld concrete breakers and picks,[65] hydraulic excavators, rope-operated excavators, dozers, loaders and excavator-loaders.[66] A separate directive lays down maximum noise levels for new lawnmowers and provides for them to be labelled accordingly.[67]

All these directives are again based on Article 94 (ex 100) E.C. and only refer to new equipment. The noise emission limit values vary between 100 and 106dB(A), with 96dB(A) for new lawnmowers. There is no requirement to maintain the noise level during the lifetime of the equipment. Member States may not prevent the placing on the market of machines that comply with the requirements of the directives but are, of course, free to fix sensitive areas, where the equipment may not be used or where it may only be used during certain hours.

8—81   In 1998, the Commission proposed a framework directive in order to cover noise levels of all outdoor machines, construction plant, garden equipment and equipment used on specific vehicles.[68] The proposal aims at replacing the existing directives, but does not intend, as a rule, to fix new emission limit values for other machines. All new machinery is to be labelled as regards its noise levels.

New household equipment is subject of another framework directive, which leaves Member States the freedom to fix emission limit values, but fixes a frame for such requirements.[69] No such measures have been taken to date, and are not planned. However, the energy labels fixed for certain household appliances provide for an indication of the noise level.[70]

The Community has not so far fixed quality objectives for noise emissions in sensitive areas such as, for instance, urban centres, residential areas, near airports, hospitals or schools; in the same way, prohibitions for night flights or Sunday traffic for lorries have neither been suggested nor adopted. The Commission's announcement in 1992 that it would consider proposals for quality standards in the vicinity of airports[71] was not repeated in the Greenbook on noise of 1996.[72]

Overall, observation of the noise levels within the Community are highly inadequate and the Community measures protecting against excessive noise levels also seem inadequate. This protection, by fixing quality standards, tends to be left to Member States.

(d) Electromagnetic waves

8—82   There are no Community provisions on electromagnetic waves from electrical power lines and other sources which are thought, sometimes, to cause problems to the health of people living next to such power lines. The Commission

---

[61] Dir. 84/533 [1984] O.J. L300/123.
[62] Dir. 84/534 [1984] O.J. L300/130.
[63] Dir. 84/535 [1984] O.J. L300/142.
[64] Dir. 84/536 [1984] O.J. L300/149.
[65] Dir. 84/537 [1984] O.J. L300/156.
[66] Dir. 86/662 [1986] O.J. L384/1.
[67] Dir. 84/538 [1984] O.J. L300/171.
[68] [1998] O.J. C124/1.
[69] Dir. 86/594 [1986] O.J. L344/24.
[70] See above, para. 6–62.
[71] Commission, Whitebook (n. 60).
[72] COM (96) 540 (n. 44).

stated that there was no "convincing scientific evidence" of electromagnetic fields causing cancer.[73]

Directive 85/337 on the environment impact assessment of certain projects was amended by Directive 97/11,[74] which now requires an environment impact assessment for electrical power lines of more than 15 kilometres in length; however, the competent authorities remain free to decide on such projects, whatever the outcome of the assessment.[75]

8—83   In 1998, the Commission proposed a Council recommendation, based on Article 152 (ex 129) E.C., on "the limitation of exposure of the general public to electromagnetic fields",[76] where essentially Member States are invited to take action in order to limit exposures to electromagnetic fields. Electrical power lines are not specifically addressed. The Council adopted this recommendation in 1999.[77]

BIBLIOGRAPHY

Alcovér Sampedro, A.: "La protección del medio atmosferico" in M. Campins i Eritja and I. Pont i Castejón (eds), *Perspectives de dret comunitari* (Bellaterra, 1997), p. 239

Aubin, A.: *La Communauté europénne face á la pollution atmosphérique* (Rennes, 1993)

Bartaire, G.. "Nociones de contaminación atmosferica" in L. Parejo Alfonso and L. Krämer (eds), *Derecho medioambiental de la Unión Europea* (Madrid, 1996), p. 297

Bennett, G.: (ed.): *Air pollution control in the European Community* (London, 1991)

Breier, S.: "Die öffentliche Beschaffung umweltfreundlicher KFZ und Kraftstoffe aus europarechtlicher Sicht", *Umwelt- und Planungsrecht* (1995), p. 128

Caspari, S.: *Die Umweltpolitik der Europäischen Gemeinschaft. Eine Analyse am Beispiel der Luftreinhaltepolitik* (Baden-Baden, 1995)

Clair, V.: *La lutte contre le bruit en droit communautaire* (Paris, 1997)

Davies, P. and Goh, J.: "E.C. law on aircraft noise: recent developments", *European Environmental Law Review* (1993), p. 229

Gallas, A.: "Aspekte der Luftreinhaltepolitik" in P. Behrens and H. Koch (eds), *Umweltschutz in der Europäischen Gemeinschaft: Spannungsfelder zwischen nationalem und europäischem Gemeinschaftsrecht* (Baden-Baden, 1991), p. 98

Gebers, B. and Robesin, M. (eds): *Licensing procedures for industrial plants and the influence of E.C. directives* (Frankfurt/M., 1993)

Giesberts, L.: "Die CO_2-Energiesteuer der EG. Anmerkungen zum geänderten Richtlinienvorschlag der Europäischen Kommission", *Recht der Internationalen Wirtschaft* (1995), p. 847

Jahns-Böhm, J.: "Güterkraftverkehrspolitik und Umweltschutz im EWG-Vertrag", *Europäische Zeitschrift für Wirtschaftsrecht* (1991), p. 523

Jahns-Böhm, J.: *Umweltschutz durch Europäisches Gemeinschaftsrecht am Beispiel der Luftreinhaltung* (Berlin, 1994)

Klocke, U.: *Klimaschutz durch ökonomische Instrumente* (Baden-Baden, 1995)

Koch, H.: "Luftreinhalterecht in der Europäischen Gemeinschaft", *Deutsches Verwaltungsblatt* (1992), p. 124

Koch, H.: "Luftreinhalterecht in der Europäischen Gemeinschaft" in P. Behrens and H. Koch

---

[73] Written Questions E-1387/97 (Baldi) [1997] O.J. C373/115; E-4190/97 (Caccavale) [1998] O.J. C196/96; E-1788/98 (Sierra Gonzalez *et al.*) [1999] O.J. C50/93.
[74] Dir. 85/337 [1985] O.J. L175/40; amendment Dir. 97/11 [1997] O.J. L73/5.
[75] See generally, paras 4–10 *et seq.*, above.
[76] Commission, COM (1998) 268 of June 11, 1998.
[77] Rec. 1999/519 [1999] O.J. L199/59.

(eds), *Umweltschutz in der Europäischen Gemeinschaft. Spannungsfelder zwischen nationalem und europäischem Gemeinschaftsrecht* (Baden-Baden, 1991), p. 75

Lavrijsen, L.: "De Europese reglementering betreffende de verbranding van huishoudelijke en gevaarlijke afvalstoffen", in Brussels Instituut voor milieubeheer (ed.), *De laatste ontwikkeling van de Europese reglementering inzake afvalstoffen* (Brussels, 1995), p. 89

McManes, F. and Burns, T.: "The impact of E.C. law on noise law in the United Kingdom", in J. Holder (ed.), *The impact of E.C. environmental law in the United Kingdom* (Chichester, 1997), p. 183

Offermann-Clas, C: "Das Luftreinhalterecht der Europäischen Gemeinschaft—Fortschritte seit dem Jahre 1983", *Neue Juristische Wochenschrift* (1986), p. 1388

Pagh, P.: "Luftforurenigsbekaempelsen i retlig belysning", *Ugeskrift for Retsvaesen* (1992), p. B361

Renaudière, P.: "De nouveaux instruments: la taxe CO_2-énergie et l'écofiscalité" in P. Renaudière and P. van Pelt (eds), *Développements récents du droit communautaire de l'environnement* (Diegem, 1995), p. 29

Rhode, B. (ed.): *Air pollution in Europe. Vol. 1: Western Europe* (Vienna, 1988)

Schröder, M.: "Instrumente zur Bekämpfung der neuartigen Waldschäden nach deutschem und europäischem Recht", *UPR* (1989), p. 49

Van Calster, G.: "E.C. noise legislation and policy", *European Environmental Law Review* (1997), p. 174

CHAPTER 9
Waste

1. WASTE MANAGEMENT POLICY AND LAW

9—01 Waste management issues played a role in Community environmental policies from its very beginnings. The Commission's communication of 1972 mentioned the necessity of preventing waste generation and to promote waste recovery.[1] The first environmental action programme discussed the question of what action on waste management could usefully be tackled at Community level and announced the harmonisation of legislations.[2] The second action programme declared that a comprehensive waste management policy was necessary, which should include measures for prevention, reclamation and disposal of waste.[3] The third action programme repeated the intentions of the second programme in similar form and announced promotional measures for waste prevention and recovery.[4]

The Community dimension of waste management problems fully came into the open when the incident of the Seveso barrels occurred in 1982. 41 barrels containing highly toxic waste, which stemmed from a major industrial accident in Seveso in 1976, were shipped, with the consent of Italian public authorities, but in contradiction to the provisions of Directive 78/319,[5] from Italy abroad, and disappeared. Numerous Community Member States were afraid that the waste might have secretly been brought to their territory.[6] The European Parliament set up, for the first time, an inquiry committee and, in its final conclusions, criticised the Commission for not having properly exercised its role as guardian of the Treaty. It expressly asked for the elaboration of a Community waste policy.[7]

9—02 The fourth action programme confirmed the previous policy objectives and underlined, in particular, the importance of promoting clean technologies and recycling of waste; it also announced a specific communication on a waste management strategy.[8]

This strategy communication was finally made in 1989.[9] It essentially fixed five strategic guidelines:

(1) Prevention of waste generation. The strategy advocated, on the one hand, clean technologies that could by financially assisted by the Commission[10] and, on the

---

[1] [1972] O.J. C52/1, p. 12.

[2] First environmental action programme (1973–1977) [1973] O.J. C112/1, chapter 7, section 1.

[3] Second environmental action programme (1977–1982) [1977] O.J. C139/1, paras 174–201.

[4] Third environmental action programme (1983–1986) [1983] O.J. C46/1, para. 29.

[5] Dir. 78/319 on toxic and dangerous waste [1978] O.J. L84/43.

[6] The wastes were later found back on a non-authorised storage site in France, transported to Switzerland and, it was reported, incinerated there.

[7] European Parliament Res. of June 8, 1983 [1983] O.J. C184/50; Res. of March 16, 1984 [1984] O.J. C104/147; Res. of April 11, 1984 [1984] O.J. C127/67. See also Economic and Social Committee [1984] O.J. C206/62.

[8] Fourth environmental action programme (1987–1992) [1987] O.J. C328/1, para. 5.3.

[9] Commission, "A Community strategy for waste management" SEC (89) 934 of September 18, 1989.

[10] Through financial assistance schemes which were later substituted by the LIFE instrument: Reg. 1973/92 [1992] O.J. L206/1. See also para. 5–19.

other hand, environmentally "better" products, for which it particularly requested an ecological labelling scheme[11];

(2) The promotion of recycling and reuse, which should be promoted through research and development, the improvement of collection and sorting schemes, the reduction of external costs and the creation of outlets for recycled and reused products. The Commission announced financial assistance for waste reuse and recycling technologies and proposals for directives on plastic waste and metal packaging;

(3) Optimisation of final disposal, where the Commission announced proposals for the dumping of waste and on the incineration of hazardous waste;

(4) Transport of waste, where the Commission only referred to existing work at national and international level;

(5) Remedial action: the Commission announced research on the clean-up of contaminated sites and studies on financial instruments for remedying the damage caused by waste in abandoned landfills.

9—03   In concluding chapters the Commission stated the objective that "as far as possible waste is disposed of in the nearest suitable centres", but that the situation was "different with waste to be recycled". Furthermore, it confirmed that "waste arising within the Community which cannot be recycled should be treated within the Community where possible and exported only in exceptional cirucumstances". These statements consituted the basis of the proximity and self-sufficiency principles, which were later laid down in Article 5 of the amended Directive 75/442.[12] The Council and the European Parliament both welcomed and supported the communication and made a considerable number of detailed proposals for future action.[13]

The waste management strategy did not include questions of radioactive waste, which were handled completely separately at Community level and monitored under the Euratom Treaty. By 1980, the Council had already approved a Community action plan in the field of radioactive waste (1980–1992).[14] In 1994, the Commission submitted a new communication for a strategy on radioactive waste management,[15] which the Council endorsed in the form of a Resolution.[16]

9—04   The fifth environmental action programme referred back to the 1989 strategy[17]; it repeated its guiding principles and announced rather ambitious waste management targets for the year 2000.[18] These targets were made somewhat less ambitious by the 1996 review of the waste management strategy of 1989,[19] which confirmed the hierarchy of principles while stating that, within the recovery principle, "where environmentally sound, preference should in general be given to the recovery of

---

[11] See para. 4–34.

[12] Dir. 75/442 on waste, as amended by Dir. 91/156 [1991] O.J. L78/32.

[13] Council Res. of May 7, 1990 [1990] O.J. C122/2; European Parliament Res. of February 19, 1991 [1991] C72/34.

[14] [1980] O.J. C51/1; see also the progress reports made by the Commission COM (83) 262 of May 16, 1983, COM (87) 312 of July 29, 1987 and COM (93) 88 of April 1, 1993.

[15] COM (94) 66 of March 2, 1994.

[16] Res. of June 15, 1992 [1992] O.J. C158/2.

[17] Fifth environmental action programme [1993] O.J. C138/5, para. 5.4.

[18] Amongst others, a stabilisation of quantities of waste generated at 300 kg per capita and year; a recycling/reuse rate of paper, glass and plastics of at least 50 per cent; markets for recycled materials; reliable E.C. data on waste generated, collected and disposed; a functioning system of liability for hazardous waste; and an inventory of risks for hazardous waste.

[19] Commission, COM (96) 399 of July 30, 1996.

material over energy recovery operations. This reflects the greater effect on the prevention of waste produced by material recovery rather than by energy recovery."

The reviewed strategy, which again did not include radioactive waste, tried to place waste management concepts into the context of the internal market and introduced the principle of producer responsibility for waste management issues. This strategy review was also the subject of extensive comments from the other Community institutions, which made a number of proposals for concrete Community measures.[20]

These different statements have, to date, left open three basic policy decisions which very considerably influence waste management policy and legislation at Community level:

9—05   (1) Waste prevention was and continues to be the first and most important objective in Community waste management policy, confirmed by all statements.[21]

Preventing the generation of waste, however, means that a product policy is followed which is more than a curing of symptoms. While it seems neither desirable nor realistic to suggest that basis of consumer society should be changed because of waste considerations, a very useful step would be systematically to reduce the presence of dangerous substances in products, wherever alternatives are available.[22] No such systematic attempts exist at Community level at present. Since waste management is an end-of-the-pipe management, its conception and implementation must necessarily be influenced by actions or omissions that are taken "upstream".

9—06   (2) The waste strategy of 1996 declared that, in principle, material recycling of waste should have priority over waste incineration with energy recovery.[23] This priority was also established in several Community directives.[24]

In practice, however, the Community takes measures to promote waste incineration (with energy recovery) rather than waste recycling. This manifests itself particularly in four areas: as regards energy policy, waste is considered a source of energy which is sometimes available at a low price and used as a substitute for fossil fuels; in its statements on renewable energies, the Commission went so far as to consider the incineration of municipal waste a renewable source of energy.[25] Agricultural policy is likewise interested in seeing agricultural waste (called "bio-mass") recognised as a renewable source of energy, tax relief given on a "biofuel", and wishes, at the same time, for the considerable quantities of agricultural waste to be reduced by incineration. Next, Community research policy has a tendency to

---

[20] Council Res. of February 24, 1997 [1997] O.J. C76/1; European Parliament Res. of November 14, 1996 [1996] O.J. C362/241; Economic and Social Committee [1997] O.J. C89/2; Committee of the Regions [1997] O.J. C116/74.

[21] See Council Res., February 24, 1997 (n. 20), paras 16 and 17: "Reiterates its conviction that waste prevention should be first priority for all rational waste policy, in relation to minimising waste production and the hazardous properties of waste; considers that efforts made in this respect need to be increased, *inter alia*, by improving the environmental dimension of technical standards, by reducing the presence of dangerous substances where less dangerous alternatives are available . . ."

[22] See also above, paras 6.21 *et seq.*

[23] See above, para. 9–04. See also Council Res., February 24, 1997 (n. 20), which is, to say the least, ambiguous: "[The Council] recognises, as regards recovery operations, that the choice of option in any particular case must have regard to environmental and economic effects, but considers that at present, and until scientific and technological progress is made and life-cycle analyses are further developed, reuse and material recovery should be considered preferable where and insofar as they are the best environmental option."

[24] Dir. 75/442 (n. 12), Art. 3(1)(b)(i) and (ii); Dir. 94/62 on packaging and packaging waste [1994] O.J. L365/10.

[25] See COM (96) 576 of November 20, 1996 and COM (97) 599 of November 26, 1997.

promote high-technology and large-scale projects such as the incineration of (hazardous) waste rather than the small-scale technology of material recycling or composting of waste. A similar tendency can be observed, finally, in the context of regional policy: the Cohesion Fund has as its aim mainly to finance big projects, which gives an advantage to incineration installations with regard to recycling projects.[26]

(3) A consistent Community waste management policy has also not been developed because it is not clear to what extent waste management strategies, policies and measures are to be established at Community or at national level. Member States generally prefer to keep responsibility for management options, including questions on investments into cleaner technologies, clean-up and others, at national level.

9—07   The Court of Justice decided, in 1992, that waste materials are, in the Community terminology, products, though of a specific nature, to which Article 28 (ex 30) E.C. applies.[27] This judgment ended a long controversy as to whether waste issues came under the provisions of the free circulation of goods, the freedom to provide services or whether they were not covered by the E.C. Treaty at all. However, the discussion continues at all levels as to what extent the specific nature of waste justifies a limitation of the provisions of Articles 28 et seq. (ex 30 et seq.) E.C., in other words, to what extent Member States are entitled to set national standards for waste. While Community waste legislation between 1975 and 1987 was based on Articles 94 and 308 (ex 100 and 235) E.C.,[28] the Commission, since 1987, has based all its proposals for waste legislation on Article 95 (ex 100a) E.C. Only when the Court of Justice declared, in 1993, that Directive 91/156, which amended Directive 75/442 on waste, was rightly based on Article 175 (ex 130s),[29] did this Treaty provision prevail and did the Commission recur to that Article. Subsequently, most waste measures were based on that provision, except two product-related waste directives.[30] It is obvious, though, that Article 175 (ex 130s) E.C. leaves Member States greater discretion for national measures, since Article 95 (ex 100a) E.C. primarily aims at establishing the internal market which requires uniform rules, while Article 175 (ex 130s) E.C. primarily aims at protecting the environment. This leads, in practice, to measures adopted at a common denominator, which is relatively low, since Member States that wish to see higher provisions adopted can easily be referred to the provision of Article 176 (ex 130t) E.C.

9—08   Also, to give some examples of political divergency within the Community, the preference for material recycling over incineration with energy recovery, which was laid down in the Community strategy, was also discussed in Germany and the United Kingdom, but was, in these two Member States, finally not established in the relevant political and legal documents. Scandinavian Member States, the Netherlands, France and others, strongly promote the incineration of at least municipal waste. The general scarcity of sites for landfills favours waste incineration, unless a very active waste prevention, reuse and recycling policy is pursued; this again presupposes a product policy, which predominantly comes into the realm of Community policy. Other

---

[26] Reg. 1164/94 establishing a Cohesion Fund [1994] O.J. L130/1, Art. 10: "Projects . . . shall be of a sufficient scale to have a significant impact in the field of environmental protection . . . In any event, the total cost of projects or groups of projects may in principle not be less than ECU 10 million."
[27] Case C-2/90 Commission v. Belgium [1992] E.C.R. I-4431.
[28] An exception was Dir. 85/339 on liquid beverage containers [1985] O.J. L176/18, which was adopted on the basis of Article 308 (ex 235) E.C. alone.
[29] Case C-155/91 Commission v. Council [1993] E.C.R. I-939.
[30] Dir. 91/157 on batteries [1991] O.J. L78/38; Dir. 94/62 (n. 24).

uncertain aspects concerning whether waste management measures are to be taken at Community or at national level involve radioactive waste, the shipment of waste to third countries, contaminated land and old landfills, provisions on liability and monitoring measures.

In 1995, the Commission reported on its efforts to set up an integrated waste management policy, where it identified the following difficulties for such a policy[31]: technical and administrative implementation of Community provisions; lack of reliable basic statistical, technical and economic data[32]; the imprecision of legal acts and the ambiguity of some of the concepts; and poor functioning of collective consultation.

2. WASTE INSTALLATIONS

(a) Siting

9—09　There are no Community provisions on the siting of waste treatment or disposal installations. The directives on the incineration of waste[33] are silent on the question of siting; the proposal for a directive on the landfill of waste[34] stipulated that landfills had to be placed at a distance from residential areas, waterways, water bodies, etc., of 0.5 kilometres in the case of municipal landfills and 2 kilometres from residential areas in the case of hazardous landfills. The Directive, adopted in 1999, deleted any precise minimum distance requirement and limited itself to general considerations, which had to indicate that the landfill does not pose a serious environmental risk.[35] Finally, no specific provisions exist for the siting of installations for radioactive waste.

9—10　Community restrictions for the siting of a waste installation flow from Articles 4(4) of Directive 79/409[36] and 6(2) of Directive 92/43,[37] where such installations could constitute a significant disturbance of the species protected in those habitats. Furthermore, a site may—at least de facto—not be chosen where the operation of the installation would, despite precautionary measures that are eventually taken, lead to a breach of the requirements of Article 4 of Directive 75/442.[38] In extreme cases, the siting of an installation may injure human rights,[39] which the Community institutions and national courts must also safeguard.

Before they are authorised, hazardous waste disposal installations must be the subject of an environmental impact assessment; the same requirement applies to incineration installations for the disposal of non-hazardous waste that have a capacity of more than 100 tonnes per day.[40] For other waste installations, Member States must

---

[31] COM (95) 522 of November 8, 1995, p. 16.

[32] See now "Proposal for a Council Regulation on statistics on waste management", based on Article 284 (ex 213) E.C. [1999] O.J. C87/22.

[33] Dir. 89/369 on the prevention of air pollution from new municipal waste incineration plants [1989] O.J. L163/32; Dir. 89/429 on the reduction of air pollution from existing muncipal waste incineration plants [1989] O.J. L203/50; Dir. 94/67 on the incineration of hazardous waste [1994] O.J. L365/34.

[34] [1997] O.J. C156/19, annex I, para. 1 (1.1.a).

[35] Dir. 1999/31 [1999] O.J. 182/1, annex I, para. 1 (1.1.a).

[36] Dir. 79/409 on the conservation of wild birds [1979] O.J. L103/1.

[37] Dir. 92/43 on the conservation of natural habitats and of wild fauna and flora [1992] O.J. L206/7.

[38] Dir. 75/442 (n. 12), Art. 4: "Member States shall take the necessary measures to ensure that waste is recovered or disposed of without endangering human health and without using processes or methods which could harm the environment and in particular: without risk to water, air, soil and plants and animals; without causing a nuisance through noise or odours; without adversely affecting the countryside or places of special interest."

[39] See European Court on Human Rights, Lopez Ostra v. Spain, judgment of December 9, 1994 (41/1993/436/515), where an installation was established at a distance of 12 metres from a private home.

[40] Dir. 85/337 on environmental impact assessment [1985] O.J. L175/40, as amended by Dir. 97/11 [1997] O.J. L73/5.

either examine case by case whether an environmental impact is necessary, or fix thresholds beyond which such an assessment is necessary.[41]

For sites where leaching of dangerous substances that are listed in annex II of Directive 80/68[42] to groundwater may occur, a prior investigation must be made; an authorisation for the installation may be granted "provided that all the technical precautions for preventing groundwater pollution by these substances are observed".[43]

(b) The choice of a type of waste legislation

9—11 The choice of the waste installation—landfill, composting plant, recycling plant, incineration plant with or without energy recovery—is at the complete discretion of Member States. It is true that Article 3 of Directive 75/442 provides for a waste "hierarchy".[44] However, this hierarchy is, legally speaking, a recommendation ("encourage"); and it is obvious that endless legal disputes could take place on the question whether a Member State really has done enough as regards waste prevention. If waste prevention were a legal obligation, the Commission would be obliged, under Article 211 (ex 155) E.C., to take legal action against Member States which did not do enough for waste prevention; the same would apply where a Member State favoured landfills over incineration of waste.[45] In reality, such an action has never been taken or even considered by the Commission.

(c) Permits

9—12 The permitting of waste treatment and disposal plants is, in general, subject to provisions of national legislations. For some[46] installations, Directive 96/61 on integrated prevention and pollution control[47] has been applicable since its entry into effect in 1999; it requires the permit to provide for the use of the best available technique and the setting of specific conditions and, in particular, emission limit values for pollutants.[48]

While there are no specific provisions on facilities for the treatment, and in particular the incineration, of nuclear waste, specific requirements apply to (non-nuclear) waste incineration installations, which are laid down in Directives 89/369 and 89/429 on municipal waste and 94/67 on hazardous waste.[49] The Directives, and in particular Directive 94/67, set emission limits for certain heavy metals and other

---

[41] As regards Dir. 85/337, see also para. 4–10, above.
[42] Dir. 80/68 on the protection of groundwater against pollution caused by certain dangerous substances [1980] O.J. L20/43.
[43] Ibid., Art. 5(1).
[44] Dir. 75/442 (n. 12), Art. 3(1): "Member States shall take the appropriate measures to encourage: (a) firstly, the prevention or reduction of waste production and its harmfulness, in particular by: the development of clean technologies more sparing in their use of natural resources; the technical development and marketing of products designed so as to make no contribution or to make the smallest possible contribution, by the nature of their manufacture, use or final disposal, to increasing the amount or harmfulness of waste and pollution hazards; the development of appropriate techniques for the final disposal of dangerous substances contained in waste destined for recovery; (b) secondly: (i) the recovery of waste by means of recycling, reuse or reclamation or any other process with a view to extracting secondary raw materials, or (ii) the use of waste as a source of energy."
[45] Greece and Ireland have no waste incineration installations.
[46] Essentially, installations for the recovery or disposal of hazardous waste with a capacity exceeding 10 tonnes per day, municipal waste incinerators with a capacity of more than 3 tonnes per day, installations for disposal of non-hazardous waste (biological and chemical process) with a capacity of more than 50 tonnes per day, landfills with a capacity of more than 25,000 tonnes or receiving more than 10 tonnes per day.
[47] Dir. 96/61 [1996] O.J. L257/26; see also above, para. 4–16.
[48] See above, paras 4–16 et seq.
[49] Dirs 89/369, 89/429 and 94/67 (n. 33); see also above, para. 8–41.

pollutants; Directive 94/67 also sets limits for emissions of dioxins.[50] They also provide for detailed conditions on the operation of the incinerators, such as minimum temperature of the burner and measures for cases of operation disturbance.

9—13 In 1998, the Commission suggested an amendment to the municipal incinerator directives,[51] under the assumption that from the point of view of the environment it is irrelevant whether the dangerous emissions stem from one or the other type of incinerator. Once these amendments are in place, they will prevail over the requirements of Directive 96/61.

Directive 94/67 does not apply to incinerators for animal carcasses or remains. Animal waste is regulated under Directive 90/667,[52] which was based on Article 37 (ex 43) E.C. Where such animal waste constitutes a high risk (that concept is not defined, but described in Directive 90/667; it includes, among other things, BSE carcasses), the waste must be burnt at temperatures of at least 133°C for 20 minutes. Directive 90/667 also sets a number of hygiene requirements for animal waste treatment or incineration plants. Once Directive 96/61 on integrated pollution prevention and control[53] enters into effect, it will also apply to installations for the recycling or disposal of animal carcasses and animal waste with a capacity of more than 10 tonnes per day.

Installations that co-incinerate waste together with other fuels—at present, in particular, power plants, cement kilns and steel plants—are regulated by the general provisions of Directive 96/61, as long as they do not incinerate hazardous waste.[54] In this latter case, Article 3(3) of Directive 94/67 applies to them, which allows less severe emission limit values than for ordinary incinerators of hazardous wastes, as long as the part of hazardous waste does not exceed 40 per cent of the fuels used; details are fixed in Directive 94/67.

(d) Landfills

9—14 As regards landfills, the Commmission submitted a proposal for a directive in 1991.[55] In May 1996, the European Parliament rejected the Council's common position on the proposal[56] with the argument that it contained too many derogations. The Commission then submitted a new proposal,[57] which the Council adopted in 1999.[58] The Directive has the same field of application as the framework directive 75/442; thus, it also applies to radioactive waste landfills, for which at present no specific Community provisions exist.

The Directive applies to all authorised or non-authorised landfills that are in operation; where existing landfills do not comply with its requirements, they shall have to be adapted by 2009 at the latest or shall have to be closed. In principle, any storage of waste on land or into land—thus also under ground—is considered a landfill; however, temporary storage prior to disposal operations that does not exceed one year, or three years prior to treatment operations, is excluded from the notion of

---

[50] See in more detail above, paras 8–41 et seq.

[51] [1998] O.J. C372/11.

[52] Dir. 90/667 laying down the veterinary rules for the disposal of animal waste, for its placing on the market and for the prevention of pathogens in feedstuffs of animal or fish origin and amending Dir. 90/425 [1990] O.J. L363/51.

[53] Dir. 96/61 (n. 47).

[54] In particular, Dir. 88/609 on large combustion plants [1988] O.J. L96/25 does not prohibit the incineration of waste in large combustion plants.

[55] [1991] O.J. C190/1.

[56] [1996] O.J. C59/1.

[57] [1997] O.J. C156/10.

[58] Dir. 1999/31 on the landfill of waste [1999] O.J. 182/1.

landfill. The Directive introduces three classes of landfills: for hazardous waste, for non-hazardous waste and for inert waste. It lays down detailed provisions for the permitting of landfills and the conditions accompanying a permit, and in particular for water control and leachate management, the protection of soil and water, gas control, stability and barriers to free access.

(e) Decommissioning of installations

9—15 There are no specific Community provisions on the decommissioning of waste installations or, indeed, other industrial installations such as, for instance, nuclear power plants. The demolition of buildings, structures or installations leads to the generation of (movable) waste, for which the general provisions apply. Where such installations contain asbestos, Article 7 of Directive 87/217[59] applies, which provides that the release of asbestos fibres does not cause "significant asbestos pollution"—whatever that means. For the rest, the general provision of Article 4 of Directive 75/442[60] also applies to decommissioning of installations.

The decommissioning of offshore oil platforms was the subject of a decision under the OSPAR Convention, taken in 1998,[61] which provides for a prohibition of putting such installations into the sea or maintaining them there after use; the decision allows contracting parties to grant, under certain conditions, a derogation. The Commission proposed that the Community approve this decision[62]; if the European Parliament and the Council adopt this proposal, the OSPAR decision will be binding on the E.C. Member States that are members of OSPAR, but not on the other Member States.[63]

(f) Decontaminated land

9—16 The Directive on landfills does not deal with issues of contaminated land, such as closed landfills, unauthorised discharges, abandoned military or industrial sites and so on. No Community inventory of such contaminated land sites exists, but some Member States set up national inventories. Thus, in Germany, the number of suspected contaminated sites registered is about 190,000; this figure does not include military sites and sites for the production of armaments. The total number is thought to be well over 240,000. Austria has a list of 2,584, Finland of 10,400 contaminated sites. In the United Kingdom, estimations go from 50,000 to 100,000,[64] while France sometimes quotes a figure of about 1,000 contaminated sites.[65] Based on Member States' data and estimations, the European Environmental Agency estimated the total number of contaminated sites in the Community to be about 750,000 sites.[66]

In its waste strategy review of 1996, the Commission expressed the opinion that the identification and rehabilitation of contaminated sites was primarily the task of

---

[59] Dir. 87/217 on the prevention and reduction of environmental pollution by asbestos [1987] O.J. L85/40.
[60] See n. 12, above.
[61] OSPAR Decision 98/3 on the disposal of disused offshore installations [1998] O.J. C158/11. As regards OSPAR in general, see para. 7–38, above.
[62] [1999] O.J. C158/10.
[63] It should be noted that Denmark, Finland, France, Germany, Greece, Ireland, the Netherlands, Portugal, Spain, Sweden and the United Kingdom have ratified the United Nations "Convention on the Continental Shelf" of April 29, 1958. This Convention provides in Article 5(5) with regard to platforms: "Any installations which are abandoned or disused must be entirely removed."
[64] National Westminster Bank, Contaminated land: counting the cost of our past (London, 1992), p. 3.
[65] See, for instance, Le Monde, April 7, 1998, p. 10: "Le gouvernement relance l'inventaire des sites pollués . . . la France compte officiellement 896 lieux contaminés. En réalité, il en existe 200,000 à 300,000, de nature et d'impact différents."
[66] European Environmental Agency, Europe's environment, the second assessment (Aarhus, 1998), p. 192.

Member States.[67] No official work is done at Community level concerning the identification of sites, classification, prioritisation and so on. However, in the context of its research policy, the Commission set up, in 1996, a "Concerted action on risk assessment for contaminated sites" (CARACAS) and two other similar networks, NICOLE (1996) and CLARINET (1998).

(g) Port reception facilities

9—17 In mid-1998, the Commission submitted a proposal for a directive on port reception facilities for ship-generated waste and cargo residues[68]; the proposal was based on Article 80(2) (ex 84(2)) E.C. Member States are required to ensure that there are facilities in ports for the reception of waste from ships; for that purpose, each port is obliged to establish a waste reception and handling plan. All ships that use a port of a Member State shall deliver all ship-generated waste to a port reception facility. In order to avoid the waste being discharged into the sea, the proposal provides that ships have to pay a fee for the port reception facilities, "irrespective of actual use of the facilities"; whether this is helpful seems doubtful, since this might now start competition among the ports as to the amount of the fee. There are no specifications set for the reception facilities.

The proposal is not likely to be adopted before the year 2000.

3. WASTE MATERIALS

(a) Framework directive on waste

9—18 Reliable and up-to-date figures on the quantity of waste generated within the Community are rarely available. The 1996 waste management strategy review,[69] quoting sources from the Commission's Statistical Office, indicated that in 1990 an overall amount of 910 million tonnes of waste was generated per annum, out of which 352 million tonnes were from mining and quarrying, 336 million tonnes from manufacturing industry, 132 million tonnes municipal waste, 57 million tonnes of waste from energy production and 33 million tonnes from other economic sectors. To this have to be added about 680 million tonnes of agricultural waste. About 22 million tonnes of this waste was classified as hazardous. According to the same source, 68 per cent of the municipal waste is landfilled, 18 per cent incinerated, 5 per cent composted and 2 per cent recycled.

As regards radioactive waste, the Commission generally differentiates between low-, medium- and high-level waste.[70] About 160,000 tonnes of radioactive waste were thought, in 1994, to be produced annually within the Community, 90 per cent of it low or medium level.[71] Considerable quantities of radioactive waste, including all high-level waste, are placed in what is called "interim storage", sometimes for years, as no final landfill site for high-level waste has as yet been decided upon within the Community.

9—19 The basic legal instrument for waste materials is Directive 75/442, which was fundamentally reviewed in 1991 and constitutes the framework for waste legislation

---

[67] Commission (n. 19), para. 56.
[68] [1998] O.J. C271/1; amended [1999] O.J. C148/7.
[69] See above, para. 9–04.
[70] Low, medium and high refer to the concentration of radionucleides in the radioactive waste and hence to the intensity of the emitted radiation.
[71] COM (94) 66 of March 2, 1994.

at Community level.[72] The Directive defined waste, established a hierarchy for waste management (prevention—recovery—safe disposal) and basic requirements for all waste management activities, introduced a licensing requirement for all persons who are active in waste treatment, disposal and management operations, and requested that Member States draw up waste management plans and regularly report on its transposition and implementation.

9—20   The amended Directive, which is based on Article 175 (ex 130s) E.C., has not led to the alignment of waste management policies and provisions within the Community, which it had tried to achieve. Member States were keen to maintain their different national approaches to waste management, whether these were active or less active. The lack of reporting on the implementation of the Directive had, as a consequence, that the Commission published the first report on the implementation of Directive 75/442 in 1997, covering the period 1989–1994 and based on reports from nine of the twelve Member States.[73]

The main findings were a great variety of definitions of waste, a transposition of the waste hierarchy into national legislation that was far from satisfactory, an enormous variety of waste management plans as regards, for example, authors (local authorities, regions, districts or national governments), content, territorial coverage, duration and waste covered. The Commission noted "a certain reticence on the part of the Member States to actually implement the Directive or some of its provisions . . . [The instrument of management plans] which is of capital importance in any waste management policy, has only very recently been deployed by the Member States, and only in piecemeal fashion."[74]

9—21   The definiton of what constitutes waste continues to raise concern. In 1975, a Community definition on waste had been established,[75] but, subsequently, this definition was considered to be not precise enough. Therefore, in 1991, it was replaced by a new definition, which referred to a set of categories that were laid down in an annex.[76] However, annex I listed 16 categories of waste, the last of which being "any materials, substances or products which are not contained in the above categories". This general clause thus referred back to the definition of Article 1.

Article 1 further requested the Commission to draw up "a list of wastes belonging to the categories listed in annex I. This list will be periodically reviewed and, if necessary, revised . . ." This list was established in 1994; at present it contains some 650 entries.[77]

9—22   The field of application of Directive 75/442 is very broad. The only item that is excluded from its field of application is "gaseous effluents emitted into the atmosphere", obviously for the reason that, for such emissions, air pollution provisions would apply. Furthermore, Directive 75/442 does not cover a number of waste items[78] "where they are already covered by other legislation". This terminology clearly shows that these items are considered waste. "Other legislation" can only refer to other Community legislation, otherwise local or regional legislation in one Member

---

[72] Dir. 75/442 on waste [1975] O.J. L194/47, amended by Dir. 91/156 [1991] O.J. L78/32.

[73] COM (97) 23 of February 27, 1997; Ireland, Italy and Greece did not report.

[74] Commission (n. 73), pp. 16 and 17.

[75] Dir. 75/442 on waste [1975] O.J. L194/39, Art. 1 (a): "'waste' means any substance or object which the holder disposes of or is required to dispose of pursuant to the provisions of national law in force".

[76] Dir. 91/156 (n. 72 above), Art. 1(a): "'waste' shall mean: any substance or object in the categories set out in annex I which the holder discards or intends or is required to discard".

[77] Commission Dec. 94/3 [1994] O.J. L5/15.

[78] Dir. 75/442 (n. 72), Art. 2(1b): "radioactive waste; waste resulting from prospecting, extraction, treatment and storage of mineral resources and the working of quarries; animal carcasses and the following agricultural waste: faecal matter and other natural, non-dangerous substances used in farming; waste waters, with the exception of waste in liquid form; decommissioned explosives".

State would lead to the inapplicability of the Directive in that local authority or region, an impossible result since Directive 75/442 would then apply in some parts of a Member State but not in others. The word "already" indicates that the Community legislation must have existed at the time of adoption of Directive 75/442; clearly it was thought that later Community provisions would expressly clarify their relationship with Directive 75/442.[79]

It is obvious that the definition of waste is a legal creation and therefore exposed to criticism; as does any definition, it contains an arbitrary element. Whether a corporal object is called a good, product, substance, residue, pollutant, discharge (of pollutants), emission or waste, is a question of legal agreement.[80] From the point of view of environmental protection, the name which is given to a specific object is not very relevant; what matters is the contamination or pollution that object causes or risks causing.

9—23   The criticism against the—unanimously agreed—Community definition for waste aimed, and continues to aim, particularly at not having certain production items subjected to the waste legislation, which is considered too stringent, too restrictive, to give a negative image or to present other disadvantages. Attempts at change concentrate on recyclable or recoverable items, for the obvious reason that such items have a certain economic value. The following discussion concentrates on the questions concerning when a product becomes waste; questions on when, in a recovery or a recycling process, a waste becomes a product again, will be discussed below, at paragraph 9–32.

Legally, there can be no doubt that the Community concept of waste also includes recoverable or recyclabe waste[81]: Directive 75/442 in its 1975 version declared as operations for the disposal of waste "the collection, sorting, transport and treatment of waste . . . the transformation operations necessary for its reuse, recovery or recycling".[82] And the enumeration of recovery operations in the annex to Directive 75/442 on waste—not on products!—would not make sense, if waste that is destined for a recovery operation was not covered by that Directive.

Directive 75/442 did not prevent Germany from adopting, in 1986, legislation that declared in essence that recoverable items were not waste but secondary raw materials. It was only after the Court of Justice stated, nine years later, that this provision was incompatible with Community law,[83] that Germany changed its legislation; the Court expressly found that the new definition of waste under Directive 91/156[84] had not changed the situation. A similar provision was then, in 1996, introduced by Italy, which led to the same verdict by the Court of Justice.[85]

9—24   Since this way of proceeding is not really promising, discussions subsequently concentrated on the concept of "discard", which replaced the previous "disposes of", but which is not defined. All products become waste, which normally occurs at the end of their useful lifetime. This question has nothing to do with the economic value that the item eventually still has: where a new television set is, after two months' use, thrown away or dumped in the street, it is discarded, even if

---

[79] This has indeed happened: see, for instance, Dir. 94/62 on packaging and packaging waste [1994] O.J. L365/10 or Dir. 94/67 (n. 33).

[80] In the United States, air emissions are considered "goods", for which, under the uniform commercial clause, federal competence exists.

[81] See, however, Written Question E-1734/97 (Seppänen) [1998] O.J. LC45/92, where the Commission declares, as regards radioactive waste, that recyclable radioactive waste were products. The Commission does not explain this reasoning.

[82] Dir. 75/442 (n. 12), Art. 1(b).

[83] Case C-422/92 Commission v. Germany [1995] E.C.R. I-1097.

[84] Dir. 91/156 (n. 12).

[85] Case C-304/94 Tombesi [1997] E.C.R. I-3561.

somebody comes past, takes the television and uses it for several years. Horse manure might be an excellent fertiliser for the garden: it remains true that where it is left on the road, it constitutes—a real production residue—waste.

Since recovery (recycling) is considered a waste management activity,[86] it is logical that an item can be discarded, even where it is collected or transported with a view to being recycled or recovered. This is, *de lege lata* and *de lege ferenda*, heavily argued about, in particular where residues of production are at stake.[87] Admittedly, the borderline between residues of production, which the Community considers waste, and the generation of two products, is not always easy to make. Thus, where steel is cut to make the body of a car, gold is worked on to make a golden ring or wood is cut, the residues—steel scrap, gold dust and wood chips—are discarded and thus constitute waste. Where chemical substances are processed to produce two chemical preparations, one of these cannot be considered the residue of the other; normally, thus, they are both products.

9—25   As with all borderline cases, the final decision is to be made on a case-by-case basis. In the end, the Court of Justice will be the final arbiter, and has started, in a number of judgments, to be so.[88]

In summer 1998, the OECD published a guidance document to facilitate the distinction between products and wastes.[89] This guidance document wants to facilitate the use of the OECD concept of waste, which is different from the Community definition[90]; in particular, "the intended destination of a material is the decisive factor in the OECD definition".[91] The document lists 17 questions to be put in order to find an answer to whether an item is a waste or a product, before concluding that no weighting can be assigned to these questions and that the decision has to be made on a case-by-case basis.[92] It will be up to the Community to consider whether it will take the discussion on the definition of waste up again, redefine waste, issue a Community guidance document or act in another way.

9—26   Another central provision of Directive 75/442 is Article 4,[93] which requests that waste management operations not harm the environment. The Court of Justice ruled that this provision was of a somewhat political nature and had to be materialised in the context of the other provisions of the Directive.[94] I am rather of the opinion that Article 4 is directly applicable. The wording, the objective and the general purpose of the provision as of the Directive itself plead for this interpretation. In particular, it is

---

[86] Dir. 75/442 in the version of Dir. 91/156 (n. 12), Art. 1(d): "'management' shall mean: the collection, transport, recovery and disposal of waste . . .".

[87] A good example is the Resolution on (steel) scrap, adopted by the Consultative Committee of CECA on October 10, 1997 [1997] O.J. C356/8.

[88] Joined cases C-206 & 207/88 *Vessoso and Zanetti* [1990] E.C.R. I-1461; C-359/88 *Zanetti* [1990] E.C.R. I-1509; C-422/92 *Commission v. Germany* (n. 83); C-304/94 *Tombesi* (n. 85); C-129/96 *Inter-Environnement Wallonie* [1997] E.C.R. I-7411; C-192/96 *Beside* [1998] E.C.R. I-4029; C-203/96 *Dusseldorp* [1998] E.C.R. I-4075.

[89] Organisation for Economic Co-operation and Development (Environment Policy Committee, Waste Management Policy Group), Final guidance document for distinguishing waste from non-waste (Paris, April 23, 1998).

[90] The OECD definition of waste, laid down in OECD Decision C (88) 90 is: "materials other than radioactive materials intended for disposal for reasons specified in Table 1".

[91] OECD, guidance document (n. 89), p. 2.

[92] *Ibid.*, paras 22 and 23.

[93] Dir. 75/442 (n. 12), Art. 4: "Member States shall take the necessary measures to ensure that waste is recovered or disposed of without endangering human health and without using processes or methods which could harm the environment, and in particular: without risk to water, air soil and plants and animals; without causing a nuisance through noise or odours; without adversely affecting the countryside or places of special interest. Member States shall also take the necessary measures to prohibit the abandonment, dumping or uncontrolled dispoal of waste."

[94] Case C-236/92 *Comitato di Difesa v. Lombardia* [1994] E.C.R. I-483.

not possible to understand why a licensed waste operator, under Article 9 of the Directive, would have to respect these requirements, whereas a person who acts without a licence would have no such obligation.

If Article 4 were properly enforced by Member States, it would have a considerable impact on unauthorised landfills, illegal dumps and other waste practices. Indeed, it is clear that most of the environmental impacts that are described in Article 4 continue to occur as long as an unauthorised landfill exists; the mere stopping of the landfilling itself would not remove the environmental impairment. This can only be achieved via the retrofitting of the landfill or the taking away of the waste which was disposed of. To date, no such consequence has been drawn from this provision.

(b) Hazardous waste

9—27   Council Directive 78/319 on toxic and dangerous waste[95] was substituted, in 1991, by Directive 91/689.[96] This Directive defined hazardous waste, introduced a licensing requirement for installations which process hazardous waste, and requested management plans for hazardous waste to be drawn up and regular information on installations which handled hazardous waste. Member States had to report regularly on the implementation of the Directive.

On the implementation of Directive 78/319 the Commission reported for the first time in 1997, based on reports from six Member States.[97] The report showed "a very low level of harmonisation of the national legislations"; the definitions of toxic and dangerous waste greatly varied. The number of plans was so small that the required comparison between them was not made. The Commission concluded that "Directive 78/319 was probably drafted in too general terms to ensure a high degree of integration".[98]

As with the notion of "waste", difficulties appeared as regards the concept of "dangerous waste". The Directive of 1978 gave a definition of dangerous waste[99] that was soon considered to be too vague. For that reason, it was replaced, in Directive 91/689,[1] by a "listing approach": hazardous was a waste which was listed in a Community positive list.[2] Since then, this list has been established.[3] At present, a major review of the list is ongoing, since Member States notified overall a further 500 wastes that they wanted to see inserted into the list.

9—28   The main problems linked to the Community definition of hazardous waste are that Member States use, in their national legislation, different terminology, such as "special waste", "chemical waste", "specially controlled waste", and so on. Since

---

[95] Dir. 78/319 on toxic and dangerous waste [1978] O.J. L84/43.

[96] Dir. 91/689 on hazardous waste [1991] O.J. L377/20.

[97] COM (97) 23 of February 27, 1997; Luxembourg, Italy, Ireland, Portugal, Greece and Belgium (Brussels and Wallonia) had not reported.

[98] Commission (n. 97), p. 33.

[99] Dir. 78/319 on toxic and dangerous waste [1978] O.J. L84/43, Art. 1(b): "'toxic and dangerous waste' means any waste containing or contaminated by the substances or materials listed in the Annex to this Directive of such a nature, in such quantities or in such concentrations as to constitute a risk to health or the environment".

[1] Dir. 91/689 on hazardous waste [1991] O.J. L377/20; the word "hazardous" was presumably preferred to "dangerous", because the Basel Convention on the shipment of waste used this terminology; in substance, the concepts are equivalent.

[2] Ibid., Art. 1(4): ". . .'hazardous waste' means: wastes featuring on a list drawn up . . . on the basis of Annexes I and II to this Directive . . . These wastes must have one or more of the properties listed in Annex III. The list shall take into account the origin and composition of the waste and, where necessary, limit values of concentration . . .; any other waste which is considered by a Member State to display any of the properties listed in Annex III. Such cases shall be notified to the Commission and reviewed . . . with a view to adaptation of the list."

[3] Dec. 94/904 [1994] O.J. L356/14.

Directive 91/689 is based on Article 175 (ex 130s) E.C., these different definitions make it possible to establish national waste lists that are different from the Community list. To complicate things further, the Basel Convention on the shipment of hazardous waste and the OECD have established hazardous waste lists, which are different from the Community list, a legal situation that generates difficulties, inconsistencies, grey markets and illegal practices.[4]

(c) Waste recovery

9—29 Waste recovery includes reuse, material recycling and incineration with energy recovery. Community terminology is not quite consistent in this regard.[5] It is not entirely clear to what extent the reuse of an object constitutes a waste operation. Probably, a differentiation has to be made: where an object is reused after having been discarded—a piece of furniture has been placed on the roadside to be taken away by the waste services—its taking up by a person and its continued use constitutes a recovery operation. However, where an object is reused without having been discarded—a friend, visiting a home, discovers a pair of shoes in a corner which are disused, takes them and wears them—the object has never become waste, so no waste recovery operation is involved. Reuse of packaging, such as empty bottles, normally comes into the second category, so the classification of reusable packaging as products by Directive 94/62 is correct.

9—30 At present, only a small percentage of all municipal waste is actually recycled, and one of the principal objectives of any national or Community waste management policy consists of promoting the recycling of waste.[6] The definition of recycling does not always make it clear whether, for instance, pyrolysis or the gasification of plastics are recycling or recovery operations.[7] The difference is important, as more and more precise and legally binding recycling targets are being set; an example is Directive 94/62,[8] which provides for (national) recovery targets of 50 to 65 per cent per packaging material, and a minimum recycling target of 15 per cent for each packaging material.[9] The trend is towards not considering these techniques as recycling operations; however, the final decision is very much a political one.

Directive 75/442 lists in annex IIB waste recovery operations. Annex IIB states that the list reflects the operations "in practice". It is clear, however, that the list is of a legal nature and that it enumerates those recovery operations that are at present practised in the Community. Indeed, Article 10 of Directive 75/442 requires any installation which carries out an operation of annex IIB to have a permit. If other operations were also considered to be recovery operations, such installations would not need a permit. In the case of shipments from one Member State to the other, this would

---

[4] For shipment questions see below, para. 9–36.

[5] See Dir. 75/442 (n. 12), Art. 3 (1b) on the one hand, Dir. 94/62 on packaging and packaging waste [1994] O.J. L365/10, Art. 1(5)–(9) where a reusable packaging is not considered to be waste, on the other hand.

[6] Commission, Communication on the competitiveness of the recycling industries COM (1998) 463 of July 22, 1998.

[7] See on the one hand Dir. 94/62 (n. 5)—"recycling shall mean the reprocessing in a production process of the waste materials for the original purpose or for other purposes including organic recycling but excluding energy recovery" (energy recovery is defined as a means to generate energy through direct incineration with recovery of the heat)—and, on the other hand, the proposal for end-of-life vehicles [1997] O.J. C337/3, Art. 2(7): "Recycling shall mean the reprocessing in a production process of the waste materials for the original purpose or for other purposes excluding the processing for use as fuel or as other means of generating energy."

[8] See in more detail, para. 9–49, below.

[9] See for more details, below, para. 9–49.

make the prior informed consent procedure developed under the provisions for the shipment of waste impossible.[10]

9—31 The greatest discussions are provoked by the operation to "use principally as a fuel or other means to generate energy". Several Member States have, in their national legislation, established calorific values below which a waste could not be considered to come under this process. While it might be necessary to specify under which circumstances a waste principally serves as a fuel, it is clearly not legal to set these conditions at national level. The phrase in question is part of Community law; therefore, its interpretation cannot but be the same throughout the Community. Allowing calorific values to be fixed at national or even regional level—in Belgium, Spain and possibly in other Member States, such a value would have to be fixed at regional level—would lead to different applications of this Community concept: at present, Germany practises a calorific value of 11,000 kJ, France of 5,000, Austria of 6,000 and the Netherlands of 13,000. This has the effect that, for instance, a shipment of waste with a calorific value of 8,000 kJ from France to Germany would be a shipment for recovery in France, but a shipment for disposal in Germany. It remains the fact that the clear jurisprudence of the Court of Justice as regards the interpretation of Community law is deliberately ignored in such cases.[11]

9—32 It remains correct, however, that to date the Community has not fixed provisions on the quality of recycling: where 10 kg of materials out of 1,000 tonnes of waste are extracted and recycled, it is obviously not possible to consider the whole process—shipment, storage, extraction—a recycling operation. Community specifications are urgently required.

Above, at paragraphs 9–23 et seq., the question was discussed as to under what circumstances a product becomes waste; at least as controversial is the question of when a waste becomes a product again. It has already been mentioned that business representatives continue to argue that a waste which is destined for recovery or recycling should not be considered a waste any more and not be subjected to waste legislation. However, this opinion would lead to a complete erosion of the concept of "waste", which might be illustrated by the facts of case C-206/88[12]: an Italian truck driver was stopped by the police, who found quantities of hazardous waste in his truck. The driver did not have the required papers that authorised the shipment of this waste. He defended himself by arguing that he was on his way to a waste incinerator where the waste was to be burned with energy recovery; thus, it did not constitute waste any more, but a product.

9—33 Since Directive 75/442 is now based on Article 175 (ex 130s) E.C., Member States are entitled, under Article 176 (ex 130t) to identify recovery operations other than those listed in annex IIB. They are then obliged to notify the Commission. This leads to a decision by way of a committee procedure under Directive 75/442 to adapt annex IIB to the new situation.

It is apparent that this reasoning could apply to all waste and to practically all operations. Furthermore, it has to borne in mind that almost every object can be recycled or recovered, if the economic costs are disregarded. The possibility or intention of recovering or recycling can therefore not be decisive.

Therefore, waste becomes a product again once the recovery/recycling process is finished. The glass bottle in a bottle bank is thus waste, even where the bottle bank is the property of a specific company which uses its contents to produce new (recycled) bottles. The transport from the bottle bank to the (recycling) plant is a transport of

---

[10] As regards the shipment of waste, see below, para. 9–36.

[11] See, for instance, case C-72/95 Kraaijeveld [1996] E.C.R. I-5403.

[12] Joined cases C-206 & 207/88 Vessoso and Zanetti (n. 88).

waste, not of products; the storage of the old glass bottles on the ground of the plant is storage of waste, and so on.

In recent times, economic operators have sometimes tried to mix waste with products—oil, coal, sawdust—and to consider the mixture as a new form of fuel, and thus as a product. However, the process lacks the essential element of recycling, namely the reprocessing. Furthermore, the consistency of the composition of the new object is not ensured, and thus such mixtures do not constitute new products.

(d) Disposal of waste

9—34 Directive 75/442 also contains in annex IIA a list of operations that are classified as disposal operations.[13] The legal status of this list is the same as the list in annex IIB for recovery operations, so the reader can be referred to the remarks above, paragraph 9–30.

The specific disposal operations are not frequently contested. Germany normally considers the placing of waste into old mines and other underground cavities as recovery operations, since this disposal would prevent the cavities from caving in. This interpretation contradicts several operations in annex IIA of Directive 75/442.[14] The German interpretation is explained by the fact that, under German mining law, less stringent provisions apply for underground storage than for waste disposal operations.

9—35 At present, Community law does not prohibit certain waste from being disposed of. Article 4(2) of Directive 75/442 only prohibits the uncontrolled disposal of waste. For this reason, there is no ban on, for instance, disposing of nuclear waste,[15] shipping waste into space, burying BSE-infected cattle, providing for seabed insertions of waste or the dumping of ships or offshore installations into the sea. There are also no restrictions in Community law as regards the incineration of waste. In future, the Directive on landfills, adopted in mid-1999,[16] will ban the landfilling of liquid waste, explosive, corrosive, oxidising, highly flammable or flammable waste, infectious hospital waste and of whole and shredded used tyres; furthermore, the landfilling of biodegradable municipal waste will be considerably reduced.

(e) Shipment of waste

9—36 Directive 78/319[17] had laid down some general requirements on the shipment of waste. Subsequent to discussions which took place within the framework of the OECD and which also concerned the shipment of waste between the United States and the Community, the Commission proposed, in the early 1980s, a Community directive on the shipment of waste.[18] This proposal, for the first time, introduced into waste law a differentiation between shipments in the Community that crossed the frontier of a Member State and other shipments, a clear departure from the concept of the single Community market and of the common transport policy, as laid down in Articles 3(f), 70 and 94 (ex 3(f), 74 and 100) E.C. in its version applicable at that time.

---

[13] It should be noted that Dir. 75/442 originally also included recovery and recycling operations in the word "disposal". The differentiation was introduced into Community law by Dir. 91/156 in 1991.

[14] Dir. 75/442 (n. 12), annex IIA, D1: "Tipping above or underground (e.g. landfill, etc.)"; D3: "Deep injection (e.g. injection of pumpable discards into wells, salt domes or naturally occurring repositories, etc.)"; D12: "Permanent storage (e.g. emplacement of containers in a mine, etc.)".

[15] The OSPAR Convention—see para. 7–38 above—provides for a ban of nuclear waste disposal at sea. This ban is binding for those E.C. Member States that are also members of OSPAR.

[16] See above, para. 9–14.

[17] Dir. 78/319 (n. 99).

[18] [1983] O.J. C53/3.

The Council adopted the proposal in 1984,[19] and it was then, in 1986, amended in order to cover the shipment of hazardous waste to third countries, too.[20]

9—37   Directive 84/631 introduced a system of prior informed consent for shipments of hazardous waste: the holder of waste had to notify the competent authority of the Member State where he wanted to ship the waste, and to use a standardised consignment note in which he had to specify details of the waste, its destination and details of the shipment. The authority had to acknowledge receipt of the notification before the shipment could be effected. The same procedure was to apply to shipments to third countries, where agreement was necessary from that third country; in such a case, the authority of the Member State of dispatch had, amongst other things, to examine whether the final destination of the waste possessed "adequate technical capacity for the disposal of the waste in question under conditions presenting no danger to human health or the environment"[21]—a provision which would have allowed broad assessments of waste management in third countries but which remained, of course, largely a dead letter.

The adoption of the 1989 Basel Convention on shipments of hazardous waste[22] followed a number of serious incidents concerning illegal shipments from industrialised to developing countries; this Convention and OECD measures on waste shipments adopted in reaction to that Convention led the Community completely to review its provisions and to adopt, in 1993, a Regulation that was based on Article 175 (ex 130s) E.C. and concerned all waste shipments.[23] Following an important amendment in 1997, which largely stopped the export of hazardous waste to third countries, the legal situation is, at present, as follows.[24]

(i) Waste shipments to and from third countries

9—38   The first distinction to be made is between hazardous and non-hazardous waste. This distinction does not follow the lines of Directives 75/442 and 91/689 and the lists on waste and on hazardous waste that had been adopted at Community level.[25] Rather, the Council, when adopting Regulation 259/93, decided to take over a listing system, which the OECD had developed. Annex II to Regulation 259/93 thus contained a green list for (non-hazardous) waste, annexes III and IV an amber and red list for (hazardous) waste; in this way, Community law had and still has a list of hazardous waste[26] and another list for the shipment of hazardous waste—a model of non-transparency.

A second distinction is made by the Regulation between whether the shipment is made for disposal or for recovery purposes; for these, the definitions in Directive 75/442 apply.[27]

9—39   Imports of waste for disposal of any kind into the Community are prohibited, with the exception of imports from countries that are parties to the Basel Convention

---

[19] Dir. 84/631 on the supervision and control within the European Community of the tranfrontier shipment of hazardous waste [1984] O.J. L326/31; see also below regarding the question of environmental liability for damage caused by (the shipment of) waste.

[20] Dir. 86/279 [1986] O.J. L181/13.

[21] Dir. 84/631 (n. 19) in its version amended by Dir. 86/279 (n. 20), Art. 3(3).

[22] Basel Convention on the control of transboundary movements of hazardous wastes and their disposal, 1989; the Community adhered to the Convention by Dec. 93/98 [1993] O.J. L39/1.

[23] Reg. 259/93 on the supervision and control of shipments within, into and out of the European Community [1993] O.J. L30/1.

[24] Reg. 120/97 [1997] O.J. L22/14; Reg. 2408/98 [1998] O.J. L298/19.

[25] See above, paras 9–21 and 9–27.

[26] Dec. 94/904 (n. 3).

[27] See above, paras 9–23 et seq.

or where specific import agreements have been made either by the Community or by Member States. The import of non-hazardous (green list) waste for recovery is not restricted. Hazardous (amber and red list) waste may be imported for recovery from countries which apply the OECD decision on waste shipment and from other countries with which specific agreements have been made.[28]

Export of non-hazardous (green list) waste to third countries for disposal purposes is prohibited. An exception is made for EFTA countries, which are also parties to the Basel Convention. Shipments for recovery of non-hazardous (green list) waste were to be the subject of a complicated procedure. The Commission was to ask each third country, for all types of non-hazardous (green list) waste, whether it was ready to accept such waste, and, if yes, which kind of control procedure it wished to see applied. As there are some 140 types of waste listed in the green list of annex II and there are more than 140 countries which had to be addressed, and with some of these countries not answering at all, giving incomplete answers or subsequently changing their position, the Council only decided in mid-1999 which waste can be shipped to what country and under what control conditions.[29]

9—40 This delay was also due to the fact that the Commission had based its proposal on the trade provision of Article 133 (ex 113) E.C. and had proposed that those third countries that had indicated that they did not wish to receive green list waste should nevertheless be able to obtain such waste, though under the control procedure which applied to (red list) hazardous wastes; the Commission had argued that some of these countries "may not be fully aware of the significance of their decision for those parts of their industrial sector which can use 'green' list waste for transformation and further processing".[30] This approach was, under pressure from the European Parliament, abandoned in the Commission's amended proposal and not taken up by the Council.

As regards exports of hazardous waste, all exports for disposal are prohibited, except to EFTA countries which are also party to the Basel Convention. Furthermore, the Community decided in January 1997[31] that as of January 1, 1998 all shipments for recovery to third countries were also prohibited, with the exception of industrialised countries.[32] This measure was a follow-up to a decision of 1995 under the Basel Convention to ban the shipment of waste for recovery to non-industrialised third countries.[33]

9—41 As regards the waste that comes under this export ban, the Community follows first of all the Basel Convention, which, in 1997, had again been amended in order to establish two lists, one that listed those wastes that came under the export ban (A-list) and another one that listed wastes that did not come under the export ban, although they might be hazardous (B-list). The Community export ban applies to A-list wastes, but not to B-list wastes. Where a specific waste appears neither on the A- nor on the B-list, the export ban applies if it is listed in Decision 94/904 on hazardous wastes or in annexes III or IV (amber and red list waste) of Regulation 259/93.[34]

---

[28] See for details Reg. 259/93 (n. 23), Arts 19–22.
[29] Reg. 1420/1999 [1999] O.J. 166/6; Commission proposal COM (94) 678 of February 8, 1995, amended by COM (97) 685 of January 26, 1998.
[30] Commission, COM (94) 678 (n. 29), para. 11.
[31] Reg. 120/97 (n. 24), amended by Reg. 2408/98 (n. 24).
[32] Formally, the exception was made for countries which apply the OECD decision of March 30, 1993 on the shipment of waste for recovery.
[33] See Dec. 97/640 adhering to this Basel Convention Decision [1997] O.J. L272/45.
[34] See Dec. 94/904 (n. 3); Reg. 2408/98 (n. 24) deleted some wastes from annex III of Reg. 259/93, which thus do not come under the export ban.

The list of hazardous waste set up by Decision 94/904,[35] and also the amber and red lists of hazardous waste, that form annexes III and IV of Regulation 259/93,[36] list waste, that is either not on the A-list of the Basel Convention or that is expressly listed on the B-list as not being subjected to the export ban. In principle, the Basel Convention provides in Article 4(11) that contracting parties may adopt provisions "in order better to protect human health and the environment". Thus, theoretically, the Community could argue that all waste that is listed as hazardous under Community law—the waste listed in Decision 94/904 and the waste listed in annexes III and IV of Regulation 259/93—should be subjected to the Community export ban. However, this was not in the interest of some Member States and of economic operators. The compromise was therefore that waste that the Basel Convention has listed as not coming under the export ban—the B-list waste—would not be banned from export from the Community either. This means in practice that some wastes which are classified hazardous in Community law are not subject to the export ban. The longer this list is, the greater the risk of the Community being accused of applying double standards.

As regards the revision of these lists, the interdependency between the Basel lists, the OECD lists and the Community lists is at present under discussion between the different organisations.

(ii) Shipments between Member States

9—42 Non-hazardous (green list) wastes that are destined for recovery may freely circulate between Member States; their shipment need not be notified. Directive 75/442 allows a Member State to take the necessary measures to prevent movement of wastes that are not in accordance with their waste management plans,[37] a provision that has until now not been used frequently.

Shipments of green list waste for disposal are subject to the principles of proximity and self-sufficiency,[38] principles that only apply to waste disposal, not to waste recovery shipments.[39] Member States may prohibit generally or partially or object systematically to waste shipments; furthermore, they may also object to individual shipments.[40]

A Member State may systematically object to the shipment of hazardous waste for disposal; the reasons for objection are the same as for the shipment of non-hazardous waste for disposal. Such shipments are allowable where the person who intends to ship the waste has first notified the administrations of destination and of dispatch of his intention to ship waste by means of a standardised consignment note and has informed them of details of the waste, the shipment and the consignee. The notifier then receives, within three weeks, the authorisation from the administration to effect the shipment, sometimes, as the case may be, accompanied by certain conditions concerning the shipment.

9—43 Shipments of hazardous waste for recovery may not be objected to systematically. Rather, the grounds for objection are laid down in Article 7(4) of Regulation 259/93 and may also not be extended by a Member State that invokes its right, under Article 176 (ex 130t) E.C., to set more stringent requirements.[41] Again, the

---

[35] Dec. 94/904 (n. 3).

[36] Reg. 259/93 (n. 23).

[37] Dir. 75/442 (n. 12), Art. 7(3).

[38] Ibid., Art. 5: "Member States shall . . . establish an integrated and adequate network of disposal installation. The network must enable the Community as a whole to become self-sufficient in waste disposal and the Member States to move towards that aim individually . . . The network must also enable waste to be disposed of in one of the nearest appropriate installations . . ."

[39] Case C-203/96 Dusseldorp (n. 88).

[40] Reg. 259/93 (n. 23), Art. 4(3).

[41] Case C-203/96 Dusseldorp (n. 88).

details of the intended shipment must be notified to the competent authorities, which may, in the case of amber list waste, give tacit consent, but must agree in writing to the shipment of red list hazardous waste.

Overall, these provisions are rather sophisticated and might seem bureaucratic. They must be understood as a reaction to several abuses of previous provisions, in particular those of Directive 84/631. The main problems at present concern different standards that exist in Member States for recovery (incineration) activities: where Germany, for instance, considers waste that has a calorific value of less than 11,000 kJ not to be capable of being incinerated with energy recovery, it will classify shipments of such wastes as shipments for disposal, whereas Belgium, which does not have the same rule, will classify the shipment as being for recovery.

(iii) Shipments within Member States

9—44 Shipments of waste within Member States are barely regulated at all by Regulation 259/93. The Regulation limits itself to stating that Member States shall establish an appropriate control and supervision system, which shall take into account the necessary coherence with the Community system; they shall inform the Commission thereof (Article 13).

All Member States have taken measures to transpose Regulation 259/93 into national law, where necessary, and to create the necessary administrative infrastructure to deal with waste shipments. Despite this, information on the implementation and practical application of the Regulation is vague; in particular, there is a lack of precise data on shipments between Member States and on exports and imports.[42]

(iv) Shipment of radioactive waste

9—45 Directive 92/3, which is based on Articles 31 and 32 of the Euratom Treaty, deals with the shipment of radioactive waste[43]; it was largely inspired by Directive 84/631 on the shipment of waste,[44] which had, however, been replaced in the meantime by Regulation 259/93. Consequently radioactive shipments are dealt with by way of a directive, whereas shipments of non-hazardous and hazardous waste are the subject of a regulation; normally, one would expect the more stringent form of the regulation to apply to materials which present the higher risk.

Radioactive waste is defined as "any material which contains or is contaminated by radio-nucleides and for which no use is foreseen", a definition which implies that recyclable or recoverable radioactive waste is—for shipment purposes—not waste. In that, the definition is not in line with that of Directive 75/442.

9—46 Shipments between Member States require the agreement of the authorities of the country of dispatch and of destination; normally, the absence of an answer within two months is considered to show tacit consent to the shipment. Exports of radioactive waste require the authorisation of the authorities of the dispatching country, which have to make contact with the country of destination. No export is allowed to countries of the Lomé Convention, to Antarctica and to countries that are not able properly to manage radioactive waste; the assessment is made by the authorities of the exporting Member State.

The Directive does not contain any provision concerning the possibility of Member

---

[42] See COM (1998) 475 of July 28, 1998 on the application of Reg. 259/93.
[43] Dir. 92/3 [1992] O.J. L35/24.
[44] Dir. 84/631 (n. 19).

States adopting a partial or total ban on the import of nuclear waste, though some Member States have banned the import of nuclear waste unilaterally.

The Directive had to be transposed into national law by the end of 1993; only Denmark, the Netherlands and the United Kingdom respected this timescale.[45] By the end of 1994 six, the end of 1995 10, and the end of 1998 all 15 Member States had transposed the Directive.[46] For 1994/1995, the Member States reported that out of 60 transboundary shipments, four of them had had authorisation refused.[47]

Overall, Directive 92/3 is less stringent than Regulation 259/93. Also, conditions for authorising an export to third countries are less stringent than those for a shipment between Member States. Finally, an export ban of radioactive waste to other than OECD countries, as for hazardous waste, is not foreseen.

(v) Shipment of animal waste

9—47   Directive 90/667[48] contains some general rules for the transport of animal waste, which provide for the prevention of leakages and set general hygiene conditions. No specific provisions exist, for instance, on the shipment of BSE waste or of waste from biotechnology processes.

4. SPECIFIC WASTE STREAMS

9—48   The Community has regulated a number of waste streams. The purpose of the provisions is to promote waste recycling and recovery, safe disposal of waste and to ensure that different national provisions on waste management do not unnecessarily affect the integrated rules on the free circulation of goods.

(a) Packaging

9—49   Packaging waste is thought to constitute up to 40 per cent of municipal waste. As early as the first environmental action programme it was announced that packaging issues would be looked at more closely; however, the Commission's initiative met with considerable hostility from economic operators, which were of the opinion that the Community would be better to abstain from this area. The Directive, which the Community finally adopted in 1985, was based on Article 308 (ex 235) E.C. and was limited to liquid beverage containers.[49] It asked Member States to set up programmes for reducing the volume of liquid beverage containers. These programmes could even be implemented by voluntary agreements, which showed the Directive's limited objective. Implementation of this Directive had only very limited success.[50]

A number of Member States had adopted national measures on regulating packaging; attempts to have these measures declared void by the Court of Justice

---

[45] Commission, COM (95) 192 of May 24, 1995, p. 7.
[46] Commission, Second report on the application of Directive 92/3, COM (1998) 778 of December 22, 1998, p. 3.
[47] Ibid., pp. 13 et seq.; shipments took place from Belgium (14), Germany (15), France (4), Luxembourg (1), Austria (1), Finland (1) and Sweden (20); in comparison to that, the United Kingdom reported more than 3,600 shipments within the United Kingdom.
[48] Dir. 90/667 (n. 52).
[49] Dir. 85/339 on containers of liquids for human consumption [1985] O.J. L176/18.
[50] In 1990, five Member States had not yet transposed the Directive: see Commission, 8th report on monitoring application of Community law (1990) [1991] O.J. C338/1, p. 160. The Court of Justice gave judgments in the following cases: C-252/89 Commission v. Luxembourg [1991] E.C.R. I-3973; C-192/90 Commission v. Spain [1991] E.C.R. I-5933; C-255/93 Commission v. France [1994] E.C.R. I-4949.

failed.[51] Since Germany also introduced measures on packaging, the Commission proposed a general directive on packaging waste, which was adopted in 1994.[52] The Directive, based on Article 95 (ex 100a) E.C., tried to lay down uniform provisions on the free circulation of packaging as well as on the protection of the environment. It asked Member States to promote prevention, reuse and recycling of packaging, to set up collection systems for packaging waste, and established recovery and recycling targets for the different packaging materials.[53] Furthermore, the Directive asked for standards for packaging, limited the content of heavy metals, and requested Member States to draw up management plans for packaging and to report regularly on the implementation measures.

9—50   Since most Member States were late in transposing the Directive, it is too early for an assessment. The integration of the environmental and internal market requirements, though, seems to have been only partly successful: imprecise drafting[54] and a loose reference to standards,[55] which is unlikely to fulfil the commitments of the Directive, places the responsibility of achieving the Directive's objective on reducing quantities and promoting reuse and recycling of packaging back on to Member States: while the Directive allows (national) environmental measures, it does not impose them; this favours divergency, not harmonisation.

(b) Batteries

9—51   A second Directive, based on Article 95 (ex 100a) E.C., regulated batteries.[56] The Directive limited the content of some heavy metals—mercury, cadmium and lead—in some batteries. These batteries also had to carry a mark—a crossed-out dustbin[57]—indicating that they should not be thrown out with ordinary household waste; Member States had to organise a separate collection system for the batteries under the Directive. After an amendment of 1998, the use of batteries that contain mercury has been almost completely forbidden.[58]

As the Directive only referred to some batteries, Member States had difficulties in getting it off the ground.[59] A major revision is envisaged.

---

[51] Cases C-302/86 *Commission v. Denmark* [1988] E.C.R. 4607, where a deposit and return system for packaging was attacked; and C-380/87 *Enichem v. Cinisello Balsamo* [1989] E.C.R. 2491, where tax measures on non-biodegradable plastic packaging were in question.

[52] Dir. 94/62 on packaging and packaging waste (n. 24).

[53] *Ibid.*, Art. 6, provides that, by the year 2001, between 50 and 65 per cent of packaging waste must be recovered and 25 to 45 per cent must be recycled; the minimum per centage for each packaging material is 15 per cent. Less stringent requirements were fixed for Greece, Ireland and Portugal.

[54] See, for instance, Art. 5: "Member States may encourage reuse systems of packaging, which can be reused in an environmentally sound manner, in conformity with the Treaty"; the relationship to the recycling targets of Art. 6 is not clear. Another example is Art. 6 itself, which sets targets but does not establish measuring methods. Under certain conditions, Member States may even fix more stringent targets than those of Art. 6: see Art. 6 (6) and Commission Dec. 1998/3940, [1999] O.J. L14/25.

[55] Under Art. 9, Member States shall admit only such packaging on their markets that comply with all essential requirements of annex II. Annex II provides that packaging shall be designed, produced and commercialised in a way as to minimise its environmental impact when it is disposed of. Furthermore, packaging shall be so manufactured that the presence of noxious substances is minimised with regard to their presence in emissions, ash or leachate when packaging is incinerated or landfilled. This might easily lead to national measures as regards metal cans, aerosols, non-biodegradable or PVC-containing packs, etc., with endless debates about whether such measures are permissible.

[56] Dir. 91/157 on batteries and accumulators containing certain dangerous substances [1991] O.J. L78/38.

[57] Introduced by Dir. 93/86 [1993] O.J. L264/51.

[58] Dir. 98/101 [1999] O.J. L1/1.

[59] Cases C-303/95 *Commission v. Italy* [1996] E.C.R. I-3859; C-218–222/86 *Commission v. Belgium* [1996] E.C.R. I-6817; C-282 & 283/96 *Commission v. France* [1997] E.C.R. I-2929; C-236/96 *Commission v. Germany* [1997] E.C.R. I-6397; C-298/97 *Commission v. Spain*, judgment of May 28, 1998 (not yet reported).

(c) Used oils

9—52   Directive 75/439, the very first environmental directive,[60] which is based on Articles 94 and 308 (ex 100 and 235) E.C., provided for the safe collection, treatment, storage and disposal of waste oils. Member States had to give priority to the recycling (regeneration) of waste oils, "where technical, economic and organisational con-straints so allow". The discharge of waste oils into waters and drainage systems was prohibited. Activities concerning the collection, treatment and disposal of waste were to be licensed. Waste oils may not contain more than 50 parts per million of PCB/PCT.

Member States all transposed the Directive into national law, though sometimes with a considerable delay.[61] Its application only had limited success: the recycling clause did not fulfil expectation; most waste oils are incinerated; recycling has remained a subordinate activity.[61a] A revision of the Directive is in preparation.

(d) PCB/PCT

9—53   Directive 76/403[62] contained provisions to control the disposal of PCB/PCT. As these provisions were considered to be not sufficiently protective, the Directive was replaced, in 1996 and after eight years of negotiations, by Directive 96/59,[63] which provided for the decontamination and disposal of all products containing PCB/PCT. This equipment must be inventoried, labelled and reported. Member States are obliged to set up, by September 1999, disposal plans and ensure that PCB/PCT is removed from the environment by 2010 at the latest.

(e) Sewage sludge

9—54   Directive 86/278, based on Articles 94 and 308 (ex 100 and 235) E.C., deals with the use of sewage sludge in agriculture.[64] The Directive fixed maximum limit values for concentrations of heavy metals in the sludge and in soil and defines conditions for the use of sewage sludge. Sludge and the soil on which it is used must be regularly analysed in order to make sure that the heavy metal concentrations are not exceeded.

Member States were expressly allowed to set more stringent requirements. Presum-ably in view of that, the values fixed by the Directive were not too severe. Several Member States adopted more stringent requirements at a national level.[65] The use of sewage sludge in agriculture has met increasing objections from farmers and the food industry, who are afraid of food contamination.

---

[60]   Dir. 75/439 on the disposal of waste oils [1975] O.J. L194/23.

[61]   See cases C-21/79 *Commission v. Italy* [1980] E.C.R. 1; C-30–34/81 *Commission v. Italy* [1981] E.C.R., 3379; C-70/81 *Commission v. Belgium* [1982] E.C.R. 175; C-172/82 *Inter-Huile* [1983] E.C.R. 555; C-295/82 *Rhone Alpes Huiles* [1984] E.C.R. 575; C-173/83 *Commission v. France* [1985] E.C.R. 491; C-240/83 *Procureur de la République v. Assoc. de Défense de Bruleurs de Huiles Usagées* [1985] E.C.R. 531; C-162/89 *Commission v. Belgium* [1990] E.C.R. 2391; C-366/89 *Commission v. Italy* [1993] E.C.R. I-4201; C-37/92 *Vanacker and Lesage* [1993] E.C.R. I-4947.

[61a]   See now case C-102/97 *Commission v. Germany,* judgment of September 9, 1999, where Germany was condemned because it had not given priority to the recycling of used oils.

[62]   Dir. 76/403 on the disposal of PCB/PCT [1976] O.J. L108/41.

[63]   Dir. 96/59 on the disposal of PCB/PCT [1996] O.J. L243/31.

[64]   Dir. 86/278 on the protection of the environment, and in particular of the soil, when sewage sludge is used in agriculture [1986] O.J. L181/6.

[65]   See also case C-260/93 *Commission v. Belgium* [1994] E.C.R. I-1611.

(f) Animal waste

9—55   Directive 90/667 laid down hygienic provisions for the disposal and processing of animal waste.[66] The Directive was an early Community reaction to BSE ("mad cow disease"); it introduced "high-risk" and "low-risk" animal waste and stated that high-risk waste had to be adequately incinerated or buried in order to prevent environmental impairment. The Directive was mainly targeted at ensuring disposal of BSE waste without causing problems for humans or the environment. To date, no problems have arisen that have been known to be linked to the disposal of BSE waste.

(g) Other waste streams

9—56   Besides these measures, to which asbestos waste questions should be added,[67] Community institutions have considered or started to take action in regulating other specific waste streams. A proposal for a directive on end-of-life vehicles establishes targets for the increased recyclability of cars and car parts,[68] following to some extent the model of Directive 94/62 on packaging; it might be adopted in the year 2000. A proposal for a directive on electrical and electronic waste, again following this model, is in preparation. The Commission is looking into questions of composting, PVC products and waste, health-care waste, and construction and demolition waste.

A Council Recommendation on waste paper from 1981 tried to promote the recycling of waste paper,[69] but has remained largely unacknowledged. Its impact on economic or administrative practices was small.

BIBLIOGRAPHY

Bartlsperger, R.: "Die Entwicklung des Abfallrechts in den Grundfragen von Abfallbegriff und Abfallregime", *Verwaltungsarchiv* (1995), p. 32

Bouckaert, J.: "Artikel 130s EEG als juridische basis voor de afvalrichtlijn", *Tijdschrift voor Milieu en Recht* (1993), p. 226

Campins Eritja, M.: *La gestion de los residuos peligrosos en la Comunidad Europea* (Barcelona, 1994)

Cheyne, I. and Purdue, M.: "Fitting definition to purpose: the search for a satisfactory definition of waste", *Journal of Environmental Law* (1995), p. 149

Christiansen, P.: "Waste—a national aspect" in B. Wenzel (ed.), *First Nordic conference on EU environmental law* (Copenhagen, 1994), p. 79

Demey, T., Hannequart, J. and Lambert, K.: *Packaging Europe. A directive standing up to transposition into 15 national laws* (Brussels, 1996)

De Sadeleer, N.: "La circulation des déchets et le marché unique", *Revue du Marché Unique Européen* (1994), p. 71

De Sadeleer, N.: *Le droit communautaire et les déchets* (Paris and Brussels, 1995)

De Villeneuve, C.: "Les mouvements transfrontières de déchets dangereux", *Revue du Marché Commun* (1990), p. 568

---

[66] Dir. 90/667 laying down the veterinary rules for the disposal and processing of animal waste, for its placing on the market and for the prevention of pathogens in feedstuffs of animal or fish origin, and amending Dir. 90/425 [1990] O.J. L363/51.
[67] See above, para. 4–08.
[68] [1997] O.J. C337/97, explanatory memorandum COM (97) 358 of July 9, 1997; amended proposal [1999] O.J. C156/5.
[69] [1981] O.J. L355/56.

Dieckmann, M.: *Das Abfallrecht der Europäischen Gemeinschaften* (Baden-Baden, 1994)

Douma, W.: "Wallooon waste import ban", *European Business Law Review* (1993), p. 32

Ermacora, F.: "Community legislation and jurisprudence in the area of waste management: recent developments", *Review of European Community and International Environmental Law* (1998), p. 274

Fluck, J.: "Zum Abfallbegriff im europäischen, im geltenden und im werdenden deutschen Abfallrecht", *Deutsches Verwaltungsblatt* (1993), p. 590

Fluck, J.: "Zum EG-Abfallrecht und seiner Umsetzung in deutsches Recht", *Europarecht* (1994), p. 71

Geradin, D.: "The Belgian waste case", *European Law Review* (1993), p. 144

Haigh, N. (with G. Bennett, P. Kromarek and T. Lavoux): *Comparative report: water and waste in four countries* (London, 1986)

Hannequart, J.: "Le règlement européen sur les mouvements de déchets", *Aménagement-Environnement* (1993), p. 67

Hannequart, J.: *European waste law* (London, The Hague and Boston, 1998)

Jadot, B.: "Mesures nationales de police de l'environnement, libre circulation des marchandises et proportionnalité", *Cahiers du droit européen* (1990), p. 408

Jans, J.: "Waste policy and European Community law: does the EEC Treaty provide a suitable framework for regulating waste?", *Ecology Law Quarterly* (1993), p. 165

Jans, J.: "Self-sufficiency in European waste law?" in B. Wenzel (ed.), *First Nordic conference on EU environmental law* (Copenhagen, 1994), p. 71

Jarass, H.: "Die Beschränkung der Abfallausfuhr und EG-Recht", *Natur und Recht* (1998), p. 397

Klett, W. and Enders, R.: "Gefährliche Abfälle—Umsetzungsdefizite europarechtlicher Vorgaben", *Betriebsberater* (1997), Beilage 4.1

Konzak, O.: "Inhalt und Reichweite des europäischen Abfallbegriffs", *Natur und Recht* (1995), p. 130

Krämer, L.: "Le déversement des déchets en mer et le droit communautaire", *Revue du Marché Commun* (1988), p. 328

Krämer, L.: "Droit à l'environnement et installations de déchets" in M. Prieur and C. Lambrechts (eds), *Mankind and the environment; études en hommage à Alexandre Kiss* (Paris, 1998), p. 353

Krämer, L.: "Die Europäische Union und der Export von Abfällen in die Dritte Welt", *Kritische Justiz* (1998), p. 345

Krings, M.: "Der Abfallbegriff nach geltendem und künftigem Abfallrecht aus europäischer und nationaler Sicht", *Wirtschaftsverwaltung* (1995), p. 103

Kummer, K.: "The international regulation of transboundary traffic in hazardous wastes: the 1989 Basel Convention", *International and Comparative Law Quarterly* (1992), p. 530

Lavrijsen, L.: "De Europese reglementering betreffende de verbranding van huishoudelijke en gevaarlijke afvalstoffen" in Brussels Instituut voor milieubeheer (ed.), *De laatste ontwikkelingen van de Europese reglementering inzake afvalstoffen* (Brussels, 1995), p. 89

Layard, A.: "The 1994 Directive on the incineration of hazardous waste, 'substitute fuels' and trans-scientific choices", *European Environmental Law Review* (1997), p. 16

Levis, L.: "The European Community's internal regime on trade in hazardous wastes: lessons from the U.S. regime", *Review of European Community and International Environmental Law* (1998), p. 283

London, C. and Llamas, M.: *E.C. law on protection of the environment and the free movement of goods* (London, Dublin and Edinburgh 1995)

Morgan de Rivery, E.: "Réglementation communautaire des déchets", (Paris) *Juris-Classeurs* (1995), Fasc. 805

Pernice, I.: "Environment and trade in the field of waste: a legal assessment", *Jahrbuch des Umwelt- und Technikrechts* (1995), p. 135

Picheral, C.: "L'ambivalence de la notion de déchet dans la jurisprudence de la CJCE", *Revue juridique de l'environnement* (1995), p. 559

Pocklington, D.: "An assessment of the proposed European legislation for end-of-life vehicles", *European Environmental Law Review* (1998), p. 138

Rehbinder, E.: "Take-back and recovery obligations in the light of the E.C. Treaty" in M. Prieur and C. Lambrechts (eds), *Mankind and the environment; études en hommage à Alexandre Kiss* (Paris, 1998), p. 367

Sander, A. and Küppers, P. (eds): *Environmentally sound waste management* (Frankfurt/M., 1993)

Schink, A.: "Die Deponie-Richtlinie der EU und die Abfallentsorgung in der Bundesrepublik Deutschland", *Abfallrechtliche Praxis* (1999), p. 3

Schliessner, U.: "Entwurf einer EG-Richtlinie über Verpackungen und Verpackungsabfall", *Europäische Zeitschrift für Wirtschaftsrecht* (1993), p. 52

Schmidt, A.: "Transboundary movements of waste under E.C. law. The emerging regulatory framework", *Journal of Environmental Law* (1992), p. 61

Schröder, M.: "Aktuelle Konflikte zwischen europäischem und deutschem Abfallrecht", *Die Öffentliche Verwaltung* (1991), p. 910

Schröder, M.: "Die steuernde und marktbegrenzende Wirkung umweltschutzrelevanter Prinzipien des EG-Vertrages am Beispiel des Abfallexportes", *Neue Zeitschrift für Verwaltungsrecht* (1996), p. 833

Sommer, J.: "Les déchets, de l'autosuffisance et de la libre circulation des marchandises", *Revue du Marché Commun et de l'Union Européenne* (1994), p. 246

Stuyck, J.: "Le traitement des déchets dans la (non-) réalisation du marché intérieur", *Journal des tribunaux—droit européen* (1994), p. 10

Vandemeersch, D.: "Het vrije verkeer van afvalstoffen binnen de Europese Gemeenschap", *Tijdschrift voor Milieurecht* (1992), p. 78

Van der Mensbrugghe, Y.: "Les frontières maritimes de la CE (observations à propos de la directive 84/631 sur les transferts transfrontaliers de déchets dangereux", *Revue du Marché Commun* (1989), p. 360

Veldkamp, A.: *Overbrengen van afvalstoffen; (trans) nationale uitvoering en handhaving* (Utrecht, 1998)

Von Köller, H., Klett, W. and Konzak, O.: *EG-Abfallverbringungsverordnung* (Berlin, 1994)

Von Wilmowsky, P.: "Grenzüberschreitende Abfallentsorgung: Ressourcenkonflikte im gemeinsamen Markt", *Neue Teitschrift für Verwaltungsrecht* (1991), p. 1

Von Wilmowsky, P.: "Abfall und freier Warenverkehr: Bestandsaufnahme nach dem EUGH-Urteil zum wallonischen Einfuhrverbot", *Europarecht* (1992), p. 414 (English version *Common Market Law Review* (1993), p. 541)

Von Wilmowsky, P. and Roller, G.: *Civil liability for waste* (Frankfurt, Berlin, Bonn, New York, Paris and Vienna, 1992)

Wendenburg, H.: "Die Umsetzung des europäischen Abfallrechts", *Neue Zeitschrift für Verwaltungsrecht* (1995), p. 833

Wiggers-Rust, L.: "Is waste law still only a national affair?", *European Business Law Review* (1991), p. 282

Winter, G.: "Notifizierung und Andienung bei grenzüberschreitender Verbringung von gefährlichen Abfällen zur Verwertung", *Natur und Recht* (1998), p. 233

CHAPTER 10
Legal Aspects of Integrating Environmental Requirements into other Policies

10—01 The new Article 6 (ex 3c) E.C. requires that environmental protection requirements are incorporated into other Community policies.[1] This message has been part of the E.C. Treaty since 1987, when for the first time provisions on environmental protection were incorporated into the Treaty. Indeed, it was clear by then, and it is now even more evident than ever, that the relatively few environmental regulations and directives which the Community has adopted since 1975 will not, in themselves, protect, preserve and improve the quality of the environment or avoid its deterioration. The use of chemicals, the growth of transport and the use of fossil or nuclear fuels continues and even increases. Directives on car emissions will help little in making transport sustainable, since besides the emissions the cars themselves are also the problem. Without specific environmental provisions the environment would probably be in a much worse state; however, this does not necessarily mean that quality of life, in urban centres or elsewhere, has improved, that the progressive disappearance of fauna and flora species has stopped or that climate change problems, tropical forest decline or other environmental problems generally have become insignificant.

The concept of sustainable development, now also used in Articles 2 of the Treaty on European Union and 2 and 6 of the E.C. Treaty, tries to assemble all the opposing interests between environmental protection and economic progress into one formula, in order to find a political compromise to which everybody can agree. This attempt is doomed to failure, because the concept of sustainable development is void of sense and is given political content according to the political actor who uses it.[2]

10—02 The integration requirement of Article 6 E.C. is nevertheless the most important of the principles which govern environmental policy,[3] since it constitutes the bridge between environmental policy and all the other policies at Community level. Any effort to describe the legal achievements of the integration of environmental requirements into the other policies runs the risk of describing the policies, not the legal aspects of integration. Since the present study does not try to examine policies themselves, but to describe legal measures, its presentation of the other policies will necessarily remain limited and even rudimentary. Some indication as to the necessity of an approach to integration which combines political, legal, economic and strategic action might appear from the list of criteria which the European Environmental Agency established for assessing the integration of environmental actions into sectoral policies[4]:

---

[1] Art. 6 (ex 3c) E.C.: " Environmental protection requirements must be integrated into the definition and implementation of Community policies and activities referred to in Article 3, in particular with a view to promoting sustainable development."

[2] See above, para. 1–11.

[3] See for this and the other principles, para. 1–16, above.

[4] European Environmental Agency, *Europe's environment, the second assessment* (Aarhus, 1998), chapter 14.

1. Is there qualitative identification of all environmental costs/benefits?

2. Is there quantification of environmental costs/benefits?

3. Are all external costs internalised into market prices (part of the polluter-pays principle)?

4. Are economic instruments designed to achieve behaviour change rather than just revenue raising?

5. Are environmentally damaging subsidies being withdrawn?

6. Is there an environmental impact assessment of projects before implementation?

7. Is there strategic environmental impact assessment of policies, plans and programmes at different spatial levels?

8. Is environmental procurement a cornerstone of purchasing strategy?

9. Are there environmental management measures within the sector and monitoring of their implementation?

10. Have eco-efficiency targets and indicators been developed and used to monitor progress?

10—03 Legal (binding or not binding) or political instruments for the application of these criteria have, up to now, not been developed at Community level, with the exception of a proposal for a directive on strategic environmental assessment of plans and programmes.[5] For all policies, it should be clear that the integration of environmental issues must be conceived of as a process that might take decades to achieve and does not depend on one or the other legal or political measure that is adopted; examples would be changes in transport policy, the renouncing of nuclear energy or the transition to environmentally friendly agriculture, where organic farming would be the rule, not the exception.

The Commission tried, in 1993, to organise its internal administration in such a way so as to allow it better to take into consideration environmental requirements[6]; these administrative measures were reviewed in 1997.[7] However, it is significant that it was not really attempted to give these decisions the widest publicity possible; in this way, any significant control of their implementation by the other institutions, the media or the public was lacking.

10—04 The measures provided mainly for the following actions[8]:

- all Commission proposals were assessed on their environmental effects. Where such effects are likely to occur, an environmental impact assessment is to be made;

- proposals for new legal measures should, in the explanatory memorandum, describe and explain environmental effects and environmental costs and benefits;

- the Commission work programme identifies with a green asterisk those proposals that will have significant environmental effects;

---

[5] [1997] O.J. C129/14; see also above, para. 4–15.
[6] Commission, SEC (93) 785 of June 2, 1993.
[7] Commission, Press Release IP/97/636 of July 11, 1997; the Commission's (1997) *Bulletin on European Union*, no. 7/8 is silent on this issue.
[8] Written Question E-0649/97 (Diez de Rivera Icaza) [1997] O.J. C367/33.

- in all relevant Commission departments, contact persons for the integration of environmental requirements were designated. Some departments have set up specific environmental units to deal with this task;

- an environmental network of director generals was set up, which was chaired by the director general for the environment and where the director generals of the most important departments are represented. The emphasis was laid on the total co-ordination of environmental questions and the interdependency between environmental policy and other political measures;

- a specific unit was created inside the environmental directorate general, which is directly placed under the responsibility of the director general and which is charged with the implementation of the fifth environmental action programme and the integration of environmental requirements into other political measures;

- the Commission's annual report was partly modified; it now contains, for key political areas an indication of which environmental considerations were taken into account;

- the Commission took a number of measures for recycling, waste management and its purchase policy ("green accounting"). A strategy paper was adopted in December 1995, which sets a framework for these activities;

- progress in better integrating environmental requirements into other policies are regularly assessed. The reviewed version of the fifth environmental action programme contains detailed information on the integration of environmental requirements into other Community measures.

10—05   The overall effect of these measures on the orientation of the Commission's policy seems insignificant. It is not known whether or not an environmental impact assessment had been made for any new Commission proposal. The greater accentuation of environmental requirements in the Commission's regional policy is less attributable to the above-mentioned measures, than to the more environmentally oriented approach by the Commissioner in charge of regional policy.

The fifth environmental action programme (1993) singled out five areas of activity as target sectors where particular efforts were to be made in order to integrate environmental requirements in those policies, namely the manufacturing industry, energy, transport, agriculture and tourism.[9] For three of these sectors— the manufacturing industry, energy and tourism—the Community did not even have an express competence for action.[10]

10—06   Legal measures on tourism matters are affected by the fact that the Community does not have an express competence on tourism[11]; hence objectives of tourism policy are not fixed at Community level—except for the statement that tourism should become sustainable; and no legal instruments have until now been adopted or proposed to promote this vague idea. The integrating of environmental requirements into tourist policy measures thus remains incoherent, largely based on financial assistance to pilot or demonstration projects.

In 1998, the European Council reduced the priority sectors to agriculture, transport and energy, without explaining this change.[12] It is to be expected that these three

---

[9] Fifth environmental action programme [1993] O.J. C138/1, pp. 28 *et seq.*

[10] See Art. 3(m) and 3(u) E.C.

[11] Art. 3(u) E.C.

[12] (1998) 6 *Bulletin of the European Union*, para. 1.11.

sectors will be considered as the future key sectors, whereas, according to political circumstances, the integration of environmental requirements into other policies—competition, consumer, regions, social, development, industry, information, research, and so on—will also be politically promoted.

1. AGRICULTURAL POLICY

10—07   Agricultural policy is based on Articles 32 to 39 (ex 38 to 48) E.C. Agricultural policy pursues the objectives of Article 33 (ex 39),[13] which may, in general terms or in concrete measures, conflict with the environmental objectives of Articles 2 and 174 (ex 2 and 130r) E.C.

The Commission's progress reports on integrating environmental requirements into the agricultural sector remained relatively general,[14] but recognised that the agricultural policy has not changed much.[15] The European Environmental Agency identified the agriculture/forestry sector as a principal contributor to the environmental problems[16] of climate change, chemicals, soil, waste, acidification, biodiversity, inland waters and marine and coastal zones. The Agency gave this resumé[17]:

> 10—08   "Overall, fertiliser and pesticide use in Europe has decreased since the late 1980s, owing to improved application methods in the West and reduced agricultural output and incomes in Eastern Europe. The number of cattle and pigs has fallen in Europe as a whole, although animal manure remains a pollution problem in north-western Europe and is causing increasing problems in southern Europe. Water use for irrigation has increased, causing wetland loss and supply shortages in some areas. Soil compaction and other forms of soil degradation caused by agricultural practices (for example desertification and salinisation) are still widespread, especially in southern Europe and in the Newly Independent States.
>
> Habitats and species are under increasing threat from intensive agriculture in all parts of Europe, but particularly in the European Union due to current Common Agricultural Policy priorities that continue to place emphasis on increasing yields. In parts of Central and Eastern Europe, there has been an increase in chemical-free food production, for economic reasons. In the European Union, organic agriculture, because of ideological reasons, grew from 1.5 per cent to 6 per cent of total agricultural land between 1990 and 1995."

---

[13] Art. 33(1) E.C.: "The objectives of the common agricultural policy shall be: (a) to increase agricultural productivity by promoting technical progress and by ensuring the rational development of agricultural production and the optimum utilisation of the factors of production, in particular labour; (b) thus to ensure a fair standard of living for the agricultural community, in particular by increasing the individual earnings of persons engaged in agriculture; (c) to stabilise markets; (d) to assure the availability of supplies; (e) to ensure that supplies reach consumers at reasonable prices."

[14] Commission, Interim review of implementation of the European Community programme on policy and action in relation to the environment and sustainable development, COM (94) 453 of November 30, 1994, p. 23; Progress report from the Commission on the implementation of the European Community programme on policy and action in relation to the environment and sustainable development, COM (95) 624 of January 10, 1996, p. 34.

[15] Commission, Interim review (n. 14), p. 23: "the core of CAP, *i.e.* the Common Market Organisations, remains to a large extent unchanged as regard environmental provisions"; Progress report (n. 14): "there has not been a lot of progress in assessing the environmental effects of new proposals in CMOs or in monitoring those effects on existing regimes"; p. 41: "improvement in Common Market Organisation schemes are limited and still weak".

[16] European Environmental Agency (n. 4), chapter 14.1.

[17] *Ibid.*, chapter 14.2.

10—09 The objectives of agricultural policy, laid down in Article 33 (ex 39) E.C., have not changed since the beginning of the European Community (1958). Environmental considerations came only very slowly into perspective. A 1985 Green Paper devoted, for the first time, a special section to the environmental effects of agriculture.[18] In 1988 a communication on "agriculture and the environment" followed, which was based on the assumption that the common agricultural policy was already under pressure anyway and did not need supplementary pressure.[19] The general problems of agricultural policy led in 1992 to a substantial reform of the common agricultural policy; although environmental improvement was not among the main objectives of this reform, increased efforts were taken subsequently to ensure income to farmers by progressively considering them to be nature conservationists, with access to environmental money. In pursuance of this policy, measures were gradually introduced to grant financial aid for environmental services provided by agriculture, such as the production of energy, forest-fire prevention, water protection, stabilisation of carbon dioxide and other greenhouse gas emissions, recycling of organic waste, nature conservation and biodiversity management, tourism and recreation, soil conservation, landscape management, the setting aside of land, less intensive production methods or afforestation. The principal objective remained, however, financial aid to farmers.

10—10 A Regulation of 1986 aimed to protect forests against air pollution, by providing for reliable data collection and financial support for forest conservation measures.[20] Regulation 2080/92 introduced a system of financial aid for afforestation.[21] Regulation 2092/91 established and defined rules on ecological agriculture and the labelling of products thereof[22]; in 1996, the Commission made a proposal for completing the Regulation by including animal production in it, which the Council adopted in 1999.[23] Regulation 2078/92 on agricultural production methods compatible with the requirements of environmental protection and the maintenance of the countryside[24] introduced a system of financial aid which aimed at the reduction of pollution caused by agriculture and at the promotion of farmers as nature conservationists and protectors of the landscape. The Regulation's role has become increasingly important for the efforts to integrate environmental requirements into agriculture; in 1996, aid distributed by it covered 4.3 billion ECU, about 3 per cent of the Community's agricultural budget,[25] though, of course, a number of aid schemes only paid lip-service to environmental concerns. For rural development measures that have the protection of the environment as their main aim, the Community made available, under its Structural Funds, 776 million ECU, about 11 per cent of that Fund (in the period 1994–1999).

Community measures that directly affect agriculture mainly stem from environmental policy, such as the protection of waters against nitrates from agricultural sources,[26] the use of sewage sludge in agriculture[27] or the environmental impact assessment of agricultural projects.[28]

10—11 Agricultural prices, which are fixed by the Community institutions, do not reflect environmental costs at all. For a number of years political pressure has tried to

---

[18] Commission, Perspectives for the common agricultural policy, COM (85) 333 of July 23, 1985.
[19] COM (88) 338 of June 28, 1988.
[20] Reg. 3529/86 [1986] O.J. L326/5.
[21] Reg. 2080/92 [1992] O.J. L215/96.
[22] Reg. 2092/91 [1991] O.J. L198/1.
[23] Reg. 1804/99 [1999] O.J. L222/1.
[24] Reg. 2078/92 [1978] O.J. L215/85.
[25] Commission, Progress report (n. 14), p. 38.
[26] Dir. 91/676 [1991] O.J. L375/1; see above, para. 7–18.
[27] Dir. 86/278 [1986] O.J. L181/6; see above, para. 9–54.
[28] Dir. 85/337 [1985] O.J. L175/40; see above, para. 4–10.

align these prices with global prices for agricultural products; however, it is implicitly accepted that a price system for agricultural products could not simultaneously reflect environmental costs and align to world market prices. Hence, the more the polluter-pays principle is applied in agriculture, the greater will be the need to avoid competition with agricultural products from the world market, since products from many regions in the world—quite apart from labour costs—do not take environmental concerns into account.

2. TRANSPORT POLICY

10—12   The Community transport policy (Articles 70 to 80 (ex 74 to 84) E.C.) is also constructed as a common policy, which should, in theory, mean that there is only one Community, but practically no national, transport policy. This construction by the E.C. Treaty has never been realised; national transport policies continued to exist and were—and still are—in large areas much more relevant than Community transport policy. The Community transport policy was for long time targeted towards realising the four Treaty freedoms for goods and services, capital and labour. The introduction of an environmental Chapter into the Treaty has not yet fundamentally changed this situation.

10—13   Transport policy contributes to the environmental problems linked with climate change, acidification, tropospheric ozone, biodiversity, urban environment and technological and natural hazards[29]; this list at best touches issues such as land use, noise, waste generation and marine pollution only marginally. Subsequent to the different environmental action programmes, which mentioned the problems of the environment, the Commission first issued a Greenbook in 1992 on environmental problems linked to transport,[30] which was quite quickly followed by a Whitebook.[31] The Whitebook denounced the increase of environmental constraints over the last 20 years and proclaimed that the consideration of environmental aspects was an integral part of a common transport policy. In order to reduce the environmental impact of transport, the Whitebook pleaded for the adoption of strict standards for exhaust emissions, energy consumption and noise emissions, as well as standards on technical controls for cars, the establishing of noise level limits around airports, and environmental impact assessments for infrastructure plans and projects, including cost-benefit analyses. It pleaded for the promotion of public transport, bicycles and electric cars, the reduction of private car use and the reduction of land use for transport infrastructure projects.

10—14   The fifth environmental action programme stated that "because of the projected increases in the volume of cars used, the mileages driven and increases of road freight traffic, the transport . . . will offset any potential reduction attributable to the introduction of new emission standards". Its suggestions were to "reduce operational pollution, limit the infrastructural development of land use, reduce traffic and congestion and prevent or reduce risks inherent in the transport of dangerous goods and wastes." It suggested, in particular, road taxes, road pricing, regulation and fiscal incentives for fuels and vehicles and a change in user behaviour.[32] In 1995, the Commission adopted an action programme on transport 1995–2000[33] and a Greenbook on

---

[29] European Environmental Agency (n. 4), chapter 14.
[30] Commission, Greenbook on the impact of transport on the environment, COM (92) 46 of April 6, 1992.
[31] Commission, Whitebook on a Community strategy on sustainable mobility, COM (92) 494 of December 2, 1992.
[32] Fifth environmental action programme [1993] O.J. C138/5, para. 4.3.
[33] COM (95) 302 of July 12, 1995.

fair and efficient prices in the transport sector.[34] Overall, there is an impressive number of opinions, statements, resolutions and other political measures on the environmental impact of transport, that have been adopted by the different Community institutions, most recently statements from a joint environment/transport council in June 1998.

10—15   Legally, the most important measures are the efforts to limit the pollution emissions by cars and trucks.[35] The Community has never, in the transport sector, managed to introduce economic (fiscal or other), instruments, such as fees for the use of motorways,[36] roads or airports, incentives for the use of less-polluting vehicles, fiscal advantages for public transport, or even simply the comprehensive promotion of electric cars.[37] Also, the recurrence to eco-points, used in the agreement with Austria on the Alp transit,[38] has never been used as a model for measures within the Community. There seems to be only very limited political determination, at Community level and at the level of Member States, to introduce the necessary changes in the form of a coherent strategy and legally binding acts. Only a minority of Member States pursue a national transport policy that integrates environmental requirements. Attempts to increase car production and to create a more efficient transport infrastructure—motorways, roads, railway lines, airports and so on—are at the centre of transport policy practically everywhere; the necessity of creating this corresponding infrastructure reduces the efficiency of environmental measures, where they are taken.

Forecasts for the year 2010 show increases of 40 per cent in passenger road traffic, 182 per cent of aviation traffic and a doubling of road traffic.[39] It is thus unsurprising that the Commission expects a substantial increase of carbon dioxide emissions from transport and concludes generally that transport, at present growth rates, is not sustainable.[40]

3. Energy policy

10—16   As mentioned, Community energy policy operates without an express legal basis in the Treaty; the 1997 amendment of the Treaty has not changed this situation, despite considerable political efforts by the Commission: Article 3 E.C. only provides for "measures" in the area of energy. The lack of an express Treaty competence on energy does not prevent Articles 154 to 156 (ex 129b to 129d) E.C. from providing for the creation, under the E.C. Treaty, of trans-European networks, amongst other things, in the area of energy infrastructure.

Community energy policy has the following three main objectives: (1) security of energy supply; (2) improvement of competitiveness; and (3) quality of life of citizens and protection of the environment[41]; thus, the environment has at least been identified as one of the objectives of Community energy policy measures, which is not the case in any other Community policies.

---

[34] COM (95) 691 of December 20, 1995.

[35] See above, chapter 7.

[36] See, for instance, Proposal for a directive to introduce charges for the use of certain transport roadways by heavy trucks [1996] O.J. C59/9, which is not yet adopted; this proposal is meant to replace Dir. 93/89 [1993] O.J. L316/19, which had been annulled by the Court of Justice: case C-21/94 *Parliament v. Council* [1995] E.C.R. I-1827.

[37] See European Parliament Res. of January 22, 1993 [1993] O.J. C42/256.

[38] See Reg. 3637/92 [1992] O.J. L373/1; Dec. 92/577 [1992] O.J. L373/4.

[39] European Environmental Agency, *Environment in the European Union 1995* (Luxembourg, 1995), p. 32.

[40] COM (96) 624 (n. 14), p. 32.

[41] See, for instance, Council Res. of November 23, 1995 [1995] O.J. C327/3 and the—rather prudently formulated—Council Res. of July 8, 1996 concerning the Whitebook on "an energy policy for the European Union" [1996] O.J. C224/1.

Within the framework of these objectives, the Commission identified, in 1997, three vital points on which Community energy measures must act: reduce dependence on supplies from energy sources outside the Community, ensure more competitive prices for energy products and make energy markets more compatible with environmental objectives.[42] One reason for slow progress in reaching these objectives is that Member States rely heavily on national sources of energy—oil in the United Kingdom, gas in the Netherlands, nuclear energy in France and Belgium, coal in Germany, for example—and wish to keep national responsibility for energy policy measures.

10—17 The E.C. Treaty, the Coal and Steel Treaty and the Euratom Treaty all provide for energy measures. The Euratom Treaty was conceived in order to promote the peaceful use of nuclear energy, but very largely lost its political *raison d'être* when in the 1960s France refused to integrate nuclear policy into the Community mechanisms and Germany also went its own way. At present, seven Member States—Greece, Italy, Portugal, Ireland, Denmark, Luxembourg and Austria—do not have nuclear energy production on their territory, mainly for environmental reasons. This influences Community energy decisions on nuclear or non-nuclear matters, including those relating to climate[43] or to the internal market. Energy measures which are based on the Euratom Treaty, in particular on Articles 30, 31, 34 and 37, do not discuss the impact of nuclear energy on the environment in any significant way; they mainly consider effects of nuclear energy on human health, but not on fauna and flora or other environmental assets, and even there the approach is not consistent.[44]

10—18 The Treaty on Coal and Steel was signed in 1951 and entered into effect in 1952; it has a duration of 50 years. It mainly provides for measures on coal, though measures on lignite may also be taken under certain conditions. The function of coal as the main energy resource in the Community—which had taken over from wood in the nineteenth century—had already, at the end of the 1950s, been replaced by oil. The serious adaptation problems caused by this change continue to exist and have contributed to reducing the discussions on environmental problems linked to coal.

All other energy resources are subject to the provisions of the E.C. Treaty. Energy use is accounted for significantly contributing to climate change and air pollution, acidification, tropospheric ozone creation, waste generation, soil degradation, marine and coastal zone problems and technological hazards issues.[45] Again, this neglects a number of other impacts of energy use, such as land use by installations and networks, water pollution and light pollution. As some of these environmental problems do not occur with the use of nuclear energy, the ongoing discusssion on climate change leads to certain attempts to promote nuclear energy, although this energy is economically not competitive—except in France, where it has been subventioned for decades—and has solved neither the problem of disposal of nuclear waste nor of decommissioning of nuclear installations. The problem of the negative perception of nuclear technology by the population is another unsolved problem.

10—19 As regards environmental measures, most provisions were based on Articles 175 (ex 130s) or 308 (ex 235) E.C. Article 175(3) expressly maintained a veto right for Member States in important energy matters, by providing for unanimous

---

[42] COM (97) 167 of April 23, 1997.

[43] For climate change issues, see also para. 8–54, above.

[44] See, for instance, Commission Opinion [1997] O.J. C291/5 on the discharge of radioactive substances from Sellafield (U.K.). The Opinion, based on Article 37 of the Euratom Treaty, did not discuss at all the impact of such discharges on the Irish Sea, on the United Kingdom environment, or on marine fauna and flora. When the Commission examined the effects of French nuclear tests in Mururoa, it looked at their effects on people in other states (the Pitcairn Islands, U.K.), but neither on French citizens nor on the environment.

[45] European Environmental Agency (n. 4), p. 418.

decisions in such cases.[46] Since the end of the 1980s, a number of political, not legally binding statements were made on the relationship between energy and the environment,[47] including the statement to stabilise carbon dioxide emissions by the year 2000 at the level of 1990, in order to combat the greenhouse effect.[48]

Of the different action taken in pursuance of the energy policy, measures on energy saving, energy taxes and on renewable energies are—next to the measures to combat climate change[49]—of particular interest here. The following measures on energy saving and on renewable energies were adopted: Directive 93/76 (SAVE I), which aimed at an improvement of energy efficiency in housing, of cars and industrial companies[50]; Decision 91/565, which provided for financial assistance for energy-saving measures[51]; Decision 93/500 (ALTENER), which promoted, particularly through financial incentives, renewable sources of energy[52]; and Decision 96/737 (SAVE II) to grant further financial assistance for energy-saving measures.[53] Generally, the amount of financial assistance that is made available by these measures is modest.[54] A coherent, systematic policy on energy saving is not pursued, since low energy prices make such a policy politically difficult.

10—20   As regards taxes, the Commission proposed, in 1992, a tax on carbon dioxide emissions and energy.[55] The proposal was intended, in particular, to combat the greenhouse effect. It provided for an exception of renewable energies[56] and stated that "in order to safeguard the competitiveness of Community industry, the tax arrangements cannot be applied in the Member States until such time as other member countries of the OECD have brought in a similar tax or measures having an equivalent financial impact".[57] This announcement condemned the proposal, since Japan and the United States, in particular, clearly indicated that they had no intention of introducing a similar tax. The amended proposal,[58] which was, by the end of 1999, still not adopted by the Council, provided for some conditions for the introduction of the tax, but left it entirely to the discretion of Member States whether they wished to introduce an emission/energy tax. Such a tax has been introduced by Scandinavian states and the Netherlands; several states have signalled that they would be ready to increase the tax, but abstained from it in order not to expose their industry to competitive disadvantages in comparison with other Community Member States

10—21   Directive 92/81[59] obliged Member States to introduce an excise duty (tax)

---

[46] Art. 175(3) (ex 130s(3)) E.C.: "[The Council shall unanimously adopt] . . . measures significantly affecting a Member State's choice between different energy sources and the general structure of its energy supply." See also para. 2–89.

[47] Commission, COM (88) 174 of April 6, 1988; Energy and the environment, COM (89) 369 of February 8, 1990.

[48] (1990) 10 E.C. Bulletin, para. 1.3.77; this commitment was made in a form of Council conclusions, i.e. in a political and unpublished form.

[49] See above, paras 8–64—8–73.

[50] Dir. 93/76 [1993] O.J. L237/28; see also the Commission's proposal COM (92) 182 of June 26, 1992, which had proposed going considerably further.

[51] Dec. 91/565 [1991] O.J. L307/34.

[52] Dec. 93/500 [1993] O.J. L235/14; the Council adopted a Common Position on ALTENER II, which contains a multiannual programme to promote renewable energies [1998] O.J. C62/31.

[53] Dec. 96/737 [1996] O.J. L335/50.

[54] 45 million euro for four years for SAVE II (n. 52), 22 million euro for ALTENER II for two years (n. 52).

[55] [1992] O.J. C196/1; see also paras 8–64—8–73.

[56] Renewable energies were not defined; the proposal provided for exemptions for fuel wood and wood charcoal, products resulting from the distillation or processing of wood, and, furthermore, any product of agricultural or vegetable origin and crude or esterified vegetable oils.

[57] Commission (n. 55), 10th considerant; it is to be noted that Germany had declared itself ready to introduce a carbon dioxide/energy tax, but only in concert with the other Community Member States.

[58] COM (95) 172 of May 10, 1995.

[59] Dir. 92/81 on the harmonisation of the structure of excise duties on mineral oils [1992] O.J. L316/15.

on mineral oils, but left the fixing of the rate to Member States. Directive 92/82[60] set minimum rates for the excise duties on mineral oils, but allowed this minimum rate to be zero for liquid petroleum gas and kerosene used for heating purposes. Both Directives provided for numerous exemptions and derogations; Directive 92/81 even contained the remarkable provision that a Member State could be authorised by unanimous Council decision, to apply an exemption or reduction on mineral oils "for specific policy considerations". In such a case, the Member State had to inform the Commission; if neither the Commission nor another Member State had then objected within two months, "[the] Council shall be deemed to have authorised the exemption or reduction proposed".[61]

These Directives thus provided, for instance, for different minimum taxes for leaded and unleaded petrol. However, Member States remained completely free as to whether they wanted to introduce such a tax differentiation or not. Overall, therefore, it remained in the hands of Member States if they wanted to use energy taxes in order to promote environmental purposes.

10—22 Renewable energies—wood, solar, water geothermal and wind energy— played, until very recently, a modest role at Community level. This sector accounted for 1.6 per cent of energy supply in 1973 and 1.5 per cent in 1989.[62] Its share has risen since, also by virtue of the accession of Sweden and Austria, which have considerable water energy supplies; at present, it accounts for about 6 per cent. In 1996, the Commission adopted a Greenbook and, subsequently, in 1997, a Whitebook on renewable energies, where it announced its objective to reach a market share of 12 per cent by the year 2010.[63] The Commission included biomass in the list of renewable sources and clearly stated its intention to promote waste incineration under the flag of renewable energies.[64] Agricultural residues, straw, crops, residues, organic fraction of municipal household waste, separated household waste, sewage sludge, wood residues and residues from the wood working industries, used vegetable oils, and biogas used as motor fuel, are all claimed to be "biomass", i.e. renewable sources of energy.[65]

10—23 The Council agreed politically to the promotion of renewable energies, but was prudent when making commitments.[66] Most measures will have to be taken in the coming years to approach or reach the non-mandatory target of 12 per cent by 2010. Again, low prices for traditional energy (fuels and others) make the recurrence to renewable energies, which would probably need financial support for several years in order to become competitive, not very attractive.

The European Parliament had already since, by early 1990s, asked for more measures to promote renewable energies,[67] amongst others to consider the conclusion of a new

---

[60] Dir. 92/82 on the approximation of the rates of excise duties on mineral oils.

[61] Dir. 92/81 (n. 59), Art. 8(4).

[62] Nuclear energy had, in 1973, almost the same market share (1.9 per cent); this had risen to 14.2 per cent in 1989 and to 17 per cent at present, see COM (90) 1428 of September 14, 1990.

[63] Commission, "Energies for the future: renewable sources of energy": Greenbook, COM (96) 576 of November 20, 1996; Whitebook, COM (97) 599 of November 26, 1997.

[64] Commission, Greenbook (n. 63), p. 7: "Municipal and other organic waste, although depletable, is normally also classified as a renewable source of energy . . . Biomass comprises material either specifically cultivated as energy crops or derived from agriculture and forestry operations and can be used to produce solid, liquid or gaseous fuels. Waste from the agricultural sector can be treated thermally or biologically to produce energy. Treatment of municipal waste has to respect the overall waste strategy which gives priority to prevention of waste and recycling. The residual municipal waste can—depending on the waste stream composition and other circumstances—be considered as a source of renewable energy."

[65] Whitebook (n. 63), pp. 37 and 38.

[66] Res. of June 8, 1998 [1998] O.J. C198/1.

[67] Res. of January 19, 1993 [1993] O.J. C42/31; Res. of May 28, 1993 [1993] O.J. C176/216; Res. of July 4, 1996 [1996] O.J. C211/27; Res. of November 14, 1996 [1996] O.J. C362/279; Res. of May 15, 1997 [1997] O.J. C167/60.

Community Treaty along the model of the Euratom Treaty, but dealing with policies and measures on renewable energies; to consider spending as much money for the promotion of renewable energies as was spent for research on nuclear fusion (840 million euro). To date, such ideas have not found an echo among Community institutions or among Member States.

4. TRADE POLICY

10—24   Community trade policy is mainly based on Articles 131 to 135 (ex 110 to 116) E.C., which give exclusive competence to the Community in matters of commercial policy. The Council and Member States interpret these provisions narrowly and accept the Community's exclusive competence only where no other matters than commercial issues are discussed which deal with products. This considerably limits the area of exclusive Community competence, because most international agreements also concern other issues of foreign economic policy, such as economic co-operation, investments, financial and technical assistance, and exchange of advisers or experts; according to the Council, agreements that include such aspects do not come under Articles 131 to 135 (ex 110 to 116) E.C.

10—25   Community decisions to adhere to international environmental conventions which contain trade elements are normally based on Article 175 (ex 130s), not Article 133 (ex 113) E.C. Examples are decisions to adhere to the Montreal Protocol on ozone-depleting substances[68] or to the Basel Convention on the shipment of hazardous waste[69]; Regulation 338/97 should also be mentioned here,[70] which transposes the provisions of the CITES Convention on trade in endangered species of fauna and flora into Community law. The Community is not a member of the Convention itself, since that Convention is open only to nation states, and an amendment that would allow the adhering of the Community has not yet entered into force.

Community environmental measures are affected more and more by the globalisation of economies. In 1994, a new World Trade Organisation (WTO) was set up, which replaced the General Agreement on Tariffs and Trade (GATT) and has the objective of promoting international trade.[71] The WTO took over the GATT rules, which had been drafted in 1947 and did not expressly address environmental issues, and follows, in general, the objective of promoting free international trade; environmental measures are mainly seen and treated as being barriers to trade. In a half-hearted attempt to discuss ways for reconciling trade and environmental issues, the WTO set up a Committee on Trade and Environment, which should discuss environmental and trade aspects, though it did not have any power to set up rules or provide for concrete proposals. The WTO statutes also provide for a dispute settlement system to solve conflicts between, amongst others, environment and trade; decisions by the WTO in this area are binding upon the contracting parties and financial sanctions are foreseen in the case of non-compliance.

10—26   As in the case of the relationship between the Community and its Member States,[72] the questions concerning whether the Community environmental measures affect the rules of free international trade have to differentiate between situations

---

[68] Dec. 88/540 [1988] O.J. L297/8.
[69] Dec. 93/98 [1993] O.J. L39/1.
[70] Reg. 338/97 [1997] O.J. L61/1, see also para. 5–25, above.
[71] The Community adhered to WTO by Dec. 94/800 [1994] O.J. L336/1.
[72] See paras 3–04 et seq., above.

where no international environmental measures have been taken, and those cases where international conventions on the protection of the environment exist.

Where no international environmental agreements exist, a Community measure which endeavours to protect the environment is, in principle, compatible with GATT/WTO rules, if it does not constitute a means of arbitrary or unjustifiable discrimination and where it is "necessary", amongst other things, "to protect human, animal or plant life or health" (GATT Agreement, Article XX(b)) or relating "to the conservation of exhaustible natural resources" (Article XX(g)). Different GATT/WTO panels used the word "necessary" in Article XX to introduce a proportionality test into measures by contracting parties. This thus makes the WTO provisions similar to those of Article 30 (ex 36) E.C.—except that the European Court of Justice's interpretation of Article 28 (ex 30) E.C., which also allows legitimate national environmental protection measures to restrict trade, has, as yet, no counterpart in the WTO provisions.

10—27   Of particular concern is the discussion as to whether WTO rules allow contracting parties to take trade-restricting environmental measures which protect the environment outside their own jurisdiction. Such measures may either concern the environment in other contracting states such as tropical rainforests or endangered species (tigers, elephants) or the so-called "global commons" that do not belong to the jurisdiction of anybody, such as the high sea, its resources and its fauna, the climate, the ozone layer and so on.

In 1991 and 1994, two different GATT panels considered U.S. restrictions on imports of tuna fish caught with so-called purse-seine nets, which also trapped and killed large numbers of dolphins. The United States had prohibited the use of those nets and had, furthermore, banned the import of tuna that was caught with capturing methods which did not correspond to the United States legislation. The first panel denied that the measures were compatible with Article XX(b), since they had extraterritorial effects[73]; the second panel expressly stated that GATT also allowed extra-territorial measures,[74] but was of the opinion that the measures were disproportionate. Neither finding has been approved by the relevant WTO/Gatt Council and have therefore remained unofficial.

10—28   Until now, Community environmental measures have not, as yet, been examined under WTO procedures; the international debate is rather politicised and might well lead, within a short time, to such an examination. Possible measures that might come under such examination are: the Community provisions on eco-labelling,[75] which developing countries, in particular, consider to constitute trade barriers; the import restrictions on fur of animals caught with leghold traps[76]; and also packaging, labelling and recycling, the ban of certain substances, products or production methods and eco-taxes.

My own opinion is that environmental measures under WTO rules are permitted, even where they aim at protecting the environment outside the jurisdiction of the state. The basic justification of this is that life, health and natural resources—which are a short formula equivalent to the environment[77]—are not available in unlimited

---

[73] "The record indicates that the concerns of the drafters of Article XX(b) focused on the use of sanitary measures to safeguard life or health of humans, animals or plants within the jurisdiction of the importing country."

[74] "The panel further observes that, under general international law, states are not in principle barred from regulating the conduct of their nationals with respect to persons, animals, plants and natural resources outside of their territory . . ."

[75] Reg. 880/92 [1992] O.J. L99/1; see above, para. 4–34.

[76] Reg. 3254/91 [1991] O.J. L308/1; see above, para. 5–36.

[77] The details of this equivalence under GATT/WTO rules, which were laid out in 1947 when the concept of "environment" did not yet exist, cannot be elaborated here.

quantities. Where measures are taken to protect the environment, which are neither discriminating nor disproportionate, such measures are also allowed, under WTO rules, to restrict international trade; and the differentiation between production and production standards cannot really lead to different results in this regard. It seems clear to me that, for instance, the United States measures in the above-mentioned tuna–dolphin case contained an element of protectionism (discrimination).

10—29   The problem with weighing the interests between trade and environment at international level lies in the fact that trade and economic interests prevail quantitatively and qualitatively in international discussions, particularly in developing countries.[78] There is hence all the more need for tribunals or dispute-settlement bodies where environmental considerations are given the same amount of attention as trade matters—which does not seem to be the case at present. Indeed, if one looks at the different reactions of GATT and WTO panels, where environmental and/or health matters were discussed, environmental matters do not have the same weight. In international discussions, outside concrete cases, even the European Community has a tendency to let trade interests prevail over environmental interests, for instance by arguing that measures to protect the environment outside the jurisdiction of the acting state should only be allowed where they are in conformity with internationally agreed measures.[79]

The necessity of avoiding, on the one hand, protectionist measures that take the formal appearance of environmental protection (green protectionism) and, on the other hand, of allowing legitimate environmental protection measures, is likely to find some compromise solutions only gradually; it is not surprising that legal writers look particularly to regional solutions, such as the European Union or the North America Free Trade Area (NAFTA), in order to find solutions for the problems of integrating environmental requirements into international trade rules. Article 95(7) (ex 100(7)) E.C., recently introduced into the E.C. Treaty, shows a possible future solution: much of the pressure on dolphins, sea turtles and other environmental assets would be avoided if the world community were willing and able to adopt worldwide measures to ensure adequate protection of dolphins or turtles.

10—30   Where environmental measures have been taken at international level, their compatibility with WTO/GATT rules is nevertheless contested. In particular there is considerable discussion as to whether the three above-mentioned conventions on trade in endangered species, in ozone-depleting substances and in hazardous waste are in conflict with the general WTO rules, though these questions have not yet been examined by a WTO dispute settlement panel or the European Court of Justice.

The legal question over which international agreement should prevail—the WTO agreement or the specific environmental conventions—will have to be decided politically. Under the existing rules of international law, it is not possible to solve this question. Since all three conventions have been elaborated under the auspices of the United Nations, it appears to be a consequent to assume that measures which are adopted by states or by the European Community, and which are in compliance with these international conventions, cannot be tackled under WTO rules. The fact that such trade restriction measures are also to be applied against states which have not ratified these specialised conventions, is not decisive.

10—31   The Montreal Protocol, the Basel Convention and the CITES Convention

---

[78] This is a matter of human behaviour which goes beyond environmental issues: "Ventre affamé n'a pas d'oreille" (J. de la Fontaine); "Erst kommt das Fressen und dann die Moral" (B. Brecht).
[79] COM (96) 54 of February 28, 1996; see also the reproach by the European Parliament, Res. of May 24, 1996 [1996] O.J. C166/260.

all allow the contracting parties to adopt more stringent provisions than those of the conventions, in order to protect the environment[80]; and the Community has, in the different areas coming under those three conventions, made use of this possibility. The question then is whether such additional domestic measures that are taken at Community or at national level are also compatible with WTO rules. The problem has not yet been discussed in detail in legal literature. My own opinion is that such measures are also compatible with WTO rules, since they rest on an express authorisation of the conventions, which expresses the wish to improve environmental protection as far as possible. It is self-evident, though, that here, again, a careful examination has to take place in order to avoid such measures being discriminating or disproportionate.

BIBLIOGRAPHY

Calliess, C.: "Ansatzpunkte für eine umweltverträgliche Verkehrspolitik im europäischen Binnenmarkt—unter besonderer Berücksichtigung der Querschnittsklausel des Art. 130r Abs.2 S.3 EGV", *Zeitschrift für angewandte Umweltforschung* (1994), p. 322

Churchill, R. and Kütting, G.: "International environmental agreements and the free movement of goods in the EC: the case of the Montreal Protocol", *European Environmental Law Review* (1994), p. 329

Demaret, P.: "Trade-related environmental measures (TREMs) in the external relations of the European Community" in M. Maresceau (ed.), *The European Community's commercial policy after 1992: the legal dimension* (Deventer, 1993), p. 315

Epiney, A.: *Verkehrspolitik und Umweltschutz in der Europäischen Union: zur Einbeziehung ökologischer Aspekte im Bereich des Strassen- und Schienenverkehrs* (Fribourg, 1997)

Esty, D. and Geradin, D.: "Environmental protection and international competitiveness", *Journal of World Trade* (1998), no. 3, p. 5

García Burgués, J. and Insausti Muguruza, M.: "Trade and the environment in the WTO: the European Community's participation in the Committee on Trade and Environment", *Review of European Community and International Environmental Law* (1997), p. 163

Geradin, D.: "Trade and environmental protection: Community harmonisation and national environmental standards", *Yearbook of European Law* (1993), p. 151

Geradin, D.: *Trade and the environment—a comparative analysis of E.C. and U.S. law* (Cambridge, 1997)

Ginzky, H.: "Umweltschutz und der internationale Handel mit Waren", *Zeitschrift für Umweltrecht* (1997), p. 124

Götz, V.: "Agrarumweltrecht der Europäischen Gemeinschaft" in H. Rengeling (ed.), *Umweltschutz und andere Politiken der Europäischen Gemeinschaft* (Cologne, Berlin, Bonn and Munich, 1993), p. 173

Grawe, J.: "Umweltschutz und Energiepolitik" in H. Rengeling (ed.), *Umweltschutz und andere Politiken der Europäischen Gemeinschaft* (Cologne, Berlin, Bonn and Munich, 1993), p. 87

Hancher, L.: "Energy and the environment: striking a balance?" *Common Market Law Review* (1989), p. 669

Hailbronner, K.: "Verkehrspolitik und Umweltschutz" in H. Rengeling (ed.), *Umweltschutz und andere Politiken der Europäischen Gemeinschaft* (Cologne, Berlin, Bonn and Munich, 1993), p. 149

Hedemann-Robinson, M.: "E.C. law, the environment and consumers: addressing the challenge

---

[80] Basel Convention (n. 69, above), Art. 3(11); CITES Convention [1982] O.J. L384/1, Art. XIV. The Montreal Protocol (n. 68, above) is formally a Protocol of the Vienna Convention on the protection of the ozone layer, to which the Community became a party in 1988 (Dec. 88/540 [1988] O.J. L297/8); Art. 2 of that Convention allows additional domestic measures.

of incorporating an environmental dimension to consumer protection at Community level", *Journal of Consumer Policy* (1997), p. 1

Hession, M. and Macrory, R.: "Balancing trade freedom with the requirements of sustainable development" in N. Emiliou and D. O'Keeffe (eds), *The European Union and world trade law* (Chichester, 1996), p. 181

Jahns-Böhm, J.: "Güterkraftverkehrspolitik und Umweltschutz im EWG-Vertrag", *Europäische Zeitschrift für Wirtschaftsrecht* (1991), p. 523

Krämer, L.: "Die Integrierung umweltpolitischer Erfordernisse in die gemeinschaftliche Wettbewerbspolitik" in: H. Rengeling (ed.), *Umweltschutz und andere Politiken der Europäischen Gemeinschaft* (Cologne, Berlin, Bonn and Munich, 1993), p. 47

Leclerc, S.: *Politique agricole commune et environnement* (Rennes, 1993)

Maresceau, M. (ed.): *The European Community's commercial policy after 1992: the legal dimension* (Deventer, 1993)

Marx, A.: "Towards sustainability? The case of tourism and the E.U.", *European Environmental Law Review* (1997), p. 181

Organisation for Economic Co-operation and Development: *Trade measures in multilateral environmental agreements: synthesis report of three case studies*, COM/ENV/TO (98) 127 (Paris, 1998)

Pâques, M. and Renaudière, P.: "Agriculture et environnement dans le droit communautaire, quelques questions", *Aménagement* (1992), special issue on "agriculture", p. 44

Pernice, I.: "Umweltschutz und Energiepolitik", *Recht der Energiewirtschaft* (1993), p. 45

Rengeling, H. (ed.): *Umweltschutz und andere Politiken der Europäischen Gemeinschaft* (Cologne, Berlin, Bonn and Munich, 1993)

Sands, P.: "Danish bottles and Mexican tuna", *Review of European Community and International Environmental Law* (1992), p. 18

Schröder, M.: "Die Berücksichtigung des Umweltschutzes in der gemeinsamen Agrarpolitik der Europäischen Union", *Natur und Recht* (1995), p. 117

Schweitzer, M.: *Alpentransit und Europäische Verkehrspolitik*, Zentrum für Europäisches Wirtschaftsrecht Bonn no. 47 (1995)

Seidl-Hohenveldern, I.: *LKW-Transit durch Österreich und die EG* (Saarbrücken, 1996)

Steinberg, R. and Britz, G.: "Die Energiepolitik im Spannungsfeld nationaler und europäischer Regelungskompetenz", *Die Öffentliche Verwaltung* (1993), p. 313

Ward, H.: "Trade and environment issues in voluntary eco-labelling and life cycle analysis", *Review of European Community and International Environmental Law* (1997), p. 139

Winter, G.: "On integration of environmental protection into air transport law: a German and E.C. perspective", *Air and Space Law* (1996), p. 132

CHAPTER 11
Implementation

1. OBLIGATIONS OF MEMBER STATES TO APPLY COMMUNITY LAW

(a) Treaty provisions

11—01 The E.C. Treaty does not contain environmental provisions which Member States would have to transpose into, or to apply in, their national legal order. Article 10 (ex 5) E.C. states that Member States shall align to the Community objectives and tasks.[1] However, this does not mean that they would have to place in their national legislation the objective of attaining a high level of environmental protection or the aim that environmental requirements are incorporated into the other policies pursued at national level. In contrast, Article 10 (ex 5) E.C. requires Member States to abstain from any measures at national level, which would make it more difficult or impossible for the Community to move towards a high level of environmental protection or to make the different Community policies "greener", *i.e.* environmentally more friendly.

The environmental provisions of the E.C. Treaty are not formulated in such a way that they are self-executing or, in Community terminology, directly applicable. While Article 28 (ex 30) prohibits barriers to trade within the Community, Article 81 (ex 85) trade-distorting agreement between undertakings, Article 82 (ex 86) abuses of dominant positions and Article 87 (ex 92) state aids, no corresponding provision exists in environmental law, for instance forbidding environmental pollution. National enforcement bodies or courts therefore do not have to align Member States' laws to instructions that come from Community primary law.

(b) Secondary legislation

11—02 The situation is completely different as regards secondary Community environmental law. Under Article 175(4) (ex 130s(4)) E.C., it is, in principle, the Member States that have to implement the different measures which have been adopted in pursuance of Community environmental policy. This provision is somewhat superfluous, since in other Community policies, too, where no such provision exists, the implementation of measures is up to Member States. Community directives and decisions address Member States; Community regulations apply in all Member States without even any transposing act (Article 249 (ex 189) E.C.). In no situation is there any decision by a national Parliament or regulating body required or admitted to accept or not to accept Community secondary law provisions. This then is the fundamental difference that distinguishes Community environmental law from public international law, which requires, in order to become valid, an express act by the national legislative body.

---

[1] Art. 10 (ex 5) E.C.: "Member States shall take all appropriate measures, whether general or particular, to ensure fulfilment of the obligations arising out of this Treaty or resulting from action taken by the institutions of the Community. They shall facilitate the achievement of the Community's tasks. They shall abstain from any measure which could jeopardise the attainment of the objectives of this Treaty."

Regulations directly apply in each Member State (Article 249(2) (ex 189) E.C.); and while environmental regulations frequently contain specific provisions that require Member States to take action—such as the appointing of responsible authorities, the publication of reports or even the taking of executive provisions—their general attribute of being directly applicable remains unchanged; the specific provision then has the characteristics of a provision of a directive and needs to be implemented, unless it is, in substance, a recommendation. Similar observations apply to decisions, which normally deal with a specific, concrete situation; where a specific provision in a decision is, in substance, that of a directive, it would require implementation as if it were a directive.[2]

11—03 "A directive shall be binding, as to the result to be achieved, upon each Member State to which it is addressed, but shall leave to the national authorities the choice of form and methods" (Article 249(3) (ex 189) E.C.). As Community legislation must be applied by Member States—this follows from Articles 10 and 211 (ex 5 and 155) E.C.[3]—Member States have two main obligations as regards Community environmental directives: they must incorporate the provisions of the directive into their national law and they must ensure that these provisions are actually complied with.

(i) Transposition

11—04 Practically all[4] environmental directives contain a provision that requests Member States to transpose the directive's provisions into national law.[5] Generally, such a transposition into national law has to be done by an express binding legislative or regulatory provision, "in order to secure full implementation of directives in law and not only in facts".[6] The Court of Justice has, on numerous occasions, rejected Member States' attempts to transpose the requirements of an environmental directive into national law by means of a multiannual plan, an administrative circular or a similar instrument.[7] Its main argument was the absence of legal certainty for individual persons and undertakings that was created by such a transposition.[8] Since the Court of Justice is of the opinion that directives which fix quality standards also give certain

---

[2] See, more generally, above, paras 2–36 et seq.

[3] Art. 211 (ex 155) E.C.: "In order to ensure the proper functioning and development of the common market, the Commission shall ensure that the provisions of this Treaty and the measures taken by the institutions pursuant thereto are applied . . ."

[4] The only exception is Dir. 76/464 on pollution caused by certain dangerous substances discharged into the aquatic environment of the Community [1976] O.J. L129/23, where this clause was probably forgotten.

[5] See, for instance, Art. 23 of Dir. 92/43 on the conservation of natural habitats and of wild fauna and flora [1992] O.J. L206/7: "1. Member States shall bring into force the laws, regulations and administrative provisions necessary to comply with this Directive within two years of its notification. They shall forthwith inform the Commission thereof. 2. When Member States adopt such measures, they shall contain a reference to this Directive or be accompanied by such reference on the occasion of their official publication. The methods of making such a reference shall be laid down by the Member States. 3. Member States shall communicate to the Commission the main provisions of national law which they adopt in the field covered by this Directive."

[6] Case C-131/88 Commission v. Germany [1991] E.C.R. I-825, para. 8.

[7] Cases C-96/81 Commission v. Netherlands [1982] E.C.R. 1791; C-131/88 Commission v. Germany (n. 6); C-361/88 Commission v. Germany [1991] E.C.R. I-2567; C-13/90 Commission v. France [1991] E.C.R. I-4327; C-58/89 Commission v. Germany [1991] E.C.R. 4983; C-262/95 Commission v. Germany [1996] E.C.R. I-5729.

[8] See, for instance, case C-131/88 (n. 7), para. 6: "The transposition of a directive into domestic law does not necessarily require that its provisions be incorporated formally and verbatim in express, specific legislation; a general legal context may, depending on the content of the directive, be adequate for the purpose provided that it does indeed guarantee the full application of the directive in a sufficiently clear and precise manner so that, where the directive is intended to create rights for individuals, the persons concerned can ascertain the full extent of their rights and where appropriate, rely on them before the national courts."

legal rights to individuals, most of the provisions of a directive will have to be transposed into national law by a binding provision. This applies even to the establishment of the requirement to set up clean-up programmes or waste management programmes[9]; indeed, such programmes also contain informations for individuals about future objectives, about measures taken and envisaged and so on.

11—05   Exceptions apply only to those provisions which provide for obligations of the Council, the Commission or other institutions, and, in addition, to provisions which exclusively concern the Member States' relations to the Community administration and ask them, for instance, to send a report regularly to the Commission. Even in such cases, though, the limits to Member States' obligations are not altogether clear: the Court of Justice held that a provision that requires regional or local authorities in border regions to consult with authoritites from the adjacent Member State, had to be transposed into national law.[10] The same applied to a provision where a Member State was allowed to grant a derogation under a directive, but had to inform the Commission thereof; where that Member State delegated the right to grant derogations to regional or local authorities, it had expressly to ensure that it was informed of the granting of derogations in order to be able to comply with its own requirements towards the Commission.[11] In the same way, it could also be argued that a Member State's report to the Commission ensures transparency of implementation and compliance, allows individuals to take action themselves or otherwise orient their behaviour, and so on.

11—06   The Court of Justice has not yet had to decide on the transposition of definitions of a directive into national law. The necessity of transposing definitions probably depends on the subject-matter that is regulated: the more directly individual rights and obligations might be affected by a definition, the greater the need to transpose a directive's definition into national law. Good examples are the definitions of "waste" and "hazardous waste" under Directives 75/442 and 91/689[12]: Member States' legislation often does not use the words "hazardous waste", but "specific waste", "waste which is to be controlled", "chemical waste", "industrial waste" and other definitions. These linguistic differentiations have consequences as regards monitoring, surveillance, statistics, customs and police controls and other administrative matters, which impinge in turn on private agents, individuals or administrations. For this reason the Commission has adopted the position that the definitions for waste and for hazardous waste had to be transposed literally into national laws.

11—07   The transposition of an environmental directive, which contains mandatory requirements, cannot be made by non-binding national measures, in particular by administrative provisions, since "mere administrative practices, which by their nature may be changed at will by the authorities, cannot be regarded as constituting proper compliance with the obligation on Member States to which a directive is addressed".[13] For this reason, implementation of an environmental directive through an environmental agreement is not possible, unless the Community directive expressly so provides[14]; this has not yet taken place.[15] As environmental agreements only apply

---

[9] In the same sense, J. Jans, *European environmental law* (The Hague, London and Boston, 1995), p. 125.
[10] Case C-186/91 *Commission v. Belgium* [1993] E.C.R. I-851.
[11] Case C-237/90 *Commission v. Germany* [1992] E.C.R. I-5973.
[12] Dir. 75/442 on waste [1975] O.J. L194/47; Dir. 91/689 on hazardous waste [1991] O.J. L377/20.
[13] Case C-429/85 *Commission v. Italy* [1988] E.C.R. 843; case C-339/87 *Commission v. Netherlands* [1990] E.C.R. I-851.
[14] In the same sense, Commission Recommendation concerning environmental agreements implementing Community directives [1996] O.J. C333/59.
[15] Dir. 85/339 on liquid beverage containers [1985] O.J. L176/18, which is often quoted as allowing implementation of directives by environmental agreements, is not relevant: indeed, the Directive requires Member States to set up packaging reduction programmes and then allows the implementation of such programmes by non-binding measures.

to contracting bodies, the equality of citizens with regard to rights or obligations that a directive grants is not ensured. Transposition of a directive by environmental agreements that are not generally binding is therefore not possible.

A transposition is also necessary in those cases where the Member State in fact already complies with the requirements of a directive. The legal certainty that economic operators and individuals are entitled to expect would be completely undermined if the local, regional or national administration could argue that the factual situation corresponds to the requirements of the directive and places the burden of proof that this is not the case on the person arguing that transposition is necessary.[16]

11—08   No obligation to transpose the requirements of a directive exists where it is physically impossible that the problem dealt with by the directive could ever occur in a Member State. Thus, Luxembourg or Austria would not be obliged to transpose requirements of a directive on coastal waters or (sea) port reception facilities. In contrast, these Member States would normally be obliged to transpose the directive on (the sea discharge of) waste from the titanium dioxide industry,[17] even if they had no such industry on their territory, as this situation could change and, furthermore, titanium dioxide waste from other Member States might be transported to states that do not have such an industry.[18]

The transposition measures must cover the whole of the territory of a Member State. This observation sounds more trivial than it is. Indeed, in many Member States responsibility for environmental issues lies at least partly with regional authorities; this is the case for Austria, Belgium, Germany, Italy and Spain. But in other Member States, too, environmental legislation is partially split; thus, environmental regulations in the United Kingdom are partly taken in or for Wales, Scotland, Northern Ireland or Gibraltar, and in Finland the Aaland Islands have a specific legislative status. Finally, waste management plans in Sweden and the United Kingdom are traditionally set up at local level.

From the point of view of the Community it is not relevant whether a provision of Community law is transposed by one single act at national level or by a number of regional regulations, as long as the transposition measures cover the whole of the territory.

11—09   It is much more difficult to comply with the second substantive requirement for the transposition measure; that is, that the Community environmental requirement is correctly transposed. First, a Member State may not rely on the wording in which a specific directive is drafted in the Member State's language—all Community languages have the same legal value (Article 314 (ex 248) E.C.) and that wording may differ from one language to the other. For that reason, the true sense of a provision has to be discovered, which may well vary between specific linguistic versions.[19] Secondly, it has already been mentioned in paragraph 3–02, above, that Community law is autonomous and has to be interpreted without recurring to identical or similar notions that exist in national law. Thus, the same word might be used in Community environmental law and in national law and yet the two meanings are quite different: this potential conflict is increased by the fact that Community law prevails over national law. However, since Community law stems from a source of law other than national law, it might carry different concepts, theories or structures that do not fit into the national

---

[16]   Case C-339/87 (n. 13).
[17]   Dir. 78/176 [1978] O.J. L54/19.
[18]   In practice, the Commission has accepted that Member States that do not have a titanium dioxide industry formally commit themselves to transposing the Directive as soon as such an industry is established on their territory or where waste from such industry is shipped into their country; legally, this practice is dubious..
[19]   Case C-72/95 *Kraaijeveld* [1996] E.C.R. I-5403; the case concerned the interpretation of Dir. 85/337 on environment impact assessment.

legal or administrative infrastructure. An example is Article 9(2) of the Directive on the conservation of wild birds,[20] which provides that local nature protection authorities may give derogations from trading, hunting and other bans under the Directive, after having examined the local situation; however, such local nature protection authorities do not exist in Ireland.

11—10   Another complication is that Community environmental law provisions normally come up against a structured and elaborate system of national rules that have been built up over years or decades, and into which the provisions then have to be integrated. The Community provision is then perceived—and all too often also treated—as an immigrant, if not as an intruder.

Where the Community environmental law provision sets numerical values such as emission limit values, quality standards or targets, national legislation will have to adopt these numerical values. Economic operators and individuals must have the opportunity to find out what these numerical values are in the national legislation.[21] The same applies to bans on substances or products. For other provisions, it is normally difficult to establish fixed rules, since it follows from Article 249 (ex 189) E.C. that a word-by-word transmission of the Community provision is not required.

11—11   A correct transposition also requires the establishing of sanctions for non-compliance with the Community provisions.[22] It is correct that Community directives do not contain provisions on sanctions for non-compliance, and regulations, too, remain very general. The reason for this is that sanctions are in many countries understood as criminal or quasi-criminal sanctions and that the Community has no specific competence in criminal matters; even where administrative sanctions could be used, there is considerable self-restraint used by the Community when addressing the details of sanctions. This also applies to environmental regulations, though it follows from Article 229 (ex 172) E.C. that regulations could contain penal sanctions.[23] The Court of Justice interpreted Article 10(2) (ex 5(2)) E.C. to mean that national sanctions for non-compliance with Community law must be equivalent to sanctions for breach of equivalent national law provisions; furthermore, they must be effective, adequate and act as a deterrent.[24]

(ii) Application

11—12   Finally, Member States are under an obligation to ensure the practical application of Community environmental law. The transposition itself is only a formal legal act, whereas the protection of the environment begins when emissions are reduced, substances no longer put on the market or (the equivalent) into the environment, habitats protected, and so on. The practical application of environmental provisions is the most serious problem that national, Community and international environmental law faces. Even a piece of national legislation that copies a directive word for word will remain a mere piece of paper unless it is applied.

Some unique features which seriously affect the full application of Community environmental law in practice, must be remembered. Since environmental provisions try to protect the general interest of the Community, they differ markedly from

---

[20] Dir. 79/409 on the conservation of wild birds [1979] O.J. L103/1.

[21] See case C-361/88 (n. 7): "It is clear that legal certainty also requires the specific transposal of individual limit-values, maximum permissible concentrations and emision values into national legislation. A general reference to Community legislation is not permitted."

[22] Case C-68/88 *Commission v. Greece* [1989] E.C.R. 2965.

[23] Art. 229 (ex 172) E.C.: "Regulations . . . may give the Court of Justice unlimited jurisdiction with regard to the penalties provided for in such regulations."

[24] Case C-68/88 (n. 22).

agricultural, transport or industry legislation, which primarily affects specific vested interests. Where vested interests are in question, law making and law enforcement take place, in Western Europe, in constant public—and sometimes not so public—discussions with the representatives of those vested interests; this discussion also continues within the various administrations, parliaments and decision-making bodies. Vested interest groups are also used to ensure the transmission of knowledge on the specific legislation and in this way contribute either to ensuring compliance with the legal rule or bringing about concerted action against that rule, often even preventing its generation. This lobbying function of vested interest groups has become an integrated factor of decision-making at Community level and at the level of Member States.

11—13 The general interest "environment" has no vested interest defender. Environmental organisations in Western Europe are structurally and financially too weak to defend environmental interests effectively over a long period of time. While there is consensus that the environment needs adequate protection and that economic development should be "sustainable", the implementation of concrete, legally binding measures proves difficult wherever other, diverging interests appear. The environment, without a voice and without strong lobby groups, loses out in almost every specific conflict of interests. Since, furthermore, local, regional and national administrations in the 15 Member States are not all convinced to the same extent that Community environmental standards are to be enforced, complied with and applied in practice, practical application of environmental provisions varies within the Community.

General features also contribute to this situation. In a number of Member States, particularly in the south, environmental problems are perceived to be the problems of affluent society; hence there is an attitude among economic operators, and also among administrations, that economic progress is of primary necessity and that environmental concerns should be tackled once the economic level of richer Member States is reached. The same phenomenon can be observed in the countries of Central and Eastern Europe that have applied for E.C. membership. To this has to be added the different enforcement culture which exists in the Community, traditional weaknesses of central government in some Member States, the lack of national environmental infrastructures such as adequate administrations at local, regional and national level, and a lack of environmental information and education, of general awareness, of environmental research bodies, laboratories and test or monitoring or enforcement bodies.

2. MONITORING TRANSPOSITION AND APPLICATION

(a) Implementation reports

11—14 Almost all Community environmental directives have contained, since the mid-1970s, a provision asking Member States to report on the implementation of the directive. Typically, such reports had to be made every three years.[25] The Commission was charged with producing, on the basis of these national reports, a Community report on the implementation of the directive in question; the normal period for these reports was, similarly, every three years.

This system did not lead to the desired result, since neither the Member States' implementation reports nor the Commission's comprehensive reports were drawn up

---

[25] See, however, Dir. 76/160 on the quality of bathing water [1976] O.J. L31/1, where Art. 13 provided for a report at "regular intervals"; since 1979, this provision has been interpreted as requiring annual reports; see also Dir. 84/631 on the shipment of dangerous waste [1984] O.J. L326/1, which provided, in Art. 13, for a report every two years.

regularly. Only for the Bathing Water Directive[26] were regular reports published; however, these dealt with the state of quality of bathing water rather than the implementation of Directive 76/160. Also, monitoring of a number of parameters was omitted and the data transmitted from the Member States were, until very recently, not comparable.

11—15   In order to improve the reporting system, the Council adopted, in 1991, a Directive that restructured the reporting requirements.[27] This Directive introduced the requirement for Member States to report, every three years, on the implementation of the different directives in a given sector (for instance, water, air or waste). The reports were to be based on questionnaires which were set up by committee procedure at Community level, in order to allow the national reports to address the same issues. The reporting period was three years.

The Directive has not improved the situation. Neither the report on the water directives, due in 1997, nor those on air and chemicals, due in 1998, have so far been published; the report on waste issues was due in mid-1999. And those directives that have been adopted since 1991 have not aligned their reporting requirements to Directive 91/692. Where Member States submit reports to the Commission, these reports, together with the national implementing legislation which is at the Commission's disposal anyway, allow a relatively clear picture to be gained on the transposition of a directive into national law. However, such reports normally do not contain information on difficulties of practical application or cases of non-compliance, lacunae and omissions on the side of local, regional or national administrations, inspections, sanctions, or on specific interpretations of individual provisions.

11—16   Commission implementation reports were, overall, very disappointing, apart from the reports on the quality of bathing waters, which continue to be published annually. Directive 91/692 did not lead to a systematic attempt to improve implementation reporting, despite other announcements.[28] Generally, the Commission's different reports on the implementation of the environmental directives have, in the past, been marked by the fact that the information contained therein came almost exclusively from the (central) administration of Member States. For that reason, the Community reports, like the national reports, give a relatively reliable picture on the legal and administrative parts of implementing Community directives—for those Member States that did report. However, less information will be found on, for example, monitoring frequency and intensity, practical non-compliance and gaps and omissions of the administrations. In the future, it is intended that the assistance of the European Environmental Agency will be obtained when elaborating of the Community implementation reports.

The Commission has, it is true, conducted some studies of its own on the practical implementation of environmental directives in the Member States, although inevitably only a limited number of these studies have been undertaken. Their value is limited, though, by the fact that it has proved extremely difficult to gain access to the data held by the national, regional or local authorities; no administration would be easily persuaded to release data showing that a directive is not properly monitored or applied

---

[26] Dir. 76/160 (n. 25).

[27] Dir. 91/692 standardising and rationalising reports on the implementation of certain directives relating to the environment [1991] O.J. L377/48.

[28] Commission, Implementing Community environmental law, COM (96) 500 of October 22, 1996, para. 58: "Through the most effective use of the Reporting Directive, and close co-operation with the European Environmental Agency, the Commission will ensure that the best possible information is available on the effectiveness of Community environmental measures and can be used in the formulation of its policies on environmental measures. The Commission will launch and co-ordinate case studies to evaluate the transposition, application and enforcement of selected provisions of Community environmental law."

in practice, whether the failure is found in the frequency and results of inspections, the economic operators that were controlled, the pollution levels recorded or the respect of the conditions laid down in the licences that the administrations have granted.

(b) The Commission's monitoring function

11—17 The Commission has to ensure that Community environmental law is applied (Article 211 (ex 155) E.C.). This provision is the nucleus which has allowed the Commission to develop, over the years, a system of monitoring transposition, application and enforcement, which goes far beyond of everything that is known in the relations between states. It is this monitoring task of the Commission that has caused the Commission to be called the "guardian of the Treaty".

It should, however, not be forgotten that it is Member States which have, according to Article 175(4) (ex 130s(4)) E.C., the obligation to ensure the implementation of Community environmental law; this then means that Member States have to ensure that Community environmental law is applied. The establishment and functioning of the European Community is also the task of Member States and it is they which have to ensure that "their" constitution—the E.C. Treaty—including its environmental provisions, are properly applied.[29]

11—18 The Commission's task is to ensure that all Community primary and secondary environmental law is applied, in particular regulations, directives and decisions. As regards international conventions, it has already been stated that the Commission does not monitor their application within the Community, not even in cases, where the Community adhered to them. This self-restraint has never been justified or reasoned in public. It is legally unjustifiable. Indeed, where the Community adheres to an international environmental convention, it undertakes that it will ensure compliance with provisions of this convention throughout the territory of the Community. This obligation rests with the Community as such and pertains to the whole Community territory, even where a specific Member State has not ratified the international convention in question. Once the Community has adhered to the international convention, Member States are obliged, under Article 10 (ex 5) E.C., to take the necessary steps in order to allow the Community to respect its international commitments.

11—19 In reality, it is clear, though, that the Commission has a particular responsibility of ensuring application of Community environmental law, because the Community is the source of these provisions. The Commission does not have any structures to monitor application of environmental legal provisions; this is ensured, rather, by the general Commission administration. In particular, the Commission does not have any inspection bodies to examine whether and to what extent Community environmental law is actually complied with. Discussions on green inspectors have been emotionalised as being an intrusion on national sovereignty and, furthermore, as being incompatible with the subsidiarity principle. This criticism omits to mention that there are Commission inspectors in the areas of competition, veterinary, customs, regional and fishery policy, without questions of interference or subsidiarity ever having been raised. The Commission is very cautious in considering

---

[29] Commission (n. 28), para. 25: "The Commission simply cannot monitor the thousands of individual decisions taken each year . . . in the different parts and levels of authority within the Member States. The daily application and enforcement . . . must be fully ensured by the authorities in the Member States . . ."

the setting up of Community inspectors,[30] which are not a subject of policy for the next few years. The Council is clearly opposed to Community environmental inspectors.[31]

Since 1983 the Commission has published an annual report on monitoring the application of Community law,[32] which includes a chapter on environmental legislation; attempts in 1991/1992 to produce a specific environmental report failed. The reports publish some general data and trends on the application of Community environmental law, but do not provide complete transparency, do not establish data which are comparable over the years, and are not always completely reliable.

(c) Monitoring by other bodies

11–20 The European Parliament does not fulfil any significant function in the monitoring of Community environmental legislation. Members of the Parliament pose, it is true, a great number of written or oral questions, which include issues of application of environmental legislation; however, these initiatives remain non-systematic. Where the European Parliament receives a petition from a citizen within the Community, it does not—contrary to the practice in most Member States—itself investigate the facts which underlie the petition, but leaves the investigation to the Commission, for which the national administration is the principal interlocutor, to clarify the facts.

The European Environmental Agency, which was set up in 1990,[33] does not have any role in monitoring the application of Community environmental law. When the Agency was set up, the European Parliament had vehemently requested such a monitoring role, following, in that, the example of the United States Environmental Protection Agency. However, it could not persuade the Council, which only conceded that in Article 20 of Regulation 1210/90 a clause should be inserted according to which the Council would check "at the latest within two years" whether the Agency should be allocated tasks in the monitoring of application of Community environmental law. When the Commission submitted the corresponding proposal in 1997, it did not suggest giving monitoring tasks to the Agency,[34] and the Council did not take this issue up either.[35]

11—21 The Community ombudsman, set up under Article 195 (ex 138e) E.C., has the task of controlling complaints of maladministration in the activities of the Community institutions or bodies. This might include maladministration in the treatment of citizen complaints in environmental matters or general omissions in the monitoring of application of environmental legislation. His control activities occasionally deal with environmental issues, but try to avoid becoming a complaint instance against decisions taken by the Commission.[36]

The Commission announced, in the fifth environmental action programme, that it would set up an implementation network which would aim "primarily at exchange of information and experience and at the development of common approaches at practical level, under the supervision of the Commission".[37] However, at that time Member States had already started to set up an informal implementation network. As they

---

[30] Commission (n. 28), para. 9: "Further consideration would be given as to whether there might be a need for a limited Community body with auditing competencies."

[31] Council Res. of October 7, 1997 [1997] O.J. C321/1.

[32] See 14th report on monitoring application of Community law, (1996) [1997] O.J. C332/1; 15th report (1997) [1998] O.J. C250/1.

[33] Reg. 1210/90 [1990] O.J. L120/1; see also above, para. 2–19.

[34] [1997] O.J. C255/9, amended [1998] O.J. C123/6.

[35] Reg. 933/1999 [1999] O.J. L117/1 amending Reg. 1210/90 (n. 33).

[36] See European Ombudsman, Annual report 1996 [1997] O.J. C272/1.

[37] Commission, Fifth environmental action programme [1993] O.J. C138/5, chapter 9.

vigorously opposed any mechanism at Community level that would give the Commission more options to monitor application of environmental provisions, they accepted the Commission as a member of that network, but kept its informal nature, and, since 1993, have called it the "European Union Network for the Implementation and Enforcement of Environmental Law" (IMPEL).[38] At present, the network consists of representatives of the enforcement and monitoring bodies of Member States, and Commission representatives; however, since a number of Member States do not have specific enforcement and monitoring bodies, officials from central or regional administrations take part in the network. IMPEL mainly deals with exchange of experience on practical application and enforcement issues, exchange of staff, and the elaboration of guidelines for different aspects of application. IMPEL is financed jointly by Member States and the Commission. Its impact on the actual application of environmental directives is very limited, since it concentrates on horizontal questions.

(d) Citizen complaints

11—22 As the Commission does not have any inspectors, controllers or decentralised administrations which would inform it on the application of Community environmental law within the whole of the Community, its main source of information on possible omissions in the application of Community environmental provision is the information that comes from outside the administrations, in particular from citizens.

The Commission instituted, in the late 1960s, a complaint system for citizens, in order to obtain information on non-technical barriers to the free circulation of goods. The Commission offered to intervene with Member States' administration in order to eliminate border controls and other barriers. Since the mid-1980s, the system has developed considerably as regards environmental complaints. The fact that individuals were able to register a complaint with the Commission stimulated Community-wide awareness of the environment, demonstrated to the citizen that the Commission was also accessible to the man in the street and made it clear to the individual that he had some responsibility for his environment, that he could become active in contributing to the preservation and protection of the environment and that environmental impairment was certainly not to be accepted as an Act of God. This was particularly important for southern European Member States.

11—23 Environmental complaints to the Commission came, and come, from individuals, environmental or professional organisations, national, regional or European deputies, local administrations, political parties, ambassadors and occasionally even from environment ministers of Member States.[39]

The Commission considers a complaint to be any written statement that invokes the breach of Community (environmental) law and asks the Commission to intervene to repair this breach. The formal requirements for such a complaint are very low; the reason for this lies in the fact that the Commission has, under Article 211 (ex 155) E.C., the possibility of starting, even without having received a complaint, an inquiry into possible breaches of Community law by a Member State. Procedurally, such an official inquiry is treated in exactly the same way as a complaint. To facilitate the

---

[38] Commission (n. 28), paras 54 et seq.

[39] The evolution of the number of complaints is as follows (Commission, 8th report on monitoring application of Community law (1990) [1991] O.J. C338/1, p. 82; 12th report on monitoring application of Community law (1994) [1995] O.J. C254/1, p. 58; 15th report on application of Community law (1997) [1998] O.J. C250/1, p. 82): 1982: 10; 1983: 8; 1984: 11; 1985: 47; 1986: 197; 1987: 188; 1988: 249; 1989: 525; 1990: 522; 1991: 455; 1992: 587; 1993: 383; 1994: 359; 1995: 265; 1996: 207; 1997: 315. These figures include cases which were taken up by the Commission ex officio.

introduction of complaints, the Commission has even drawn up and published a form.[40]

11—24   The complaint is registered in a central Commission register. This has as a consequence that the complainant is kept informed as to the evolution of the complaint and that only the Commission as an institution—not an individual official—may decide on the final outcome of it.

The Commission tries to obtain as much factual information from the complainant as possible, which often overburdens the person who has introduced the complaint. For the rest of the facts, the Commission seeks to obtain factual and legal information from the (central) administration of the Member State against which the complaint is directed. In rare cases, expert advice is taken. Hearings or witnesses' testimony are never taken in environmental cases. Also, inspections in Member States do not take place; in very rare cases visits to the affected sites in the form of fact-finding missions have been organised, but not more frequently than once per year.

11—25   In the 1980s, the Commission committed itself—both on the complaint form and in different declarations towards the public—to instruct each complaint; in 1999, it indicated that its administrations would decide according to the internal rules and priorities whether they would examine a complaint or not.[41] Anyway, no sanction exists against an omission to instruct properly, except for disciplinary measures and, eventually, the intervention of the European ombudsman.[42] The complainant has no direct rights as regards the omission to examine a complaint.

At the end of the instruction period, which shall not, according to the Commission's internal instructions, extend beyond one year, the Commission decides either to file the complaint or to open formal proceedings, under Article 226 (ex 169) E.C., against a Member State.[43] Upon intervention of the European ombudsman, the Commission changed its rules in 1997; before it decides to file a complaint, the complainant is heard and has the right to present observations.[44] These procedural guarantees, however, do not give any right to a complainant as regards the final decision which the Commission takes; neither can he oppose the filing of the complaint nor can he oblige the Commission to start legal proceedings under Article 226 (ex 169) E.C. against a Member State. The complainant also does not have a right to ensure the Commission makes adequate use of its discretion or, in other words, to see that the Commission's decision is not grossly arbitrary, for instance with regard to previous Commission decisions. The Court of Justice has rejected all attempts to oblige the Commission to start proceedings under Article 226.

11—26   The Court argued that the decision under Article 226 is not a decision which can be tackled under Article 230 (ex 173) E.C., since it forms an accessory part of a subsequent Court procedure.[45] Furthermore, a complainant is not in the position of a person entitled to take action before the European courts under Article 230(4) (ex 173(4)) E.C., since a decision under Article 226 (ex 169) would not be addressed to the complainant. Finally, the Commission has a margin of discretion which cannot be questioned by individual complainants.[46] In particular the latter argument could hardly be called convincing, if one reads Article 226 ("the Commission . . . shall deliver . . .", in contrast to the fact that it "may" bring a case before the Court of Justice).

---

[40] [1989] O.J. C26/1; reviewed [1999] O.J. C119/5.
[41] See the different versions of the complaint forms (n. 40, above).
[42] See para. 11–21, above.
[43] See below, para. 11–30.
[44] Commission, 15th report on monitoring application of environmental law (1997) [1998] O.J. C250/1, p. 10.
[45] Court of First Instance, case T-126/95 *Dumez v. Commission* [1995] E.C.R. II-2863.
[46] Court of Justice, cases C-247/87 *Star Fruit v. Commission* [1989] E.C.R. I-289 and C-29/92 *Asia Motor France v. Commission* [1992] E.C.R. I-3935.

Practice has shown that an environmental complaint has a greater chance of leading to a positive result, the more the conflict between the environmental interests and the diverging economic interests is discussed in public. The mobilisation of public opinion constitutes an important element of ensuring the taking into consideration of environmental interests and demonstrates at the same time the—at least partly—political character of the complaint procedure; this political character also appears through the lack of control of the Commission's decisions, which facilitates policy interventions in the decision-making procedure.

Complaints procedures in environmental matters normally take a considerable time. Their lack of transparency and the—overall—limited results, in particular as regards large infrastructural projects, have not led to a situation where the Commission is perceived as a true complaint institution.

(e) Direct effect of environmental provisions

11—27 In an effort to make Community provisions fully operational for the individual citizen, too, the Court of Justice had, by the early years of the Community, already developed the doctrine of direct effect. It started with judgments which stated that provisions of the E.C. Treaty also had direct effects in favour of citizens, who were entitled to invoke these provisions before the courts. Later the Court extended this doctrine to provisions of directives which could also, under certain conditions, be invoked by citizens before national courts.[47] This constitutes a deviation from the provision of Article 249 (ex 189) E.C., which states that regulations, but not directives, are directly applicable and that directives must be transposed into national law in order to have legal effect. The Court justifies this decision by the fact that a Member State should not be entitled to take advantage of the fact that a directive was not or was not correctly or completely transposed into national law. For that reason this doctrine is only applied in favour of individuals, but never—for instance in criminal cases— against individual persons. Furthermore, the Court does not apply this doctrine in cases where two individuals are in dispute. This demonstrates that the direct effect of a directive is construed, by the Court, as a sanction against the deviating Member State.

11—28 The following conditions must be fulfilled for a provision of a directive to be directly applicable:

- the period for transposing a directive into national law has expired;

- a Member State has not, or has not correctly, transposed the provisions of a directive;

- the provision of a directive is unconditional, *i.e.* the provision "is not subject, in its implementation or effects, to the taking of any measure either by the institutions of the Community or by the Member States"[48];

- the provision is sufficiently precise to be relied on by an individual and applied by the court; this is the case "where the obligation which it imposes is set out in unequivocal terms"[49];

---

[47] See, for instance, case C-236/92 *Comitato di Difesa della Cava* [1994] E.C.R. I-483: "The Court has consistently held that wherever the provisions of a directive appear, as far as their subject-matter is concerned, to be unconditional and sufficiently precise, those provisions may be relied upon by an individual against the State where the State fails to implement the directive in national law by the period prescribed or where it fails to implement the directive correctly."
[48] *Ibid.*
[49] *Ibid.*

- the provision explicitly or implicitly confers rights to an individual as against a Member State. In this regard the Court of Justice held on several occasions that where a provision dealt with the relations between administrations, it did not give rights to individuals.[50] I have defended the argument that, for the test as to whether a provision of Community law grants rights to an individual, the provision has to be constructed in such a way as if it were contained in a regulation; then it would have to be checked as to whether in such a case the provision would confer an improved position, a legal advantage. It has to be admitted, though, that the question of whether a provision confers a "right" to a person is extremely difficult to answer. The Court, for instance, was of the opinion that Article 4 of Directive 75/442 on waste[51] did not have direct effect, whereas in my opinion this is certainly the case.[52]

11—29 As the Court of Justice constructs the direct effect as a sanction against a Member State which has not, or has not correctly, transposed a directive, it is only logical that it does not apply the doctrine of direct effect in favour of the state, for instance in a criminal procedure against a polluter,[53] or in relations between a citizen and a polluting installation.[54] These limitations and the general difficulties with the interpretation of when a provision has direct effect make this doctrine of rather restricted use.

3. SANCTIONS FOR NON-APPLICATION

(a) Action under Article 226 (ex 169) E.C.

11—30 By far the most important instrument at the Commission's disposal when to fulfilling its obligation under Article 211 (ex 155) E.C. is Article 226 (ex 169) E.C.[55] This provision provides for a three-stage procedure[56]:

(1) formal notice of breach of obligations to the Member State;

(2) issue of a reasoned opinion;

(3) application to the Court of Justice.

Steps (1) and (2) jointly constitute the prejudicial procedure, which has the objective of enabling the Member State to comply with its obligations under Community law or to

---

[50] Cases C-380/87 *Cinisello Balsamo* [1989] E.C.R. 2491 and C-194/94 *Security International v. Signalson* [1996] E.C.R. I-2201.

[51] Dir. 75/442 [1975] O.J. L194/39.

[52] Art. 4: "Member States shall take the necessary measures to ensure that waste is recovered or disposed of without endangering human health and without using processes or methods which could harm the environment, and in particular: without damage to water, air, soil and plants and animals; without causing detriment through noise or smell pollution; without adversely affecting the countryside or places of special interest. Member States shall also take the necessary measures to prohibit the abandoning, dumping or uncontrolled disposal of waste."

[53] Case C-168/95 *Arcaro* [1996] E.C.R. I-4705.

[54] See in this regard the leading case C-91/92 *Dori* [1994] E.C.R. I-3325.

[55] See wording of Art. 226 (ex 169) E.C.: "If the Commission considers that a Member State has failed to fulfil an obligation under this Treaty, it shall deliver a reasoned opinion on the matter, after giving the state concerned the opportunity to submit its observations. If the state concerned does not comply with the opinion within the period laid down by the Commission, the latter may bring the matter before the Court of Justice."

[56] The procedural provisions regarding Article 226 are not codified, contrary to the provisions of Article 88 (ex 93) E.C.; see Reg. 659/1999 [1999] O.J. L83/1. The Commission stated in Written Question E-2496/98 (Watson) [1999] O.J. C142/18 that the provisions regarding Article 226 had been published in the introduction to the Commission's 10th report on monitoring application of Community law (1992) [1993] O.J. C233/1, and that later amendments were published in the successive annual reports.

present its arguments to the Commission on why there is no breach of Community law. For this reason the Commission, which alone may initiate the procedure under Article 226, is obliged to specify clearly the object on which it considers the Member State's breach to have occurred (object of litigation).[57]

11—31   The formal notice to a Member State that is considered to be in breach of its obligation does not require a specific form. In practice, however, notice is always given in the form of a letter. The decision to send such a letter is taken by the Commission, after detailed preparation of the Commission services. The formal letter is agreed word by word at administrative, legal and political level, before it is formally notified to the Member State. This careful preparation is also due to the view held by the Court of Justice that the Commission's letter defines the object of litigation for any subsequent Court proceedings.[58] Thus, the Commission cannot, in any subsequent part of the procedure under Article 226 (ex 169) E.C., include any additional point of complaint against a Member State, since the Member State would not have had "the opportunity to present its observations" on such points. Since, however, the factual side of the case is normally not completely clarified, changes in the legal assessment are, of course, possible.

Normally, the Member State has two months to reply to the Commission's letter of formal notice. However, since, on average, the Commission discusses and decides on cases under Article 226 (ex 169) only once every six months, the time available to Member States for a reply is almost always much longer.

11—32   Where the Commission is not satisfied with the Member State's answer, it may decide to issue a reasoned opinion. The reasoned opinion is produced in the same form as the letter of formal notice. The facts of the dispute are supposed to have been clarified during the procedure preceding the decision to issue a reasoned opinion. The reasoned opinion gives a detailed and comprehensive description of the case as it presents itself in the opinion of the Commission, indicates the legal opinion and describes, in particular, in detail how Community environmental law has been breached. Should proceedings subsequently be initiated with the Court of Justice, the facts no longer need to be clarified and the dispute can normally be confined to legal issues.

On average, between 1995 and 1997, the timespan between the decision to send a letter of formal notice and the application to the Court of Justice was 33 months.[59]

11—33   The Commission occasionally publishes a press release on those disputes which it considers politically or environmentally important. The impact of such press releases is sometimes considerable, depending on the sensitivity of the media to the issue. However, the Commission does not make public either the letter of formal notice or the reasoned opinion. This practice, for which no explanation can be found in Article 226 (ex 169) E.C., is justified with the argument that the confidentiality of the relations between Member States and the Commission would otherwise be disturbed and a smooth solution to the problem made more difficult. This attitude seems to be neither in the interest of the environment nor of the citizen and it is not conducive to an open society.[60]

The Commission has a very large discretion to apply to the Court of Justice and, in

---

[57] Case C-266/94 *Commission v. Spain* [1995] E.C.R. I-1975.

[58] Case C-337/89 *Commission v. United Kingdom* [1992] E.C.R. I-6103.

[59] See L. Krämer, "Die Rechtsprechung der EG-Gerichte zum Umweltrecht 1995–1997", *Europäische Grundrechte Zeitschrift* (1998), p. 309; the figure refers to cases which had been submitted to the Court of Justice; between 1992 and 1994, this timespan was 35 months (author's own calculations for both periods).

[60] See Written Question E-1106/98 (Lambrias) [1998] O.J. C354/62, where the Commission explains its policy under Article 226, arguing also that it normally publishes the reasoned opinion. This appears not to correspond to normal practice.

practice, less than 10 per cent of cases where the procedure under Article 226 was initiated are actually submitted to the Court of Justice. There is no delay required in submitting the application to the Court, nor need the Commission demonstrate a specific legal interest in order to obtain a judgment.

11—34   The Court's decision under Article 226 (ex 169) E.C. states that there is a breach of Community environmental law, unless the application is dismissed. The Court neither annuls the national measures that cause the breach of Community law nor does it pronounce on the measures that have to be taken; it is up to the Member State to comply with the judgment and take the necessary measures.

Between 1976 and 1997, the Court of Justice decided 98 environmental cases under Article 226[61]; during the last three years, the average timespan, including the prejudicial procedure, has been 47 months, thus almost four years.[62]

(b) Action under Article 227 (ex 170) E.C.

11—35   Article 227 (ex 170) E.C. allows Member States to take judicial action against another Member State which has not fulfilled its environmental obligations under the E.C. Treaty. However, no such case has ever been brought before the Court in environmental matters. Member States instead rely on the Commission to take action.

(c) Action under Article 228 (ex 171) E.C.

11—36   Where a Member State does not comply with a judgment by the Court, the Commission may, under Article 228 (ex 171) E.C., start a new procedure. The justification for that is probably the continued non-compliance with Community law and, at the same time, the contempt of the Court that is enshrined in the non-execution of the judgment. The procedure is the same as under Article 226 (ex 169) E.C.; the second judgment is again of a declaratory nature.

The Maastricht Treaty of 1993 introduced a new version of Article 228 (2) (ex 169(2)) in order to address the problem that Member States do not comply with a judgment of the Court. In such a case, the Commission may make a second application to the Court; it then shall specify the amount of the lump sum or of a penalty payment to be paid by the Member State concerned. The Court may then impose a lump sum or a penalty payment.

The Commission issued two communications in 1996 and 1997 regarding the methods for calculating the penalty payments.[63] The seriousness and duration of the infringement are assessed and the deterrent effect of a financial sanction rated; the resulting figure is multiplied by a financial sum that has been fixed according to the financial capacity of the Member State in question.

11—37   The Court has not yet delivered any judgment where it has pronounced a financial sanction against a Member State. This seems to be due to the preventive effect of Article 228(2): where it becomes known that the Commission has decided to ask the Court for a specific penalty payment per day, the Member State in question seems to deploy specific efforts in complying with its environmental obligations.

The Commission has, in environmental cases, taken the following decisions to request payment[64]:

---

[61]   Author's calculations. The judgments were brought against Belgium (22), Italy (22), Germany (21), France (9), Greece, (7), the Netherlands (5), Luxembourg (4), Spain (4), Denmark (2) and the United Kingdom (2).
[62]   See Krämer, "Die Rechtsprechung" (n.59), p. 310; of the 47 months in total, 33 were used in the prejudicial procedure and 14 for the procedure before the Court of Justice.
[63]   [1996] O.J. C242/6 and [1997] O.J. C63/2.
[64]   See Written Question E-3278/98 (Kjer Hansen) [1999] O.J. C135/182.

- Italy; non-compliance with the judgment in case C-33/90[65]: 123,300 euro per day; this case was not submitted to the Court under Article 228, as the dispute was solved beforehand.

- Germany; non-compliance with the judgment in case C-131/88[66]; 264,000 euro per day; this case was not submitted to the Court under Article 228, as the dispute was solved beforehand.

- Belgium; non-compliance with the judgment in case C-247/85[67]; 7,750 euro per day; this case was not submitted to the Court under Article 228, as the dispute was solved beforehand.

- Germany; non-compliance with the judgment in case C-58/89[68]; 158,400 euro per day; Germany complied with its obligations before the Court gave its judgment under Article 228.

- Germany; non-compliance with the judgment in case C-288/88[69]; 26,400 euro per day; Germany complied with its obligations before the Court gave its judgment under Article 228.

- Greece; non-compliance with the judgment in case C-45/91[70]; 26,400 euro per day; the case under Article 228 is pending.

- France; non-compliance with the judgment in case C-252/85[71]; 105,500 euro per day; the case under Article 228 is pending.

(d) State liability

11—38   According to the Court of Justice, a Member State may also be liable for damages towards private individuals because it has breached Community law by failing to transpose a Community directive into national law.[72] The Court laid down a number of conditions for such a liability: there must be a serious breach of Community obligations; the Community directive must confer rights to individual persons; the content of these rights is identifiable by reference to the directive; and there exists a causal link between the Member State's obligations and the damage suffered by the person affected. Fault or negligence on the part of the Member State is, however, not required.

Until now, this theory has not been applied to environmental cases, though there might be some potential for such cases, all the more so since the theory also applies to cases where a directive has not correctly or completely been transposed. As the Court also considered that individuals also acquire rights from quality objectives,[73] the construction of such damages could, in future, be considerable.

(e) Financial sanctions

11—39   Financial sanctions for breach of Community environmental law exist in theory. Indeed, the different regulations for the Community Structural Funds and the

---

[65] Case C-33/90 *Commission v. Italy* [1991] E.C.R. I-5987.
[66] Case C-131/88 *Commission v. Germany* [1991] E.C.R. I-825.
[67] Case C-247/85 *Commission v. Belgium* [1987] E.C.R. 3073.
[68] Case C-58/89 *Commission v. Germany* [1991] E.C.R. I-4983.
[69] Case C-288/88 *Commission v. Germany* [1990] E.C.R. 2721.
[70] Case C-45/91 *Commission v. Greece* [1992] E.C.R. I-2509; judgment of April 7, 1992.
[71] Case C-252/85 *Commission v. France* [1988] E.C.R. 2243; judgment of April 27, 1988.
[72] Joined cases C-6 & 9/90 *Francovich v. Italy* [1991] E.C.R. I-5357; C-48/93 *Factortame* [1996] E.C.R. I-1029.
[73] Cases C-361/88 *Commission v. Germany* [1991] E.C.R. I-2567; C-131/88 (n. 66).

Cohesion Fund provide that measures which are financed or co-financed by the Community must comply with Community law, and in particular with Community environmental law.[74] Thus, according to this provision, measures may not be financed with Community funds if they fail to comply with all the provisions of Community environmental law. As a consequence of this, each measure which is undertaken in a Member State without respect of Community environmental law—an example would be the construction of a motorway without an environmental impact assessment—may lead to a refusal of financial assistance or to the recuperation of the sums paid.[75]

Subsequent to an *obiter dictum* by the Court of First Instance,[76] the Commission considers the procedures under Article 226 (ex 169) E.C. and under the provisions of the different funds that deal with the recovery of the financial assistance as independent from each other. Thus, the start of a procedure under Article 226 or even a judgment by the Court of Justice does not automatically lead to the Commission recovering the sums paid; rather, the Commission reserves the right to examine, in each individual case, what steps are to be taken.[77]

11—40   Since the Commission's decision to recover or not to recover its financial assistance cannot be attacked by any third person, and since the Commission does not publish details of cases where Community environmental law was not respected, nor any information as to how often it has suspended, refused or recovered financial assistance,[78] the main value of the provisions is likely to lie in a preventive effect: where a Member State is asked, prior to the financing of a project, whether it has complied with all Community environmental law provisions, this might lead to a more careful consideration of such provisions. From media reports, it is known that the Commission, in the past, has sometimes refused financial assistance or at least threatened to do so; however, no quantification can be given. I know of no case, and no publicly available document records any case, where financial assistance was ever definitely refused in an environmental case.

(f) Criminal sanctions

11—41   Criminal measures against a polluter or against a Member State cannot be taken by the Community institutions. Under Articles 29 to 41 (ex K1 to K13) of the Treaty on European Union, criminal sanctions are the responsibility of Member States, which have agreed far-reaching co-operation. This might include, eventually, the agreeing on criminal sanctions in cases such as the illegal shipment of waste or the pollution of the environment in excess of authorisations. However, Community environmental law does not contain any provision allowing the taking out of criminal sanctions against Community institutions.

---

[74] See, for instance, Reg. 2081/93 [1993] O.J. L193/5, Art. 7: "Measures financed by the Structural Funds or receiving assistance from the EIB or from another existing financial instrument shall be in conformity with the provisions of the Treaties, with the instruments adopted pursuant thereto and with Community policies, including those concerning . . . environmental protection." An almost identical provision is found in Reg. 1164/94 on the Cohesion Fund [1994] O.J. L130/1, Art. 8.

[75] Reg. 2081/93 (n. 74), Art. 24; Reg. 1164/94 (n. 74), annex II, Art. H; see also Commission, 15th report (n. 44), p. 76.

[76] Case T-461/93 *An Taisce/WWF v. Commission* [1994] E.C.R. II-733.

[77] Commission, 15th report (n. 44), p. 77.

[78] The Commission's 14th and 15th reports on monitoring application of Community law (1996 and 1997) [1997] O.J. C332/1, p. 70 and [1998] O.J. C250/1, p. 76 contain for the first time a chapter on monitoring compliance under the Structural Funds. These chapters are virtually identical, though they concern two different years, and remain very abstract. For 1996, the Commission states that Community environmental law was not respected in 23 cases, for 1997 in 25 cases. There is neither an indication on the different cases nor is there any information on whether financial assistance was suspended, refused or recovered.

(g) Interim measures

11—42　Article 243 (ex 186) E.C. provides that the Court of Justice may prescribe any necessary interim measure in cases before it. This provision does not state whether the Commission may also take interim measures as soon as it discovers a breach of Community law. However, it is now generally accepted that the Commission has no such powers and that the decision on interim measures can only be taken by the Court of Justice. The Commission may appeal to the Court to prescribe such measures, but this can only take place where a case is pending before the Court or where it is submitted to the Court together with the request for the interim measure. The Commission has then to demonstrate the urgency and necessity of the measure, in particular if there is a risk of a serious and irreversible damage that might otherwise occur.

Attempts by the Commission to stop the construction of a dyke that would have destroyed a bird habitat were rejected, since the Commission was not able to show the urgency of such a measure.[79] An attempt by an environmental organisation to stop the construction of a tourist information centre in a natural habitat was rejected, because a national court had already stopped the project.[80] The attempt to stop, by way of interim measures, the French nuclear tests in Mururoa in 1995, was rejected as inadmissible, since the private applicants were not directly and individually concerned and had thus no standing.[81]

Generally, it can be said that it will hardly ever be possible to demonstrate the urgency and necessity of interim measures under Article 226 (ex 169) E.C., since the pre-Court stage, during which no interim measures are possible, takes almost three years.[82]

(h) Action by individuals

11—43　Community environmental law does not provide for any active role for citizens or their organisations to ensure full application of Community environmental law. The role of monitoring application is given to the Commission, though it is obvious that the Commission is not the owner or the stakeholder of the environment; however, in that respect Community environmental law is basically no different from law in most Member States and, indeed, most other industrialised countries. It seems that almost only the United States ensures that there is the possibility for its citizens and private organisations actively to monitor application of environmental law. Within the Community, the idea of having private citizens actively pursuing general interest matters such as the application of environmental law and, thereby, the protection of the environment, is not strongly developed. Member States in the tradition of Roman law resist it, as the concept of an "open society" and the activation of citizens as law enforcers has no tradition in law. In Scandinavian Member States, a concept of the modern welfare state seems to lead to the conclusion that it is best for public authorities to ensure the application of environmental law.

The complaint procedure, described in paragraphs 11–22 et seq., above, does not give citizens the possibility actively to pursue any lack of compliance with Community law. Actions against Member States can only be taken by the Commission; its decision to act or not to act under Article 226 (ex 169) E.C. cannot be challenged by citizens.

---

[79] Case C-57/89R Commission v. Germany [1989] E.C.R. 2849.
[80] Case C-407/92R An Taisce v. Commission, decision of July 6, 1993, unpublished.
[81] Court of First Instance, case T-219/95R Danielsson v. Commission [1995] E.C.R. II-3051.
[82] See above, para. 11–32.

Where the Commission itself causes environmental impairment, there is hardly any possibility for a citizen to take action against the Commission, since that citizen is seen as not being directly and individually concerned. The jurisprudence by the Court of Justice, which grants citizens some "rights" under Community environmental directives,[83] has had no influence whatsoever on individuals'—and their organisations'— right of standing under Community law.

11—44 In 1998, the Community and all Member States signed the Aarhus Convention on "access to information, public participation in decision-making and access to justice in environmental matters", which had been elaborated under the auspices of the United Nations. This Convention, which has not yet entered into force, provides for access to justice[84] for "members of the public concerned (a) having a sufficient interest or, alternatively (b) maintaining impairment of a right, where the administrative procedural law of a Party requires this as a precondition". This provision includes environmental organisations.

It will be interesting to see if and how these provisions will be transposed into Community law, as it seems that the present wording of Article 230(4) (ex 173(4)) E.C. is much narrower as regards access by individuals and environmental organisations to European courts.

11—45 The extent to which an individual can address national courts and claim there a breach of Community law is governed by national law; no general Community provisions exist.[85] At present, there has been no attempt to improve the possibilities for individuals actively to ensure the application of Community environmental law. A Commission communication of 1996 is silent in that respect[86]; the Council's resolution on that communication is no more explicit.[87]

To what extent the monitoring of application of Community environmental law should be ensured by the Community staff or should be, at least to some extent, externalised, is a question of legal and institutional policy. It is obvious that Member States—and even less actual or potential polluters—do not like to be checked as to their environmental performance. Whether the environment can indefinitely survive the present monitoring practice, which is often influenced by political or administrative intervention or private lobbying, is not a question to be dealt with here.

BIBLIOGRAPHY

Addink, G., Aland, N., Besselink, H., VanDijk, G., Grapperhaus, A. and Veltkampm B.: *Europees milieurechtspraak* (Zwolle, 1996)

Betlem, G.: "Being 'directly and individually concerned', the Schutznorm doctrine and *Francovich* liability" in H. Micklitz and N. Reich (eds), *Public interest litigation before European courts* (Baden-Baden, 1996), p. 319

Betlem, G.: "Enforcement of E.C. environmental law in the light of the 5th action programme" in N. Reich and R. Heine-Mernik (eds), *Umweltverfassung und nachhaltige Entwicklung in der Europäischen Union* (Baden-Baden, 1997), p. 119

---

[83] See above, para. 11–28.

[84] In the wording of Article 9 (2) of the Convention, this means "access to a review procedure before a court of law and/or another independent and impartial body established by law".

[85] Under Article 234 (ex 177) E.C., a national court may—and in certain cases must—ask the Court of Justice for a preliminary ruling on the validity and interpretation of Community environmental law; however, this provision only has limited functions in the application of Community environmental law.

[86] Commission, Implementing Community environmental law, COM (96) 500 of October 22, 1996. The communication mainly addresses measures at national level and considers, at Community level, better information, co-operation and consultation.

[87] Council Res. of October 7, 1997 [1997] O.J. C321/1.

Capria, A: *Direttive ambientali CEE. Stato di attuazione in Italia* (2nd ed., Milan, 1992)

Castanon i Garcia-Alix, O.: "Aplicació del dret comunitari per les Comunitats Autònomes" in M. Campins i Eritja and I. Pont i Castejón (eds), *Perspectives de dret ambiental* (Bellaterra, 1997), p. 449

Clinton-Davis, S.: "Enforcing E.C. environmental law: a personal perspective" in H. Somsen (ed.), *Protecting the European environment: enforcing E.C. environmental law* (London, 1996), p. 7

Dell'Anno, P.: "L'attuazione del diritto communitario ambientale tra supremazia delle fonti e disapplicazione amministrativa: spunit di riflessione", *Rivista trimesteriale di diritto pubblico* (1994), p. 615

Demmke, C.: *Die Implementation von EG-Umweltpolitik in den Mitgliedstaaten. Umsetzung und Vollzug der Trinkwasserrichtlinie* (Baden-Baden, 1994)

Demmke, C.: "Nationale Verwaltung und europäische Umweltpolitik—die Umsetzung und der Vollzug von EG-Umweltrecht" in C. Demmke (ed.), *Europäische Umweltpolitik und nationale Verwaltungen* (Maastricht, 1998), p. 85

Engelsberger, C.: *Der Vollzug europarechtlicher Vorschriften auf dem Gebiet des Umweltschutzes* (Berlin, 1998)

Epiney, A.: "Dezentrale Durchsetzungsmechanismen im gemeinschaftlichen Umweltrecht—dargestellt am Beispiel der UVP-Richtlinie", *Zeitschrift für Umweltrecht* (1996), p. 229

Everling, U.: "Umsetzung von Umweltrichtlinien durch normkonkretisierende Verwaltungsanweisungen", *Recht der Internationalen Wirtschaft* (1992), p. 392

Everling, U.: "Durchführung und Umsetzung des Europäischen Gemeinschaftsrechts im Bereich des Umweltschutzes unter Berücksichtigung der Rechtsprechung des EUGH", *Neue Zeitschrift für Verwaltungsrecht* (1993), p. 209

Faulks, J. and Rose, L.: "Common interest groups and the enforcement of European environmental law" in H. Somsen (ed.), *Protecting the European environment: enforcing E.C. environmental law* (London, 1996), p. 195

Fenelly, N.: "The role of Community law in controlling the transposition and excution of environmental regulations" in A. García Ureta (ed.), *Transposición y control de la normativa ambiental comunitaria* (Basauri, 1998), p. 15

García Ureta, A. (ed.): *Transposición y control de la normativa ambiental comunitaria* (Basauri, 1998)

Garzia, G.: "L'attuazione delle direttive CEE mediante regolamenti ed il diritto dell'ambiente", *Rivista giuridica edilizia* (1993) 2, p. 159

Gaskin, F.: "The implementation of E.C. environmental law", *Review of European Community and International Environmental Law* (1993), p. 335

Gellermann, M. and Szczekalla, P.: "Gemeinschaftskonforme Umsetzung von Umweltrichtlinien der EG", *Natur und Recht* (1993), p. 54

Goebel, B.: "Gemeinschaftsrechtlich begründete Staatshaftung—ein Beitrag zum Vollzug des Gemeinschaftsumweltrechts?", *Umwelt und Planungsrecht* (1994), p. 361

Hansmann, K.: "Schwierigkeiten bei der Umsetzung und Durchführung des Europäischen Umweltrechts", *Neue Zeitschrift für Verwaltungsrecht* (1995), p. 320

Heim, S.: *Unmittelbare Wirkungen von EG-Richtlinien im deutschen und französischen Recht am Beispiel des Umweltrechts* (Baden-Baden, 1999)

Henshaw, L., Aalders, M. and Molander, P.: "Implementation of the E.C. Directive on integrated pollution prevention and control (96/61): a comparative study", *Environmental Liability* (1998), p. 39

Hey, E.: "The European Community's courts and international environmental agreements", *Review of European Community and International Environmental Law* (1998), p. 4

Hilson, C.: "Community rights in environmental law: rhetoric or reality" in J. Holder (ed.), *The impact of E.C. environmental law in the United Kingdom* (Chichester, 1997), p. 51

Holder, J.: "A dead end for direct effect? Prospects for enforcement of European Community environmental law by individuals", *Journal of Environmental Law* (1996), p. 313

House of Lords, Select Committee on the European Communities: *Implementation and enforcement of environmental legislation. 9th report* (London, 1992)

Howarth, W.: "Umweltrecht und Vollzug des Umweltrechts in England und Wales" in G. Lübbe-Wolff (ed.), *Vollzug des europäischen Umweltrechts* (Berlin, 1996), p. 37

Huglo, J.: "L'application par les Etats membres des normes communautaires en matière d'environnement", *Revue trimestérielle de droit européen* (1994), p. 451

Jans, J.: "Legal protection in European environmental law: an overview" in H. Somsen (ed.), *Protecting the European environment: enforcing E.C. environmental law* (London, 1996), p. 49

Juin, D.: *L'application de la législation communautaire de l'environnement en France* (Paris, 1992)

Kahl, W.: "Der Vollzug des europäischen Umweltrechts", *Die Öffentliche Verwaltung* (1995), p. 860

Klösters, A.: *Kompetenzen der EG-Kommission im innerstaatlichen Vollzug von Gemeinschaftsrecht* (Cologne, 1994)

Köck, W.: "Vollzugsaspekte des Öko-Audit-Systems" in N. Reich and R. Heine-Mernik (eds), *Umweltverfassung und nachhaltige Entwicklung in der Europäischen Union* (Baden-Baden, 1997), p. 149

Krämer, L.: "The implementation of environmental laws by the European Economic Communities", *German Yearbook of International Law* (1991), p. 9

Krämer, L.: "Die Rechtsprechung des Gerichtshofs der Europäischen Gemeinschaften zum Umweltrecht 1992–1994", *Europäische Grundrechte Zeitschrift* (1995), p. 45

Krämer, L.: "Direct effect of E.C. environmental law" in H. Somsen (ed.), *Protecting the European environment: enforcing E.C. environmental law* (London, 1996), p. 99

Krämer, L.: "Public interest litigation in environmental matters before European courts", *Journal of Environmental Law* (1996), p. 1

Krämer, L.: "Deficits in application of E.C. environmental law and its causes" in L. Krämer, *Focus on European environmental law* (London, 1997), p. 1

Krämer, L.: "Die Rechtsprechung der EG-Gerichte zum Umweltrecht 1995–1997", *Europäische Grundrechte Zeitschrift* (1998), p. 309

Lefevre, J.: "State liability for breaches of Community law", *European Environmental Law Review* (1996), p. 237

Lewis, C.: "The role of the ECJ in the development and enforcement of environmental law" in B. Wenzel (ed.), *First Nordic conference on EU environmental law* (Copenhagen, 1994), p. 161

Lindemann, H. and Delfs, S.: "Vollzug des europäischen Umweltrechts. Lösungsansätze zur Überprüfung und Verbesserung", *Zeitschrift für Umweltrecht* (1993), p. 256

Lübbe-Wolff, G.: "Stand und Instrumente der Implementation des Umweltrechts in Deutschland" in G. Lübbe-Wolff (ed.), *Vollzug des europäischen Umweltrechts* (Berlin, 1996), p. 77

Lübbe-Wolff, G. (ed.): *Der Vollzug des europäischen Umweltrechts* (Berlin, 1996)

Macrory, R.: "The enforcement of Community environmental laws: some critical remarks", *Common Market Law Review* (1992), p. 347

Macrory, R.: "Community supervision in the field of the environment" in H. Somsen (ed.), *Protecting the European environment: enforcing E.C. environmental law* (London, 1996), p. 9

Martínez Aragón, J.: "El control del a aplicación de la normativa comunitaria en materia de medio ambiente por parte de la Comisión y los procedimientos de infracción contra el Estado espanol" in M. Campins i Eritja and I. Pont i Castejón (eds), *Perspectives de dret comunitar ambiental* (Bellaterra, 1997), p. 497

Narbona Ruiz, C.: "Aplicación de la normativa comunitaria en materia de medio ambiente por parte del Estado espanol" in M. Campins i Eritja and I. Pont i Castejón (eds), *Perspectives de dret comunitari ambiental* (Bellaterra, 1997), p. 463

Nicklas, C.: *Implementationsprobleme des EG-Umweltrechts* (Baden-Baden, 1997)

Noble, D.: "Enforcing E.C. environmental law: the national dimension" in H. Somsen (ed.), *Protecting the European environment: enforcing E.C. environmental law* (London, 1996), p. 37

Pagh, P.: "The 'direct effect doctrine' in E.C. environmental law", *Nordic Journal of International Law* (1995), p. 23

Pernice, I.: "Kriterien der normativen Umsetzung von Umweltrichtlinien der EG im Lichte der Rechtsprechung des EUGH", *Europarecht* (1994), p. 325

Pridham, G. and Cini, M.: "Enforcing environmental standards in the European Union: is there a Southern problem?" in M. Faure, J. Vervaele and A. Weale (eds), *Environmental standards in the European Union in an interdisciplinary framework* (Anvers and Appeldoorn, 1994), p. 251

Raum-Degrève, R. and de Hemptinne, F. (eds): *Le droit communautaire de l'environnement; problèmes de mise en oeuvre nationale* (Luxembourg, 1995)

Reich, N.: "Der Schutz subjektiver Gemeinschaftsrechte durch Staatshaftung", *Europäische Zeitschrift für Wirtschaftsrecht* (1996), p. 709

Sands, P.: "The European Court of Justice: an environmental tribunal?" in H. Somsen (ed.), *Protecting the European environment: enforcing E.C. environmental law* (London, 1996), p. 23

Simon, D. and Rigaux, A.: "Les contraintes de la transcription en droit francais des directives communautaires: le secteur de l'environnement", *Revue juridique de l'environnement* (1991), p. 269

Sioutis, G.: "Die Implementation der Umweltgesetzgebung der EG in Griechenland" in G. Lübbe-Wolff (ed.), *Vollzug des europäischen Umweltrechts* (Berlin, 1996)

Somsen, H. (ed.): *Protecting the European environment: enforcing E.C. environmental law* (London, 1996)

Somsen, H.: "*Francovich* and its application to E.C. environmental law" in H. Somsen (ed.), *Protecting the European environment: enforcing E.C. environmental law* (London, 1996), p. 135

Uebersohn, G.: *Effektive Umweltpolitik—Folgerungen aus der Implementations- und Evaluationsforschung* (Frankfurt/M., 1990)

Van Hoorick, G.: *Beschrijving van de EG-Richtlijnen inzake de bescherming van het leefmilieu en de stand van implementatie in het Vlaamse Gewest* (Ghent, 1993)

Wägenbaur, R.: "The European Community's policy on implementation of environmental directives", *Fordham International Law Journal* (1990–1991), p. 455

Ward, A.: "The right to an effective remedy in E.C. law and environmental protection", *Journal of Environmental law* (1994), p. 331

Wegener, B.: "Vollzugskontrolle durch Klagerechte vor mitgliedstaatlichen Gerichten" in G. Lübbe-Wolff (ed.), *Vollzug des europäischen Umweltrechts* (Berlin, 1996), p. 145

Werner, J.: "Das EU-Netzwerk für Umsetzung und Vollzug von Umweltrecht" in G. Lübbe-Wolff (ed.), *Vollzug des europäischen Umweltrechts* (Berlin, 1996), p. 131

Williams, R.: "The European Commission and the enforcement of environmental law: an invidious position", *Yearbook of European Law* (1995), p. 351

Winter, G.: "Rechtsschutz gegen Behörden, die Umweltrichtlinien der EG nicht beachten", *Natur und Recht* (1991), p. 453

Winter, G.: "Kompetenzen der Europäischen Gemeinschaft im Verwaltungsvollzug" in G. Lübbe-Wolff (ed.), *Vollzug dees europäischen Umweltrechts* (Berlin, 1996), p. 107

Woolley, J.: "The enforcement of E.C. environmental law and the role of local government" in H. Somsen (ed.), *Protecting the European environment: enforcing E.C. environmental law* (London, 1996), p. 167

Index